SKELETAL BIOLOGY OF PAST PEOPLES: RESEARCH METHODS

SKELETAL BIOLOGY OF PAST PEOPLES: RESEARCH METHODS

Editors
Shelley R. Saunders
Department of Anthropology
McMaster University
Hamilton, Ontario, Canada

M. Anne Katzenberg
Department of Archaeology
The University of Calgary
Calgary, Alberta, Canada

WILEY-LISS
A JOHN WILEY & SONS, INC., PUBLICATION
New York • Chichester • Brisbane • Toronto • Singapore

Address all Inquiries to the Publisher
Wiley-Liss, Inc., 605 Third Avenue, New York, NY 10158-0012

Library of Congress Cataloging-in-Publication Data

Skeletal biology of past peoples : research methods / editors,
  Shelley R. Saunders, M. Anne Katzenberg.
      p. cm.
    Includes bibliographical references and index.
    ISBN 0-471-56138-X
    1. Anthropometry—Research. 2. Anthropometry—Methodology.
  3. Human skeleton. I. Saunders, Shelley Rae. II. Katzenberg, Mary Anne.
  GN70.S5   1992
  573'.6'072—dc20   91-26243
                                                               CIP

To Professor F. Jerome Melbye
for encouraging future generations
of human osteologists

Contents

Contributors

Alan H. Goodman (Ph.D. University of Massachusetts, Amherst, 1984) is currently Associate Professor of biological anthropology in the School of Natural Science, Hampshire College, Amherst, Massachusetts. Specializing in biological, medical, and nutritional anthropology, his research focuses on the political economy of human biology. He has published numerous books and articles, including: "Health, adaptation, and maladaptation in past societies," in H Bush and M Zvelebil (eds.): *Health in Past Societies*, BAR International Series, Oxford, 1991; "Nutritional supplementation and enamel developmental defects in children from Tezonteopan, Mexico" (with Martinez C and Chavez A), *Am. J. Clin. Nut.*, 1991; "Dental enamel hypoplasias as indicators of nutritional status" (with Rose JC), in M Kelley and C Larsen (eds.): *Advances in Dental Anthropology*, Wiley-Liss, 1991; *Black Mesa Anasazi Health* (with Martin DL, Armelagos GJ, Magennis AL), Southern Illinois University Press, 1991; The assessment of systemic physiological perturbations from development defects of enamel and histological structures (with Rose JC), *Yrbk. Phys. Anthropol.*, 1990; Bioculture perspectives on stress in prehistoric, historical, and contemporary population research (with Thomas RB, Swedlund AC, and Armelagos GJ), *Yrbk Phys. Anthropol.*, 1988; Disease and death at Dr. Dickson's mounds (with Armelagos GJ), *Natural History*, 1985. He is the recipient of a National Institutes of Health grant to study the enamel histology of individuals of known nutrition and health status in Mexico and Egypt. He is Vice President of the Council of Nutritional Anthropology, a contributing editor of *Nutrition Reviews*, and a member of numerous other professional organizations.

Mary Jackes (Ph.D., University of Toronto, 1977; MAgEc., University of New England; B.A.,

University of Sydney) is currently an Adjunct Professor of anthropology at the University of Alberta. She has worked as an osteologist on both human and nonhuman remains in Australia, East and North Africa, Canada, and Portugal. Her current interests are paleodemography and paleopathology, and the archaeology and human biology of the Mesolithic-Neolithic transition. Her publications include: "Osteological evidence for smallpox: A possible case from seventeenth century Ontario," *Am. J. Phys. Anthropol.*, 1983; "Continuities in the Epipalaeolithic of North Africa with emphasis on the Maghreb" (with Lubell D and Sheppard P) in F Wendorf and A Close (eds): *Advances in World Archaeology, Volume 3,* 1984; "Pubic symphysis age distributions," *Am. J. Phys. Anthropol.*, 1985; "The mortality of Ontario archaeological populations," *Can. J. Anthropol.*, 1986; "Demographic change at the Mesolithic-Neolithic transition: Evidence from Portugal," *Riv. Antropol.*, 1988a; "Portuguese Mesolithic-Neolithic subsistence and settlement" (with Lubell D), *Riv. Antropol.*, 1988b. She is a member of the American Association of Physical Anthropologists and is Secretary-Treasurer of the Canadian Association for Physical Anthropology.

M. Anne Katzenberg (Ph.D., University of Toronto, 1983) is currently an Associate Professor in the Department of Archaeology at the University of Calgary. Specializing in physical anthropology, human skeletal biology, and bone chemistry, her publications include: *"Changing Diet and Health in Pre- and Protohistoric Ontario,"* MASCA Research Papers in Science and Archaeology, in press; "Stable isotopes in human skeletons of southern Ontario: Reconstructing paleodiet" (with Schwarcz HP, Melbye FJ, and Knyf M), *J. Arch. Sci.*, 1985; and *Chemical Analysis of Prehistoric Human Bone*

From Five Temporally Distinct Populations in Southern Ontario, National Museum of Man, Mercury Series, Archaeological Survey of Canada (monograph). Dr. Katzenberg is the recipient of a Fullbright Scholarship and, in cooperation with Dr. S.R. Saunders, a grant from the Social Sciences and Humanities Research Council of Canada to study bone chemistry and histomorphology in early European settlers of Canada. She is past-president of the University of Calgary Chapter of Sigma Xi, the scientific research society, and a member of the Canadian Association for Physical Anthropology, the American Association of Physical Anthropologists, the Human Biology Council, and the Paleopathology Association.

Linda L. Klepinger (Ph.D., University of Kansas, 1972) is currently an Associate Professor of anthropology at the University of Illinois at Urbana-Champaign. She specializes in skeletal biology and chemistry, forensic anthropology, and paleopathology. Her publications include: "Prehistoric dental calculus gives evidence for coca in early coastal Equador," *Nature,* 1977; "Nutritional assessment from bone," *Ann. Rev. Anthropol.,* 1984; "An elemental analysis of archaeological bone from Sicily as a test of predictability of diagenic change" (with Kuhn J and Williams WS), *Am. J. Phys. Anthropol.,* 1986; "Magnesium ingestion and bone magnesium concentration in paleodietary reconstruction: Cautionary evidence from an animal model," *J. Archaeol. Sci.,* 1990. Dr. Klepinger, currently director of the Program on Ancient Technologies and Archaeological Materials at University of Illinois, is a member of the American Association of Physical Anthropologists (and Executive Committee member), Society for Archaeological Sciences, American Association for the Advancement of Science, Paleopathology Association, a Fellow of American Anthropological Association and American Academy of Forensic Sciences, and a member of the American Board of Forensic Anthropology.

John T. Mayhall (D.D.S., Indiana University, 1963; Ph.D., University of Chicago, 1976) is a Professor of denistry and head of the Oral Anatomy Department at the Faculty of Dentistry,

University of Toronto. Specializing in dental morphology and the study of the oral health of native peoples of the artic and subartic, his publications include: "Sexual dimorphism in the three-dimensional determinations of the maxillary first molar: Cusp height, area, volume, and position" (with Alvesalo L) in P Smith (ed): *Structure, Function, and Evolution of Teeth,* Freund, 1991; "A three-dimensional analysis of the maxillary first molar crowns of Canadian Inuit" (with Kanazawa E), *Am. J. Phys. Anthropol.,* 1989; "Dimensional and discrete dental trait asymmetry relationships" (with Saunders SR), *Am. J. Phys. Anthropol.,* 1986; and "The dental morphology of the Inuit of the Canadian central artic," *Ossa,* 1979. Dr. Mayhall is a member of the American Association of Physical Anthropologists, the Canadian Association for Physical Anthropology, the Canadian Society for Circumpolar Health, the Dental Anthropology Association, the International Association for Dental Research, the Society for the Study of Human Biology, and a fellow of the Human Biology Council.

Eric Abella Roth (Ph.D., University of Toronto, 1980) is currently an Associate Professor of anthropology at the University of Victoria. He specializes in demography of traditional peoples. His publications include: "Community demography and computer simulation methodology in historic village population reconstruction," *J. Anthropol. Res.,* 1981; "Population structure and sex differences" in R Hall et al. (eds): *Male-Female Differences: A Bio-Cultural Perspective,* 1985; "Child mortality levels and survival patterns from southern Sudan" (with Kurup B), *J. Biosoc. Sci.,* 1990; "Education, tradition, and household labor among Rendille pastoralists of northern Kenya," *Human Organization,* 1991. He is a member of the American Anthropological Association, the Population Association of America, and the Society for Applied Anthropology.

Bruce M. Rothschild (M.D., New Jersey College of Medicine, 1973) is currently a Professor of mMedicine at Northeastern Ohio Universities College of Medicine, a Professor of biomedical engineering at the University of Akron, Director of the Arthritis Center of Northeast Ohio in

Youngstown, and a Research Associate at the University of Kansas Museum of Natural History. He specializes in paleopathology, antiquity of disease, and skeletal biology. His recent publications include: "Symmetrical erosive peripheral polyarthritis in the Late Archaic period of Alabama" (with Turner KR and DeLuca MA), *Science*, 1988; "Spondyloarthropathy in gorillas" (with Woods RJ), *Semin. Arthritis Rheum.*, 1989; "Rheumatoid arthritis "in the buff:" Erosive arthritis in representative defleshed bones" (with Woods EJ and Ortel W), *Am. J. Phys. Anthropol.*, 1990; "Spondyloarthropathy: Erosive arthritis in representative defleshed bones" (with Woods EJ and Ortel W), *Am. J. Phys. Anthropol.*, 1991; "Arthritis in an early 20th Century geriatric population" (with Woods R), *Age*, 1991. He is a member of the American Association of Physical Anthropology, American College of Rheumatology, Society of Skeletal Radiology, Society of Vertebrate Paleontology, and Sigma Xi.

Christopher Ruff (Ph.D., University of Pennsylvania, 1981) is currently an Associate Professor in the Department of Cell Biology and Anatomy at Johns Hopkins University School of Medicine. He specializes in musculoskeletal biomechanics, comparative primate functional anatomy, hominid evolution, North American prehistory, and the biology of skeletal aging. His publications include: "Sexual dimorphism in human lower limb bone structure: Relationship to subsistence strategy and sexual division of labor," *J. Hum. Evol.*, 1987; "New approaches to structural evolution of limb bones in primates," *Folia Primatol.*, 1989; "Postcranial biomechanical adaptations to subsistence changes on the Georgia coast" (with Larsen CS), *Anth. Pap. Am. Mus. Nat. Hist.*, 1990; *Aging and Osteoporosis in Native Americans From Pecos Pueblo, New Mexico: Behavioral and Biomechanical Effects*, New York: Garland Press. He is a member of the American Association of Physical Anthropologists, the American Anthropological Association, the American Association for the Advancement of Science, the Orthopaedic Research Society, and the Maryland State Anatomy Board (vice chairman), and is an Associate Editor for the *American Journal of Physical Anthropology*.

Mary K. Sandford (Ph.D., University of Colorado, 1984) is currently an Assistant Professor of anthropology at the University of North Carolina at Greensboro. Specializing in paleopathology, skeletal biology, and chemical analyses of archaeological bone and hair, she is the editor of the volume *Investigations of Ancient Human Tissue: Chemical Analysis in Anthropology*, Gordon and Breach, Science Publishers, in press. Her dissertation research, funded by a National Science Foundation dissertation improvement grant, is one of only few studies in which elemental analyses have been performed on hair samples taken from an archaeological population. Her publications in the area of trace element analysis include: "Elemental hair analysis: New evidence on the etiology of Cribra Orbitalia in Sudanese nubia" (with Van Gerven DP and Meglen RR), *Hum. Biol.*, 1983; and "Element analysis of human bone from Carthage: A pilot study" (with Repke DB and Earle AL), in JH Humphrey (ed): *The Circus and a Byzantine Cemetery at Carthage*, University of Michigan Press, 1988. She is a member of the American Association of Physical Anthropologists, the American Anthropological Association, the Paleopathology Association, the New York Academy of Sciences, and Sigma Xi.

Shelley R. Saunders (Ph.D., University of Toronto, 1977) is currently an Associate Professor in the Department of Anthropology, McMaster University, Hamilton, Ontario. She specializes in physical anthropology, human skeletal biology, and evolutionary theory. She has worked on human skeletal remains from eastern North America, Alaska and the Aleutian Islands, southwest France, and Egypt. Her publications include: "Can revisionism in evolutionary biology help in formulating hypotheses about hominid evolution?" *Hum. Evol.*, in press; "Nonmetric skeletal variation," in MY Iscan and KAR Kennedy (eds): *Reconstruction of Life From the Skeleton*, Alan R. Liss, Inc., 1989; "Transformation and disease: Precontact Ontario Iroquoians" (with Ramsden P and Herring A), in: *Disease and Contact*, Smithsonian Institution, in press; "Subadult mortality and skeletal indicators of health in Late Woodland Ontario Iroquoians" (with Melbye FJ), *Can. J. Archaeol.*,

1990; "The inheritance of acquired characteristics: A concept that will not die," in LR Godfrey (ed): *What Darwin Began,* Alley & Bacon, 1985. In cooperation with Dr. M.A. Katzenberg, she is a recipient of a grant from the Social Sciences and Humanities Research Council of Canada to study bone chemistry and histomorphometry in early European settlers of Canada as well as further detailed studies of skeletal representativeness from the St. Thomas Church Cemetery in Belleville, Ontario. Among other associations, she is a member of the Canadian Association for Physical Anthropology, the American Association of Physical Anthropologists, the Human Biology Council, and the Canadian Association of Forensic Sciences.

Willem Schaafsma (Ph.D. University of Groningen, 1966) is professor of mathematical statistics at Groningen University. He works on the foundations of his science by cooperating with and learning from research workers in various fields (e.g. physical anthropology). Recent interests are indicated by the title "Standard Errors of Posterior Probabilities and How to Use Them" of a paper in PR Krishnaiah (ed): *Multivariate Analysis VI,* 1985. He is a member of the ISI, IMS, and Bernoulli Society.

Mark Skinner (Ph.D., University of Cambridge, 1978) is an Associate Professor in the Department of Archaeology at Simon Fraser University, Vancouver, British Columbia. He specializes in paleoanthropology and forensic anthropology. His publications include: "Individualization and enamel histology: Case report in forensic anthropology" (with Anderson GS), *J. Forensic Sci.,* 1991; "Cranial asymmetry and muscular torticollis in prehistoric Northwest Coast natives from British Columbia, Canada" (with Barkley J and Carlson RL), *J. Paleopathol.,* 1989; "Social and biological correlates of localized enamel hypoplasia of the human deciduous canine tooth" (with Hung JTW), *Am. J. Phys. Anthropol.,* 1989; Enamel hypoplasia in sympatric chimpanzee and gorilla," *Hum. Evol.,* 1986; and *Atlas of Radiographs of Early Man* (Editor, with GH Sperber), Alan R. Liss, 1982. Dr. Skinner is an Associate Editor of the American Journal of Physical Anthropology and a Diplomate of the American Board of Forensic Anthropology.

Sam D. Stout (Ph.D., Washington University, St. Louis, 1975) is currently a Professor of Anthropology at the University of Missouri, Columbia. Specializing in skeletal biology, bone histomorphometry, and forensic anthropology, he was a member of the scientific team commissioned by the government of Peru to authenticate the remains of Francisco Pizarro. His publications include: "Percent osteonal bone vs osteon counts: The variable of choice for estimating age at death" (with Stanley SC), *Am. J. Phys. Anthropol.,* 1991; "Bone fragments a body can make" (with Ross L), *J. Forensic Sci.,* 1991; "A unique case of congenital bilateral absence of parietal bones in an infant" (with Dunn R), *J. Forensic Sci.,* 1991; "Histomorphometric analysis of human skeletal remains," MY Iscan and KAR Kennedy (eds): *Reconstruction of Life From the Skeleton,* New York: Alan R. Liss, 1989. Dr. Stout is a member of the American Association of Physical Anthropologists, the American Academy of Forensic Sciences, and the American Association for the Advancement of Science.

Gerrit N. van Vark (Ph.D., University of Groningen, 1970) is currently Professor of anatomy and embryology at the University of Groningen. His research specializations are human evolution, development and application of multivariate statistical and data-analytic methods for human skeletal research. His recent publications include: "The investigation of human cremated skeletal material by multivariate statistical methods: I. Methodology," *Ossa,* 1974; "New discrimination and classification techniques in anthropological practice" (with van der Sman PGM), *Z. Morophol. Anthropol.,* 1982; *Multivariate Statistical Methods in Physical Anthropology,* (with Howells WW, editor), Reidel, 1984; "A further study of the morphological affinities of the Border Cave 1 cranium, with special reference to the origin of modern man" (with Bilsborough A and Dijkema J), *Bull. Soc. Roy. Belge Anthropol. Prehist.,* 1989; He is President of the Dutch Society of Physical Anthropologists and Editor of *Ossa,* International Journal of Skeletal Research.

Preface

Shelley R. Saunders and M. Anne Katzenberg, *Editors*

The Martian troops, moreover, had no control over where their ships were to land. Their ships were controlled by fully automatic pilot-navigators, and these electronic devices were set by technicians on Mars so as to make the ships land at particular points on Earth, regardless of how awful the military situation might be down there. The only controls available to those on board were two push-buttons on the center post of the cabin—one labeled on and one labeled off. The on button simply started a flight from Mars. The off button was connected to nothing. It was installed at the insistence of Martian mental-health experts, who said that human beings were always happier with machinery they thought they could turn off.—Kurt Vonnegut Jr.

Vonnegut, an anthropologist and writer, chose people's relationship with machines as a theme in many of his writings in the 1950s and 1960s in an increasingly mechanized North America. Machines were developed, in Vonnegut's world, to help the human condition but in the end they turned out to be cold and impersonal and they usually wrought destruction through some unintended twist in their programming. Writers of this time who satirized our relationship with technology appeal to us because so many people are intimidated by technology and see it as "other". The opposite situation is one in which the application of sophisticated technology to a simple question somehow elevates the importance of the answer. An example from the earlier history of physical anthropology is the tremendous emphasis placed on measurements of bones for determining past human diversity. Anthropometry was seen as more scientific than anthroposcopy, since it involved measuring devices and numbers. The many scientific inventions and advancements that have appeared in this century have often been misinterpreted as representing the advancement of science to the neglect of the truly important conceptual changes that have occurred along with the technological achievements. As has been expressed so aptly by Jacquard (1985),

the newest and most innovative concepts have been camouflaged by the plethora of technological successes, which often pass for science. . . . The most decisive scientific advances are those which give us the means of asking better questions. (p.9)

In physical anthropology, where there is a long tradition of working with machines, it may seem that researchers are driven by new technology. That is, the questions are designed so that some new technique can be used in the study of human evolution. Alternatively, perhaps researchers seek out and create, or modify, the new technology required to answer existing questions and this may, in turn, lead to new questions. We believe the second concept is more generally the rule. As with other sciences, physical anthropology advances through the formulation of new questions. There are many examples where the need to ask certain questions has generated the application or development of some new technological application. Advances in quantitative analysis are a good illustration: The desire to understand complex skeletal form and to deal with a large number of measurements and observations promoted appropriate modifications to existing quantitative techniques and the development of new ones. Paleoanthropologists have sought to improve methods of examining fossilized hominid bones, from gross visual examination, through X-ray analysis, to chemical, microscopic, and biomechanical analyses. CAT scanning simply provides one new option for understanding skeletal morphology.

In putting together this book, we hope to show how technological advances can be used to learn more about past peoples and it is one of our goals to do this in a way that is instructive rather than intimidating to the reader. It has become increasingly difficult for any single researcher to be familiar with the various methods used to reconstruct past peoples from bones and teeth. Yet many of the studies employing these methods ask the same questions, so it is essential to have the ability to evaluate results in a critical manner.

The biology of prehistoric peoples is studied in large part through analyses of hard tissues. Studies in human osteology and odontology can be recognized to have advanced rapidly with the development of new techniques in science and medicine such as computed axial tomography, scanning electron microscopy, stable isotope analysis by mass spectrometry and computer simulation. The background to new techniques, the theoretical basis for their use, and therefore the basic understanding of their application in physical anthropology are beyond the scope of most courses in human osteology and odontology. Yet students and professionals are faced with a growing literature in which these techniques are applied to the problems of interest to their research areas. The purpose of this volume is to provide a comprehensive collection of articles on recently developed analytical and methodological approaches to prehistoric hard tissue analysis. We have brought together the practical experience of fourteen scholars of human osteology and odontology. Each contributor was asked to provide the following with reference to their particular research area: a review of the literature, a description of analytical techniques that includes underlying assumptions and technical difficulties, prevailing theoretical views, the impact of methodological advancements on the development of the theories, and predictions of the directions of future research.

Our two main goals are (1) to provide adequate background information to allow advanced students and professionals in physical anthropology and archaeology to critically evaluate studies employing newer techniques, and (2) to provide basic information for individuals beginning their own research programs in the areas discussed herein.

There are several themes that become manifest through the writings of the various authors. For example, there is the contrast between experimentation and application of techniques di-

rectly to skeletal samples. Several of the topics discussed, including enamel hypoplasia, growth and development, and bone chemistry, show a trend towards designing studies on the living in order to aid in the interpretation of studies of past peoples. Another overriding theme is that of preservation of skeletal remains. Studies of diagenesis, or changes that occur in the burial environment, have become important to almost every area of study of skeletal remains. Preservation of the bones of infants and children, of histological structures, of biogenic chemical composition, and of DNA are essential to the application of various methods of analysis. Since postdepositional processes act at all of these levels of study, it is crucial to our interpretations of results to understand how they work, and how they alter bones and teeth.

Finally, there are the two different approaches to material analysis of morphology, visual versus metric. The two are contrasted in the chapter on quantitative analysis. Van Vark and Schaafsma criticize nonquantitative analysis of visual data but point out that there are methods for carefully evaluating the variability and manifestation of both continuous, ordinal, and dichotomous variables. On the other hand, Ruff uses the same comparison to introduce a third approach to examining skeletal remains, which he calls the functional approach. Here, the difference is that the analyses are seen to directly reflect functional activities.

We have organized the various approaches to studying human skeletal and dental remains into four areas: morphological analyses, chemical analyses, evidence of health and disease, and population studies and quantitative methods. There are four chapters that cover morphological analyses. Saunders reviews the analysis of immature human bones for the purpose of studying the processes of growth and development in prehistory and evaluating health status. She discusses the potential for determining sex from subadult bones and improvements to methods of estimating age at death. These methodological efforts are crucial to meaningful analyses of the growth and health status of past populations. She stresses that one aspect of studying mortality samples that we must come to understand better is the nature of mortality bias or the extent to which subadult mortality samples are skeletally different from those who would have survived to adulthood.

The second chapter, by Stout, focuses on histological methods for determining age at death using bone microstructure. He summarizes and critically evaluates the various regression equations that have been devised for estimated adult age at death from cortical bone thin sections. There is a firm recognition that pathological alterations to the process of bone remodeling, which is the process that is being evaluated by the technique of microstructure counting, can compromise estimates of age at death. However, Stout also points out that improvements to histological age estimations come with some control over intrabone variability in remodeling. If workers study several entire cross sections from different bones, they improve their chances for achieving more accurate age estimates.

Ruff covers the subject of biomechanical analyses of bone with a focus on the application of the engineering beam model and the use of computerized tomography as a nondestructive means of characterizing the geometric properties of long bones. By taking cross sections perpendicular to the long axis of the beam (bone) various geometric properties can be determined from the amount and distribution of bone in the sections. This approach can be applied to growth, development, genetic variation, and occupational stress. Ruff emphasizes that technological advances have allowed for the faster collection of data and larger-scale demographic and comparative studies, meaning that the interesting kinds of questions that can be asked include investigations of transitions in subsistence strategy and general long-term trends in human behavior.

Mayhall presents new techniques in dental anthropology including photographic techniques for quantitative analyses of tooth size and tooth surfaces, advances in sex determination using the teeth, improved means of studying dental morphological variation and the impact of oral pathology on dental morphological analyses. He points out that the relatively simple technique of collecting dental stone models is still extremely useful for obtaining copies of dentitions from past groups and that these accurate models can be used in conjunction with the newer, advanced techniques to expand upon our questions about human biological variation and evolution.

The second area includes two chapters on bone chemical analysis. Sandford discusses the development of trace element analysis for paleodiet reconstruction with attention to the problems of postmortem alteration in buried bone. She focuses on the recent trend toward experimentation in trace element studies wherein the nature of chemical exchange under varying conditions is explored in the hopes that biogenic composition of bone can be distinguished from diagenetic changes. Explanations of the various analytical techniques used to study trace element composition are provided, including atomic absorption, X-ray fluorescence, neutron activation and inductively coupled plasma emission spectrometry.

Katzenberg covers the development of stable isotope analysis in paleodiet reconstruction. The principals that are applied in using carbon isotopes to distinguish plant use, carbon and nitrogen isotopes to distinguish marine from terrestrial diets, and nitrogen isotopes for distinguishing protein source are discussed. Basic information on instrumentation and isolation of bone protein is provided. New applications of isotope data are presented, including identification of residence patterns and, possibly, age at weaning.

Chapters on prehistoric health and disease include those on bone chemistry, bone physiology, and the development of the science of paleopathology. Klepinger takes bone chemical analysis beyond paleodiet reconstruction to explore applications in paleopathology. In conjunction with histological techniques, bone chemistry may be used to determine protein intake and diseases related to protein overload or deficiency. She emphasizes that the new technologies are not, in themselves, the guidebooks to the past but that the interpretations that the anthropological researchers make of these data are crucial.

Rothschild, in a chapter on paleopathological diagnosis, discusses newer techniques for studying pathology in dry bone, such as radioabsorption, computed axial tomography, and magnetic resonance imaging. Microscope techniques such as scanning electron microscopy in conjunction with the electron probe can also aid in diagnoses of pathological conditions. He also presents an informative discussion of efforts to identify and characterize DNA from ancient bone and tissue samples. One particularly noteworthy technique that he discusses is an immunological method of analyzing antibodies in prehistoric bone. This method can potentially detect specific diseases such as treponemal infection and possibly tuberculosis. Rothschild is optimistic about the potential for diagnosing diseases in paleopathology, but he cautions that researchers need a strong dose of common sense in developing their diagnoses. They must also be aware of the epidemiological consequences of the invasion and spread of infection by disease organisms.

Skinner and Goodman address the topic of enamel hypoplasia and what this indicator of growth disturbance can reveal about past growth, health, and disease. They provide detailed information on the formation of teeth, specifically enamel, and they contrast microscopic and grossly observable enamel defects with reference to the timing of growth disturbances. They caution against estimating specific ages for growth disruption, since there is a lag between enamel matrix formation and mineralization.

The fourth area deals with the management of data obtained from techniques for determining morphology, age at death, sex, diet and pathology. Roth addresses the study of prehistoric population dynamics as a specialized subfield of demography with emphasis on the application of demographic models developed on well-documented contemporary populations. The use of demographic models of fertility and mortality and the application of computer simulations are explained. Roth sees anthropological demography as a major link between demography and paleodemography, and he finds paleodemography to be a stronger field today as a result of the criticisms launched against it in the recent past and the research that addresses those criticisms.

Jackes discusses paleodemography from the perspective of the skeletal data, specifically techniques for the determination of adult age at death and excavation techniques that may bias a sample. She details explicitly the methodological problems of morphological estimation of adult age at death and points out that one of the most basic problems that hampers the application of various techniques, morphological and histological, is the degree of preservation of skeletal and dental remains. In fact, she is pessimistic about many of the developed

methods, perhaps more so than other researchers may wish to be. However, she notes that there is some potential for developing a more complex system of adult age estimation from a combination of dental wear and dental measurement that would be particularly applicable to fragmentary samples. She is also strongly critical of paleodemographic applications of age estimation data but offers one hopeful solution, which is the use of childhood mortality data alone as an indicator of population dynamics.

Van Vark and Schaafsma cover the subject of quantitative analysis of bone measurement data. They argue for the development and use of multivariate statistical methods designed specifically for anthropological problems. Their chapter introduces the two different uses of the term *population*, a biological definition and a statistical one. They point out that a statistical population generally characterizes individuals living in a certain area at a certain time as opposed to one defined as a biological population, a term that is more restrictive in attempting to characterize interbreeding groups. Consequently, there has been an attempt to maintain some continuity throughout all of the chapters with respect to the use of the terms *population* and *sample*. Van Vark and Schaafsma's chapter is of particular value in that they discuss common errors and assumptions that are made in current quantitative analyses. They also propose several innovative ways of dealing with incomplete samples and of more accurately estimating sex from large samples. Finally, they propose some useful quantitative approaches to combined analyses of metric and nonmetric skeletal variables.

It is our hope that the chapters presented herein will provide students and professionals with an understanding of some of the currently employed advanced techniques in osteology and odontology so that they may better follow the work of their colleagues, and formulate new questions that will ultimately extend our knowledge of past populations.

REFERENCES

Jacquard, A (1985): "Endangered by Science?" New York: Columbia University Press.

Vonnegut, Kurt Jr (1959) "The Sirens of Titan." New York: Dell Publishing Co, p 167.

Acknowledgments

We would like to acknowledge the hard work, patience, and cooperation of the contributors to this volume. Thanks also to our students, past, present, and future, who we hope will benefit from these efforts. The students in the graduate seminars, Advanced Osteology at the University of Calgary and Advanced Skeletal Biology at McMaster University read most of the chapters and provided helpful comments and suggestions.

Shelley R. Saunders
M. Anne Katzenberg

Skeletal Biology of Past Peoples: Research Methods
pages 1–20 © 1992 Wiley-Liss, Inc.

Chapter 1

Subadult Skeletons and Growth Related Studies

Shelley R. Saunders

Department of Anthropology, McMaster University, Hamilton, Ontario, Canada L8S 4L9

INTRODUCTION

In 1968, Johnston was justified in claiming that physical anthropologists studying the skeletal biology of earlier human populations concentrated upon adults and almost completely excluded infants and children from their research (Johnston, 1968). This neglect was all the more surprising since typical mortality curves for nonindustrial and pre–nineteenth–century groups graphically portrayed the precariousness of the growth period with its great nutritional requirements and susceptibility to disease. However, since the 1960s, and in large part influenced by Johnston's early efforts (Johnston, 1961, 1962, 1969) on the Indian Knoll skeletal sample from Kentucky, there have been a number of attempts to redress the oversight and look for prehistoric population differences in child growth and development.

In addition, the assessment of general population health has become a fundamental part of the interpretation of the lifeways of extinct or past populations, which was accompanied by a shifting focus on multiple rather than single indicators of physiological stress (Mensforth et al, 1978; Buikstra and Cook, 1980; Goodman et al., 1988). There is a general confidence that it is now possible to test hypotheses and assess the relationship between a population and its environment from the study of cemetery skeletal remains (Johnston and Zimmer, 1989). But the question remains, Is this confidence justified?

This chapter examines in some detail the practical problems of characterizing immature individuals from archaeological skeletal samples and whether these problems are surmountable. It examines questions of sampling, the determination of sex, and methods of estimating age. The remainder of the chapter focuses on the assessment of growth and development using population comparisons, studies of growth rates, and the influence of environmental factors on growth. It is made clear that there are certain theoretical difficulties that cannot be overcome. Since this is so, what is possible? The chapter concludes with recommendations for future research.

SAMPLING

First and foremost in any study of skeletal samples is the question of bone preservation. It is widely believed that infants' and childrens' bones, because they are small and fragile, will not preserve as well as adult bones and therefore will be lost to the excavator (Johnston and Zimmer, 1989). Certainly, it is known that the bones of young individuals are relatively less dense, having higher organic and lower mineral content, which makes them more susceptible to decay (Currey and Butler, 1975; Specker et al., 1987). Gordon and Buikstra (1981) found soil pH to be significantly correlated with bone preservation in children's skeletons although pH alone explained only 23% of the preservational variation. Nevertheless, the steeper slope and larger intercept of the regression equation for immature bones suggested to these authors that preservation declines more rapidly with decreasing pH in juvenile bones than adult bones.

But other factors might be more important to intracemetery bone preservation. Sundick (1978) argues that even the smallest of the epiphyses and the most fragile of the flat bones of the vault of the skull or the scapula of the subadult skeleton can be as well preserved as the bones of the robust adult skeleton. He attributes any incompleteness to the deficiencies of skill of the excavators and a limited abllility to recognize subadult bones.

Waldron (1987) has examined adult skeletal remains from a Romano-British site and found a reasonably consistent relationship between bone size and survival as well as some evidence that anatomical position may influence bone survival. The bones least well represented in his study included the phalanges of the hands and feet, the carpals, the coccyx, and the smaller tarsal bones. There was also an underrepresentation of bones occupying an anterior position (i.e., sternum, pubic bone, and patella) in these extended, prone burials. What seems relevant to skeletal analyses is the degree of preservation of important age– and sex–determining criteria in subadult in comparison with adult skeletons. In intracemetery comparisons, are infants and juveniles always less likely to be found and are identification criteria of subadult skeletons really less well preserved than for adult skeletons?

As a test of these questions, an examination of the degree of preservation of subadult bones compared with adult bones was carried out on a historic nineteenth century cemetery skeletal sample. In 1989, archaeologists excavated 597 skeletons of individuals buried in the St. Thomas Anglican Church cemetery in Belleville, Ontario (McKillop et al., 1989; Saunders and Herring, 1991). The cemetery was used during the period 1821–1874 and the 1989 excavation recovered 40% of total interments. The general conditions of bone preservation were considered excellent; all excavated individuals had been buried in wooden coffins and intracemetery soil variability was minimal (neutral pH).

It was possible to compare the proportions of excavated skeletons in this study with known interments because all burials in the cemetery had been recorded by successive church rectors. The burial records were checked for completeness by means of a standard demographic protocol (Drake, 1974) and it was evident from the inscriptions that the few individuals buried elsewhere could be distinguished in the records. Figure 1 shows that the estimated proportions of subadults to adults in the (smaller) skeletal sample matched very closely with the known proportions tallied from the burial records. In addition, Table 1 shows that, in fact, a similar or even better proportion of the subadults (individuals aged under 16 years although most are under 6 years) preserved usable age indicators. Ninety-eight percent of subadult skeletons preserved either dental, diaphyseal, or both indicators sufficient for age estimation. This suggests that factors such as *differential burial practices* and *inexperience on the part of excavators* can prove more important to subadult skeletal preservation than differential tissue survival.

There is considerable evidence for differential burial practices that will frequently bias against infants and children or alter the proportions of subadult and adult skeletons from a cemetery. The practice of infanticide has been and still is widespread and relatively common among many human cultures (Scrimshaw, 1984). Both the deliberate killing of babies and "passive infanticide" in the form of neglect or by increasing the risks to infant survival decrease the likelihood that a deceased infant will receive formal cemetery burial. In addition, the definition of life after birth is usually dependent upon a cultural definition of when life begins. Some groups acknowledge infant life several days after birth, while others do not consider children fully human for several years (Scrimshaw, 1984)

Infants are frequently buried far away from cemeteries, in house floors, entryways or in other contexts. *Taran* is a well–known term in Gaelic that refers to the ghosts of unbaptized babies who were usually buried outside of normal cemeteries. The burial practices of prehistoric Iroquoians of southern Ontario are another illustration. Ethnohistoric sources refer to the burial of infants along pathways so that

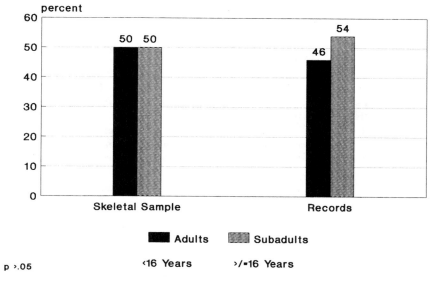

Fig. 1. A comparison of the proportions of adults and nonadults (or subadults) for the skeletal sample and for the parish burial records of St. Thomas' Anglican Church, Belleville.

TABLE 1. Frequency of Usable Preserved Age Estimation Indicators for Subadult Skeletons and Adult Skeletons From the St. Thomas' Anglican Church Sample

Age	Frequency	Percentage
Subadults		
Dental and/or Diaphyseal data	275/281	97.9
Dental calcification data	240/281	85.4
Diaphyseal data	242/281	86.1
No information for age	6/281	2.1
Adults		
Auricular surface data	238/278	85.6
Pubic symphysis data	171/278	61.5
Intact cranium (analyzable)	232/278	83.5
Postcranial measurements	255/278	91.7

their souls might reenter the womb of a woman passing by (Thwaites, 1896–1901). Modern excavations of Iroquoian village sites have uncovered high proportions of newborn infants buried in longhouse floors (Saunders and Spence, 1986), and it appears that the choice of the central corridor of the longhouse often represented the "path" along which an appropriate woman might walk (Saunders and Fitzgerald, 1988).

While it might be widely accepted, then, that infants will be underrepresented in skeletal samples (the term *infant* refers to individuals under 1 year of age), there is a broad but mistaken assumption that mortality rates will be highest at birth and slowly decline thereafter so that we should expect mostly newborn deaths in any mortality sample. Demographers normally divide infant death rates into several categories:

1. Neonatal mortality rate: the number of deaths in the first 4 weeks per 1,000 *live* births.

2. Postneonatal mortality rate: The number of deaths between the end of the fourth week and the end of the first year per 1,000 *live* births.

3. Stillbirths (or late fetal mortality rate): Number of infants born dead after the 28th week of pregnancy per 1,000 *total births*.

Postneonatal mortality exceeded neonatal mortality in industrialized countries up until the 1930s (Forfar and Arneil, 1978). In many developing countries this situation still applies and might be extrapolated to prehistoric societies. Postneonatal mortality is largely caused by environmental factors such as poor sanitation and poor nutrition, whereas neonatal mortality is largely due to physiological and organic weaknesses of infants. However, when stillbirth mortality is added to neonatal mortality (the total is called perinatal mortality), the rates almost always exceed those of postneonatal mortality. Theoretically, in an unbiased skeletal sample of infants it should be possible, with good age estimation techniques, to separate these classes of mortality to determine their relative frequency. On the other hand, if the excavator recovers relatively larger proportions of neonatal deaths compared to the rest of the infants then there is some justification for arguing that this is further evidence of biased mortuary practices (Saunders and Spence, 1986).

SEX DETERMINATION

One overarching problem presents itself with the study of subadult skeletons: The apparent inability to determine sex (Workshop of European Anthropologists, 1980). Determination of sex has a bearing on determination of age because of sex variability in growth. The fact that females grow at different rates than males influences age estimation and makes age estimates for subadults broader than they might be.

The differentiation between the sexes is in large part determined by the testes, because if cells are not masculinized by the presence of androgen, they develop along ovarian lines (Stini, 1985). This is illustrated by the fact that fetal testosterone is present by the 10th week, peaks around the time of major sexual differentiation, and decreases again until just before puberty (Weaver, 1980). Multiple loci have been implicated in the ultimate genetic control of sex differentiation. Endocrine function then contributes to producing human sexual dimorphism. Before the onset of puberty, male infants and children are, on the average, larger than females for such features as head-for-weight index (Ounsted et al., 1981), bone thickness, and bone density (Mazess and Cameron, 1972; Specker et al., 1987). But, in addition, from the 20th week of life in utero the female fetus is approximately 10% more mature than the male and this will persist until the attainment of full maturity (Stini,1985). This difference in maturation rate is presumably influenced by a different complex of factors.

Because of the sex difference in maturation, the sex of subadolescent human skeletons might be inferred by comparing dental development with postcranial development in the same individual, since males mature more slowly skeletally than females, while their rates of dental calcification are more similar (Hunt and Gleiser, 1955). The procedure is to estimate age independently from dental and skeletal remains, applying both male and female standards. If the dental and skeletal age estimates from male standards are closer to one another than those found for female standards, then the unknown individual would be male. A test of this method using dental and skeletal radiographs from living children obtained accuracy levels of 73%–81% (Hunt and Gleiser, 1955). However, skeletal ages were based on carpal bone maturation, a method that cannot be applied readily to excavated skeletons. While Sundick (1977) achieved apparent success by applying this method to skeletons of individuals over 12 years and confirming sex by pelvic morphology and estimating skeletal age from diaphyseal lengths, it has apparently not been tested widely on skeletons of documented sex. There are other problems. The only standards for postnatal long–bone growth when the sexes are separated come from radiographs of healthy white North Americans and one small sample of American blacks (Kelly and Reynolds, 1947; Anderson and Green, 1948; Anderson et al., 1963; Ghantus, 1951; Maresh, 1955, 1970; Gindhart, 1973). In addition, any large discrepancy between estimated dental age and skeletal age based on diaphyseal lengths must contend with the additional effects of pathological stress which may significantly affect long bone growth.

Choi and Trotter (1970) used long bone weight and length ratios to produce a sex classification accuracy of 72% for fetal skeletons, but the use of bone weights makes this method presently inapplicable for exhumed bones. Furthermore, the classification accuracy is low; a minimum criterion for classification accuracy should be 50% better than chance or at least 75% (De Vito and Saunders, 1990).

Since the pelvis is the most sexually dimorphic part of the adult skeleton, it would make sense to look for dimorphism in the subadult pelvis; there is a long literature on this subject (Thomson, 1899; Reynolds, 1945, 1947; Boucher, 1955, 1957), with some demonstration of differences through radiographic study. Infant males are said to have longer ilia, ischia, and femoral necks and females to have longer pubic bones and greater sciatic notches. Weaver (1980) reevaluated some of the earlier metric methods, using a large fetal dry bone sample of known sex but found almost no significant sex differences for measurement indices. Schutowski (1987) has also used the raw data from hip and femur dimensions of fetuses and neonates gathered by Fasekas and Kósa (1978) to examine sex differences. Discriminant functions were derived from these measurements, but the maximum classification accuracy was only 70%.

Weaver (1980, 1986) has also proposed that subjectively recorded variation in the height of the iliac auricular surface is sex–dependent in fetal and infant skeletons. He tested this nonmetric trait (raised vs. non-raised) on the known sample he was studying and obtained a classification accuracy of 43%–75% for females and 73%–92% for males. Recently, a further attempt to test the reliability of the trait was conducted in an indirect fashion. Hunt (1990) compared the ratio of raised to nonraised auricular surfaces with a 1:1 expected sex distribution in a large sample of subadult ilia from several archaeological sites. Although biased burial practices and other epidemiological factors could alter an expected 1:1 infant sex ratio in archaeological samples, Hunt found severely unrealistic sex ratios including an age-related shift from 6:1 raised/nonraised auricular surface ratio in newborns (where females would then be strongly predominant) to a 1:4 ratio in young adolescents. This test suggests that auricular surface morphology is related to aspects of shape and morphology in pelvic growth and not sex.

The fact that significant sexual dimorphism occurs in the permanent dentition has prompted the claim that, for children, the teeth might represent the only factor useful for sex diagnosis (Workshop of European Anthropologists, 1980). But the magnitudes of dimorphism are small (2%–6%) (see Mayhall, Chapter 4, this volume for more on this subject) and most data come from permanent teeth which are not applicable to the large samples of young infants coming from archaeological sites. Several studies have determined that a small but significant dimorphism does exist in the deciduous dentition but only two studies have employed classificatory procedures for separating the sexes. One of these (Black, 1978) concluded that the deciduous dentition displays much less dimorphism than the permanent dentition and that discriminant functions calculated from the diameters of deciduous teeth are much less accurate for sex classification. More recently, De Vito and Saunders (1990), using three to five measurements of deciduous teeth as well as combinations of deciduous and permanent measurements, produced discriminant functions in which 76%–90% of holdout samples were correctly classified by sex, which means that the level of classification accuracy of the deciduous teeth at least approaches the levels achieved by using the permanent teeth. However, the pattern and degree of sexual dimorphism reported for various groups shows considerable population variation. As is generally the case (with all kinds of studies), the discriminant functions derived from a Canadian group of children of mainly British origin can only be applied to similar groups (Table 2).

Recently, a test of these discriminant function equations was conducted with personally identified skeletons of children from two historic nineteenth century pioneer cemeteries in southern Ontario: the St. Thomas, Belleville Site and the Harvie Site (Saunders and Lazenby, 1991). The 15 individuals, born between 1850 and 1874, represented the offspring of English and Scottish immigrants to Upper Canada. This is comparable in ethnic constitution to the later twentieth century sample from which the functions were derived. The skeletons were identified on the basis of inscribed coffin plaques and reference to burial records in church archives. Of the seven females represented, six were correctly classified but of the eight males only three were correctly classified. This might suggest that the teeth of individuals from archaeological samples are smaller than the living Canadian reference sample and that males will more often be assessed as females. This is borne out most clearly in the small measurements of the canines of these individuals (Fig. 2). It further suggests that there may be a bias against size and/or maturity in the skeletal sample that is influenced by mortality bias.

At times hopes have been expressed for methods of chemical or elemental identifica-

TABLE 2. Discriminant Function Equations for Distinguishing Males From Females by Various Combinations of Deciduous and Permanent Tooth Dimensions[a,b,c]

Group/Equation

4 Maxillary and 1 Mandibular Variables

A   1.500 (FL R max li) + 1.091 (FL R max ci) + 0.654 (FL L max dm2) − 1.489 (FL L max c) + 1.640 (MD R mand c) − 20.342

B   1.380 (FL R max li) + 0.896 (FL R max ci) + 0.357 (FL L max dm2) − 1.474 (FL L max c) + 2.266 (MD R mand c) − 19.736

3 Maxillary and 1 Mandibular Variables

D   1.899 (FL R max li) + 1.174 (FL L max dm2) − 1.750 (FL L max c) + 1.653 (MD R mand c) − 20.138

4 Maxillary Variables

A   1.625 (FL R max li) + 1.239 (FL R max ci) + 1.135 (FL L max dm2) − 1.141 (FL L max c) − 18.564

B   1.690 (FL R max li) + 0.967 (FL R max ci) + 1.184 (FL L max dm2) − 1.097 (FL L max c) − 18.192

3 Maxillary Variables

D   2.084 (FL R max li) + 1.688 (FL L max dm2) − 1.353 (FL L max c) − 18.425

1 Mandibular Variable

A   3.079 (MD R mand c) − 18.861

B   3.051 (MD R mand c) − 18.699

D   3.000 (MD R mand c) − 18.407

4 Deciduous and 3 Permanent Maxillary and Mandibular Variables

C   0.542 (FL R max li) + 0.279 (FL L max dm2) − 0.723 (FL L max c) + 1.058 (MD R mand c) + 1.837 (FL L max M1) + 0.628 (MD L mand M1) − 1.692 (FL L mand M1) − 17.423

3 Deciduous and 1 Permanent Maxillary Variable

C   0.574 (FL R max li) + 0.393 (FL L max dm2) − 0.371 (FL L max c) + 1.521 (FL L max M1) − 21.314

1 Deciduous and 2 Permanent Mandibular Variables

C   2.049 (MD R mand c) + 0.887 (MD L mand M1) − 0.516 (FL L mand M1) − 16.872

[a]Reproduced from De Vito and Saunders (1990), with permission of the publisher.
[b]Abbreviations: FL, faciolingual; MD, mesiodistal; L, left; R, right; max, maxillary; mand, mandibular.
[c]Results above 0 are male and those above 0 are female.

tion of sex from the skeleton (Lengyel, 1968; Dennison, 1979; Beattie, 1982; Gibbs, 1985). However, to date, any sex differences in bone composition are dependent upon behavioral and postpubertal physiological differences. For example, some interest has been sparked in sex–dependent bone citrate concentrations. But these concentrations depend on the expectation that the monthly menstrual cycle in females beginning at puberty will discriminate against citrate in bone. Hence, the method would not be applicable to subadult bones. In fact, its applicability to adults has been convincingly rejected by recent research (Gibbs, 1991).

AGE ESTIMATION

Most critical, of course, to the identification of immature individuals from skeletal samples is age estimation. Estimations of subadult age at death can be considered more accurate than age estimations of adults because of the tele-

scoped time span of human growth relative to the total life–span over which age variability is assessed. But, of course, the present difficulties with determining sex in subadults increase the range of error.

Age estimation of the skeleton involves establishing physiological age (developmental changes in the tissues) and then attempting to correlate this with chronological age at death. Because of the difference between physiological and chronological age there are additional sources of error in age estimates. They include (1) random individual variation in maturation and (2) the systematic effects of environmental and genetic factors on growth.

Tooth emergence, a piercing of the gum or alveolar bone by the developing tooth, has been studied extensively and used widely in archaeological and forensic efforts to estimate age at death of unknown skeletons. However, many local factors can affect tooth emergence, for example, infection or premature extraction

Burlington Growth Sample
Mandibular Canine Mesiodistal Dimension

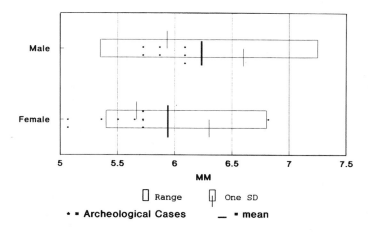

Fig. 2. Study of deciduous tooth size from the Burlington Growth Study (De Vito and Saunders, 1990). The archaeological cases of known individuals are plotted over the Burlington **sample** ranges.

of the deciduous predecessor (Demirjian, 1978; El-Nofely and İşcan, 1989). Consequently, dental calcification is a better measure of physiological maturity. Developing teeth show morphologically distinct stages of formation and mineralization that can be identified with radiography and histologically. Human biologists studying growth in living children started in the middle of this century to use dental formation or calcification rather than emergence as a maturity indicator. There are two major advantages to using dental calcification as an indicator of age in archaeological samples. First of all, dental calcification or formation is independent of skeletal maturity and most closely approximates chronological age (Garn et al., 1958; Lewis and Garn, 1960; Nolla, 1960; Moorrees et al., 1963a; Demirjian et al., 1973). In addition, the dental system is the only system that is uniformly applicable for estimating age from prenatal stages to late adolescence, because calcification is a continuous process (Demirjian, 1978).

It is important to ask then, what methods should be followed to record dental maturation and what standards exist for estimating chronological age from dental age. Since skeletal biologists studying archaeological samples

now seem to recognize that dental calcification is the preferred method for age estimation, it is important that careful methodologies be employed. Obtaining good radiographs of all subadult dentitions from cemetery samples should be common practice. Many researchers now have their own X-ray facilities and most have ready access to medical or dental X-ray services. Even small, portable X-ray units with independent power sources are becoming more widely available for those having to work in difficult field situations. Besides their value for comparing tooth calcification with existing standards, which are all based on X-rays, the films themselves serve as primary data sources for future, more complex analyses even when skeletons must be reburied.

At present, the limitations of the published standards for tooth calcification are that they are group-specific and mainly derived from samples of white North American and northern European children, although even these standards are relatively few (Moorrees et al., 1963a,b; Demirjian et al., 1973; Anderson et al., 1976; Haavikko, 1970; Nielsen and Ravn, 1976). There is very little information on blacks, Native Americans, Inuit, or other populations, although there are some recent efforts in this direction (Trodden, 1982; Loevy, 1983; Nichols et al., 1983; Harris and McKee, 1990).

Lovejoy and colleagues (1990) have attempted to numerically correct for population differences in chronological age estimation of a prehistoric native sample from Ohio by comparing data on gingival emergence for Euroamericans with data for Amerindians. The average absolute time of emergence is earlier in Amerindians and the discrepancy appears to increase with increasing age. Since the average discrepancy was calculated as 0.69 years at age 12, these authors applied a sliding scale of correction of 0.69/12 or 0.0575 years of delay per year to both deciduous and permanent tooth evaluations of developmental age using calcification. Though ingenious, some of their assumptions are in error. For one, dental emergence is not closely correlated with dental development and can be strongly affected by premature tooth loss, which is itself, exacerbated by high rates of dental pathology (Brauer and Bahador, 1942; Garn et al., 1960).

In fact, few skeletal biologists are aware of the pioneering efforts to examine dental calcification in North American native and Inuit children by Trodden (1982). Using cross-sectional radiographs, she studied all permanent teeth and did find the mean age for each calcification score to be younger in both Indian and Inuit samples compared with white populations, as well as some indication of an increase in the difference with increasing age. However, the average difference between native Americans and whites for tooth calcification was smaller than that calculated for tooth emergence (an overall average of 0.21 years or 0.0191 years of delay per year) with almost no difference between natives and whites for the permanent mandibular incisors and first premolar. In fact, any such estimates of difference should be treated with caution for the present, since they are strongly dependent upon sample size and may vary over the growth period (Nichols et al., 1983). A further problem is that the majority of the standards that exist are for permanent teeth only. Deciduous tooth formation standards are needed to estimate age for individuals from before birth to 4 years, an age period that is often heavily represented in skeletal samples. Only the studies by Moorrees et al. (1963a,b) combine data on deciduous and permanent teeth for the same sample: children in the Fels growth study from Ohio. An examination of the various studies illustrates certain methodological problems that warrant further investigation in and of themselves.

During tooth maturation a series of morphological stages are recognizable, beginning with actual formation of the tooth crypt and ending with closure of the apex of the fully formed root. Every tooth follows the same sequence but in order to study the process some system of mensuration is required. All researchers have chosen ordinal or ranked systems of observation but the numbers of tooth formation stages in the different systems have ranged from three to 20 (Table 3) (see Demirjian, 1978, for a detailed discussion of these systems). Difficulties with this type of observation include problems of definition of stages and subjectivity in identifying stages such as the difference between ¼ and ½ calcification of root length (Jackes, this volume, Chapter 11, also comments on interobserver error and recording calcification stages, but also see Saunders and MacKenzie-Ward, 1988). On the other hand, absolute or continuously measured lengths of developing teeth are inappropriate because of substantial individual variability in total tooth length. Demirjian and Goldstein (1976) have partially solved this problem by carefully defining eight stages of calcification by using X-ray pictures, diagrams and written criteria. However, these standards are naturally population–specific, because they come from a sample of French Canadian children, they apply to permanent teeth only (though the total age range examined might be 2–20 years), and they require a minimum of four different tooth types to assign a maturity score. The published systems of dental developmental aging have utilized several methods of reporting their results. Most commonly the average age of attainment for each mineralization stage along with standard deviations is given, for males and females separately. The values are usually reported in regular decimal scale, although growth researchers have shown that some statistical advantages are gained by log–transforming the values to avoid the effects of positive skewing (Tanner, 1962). The articles by Moorrees et al. (1963a,b) present ages of attainment graphically in the form of box and whisker

TABLE 3. Comparative Table of "Stages of Dental Formation" According to Different Authors[a]

	Fanning (1961)	Moorrees et al. (1963a)	Hunt and Gleiser (1955)	Nanda and Chawla (1966)	Nolla (1960)	Demirjian et al. (1973)	Garn et al. (1958)
Presence of crypt	1	—	—	—	1	—	—
Initial cusp formation	2	1	—	—	2	1(A)	1
Coalescence of cusps	3	2	1	—	—	—	—
Occlusal surface completed	4	3	2	1	—	2(B)	—
Crown ⅓	—	—	—	—	3	—	—
Crown ½	5	4	3	2	—	3(C)	—
Crown ⅔	6	—	4	—	4	—	—
Crown ¾	—	5	—	3	5	—	—
Crown formation completed	7	6	5	4	6	4(D)	—
Initial radicular formation	8	7	6	5(⅛)	—	—	2
Initial radicular bifurcation	8 A,B	8	—	—	—	—	—
Root ¼	9	9	7	6	—	5(E)	—
Root ⅓	10	—	8	7(⅜)	7	—	—
Root ½	11	10	9	8	—	—	—
Root ⅔	12	—	10	9(⅝)	8	6(F)	—
Root ¾	13	11	11	10	—	—	—
Root completed	14	12	12	11(⅞)	9	7(G)	—
Apex ½ closed	—	13	—	—	—	—	—
Apex closed[b]	15	14	13	12	10	8(H)	3

[a]Reproduced from Demirjian (1978), with permission of the publisher.
[b]Apex closure: ¼; ½; ¾.

plots, thereby forcing secondary calculations of average ages of attainment from the graphs, but these calculations are not easily derived (Fig. 3). Demirjian and Goldstein (1976) present their results in the form of dental maturity scores on percentile charts so that "dental age" is determined by finding the age at which the 50th centile equals the maturity score (Fig. 4). In any event, skeletal researchers are obliged to calculate mean age estimates along with total estimate ranges based on the sum of male and female values. There is also a bias effect from the reference samples that superimposes further variability on the age estimations of archaeological samples. Figure 5 illustrates that when different standards are used to calculate age for fetuses and newborns there will be tendencies to under– or over–estimate age (Saunders and Spence, 1986).

Age evaluation for the prenatal and perinatal periods is generally based on fewer standards produced from much smaller samples. Kraus

and Jordan (1965) produced standards for very early crown coalescence from a sample of 737 human fetuses examined between 1954 and 1963. These standards have been applied to archaeological specimens in several cases known to this author (Spence, 1986; Saunders and Spence, 1986). Deutsch and colleagues (1985) have also provided data on deciduous anterior tooth crown length measurements and weights from a sample of 50 anatomically normal fetuses and infants aged 0–46 weeks. Obviously, only the developing crown length standards can be used on archaeological samples (see Skinner and Goodman, this volume, Chapter 9, for a more complete discussion of the inadequacy of existing standards of tooth formation).

Physiological age of the immature skeleton, sans teeth, must be assessed from either the appearance and union of bony epiphyses or from bone size. It is well known that there is considerably more potential for variability in

Fig. 3. Illustration of the norms of tooth formation for deciduous canines and molars, demonstrating that numeric estimates of dental age must be extrapolated from the charts. Reproduced from Moorrees et al. (1963a), with permission of the publisher.

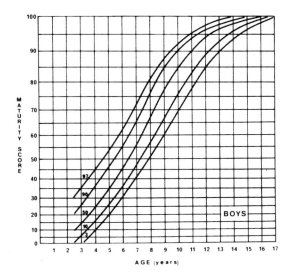

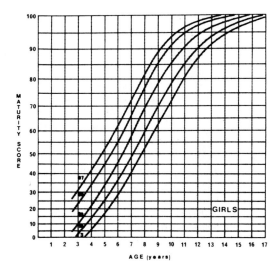

Fig. 4. Dental maturity percentiles given in tooth maturation scores based on four permanent teeth (M_2, M_1, PM_2, PM_1), illustrating that numeric dental age estimates must also be extrapolated from the charts. Reproduced from Demirjian and Goldstein (1976), with permission of the publisher.

skeletal age in comparison with dental age because of the stronger environmental influences on the developing long bones (Fig. 6) (Demirjian, 1978). Diaphyseal length measurements are the common sources of skeletal age estimates from before birth to midteens because long–bone epiphyses are assumed to be frequently lost at excavation. Even if they are recovered, trying to attach them to separate diaphyses would simply introduce more error into the measurements. This limits the bone size technique of skeletal age estimation to a shorter portion of the total growth period, approximately late fetal to 12 years.

Since epiphyseal appearance is not readily applicable to excavated skeletons because of recovery problems, epiphyseal union becomes the favored method in the midteens when the process of gradual union of the epiphyses begins. Ubelaker (1989) provides a thorough discussion of the various standards available for age estimation from epiphyseal union. Important points to bear in mind are that sex differences also exist in the timing and sequence of epiphyseal union, there is a failure of many published studies to report full ranges of variation for the timing of union of epiphyses, and there are methodological problems with observation of the process and duration of union. Several years can elapse between the beginning and final closure of an epiphysis (McKern and Stewart, 1957), so that various "stages" of union can be defined. However, others have shown that interobserver error increases with the number of ranked stages of union defined for any one epiphysis (Webb and Suchey, 1985). There are some studies that have proposed using specific examples of growth center appearance, size increase and early union for estimating skeletal age of infants and young children. These include the mandibular symphysis (Becker, 1986) the tympanic plate of the temporal (Weaver, 1979; Curran and Weaver, 1982), and development of the occipital bone (Redfield, 1970), but the age ranges appropriate to these criteria are relatively limited.

Diaphyseal length is often used as an estimate of skeletal age when calcifying teeth are missing. Growth studies using skeletal samples require both dental and skeletal data so that dental age may be treated as the closest approximation to chronological age while skele-

Estimated Ages of Burials
Three Age Methods, Same Sample

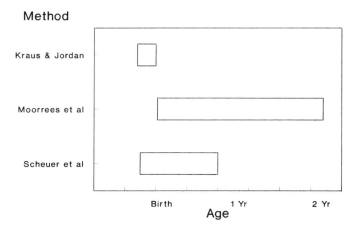

Fig. 5. Illustration of the ranges in estimated ages for the same sample of young infants, that result from using three different methods: Fetal dental development (Kraus and Jordan, 1965), postnatal dental development (Moorrees, et al., 1963a) and diaphyseal length (Scheuer et al., 1980).

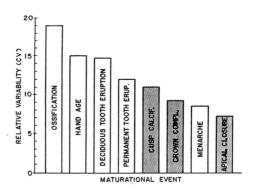

Fig. 6. Illustration of the relative amount of variability for various processes of maturation, demonstrating that dental calcification has very low variability compared with other criteria. Reproduced from Lewis and Garn (1960), with permission of the publisher.

tal age serves as a marker for alterations and defects of growth. Sources of diaphyseal length data include the radiographic samples mentioned above and dry bone measurements taken from archaeological samples (Johnston, 1962; Sundick, 1972; Armelagos et al., 1972; y'Edynak, 1976; Merchant and Ubelaker, 1977; Hoffman, 1979; Hummert, 1983a; Mensforth, 1985). The purpose of recording diaphyseal

measurements from archaeological samples by using dental development as an approximation of chronological age (true chronological age is unknown) is to try to account for population variation in bone size as well as to attempt assessments of population variation in growth. Ubelaker (1989b) has shown that the calculated age at death from femur diaphyses keyed to a number of different population standards varies widely. The total number of years within the range of estimates he calculated varies from 3.5 to 8.5 years and increases with increasing size of the bone. Consequently, it is important to choose skeletal age standards appropriate for the known or suspected population affiliation of the individual or sample because this will greatly increase accuracy.

There also exist specific bone size standards for estimating fetal and perinatal age (Olivier and Pineau, 1960; Fasekas and Kósa, 1978; Malinowski and Młodziejowski, 1978; Scheuer et al., 1980; Kósa, 1989).[1] Here again, population variation is a factor (Scheuer et al., 1980). Ubelaker has shown that there is a

---

1. Malinowski and Młodziejowski provide a useful review of previous studies of the size of limb bones of fetuses and infants.

considerable range of variation in fetal age estimations, exceeding one-half lunar month, when the Fazekas and Kósa regression equations are used. One other potential source of data for fetal and perinatal age estimation is fetal femur length measured by ultrasound (O'Brien and Queenan, 1981). An examination of mean ultrasound femur length at term is very close to mean length based on cadaver samples (Olivier and Pineau, 1960; Fasekas and Kósa, 1978).

Other Age Estimation Methods

While the dental and skeletal methods described above are the main means of estimating age, there is also the possibility of using histological methods with subadult bones. Several important studies of cortical bone histology have included assessments of infants and children (Amprino and Bairati, 1936; Jowsey, 1960; Kerley, 1965). Bone turnover in the growing skeleton is usually seen as too complex to be used in age estimation because of the superimposition of bone modeling over remodeling of cellular–based structures (see Stout, this volume, Chapter 2). Nevertheless, there may be some useful applications in the future (Saunders and DeVito, 1990).

One other possibility is the use of a modification of the method of functional dental wear developed by A.E.W. Miles (1962, 1963, 1978). The advantage of this method is that it is specifically tailored to each population to which it is applied. One begins with dental age estimates from calcification and eruption of preadult dentitions, which are then seriated from youngest to oldest. The degree of occlusal molar wear observed on permanent molars of age–estimated children and adolescents is then used to assign ages to the adults in a sample. The method is based on the premise that the first permanent molar will average six more years of wear than the second permanent molar, and so on. *Functional molar age* is then defined as the number of years for which the molar had been in use. Functional dental age estimates based on wear might be applied to older children and adolescents while deciduous tooth wear could also be examined as a check on dental age variability among individuals. Jackes (this volume, Chapter 11) indicates that wear assessments for

estimating age should be supplemented with dental measurements.

GROWTH STUDIES OF ARCHAEOLOGICAL SKELETAL SAMPLES

While he was one of the first to attempt to study growth from archaeological skeletal samples, Johnston (1962) was also the first to caution that these samples do not represent the normal, healthy children in the population who lived but those who died and became part of a biased, mortality sample. On the other hand, Lovejoy and colleagues (1990) have argued that most infant deaths among earlier groups were the result of not chronic but acute diseases, which should not drastically alter dental or osteological maturation. They claim as does Sundick (1978), that skeletal samples compare favorably with their counterparts who survived to adulthood. Other researchers are more conservative, arguing that deceased juveniles represent the minima rather than the modes of those who survived to adulthood (Buikstra and Cook, 1980). To some, differential selection at death and the heterogeneity of mortality samples is a given (Whittington, 1991). There is little in the way of an answer to this question at the moment. It presents a fertile area for further enquiry for interested researchers, but it also diminishes the validity of current intersample comparisons until more data are forthcoming.

One of the difficulties with the earliest growth-related studies is that chronological age was often estimated from combinations of dental and osseous criteria or from dental emergence alone (Johnston, 1962; Armelagos et al., 1972; Lallo, 1973; y'Edynak, 1976) (see Table 4). Some early researchers also attempted to separate male and female juveniles without any methodological justification. A turning point came with the use of dental development to estimate chronological age at death (Sundick, 1972; Merchant and Ubelaker, 1977). Nevertheless, because of constant efforts to "tinker" with age estimation methodologies, very few existing publications are comparable even if we ignore the problem of mortality bias. Yet there are several other notable methodological advancements including Cook's (1984) choice of examing only individuals under 6 years in a study of prehistoric Il-

TABLE 4. Various Studies of Growth-Related Features of Archaeological Skeletal Samples, Their Size, Age Range, and Method(s) Used to Estimate Age

Source	Sample	Size	Age range	Method
Johnston, 1962	Indian Knoll, Kentucky, Archaic Period, 3000 B.C.	165	Fetal–5.5 yrs	Dental erupt. & osseous
Mahler, 1968 (see Armelagos et al., 1972)	Nubians, Wadi Halfa, 350 B.C.–1350 A.D.	115	6 mos.–31 yrs.	Dental erupt. & osseous
Walker, 1969	Late Woodland, Illinois	43	nb–12 yrs.	Dental development
Sundick, 1972	Indian Knoll, Kentucky, Archaic Period, 3000 B.C.	128	nb–18 yrs.	Dental development
Lallo, 1973 (see Goodman et al., 1984)	Dickson Mounds, Woodland, Mississippian	557	nb–35 yrs.	Multiple
y'Edynak, 1976	Eskimo and Aleut	109	nb–20 yrs.	Dental erupt. & osseous
Merchant and Ubelaker, 1977	Mobridge Site, Arikara, 1700–1750 A.D.	193	nb–18.5 yrs.	Dental development
Sundick, 1978	Altenerding, W. Germany, 6–7th centuries A.D.	82	nb–18 yrs.	Dental development
Jantz and Owsley, 1984b	Arikara, seven samples	~500	n.b.–12 yrs.	Adjusted dental development
Hummert, 1983a	Kulubnarti, Nubia, early and late Christian 550–1450 A.D.	180	nb–16 yrs.	Dental development
Cook, 1984	Illinois Valley, Woodland and Mississippian	~244	nb–6 yrs.	Dental development
Mensforth, 1985	Libben Late Woodland and Bt-5 Archaic	85 45	nb–10 yrs.	Dental development
Saunders and Melbye, 1990	Late Ontario Iroquois, 1615 A.D.	147 146	n.b.–15 nrs.	Dental development
Lovejoy et al., 1990	Libben Site, Ohio, Late Woodland, 800–1100 A.D.	152	nb–12 yrs.	Dental development

linois populations and thereby minimize sampling problems. In addition, she also chose regression analysis to look at increments in femur length and the natural log of conception-corrected dental age in months to give a linear fit to the data. Her comparison of three temporal periods showed that the Late Woodland groups in Illinois differed from both earlier and later groups in having shorter femurs for dental age, or apparent growth retardation. Jantz and Owsley (1984a,b) also applied regression analysis to an examination of inter-sample long–bone size variation among South Dakota historic Arikara, as did Lovejoy and colleagues (1990) for data smoothing. They also normalized diaphyseal lengths by average adult long bone length.

Measures of diaphyseal length, when compared with estimated dental age in archaeolog-ical samples, are necessarily cross-sectional but have the superimposed problems of sex and age estimation. Longitudinal growth studies of living children, which follow a series of individuals continuously over substantial periods of time, can examine individual growth patterns, the timing of significant growth events, and the relative velocities of growth. Only longitudinal growth studies can adequately examine individual variability in growth rates and patterns. Many who have studied juvenile long bone size in archaeological samples persist in referring to their results as growth curves. It must be remembered that these are not true growth curves in the sense that they are used in living growth studies, either cross-sectional or longitudinal since, of course, the dimensions represent deceased individuals who never reached maturity. There have even been attempts to examine the relative increase in percentage diaphyseal size by dental age group as a means to plot "growth in velocity." Again, these are analyses of velocity changes in long bone size, not true velocity curves as growth researchers use them.

In consideration of the above limitations, studies of growth–related change in archaeological samples have been restricted to examining the adequacy of growth of children as an index of overall community health or the adaptation of the population to its environment (Johnston and Zimmer, 1989). No one has discovered any major differences in the direction or apparent pattern of skeletal size in the past. It could be argued that this means there have not been any major changes in human growth patterns over time, but such changes would have to be drastic to be detected in archaeological skeletal samples. Most or all skeletal samples of past groups appear shorter for age than modern groups. Might this represent genetic differences (see y'Edynak, 1976) or the effects of a harsh environment on the growth of disadvantaged children (Johnston and Zimmer, 1989)? Given what is known about the effects of the environment on the growth of the skeleton, we would expect that most cases represent environmental effects, that is, populations suffering from nutritional and disease-related stress.

There are several ways of assessing alterations to the growth process in skeletal samples. One can look for temporal changes that reflect changes in environmental quality within groups, or possibly changes in comparison with modern samples with adequate control of population factors (age estimation, etc.). As long as we know that population migration was minimal, rapid changes over relatively short time periods are easily attributable to environmental changes since genetic change takes place much more slowly. Several studies have identified temporal changes in growth-related bone size. Jantz and Owsley in their series of papers on the Arikara (Jantz and Owsley, 1984a,b; Owsley and Jantz, 1985) showed that the latest group (in the late eighteenth and early nineteenth centuries) experienced the lowest rates of diaphyseal increase in size, particularly in late childhood and in the perinatal group (late fetal/early neonatal) of the archae-

ological samples. This is attributed to undernutrition, introduction of epidemic diseases, depopulation and intertribal conflict, and especially stress effects on the mother that were later reflected in the perinatals. One might ask here how epidemic diseases would influence altered growth characteristics in the later samples, since most contact period epidemics were acute and not chronic.

It is also possible to look for an association between smaller individuals in specific growth periods and other skeletal indicators of bone pathology. Hummert and associates (Hummert and Van Gerven, 1983; Hummert, 1983a,b) have examined the relationship between diaphyseal lengths and cortical bone volume, Harris lines and histomorphology in two medieval period samples from Sudanese Nubia. They identified differences between the early and late samples. However, while increases in bone lengths appear to have been fairly well maintained, percentage cortical area revealed excessive endosteal resorption. This was attributed to nutrition–related stress. However, a later study of the geometric properties of these bones (Van Gerven et al., 1985; see also Ruff, this volume, Chapter 3) suggested that the reduction in percentage cortical area could just as easily be interpreted as a response to increased bending strength (developed as the children grew normally) and that there might not be any evidence of environmental stress on growth at all. On the other hand, there is definite evidence that bone growth in length will be maintained at the expense of growth in cortical thickness in the face of nutritional and disease stress (Himes, 1978; Huss-Ashmore, 1981). These kinds of comparisons require further study.

Several examinations of temporal and within–site variations in growth-related features have also been conducted by Mensforth (1985) and Lovejoy and colleagues (1990) on prehistoric sites in Kentucky and Ohio. Mensforth (1985) identified early long–bone growth retardation in the later Woodland Libben sample, specifically in the 6 month to 4 year age range and suggested high levels of infectious disease in the first years of life as the implicating factor. This was based on the identification of a high incidence of periosteal reactive bone in the subadults, indicating infection. Lovejoy and coworkers (1990) appear to have provided further documentation of this situation in their study of the normalized values for the Libben sample, compared with healthy Euroamerican children. Both studies note that there is evidence that the Libben people ate a nutritionally adequate diet. They attribute the elevated disease loads to higher population density and a greater degree of sedentism compared with seasonally mobile hunter–gatherers. While, generally speaking, this is true, this hypothesis is still in the realm of speculation. Concrete evidence for a strong relationship between the above–mentioned population factors and disease loads would be needed. To reiterate an earlier comment, at this stage none of the growth researchers can satisfactorily resolve the question of what proportion of the differences might also be attributed to mortality bias.

SUGGESTIONS FOR FUTURE RESEARCH
Sex Determination

Logic says that there should be sufficient dimorphism for sex separation in fetal and early infant skeletons because of the presence of high levels of testosterone. Dimorphism should increase again at adolescence as pubertal changes begin to occur. But the percentages of observed subadult skeletal dimorphism are believed to be low compared with levels observed in the adult pelvis. In Weaver's (1980) study of hip bones two indices, although they are not significantly different between the sexes but do fit expected patterns, showed percentage dimorphism ranging from 0.2% to 9.9%. Specker and colleagues (1987) in their analysis of bone mineral index in 5– 7–year–old children observed 17.7% dimorphism, which is surprisingly high. The ranges of percentage dimorphism for a variety of adult pelvic indices (Kelley, 1979; Schulter-Ellis, et al., 1983; MacLaughlin and Bruce, 1986) are between 10% and 26%, the highest levels deriving from Kelley's sciatic notch/acetabular index.

The teeth, because of their constancy of size after development, should be good indicators of subadult sexual dimorphism. However, the magnitude of tooth dimorphism is also fairly low, as indicated above. Here, dimorphism is attributed to protracted amelogenesis in the developing male tooth crowns, which results in

thicker enamel, a process that will also be affected by individual variability (Moss and Moss-Salentijn, 1977). There has been some success with sex discrimination by means of measurements of the permanent teeth (see Mayhall, this volume, Chapter 4) and more recently with combinations of permanent and deciduous teeth and even deciduous teeth alone (DeVito and Saunders, 1990). But population variation in both tooth size and dimorphism remain stumbling blocks to the application of discriminant functions derived from specific groups. It should also be pointed out that population differences in tooth size are independent of population differences in tooth size dimorphism, further complicating the issue (DeVito, 1989). Problems of tooth preservation and postmortem damage are less of an issue here. Interest in permanent tooth dimorphism as an indicator of sex was generated from a desire to characterize fragmentary samples where teeth are the best preserved or least destroyed elements. However, if deciduous tooth dimorphism could be used with some reliability, it would be applicable to teeth which are generally in better condition than permanent teeth, less affected by caries, wear and other trauma. Here, careful excavation is crucial since it is certainly possible to recover incompletely calcified tooth crowns still in their crypts.

It would help if future osteoarchaeological researchers could have access to large samples of subadult skeletons of known sex and age, be they accumulations of data from forensic cases (which are, fortunately, still rare) or, more likely, from identified individuals excavated from historically documented cemeteries. With such samples, there could be examinations of the sex–discriminating ability of combinations of dental and skeletal measurements and further studies of sex–related dental variation could be done on living samples that would serve as useful explorations of newer techniques of measurement (see Mayhall, this volume, Chapter 4) and the problem of mortality bias.

Age Estimation

There is still a need for further examination of dental development in a variety of population groups. In particular, we need information on deciduous tooth development gathered from living individuals. While there will not be much in the way of longitudinal tooth development data in future, since the widespread use of research X-rays has been curtailed, there is still the possibility of amassing large samples of cross-sectional data from clinical radiograph databases (Trodden, 1982). Yet archaeological samples themselves may be the best sources of data for devising and improving on methods of skeletal and even dental age estimation. No one has yet applied the Demirjian and Goldstein (1976) standards of dental calcification age estimation to archaeological skeletal samples, despite their methodological superiority (the Ubelaker, 1989a, chart is useful for generalized age estimation but not in the application of subadult skeletal samples in growth investigations).

Identified cases from historical archaeological sites can, again, act as a database for exploring deciduous crown and root development, dental wear as a subadult age estimation technique, and histological age changes in cortical and possibly even trabecular bone.

Growth Related Research

To continue to pursue growth related research on archaeological skeletal samples we need some solutions to the problems identified above. Pragmatically, the most useful research at present would be to utilize ranges established for population variation in growth and development in the kinds of living groups that are comparable to the archaeological samples we are studying. We will never be able to conduct longitudinal studies of growth in the past, but we can refine our cross-sectional comparisons between archaeological samples and modern group data.

Since there is little likelihood of examining the skeletons of willed bodies of subadults, occasional forensic cases of immature individuals serve as very important sources of data for improving our methods of identification. One other source that has considerable potential is the recovery of identified individuals from historical cemeteries with associated documentation. Stored databases of clinical radiographs might also prove useful in this regard.

This survey has been cautionary, but it is not pessimistic. There is considerable potential for the analysis of growth related phenomena in archaeological skeletal samples. Studies of historical samples, especially those with associated documentation, may allow us to test some of our assumptions about the nature of human mortality samples so that we can reach confident conclusions about prehistoric people.

ACKNOWLEDGMENTS

Work conducted on the St. Thomas', Belleville sample was carried out thanks to the research association provided by Dr. Heather McKillop and thanks to the permission for study provided by St. Thomas' Anglican Church. The skeletal research on the St. Thomas' sample has been supported by grants from the Ontario Heritage Foundation, the Bridge St. Foundation and the Arts Research Board, McMaster University. A special thanks is extended to Gerry Boyce and Ann Herring for their collaboration.

REFERENCES

Amprino J, Bairati EA (1936): Processi di reconstruzione e di riassorbimento nella sostansa compaata delle osa dell nomo. Richerche see cento soggetto della nascita sino a tarda eta. Z Zellforsch Mikrosk Anat 24:439–511.

Anderson DL, Thompson GW, Popovich F (1976): Age of attainment of mineralization stages of the permanent dentition. J Forensic Sci 21:191–200.

Anderson M, Green WT (1948): Lengths of the femur and the tibia. Am J Dis Child 75:279–290.

Anderson M, Messner MB, Green WT (1963): Distribution of lengths of the normal femur and tibia in children from one to eighteen years of age. J Bone Joint Surg 46A:1197–1202.

Armelagos GJ, Mielke JH, Owen KH, Van Gerven DP (1972): Bone growth and development in prehistoric populations from Sudanese Nubia. J Hum Evol 1:89–119.

Beattie O (1982): An assessment of X-ray energy spectroscopy and bone trace element analysis for the determination of sex from fragmentary human skeletons. Can J Anthropol 2:205–215.

Becker MJ (1986): Mandibular symphysis (medial suture) closure in modern Homo sapiens: Preliminary evidence from archaeological populations. Am J Phys Anthropol 69:499–501.

Black TK (1978): Sexual dimorphism in the tooth-crown diameters of the deciduous teeth. Am J Phys Anthropol 48:77–82.

Boucher BJ (1955): Sex differences in the foetal sciatic notch. J Forensic Med 2:51-54.

Boucher BJ (1957): Sex differences in the foetal pelvis. Am J Phys Anthropol n.s. 15:581–600.

Brauer JC, Bahador MA (1942): Variation in calcification and eruption of the deciduous and permanent teeth. J Am Dent Assoc 29:1373.

Buikstra JE, Cook DC (1980): Paleopathology: An American account. Annu Rev Anthropol 9:433–470.

Choi SC, Trotter M (1970): A statistical study of the multivariate structure and race–sex differences of American

White and Negro fetal skeletons. Am J Phys Anthropol 33:307–312.

Cook DC (1984): Subsistence and health in the Lower Illinois Valley: Osteological evidence. In Cohen MN, Armelagos GJ (eds): "Paleopathology at the Origins of Agriculture." Orlando, FL: Academic Press, pp 237–271.

Curran BK, Weaver DS (1982): The use of the coefficient of agreement and likelihood ratio test to examine the development of the tympanic plate using a known-age sample of fetal and infant skeletons. Am J Phys Anthropol 58:343–346.

Currey JD, Butler G (1975): The mechanical properties of bone tissue in children. J Bone and Joint Surg 57A:810–814.

Demirjian A (1978): Dentition. In Falkner F, Tanner JM (eds): "Human Growth, Vol 2: Postnatal Growth." New York: Plenum Press, pp 413–444.

Demirjian A, Goldstein H (1976): New systems for dental maturity based on seven and four teeth. Ann Hum Biol 3:411–421.

Demirjian A, Goldstein H, Tanner JM (1973): A new system of dental age assessment. Hum Biol 45:211–228.

Dennison J (1979) Citrate estimation as a means of determining the sex of human skeletal remains. Arch Phys Anthropol Oceania 14:136–143.

Deutsch D, Tam O, Stack MV (1985): Postnatal changes in size, morphology and weight of developing postnatal deciduous anterior teeth. Growth 49:202–217.

De Vito C (1989): Discriminant Function Analysis of Deciduous Teeth to Determine Sex. MA dissertation, McMaster University.

De Vito C, Saunders SR (1990): A discriminant function analysis of deciduous teeth to determine sex. J Forensic Sci 35:845–858.

Drake M (1974): "Historical Demography: Problems and Prospects." Milton Keynes, England: The Open University Press.

El-Nofely A, İşcan MY (1989): Assessment of age from the dentition in children. In İşcan MY (ed): "Age Markers in the Human Skeleton." Springfield, IL: Charles C Thomas, pp 237–254.

Fanning EA (1961): A longitudinal study of tooth formation and root resorption. NZ Dent J 57:202.

Fasekas IG, Kósa F (1978): "Forensic Fetal Osteology." Budapest: Akadémiai Kiadó.

Forfar JO, Arneil GC (1978): "Textbook of Pediatrics." Edinburgh: Churchill Livingstone.

Garn SM, Lewis AB, Koski PK, Polachek DL (1958): Variability of tooth formation. J Dent Res 38:135.

Garn SM, Lewis AB, Polachek DL (1960): Interrelations in dental development. 1. Interrelationships within the dentition. J Dent Res 39:1049.

Ghantus MK (1951): Growth of the shaft of the human radius and ulna during the first two years of life. Am J Roentgenol Radium Ther 65:784–786.

Gibbs LM (1985): Preliminary Report on the Use of Citrate Levels From Human Skeletal Remains as a Possible Determinant of Sex. Paper presented at the 13th Canadian Association for Physical Anthropology Meetings, Thunder Bay, Ontario.

Gibbs LM (1991): Citrate, Sex and Skeletal Remains. MA Thesis, McMaster University.

Gindhart PS (1973): Growth standards for the tibia and radius in children aged one month through eighteen years. Am J Phys Anthropol 39:41–48.

Goodman AH, Lallo J, Armelagos GJ, Rose JC (1984): Health changes at Dickson Mounds, Illinois (A.D. 950–1300). In Cohen MN, Armelagos GJ (eds): "Paleopathology at the Origins of Agriculture." Orlando, FL: Academic Press, pp 271–306.

Goodman AH, Thomas RB, Swedlund AC, Armelagos GJ (1988): Biocultural perspectives on stress in prehistoric, historical and contemporary population research. Yearb Phys Anthropol 31:169–202.

Gordon CC, Buikstra JE (1981): Soil pH, bone preservation, and sampling bias at mortuary sites. Am Antiq 48:566–571.

Haavikko K (1970): The formation and the alveolar and clinical eruption of the permanent teeth. Suomen Hammaslaak Toim 66:103–170.

Harris EF, McKee JH (1990): Tooth mineralization standards for Blacks and Whites from the Middle Southern United States. J Forensic Sci 35:859–872.

Himes JH (1978): Bone growth and development in protein-calorie malnutrition. World Rev Nutr Diet 28:143–187.

Hoffman JM (1979): Age estimations from diaphyseal lengths: two months to twelve years. J Forensic Sci 24:461–469.

Hummert JR (1983a): Childhood Growth and Morbidity in a Medieval Population from Kulubnarti in the Batn El Hajar of Sudanese Nubia. PhD Dissertation, University of Colorado at Boulder.

Hummert JR (1983b): Cortical bone growth and dietary stress among subadults from Nubia's Batn el Hajar. Am J Phys Anthropol 62:167–176.

Hummert JR, Van Gerven DP (1983): Skeletal growth in a medieval population from Sudanese Nubia. Am J Phys Anthropol 60:471–478.

Hunt DR (1990): Sex determination in the subadult ilia: An indirect test of Weaver's nonmetric sexing method. J Forensic Sci 35:881–885.

Hunt EE, Gleiser I (1955): The estimation of age and sex of preadolescent children from bones and teeth. Am J Phys Anthropol 13:479–487.

Huss-Ashmore R (1981): Bone growth and remodeling as a measure of nutritional stress. In Martin DL, Bumsted MP (eds): "Biocultural Adaptation: Comprehensive Approaches to Skeletal Analysis." Research Reports No. 20. Amherst, MA: Department of Anthropology, University of Massachusetts, pp 84–95.

Jantz RL, Owsley DW (1984a): Temporal changes in limb proportionality among skeletal samples of Arikara Indians. Ann Hum Biol 11:157–164.

Jantz RL, Owsley DW (1984b): Long bone growth variation among Arikara skeletal populations. Am J Phys Anthropol 63:13–20.

Johnston FE (1961): Sequence of epiphyseal union in a prehistoric Kentucky population from Indian Knoll. Hum Biol 33:66–81.

Johnston FE (1962): Growth of the long bones of infants and young children at Indian Knoll. Am J Phys Anthropol 20:249–254.

Johnston FE (1968): Growth of the skeleton in earlier peoples. In Brothwell DR (ed): "The Skeletal Biology of Earlier Human Populations." Oxford: Pergamon Press, pp 57–66.

Johnston FE (1969): Approaches to the study of developmental variability in human skeletal populations. Am J Phys Anthropol 31:335–341.

Johnston FE, Zimmer LO (1989): Assessment of growth and age in the immature skeleton. In İşcan MY, Kennedy KAR (eds): "Reconstruction of Life from the Skeleton." New York: Alan R. Liss, pp 11–22.

Jowsey J (1960): Age changes in human bone. Clin Orthop 17:210–218.

Kelly HJ, Reynolds L (1947): Increases in the body dimensions of White and Negro infants. Am J Roentgen Radiol 57:477–516.

Kelley MA (1979): Sex determination with fragmented skeletal remains. J Forensic Sci 24:154–158.

Kerley ER (1965): The microscopic determination of age in human bone. Am J Phys Anthropol 23:149–163.

Kósa F (1989): Age estimation from the fetal skeleton. In İçan MY (ed): "Age Markers in the Human Skeleton." Springfield, IL: Charles C Thomas, pp 21–54.

Kraus BS, Jordan RE (1965): "The Human Dentition Before Birth." Philadelphia: Lea & Febiger.

Lallo J (1973): The Skeletal Biology of Three Prehistoric American Indian Societies from Dickson Mounds. PhD Dissertation, Amherst, MA: Department of Anthropology, University of Massachusetts.

Lengyel (1968): Biochemical aspects of early skeletons. In Brothwell DR (ed): "Skeletal Biology of Earlier Human Populations." Oxford: Pergamon Press, pp 271–278.

Lewis AB, Garn SM (1960): The relationship between tooth formation and other maturational factors. Angle Orthod 30:70.

Loevy HT (1983): Maturation of permanent teeth in Black and Latino children. J Dent Res 62A:296.

Lovejoy CO, Russell KF, Harrison ML (1990): Long bone growth velocity in the Libben Population. Am J Hum Biol 2:533–542.

MacLaughlin SM, Bruce MF (1986): The sciatic notch/acetabular index as a discriminator of sex in European skeletal remains. J Forensic Sci 31:1380–1390.

Malinowski A, Młodziejowski B (1978): Development of long bones of lower limbs in human fetuses. Collegium Anthropologicum 2:196–205.

Maresh MM (1955): Linear growth of long bones of extremities from infancy through adolescence. Am J Dis Child 89:725–742.

Maresh MM (1970): Measurements from roentgenograms. In McCammon RW (ed): "Human Growth and Development." Springfield, IL: Charles C Thomas pp 157–200.

Mazess RB, Cameron JR (1972): Growth of bone in school children: Comparison of radiographic morphometry and photon absorptiometry. Growth 36:77–92.

McKern TW, Stewart TD (1957): Skeletal age changes in young American males analyzed from the standpoint of age identification. Environ Protection Res Div, Quartermaster Res. and Dev. Center, and U.S. Army, Tech Report EP-45, 1957.

McKillop H, Marshall S, Boyce G, Saunders S (1989): Excavations at St. Thomas Church, Belleville Ontario: A Nineteenth Century Cemetery. Paper presented at the Ontario Archaeological Symposium, London, Ontario.

Mensforth RP (1985): Relative tibia long bone growth in the Libben and Bt-5 prehistoric skeletal populations. Am J Phys Anthropol 68:247–262.

Mensforth RP, Lovejoy CO, Lallo JW, Armelagos GJ (1978): The role of constitutional factors, diet, and infectious disease in the etiology of porotic hyperostosis and periosteal reactions in prehistoric infants and children. Med Anthropol 2:1–59.

Merchant VL, Ubelaker DH (1977): Skeletal growth of the protohistoric Arikara. Am J Phys Anthropol 46:61–72.

Miles AEW (1962): Assessment of the ages of a population of Anglo–Saxons from their dentitions. Proc R Soc Med 55:881–886.

Miles AEW (1963): The dentition in the assessment of individual age in skeletal material. In Brothwell DR (ed): "Dental Anthropology." New York: Pergamon Press, pp 191–209.

Miles AEW (1978): Teeth as an indicator of age in man. In Butler PA, Joysey KA (eds): "Development, Function and Evolution of Teeth." London: Academic Press, pp 455–464.

Moorrees CFA, Fanning EA, Hunt EE (1963a): Age variation of formation stages for ten permanent teeth. J Dent Res 42:1490–1501.

Moorrees CFA, Fanning EA, Hunt EE (1963b): Formation and resorption of three deciduous teeth in children. Am J Phys Anthropol 21:205–213.

Moss ML, Moss-Salentijn L (1977): Analysis of developmental processes possibly related to human sexual dimorphism in permanent and deciduous canines. Am J Phys Anthropol 46:407–414.

Nanda RS, Chawla TN (1966): Growth and development of dertitions in Indian children. I. Development of permanent teeth. Am J Orthod 46:363.

Nichols R, Townsend E, Malina R (1983): Development of permanent dentition in Mexican American children. Am J Phys Anthropol 60:232.

Nielsen HG, Ravn JJ (1976): A radiographic study of mineralization of permanent teeth in a group of children aged 3–7 years. Scand J Dent Res 84:109–118.

Nolla CM (1960): The development of the permanent teeth. J Dent Child 27:254.

O'Brien GD, Queenan JT (1981): Growth of the ultrasound fetal femur length during normal pregnancy. Am J Obstet Gynecol 141:833–837.

Olivier G, Pineau H (1960): Nouvelle determination de la taille foetale d'aprés les longueurs diaphysaires des os longs. Ann Med Leg 40:141–144.

Ounsted M, Scott A, Moar V (1981): Proportionality and gender in small-for-dates and large-for-dates babies. Early Hum Devel 5:289–298.

Owsley DW, Jantz RL (1985): Long bone lengths and gestational age distributions of post-contact period Arikara Indian perinatal infant skeletons. Am J Phys Anthropol 68:321–329.

Redfield A (1970): A new aid to aging immature skeletons: Development of the occipital bone. Am J Phys Anthropol 33:207–220.

Reynolds EL (1945): The bony pelvic girdle in early infancy. Am J Phys Anthropol n.s. 3:321.

Reynolds EL (1947): The bony pelvis in prepuberal childhood. Am J Phys Anthropol n.s. 5:165–200.

Saunders SR, DeVito C (1990): Variability in cortical bone microstructure in the subadult human femur. Am J Phys Anthropol 81:290–291.

Saunders SR, Fitzgerald W (1988): Life and Death in Sixteenth Century Ontario. Paper presented to the McMaster Symposium, Hamilton, Ontario.

Saunders SR, Herring DA (1991): Testing Theory and Method in Paleodemography: The St. Thomas Anglican Church Cemetery. Paper presented at the Canadian Archaeological Association Meetings, St. John's, Newfoundland.

Saunders SR, Lazenby R (1991): "The Links That Bind: The Harvie Family Nineteenth Century Burying Ground. Dundas, Ontario: Copetown Press.

Saunders SR, MacKenzie-Ward D (1988): The Reid Site burials. Kewa 88–4:21–26.

Saunders SR, Melbye FJ (1990) Subadult mortality and skeletal indicators of health in Late Woodland Ontario Iroquois. Can J Archaeol 14:61–74.

Saunders SR, Spence MW (1986): Dental and skeletal age determinations of Ontario Iroquois infant burials. Ontario Archaeol 46:21–26.

Scheuer JL, Musgrave JH, Evans SP (1980): The estimation of late fetal and perinatal age from limb bone length by linear and logarithmic regression. Ann Hum Biol 7:257–265.

Schulter-Ellis FP, Schmidt DJ, Hayek LA, Craig J (1983): Determination of sex with a discriminant analysis of new pelvic bone measurements: Part 1. J Forensic Sci 28:169–179.

Schutowski H (1987): Sex determination of fetal and neonate skeletons by means of discriminant analysis. Int J Anthropol 2:347–352.

Scrimshaw SCM (1984): Infanticide in human populations: Societal and individual concerns. In Hausfater G, Hrdy SB (eds): "Infanticide; Comparative and Evolutionary Perspectives." New York: Aldine, pp 439–462.

Specker BL, Brazerol W, Tsang RC, Levin R, Searcy J, Steichen J (1987): Bone mineral content in children 1 to 6 years of age. Am J Dis Child 141:343–344.

Spence MR (1986): The Excavation of the Keffer Site Burials. Report on file at the Museum of Indian Archaeology, London, Ontario.

Stini WA (1985): Growth rates and sexual dimorphism in evolutionary perspective. In Gilbert RI, Mielke JH (eds): "The Analysis of Prehistoric Diets." Orlando, FL: Academic Press, pp 191–226.

Sundick RI (1972): Human skeletal growth and dental development as observed in the Indian Knoll population. PhD. dissertation, Toronto, Ontario: University of Toronto.

Sundick RI (1977): Age and sex determination of subadult skeletons. J Forensic Sci 22:141–144.

Sundick RI (1978): Human skeletal growth and age determination. Homo 29:228–249.

Tanner JM (1962): "Growth at Adolescence" (2nd ed). Oxford, UK: Blackwell Scientific Publications.

Thomson A (1899): The sexual differences of the foetal pelvis. J Anat Phys 33:359.

Thwaites RG (ed).(1896–1901): "The Jesuit Relations and Allied Documents." 73 volumes. Cleveland, OH: Burrows Brothers.

Trodden BJ (1982): "A Radiographic Study of the Calcification and Eruption of the Permanent Teeth in Inuit and Indian Children." National Museum of Man Mercury Series, Archaeological Survey of Canada, Paper No. 112.

Ubelaker DH (1989a): "Human Skeletal Remains: Excavation, Analysis, Interpretation." Taraxacum, Washington.

Ubelaker DH (1989b): The estimation of age at death from immature human bone. In İşcan (ed): "Age Markers in the Human Skeleton." Springfield, IL: Charles C Thomas, pp 55–70.

Van Gerven DP, Hummert JR, Burr DB (1985): Cortical bone maintenance and geometry of the tibia in prehistoric children from Nubia's Batn el Hajar. Am J Phys Anthropol 66:275–280.

Waldron T (1987): The relative survival of the human skeleton: implications for paleopathology. In Boddington A, Garland AN, Janaway RC (eds): "Death, Decay and Reconstruction. Approaches to Archaeology and Forensic Science." Manchester, England: Manchester University Press, pp 55–64.

Walker PL (1969): The linear growth of long bones in Late Woodland Indian children. Proc Ind Acad Sci 78:83–87.

Weaver DS (1979): Application of the likelihood ratio test to age estimation using the infant and child temporal bone. Am J Phys Anthropol 50:263–270.

Weaver DS (1980): Sex differences in the ilia of a known sex and age sample of fetal and infant skeletons. Am J Phys Anthropol 52:191–195.

Weaver DS (1986): Forensic aspects of fetal and neonatal skeletons. In Reichs KJ (ed): "Forensic Osteology." Springfield, IL: Charles C Thomas, pp 90–100.

Webb PAO, Suchey JM (1985): Epiphyseal union of the anterior iliac crest and medial clavicle in a modern multiracial sample of American males and females. Am J Phys Anthropol 68:457–466.

Whittington SL (1991): Detection of significant demographic differences between subpopulations of prehispanic Maya from Copan, Honduras, by survival analysis. Am J Phys Anthropol 85:167–184.

Workshop of European Anthropologists (1980): Recommendations for age and sex diagnoses of skeletons. J Hum Evol 9:517–549.

y'Edynak G (1976): Long bone growth in western Eskimo and Aleut skeletons. Am J Phys Anthropol 45:569–574.

Skeletal Biology of Past Peoples: Research Methods
pages 21–35 © 1992 Wiley-Liss, Inc.

Chapter 2

Methods of Determining Age at Death Using Bone Microstructure

Sam D. Stout

Department of Anthropology, University of Missouri, Columbia, Missouri 65211

INTRODUCTION

Beyond the obvious fact that bone is the tissue most likely to survive after death, it is also a valuable source of information about the biology of past peoples. Bone possesses the unique property of providing a "living, dynamic and durable record" of past metabolic events encoded in its microstructure (Pirok et al., 1966). Histomorphometric (quantitative histological) studies of ancient bone can, therefore, go beyond merely identifying histomorphological features that are pathognomonic of specific diseases, and provide information relating to age at death, bone remodeling rates, and levels of physical activity (biomechanics). This chapter will discuss the use of bone histomorphometry to estimate age at death.[1] I will begin with a brief review of the historical background of paleohistology, followed by a discussion of the physiological basis for the histomorphological variables currently used to estimate age and a summary of several of the more commonly used histological age estimating methods, and will conclude with a discussion of how to maximize the accuracy and reliability of histomorphometric age estimates.[2]

HISTORICAL BACKGROUND

The term *paleohistology* was first suggested some 40 years ago (Graf, 1949). However, the fact that histomorphology is often preserved in bones of considerable antiquity has been established for nearly 150 years. As early as 1849, Queckett identified many gross histological features in animal fossils (cited by Graf, 1949). Some three decades later, Aeby (1878) published the results of an extensive histological analysis of bones and teeth, in which he identified characteristic canals and lacunae in the fossilized bones of a variety of genera. For discussions of the preservation of histological structure in ancient bone the reader is referred to Stout (1978), Garland (1987), and Hanson and Buikstra (1987).

Current histological age estimating methods trace their origins to several seminal reports describing age associated variations in cortical bone histomorphology.[3] Amprino and Bairati (1936) provided a qualitative study that illustrated the age–associated changes in cortical bone microstructure. Some 20 years later, Jowsey (1960) published a "semiquantitative analysis" of the variation in the appearance of normal cortical bone with age. In a more quantitative study, Currey (1964) reported an increase in the number of intact and fragmentary

---

1. For more general discussion of the use of histomorphometry in anthropological research the reader is referred to Stout and Simmons (1979), Stout (1989b), Simmons (1985) and Frost (1985).

2. For an earlier discussion of the use of cortical bone histology to estimate age at death see Stout (1989a).

3. Although essentially the same processes obtain for cancellous or trabecular bone, its complex geometry and fragility render it less suitable for paleohistology.

Haversian systems per unit area of cortical bone.

REMODELING: THE METABOLIC BASIS FOR CORTICAL BONE HISTOMORPHOMETRY

Anyone attempting to undertake histological analysis of ancient bone, whether it be for the purpose of estimating age at death or determining bone remodeling rates, must be familiar with the metabolic basis for the histomorphological features that are to be employed.

The vertebrate skeleton is not merely an inert column of mineral, but a system of organs composed of a specialized connective tissue. The individual bones of the skeleton are its organs, and bone is the specialized connective tissue. Bone is composed of a collagenous protein fiber matrix and ground substance impregnated with a carbonate-containing analog of the mineral hydroxyapatite (Teitelbaum and Bullough, 1979). Through the action of specialized cells, primarily osteoblasts, and osteoclasts, bone is capable of growth, modeling, remodeling, and repair.

Growth and Modeling

These two processes work in concert to produce bones of the size and shape that are characteristic of the skeleton of a species. Growth is the process through which tissues and structures increase in size by increasing the number of cells and amounts of intracellular materials in them. Modeling, through the polarized distribution of osteoblastic and osteoclastic activity, sculpts the bones to produce their species characteristic shapes, which are designed to meet the biomechanical demands placed upon them.

Although growth and modeling essentially cease once skeletal maturity is reached, one must be aware of their effects on histomorphology. The "effective" age of adult compact bone is actually less than the chronological age. This is because the cortical drift patterns associated with the size and shape changes that occur during growth result in a mosaic of ages within the adult compacta (Fig. 1). Although the pattern of the mosaic is generally consistent for particular bones of a species, a large amount of variability results from factors such

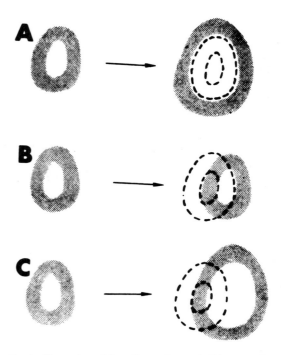

Fig. 1. Illustration of the effects of growth (A), cortical drift (B) and growth and drift combined (C) on the histomorphology of the rib.

as disease and biomechanics, which can affect observed osteon population density in adult bones (Table 1). It is because of these factors that the selection of field location and size is so critical to the histological aging methods discussed below.

Another factor related to modeling that can affect histomorphometry is the regional acceleratory phenomenon (RAP). The effects of RAP on bone histomorphometry have been known for some 30 years (Frost, 1983), but its importance as a source of variability has generally gone unrecognized. RAP consists of an acceleration of most ongoing normal vital tissue processes, and it is regional in its anatomical distribution (Frost, 1983). It can be produced by any regional noxious stimulus of significant magnitude (Table 2). Histomorphometrics from regions of bone affected by RAP will reflect their much higher bone turnover relative to nonaffected adjacent areas. The consequences of attempting to estimate age from such regions should be obvious. Although

TABLE 1. Factors Known to Influence Osteonal Remodeling and Accumulated Osteon Populations[a]

Age, chronological	Regional trauma
Life span	Paralysis
Sex	Mechanical usage
Maturation, skeletal	Acute mechanical disuse
Species	Nutrition
Hormones	Metabolic alkalosis
Electrolyte disorders	Metabolic acidosis
Metabolic	Vitamins
Genetic disorders	Genetic structural disorders
Toxic agents	Microdamage
Radiation damage	Drugs
Bone growth	Mean tissue age
Bone-remodeling patterns	Mechanical strain

[a]Reproduced from Frost (1985).

TABLE 2. Factors That Can Produce the Regional Acceleratory Phenomenon (RAP)[a]

Crushing injury
Fracture
Bone operations
  Osteotomy
  Drilling
  Internal fixation
  Periosteal stripping
  Implantation of fixation devices and irritating
    materials
Arthrotomy
Arteriotomy
Burns
Acute denervation
Acute paralysis
Infarcts
Soft tissue and bone infections
Noninfectious inflammatory processes
  Arthritis
  Rheumatic fever
  Reiter's disease

[a]Reproduced from Frost (1983), with permission of the publisher.

Samson and Branigan (1987) found no significant differences in Haversian canal measurements and numbers among sections taken at 1-cm intervals along a 9-cm length from the femur midshaft, the use of only small core samples, small numbers of fields, single sections of bone, or even single bones to estimate age increases the risk of arriving at nonrepresentative histomorphometrics because of the influence of RAP.

Remodeling

Remodeling is the sequential removal (resorption) and replacement (formation) of older lamellar bone with new lamellar bone.[4] This turnover occurs throughout life in large and long-lived animals such as humans. The histomorphological features that are the basis for the histomorphometric aging methods discussed above represent the durable record of remodeling events that occur prior to death. An understanding of the remodeling process, therefore, is essential for anyone attempting to employ these methods. The following is a brief discussion of cortical bone remodeling and its relationship to the histomorphometric parameters employed to estimate age at death. For more detailed discussions of bone remodeling the reader is referred to Frost (1973), Lacroix (1971), and Parfitt (1983).

The remodeling process begins with the focal activation of bone-resorbing cells called *osteoclasts* from precursor cells.[5] These cells, working together as a unit, resorb packets of relatively constant bone volume, thus determining the location, shape, and size of the future bone structural unit (BSU) (Parfitt, 1983). The histomorphological hallmark of this process is the resorptive bay or cutting cone with its characteristic scalloped surface which results from the presence of Howship's lacunae (Fig. 2).

The resorption phase of remodeling is followed by a quiescent interval or reversal phase of variable duration, during which the scalloped bone surface of the resorptive bay is smoothed off and an electron-dense, collagen-free connective tissue, which is seen histologically as a cement line, is laid down (Parfitt, 1983). Cement lines formed during such reversal phases are called *reversal lines* and are important to our discussion because their presence distinguishes secondary osteons from other, similar structures such as primary osteons (Figs. 3 and 4). Reversal lines can also be found within osteons. Believed to be the result of short term and limited magnitude intraosteonal remodeling, this kind of cement line cir-

---

4. Prior to about 1966, the term remodeling included the process of modeling discussed above.

5. The precursor cells are probably both local and blood borne.

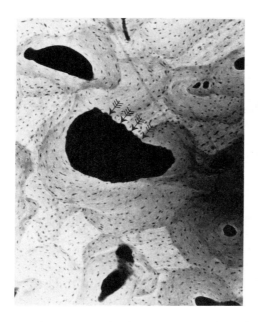

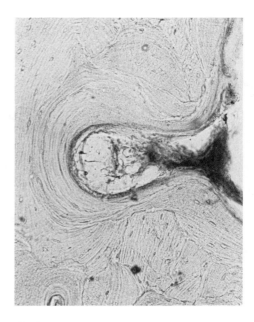

Fig. 2. Photomicrograph of transverse section from the femur of a 39 year old female, illustrating a resorptive bay or cutting cone with its characteristic scalloped border due to the presence of Howship's lacunae (arrows). Undecalcified, unstained, 10×.

Fig. 4. Photomicrograph of a transverse section of a rib from a 29-year-old female, illustrating a type of primary osteon often encountered at the endosteal border. It results from formation that was not preceded by a resorptive phase and should not be counted as a secondary osteon. Undecalcified, unstained, 10×.

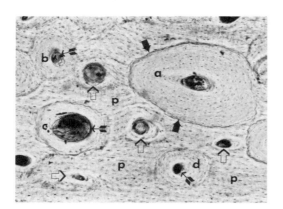

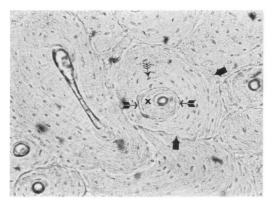

Fig. 3. Photomicrograph of a transverse section of a rib from a 29-year-old female. **a–d,** Typical secondary osteons (Haversian systems). Solid darts indicate reversal lines; open darts primary vascular canals; arrows indicate Haversian canals; and p's overlay primary lamellar bone. Undecalcified, unstained, 10×.

Fig. 5. Photomicrograph of a transverse section of a rib from a 29-year-old female, illustrating a type II osteon (×). Note the presence of a reversal line (arrows) within the reversal line of the "parent" osteon (darts). Smaller dart indicates an osteocytic lacuna. Undecalcified, unstained, 20×.

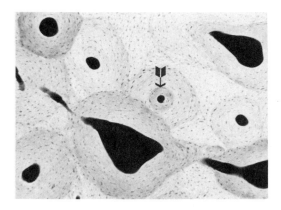

Fig. 6. Photomicrograph of a transverse section of the femur of a 39-year-old female, illustrating a double zonal osteon (arrow). Microradiograph, $10 \times$.

cumscribes what have been described as type II osteons (Jaworski et al., 1972; Ortner, 1974; Richman et al., 1979)(Fig. 5).

The reversal phase is followed by the replacement of most, but not all of the resorbed bone by cells called *osteoblasts*. As formation proceeds centripetally, some of the osteoblasts are trapped within their lacunae in the matrix to form concentric layers of cells destined to become the bone cells referred to as *osteocytes* (Fig. 5). The formation process sometimes undergoes periods of temporary inactivity, producing a type of cement line called an *arrest line*. It can be distinguished from the reversal line by its smooth surface and continuity with the concentric lamellae and osteocytes of the BSU. Arrest lines may be the microscopic equivalent of Harris lines (Stout and Simmons, 1979). When they occur within osteons, a zonal osteon (Fig. 6) is created (Pankovich et al., 1974). Zonal osteons are distinguished from type II osteons on the basis of their synchronization with the lamellae and osteocytic lacunae of the osteon in which they occur. Type II osteons, in contrast, disrupt the pattern of lamellae and osteocytic lacunae. Arrest lines also circumscribe primary osteons, since they are formed by the apposition of concentric lamellae of bone around a longitudinal vessel without being preceded by resorption and a reversal phase.

AGE-ESTIMATING METHODS
The Kerley Method

Ellis Kerley (1965) pioneered the use of histomorphometry to estimate age at death. The method is applicable only if one has transverse bone sections from midshaft femur, tibia, and fibula. It is based upon age associated changes in the number of osteons (Haversian systems), the number of fragments of old osteons, the percentage of circumferential lamellar (primary) bone, and the number of non-Haversian (primary vascular) canals. These histomorphological variables are quantified at a magnification of 100 (10× objective and 10× eyepiece) for four circular fields per bone section. The fields are selected from anterior, posterior, medial, and lateral quadrants, such that the outer border of the circular field is tangential to the periosteal border of the bone and is "fairly representative of that particular anatomical area of the section being examined" (Kerley, 1965).

As with any method, one must pay close attention to the definitions of the variables that are to be quantified. Kerley's independent variables are defined as follows:

Secondary osteons are distinguished from fragments on the basis of being over 80% complete, that is, not exhibiting significant remodeling by subsequent generations of osteons, and having an intact Haversian canal. Osteon counts do not include what are termed primary osteons or pseudo-Haversian systems, which are discussed below.

Circumferential lamellar bone consists of the concentric bands of unremodeled primary lamellar bone that was formed during growth and through osteoblastic drift. The percentage of each field that is composed of this primary bone can be simply estimated by eye, or using a point count technique with the aid of an ocular grid (Kimmel and Jee, 1983), or measured directly by an image analysis system.

Non-Haversian canals include all vascular canals except those found in Haversian systems or secondary osteons. These include primary vascular canals as well as pseudo-Haversian systems (primary osteons). Primary vascular canals surround small peripheral blood vessels that were included in the formation of the original primary circumferential lamellar bone.

Pseudo-Haversian systems are osteon-like in appearance, but since they are the result of centripetal bone formation that has not been preceded by resorption, they lack the characteristic reversal line of secondary osteons.

Each of the four variables is summed, not averaged, over the four microscopic fields for each bone. Structures are counted even if partly obscured by the periphery of the field. This often requires changing to a lower-magnification objective to ascertain whether one is dealing with a fragment or a complete osteon when counting directly from the microscope. Note that the numbers of osteons, fragments, and non-Haversian canals are expressed in terms of absolute counts, rather than per unit area. Field size,[6] therefore, is important. This was not recognized in the original article by Kerley (1965). Kerley and Ubelaker (1978) subsequently published revisions to this method that describe a correction factor for field sizes that is different from that used to develop the original method. Correction involves simply dividing one's own particular field size into Kerley's estimated original field size of 2.06 mm². Stout and Gehlert (1982) caution that since the histomorphological structures are not randomly distributed within cortical bone cross sections (Amprino and Marotti, 1964; Frost, 1969), merely adjusting counts in proportion to differences from Kerley's original field size may have limitations. The use of field sizes as close as possible to 2.06 mm² is recommended. The problems of field size and interpreting structures in the periphery of the field can be circumvented if counts are made from photomicrographs that include the required field size and location. Circumscribing the correct field size and location on the photomicrograph provides a permanent record of each microscopic field, and structures in the periphery of the field can readily be evaluated. We recommend actually tracing the outlines of the structures identified within the circumscribed fields with a marker pen. By referring to the photomicrograph and the actual section when reading each field, a much greater accuracy is attained.

Kerley (1965) recommends the use of polarized light. Polarized light often enhances the ability to distinguish histomorphological features, especially when dealing with bone sections that are not the ideal thickness of 50–100μm or are less than well preserved. It has been this author's experience that it can also introduce optical artifacts which result in the perception of osteon fragments where they do not exist. Counts are best made after viewing the field with both natural and polarized light.

Age estimations can be derived from any one of the four variables for the femur, tibia, or fibula with the appropriate regression equation provided by Kerley and Ubelaker (1978) (Table 3), or the absolute limits of the age curve graphs provided by Kerley (1965).[7] Kerley (1965) suggests that greater reliability is gained when multiple factors and bones are used. To this end he provides a profile chart that was devised to determine age from the four factors in all or any of the three anatomical sampling sites. In their study of the relative accuracy and reliability of histological aging methods, Stout and Gehlert (1980) found the greatest accuracy and reliability was achieved when age estimates were based upon averaging the results from the regression equations.

Ahlqvist and Damsten

Ahlqvist and Damsten (1969) describe a modification of Kerley's (1965) method. Their intent is to simplify Kerley's original method. Modifications are as follows. In order to avoid the linea aspera region, the microscope fields are located half way between those used in Kerley's method. An eyepiece reticule measuring 1 mm² at the level of the section, and containing a 100–square grid is employed. Ahlqvist and Damsten specify a square rather than a circular field, claiming that the square configuration better covers the subperiosteal regions of the cortex, which is where the most significant age-associated changes in the percentage of osteons and osteon fragments occur.

Using polarized light, the percentage of the square grid that is occupied by osteonal (Hav-

---

6. Field size can be easily determined with the use of a stage micrometer (see Kimmel and Jee, 1983).

7. Kerley and Ubelaker (1978) provide these revised regression equations which should be used in place of those presented in the original article (Kerley, 1965).

TABLE 3. Kerley's Revised Regression Formulas for Calculating Age at Death (Y) From Cortical Microstructure[a]

Factor	Predicting equation	SEE[b]
Femoral osteons	$Y = 2.278 + 0.187X + 0.00226X^2$	9.19
Femoral fragments	$Y = 5.241 + 0.509X + 0.017X^2 - 0.00015X^3$	6.98
Femoral lamellar	$Y = 75.017 - 1.790X + 0.0114X^2$	12.52
Femoral non-Haversian	$Y = 58.390 - 3.184X + 0.0628X^2 - 0.00036X^3$	12.12
Tibial osteons	$Y = -13.4218 + 0.660X$	10.53
Tibial fragments	$Y = -26.997 + 2.501X - 0.014X^2$	8.42
Tibial labellar	$Y = 80.943 - 2.281X + 0.019X^2$	14.28
Tibial non-Haversian	$Y = 67.872 - 9.070X + 0.0440X^2 - 0.0062X^3$	10.19
Fibular osteons	$Y = -23.59 + 0.74511X$	8.33
Fibular fragments	$Y = -9.89 + 1.064X$	3.66
Fibular lamellar	$Y = 124.09 - 10.92X + 0.3723X^2 - 0.00412X^3$	10.74
Fibular non-Haversian	$Y = 62.33 - 9.776X + 0.5502X^2 - 0.00704X^3$	14.62

[a]Reproduced from Kerley and Ubelaker (1978).
[b]Standard error of estimate for the regression (i.e., square root of the mean-square residual). Correlation coefficients are not provided for the revised formulas.

ersian) bone is estimated. The percentages for the four fields are then averaged. The authors claim that this average percentage osteonal bone simultaneously reflects osteon counts, which increase with age, and primary (non-Haversian) bone, which decreases with age. Age is estimated by inserting the mean percentage osteonal bone for the four fields into either of two regression equations (Table 4). The method has so far been developed for only the femur. Ahlqvist and Damsten (1969) suggest that their method might be more accurate when developed for other bones, such as the tibia and fibula. However, a comparison between the correlation of osteon counts with age and correlation of percentage Haversian bone with age, based on the radius, tibia, and fibula, found that while osteon counts showed significant correlations with age for all bones, percentage Haversian bone tended to exhibit a poor to nonsignificant association with age (Stout and Stanley, 1991).

Bouvier and Ubelaker (1977) compared Kerley's method for femoral complete osteons with the method of Ahlqvist and Damsten (1969). They found Kerley's method to produce more accurate age estimates. It should be noted that the test sample was derived from Kerley's original sample, and that the earlier (Kerley, 1965) regression formula, rather than the revised formula (Kerley and Ubelaker,

1978), was used to estimate age from femoral osteons. Also, a field 1.45 mm in diameter was employed for Kerley's method, rather than either the 1.25 mm in the original 1965 study or the 1.62 mm reported by Kerley and Ubelaker (1978) in their later revisions. Stout and Gehlert (1980), however, using an independent sample, confirmed the apparent superiority of the Kerley method for most bones and variables (Table 5).

Stout and Paine

Stout and Paine (1991) have developed a histological aging method based upon the histomorphometry of the middle third of the 6th rib and midshaft clavicle. These two sampling sites were selected for several reasons. Most of the other histological methods involve sampling major long bones (e.g. femur, tibia, fibula). Because of the invasive nature of histological analysis, there is an understandable reluctance to apply the methods. Currently there are no important osteological methods that require intact ribs and clavicles. The relatively recent aging method developed by İşcan and Loth (Loth and İşcan, 1989), which is based upon the metamorphosis at the sternal rib, would not be affected, since the sternal ends are not altered by this histological analysis. Ribs are also particularly appropriate, because they are commonly sampled in isotopic and trace ele-

TABLE 4. Age-Predicting Equations for the Ahlqvist and Damsten (1969) Method

Bone	Predicting equation	Statistics
Femur	$Y = 4.96 + 0.991X$	$SE = 6.71$, $p = 0.965$
	$Y = -0.99 + 0.783X$ $+ 0.00206X^2$	$SE = 6.79$ $p = 0.962$

TABLE 5. Evaluation of the Accuracy and Reliability of Histological Aging Methods of Kerley and of Ahlqvist and Damsten With an Independent Sample[a,b]

Rank	Method/formula
1	Mean regression[c]
2	Femur osteon fragments regression formula
3	Femur intact osteons regression formula
4	Fibula osteon fragments regression formula
5	Kerley's (1965) profile method
6	Tibia intact osteons regression formula
7	Ahlqvist and Damsten (1969)
8	Fibula intact osteons regression formula
9	Tibia fragments regression formula

[a]Data from Stout and Gehlert (1980).
[b]The sample consisted of femurs, tibias, and fibulas from 13 cadavers ranging in age from 13 to 103 years.
[c]Mean regression age is the average of the ages derived from each of Kerley and Ubelaker's (1978) regression formulas.

ment research (Sanford and Katzenberg, this volume, Chapters 5 and 6), and it has been suggested that histological evaluation of diagenesis should be a necessary prerequisite to such noninvasive methods of analysis (Stout, 1978; Hanson and Buikstra, 1987).

The rib and clavicle represent the only non-axial skeletal sampling sites. They therefore provide a means to estimate age for fragmentary skeletal remains when the major long bones are absent or the midshaft regions are not available. Since these bones are not directly involved in locomotion, they are probably less subject to non-age-related variability due to biomechanical factors than bones such as the femur and tibia. Finally, when used in addition to those methods already available, these methods provide additional sources of data with which to derive age estimates.

This method is based upon the association between age at death and the number of ob-

TABLE 6. Age-Predicting Equations for the Stout and Paine (1991) Method[a]

Bone	Predicting equation[b]	Statistics[c]
Rib	$L_nY = 2.343$ $+ 0.050877X_r$	$s_{yx} = L_n0.231$ $\bar{x} = 18.03$ $s^{2x} = 51.696$ $r^2 = 0.7211$
Clavicle	$L_nY = 2.216$ $+ 0.070280X_c$	$s_{yx} = L_n0.239$ $\bar{x} = 14.86$ $s^{2x} = 26.256$ $r^2 = 0.6989$
Rib and clavicle	$L_nY = 2.195$ $+ 0.029904X_r$ $+ 0.035430X_c$	$s_{yx} = L_n0.209$ $r^2 = 0.7762$

[a]$N = 40$; age range = 13–62 years; mean age = 28.6 years, $s = 12.9$ years.
[b]X in these equations is the total visible osteon density (i.e., intact + fragmentary osteons per 1 mm^2). Note that the dependent variable Y is natural log age.
[c]$t_{0.05} = 2.0244$.

servable osteons per unit area in a cross section of bone. The number of intact and fragmentary osteons per unit area is calculated for each bone. For this method, intact osteons are defined as those secondary osteons for which the Haversian canals are at least 90% complete; all other forms of secondary osteons are classified as fragments. In order to minimize the sampling error that can exist between even serial sections from the same bone (Frost, 1969), these variables are calculated on the basis of at least two sections for each bone. Sections are read such that all major topographical regions of the cross section are sampled. Total visible osteon density, the sum of the number of intact and fragmentary osteons per unit area, serves as the independent variable, which is then inserted into the appropriate regression formula (Table 6). Determining the number of osteons and their fragments per unit area can be accomplished by simply employing a point count technique with the aid of a counting reticule (Kimmel and Jee, 1983; Stout 1989a). The advantages to this sampling procedure and the use of osteon counts per unit area, rather than absolute counts, are that any magnification can be used and field selection is less rigid.

The following methods employ less than a complete cross section of bone in order to min-

TABLE 7. Age-Predicting Equations for the Singh and Gunberg (1970) Method

Bone	Predicting Equation	Statistics
Mandible	$Y = 20.82 + 0.85X_1 + 0.87X_2 - 0.22X_3$	$R = 0.979, s_{yx} = 2.55$
	$Y = -18.99 + 1.13X_1 + 1.76X_2$	$R = 0.976, s_{yx} = 2.69$
	$Y = 32.23 + 0.92X_1 - 0.30X_3$	$R = 0.978, s_{yx} = 2.58$
	$Y = 74.73 + 1.52X_2 - 0.45X_3$	$R = 0.969, s_{yx} = 3.04$
	$Y = -28.24 + 1.68X_1$	$R = 0.969, s_{yx} = 3.02$
	$Y = 5.31 + 5.00X_2$	$R = 0.950, s_{yx} = 3.83$
	$Y = 103.99 - 0.63X_3$	$R = 0.966, s_{yx} = 3.16$
Femur	$Y = 27.65 + 0.65X_1 + 0.78 + X_2 - 0.26X_3$	$R = 0.958, s_{yx} = 3.24$
	$Y = -14.69 + 1.13X_1\ 1.11X_2$	$R = 0.948, s_{yx} = 3.55$
	$Y = 29.59 + 0.79X_1 - 0.28X_3$	$R = 0.957, s_{yx} = 3.25$
	$Y = 61.25 + 1.74X_2 - 0.44X_3$	$R = 0.949, s_{yx} = 3.52$
	$Y = 16.10 + 1.38X_1$	$R = 0.945, s_{yx} = 3.60$
	$Y = 2.00 + 5.16X_2$	$R = 0.889, s_{yx} = 5.01$
	$Y = 89.01 - 0.62X_3$	$R = 0.937, s_{yx} = 3.82$
Tibia	$Y = 43.52 + 0.291X_1 + 0.147X_2 - 0.34X_3$	$R = 0.964, s_{yx} = 3.02$
	$Y = -3.40 + 0.67X_1 + 2.27X_3$	$R = 0.936, s_{yx} = 3.93$
	$Y = 48.61 + 0.53X_1 - 0.38X_3$	$R = 0.957, s_{yx} = 3.22$
	$Y = 54.79 + 2.19X_2 - 0.4X_3$	$R = 0.960, s_{yx} = 3.12$
	$Y = -4.76 + 1.15X_1$	$R = 0.919, s_{yx} = 4.33$
	$Y = 5.10 + 4.88X_2$	$R = 0.908, s_{yx} = 4.59$
	$Y = 91.32 - 0.64X_3$	$R = 0.935, s_{yx} = 3.88$

imize the destructive nature of the sampling procedure.

Singh and Gunberg

In the Singh and Gunberg (1970) method, 1-cm^2 bone samples are taken from the anterior quadrant of the femur and tibia and the posterior border of the mandibular ramus. Two microscopic fields measuring 2 mm in diameter are selected at random from the periosteal third of the each bone sample. It is recommended that the fields be derived from different sections for each bone whenever possible. Although the Singh and Gunberg study involved only males ($N = 52$), a small sample of 7 females was used to test the model and make preliminary observations regarding possible sex differences. Significant sex differences were not observed, a finding that is in agreement with Kerley (1965).

Three independent variables are measured:

1. X_1, the total number of complete secondary osteons contained in the two fields. Complete osteons are defined on the basis of the presence of a complete Haversian canal.

2. X_2, the average number of lamellae per osteon, based upon all osteons encountered in the two fields.

3. X_3, the average Haversian canal diameter, based upon the smallest diameter of all Haversian canals encountered in the two sections, excluding tangentially cut canals that are three or more times longer than wide.

Seven age-predicting equations, representing possible combinations of the three dependent variables, are provided for each sampling site (Table 7). Errors are reported to be least when all three predicting variables are used to estimate age, and greatest when average number of lamellae per osteon alone is employed. The authors report that age at death can be estimated to within 6 years of the true value in 95% of cases in human males. In addition, a nomograph for the estimation of age is provided that employs total number of osteons (X_1) and average Haversian canal diameter (X_3) for the mandible only. The nomograph is reported to have a standard error of estimate of ±2.58 years for 67% of the subjects and ±5.16 years for 95% of the subjects. It should be noted that, as is typical of samples derived from dissecting room populations, Singh and Gunberg's sample is skewed towards older ages. Mean ages for the three bones range from 64.25 years for the mandible to 62.33 years for the femur and tibia.

TABLE 8. The 19 Variables and Their Abbreviations Used in Thompson's (1979) Age-Predicting Formulas

Variable	Abbreviation	Variable description
1. Cortical thickness, mm	CTHICK	Measured from intact core with calipers
2. Core weight, g	COREWT	Wet weight of refinished core
3. Cortical bone density, g/em^3	CDEN	Weight of core per unit volume of core
4. Mineral content, g/em	CMC	Measured in cores by Bone Mineral Analyzer
5. Mineral index, g/em^2	CMCC	Mineral context/refinished core length
6. Aggregate osteon lamellae area, %	OSTA	Percentage of area of fields containing osteon lamellae
7. Aggregate Haversian canal area, %	HCA	Percentage of area of fields containing canals
8. Osteon area, %	OSTHC	Aggregate osteon lamellae plus Haversian canal area
9. Secondary osteon number	NUMOST	Number of secondary osteons in a field
10. Haversian canal number	NUMHC	Number of canals and primary osteons in a field
11. Individual osteon lamellae area, %	INDOSTA	Osteon lamellae area/secondary osteon number
12. Individual Haversian canal area, %	INDHCA	Haversian canal area/Haversian canal number
13. Aggregate osteon perimeter, mm	OSTBA	Total osteon perimeter length in a field
14. Aggregate Haversian canal perimeter, mm	HCBA	Total Haversian canal perimeter length in a field
15. Individual osteon perimeter, mm	IOSTBA	Aggregate osteon perimeter/osteon number
16. Individual Haversian canal perimeter, mm	IHCBA	Aggregate canal perimeter/canal number
17. Ratio 1	RATIOA	Aggregate Haversian canal area/aggregate secondary osteon: lamellae area
18. Ratio 2	RATIOB	Aggregate Haversian canal perimeter/aggregate osteon perimeter
19. Ratio 3	RATIOC	Individual canal perimeter/individual osteon perimeter

It should also be noted that both 30– to 50–μm ground sections and 10–μm decalcified thin sections were used in the study. Since it has been demonstrated that section thickness can affect histomorphometrics (Frost, 1962), the comparability of counts from thin and ground sections may come into question. Considering the size of the histomorphological features that serve as variables in this method, probably only X_2, average number of lamellae per osteon would be affected. Samson and Branigan (1987) found no difference in measurements of Haversian canal diameters and numbers per unit area among 50–, 100–, and 150–μm–thick sections.

D.D. Thompson

A method also designed to minimize the extent of the destruction to bones was developed by D.D. Thompson (1979). An additional advantage of this method is its applicability to bones of the upper extremity. This method requires the removal of only a 0.4-mm-diameter core of bone with a specially designed corer mounted on a high speed Dremel drill.

In Thompson's (1979) original study, cores were removed from the anterior surfaces of the midshafts of the femur, the medial surface of the anterior tibia, the midshaft of the humerus medial to the deltoid tuberosity, and the lateral surface of the ulna approximately one third of the distance from the distal end. Both left and right sides were included. The study sample consisted of 116 human cadavers with an age range of 30–97 years for males and 43–94 years for females.

Nineteen age-associated variables (Table 8) were subjected to stepwise linear regression to select the variable or combination of variables that, on the basis of standard error of estimate and coefficient of determination (r^2), best estimate age at death. Regression was performed on 28 groups, including the whole sample and subsamples based on side, sex, and "nonpathological" criteria for the femur and tibia; because of sampling factors, the upper extremity

TABLE 9. Selected Age-Predicting Formulas From D.D. Thompson (1979)

Bone[a]	Formula[b,c]	r^2	s_{yx}
Femur	$Y = 12.409 + 91.936(OSTHC)$	0.6221	7.8789
	$Y = 35.747 + 100.985(OSTHC) - 26.752(IOSTBA)$	0.6807	7.3760
	$-1.194(CTHIC) - 2.791(OSTBA) + 1.058(NUMOST)$		
Tibia	$Y = 20.632 + 82.475(OSTHC)$	0.5537	8.6822
	$Y = 104.964 + 120.319(OSTHC) - 95.279(IOSTBA)$	0.6692	7.5778
	$-3.000(OSTBA) - 68.935(CMCC)$		
Humerus	$Y = -22.785 + 146.989(OSTHC)$	0.5322	9.4605
	$Y = -35.652 + 146.910(OSTHC) - 139.160(COREWT)$	0.7090	7.8804
	$+ 117.071(RATIOC) - 106.455(RATIOA)$		
Ulna	$Y = -1.575 + 118.104(OSTHC)$	0.4277	10.5699
	$Y = 74.264 + 223.558(OSTHC) - 8.560(OSTBA)$	0.5965	9.3731
	$-94.535(IOSTBA) - 138.297(COREWT)$		

[a]Equations for both the left and the right sides are provided by Thompson (1979). Since the r^2 values are not significantly different between sides, only those for the right side, which represent the larger sample size, are presented here.
[b]Thompson's original (1979) article provides equations for five combinations of variables resulting from stepwise regression for each of five groups. Because of the small differences among r^2 values, only equations for the best single age indicator and the last step are presented here.
[c]See Table 8 for a definition of the abbreviations for the independent variables.

was not subdivided beyond left and right. The results of the stepwise regression analysis are 118 predicting equations for various combinations of the 19 variables for 28 sample subgroups.

The nonhistological variables cortical thickness and bone mineral content did not contribute to the reduction of the standard error of estimate. Osteon area, with standard errors of estimate ranging from a high of 10.57 for the left ulna to a low of 7.07 for the male right femur, was found to be the single best variable for predicting age. The overall best prediction of age was gained by using osteon area, core weight, individual Haversian canal perimeter, cortical bone density, and aggregate osteon perimeter for the left humerus ($N = 29$) as independent variables. For the lower extremity, the best age prediction is gained from using percentage osteon area, individual osteon perimeter, percentage individual osteon lamellae area, Haversian canal numbers, and cortical thickness for nonpathological female right tibias as predictors. Table 9 provides the best predicting equations generated for the whole sample and selected subsamples for the 4 bone-sampling sites.

A test of the method using 8 forensically derived cases of known age at death produced good results, with a mean absolute difference from known age of 3 years (Thompson, 1979).

It should be noted that three of these cases fall below the age range of the sample from which the formulas were derived. In a later study, Thompson and Gunness-Hey (1981) generated age estimates for larger forensic series of 28 individuals. The mean absolute difference between known age and predicted age is 7.6 years. It is curious that in this study the authors estimated age histologically by using area in square millimeters of a femoral section containing secondary osteons. They do not provide the formula but refer to Thompson (1979). No such variable is provided in the 1979 article. Indeed, it is not clear which formulas are being used to generate the age estimates for the forensic test cases in either article.

Ericksen

More recently, M.F. Ericksen (1991) has developed another method designed to minimize the destruction involved in obtaining the bone sample used for histological age estimation. It is based upon a sample of 328 documented individuals obtained from a U.S. dissecting room, two modern cemeteries in the Dominican Republic, and autopsies performed in a Chilean hospital. The age range of her sample is 14–97 years.

A small wedge of bone at least 1 cm in transverse width is removed from the anterior fe-

TABLE 10. Selected Age-Predicting Equations for Ericksen's (1991) Method for the Femur

Predicting equation[a,b]	r^2	s_{xy}
Sexes combined ($N = 328$)		
$Y = 75.49 - 0.53X_6$	0.51	12.21
$Y = 53.12 + 0.60X_3 - 2.67X_5$	0.63	10.66
$Y = 44.06 + 0.68X_1 + 0.60X_3 - 2.05X_5$	0.65	10.43
$Y = 43.54 + 0.61X_1 + 2.01X_2 + 0.52X_3 - 1.97X_5$	0.66	10.25
Females ($N = 154$)		
$Y = 77.91 - 0.61X_6$	0.60	11.58
$Y = 52.63 + 0.58X_3 - 2.98X_5$	0.68	10.45
$Y = 50.69 + 2.40X_2 + 0.50X_3 - 2.77X_5$	0.69	10.25
$Y = 56.54 + 2.38X_2 + 0.39X_3 - 1.75X_5 - 0.19X_6$	0.70	10.10
$Y = 53.12 + 2.89X_2 + 0.32X_3 + 1.28X_4 - 1.83X_5 - 0.19X_6$	0.71	10.00
Males ($N = 174$)		
$Y = 44.37 + 0.97X_3$	0.48	12.04
$Y = 51.94 + 0.70X_3 - 2.30X_5$	0.59	10.70
$Y = 40.02 + 0.97X_1 + 0.66X_3 - 1.54X_5$	0.62	10.24
$Y = 39.68 + 0.93X_1 + 1.66X_2 + 0.56X_3 - 1.49X_5$	0.64	10.11

[a]Only equations in which increasing the number of variables leads to an increase in r^2 are included here. Equations that include highly correlated variables (e.g., osteons per 1 mm^2 and average percentage osteonal bone) have also been omitted, since they add little new information and led to no significant increase in r^2.
[b]Descriptions of the variables are provided in the discussion of this method.

mur at midshaft. Numbers (per square millimeter) of secondary osteons, type II osteons (see discussion of resorptive phase in bone remodeling above), osteon fragments, resorption spaces, and non-Haversian canals, as well as average percentage unremodeled bone, average percentage osteonal bone, and average percentage fragmental bone are recorded in five 0.886-mm^2 fields located "as close to the periosteal edge as possible." Based upon the recommendation of Ortner (1970), histomorphological structures are recorded directly on photographs, while the fields are simultaneously viewed through the microscope. Percentages are determined with a 100-space grid superimposed upon the photographs. This is an excellent way to keep track of the various structures and their counts, and it provides a record of each field for future reference.

Stepwise linear regression of the variables with age as the dependent variable produced three sets of predicting equations, representing the combined sexes and males and females separately. Standard error of estimates for the regression equations range from 9.96 to 12.21, and r^2 values from 0.48 to 0.72. The use of sex-specific equations is recommended whenever possible, although the r^2 and SEE figures do not appear to differ significantly (Table 10).

The iliac crest, because of its widespread clinical use, has well established modern age associated histomorphometrics. Two methods involving the iliac crest warrant mentioning. G. Boivin, A. Schoenboerner, and C.A. Baud (1981) of the Institute de Morphologie of the University of Geneva's Centre Medical Universitaire have reported data that suggest that the number of intact and fragmentary osteons per 1mm^2 in iliac crest cortical bone may be useful in estimating age. Also using the iliac crest, Weinstein et al. (1981) have demonstrated the use of trabecular bone volume to estimate age in a Peruvian mummy. Because of the fragile nature of most archaeological remains, the application of trabecular bone histomorphometry may be limited to only specimens that exhibit substantial preservation, such as are encountered with mummified remains. The development of embedding procedures that can stabilize trabecular bone prior to sectioning may allow application to mere skeletal remains.

The following methods would be applicable to extremely fragmentary and weathered bone.

Samson and Branigan

Samson and Branigan (1987) have developed a histological age estimation method that is designed for use on extremely fragmentary and weathered bone such as is often encountered with archaeological skeletal remains. The femur was chosen for the method because it has been reported to be the bone most likely to survive archeologically (Waldron, 1987). Examination of various archaeological specimens revealed that, although preservation of histological structure varies considerably, Haversian canals are usually preserved in measurable form.

The Samson and Branigan sample consisted of 58 "Caucasian individuals" that ranged in age from 16 to 91 years[8], and included 31 males and 27 females. Mean cortical thickness (MCORTK), mean minimum Haversian canal diameter (MHCD), and number of Haversian canals per unit area of bone (NHC) were analyzed as independent variables. MCORTK was based upon 8 equally spaced measurements taken around the section and avoiding the linea aspera. MHCD and NHC were determined from two 1-cm^2 ground sections, 150μm thick that had been removed from the anteriomedial and anterolateral areas of the cross sections. A significant correlation with age was found only for NHC from males. Although the statistics are not provided, the authors reported a standard error of ±8 years for the linear regression of NHC against age. They further reported that a "transformation" resulting from the product of NHC and MHCD produced a standard error of ±6 years.

This study failed to predict age in females with an error less than ±16 years. The authors suggest that this is due to sexual dimorphism in bone remodeling, perhaps because of increased resorption resulting from the drop in estrogen levels in older females. They also suggest that increased resorption would lead to no further increase, or even a decrease, in the number of Haversian canals. If the increased resorption were related to an increase in intracortical remodeling, however, the number of Haversian systems per unit area could actually

TABLE 11. Age-Associated Ratios of Cortical to Total Area (C/T) for the Middiaphysis of the Sixth Rib[a]

Age range (years)	Mean age (years)	C/T[b]
0.0–0.9	0.33	0.69 ± 0.2
1.0–9.0	4.5	0.61 ± 0.2
10–19	16.0	0.53 ± 0.2
20–29	24.0	0.48 ± 0.2
30–39	35.0	0.40 ± 0.15
40–49	44.0	0.40 ± 0.15
50–59	55.0	0.36 ± 0.15
60–69	64.0	0.34 ± 0.1
70–89	75.0	0.28 ± 0.1

[a]Data from Frost (1969) based upon a sample size of 356.
[b]Cortical area divided by total area within the periosteal border. For sex-specific values see Takahashi and Frost (1966).

increase, since the increased resorption would reflect an increased activation frequency.

Finally, age associated changes in the ratio of cortical to total area of the rib (Takahashi and Frost, 1966; Sedlin et al., 1963; Frost, 1969) might also be used to make rough estimates of age in cases in which the skeletal remains are extremely fragmentary and lack the degree of microstructural preservation necessary to permit the use of the above histomorphometric methods (Table 11). The ratio of cortical to total area (C/T) is determined by dividing the total cross-sectional area contained within the periosteal border into the area of cortical bone, that is, the total area excluding the marrow cavity and any trabecular bone. The reliability of age estimates derived from these data remains to be established.

ACCURACY AND RELIABILITY IN HISTOLOGICAL AGE ESTIMATION

Given the possible sources of variability in bone remodeling identified by Frost (1985), and the variation in histomorphometry that can exist between one unit of bone tissue and an adjacent comparable unit (Frost, 1969)— for example, serial sections— it is hard to imagine how methods employing only a single section, let alone only a wedge or core of bone, can produce reliable age estimates. Kerley (1965) recognized this problem and recommended the use of multiple factors and more

---

8. It is unclear as to why the authors report this age range for the sample, yet later state that although the sample did not include individuals over 76 years of age, the method should be applicable to older individuals.

than one skeletal sampling site when estimating age histologically.

The future lies in minimizing the amount of bone required for estimating age through reducing the number of fields required. This would entail choosing the location of microscopic fields from which age-associated histomorphometrics are to be determined on the basis of mean tissue age. Frost (1987) discusses the issue of mean tissue age and how it might be determined for a particular bone. By selecting microscopic fields that include bone of greatest mean tissue age within a cross section of bone, it should be possible to reduce the number of fields read, yet increase reliability. This could ultimately lead to the use of small cores or wedges of bone, the location of which will include the maximum mean tissue age for particular bone-sampling sites.

A final matter that should be considered when predicting age by linear regression is the age range that should be reported for an estimate. In the past, most age estimates have used the standard error of estimate for the regression. This is merely the square root of the mean square error and may not be appropriate for a single specific predicted age, since the actual confidence interval around a regression line is not linear, but expands as the regression line extends from the mean (Sokal and Rohlf, 1981). Maples and Rice (1979) recognized this problem but noted that computation of a confidence interval band for a regression equation is tedious and rarely used. Giles and Klepinger (1988) described the method by which the computation is significantly reduced by obtaining the confidence interval for a single predicted value of Y from a known X. The procedure for multiple regression is more complex and the reader is referred to standard statistical texts such as Sokal and Rohlf (1981) and Neter et al. (1990). The information that is required to calculate confidence intervals for predicted values is routinely provided by computer generated regression analysis programs.

The purpose of this chapter has been to provide a critical discussion of some of the major histological age- estimating methods currently available. Choice of methods, of course, will often be dictated by the condition of the skeletal remains at hand. In general, this author feels that methods that sample entire cross sections of bones, rather than cores or wedges, should be the most reliable. It is also recommended that the histomorphometrics used to estimate age at death be based upon the analysis of at least two sections per bone to avoid the affects of spatial variation and focal remodeling activity. For similar reasons, one should average the results from methods utilizing as many different sampling sites as possible.

Finally, histological age predicting methods should be applied only by someone with the laboratory facilities necessary to prepare undecalcified bone sections for microscopic analysis, and sufficient background in bone biology to adequately interpret the histomorphology.

REFERENCES

Aeby C (1878): Das histologische verhalten fossilen knochen- und zahngewebes. Arch Mikrosk Anat 15:371–382.

Ahlqvist J, Damsten O (1968): A modification of Kerley's method for the microscopic determination of age in bone. J Forensic Sci 14:205–212.

Amprino J, Bairati EA (1936): Processi di reconstruzione e di riassorbimento nella sostansa compatta delle osa dell nomo. Richerche see cento soggetti della nascita sino a tarda eta. Z Zellforsch Mikrosk Anat 24:439–511.

Amprino R, Marotti G (1964): A topographic quantitative study of bone formation and reconstruction. In Blackwood HJJ (ed): "Bone and Tooth Symposium." New York: MacMillan, pp 21–33.

Boivin G, Schoenboerner A, Baud CA (1981): Human compact bone: Structural changes with aging (abstract). Acta Anat 110:81.

Bouvier M, Ubelaker DH (1977): A comparison of two methods for microscopic determination of age at death. Am J Phys Anthropol 46:391–394.

Currey JD (1964): Some effects of aging in human Haversian systems. J Anat 98:69–75.

Ericksen MF (1991): Histological estimation of age at death using the anterior cortex of the femur. Am J Phys Anthropol 84:171–179.

Frost HM (1962): Microscopy: Depth of focus, optical sectioning and integrating eyepiece measurement. Henry Ford Hosp Med J 10:267–285.

Frost HM (1969): Tetracycline-based histological analysis of bone remodeling. Calcif Tissue Res 3:211–237.

Frost HM (1973): "Bone Remodeling and Its Relationship to Metabolic Bone Disease." Springfield, IL: Charles C. Thomas.

Frost HM (1983): The regional acceleratory phenomenon: A review. Henry Ford Hosp Med J 31:3–9.

Frost HM (1985): The "new bone": Some anthropological potentials. Yearb Phys Anthropol 28:211–226.

Frost HM (1987): Secondary osteon populations: Algorithm for determining mean bone tissue age. Yearb Phys Anthropol 30:221–238.

Garland AN (1987): A histological study of archaeological bone decomposition. In Boddington A, Garland AC, Janaway RC (eds): "Death, Decay and Reconstruction: Approaches to Archaeology and Forensic Science." Manchester, UK: Manchester University Press, pp 109–126.

Giles E, Klepinger LL (1988): Confidence intervals for estimates based on linear regression in forensic anthropology. J Forensic Sci 33:1218–1222.

Graf W (1949): Preserved histological structure in Egyptian mummy tissues and ancient Swedish skeletons. Acta Anat 8:236–250.

Hanson DB, Buikstra JE (1987): Histomorphological alteration in buried human bone from the lower Illinois Valley: Implications for paleodietary research. J Archaeol Sci 14:549–563.

Jaworski ZFG, Meunier P, Frost HM (1972): Observations on two types of resorption cavities in human lamellar cortical bone. Clin Orthop 83:279.

Jowsey J (1960): Age changes in human bone. Clin Orthop 17:210–218.

Kerley ER (1965): The microscopic determination of age in human bone. Am J Phys Anthropol 23:149–164.

Kerley ER, Ubelaker DH (1978): Revisions in the microscopic method of estimating age at death in human cortical bone. Am J Phys Anthropol 23:149–164.

Kimmel DB, Jee SS (1983): Measurements of area, perimeter and distance: Details of data collection in bone histomorphometry. In Recker RR (ed): "Bone Histomorphometry: Techniques and Interpretations." Boca Raton, FL: CRC Press, pp 89–108.

Lacroix P (1971): The internal remodeling of bones. In Bourne HC (ed): "The Biochemistry and Physiology of Bone, Vol 3." New York: Academic Press, pp 119–144.

Loth SR, İşcan MY (1989): Morphological assessment of age in the adult: The thoracic region. In İşcan MY (ed): "Age Markers in the Human Skeleton." Springfield, IL: Charles C Thomas, pp 105–135.

Maples WR, Rice PM (1979): Some difficulties in the Gustafson dental age estimations. J Forensic Sci 24:168–172.

Neter J, Wasserman W, Kutner MH (1990): "Applied Linear Statistical Models." Homewood, IL: Richard D. Irwin.

Ortner DJ (1970): The effects of aging and disease on the micromorphology of human compact bone. PhD dissertation, Universitry of Kansas, Lawrence.

Ortner DJ (1974): Aging effects on osteon remodeling. Calcif Tissue Res 18:27–36.

Pankovich AM, Simmons DJ, Kulkarmi VV (1974): Zonal osteons in cortical bone. Clin Orthop 100:356–363.

Parfitt AM (1983): Stereologic basis of bone histomorphometry; theory of quantitative microscopy and reconstruction of the third dimension. In Recker RR (ed): "Bone Histomorphometry: Techniques and Interpretation." Boca Raton, FL: CRC Press, pp 53–87.

Pirok DJ, Ramser JR, Takahashi H, Villanueva AR, Frost HM (1966): Normal histological tetracycline and dynamic parameters in human mineralized bone sections. Henry Ford Hosp Med Bull 14:195–218.

Richman EA, Ortner DJ, Schulter-Ellis FP (1979): Differences in intracortical bone remodeling in three aboriginal American populations: Possible dietary factors. Calcif Tissue Int 28:209–214.

Samson C, Branigan C (1987): A new method of estimating age at death from fragmentary and weathered bone. In Boddington A, Garland AN, Janaway RC (eds): "Death, Decay and Reconstruction: Approaches to Archaeology and Forensic Science." Manchester, UK: Manchester University Press, pp 101–108.

Sedlin ED, Frost HM, Villanueva AR (1963): Variations in cross-section area of rib cortex with age. J Gerontol 18 (1):9–13.

Simmons DJ (1985): Options for bone aging with the microscope. Yearb Phys Anthropol 28:249–263.

Singh IJ, Gunberg DL (1970): Estimation of age at death in human males from quantitative histology of bone fragments. Am J Phys Anthropol 33:373–382.

Sokal RR, Rohlf FJ (1981): "Biometry." New York: WH Freeman.

Stout SD (1978): Histological structure and its preservation in ancient bone. Curr Anthropol 19:601–603.

Stout SD (1989a): The use of cortical bone histology to estimate age at death. In İşcan MY (ed): "Age Markers on the Human Skeleton." Springfield, IL: Charles C. Thomas, pp 195–207.

Stout SD (1989b): Histomorphometric analysis of human skeletal remains. In İşcan MY, Kennedy KAR (eds): "Reconstruction of Life from the Skeleton." New York: Alan R. Liss, pp 41–52.

Stout SD, Gehlert SJ (1980): The relative accuracy and reliability of histological aging methods. Forensic Sci Int 15:181–90.

Stout SD, Gehlert SJ (1982): Effects of field size when using Kerley's histological method for determining age at death. Am J Phys Anthropol 58:123–125.

Stout SD, Paine RR (1991): Histological age estimation using rib and clavicle. Am J Phys Anthropol:in press.

Stout SD, Simmons DJ (1979): Use of histology in ancient bone research. Yearb Phys Anthropol 44:263–270.

Stout SD, Stanley SC (1991): Percent osteonal bone US osteon counts: The variable of choice for estimating age at death. AM J Phys Anthropol in press.

Takahashi H, Frost HM (1966): Age and sex related changes in the amount of cortex of normal human ribs. Acta Orthop Scandinav 37:122–130.

Teitelbaum SL, Bullough PG (1979): The pathophysiology of bone and joint disease. Am J Pathol Teach Monogr

Thompson DD (1979): The core technique in the determination of age at death in skeletons. J Forensic Sci 24: 902–915.

Thompson DD, Gunness-Hey M (1981): Bone mineral-osteon analysis of Yupik-Inupiaq skeletons. Am J Phys Anthropol 55:1–7.

Waldron T (1987): The relative survival of the human skeleton: Implications for paleopathology. In Boddington A, Garland AC, Janaway RC (eds): "Death, Decay and Reconstruction: Approaches to Archaeology and Forensic Science." Manchester, UK: Manchester University Press, pp 55–64.

Weinstein RS, Simmons DJ, Lovejoy CO (1981): Ancient bone disease in a Peruvian mummy revealed by quantitative skeletal histomorphometry. Am J Phys Anthropol 54:321–326.

Skeletal Biology of Past Peoples: Research Methods
pages 37–58 © 1992 Wiley-Liss, Inc.

Chapter 3

Biomechanical Analyses of Archaeological Human Skeletal Samples

Christopher Ruff

Department of Cell Biology and Anatomy, Johns Hopkins University School of Medicine, Baltimore, Maryland 21205

BIOMECHANICAL MODELS

A common goal of virtually all osteological comparisons between individuals or population samples is to reduce the complex morphology of bones to simpler quantifiable variables more amenable to analysis and interpretation. One possible approach is to limit the analysis to apparently "discrete" morphological features, for example, nonmetric or epigenetic cranial traits (Corruccini, 1974). A similar tactic is to divide continuously variable morphological characteristics into two or more discrete classes as is common, for example, in cladistic analyses (e.g., Skelton et al., 1986). Some of the problems inherent in such approaches, including the definition of variables and choosing of classes or categories for analysis, have been recently discussed by Trinkaus (1990). Another strategy is to include a relatively large number of metric data but to reduce these to a few underlying factors or components by multivariate statistical techniques, and then carry out comparisons with respect to these components rather than the raw data. This method, too, has been criticized on several grounds, including difficulty in interpreting the resulting factors and a tendency towards typological thinking (Armelagos et al., 1982).

An alternative approach is to start with a functional rather than statistical model of a bone and attempt to measure and compare those aspects of morphology that are relevant to the model. If a relatively simple model can be shown to be appropriate, this approach has the great advantage of directly relating form and function of skeletal elements in a readily interpretable way.

Fortunately, there does exist a relatively simple mechanical model that can be applied appropriately to the analysis of at least some skeletal elements. This is a *beam model*, the same type of model that is used by engineers to design and analyze many man-made structures (Timoshenko and Gere, 1972). A beam model is generally appropriate when the structure is long relative to its width, and when certain other requirements are met (Ruff, 1989). It is particularly applicable to the analysis of long bone diaphyses (Ruff, 1989), and has also been applied to certain other skeletal regions such as the mandibular corpus (Hylander, 1979; Daegling, 1989; Biknevicius, 1990) and the femoral neck (Phillips et al., 1975; Beck et al., 1990).

In a beam model analysis, cross sections are taken perpendicular to the long axis of the beam (bone), and certain geometric properties are determined from the amount and distribution of material (bone) in the section. These properties are direct measures of the mechanical characteristics of the bone at that section— that is, they reflect how strong (or rigid) the bone is at that location for resisting mechanical forces placed upon it. These forces, or more generally "loadings," derive from the action of gravity and muscles on the bone, and can vary owing to a number of factors, including differences in body

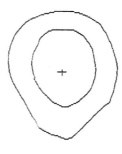

```
001GPF

Cortical Properties

TA    :       454.96
CA    :       287.26
Xbar  :        19.40
Ybar  :        31.74
Ix    :     16468.40
Iy    :     12422.80
Theta:         97.48
Imax  :     16539.40
Imin  :     12351.80
J     :     28891.20
```

User scale points @ (10 , 10) (30 , 10)

Fig. 1.   Cross section of a midshaft femur from an archaeological sample, computer reconstructed with program SLICE (also see Fig. 2). Cross indicates position of section centroid;
scale bar is oriented along x (mediolateral) axis. Geometric section properties: TA: total
subperiosteal area; CA: cortical area; Xbar, Ybar: centroid coordinates; I_x, I_y: second moments
of area about x and y axes; theta: orientation of greatest bending rigidity (major axis of
section), measured counterclockwise from the x axis; I_{max}, I_{min}: maximum and minimum
second moments of area; J: polar second moment of area. Centroid coordinates in mm, areas
in mm^2, SMA's in mm^4, theta in degrees.

mass (weight), body proportions, habitual pos-
tures, and activity types and levels. It is known
that bone tissue will adapt itself during life to
the kinds of mechanical loadings placed upon it
(Wolff, 1892; Lanyon, 1982; Cowin et al., 1985).
It is also assumed that through natural selection
some relatively optimal arrangement of bone
will evolve in order to best serve the functional
needs of the organism (e.g., Smith and Savage,
1956). Therefore, beam model properties of an
archaeological specimen should reflect the mechanical loadings of the specimen while it was
alive, and thus the biological and behavioral
characteristics of the individual that produced
those loadings.

A computer-reconstructed femoral cross
section (see below) from a human archaeological specimen is shown in Figure 1, together
with its geometric section properties. Cortical
area (CA) is a measure of strength of the section in pure axial compression or tension,
which would result from the application of two
forces perpendicular to and at the center of the
section towards or away from each other, respectively. Pure axial compressive or tensile

loadings are relatively uncommon in long
bones, however, because of the normal longitudinal curvature of bones, the ways in which
muscles act across bones, and other factors.
More important types of mechanical loadings
are bending and torsion (twisting). To investigate the adaptation of a bone to these kinds of
loadings, other geometric section properties
referred to as second moments of area, SMA's
(or area moments of inertia), must be determined. These are calculated as the product of
small unit areas of the cross section and the
squared distances of these areas from either an
axis running through the section or the center
of the section; thus, SMA's are expressed in linear dimensions to the fourth power (e.g.,
mm^4); for illustrations of the calculations involved see, for example, Burr et al. (1981) or
Sumner et al. (1985). SMA's used to measure
bending strength are calculated about an axis
(the "neutral axis") and are referred to as I
together with a subscript referring to that axis.
For example, I_x refers to the SMA about the x
axis (in Fig. 1, the mediolateral axis). The SMA
used to measure torsional strength is calcu-

Fig. 2. Digitizer with back-projected photographic slide of bone cross section for manual tracing; section reconstruction by SLICE shown on screen at left (note: not the same section as shown in Fig. 1).

lated about the center (centroid) of the section and is referred to as J, the polar second moment of area. Other section properties are listed and identified in Figure 1; for further discussion see, for example, Lovejoy et al. (1976) and Ruff and Hayes (1983a).

The two major difficulties in calculating such section properties of intact bones are, first, obtaining accurate outer (periosteal) and inner (endosteal) boundaries and, second, doing the mathematical integration (or equivalent) of the bone area necessary to actually calculate the parameters. For these reasons, earlier studies utilizing a biomechanical beam approach on long bones were limited to small to moderate sample sizes (Koch, 1917; Amtmann, 1971; Kimura, 1971a, 1974; Minns et al., 1975; Lovejoy et al., 1976; Piziali et al., 1976; Martin and Atkinson, 1977; Miller and Piotrowski, 1977; Jungers and Minns, 1979). However, both of these problems have been largely eliminated by the development and increasing accessibility of new technologies over the past decade. New methods of noninvasive imaging, particularly computed axial tomography (CAT) scanning, now allow rapid accurate reconstruction of section contours without destructive analysis (Ruff and Leo,

1986). New automated methods of calculating section properties from these images, one of which is described below, have tremendously reduced data acquisition time. A fuller account of the various techniques now available has recently been presented elsewhere (Ruff, 1989). With such techniques, it has been possible to carry out larger scale, truly demographic studies of archaeological samples (Ruff and Hayes, 1983a,b; Ruff et al., 1984; Sumner, 1984; Martin et al., 1985; Van Gerven et al., 1985; Brock and Ruff, 1988; Bridges, 1989a,b; Ruff and Larsen, 1990).

The technique we have used in the past to calculate long bone section properties is based on the SLICE program algorithm originally described by Nagurka and Hayes in 1980. A cross section image is obtained through one of several techniques—use of fortuitous breaks (Ruff et al., 1989), direct sectioning (Ruff and Hayes, 1983a,b, 1988; Ruff et al., 1984), or CAT scanning (Ruff, 1987a)—and a magnified photographic slide of the image back-projected onto a digitizer screen (Fig. 2). The periosteal and endosteal boundaries of the section are then manually traced with the digitizer stylus, with x,y boundary coordinates at a specified interval (typically 1 mm) input to the program, which runs on a microcomputer.[1] A hardcopy printout of one section analyzed by the program is shown in Figure 1. As detailed elsewhere (Ruff, 1989), when using CAT scanning, it is also possible to eliminate the intermediate step of manual section boundary tracing and work directly from the image data stored by the scanner, although this requires careful calibration and validation procedures (Ruff and Leo, 1986; Sumner et al., 1989).

It is important to emphasize that while use of a program such as SLICE on true bone cross sections is optimal for biomechanical analyses, a general appreciation of biomechanical principles and their application to skeletal structure is more important. For example, in a previous comparative study of male and female lower limb bone structure (Ruff, 1987b; also see below), once a general pattern of differences in biomechanical properties was recognized, simpler and more widely available osteometric indices could be used to investigate the same phenomenon in other population samples. Also, if the appropriate reconstruction formulas are applied (Ruff, 1989; Biknevicius, 1990), more approximate techniques of calculating section properties (e.g., from biplanar radiographs) can often be used very effectively without resorting to CAT or other more sophisticated methods.

Some specific applications of this general approach to the analysis of human archaeological remains are given in the following sections. The emphasis here is on postcranial material, and thus on biomechanics of the limbs. However, it should be noted that the method is also applicable to other skeletal areas and other types of structure–function problems, for example, the biomechanical effects of dietary differences on the morphology of the mandibular corpus (Daegling, 1989; Biknevicius, 1990). Also, results of the beam model geometric method can be combined with other types of structural analyses, such as studies of articular structure (Ruff, 1988) or histomorphometry (Burr et al., 1990). Some examples of this type of combined analysis and suggestions for areas

of future research are given at the end of this chapter.

VARIATION AMONG POPULATIONS
Changes in Subsistence Strategy

Investigations of the effects of subsistence strategy on postcranial skeletal form have tended to concentrate on total body size and occasionally general proportions or robusticity (see references in Larsen, 1982, and Cohen and Armelagos, 1984). There has also often been an overriding concern with the direct dietary effects on the skeleton of a change in subsistence. However, changes in subsistence technology can have profound effects on behavior as well (see Ruff, 1987b). Following the line of reasoning presented above, these behavioral changes can be much better elucidated from preserved skeletal remains by using a biomechanical approach.

Changes in femoral cross-sectional geometry were examined in an Amerindian sample from the Georgia coast that spanned almost 4,000 years, including a transition from a hunting–gathering subsistence strategy to one that included corn agriculture (Ruff et al., 1984). Both raw properties and properties standardized over powers of bone length (to control for differences in general body size) were analyzed. As shown schematically in Figure 3, the agricultural sample exhibited a decrease in cross-sectional area and second moments of area (i.e., bone strength) even with size standardized (see Ruff et al., 1984, for details). The agricultural femora were also rounder in cross section than the preagricultural sample. Both of these observations strongly suggest a reduction in mechanical loading of the femur, and very likely the lower limb as a whole, in the agricultural group. This was consistent with other skeletal indices, notably arthritic patterns, that indicated a general reduction in activity level and increase in sedentism with the adoption of agriculture (Larsen, 1982).

Interestingly, when compared with an Amerindian agricultural sample from Pecos Pueblo, New Mexico (Ruff and Hayes, 1983a,b), the Georgia coast agricultural femora were significantly weaker, but similar in terms of cross-sectional shape, while the preagricultural Georgia coast sample was as strong as, but dif-

---

1. At the present time versions of SLICE have been developed to run on Hewlett-Packard 9845, Digital Equipment Pro-350, IBM 386, and Macintosh II microcomputers.

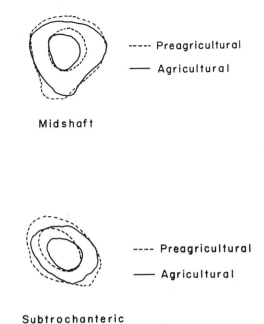

---- Preagricultural

—— Agricultural

Midshaft

---- Preagricultural

—— Agricultural

Subtrochanteric

Fig. 3. Changes in cross-sectional geometry of femora with the transition to agriculture in Georgia coast archaeological samples (outlines scaled for equal bone lengths). Agricultural femora are both relatively weaker and rounder than preagricultural femora. Reproduced from Ruff et al. (1984).

ferent in shape from, Pecos (Ruff et al., 1984: Fig. 6). This suggests that bone cross-sectional *shape* more accurately reflects *types* of mechanical loads on a bone (which would be more similar in two agricultural samples), while bone cross-sectional *size* more accurately reflects general *levels* of mechanical loads on a bone (which would be relatively high at Pecos given the rugged landscape, etc.) (also see Ruff, 1987b).

This study has recently been expanded to include the humerus as well as femur, and more recent Spanish mission cemetery samples spanning the earlier and later colonial periods on the Georgia coast (Larsen et al., 1990, in press; Ruff and Larsen, 1990). Temporal changes in the upper limb generally parallel those in the lower limb. During the colonial period, there is a reversal of the decline in bone strength noted for precontact agricultural populations, that is, native populations become

relatively stronger. However, femora generally become even rounder in the colonial period. This was interpreted as indicating a population forced to perform heavy manual labor, but at the same time becoming confined to the Spanish mission itself (with the exception of some males; see below). An increase in relative body weight to stature that resulted partly from this increased sedentism as well as a reduction in dietary quality (heavier dependence on maize) may also have contributed to the observed trends in bone cross-sectional shape. There is even evidence from these structural properties for a subgroup of males in the early colonial period who were forced into long distance travel as part of the Spanish *repartimiento* labor system (Ruff and Larsen, 1990). This example illustrates that it is sometimes possible to discern fairly specific and relatively subtle behavioral differences with this kind of analysis.

Bridges (1985, 1989a,b) reported somewhat different results in a comparison of Archaic and Mississippian samples from the Tennessee River Valley. Here some measures of relative strength of the limbs increased rather than decreased with the transition to agriculture in this region, particularly in the lower limb in males and the upper limb in females. The change in the upper limb in females was attributed to increased mechanical loads due to corn grinding. The explanation for the changes in the lower limb was not entirely clear, but these were provisionally interpreted as reflecting a general increase in activity level in the agricultural period. Thus, these results may indicate that the transition to agriculture in inland regions of the Southeastern United States was associated with a different change in behavior than that found in coastal regions. Possible explanations for this include regional differences in intensity of reliance on agriculture as well as difficulty in hoe agriculture itself, relative to prior hunting and gathering subsistence techniques. Bridges (1985) did find the same pattern of temporal change in cross-sectional bone *shape* as that documented for the Georgia coast, however. The type of change observed appears to indicate a similar increase in sedentism per se with the adoption of agriculture in this region (Ruff and Larsen, 1990). Bridges (1989b) also emphasized the need to examine changes in bone structure in multiple skeletal regions in order to distinguish local mechanical effects from general systemic effects (e.g., diet). The effects of change in subsistence strategy on bone cross-sectional properties have also been investigated in samples from three temporal periods in the American Southwest (Brock and Ruff, 1988). In this study changes in bone material as well as geometric properties were included by measuring bone densities from CAT scans[2]. The results indicated a general increase, then decrease in activity level through time, with an opposite pattern of decrease, then increase in nutritional quality. These findings were consistent with other archaeological indications of decreased sedentism and increased nutritional stress during the middle period. The intensification of agriculture in the last period produced changes in bone structure in some ways similar to those observed in the Georgia coast agricultural sample, particularly with regard to sexual dimorphism (also see below).

Finally, a recent biomechanical study of prehistoric and early historic femora from the Great Plains of North America provides evidence for skeletal adaptation to major subsistence and technological changes in a geographic region with very different environmental requirements (Ruff, in press). Early horticulturalists from this region show evidence for generally similar types of activities compared with agricultural groups from other regions of North America. However, in other respects they are more similar to hunter–gatherers, indicating that the initial adoption of food production had a minimal effect on some aspects of behavior in this region, particularly sexual division of labor. Later Plains populations who probably practiced more intensive agriculture, are more similar to agricultural populations from other areas of North America.

General Temporal Trends

In addition to the specific effects of a change in subsistence technology, a few studies have attempted to interpret more general observed temporal trends and patterns of variation in long bone structure from a biomechanical perspective.

Past investigators have commonly observed that the long bones of earlier archaeological populations tend to be less circular in cross section than those of modern industrial populations, an observation that has been interpreted in several ways (e.g., Parsons, 1914; Martin, 1928; Buxton, 1938; Brothwell, 1972). It is only relatively recently that this issue has been addressed by a true mechanical analysis, however.

One of the first of these studies was a biomechanical comparison of tibial cross-sectional shape in archaeological and modern samples by Lovejoy and colleagues in 1976.[3] On the basis of differences in relative bending and torsional strength between the samples, they hypothesized that platycnemic tibiae (i.e., those with relatively mediolaterally flattened shafts), which are prevalent among earlier pre-Neolithic and preurban populations, result from "a loading pattern [that] would include a greater proportion of anteroposterior bending strain and strain developed by external torque . . . likely to occur in active locomotion on uneven substrates" (Lovejoy et al., 1976:505). This general hypothesis was extended to a much larger archaeological sample by Ruff and Hayes (1983a; also see below), who also interpreted cross-sectional differences in shape of the fe-

---

2. Bone material properties include density, elasticity, strength, and other properties of the tissue itself (see, e.g., Burr, 1980). Both material and geometric properties affect the rigidity and strength of a structure. However, there is extensive evidence (cited in Ruff, 1989) that changes in mechanical loadings produce changes in bone geometry rather than bone material properties. Thus, measurement of geometric section properties is more appropriate for reconstructing a bone's adaptation to its mechanical environment (also see Ruff and Hayes, 1983a). In contrast, *systemic* effects such as changes in diet may affect bone composition (see Brock and Ruff, 1988). Thus, by measuring material and geometric properties of skeletal remains, it should theoretically be possible to better distinguish dietary and behavioral factors in past populations (Brock and Ruff, 1988). One potential problem in such studies is the uncertain effects of soil preservation, and so forth, on material properties; except in extreme cases these will not affect bone geometric properties.

---

3. Kimura (1971a) included some archaeological specimens in his description of tibial cross-sectional geometry, and Preuschoft (1971) determined cross-sectional properties of the Olduvai 35 hominid tibia, but neither attempted any description or explanation of general temporal trends in these properties. Endo and Kimura (1970), in their analysis of the Amud I Neanderthal postcranial skeleton, included comparative tibial cross-sectional (as well as traditional osteometric) data for a wider range of specimens, and also presented a general functional explanation for the differences observed (Endo and Kimura, 1970:350–355). However to my knowledge, Lovejoy et al. (1976) were the first to carry out a systematic detailed comparison of sections along the entire length of a bone (tibia) in archaeological and modern samples, and to postulate a specific biomechanical hypothesis explaining the sample differences.

mur and tibia to result from generally higher mechanical loadings in earlier populations. Other biomechanical studies of hominid paleontological samples (Lovejoy and Trinkaus, 1980; Trinkaus and Ruff, 1989; Ruff et al., in preparation) indicate that activity levels and/ or muscular loadings in pre-Holocene hominids were even higher than in archaeological samples, and that the general gracility of modern human long bones is a very recent phenomenon (Ruff et al., in preparation).

Lovejoy (1978, 1979) has also cautioned against the too strict application of long bone biomechanical analysis to the reconstruction of general locomotor differences among past human (and nonhuman) skeletal samples, because of the extreme phenotypic plasticity of bone tissue and its responsiveness to idiosyncratic behaviors. In fact, extending his analysis of the tibia described above, he predicted (1979: 410) that in terms of relative maximum to minimum bending rigidities of the tibia (i.e., "platycnemia"), some recent human populations might group more closely with pongids than with other human populations.

To test this proposition, as well as to illustrate some other points regarding cross-sectional shape analysis, a comparison was carried out of two section properties—the ratio of maximum to minimum bending rigidities (I_{max}/I_{min}), and the orientation of greatest bending rigidity (theta)—at five locations in the tibial diaphysis in two recent human population samples and a chimpanzee sample. In addition to their biomechanical importance, these particular geometric properties have the advantage of being size-independent. They are illustrated, along with the locations of the sections analyzed, in Figure 4. The two recent human groups are the late prehistoric and protohistoric Pecos Pueblo archaeological sample ($n = 119$; Ruff and Hayes, 1983a) and a modern U.S. white autopsy sample ($n = 42$; Ruff and Hayes, 1988). For the modern U.S. sample, only individuals under 60 years of age are included to avoid the more extreme effects of aging (osteoporosis) on bone structure properties (e.g., Martin et al., 1980; Ruff and Hayes, 1988). The chimpanzee sample consists of wild-shot museum specimens included in another study ($n = 20$; Ruff, 1987a). Sexes are combined, with about equal numbers of males

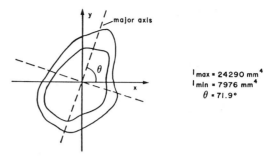

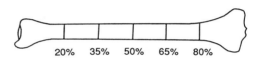

Fig. 4. Tibial cross section with maximum and minimum second moments of area (I_{max}, I_{min}) and orientation of major axis, theta (θ), and locations of tibial cross sections included in the analysis shown in Figure 5 and Figure 6. The I_{max}/I_{min} ratio of the 65% section illustrated (from Pecos Pueblo) is 3.05. A lower ratio would indicate a more circular section.

and females in each sample. The comparisons between samples are shown in Figure 5 (I_{max}/I_{min}) and Figure 6 (theta).

As shown in Figure 5, it is apparent that recent human populations can vary greatly in the ratio of maximum to minimum bending rigidity of tibial cross sections, and that one sample (U.S. white autopsy) does indeed group much more closely with chimpanzees than with the other human sample (Pecos). Thus, this particular biomechanical characteristic does *not* serve as a good indicator of general locomotor differences between species, as predicted previously (Lovejoy, 1979). However, as shown in Figure 6, despite the large difference in maximum to minimum bending rigidity in the two human samples, they are virtually indistinguishable, except in the most distal section, in the *orientation* of these bending rigidities, while chimpanzees show a completely different pattern of variation in this property. The similarity among all humans in theta (also see Ruff and Hayes, 1983a: Fig. 8) is reasonable, since this property indicates the direction of

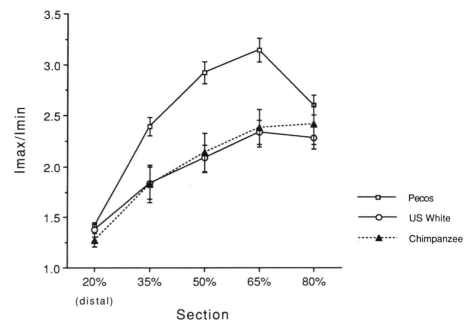

Fig. 5. Maximum-to-minimum second moments of area (bending rigidities) of five tibial cross sections in three samples: an archaeological sample from Pecos Pueblo (n = 119; Ruff and Hayes, 1983a), a U.S. white autopsy sample (n = 42; Ruff and Hayes, 1988), and a chimpanzee sample (n = 20; Ruff, 1987a) (also see text). Mean ±2 SE; sexes combined.

greatest bending loads on the tibia, which on average should be fairly consistent in a biped regardless of activity level (Carter, 1978).[4] In contrast, it is not unexpected that the orientation of greatest bending loads in the tibia would be quite different in a quadruped because of differences in limb orientation during locomotion, and so forth.

This example illustrates two points regarding the use of long bone cross-sectional properties for comparisons between groups. First, it is important, at least initially, to examine patterns of variation in *all* properties, since different properties may produce different groupings. Second, properties will vary in how informative they are in elucidating different types of relationships, depending

upon the particular research questions of interest. For example, at least for the tibia, if the major focus of a study were determining whether major adaptive (locomotor) differences existed between two early hominids, the orientation of greatest bending rigidity might be an appropriate characteristic to examine. On the other hand, if the intent of the study were to determine more minor variations in mechanical loadings, for example, differences in activity level (or frequency of long distance travel) between relatively recent human populations with the same basic locomotor mode, then the ratio of greatest to least bending strength of the tibia would be a more informative characteristic (Lovejoy et al., 1976; Ruff and Hayes, 1983a,b; Ruff, 1987b). In some cases, for example in estimating body weight from skeletal remains (Ruff, 1987a; Ruff et al., 1989), the investigator may wish to ignore *both* of these types of characteristics and concentrate on properties that are less influenced by the specific types of mechanical

---

4. The deviation between the two human samples in the most distal section is probably due to the relative circularity of this section in all samples (Fig. 5), reflecting the reduction in relative importance of bending in this region of the tibia (see discussion in Ruff and Hayes, 1983a).

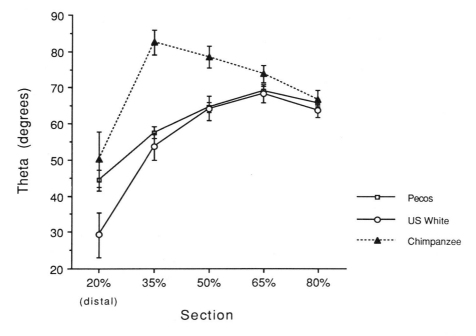

Fig. 6. Orientation of greatest bending rigidity, theta, in five tibial cross sections in three samples (see Fig. 5). Mean ±2 SE.

loadings and are more related to the overall *magnitude* of loading. In this case, cross-sectional area or a combined measure of second moments of area in all directions (J, the polar second moment of area) might be more appropriate characteristics to examine (e.g., Ruff et al., 1989).

VARIATION WITHIN POPULATIONS
Age-Related Bone Loss

Loss of bone with aging in adults that leads to increased fracture risk in old age, commonly referred to as *osteoporosis*,[5] is a major medical and societal problem in modern human popu-

lations, particularly among women in Western industrialized countries (Chalmers and Ho, 1970; Riggs and Melton, 1986). Osteoporosis has also been demonstrated in many archaeological samples, by a variety of measurement techniques (Dewey et al., 1969; Van Gerven et al., 1969; Van Gerven and Armelagos, 1970; Van Gerven, 1973; Mielke et al., 1972; Perzigian, 1973; Carlson et al., 1976; Ericksen, 1976; Ruff and Hayes, 1982, 1983b; Martin et al., 1985).

Two general conclusions can be drawn from these studies. First, basic age changes in bone mass and volume are broadly similar in all populations. Peak bone mass is reached in the third or fourth decade and declines thereafter, more rapidly in women. The etiology of osteoporosis is probably generally similar in all populations as well. Recent studies of living populations have distinguished two types of osteoporosis, one resulting from menopause and the loss of the protective effect of estrogen on bone mass (Type I), and the other a more gradual process occurring in both sexes throughout life, possibly as a result of reduced absorption of calcium

---

5. The term *osteoporosis* has historically been used in anthropology to indicate bone loss in general, usually with aging, and as such would be equivalent to *osteopenia* as often used in clinical literature. Since different types of osteopenia (e.g., preferential loss of bone mineral, or osteomalacia) could not be or at least were not distinguished in the great majority of skeletal archeological studies reviewed here, and because of its widespread usage historically, I have retained the traditional terminology of *osteoporosis* with the understanding that as used here this is synonymous to osteopenia.

or other factors (Type II) (Riggs and Melton, 1986). The two types are superimposed in women, accounting for their more rapid bone loss in the sixth and seventh decades, and are apparently characterized by different effects on bone tissue and thus fracture types: Type I preferentially affects trabecular bone (and thus fractures of primarily trabecular bone regions, such as the distal end of the radius), and Type II affects both compact and trabecular bone (and thus fractures of mixed tissue regions such as the femoral neck). It seems likely that these same general mechanisms of skeletal aging occurred in past populations as well. In fact, in a study by photon absorptiometry of two archaeological samples that included regions of primarily trabecular and primarily compact bone (Perzigian, 1973), males and females showed about equal losses of compact bone, while females showed greater losses of trabecular bone—a finding that is consistent with this model.

The second general conclusion is that measures of bone mass or volume alone are not sufficient to characterize patterns of skeletal aging. This includes both raw measures, such as bone mineral content (BMC) and cortical thickness (CT) or cortical area (CA), and various "size-standardized" measures, such as BMC divided by bone width, or CT or CA divided by bone width or total bone area (%CT or %CA). These measures are insufficient because none of them adequately reflects age changes in geometry or important bone material properties other than density (Ruff and Hayes, 1984a,b). For example, it has now been shown by several investigators that long bones continue to expand slightly on their subperiosteal surface throughout life (Smith and Walker, 1964; Garn, 1970; Carlson et al., 1976; Martin and Atkinson, 1977; Ruff and Hayes, 1982, 1983b, 1988). This tends to compensate for medullary expansion with aging, and also a decline in bone material strength, by increasing second moments of area and thus bending and torsional strength (see references above; also see Burr and Martin, 1983). Thus, measures of either raw CT or CA, or %CT or %CA, still cited in some archaeological studies (e.g., Cook, 1984), can present an incomplete and even misleading impression of bone remodeling with aging (or in response to nutritional stress; see Ruff et al., 1984, and

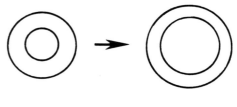

△ % Cortical Thickness:	- 33%
△ % Cortical Area:	- 33%
△ Cortical Area:	+12%
△ Second Moments of Area:	+100%

Fig. 7. Effects of subperiosteal and medullary expansion on bone cross-sectional geometric properties. The section on the right has decreased percentage cortical thickness and percentage cortical area relative to the section on the left, yet it shows a slight increase in cortical area (axial strength) and a large increase in second moments of area (bending and torsional strengths).

Bridges, 1989b). As illustrated in Figure 7, given subperiosteal expansion, a decrease in %CA may actually indicate an *increase* in bending and torsional strength. Thus, interpretation of negative trends in such measures as necessarily "detrimental" to skeletal integrity is unwarranted.

Observed differences between populations in patterns of bone loss or remodeling with aging have been attributed to both genetic and environmental factors, the latter including diet and activity levels. While some earlier studies emphasized differences in diet as a factor (Dewey et al., 1969), most subsequent studies have tended to discount direct dietary effects (Perzigian, 1973; also see Garn, 1970, and Riggs et al., 1987) and to consider variation in mechanical loadings as more important (Carlson et al., 1976; Ericksen, 1976; Ruff and Hayes, 1982, 1983b, 1988; however, see Martin et al., 1985).

Sex or population differences in bone geometric remodeling with aging may have important consequences on fracture likelihood in old age. Figure 8 is a schematic summary of geometric changes with age in the femoral and tibial cortex of the Pecos Pueblo archaeologi-

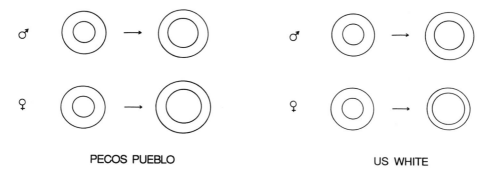

PECOS PUEBLO   US WHITE

Fig. 8. Schematic representation of geometric remodeling with age in the femoral and tibial cortices of two samples: Pecos Pueblo (Ruff and Hayes, 1982, 1983b) and a U.S. white sample (Ruff and Hayes, 1988). Males of both samples and females of the Pecos Pueblo sample show subperiosteal expansion with aging concurrent with medullary expansion, thus maintaining or even increasing bone strength (also see Fig. 7). In contrast, U.S. white females show medullary expansion but little subperiosteal expansion with aging, leading to reduced bone strength and higher susceptibility to fracture (see text).

cal sample (Ruff and Hayes, 1982, 1983a) and a modern U.S. autopsy sample (Ruff and Hayes, 1988). Males and females in both samples undergo significant endosteal resorption and medullary expansion with aging. However, Pecos males and females, and modern U.S. males, compensate for this through concurrent subperiosteal expansion, while modern U.S. females do not. This lack of geometric compensatory remodeling may contribute to the higher risk of fracture among modern U.S. women (and women in industrialized societies in general) (also see Martin and Atkinson, 1977). Interestingly, women in modern nonindustrial societies do not suffer the same increase in fracture incidence with aging (Chalmers and Ho, 1970; Barss, 1985), which is consistent with this observation. The reason for the apparent difference in skeletal remodeling and thus fracture risk is not entirely certain, but a general decline in activity level in industrialized populations leading to inadequate bone deposition during adult life, is a strong candidate (Barss, 1984; Ruff and Hayes, 1988).

Sexual Dimorphism

Comparative studies of sexual dimorphism in overall body size in past human populations have been fairly common (e.g., Frayer, 1980, 1984; Trinkaus, 1980; Hamilton, 1982; also see Armelagos and Van Gerven, 1980). Interpretations of population differences in this regard have emphasized both nutritional (Hamilton, 1982) and mechanical (Frayer, 1980, 1984) factors. However, overall size, and even general robusticity of skeletal dimensions, is a relatively imprecise (or incomplete) measure of sexual dimorphism in skeletal structure (Ruff, 1987b). More precise reconstructions of behavioral differences between males and females can be obtained from bone shape characteristics.

Sex differences in long bone cross-sectional shape, and variation among populations in the degree of this difference, have long been recognized (Hrdlicka, 1898, 1934; Parsons, 1914; Holtby, 1917; Pearson and Bell, 1919; Martin, 1928). Ruff and Hayes (1983b) found some striking differences in cross-sectional shape of the lower limb bones between males and females of the Pecos Pueblo archaeological sample. In particular, males of this sample showed an adaptation to relatively greater anteroposterior bending loads in the region from the midtibia to the midfemur, that is, around the knee.

This analysis was later extended to a modern U.S. white sample and a variety of other samples—modern, archaeological, and paleontological (Ruff, 1987b). Some of the data from this study are summarized in Figure 9, which plots sexual dimorphism in the ratios of anteroposterior (AP) to mediolateral (ML) bending strength (I_x/I_y) and AP to ML external breadths

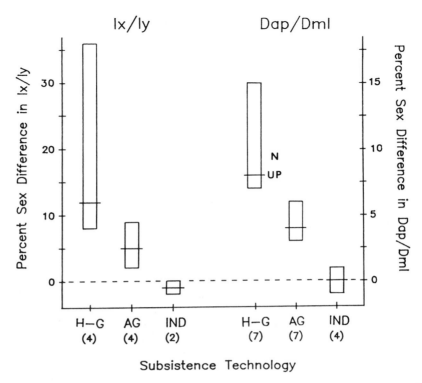

Fig. 9. Changes in sexual dimorphism of two indices of relative anteroposterior-to-mediolateral bending strength of the midshaft femur with changes in subsistence technology. I_x/I_y: ratio of second moments of area about x and y axes; D_{ap}/D_{ml}: ratio of AP to ML external diameters. Sexual dimorphism = [(males − females)/females] × 100. Ranges and medians shown for population sample means within each subsistence type: HG: hunter–gatherers; AG: agriculturalists; IND: industrial (numbers in parentheses indicate number of samples). N and UP indicate mean sexual dimorphism in Neandertal ($n = 13$) and Upper Paleolithic ($n = 19$) samples, respectively. Modifications from Ruff (1987b).

$(D_{ap}/D_{ml}$, the pilasteric index) of the midshaft femur in a number of different samples, arranged by subsistence technology (see Ruff, 1987b, for details). As shown here, the degree of sexual dimorphism in relative AP bending strength of the midshaft femur steadily declines from hunter–gatherers through agriculturalists to industrial populations. The same is true of all cross sections from the midfemur to the midtibia (Ruff, 1987b: Tables 1–4). Neandertals and early anatomically modern (Upper Paleolithic) samples show the same sexual dimorphism in shape indices as modern hunter–gatherers. This is true despite the fact that Neandertals *as a whole* exhibit some dif

ferences in lower limb bone cross-sectional shape from *Homo sapiens sapiens* (Trinkaus, 1980; Trinkaus and Ruff, 1989). More recent analyses of other population samples also strongly support these observations (Ruff, in press; Larsen et al., 1991).

This sex difference in femoral and tibial shape can be related to differences in mobility patterns between the sexes. Kinesiological studies of living humans indicate that anteroposterior bending loads on the lower limb, particularly in the region around the knee, are much greater during running or climbing than during walking (Ruff, 1987b). Ethnographic studies indicate that economic tasks that require long distance travel are almost always assigned to males, and that with increasing dependence on agriculture and technological specialization males generally tend to be assigned more sedentary tasks (Ruff, 1987b; Murdock and Provost, 1973). Thus, the observed differences in skeletal morphology appear to reflect culturally prescribed differences in behavioral patterns between the sexes. The results shown in Figure 9 also indicate that the sexual division of labor found in modern hunter–gatherers was apparently present at least as far back as the Middle Paleolithic.

Another consistent, although not as pronounced, difference between the sexes observed in this study was that females tend to have slightly less circular proximal femoral shafts than males; that is, they are relatively stronger in the mediolateral plane. This difference, unlike the difference near the knee, was relatively constant and showed no relationship to subsistence strategy. It most likely reflects differences in pelvic morphology related to obstetric requirements (females being relatively wider mediolaterally) that are also fairly constant across different populations, including those from the Middle and Upper Paleolithic.

These results also have some implications with regard to sex determination techniques that use measurements of the femoral or tibial diaphyses (Kimura, 1971b; Black, 1978; DiBennardo and Taylor, 1979, 1982; İşcan and Miller-Shaivitz, 1984; MacLaughlin and Bruce, 1985; Dittrick and Suchey, 1986). Since males in archaeological samples will tend to have relatively larger AP-to-ML dimensions from the midshaft femur to midshaft tibia, and males are larger on average in all dimensions, AP breadths should more clearly distinguish the sexes than ML breadths (as is in fact demonstrated in several of the above studies). This suggests that AP/ML shaft breadth ratios of the femur and tibia, in combination with size measures, might aid in sex determination. However, the accuracy of these determinations will depend upon the particular subsistence strategy and sexual division of labor that characterize the sample. In fact, if adequate samples are available and sexing can be accomplished independently, the relative degree of sexual dimorphism in cross-sectional shape in this skel-

etal region could be used to investigate differences in subsistence technology and mobility patterns in past populations.

Although this discussion has been limited to the lower limb, the general approach is applicable to other skeletal regions as well. For example, as noted earlier, Bridges (1989a,b) illustrated some differences in the effects of the introduction of agriculture on the cross-sectional properties of upper limb bones of males and females in Tennessee River Valley population samples. Also, the data in Figure 9 show that once a hypothesis has been formulated in mechanical terms, it is sometimes possible to test the hypothesis by using more widely available traditional osteometrics in addition to true biomechanical section properties. However, caution should be exercised here that the two are actually measuring the same thing, that is, that the simple linear measurements are adequately reflecting the significant functional characteristics of the specimen. As an example, average external breadth or circumference of long bones in early hominids are *not* good indices of their overall strengths under mechanical loadings, given the very thick cortices and small medullary cavities of most of these specimens relative to modern humans (Kennedy, 1985; Trinkaus and Ruff, 1989).

Preadult Growth and Development

Changes during preadult growth and development in bone breadths and extrapolated areas, usually of the second metacarpal, have been studied in living populations by many investigators (e.g., Smithgall et al., 1966; Frisancho et al., 1970; Himes et al., 1975). The focus of these studies, and of comparable studies of archaeological samples (e.g., Cook, 1979), has been largely on the effects of nutrition and disease on bone growth and development. Biomechanical studies of skeletal growth and development in human samples have been extremely rare.[6] One study that did examine preadult patterns of change in geometric section properties was an investigation of tibial modeling in a Medieval Nubian juvenile sample by

---

6. There have been several studies of bone *material* property changes with age during preadult growth and development in humans; for review see Currey (1984: 93–96); also see Currey and Pond (1989).

Van Gerven and colleagues (1985). Cross-sectional bone areas were measured through direct sectioning, while bone mineral content and second moments of area were derived from photon absorptiometric data (Martin and Burr, 1984). This study clearly demonstrated the danger in using periosteal area or breadth to "standardize" either cortical area (CA) or bone mineral content (BMC) (see the present Figure 7). While %CA declined during adolescence in this sample because of concurrent subperiosteal expansion, second moments of area showed large *increases* over the same age range. Also, while BMC standardized over bone width showed a continuous increase with age, BMC over true bone area remained almost constant after age 6 years (also see Ruff and Hayes, 1984a,b).[7] These observations helped resolve some apparent anomalies noted earlier in the pattern of adolescent skeletal growth and development in this sample, namely, normal growth in long bone length and bone areas but apparently "abnormal" change in %CA (Hummert, 1983).

Another interesting observation of the Nubian study was that anteroposterior to mediolateral bending strength of the midshaft tibia increased throughout childhood and adolescence; that is, the bones became less circular through time. Data reported by Sumner (1984) for a Southwestern Amerindian juvenile sample also indicate an increase in the ratio of AP/ML bending rigidity of the midfemur and distal femur during growth and development. However, concurrently with this change, the *orientation* of greatest bending rigidity in the femur remained very similar. This is interesting in relation to the hypothesis advanced earlier in this chapter that the orientation of maximum loading of the lower limb bones may be relatively constant among (modern) humans, while the relative magnitudes of maximum and minimum bending loads vary in response to particular activity types or levels. It would also be interesting to determine how early in development the pattern of sexual dimorphism in bone cross-sectional shape (and inferred behavior) noted above for adults is established in different population samples. I am currently exploring these questions in a group of juveniles from the Pecos Pueblo archaeological sample. Initial results indicate that the sex difference in bone shape around the knee is already present in middle to late adolescence in this sample.

VARIATION WITHIN INDIVIDUALS
Bilateral Asymmetry

Measuring the degree of bilateral asymmetry in limb bone dimensions present within individuals is another way to investigate the effects of mechanical loadings on skeletal structure in archaeological samples. This approach has several advantages since systemic factors, such as nutrition or overall activity level, as well as body size, are inherently controlled. Differences in the average degree of asymmetry present within populations or subsets of populations may be indicative of significant differences in behavioral characteristics.

Only a few studies of archaeological samples have directly examined bilateral asymmetry in long bone cross-sectional dimensions from a mechanical point of view, and most of these have concentrated on the upper limb bones (Bridges, 1989a; Fresia et al., 1990), although some have also examined bones from the lower limb (Ruff and Jones, 1981; Ruff and Hayes, 1983b). These have confirmed the long-standing observations that human right upper limb bones tend to be more robust (i.e., be designed to withstand higher mechanical loads) than left upper limb bones, and that, to a much less marked degree, a reverse pattern of left "dominance" is found in the lower limb bones (see references in Ruff and Jones, 1981). However, these studies have also shown that the degree and patterning of bilateral asymmetry in bone strength can vary depending upon the particular group examined.

---

7. Of course, in any such study of bone mass or density (as opposed to geometry) in archaeological samples, the possible effects of diagenesis must be considered. In a study of bone mineral content in the Pecos sample (Ruff and Hayes, 1984b) it was noted that femoral bone cores obtained from the same sample and measured directly had a rewetted density of $1.901 \pm .026$ g/cm^3 (mean $\pm$ 1 SE), which is identical to that reported for modern compact cortical bone (1.8–2.0 g/cm^3). This was taken to indicate that no significant degeneration of the material had taken place subsequent to burial, at least with regard to density and relative mineral content. Under different preservation conditions, though, reduced bone tissue density may be apparent following even a few hundred years of burial (see Ruff and Leo, 1986: Fig. 4, and discussion in text). Even here, however, variation between individuals within the same archaeological site (assuming no large differences in preservation conditions) should still be a valid index in a relative sense, of bone density variation prior to burial (Ruff and Leo, 1986).

TABLE 1. Bilateral Asymmetry[a,b] in Middistal Humeral Bending and Torsional Strengths in Three Samples

Sample[c]	Sex	n	% Difference between sides		
			I_x	I_y	J
California Amerindians	Male	30	15.6	7.0	16.3
	Female	39	6.4	5.3	6.1
Georgia Coast Amerindians	Male	19	4.5	8.9	6.1
	Female	18	1.6	8.3	4.7
Professional tennis players	Male	34	64.7	73.2	68.5
	Female	12	36.7	51.4	43.5

[a]For Amerindian samples, [(right − left)/left] · 100; for tennis players, [(playing side − nonplaying side)/nonplaying side] · 100.
[b]I_x: second moment of area about mediolateral axis (AP bending strength); I_y: second moment of area about anteroposterior axis (ML bending strength); J: polar second moment of area (torsional strength).
[c]See text for provenience of samples.

Fresia et al. (1990) clearly showed that bilateral asymmetry in humeral bone strength declined through time on the Georgia coast, first with the introduction of agriculture, and then with Spanish colonization. Furthermore, the timing of this decline differed between males and females, females showing the largest decline with the adoption of agriculture, and males with historic contact and missionization. Sexual dimorphism in humeral bilateral asymmetry was largest in the precontact agricultural period and smallest in the historic period. These observations were interpreted to indicate that agriculture had a marked effect on differential use of the upper limbs in females (leading to a more equal use of both limbs), and that the same kind of effect occurred in males only later, in the historic period. This supports the Bridges (1989a) hypothesis that the introduction of agriculture to Southeastern Amerindian populations caused a more equal distribution of mechanical loading on the left and right upper limbs owing to the requirements of maize grinding, which would be preferentially carried out by women. The evidence from the Georgia coast is also consistent with the hypothesis (Ruff and Larsen, 1990) that men were increasingly recruited to perform traditionally "female" (i.e., agricultural) tasks by the Spanish colonialists, thus leading to reduced levels of sexual dimorphism in behavioral use of the upper limb bones in this period.

The percentage differences between right and left sides in bending and torsional strengths of the middistal humerus are listed in Table 1 for three very different samples: a hunting–gathering–fishing archaeological sample from San Francisco Bay (Ruff and Jones, 1981), a historic Amerindian sample from the Georgia coast (Ruff and Larsen, unpublished data), and a sample of professional tennis players (Jones et al., 1977; Ruff et al., in preparation).[8] Cross-sectional geometric measurements of the Georgia coast sample were determined through sectioning and direct measurement, while properties of the other samples were estimated from reported subperiosteal and medullary breadths in two planes, using standard formulas and assuming an elliptical section (Fresia et al., 1990).

The hunting–gathering–fishing sample from California has higher levels of humeral asymmetry among males (16%–17%) than females (5%–6%), while the levels of asymmetry in males and females in the historic Georgia coast sample are nearly equal and low, about the level of the female California sample. This is consistent with the hypothesis advanced above

8. The Georgia coast sample is from the Santa Maria site on Amelia Island, from a somewhat later time period (A.D. 1686–1702) than the historic sample used in previous analyses (Ruff and Larsen, 1990; Fresia et al., 1990; also see Larsen et al., in press). The California Amerindian sample is from Alameda 329 site, dated to about A.D. 500–1000 (Ruff and Jones, 1981). Both samples are adult. The professional tennis players include a few juveniles under 18 years of age (girls only). Properties for this sample were recalculated from raw data originally used in another study (Jones et al., 1977); only individuals with no missing data were included in the new study (Ruff et al., in preparation).

that male and female subsistence tasks became very similar during the historic period on the Georgia coast, while prehistoric samples show more sexual dimorphism (the California sample is actually more similar in this regard to the Bridges (1989a) inland sample than the precontact Georgia coast samples). It is also consistent with the temporal decline in sexual dimorphism in lower limb bone shape discussed earlier (Ruff, 1987b).

The professional tennis players represent an extreme of bilateral asymmetry in upper limb bone strength (about 35%–50% in women and 65%–75% in men). This may represent a near limit for skeletal adaptation to variation in mechanical loads, short of pathological conditions. Interestingly, Neandertals, who have relatively robust limb bones in general (Trinkaus and Ruff, 1989), also show markedly greater bilateral asymmetry in the upper limb bones than modern human samples (Trinkaus et al., 1990). This may suggest a pattern of greater upper limb specialization of use in earlier hominids, although more data will be required to fully test this hypothesis.

Bilateral asymmetry in lower limb bone cross-sectional dimensions was also studied in the California sample (tibia; Ruff and Jones, 1981) and the Pecos Pueblo sample (tibia and femur; Ruff and Hayes, 1983b). In both samples bones from the left side were stronger than bones from the right side, and females showed more asymmetry than males. Also, in both samples bones from the left side showed adaptations to relatively greater anteroposterior bending loads. This suggests that the left lower limb may have been used to "push off" in conjunction with use of the right upper limb—the so-called "crossed symmetry" pattern observed by Schaeffer (1928). To date no comparable data have been collected for very recent industrial population samples (outside of select athletes), but given the results reported above it seems likely that both lower and upper limb bone asymmetry would be relatively small in such samples.

Intermembral Proportions

No one has yet reported actual ratios of upper to lower limb bone cross-sectional geometric properties in a human sample, although

such a study has been carried out for some nonhuman primates (Schaffler et al., 1985). Both Bridges (1989a,b) and Ruff and Larsen (1990) have reported some different patterns of change in the upper and lower limbs with the adoption of agriculture, some of which appeared to be sex-specific, but actual paired intraindividual analyses were not carried out. Such analyses will be important not only in elucidating minor behavioral shifts in relatively recent human populations, but also in providing baseline data with which to evaluate currently competing theories on upper and lower limb use, and relative arboreality/terrestriality of early hominids (e.g., Susman et al., 1985; Latimer et al., 1987).

OTHER STRUCTURAL CHARACTERISTICS

Although this review has emphasized biomechanical analysis of long bone diaphyses using a beam model, there are other types of functional approaches to skeletal structure that can yield important insights into past mechanical use. Two of these—analysis of articulations and bone histomorphometry—are briefly considered here. It is not the purpose here to review in detail the studies of archaeological material that have used these methods (also see Stout, this volume, Chapter 2). Rather, a few examples germane to the general issues discussed above, particularly where these approaches have been combined with diaphyseal analysis, will be discussed.

Articulations and Osteoarthritis

Although there is some conflicting evidence, a preponderance of studies have implicated increased mechanical loading (or overloading) of joints as a major cause of osteoarthritis (OA), or degenerative joint disease (for a review see Peyron, 1986). Based on this relationship, patterns of occurrence of osteoarthritis in skeletal samples have been used by several investigators to help reconstruct behavioral characteristics of past populations (e.g., Merbs, 1983; for an extensive review, see Larsen, 1987).

Larsen (1982; Larsen et al., 1990, in press) has documented changes in the frequency of OA through time in the same Georgia coast samples as those included in the diaphyseal analyses discussed earlier. In general, the two types of analyses produce closely concordant results. That is, during temporal periods when diaphyseal cross-sectional geometric dimensions indicate a relative increase or decrease in mechanical loadings of the skeleton, OA also increases or decreases, respectively. Thus, on the whole, the frequency of OA declines from the preagricultural to the agricultural periods in this region, then increases during the contact period. The relatively high frequency of OA in the historic period may have been the result of increased heavy lifting or other stereotypic repetitive tasks under the forced labor system imposed by the Spanish.

With respect to sexual dimorphism in activity patterns under different subsistence strategies, the OA data are again largely consistent with the long bone diaphyseal shape analyses presented earlier (Ruff, 1987b). Sexual dimorphism in OA is greatest in preindustrial populations and declines in modern Western skeletal samples (Jurmain, 1977, 1980). Even bilateral asymmetry of occurrence of OA seems to some extent to parallel asymmetry in diaphyseal dimensions. For example, Jurmain (1977) documented a higher incidence of knee OA on the left side in a sample from Pecos Pueblo, with a more marked difference among females. This corresponds exactly to the pattern of asymmetry in diaphyseal strength (and thus inferred mechanical loadings) noted earlier for lower limb bones from this sample (Ruff and Hayes, 1983b).

Thus, to a large extent degenerative joint disease and diaphyseal cross-sectional geometry seem to reflect similar variations in the mechanical environment, that is, increases or decreases in mechanical loading of a skeletal region. This follows from a consideration of the different types of constraints on bone remodeling and thus responses to mechanical loadings characteristic of articulations and diaphyses. As shown elsewhere (Ruff, 1988; Ruff et al., 1991), joints apparently cannot respond to increases in mechanical loads by increasing their size, at least in adults. The most likely response of an articulation to increased loading is to increase the density of trabecular bone underlying the joint surface (e.g., Radin et al., 1982, 1984). This in turn would be expected to

stiffen the joint surface, reducing its compliance (i.e., its ability to absorb energy), and thus increasing rather than decreasing stress in the joint cartilage, and leading eventually to cartilage failure and the development of OA. In contrast, there are no such bone remodeling constraints on bone diaphyses, which consequently respond to increased (or decreased) mechanical loadings through changes in cross-sectional size and shape.

Given this view of bone adaptation, though, it is also likely that observed changes in frequency of OA and diaphyseal cross-sectional geometry in skeletal samples, though generally paralleling each other, will not be perfectly concordant, for several reasons. First, moderate increases in mechanical loadings may be reflected in cross-sectional diaphyseal changes but may be within the "tolerance" of joints, not leading (at least immediately) to the development of OA. Second, in almost all cases OA would be expected to develop later than changes in cross-sectional geometry, so that samples of younger adults may not show as good correspondence between the two. Finally, it is possible that certain types of mechanical loadings may produce relatively greater increases in mechanical loadings of joints than of diaphyses (and vice versa). For example, activities that produce bending and torsion are probably the most significant in terms of diaphyseal remodeling (Ruff and Hayes, 1983a), while such loadings would not necessarily produce the highest loads on a joint. In terms of the first two factors above, measurement of trabecular density within articulations could be a useful addition to recording of OA for determining relative joint loadings in past populations, particularly younger populations. Both invasive (Mielke et al., 1972) and noninvasive techniques (Huddleston, 1988) are available for making such determinations.

Bone Histomorphometry

Bone microstructural analysis has been applied to archaeological skeletal samples for varied purposes, the primary being age at death determinations and identification of metabolic bone diseases, including the effects of dietary deficiencies (e.g., Richman and Ortner, 1978; Stout and Simmons, 1979; Ericksen, 1980;

Thompson and Trinkaus, 1981). Since this general topic is covered elsewhere in this volume (Stout, Chapter 2), I will limit my comments to a few cases where histomorphometry of bone has been related to mechanical factors.

It appears that adequate mechanical stress is necessary to maintain normal cortical bone microstructural remodeling (Stout, 1982), and that increases in stress may produce increases in remodeling (Bouvier and Hylander, 1981). Thus, variations in cross-sectional geometric parameters and microstructural parameters in response to variations in mechanical loading may be related. Two studies support this general hypothesis. A histomorphometric study of core biopsies from the anterior femoral cortex of the Pecos Pueblo archaeological sample (Burr et al., 1990) showed some features that appeared to be related to the more active lifestyle of this sample that had also been indicated by the cross-sectional geometric analysis described above. Specifically, males showed a greater osteon population density (OPD) and females a larger osteonal mean wall thickness than found in modern U.S. populations. The greater OPD in males indicates more frequent activation of remodeling and more rapid bone turnover in the anterior femoral cortex than in females, which may be another reflection of increased anteroposterior bending of the femoral midshaft in males of this sample, indicated by the cross-sectional geometric data (Ruff and Hayes, 1983b, Ruff, 1987b).

Lazenby (1986) reported an apparent correspondence between porosity and section properties of the midshaft femora of an autopsy sample of older Euroamericans, with apparent "compensation" for increased porosity by increased geometric resistance to bending (i.e., increased second moments of area). This is generally consistent with the observations of Martin and coworkers (Martin and Atkinson, 1977; Martin et al., 1980) and Ruff and Hayes (1982, 1983b, 1988) with regard to geometric "compensatory" skeletal remodeling with aging.

There is obviously great potential for deducing mechanical loadings from combined analysis of both macrostructural and microstructural features. Most previous histomorphometric studies have been concerned with systemic rather than localized effects on bone structure, and have thus tended to sample only one skeletal location or a very few. However, one aim of a mechanically oriented study would be to document *variation* among locations in microstructural parameters, since mechanical effects tend to be relatively localized. Thus, a prime objective of future histomorphometric studies should be to increase the number of sampling sites and to include as many types of locations under different types of mechanical loadings as possible. This approach would also be of value in studies in which the primary aim is paleopathological and dietary reconstruction, since it would help to sort out the effects of localized mechanical responses of bone from more systemic responses.

CONCLUSIONS

An approach to morphological variation that begins with a mechanical rather than statistical model of a bone can more directly relate form to function in archaeological skeletal samples. A biomechanical beam model is particularly applicable to the functional analysis of long bone diaphyses (as well as other skeletal regions such as the mandibular corpus). Advances in technology have allowed faster collection of the cross-sectional geometric data that are necessary for this kind of analysis. As a consequence, larger-scale demographic and comparative studies have become possible. This approach has recently been used to investigate several issues of traditional anthropological interest, including the effects on populations of transitions in subsistence strategy, general temporal trends in human biology and behavior during the Pleistocene, differences among populations in patterns of age-related bone loss (osteoporosis), sexual dimorphism in activity patterns, skeletal growth and development, and bilateral asymmetry. Consideration of cross-sectional geometric properties in combination with other types of skeletal features, such as articular structure and bone histomorphometry, holds even greater potential for reconstructing the biology and behavior of past human populations.

ACKNOWLEDGMENTS

Much of the earlier work reported here was carried out in collaboration with Dr. Wilson

Hayes, Orthopedic Biomechanics Laboratory, Beth Israel Hospital, Boston. I would also like to acknowledge Dr. Clark Larsen, Department of Anthropology, Purdue University, for his continuing collaboration on the Georgia coast samples. This work has been supported by research grants from the Wenner-Gren Foundation, National Science Foundation, and the National Institutes of Health.

REFERENCES

Amtmann VE (1971): Mechanical stress, functional adaptation, and the variation structure of the human femur diaphysis. Ergeb Anat 44:1–89.

Armelagos GJ, Van Gerven DP (1980): Sexual dimorphism and human evolution: An overview. J Hum Evol 9:437–446.

Armelagos GJ, Carlson DS, Van Gerven DP (1982): The theoretical foundations and development of skeletal biology. In Spencer F (ed): "A History of American Physical Anthropology: 1930–1980." New York: Academic Press, pp 305–328.

Barss P (1985): Fractured hips in rural Melanesians: A nonepidemic. Trop Geogr Med 37:156–159.

Beck TJ, Ruff CB, Warden KE, Scott WW, Rao GU (1990): Predicting femoral neck strength from bone mineral data: A structural approach. Invest Radiol 25:6–18.

Biknevicius AR (1990): "Biomechanical Design of the Mandibular Corpus in Carnivores." Thesis, Johns Hopkins University, Baltimore.

Black T III (1978): A new method for assessing the sex of fragmentary skeletal remains: Femoral shaft circumference. Am J Phys Anthropol 48:227–232.

Bouvier M, Hylander WL (1981): Effect of bone strain on cortical bone structure in macaques (Macaca mulatta). J Morphol 167:1–12.

Bridges PS (1985): "Changes in Long Bone Structure with the Transition to Agriculture: Implications for Prehistoric Activities." Thesis, University of Michigan, Ann Arbor.

Bridges PS (1989a): Changes in activities with the shift to agriculture in the southeastern United States. Curr Anthropol 30:385–394.

Bridges PS (1989b): Bone cortical area in the evaluation of nutrition and activity levels. Am J Hum Biol 1:785–792.

Brock SL, Ruff CB (1988): Diachronic patterns of change in structural properties of the femur in the prehistoric American Southwest. Am J Phys Anthropol 75:113–127.

Brothwell DR (1972): "Digging Up Bones." London: British Museum of Natural History.

Burr DB (1980): The relationship among physical, geometrical and mechanical properties of bone, with a note on the properties of nonhuman primate bone. Yearb Phys Anthropol 23:109–146.

Burr DB, Martin RB (1983): The effects of composition, structure and age on the torsional properties of the human radius. J Biomech 16:603–608.

Burr DB, Piotrowski G, Miller GJ (1981): Structural strength of the macaque femur. Am J Phys Anthropol 54:305–319.

Burr DB, Ruff CB, Thompson DD (1990): Patterns of skeletal histologic change through time: Comparison of an archaic Native American population with modern populations. Anat Rec 226:307–313.

Buxton LHD (1938): Platymeria and platycnemia. J Anat 73:31–36.

Carlson DS, Armelagos GJ, Van Gerven DP (1976): Patterns of age-related cortical bone loss (osteoporosis) within the femoral diaphysis. Hum Biol 48:295–314.

Carter DR (1978): Anisotropic analysis of strain rosette information from cortical bone. J Biomech 11:199–202.

Chalmers J, Ho KC (1970): Geographical variations in senile osteoporosis. J Bone Joint Surg 52B:667–675.

Cohen MN, Armelagos GJ, (eds). (1984): "Paleopathology at the Origins of Agriculture." New York: Academic Press.

Cook DC (1979): Subsistence base and health in prehistoric Illinois Valley: Evidence from the human skeleton. Med Anthropol 3:109–124.

Cook DC (1984): Subsistence and health in the lower Illinois valley: Osteological evidence. In Cohen MN, Armelagos GJ (eds). " Paleopathology at the Origins of Agriculture." New York: Academic Press, pp 237–269.

Corruccini RS (1974): An examination of the meaning of cranial discrete traits for human skeletal biological studies. Am J Phys Anthropol 40:425–446.

Cowin SC, Hart RT, Balser JR, Kohn DH (1985): Functional adaptation in long bones: Establishing in vivo values for surface remodeling rate coefficients. J Biomech 18:665–684.

Currey J (1984): "The Mechanical Adaptations of Bone." Princeton, NJ: Princeton University Press.

Currey JD, Pond CM (1989): Mechanical properties of very young bone in the axis deer (Axis axis) and humans. J Zool (London) 218:59–67.

Daegling DJ (1989): Biomechanics of cross-sectional size and shape in the hominoid mandibular corpus. Am J Phys Anthropol 80:91–106.

Dewey JR, Armelagos GJ, Bartley MH (1969): Femoral cortical involution in three Nubian archaeological populations. Hum Biol 41:13–28.

DiBennardo R, Taylor JV (1979): Sex assessment of the femur: A test of a new method. Am J Phys Anthropol 50:635–638.

DiBennardo R, Taylor JV (1982): Classification and misclassification in sexing the black femur by discriminant function analysis. Am J Phys Anthropol 58:145–151.

Dittrick J, Suchey JM (1986): Sex determination of prehistoric Central California skeletal remains using discriminant analysis of the femur and humerus. Am J Phys Anthropol 70:3–9.

Endo B, Kimura T (1970): Postcranial skeleton of the Amud Man. In Suzuki H, Takai F (eds): "The Amud Man and His Cave Site." Tokyo: University of Tokyo, pp 231–406.

Ericksen MF (1976): Cortical bone loss with age in three Native American populations. Am J Phys Anthropol 45:443–452.

Ericksen MF (1980): Patterns of microscopic bone remodeling in three aboriginal American populations. In Browman DL (ed): "Early Native Americans." The Hague: Mouton, pp 239–270.

Frayer DW (1980): Sexual dimorphism and cultural evolution in the late Pleistocene and Holocene of Europe. J Hum Evol 9:399–415.

Frayer DW (1984): Biological and cultural change in the European Late Pleistocene and Early Holocene. In Smith FH, and Spencer F (eds): "The Origins of Modern Humans: A World Survey of the Fossil Evidence." New York: Alan R. Liss, pp 211–250.

Fresia A, Ruff CB, Larsen CS (1990): Temporal decline in bilateral asymmetry of the upper limb on the Georgia Coast. In Larsen CS (ed): "The Archaeology of Mission Santa Catalina de Guale: 2. Biocultural Interpretations of a Population in Transition." Anthropol Pap Am Mus Nat Hist 68:121–132.

Frisancho AR, Garn SM, Ascoli W (1970): Subperiosteal and endosteal bone apposition during adolescence. Hum Biol 42:639–664.

Garn SM (1970): "The Earlier Gain and the Later Loss of Cortical Bone." Springfield, IL: Charles C. Thomas.

Hamilton ME (1982): Sexual dimorphism in skeletal samples. In Hall RL (ed): "Sexual Dimorphism in *Homo sapiens.*" New York: Praeger, pp 107–163.

Himes JH, Martorell R, Habicht J-P, Yarbrough C, Malina RM, Klein RE (1975): Patterns of cortical bone growth in moderately malnourished preschool children. Hum Biol 47:337–350.

Holtby JR (1917): Some indices and measurements of the modern femur. J Anat 7:363–382.

Hrdlicka A (1898): Study of the normal tibia. Am Anthropol 11:307–312.

Hrdlicka A (1934): The human femur: shape of the shaft. Anthropologie 12:129–163.

Huddleston AL (1988): "Quantitative Methods in Bone Densitometry." Boston: Kluwer Academic.

Hummert JR (1983): Cortical bone growth and dietary stress among subadults from Nubia's Batn El Hajar. Am J Phys Anthropol 62:167–176.

Hylander WL (1979): The functional significance of primate mandibular form. J Morphol 160:223–239.

İşcan MY, Miller-Shaivitz P (1984): Determination of sex from the tibia. Am J Phys Anthropol 64:53–57.

Jones HH, Priest JD, Hayes WC, Tichenor CC, Nagel DA (1977): Humeral hypertrophy in response to exercise. J Bone Joint Surg 59A:204–208.

Jungers WL, Minns RJ (1979): Computed tomography and biomechanical analysis of fossil long bones. Am J Phys Anthropol 50:285–290.

Jurmain RD (1977): Stress and the etiology of osteoarthritis. Am J Phys Anthropol 46:353–366.

Jurmain RD (1980): The pattern of involvement of appendicular degenerative joint disease. Am J Phys Anthropol 53:143–150.

Kennedy GE (1985): Bone thickness in *Homo erectus.* J Hum Evol 14:699–708.

Kimura T (1971a): Cross-section of human lower limb bones viewed from strength of materials. J Anthropol Soc Nippon 79:323–336.

Kimura T (1971b): Sex determination on the cross-section of human lower leg bones. Jpn J Legal Med 25:431–438.

Kimura T (1974): Mechanical characteristics of human lower leg bones. J Fac Sci University of Tokyo, Section 5, 4:319–393.

Koch JC (1917): The laws of bone architecture. Am J Anat 21:177–298.

Lanyon LE (1982): Mechanical function and bone remodeling. In Sumner-Smith G (ed): "Bone in Clinical Orthopaedics." Philadelphia: Saunders, pp 273–304.

Larsen CS (1982): The anthropology of St. Catherines Island. 3. Prehistoric human biological adaptation. Anthropol Papers Am Mus Nat Hist 57:159–270.

Larsen CS (1987): Bioarchaeological interpretations of subsistence economy and behavior from human skeletal remains. In Schiffer MB (ed): "Advances in Archaeological Method and Theory, Vol 10." New York: Academic Press, pp 339–445.

Larsen CS, Ruff CB, Griffin MC (1990): Behavioral Adaptations at Contact: Biomechanical and Pathological Evidence From the Southeastern Borderlands. Paper presented at annual meeting Am Ass Phys Anthropol, Miami.

Larsen CS, Ruff CB, Kelly RL (1991): Skeletal structural adaptations in prehistoric western Great Basin hunter–gatherers. Paper presented at annual meeting Am Ass Phys Anthropol, Milwaukee.

Larsen CS, Ruff CB, Schoeninger MJ, Hutchinson DL (in press): Population decline and extinction in La Florida. In Ubelaker DH, and Verano JW (eds): "Disease and Demography in the Americas: Changing Patterns Before and After 1492." Washington, DC: Smithsonian Institution Press.

Latimer B, Ohman JC, Lovejoy CO (1987): Talocrural joint in African hominids: Implications for *Australopithecus afarensis.* Am J Phys Anthropol 74:155–175.

Lazenby R (1986): Porosity–geometry interactions in the conservation of bone strength. J Biomech 19:257-258.

Lovejoy CO (1978): A biomechanical view of the locomotor diversity of early hominids. In Jolly CJ (ed): "Early Hominids of Africa." New York: St. Martin's Press, pp 403–430.

Lovejoy CO (1979): Contemporary methodological approaches to individual primate fossil analysis. In Morbeck ME, Preuschoft H, Gomberg N (eds): "Environment, Behavior and Morphology: Dynamic Interactions in Primates." New York: Gustav Fischer, pp 229–243.

Lovejoy CO, Trinkaus E (1980): Strength and robusticity of the Neanderthal tibia. Am J Phys Anthropol 53:465–470.

Lovejoy CO, Burstein AH, Heiple KG (1976): The biomechanical analysis of bone strength: A method and its application to platycnemia. Am J Phys Anthropol 44:489–506.

MacLaughlin SM, Bruce MF (1985): A simple univariate technique for determining sex from fragmentary femora: Its application to a Scottish short cist population. Am J Phys Anthropol 67:413–417.

Martin R (1928): "Lehrbuch der Anthropologie." Jena: Fischer.

Martin RB, Atkinson PJ (1977): Age and sex-related changes in the structure and strength of the human femoral shaft. J Biomech 10:223–231.

Martin RB, Burr DB (1984): Non-invasive measurement of long bone cross-sectional moment of inertia by photon absorptiometry. J Biomech 17:195–201.

Martin RB, Pickett JC, Zinaich S (1980): Studies of skeletal remodeling in ageing men. Clin Orthop 149:268–282.

Martin RB, Burr DB, Schaffler MB (1985): Effects of age and sex on the amount and distribution of mineral in Eskimo tibiae. Am J Phys Anthropol 67:371–380.

Merbs CF (1983): Patterns of activity-induced pathology in a Canadian Inuit population. Arch Survey Canada, Natl Mus Man Mercury Series 119.

Mielke JH, Armelagos GJ, Van Gerven DP (1972): Trabecular involution in femoral heads of a prehistoric (X-Group) population from Sudanese Nubia. Am J Phys Anthropol 36:39–44.

Miller GJ, Piotrowski G (1977): Geometric properties of paired human femurs. In Grood ES, and Smith CR (eds): "Advances in Bioengineering." New York: American Society for Testing and Minerals, pp 73–74.

Minns RJ, Bremble GR, Campbell J (1975): The geometric properties of the human tibia. J Biomech 8:253–255.

Murdock GP, Provost C (1973): Factors in the division of labor by sex: A cross-cultural analysis. Ethnology 12:203–225.

Nagurka ML, Hayes WC (1980): An interactive graphics package for calculating cross-sectional properties of complex shapes. J Biomechanics 13:59–64.

Parsons FG (1914): The characters of the English thighbone. Am J Phys Anthropol 48:238–267.

Pearson K, Bell J (1919): "A Study of the Long Bones of the English Skeleton." London: Cambridge Univervisty Press.

Perzigian AJ (1973): Osteoporotic bone loss in two prehistoric Indian populations. Am J Phys Anthropol 39:87–96.

Peyron JG (1986): Osteoarthritis: The epidemiologic viewpoint. Clin Orthop 213:13–19.

Phillips JR, Williams JF, Melick RA (1975): Prediction of the strength of the neck of femur from its radiological appearance. J Biomed Eng 10:367–372.

Piziali RL, Hight TK, Nagel DA (1976): An extended structural analysis of long bones—Application to the human tibia. J Biomech 9:695–701.

Preuschoft H (1971): Body posture and modes of locomotion in early Pleistocene hominids. Folia Primatol 14:209–240.

Radin EL, Orr RB, Kelman JL, Paul IL, Rose RM (1982): Effect of prolonged walking on concrete on the knees of sheep. J Biomech 15:487–492.

Radin EL, Martin RB, Burr DB, Caterson B, Boyd RD, Goodwin C (1984): Effects of mechanical loading on the tissues of the rabbit knee. J Orthop Res 1:221–234.

Richman EA, Ortner DJ (1978): Intracortical bone remodeling in three aboriginal populations: Possible dietary factors in differences. Am J Phys Anthropol 48:429.

Riggs BL, Melton LJ III (1986): Involutional osteoporosis. New Engl J Med 314:1676–1686.

Riggs BL, Wahner HW, Melton LJ III, Richelson LS, Judd HL, O'Fallon WM (1987): Dietary calcium intake and rates of bone loss in women. J Clin Invest 80:979–982.

Ruff CB (1987a): Structural allometry of the femur and tibia in Hominoidea and *Macaca*. Folia Primatol 48:9–49.

Ruff CB (1987b): Sexual dimorphism in human lower limb bone structure: Relationship to subsistence strategy and sexual division of labor. J Hum Evol 16:391–416.

Ruff CB (1988): Hindlimb articular surface allometry in Hominoidea and *Macaca*, with comparisons to diaphyseal scaling. J Hum Evol 17:687–714.

Ruff CB (1989): New approaches to structural evolution of limb bones in primates. Folia Primatol 53:142–159.

Ruff CB (in press): Biomechanical analysis of Northern and Southern Plains femora: Behavioral implications. In Owsley DW, and Jantz RL (eds): "Skeletal Biology in the Great Plains: A Multidisciplinary View." Washington, DC: Smithsonian Institution Press.

Ruff CB, Hayes WC (1982): Subperiosteal expansion and cortical remodeling of the human femur and tibia with aging. Science 217:945–948.

Ruff CB, Hayes WC (1983a): Cross-sectional geometry of Pecos Pueblo femora and tibiae—a biomechanical investigation. I. Method and general patterns of variation. Am J Phys Anthropol 60:359–381.

Ruff CB, Hayes WC (1983b): Cross-sectional geometry of Pecos Pueblo femora and tibiae—A biomechanical investigation. II. Sex, age, and side differences. Am J Phys Anthropol 60:383–400.

Ruff CB, Hayes WC (1984a): Age changes in geometry and mineral content of the lower limb bones. Ann Biomed Eng 12:573–584.

Ruff CB, Hayes WC (1984b): Bone mineral content in the lower limb: Relationship to cross-sectional geometry. J Bone Joint Surg 66A:1024–1031.

Ruff CB, Hayes WC (1988): Sex differences in age-related remodeling of the femur and tibia. J Orthop Res 6:886–896.

Ruff CB, Jones HH (1981): Bilateral asymmetry in cortical bone of the humerus and tibia—Sex and age factors. Hum Biol 53:69–86.

Ruff CB, Larsen CS (1990): Postcranial biomechanical adaptations to subsistence changes on the Georgia Coast. In Larsen CS (ed): "The Archaeology of Mission Santa Catalina de Guale: 2. Biocultural Interpretations of a Population in Transition." Anthropol Pap Am Mus Nat Hist 68:94–120.

Ruff CB, Leo FP (1986): Use of computed tomography in skeletal structural research. Yearb Phys Anthropol 29:181–195.

Ruff CB, Larsen CS, Hayes WC (1984): Structural changes in the femur with the transition to agriculture on the Georgia coast. Am J Phys Anthropol 64:125–136.

Ruff CB, Walker AC, Teaford MF (1989): Body mass, sexual dimorphism and femoral proportions of *Proconsul* from Rusinga and Mfangano Islands, Kenya. J Hum Evol 18:515–536.

Ruff CB, Scott WW, Liu AY-C (1991): Scaling of proximal femoral dimensions to body mass in a living human sample. Am J Phys Anthropol 86:397–413.

Ruff CB, Trinkaus E, Walker AC, Jones HH, Larsen CS (in preparation): Postcranial robusticity in *Homo*, I: Temporal trends and mechanical interpretation.

Schaeffer AA (1928): Spiral movement in man. J Morph Physiol 45:293–398.

Schaffler MB, Burr DB, Jungers WL, Ruff CB (1985): Structural and mechanical indicators of limb specialization in primates. Folia Primatol 45:61–75.

Skelton RR, McHenry HM, Drawhorn GM (1986): Phylogenetic analysis of early hominids. Curr Anthropol 27:21–43.

Smith JM, Savage RJG (1956): Some locomotory adaptations in mammals. J Linn Soc (Zool) 42:603–622.

Smith RW, Walker RR (1964): Femoral expansion in aging women: Implications for osteoporosis and fractures. Science 145:156–157.

Smithgall EB, Johnston FE, Malina RM, Galbraith MA (1966): Developmental changes in compact bone relationships in the second metacarpal. Hum Biol 38:141–151.

Stout S, Simmons DJ (1979): Use of histology in ancient bone research. Yearb Phys Anthropol 22:228–249.

Stout SD (1982): The effects of long-term immobilization on the histomorphology of human cortical bone. Calif Tissue Int 34:337–342.

Sumner DR (1984): "Size, Shape, and Bone Mineral Content of the Human Femur in Growth and Aging." Thesis, Univeristy of Arizona: Tucson.

Sumner DR, Mockbee B, Morse K, et al. (1985): Computed tomography and automated image analysis of prehistoric femora. Am J Phys Anthropol 68:225–232.

Sumner DR, Olson CL, Freeman PM, Lobick JJ, Andriacchi TP (1989): Computed tomographic measurement of cortical bone geometry. J Biomech 22:649–653.

Susman RL, Stern JT, Jungers WL (1985): Locomotor adaptations in the Hadar hominids. In Delson E (ed): "Ancestors: The Hard Evidence." New York: Alan R. Liss, pp 184–192.

Thompson DD, Trinkaus E (1981): Age determination for the Shanidar Neanderthal. Science 212:575–577.

Timoshenko SP, Gere JM (1972): "Mechanics of Materials." New York: Van Nostrand Reinhold.

Trinkaus E (1980): Sexual differences in Neanderthal limb bones. J Human Evol 9:377–397.

Trinkaus E (1990): Cladistics and the hominid fossil record. Am J Phys Anthropol 83:1–11.

Trinkaus E, Churchill SE, Ruff CB (1990): Neanderthal post-traumatic humeral asymmetry and the interpretation of fossil diaphyseal morphology. Paper presented at annual meeting Am Assoc Phys Anthropol, Miami.

Trinkaus E, Ruff CB (1989): Diaphyseal cross-sectional morphology and biomechanics of the Fond-de-Foret 1 femur and the Spy 2 femur and tibia. Bull Soc R Belge Anthropol Prehist 100:33–42.

Van Gerven DP (1973): Thickness and area measurements as parameters of skeletal involution of the humerus, femur, and tibia. J Gerontol 28:40–45.

Van Gerven DP, Armelagos GJ (1970): Cortical involution in prehistoric Mississippian femora. J Gerontol 25:20–22.

Van Gerven DP, Armelagos GJ, Bartley MH (1969): Roentgenographic and direct measurement of femoral cortical involution in a prehistoric Mississippian population. Am J Phys Anthropol 31:23–38.

Van Gerven DP, Hummert JR, Burr DB (1985): Cortical bone maintenance and geometry of the tibia in prehistoric children from Nubia's Batn el Hajar. Am J Phys Anthropol 66:275–280.

Wolff J (1892): "Das Gesetz der Transformation der Knochen." Berlin: A. Hirchwild.

Skeletal Biology of Past Peoples: Research Methods
pages 59–78 © 1992 Wiley-Liss, Inc.

Chapter 4

Techniques for the Study of
Dental Morphology

John T. Mayhall

Faculty of Dentistry, University of Toronto, Toronto, Ontario, Canada M5G 1G6

INTRODUCTION

Dental morphology may be defined as the science of the form and structure of teeth (modified from Jablonski, 1982). This chapter takes a broad view of the form of the teeth and includes topics such as mensuration and pathology along with morphology as it is more narrowly defined (see Skinner and Goodman, this volume, Chapter 9 and Ten Cate, 1989, for descriptions of tooth development and microstructure). All of these topics are related to the "look" of the teeth and are valuable in describing the dentition of skeletal samples and individual skeletons. Much of what follows is from the dental literature or the specialized volumes that deal with dental anthropology that may be read infrequently by biological anthropologists (Brothwell, 1963; Butler and Joysey, 1978; Dahlberg, 1971; Dahlberg and Graber, 1977; Kurtén, 1982; Hillson, 1986; Pedersen et al., 1967; Russell et al., 1988). The references provided are rather extensive but not exhaustive. They are intended to allow the reader to go to several sources for further study on a particular topic. Much of the primary literature on tooth development, pathology, growth, and physiology of the oral structures and data on dental morphology and mensuration is in the dental literature—a literature that may not be familiar to the anthropologist.

This chapter takes a conservative approach to the techniques that are described. The reader can be assured that the methods are ones that are easily achievable and are generally accepted. They are not esoteric ones that can be achieved only with highly specialized, very expensive equipment. This is not to suggest that there are not other methods that can be applied to the study of dental morphology but one must be careful to use methods that are comparable throughout the field of dental morphology. The reader will notice that many of the methods proposed here are criticized as well. This does not mean that the techniques are inappropriate but rather suggests that they must be carefully considered to determine if they are the correct ones for the particular goal of the researcher. As with any technique, there are deficiencies that must be considered before embarking on a particular study. The appropriate technique for one study may not be so for another.

The chapter is divided into three principal areas: tooth size, tooth morphology, and a brief synopsis of dental caries and periodontal diseases. These are not mutually exclusive. The morphology of a tooth is closely related to the size of the tooth (four-cusped molars are generally smaller than five-cusped molars). A tooth with a complex groove pattern is more likely to be carious than one with a simple pattern simply because the complex tooth has more furrows to trap food. However, the complexly patterned molar is more efficient for mastication than the simple molar. A classic example of the relationship of morphology and pathology is the shovel-shaped incisor. This

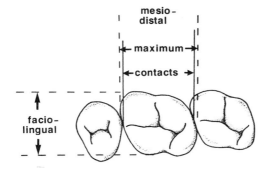

Fig. 1. Illustration of the points included in the two principal means (contact point to contact point or maximum diameter) of determining the mesiodistal dimension of the tooth. The faciolingual measurement is obtained by holding the caliper beaks perpendicular to the mesiodistal measurement (it must also be parallel to the occlusal plane).

tooth, because of its I-beam cross section, is a very strong tooth that resists chipping and breaking. However, the morphology of the lingual surface is such that there is a food trap created by the joining in the cingulum area of the extra tooth material of the marginal ridges that creates this strength. This food trap was not a problem in populations that subsisted on a noncariogenic diet but with the advent of processed foods and increased levels of caries these teeth became the nidus of early, difficult to detect decay.

TOOTH SIZE

The traditional measurement of teeth was confined to two crown measurements and from these came several indices that have been useful in describing tooth crown proportions and basic shapes. This is not to suggest that there are only two measurements; there are several that can be used to describe the entire tooth. However, the vast majority of the literature will describe the tooth crown with two measurements: the mesiodistal diameter and the faciolingual diameter. The former is the one that has to be considered very carefully before embarking on the measurement of any large sample.

In determining the mesiodistal diameter, two sets of landmarks can be used, both with their justifications. First (Fig. 1), some investigators

describe the mesiodistal diameter of the crown as the distance between the contact points of the tooth, the area where the tooth contacts its neighbor (Moorrees, 1957; Thomsen, 1951). (Even though we refer to "contact points," these are, in reality, *areas* of contact, which become larger with interproximal attrition, the wear of the enamel that occurs when the teeth move against each other during mastication.) In this case, the calipers are held parallel to the occlusal plane of the tooth and the (sharpened) beaks of the caliper are placed on the mesial and distal contact points of the crown. This method has the disadvantage that if there is any interproximal attrition, a very common situation in skeletal materials, the mesiodistal measurement will be reduced. If one uses this method the sample sizes will be reduced, sometimes drastically, by the number of rejected measurements due to mesial or distal attrition.

The latter method (Fig. 1) measures the maximum width of the crown in the mesiodistal plane (Mayhall, 1979; Pedersen, 1949). This will be wider than the former method and may be the easier method to employ. There are instances, especially in the anterior teeth, when the two methods will be using the same landmarks and derive the same values (Fig. 2). It is important to decide before the study which will be used. This will require a comprehensive literature search to determine what studies one wishes to use for comparative purposes. Both methods require the investigator to have a reasonable sense of dental morphology, especially when the teeth are not in the alveolus. Any good dental anatomy text (Jordan, et al., 1982; Osborn, 1981; Woelfel, 1984) or, more to this area of interest, works by Goose (1963) and Hillson (1986) can be of assistance if one is not sure of the morphological landmarks of the particular teeth included in the study. The landmarks may vary considerably depending on the tooth type being measured.

Once the mesiodistal measurement is determined then the faciolingual one can be ascertained (Fig. 1) by holding the calipers perpendicular to the plane that was used for the mesiodistal and determining the widest diameter of the tooth (Goose, 1963). This measurement is subject to error because, for many of the molars, the most protruding portion of the

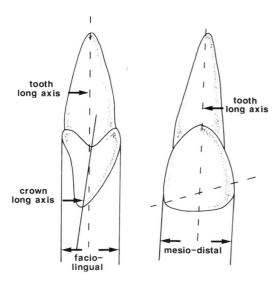

Fig. 2. The important landmarks for measuring the anterior teeth. Note that the long axis of the crown is not the same as the long axis of the tooth. The determination of the mesiodistal distance is through the contact points but it is *not* necessarily parallel to them (it is perpendicular to the long axis of the tooth).

facial aspect of the tooth will be toward the mesial and the corresponding point for the lingual will be toward the distal of the crown. This requires that the calipers be carefully positioned so as not to be anything other than perpendicular to the mesiodistal axis. As well, the two points may not be in the same plane occlusocervically. The calipers must also be held parallel to the occlusal plane. In the anterior teeth, the faciolingual measurement is difficult because the heights of contour of the facial and lingual surfaces are so disparate. It is important here, and with the premolars and canines, to ensure that the caliper beaks are parallel to the long axis of the tooth (Fig. 2), not the crown (the long axis of the crown is often not in the same plane as the axis for the entire tooth).

With these two measurements one can construct indices that crudely describe the proportions of the tooth, the approximate area of the occlusal surface, and so forth (Goose, 1963; Jacobson, 1982; Middleton Shaw, 1931; Pedersen, 1949; Selmer-Olsen, 1949). The crown index is the faciolingual diameter of the crown

divided by the mesiodistal diameter and then multiplied by 100. This index is designed to display the ratio between the two measurements and illustrate the shape of the crown. Rosenzweig (1970) used it to study sexual dimorphism and population differences of Middle Eastern groups and cautiously promoted it as a distinguishing factor. The crown module is derived by the addition of the mesiodistal and faciolingual measurements and division by 2. This is claimed to be an expression of the mass of the crown, although Pedersen (1949) correctly notes that it is "a rather imperfect one." The third index is crown robustness, which is the mesiodistal dimension multiplied by the faciolingual one (Kajava, 1912; Weidenreich, 1937). This last index has also been termed the crown area by Wolpoff (1971) and has been recently used by Lukacs (1988). Most of these indices have been overtaken by much more sophisticated techniques that are available to accurately describe not only the occlusal area but the heights of the cusps, the distance between them, and their position on the crown.

One technique that has gained popularity recently is the use of moiré fringe photography. The technique is anything but new (Takasaki, 1970, 1973) but with the advent of grids that indicate differences in contour of as little as 50 μm it is possible to quickly and accurately describe the tooth crowns of the molars and, to some extent, the other teeth. Until now, the work has concentrated on the molars because they are the easiest to orient reliably (Kanazawa et al., 1984; Mayhall and Kanazawa, 1989; Sekikawa et al., 1988).

The tooth to be analyzed is oriented with the occlusal plane parallel to a grid with inscribed parallel lines through which columnated lights and a macro lens of a 35-mm camera are aimed (see Ozaki and Kanazawa, 1984, for a detailed description). The result of the light passing through the grid and striking the uneven surface of the tooth is the production of contour lines (fringes) that are an easily determined distance apart (Fig. 3). These contour lines are captured with high speed, high-contrast film and enlarged about six to eight times normal size. The resulting photographs are then measured, and the heights of cusps can be determined by counting the number of contour lines. Distance determinations that have been

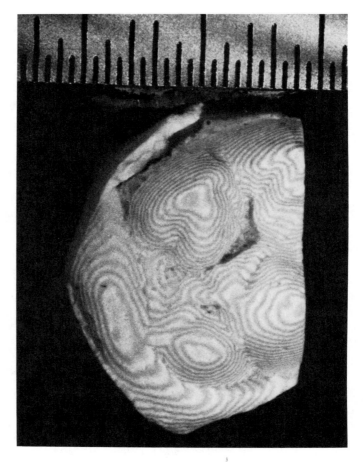

Fig. 3. Moiré contourography image of a maxillary molar (a standardized tooth sectioned through the mesial cusp tips) with the fringes at 0.2 mm intervals.

reported recently include intercuspal distances, position of the cusps on the occlusal surface, heights of the cusps, and the depths of the fossae and their positions. Moiré contourography techniques are not limited to teeth. Kanazawa (1980) has successfully used the technique for craniometry and found that many of the problems that have made craniometrics difficult can be overcome.

One further advance that has the potential to describe the basal areas of tooth crowns utilizes the moiré methodology. Until very recently researchers attempted to determine the basal area of the tooth crown by photograph-

ing the tooth from directly above (Biggerstaff, 1970; Hanihara et al., 1970a) and tracing the resultant outline of the crown with a planimeter (Williams, 1979). In this way an approximation of the area of each cusp and the entire crown could be reported. This method has one important drawback: the heights of contour of the crown are not at the same level on all surfaces of the crown. Thus, the plane that was measured might be tilted or be different for each cusp (Fig. 4).

Using moiré contourography and digital image analysis it is possible to achieve the basal areas of the crown and cusps at the same level

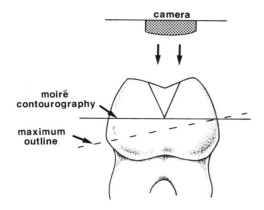

Fig. 4. Different dimensions described by moiré contourography and methods using the maximum outline of the crown. Note that the maximum measurement method measures a plane through the heights of contour, which is not perpendicular to the occlusal plane.

throughout the crown (Mayhall and Alvesalo, 1991). In other words, one can make an imaginary cross section of the crown at any distance from the occlusal plane to the heights of contour and determine the area at that level.

Townsend has photographed casts of premolars with a small pencil mark delineating each cusp tip. With a scale introduced into the photo it is possible to accurately determine the intercuspal distance. This technique is one that holds promise because of its low technical requirements. To produce accurate photos that are easily measured one needs only a camera, high contrast film, and some method of ensuring that the occlusal plane is parallel to the focal plane of the camera, plus a scale introduced into each photograph and a pencil! The distance between cusp tips is important because it is seemingly less affected by sexual differences than the "outer" measurements such as the mesiodistal and faciolingual dimensions (Mayhall and Kanazawa, 1989). The importance of this becomes obvious in measuring loose teeth when there is the possibility of a significant amount of sexual dimorphism in the mesiodistal and faciolingual dimensions but the sex of the teeth is unknown.

A rather interesting technique that incorporates a variant of photography is the use of photocopying equipment to reproduce in two dimensions the intercuspal distances and the intra-arch distances. In these cases one simply puts the cast of the arch or a tooth on the photocopying plate and reproduces it in a flat plane (Singh and Savara, 1964). McKeown (1981) suggested a photographic method for recording the three-dimensional form of individual teeth. The tooth to be analyzed is placed in a metal frame cube that allows it to be photographed from all sides. Five photographs are taken from a standard distance (5 feet) and from these the dimensions can be determined. One other technique that utilizes standardized photographs has been reported by Yamada and Brown (1988). Occlusal photographs were used to determine the contours of maxillary molars by measuring the distances from the central pit to the perimeter of the crown at 10–degree intervals. These last two determinations may suffer from the same constraints that limited earlier studies: The maximum contours of the crown are not in the same plane.

The use of standardized measurement techniques allows the skeletal biologist to accurately compare individual teeth and those of populations and various subgroups. However, it must be remembered that there is a wide range of variability in tooth size, both interpopulational (Brabant, 1973; Garn et al., 1968; Lavelle, 1970, 1971) and intrapopulational (Dahlberg, 1990). Care must be taken that the results of mensuration are accurate and comparable with other studies and that samples are of sufficient size to allow for meaningful comparisons. This last caveat is one that plagues skeletal biologists as well as other dental researchers. When beginning a study of the dentition, be prepared to lose a large proportion of the teeth to wear, pathology, and antemortem and postmortem loss. In some studies populations of several hundred revealed the number of teeth in a particular class that were usable to be less than a dozen (Mayhall, 1979). The numbers may be so reduced that studies of fluctuating asymmetry, for instance, are impossible because of a lack of suitable antimeres (Mayhall et al., 1991).

Upon determining the techniques that are appropriate to the material to be examined, the researcher is still confronted with the problem of the usefulness of the various techniques. How are these mensurational determinations to be used? Are they valuable for genetic studies?; population comparisons?; sexual dimorphism comparisons?; evolutionary studies?; asymmetry studies? While there is, obviously, no single answer to these questions it may be of value to show how dental measurements have been used in studies that include the above areas.

Genetic studies can be of a populational nature (and these will be covered when population comparisons are described) or they can be used to determine the role of genes in tooth size. Some of the results of studies by Alvesalo and his colleagues provide clues to "unusual" teeth or dentitions that may be found in skeletal samples (Alvesalo, 1985; Alvesalo and Portin, 1980; Alvesalo and Varrela, 1979; Kari et al., 1980; Kirveskari and Alvesalo, 1981, 1982; Mayhall et al., 1991). Alvesalo and co-workers have used various measurements of the tooth to describe groups of individuals with abnormalities in their sex chromosomes and to compare these with their normal first-degree relatives (Townsend et al., 1988). For instance, the greater thickness of enamel and dentin and a larger overall tooth size in 47,XYY males compared with measurement for their normal relatives supports the view that the extra Y chromosome exerts a promoting effect on the function of the ameloblasts and, possibly, on the growth of dentin (Alvesalo, 1985). By examining males with portions of the Y chromosome missing it is possible to suggest a growth-promoting gene in the nonfluorescent part of the long arm (Alvesalo, 1985). Similarly, it is now becoming clear that the X chromosome's short arm contains a gene or genes for tooth crown growth. This evidence comes from studying the tooth size of 46,X,i(Xq) females and comparing it with the size of 45,X females (Turner's syndrome) and normal female relatives. The isochromosome females have smaller teeth than the 45,X females, who in turn have smaller teeth than the normal 46,XX females (Mayhall et al., 1991). It may be worth identifying individuals in a population with extremely small tooth sizes and *speculating* about the possibility of a syndrome such as Turner's syndrome, and so on, being the cause.

Teeth have the unique asset of being comparable between skeletal samples and living populations. In living individuals one can utilize dental stone models of the dentition for accurate measurements; for teeth from archaeological sites the measurements can be done directly. Several studies have used this "crossover" ability to their advantage (Campbell, 1925; Mayhall, 1976; Pedersen, 1949), while others have compared the tooth size among skeletal groups (Brabant, 1973; Perzigian, 1976; Selmer-Olsen, 1949; Turner, 1967) or among living groups (Garn et al., 1968; Hanihara, 1977; Harris, 1977; Jacobson, 1982; Lavelle, 1970, 1971). These comparisons must be carefully examined because of the possibility that two samples of any one population may show large variation (Lavelle, 1970). By use of univariate and multivariate statistics, populations can be defined on the basis of tooth size alone.

The sexual dimorphism of tooth size has been the subject of various studies of populations as diverse as Swedish children (Lysell and Myrberg, 1982), Australian Aborigines (Brown et al., 1980; Hanihara, 1976), Ecuadorian Indians (Mayhall and Karp, 1983), and French-Canadians (Buschang et al., 1988). The Swedish study noted that "although the sex differences are small, especially in the deciduous dentition, they are statistically significant for both dentitions" (p. 113). The permanent canines displayed a 5%–6% difference in the permanent canines while the sexual dimorphism for the rest of the teeth was about 2%–4%. These figures, it is claimed, agree with results of other studies of Caucasoids. This rather small amount of dimorphism leads to a cautionary note: In most skeletal samples the numbers are small and this 2%–6% dimorphism will not be apparent. In short, it is probably not possible to use univariate analysis of the size of the teeth for any sexual discrimination. De Vito and Saunders (1990) recognized the problem of using single teeth and deciduous teeth to sex individuals. In a discriminant function analysis of deciduous teeth from the Burlington, Ontario, growth study (Canadians of British origin), they were able to reach an acceptable level of discrimination. However, they caution that the application of the discriminant functions to other populations may not be applicable owing to their variations in dimorphism.

Moiré contourography has also been used to determine the amount of sexual dimorphism in the molar crowns. This is especially valuable, because for the first time the heights of the cusps have been accurately measured and compared. Studies of a Japanese population (Sekikawa et al., 1988) have noted that the cusps of the deciduous second molars (maxillary and mandibular) and permanent first molars are consistently higher in males than in females. Kanazawa et al. (1983) found that the sex differences were found primarily around the distal cusps of the maxillary teeth; Mayhall and Kanazawa (1989) noted that the differences in Canadian Inuit were consistently higher in males for all cusps in the maxillary first molar. The broadest comparisons between populations and between males and females were in the study by Kanazawa and coworkers (1988), in which the authors claimed that the three-dimensional shape of the occlusal surface was distinguishable for four general racial populations.

In evolutionary studies, particularly microevolutionary ones, tooth size has been a valuable adjunct. Japanese studies have used tooth dimensions for analyzing geographically isolated populations (Hanihara, 1989), investigating temporal and biological relationships (Mizoguchi, 1988), and demonstrating the effects of hybridization on Japanese children's dentition (Hanihara and Ueda, 1979). Two other studies that demonstrate the use of tooth size for evolutionary studies are the works of Rosenzweig and Smith (1971), who noted that highly inbred isolates were found to display the same amount of variability as more heterogeneous groups, and Henderson and Greene's (1975) application of dental field theory to primate evolution. Some workers have attempted to use tooth size and changes in it to analyze evolutionary trends (Hinton et al., 1980; Lukacs, 1984; Perzigian, 1975, 1984). Many of the studies suggest that there has been a reduction in tooth size over time. However, the cause of these reductions is unknown at present because, as Lukacs (1984) states, there are at least two barriers to this line of research: the absence of a mechanism consistent with known evolutionary principles for producing the reduction and the absence of accurate data on many of the living and prehistoric populations. Mayhall (1977), in a study of the Eskimos of northern Alaska, noted that these people were renowned for their use of their teeth

as a "third hand" and for heavy mastication, but this role may have been exaggerated by observers. In fact, many Eskimos have functioned well both physically and reproductively without teeth while consuming frozen whale, seal, and fish, which casts doubt on the dogma that teeth were necessary for survival in prehistoric human populations. It appears premature to suggest that the mechanisms of tooth reduction are known. Lukacs (1984: 253) correctly notes, "Final determination of the precise evolutionary mechanism(s) of dental reduction will come from experimental studies of laboratory animals rather than from analysis of the fossil or skeletal record."

One final area that has been popular with those interested in tooth size is the amount of fluctuating asymmetry seen in the dentition. These random differences between antimeres may indicate an inability of an individual to buffer against disturbances in development and may be valuable to the skeletal biologist in that they could indicate local developmental disturbances. Perzigian (1977: 81), using skeletal samples, has suggested that "environmentally mediated growth disturbance may be sensitively reflected by fluctuating asymmetry." It would be of benefit in reconstructing the lifestyles of skeletal populations if we could use dental asymmetry to determine the levels of insults to the growth of the individuals in that population. However, before embarking on the study of asymmetry, one is cautioned that there are several factors that may influence the validity of the results. Townsend (1981) and Townsend and Brown (1980) warn that the methodology of the data collection is very important in comparisons. Measurement methods must be comparable between studies, the methods of quantifying the asymmetry should be the same, and the methods of obtaining the dental casts measured should be alike. Garn and coworkers (1979) and Smith and her colleagues (1982) demonstrate that large sample sizes are required to be able to make statistically valid comparisons. Garn and colleagues state: "Since most published studies on left–right dental asymmetry are based on small samples (generally below 100 and in some cases as small as 15), it is increasingly likely that apparent intergroup differences in crown asymmetry may reflect sampling limitations"

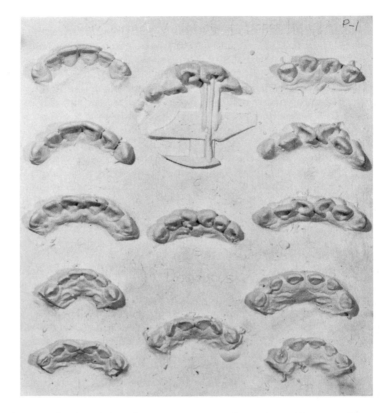

Fig. 5. The shovel-shaped permanent incisor plaque devised by A.A. Dahlberg.

(1979: 2012). Smith and coworkers summarize their research by concluding that "fluctuating asymmetry is not yet established as a useful and reliable measure of general stress in human populations" (1982: 288). Finally, Mayhall and Saunders (1985) felt that it was practically impossible to overcome the "noise" level and test recent hypotheses regarding fluctuating dental asymmetry. The case for caution should be apparent: if one is to explore the hypothesized benefits of this area, a rigorous protocol and large samples are a must.

TOOTH MORPHOLOGY

An area of dental research that has suffered from a lack of comparable observations is tooth morphology. In many instances tooth crown morphology is the only visible way of comparing large populations. Novice (and experienced) researchers in this area have been frus-

trated by the lack of standardization and an inability to observe the range of variation of dental morphological traits. They have also had the uneasy feeling that their observations were not comparable with those of others. It is not possible to alleviate these problems here, but it is possible to steer the observer toward techniques that have been used successfully by experienced researchers.

The use of dental morphology and the observation of dental morphological traits have a long history in dental anthropology. Some of the earliest pioneers, such as Campbell (1925), Dahlberg (1945, 1950, 1951, 1958, 1963, 1965) and Pedersen (1949), cautioned the researcher that there were problems in comparing results from one investigator with those from another. A.A. Dahlberg attempted to alleviate the problem by constructing a set of dental stone models that displayed the range of

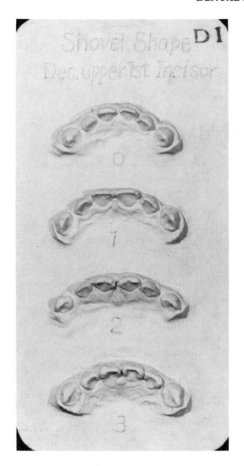

Fig. 6. Kazuro Hanihara's plaque, illustrating the shovel shape in deciduous incisors.

plaques are invaluable and should be available for consultation. These are the only three-dimensional materials generally available to reduce interobserver error in trait determinations. However, the majority of studies that have used the standards do not describe which variations of a particular trait were used or they collapse observations into a few categories, which obliterates the fine differences between traits so that it becomes difficult to compare one's studies with published materials. This deficiency in comparing population traits is usually overcome by a single investigator doing all of the observations on all the populations to be studied: a cumbersome, time consuming, and expensive process. Another way of attempting to overcome problems has been to use the presence or absence of a trait as the description for comparative purposes, but this method suffers from the lack of an accurate description of the threshold for the presence of the trait.

The use of dental morphological traits such as Carabelli's trait, shovel-shape incisors, molar cusp and groove patterns, and protostylid continues to be valuable in general population identification and comparison. It is difficult to "learn" the variation in the dozen or so traits generally used without consulting the standards above and/or working with an experienced investigator to observe the variation of the traits and their scoring. The comparison of the results of such studies is also difficult because the traits are continuous variables but the descriptions of the traits are not. Thus, many of the usual statistical tests are not applicable to these trait comparisons.

Carabelli's trait is frequently referred to as Carabelli's cusp although the range of expression encompasses variations from a pit to a groove to a cusp on the lingual surface of the mesiolingual cusp of the maxillary molar (Dahlberg, 1951; Townsend and Brown, 1981). The plaques of Hanihara (Fig. 8) for the deciduous molars and of Dahlberg (Fig. 9) and Turner for the permanent molars are invaluable for accurately describing the range of variation seen for this cusp. Probably more has been written about this trait than any other. Although this may be admirable, it has resulted in a varied and contradictory literature about such topics as the description of the expres-

variability of about a dozen morphological traits of the permanent dentition (Fig. 5 illustrates an example of his shovel-shaped incisor plaque). These "standards" are available from Dr. Dahlberg for a modest fee and they are still the most widely used materials. Soon after Dahlberg issued the permanent series Kazuro Hanihara issued a set for the deciduous dentition (Fig. 6). These plaques are not widely available and none seem to be produced at present. Christy Turner has issued a series of plaques (Fig. 7) that also deal with the permanent dentition and these are available from the Department of Anthropology, Arizona State University. If one is to do any comparative studies of dental morphological traits, the

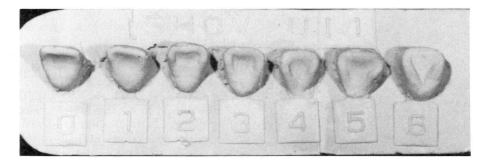

Fig. 7. Christy Turner's shovel-shaped incisor plaque.

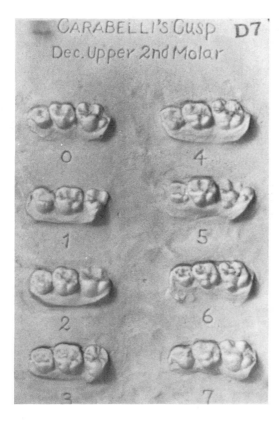

Fig. 8. Kazuro Hanihara's plaque, illustrating the range of variation of the Carabelli's trait in the deciduous maxillary second molar.

sions of the trait, the frequency of occurrence of the trait in various populations, and the role of heredity in its expression. For instance, there has been discussion about whether the

pit that is found in the same location as the cusp is a negative expression of the trait. The mode of inheritance has continued to be enigmatic, some proclaiming a simple dominant-recessive mode (Tsuji, 1958), others opting for two allelic genes with no dominance (Kraus, 1951; Turner, 1967), and still others pointing out that the simple models are just that and suggesting that the inheritance may be multifactorial (Goose and Lee, 1971; Townsend and Brown, 1981).

The interpopulation expression of the trait is confused by the lack of consistent reporting. Many of the articles report the cusp expressions only, whereas others report the incidence of the varying expressions of the trait. In general, one can state that the larger expressions such as a cusp or a bulge can be found in a high percentage of Caucasoids[1] (Dahlberg, 1963; Mayhall et al., 1982), and a high frequency of the moderate to absent expressions is found in Mongoloid groups (Mayhall, 1976; Pedersen, 1949; Tratman, 1950). In Australian Aborigines the frequency varies in trait occurrence and expression; however, Townsend and Brown (1981) note that they are comparable with that reported for Bushman and Bantu whereas the cusp frequency is similar to South African whites and Hawaiians. (These data further confirm the difficulty of comparisons between reports by different authors.)

The protostylid, or Tubercle of Bolk (DeSmet and Brabant, 1969), is found on the facial surface of the mesiofacial cusp of mandibular

---

1. For illustrative purposes the terms Caucasoid, Mongoloid and Negroid are used here to indicate broad population groupings.

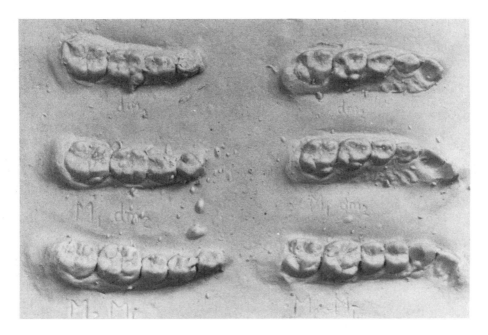

Fig. 9. Plaque from A.A. Dahlberg's series illustrating protostylid variation on permanent mandibular molars (left) and Carabelli's trait expression on permanent maxillary molars (right). There is a more detailed plaque for the Carabelli's trait expressions in Dahlberg's series.

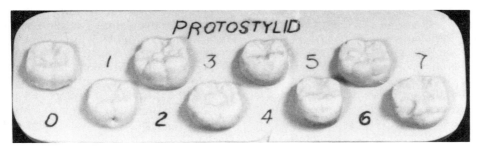

Fig. 10. Christy Turner's protostylid plaque.

molars (Fig. 10). It displays about the same range of variation in expression as does the Carabelli trait (Dahlberg, 1951, 1986). The pit expression has been difficult to characterize because it falls along the facial groove of the crown, and in some populations there is another pit (foramen caecum) that may occur at the same location. Because of this confusion some studies have reported only the bulge and cusp expressions (Hanihara et al., 1975). The figures for the frequency of occurrence of this trait are varied and subject to the same prob-

lems as were noted for expressions of the Carabelli's trait. Until 1950, the protostylid appears to have escaped scrutiny, only ten instances being reported (Dahlberg, 1950). Dahlberg reported that 31% of Pima Indians displayed the trait, which suggested that this might be a Mongoloid trait. However, subsequent studies have been only mildly supportive of this. In 1963 Dahlberg found that 42% of Old Harbor Eskimos displayed a complete absence of the trait on the first molar, while Sioux Indians and U.S. whites showed complete absence in 20% and 26% respectively. Hanihara and colleagues (1975) noted that Caucasoids displayed none of the positive expressions, but 29% of the Eskimos he studied had "swelling or tubercle type" expressions on the first molar. (Figures in Hanihara et al indicate that the expressions on the second deciduous molar are much more prevalent.) This trait is unusual in that the cusp-like expressions are more common on the third molar than on the first, a feature quite different than the usual pattern of expression (for most traits, the most mesial tooth in a group is the most stable and demonstrates the greatest expressions of a trait).

The most famous variation in crown morphology is the shovel-shaped incisor. This trait can be found on any of the incisors but is generally more highly expressed in the maxillary ones rather than the mandibulars. The range of variation (Figs. 5, 6, 7) is truly amazing (Aas and Risness, 1979a,b; Mizoguchi, 1985). The shovel is generally seen on the lingual surface of the incisors, where the lingual marginal ridges are enlarged and thus form the sides of the shovel. As well, there are double-shovel incisors where the facial marginal ridges are also enlarged, creating two areas of depression, one on the lingual and one on the facial surface. The greatest expression is the barrel-shaped incisor: The lingual marginal ridges are so enlarged that they contact on the lingual surface, creating a depression surrounded by the incisal edge and the marginal ridges, a barrel as viewed from the incisal. These generally occur on the maxillary lateral incisors.

The determination of the amount of "shoveling" can be done visually; alternatively, several researchers have successfully measured the depth of the lingual fossa by using a depth gauge (Aas, 1979, 1983; Aas and Risness, 1979a,b; Hanihara et al., 1970b; Kirveskari, 1974). When the depth is measured, it becomes clear that the visual determinations can be biased by the distance between the lingual marginal ridges. It may be that the depth of the fossa is approximately the same in the central and lateral incisors, but because the laterals are narrower mesiodistally the fossa appears to be deeper, resulting in a higher rating than for the central. The investigator must be extremely careful to use standards for visual comparisons

and to continually refer to them during any data collection.

The frequency of the occurrence of shovel-shaped incisors is generally held to be greatest in Mongoloid populations and lower in other groups. In a thorough analysis of the trait Mizoguchi (1985) has presented the data from 148 studies that used visual determination of the expression and 44 that utilized depth measurements. In general, populations native to Asia and North America have the deepest lingual fossae (larger than 0.9 mm), South American natives having intermediate depths (0.5–1.0 mm) and Europeans the shallowest (0.3–0.7 mm). If only the larger expressions (shovel and semishovel) are included, one can generalize and show that North and South American natives demonstrate an occurrence of 70%–95%, Asians about the same as the Amerindians, Melanesians approximately 6%–20%, Australian Aborigines about 60%–90%, Europeans 5%–50% and Teso and Bantu from Africa between 10% and 20% (Mizoguchi, 1985). In North America, Indians and Inuit have about the same frequency of occurrence of the trait, but the Indians have the larger expressions (Mayhall, 1972).

There has been much written about the cusp and groove patterns of the mandibular teeth. Most skeletal biologists know of the Dryopithecus or Y-5 pattern. What may be overlooked is that the number of cusps varies independently of the groove pattern. So when we describe the molar as having a +4 pattern we are really describing two phenomena, the number of cusps (in this case four) and the groove pattern (a plus). Without going into the detail that is available in Dahlberg (1945, 1951), Jorgensen (1956), or Kirveskari (1974), there are three generally recognized patterns of the primary grooves on the mandibular molars: a Y, an X, and a +. These describe the manner in which the grooves contact each other and separate the cusps from each other. The cusp number, at first glance, appears to be simple: Just count the cusps. It is not quite this easy as the number refers only to the principal cusps. This means that a five cusped tooth may have as many as seven cusps, two of them being accessory cusps. Furthermore, a four-cusped tooth may have five or six cusps for the same reason. The accurate description of the cusp and groove patterns requires a basic knowledge of crown morphology, which can be obtained from any of the dental anatomy texts mentioned earlier or several papers that deal with the trait variability (Axelsson and Kirveskari, 1981; Dahlberg, 1951). Hillson (1986) has an excellent discussion of the traits.

As noted above, mandibular molars can have accessory cusps, two of which are commonly described: the sixth cusp and the seventh cusp. The seventh cusp is also known as the tuberculum intermedium, metaconulid, tuberculum accessorium mediale internum, or c7, and the sixth as the tuberculum sextum, entoconulid, tuberculum accessorium posteriore internum, or c6 (Kirveskari, 1974). The expression of these traits can be observed from the standard plaques of Turner or Hanihara. The sixth cusp and seventh cusp have been described for such diverse groups as Canadian Eskimos (Hartweg, 1966), Skolt Lapps (Kirveskari, 1974), North American whites (Dahlberg, 1945; Mayhall et al., 1982), Australian Aborigines (Hanihara, 1976), Japanese (Suzuki and Sakai, 1955), and Ainu (Hanihara et al., 1975). Generally, it has been suggested that nonwhite and large-toothed peoples show the higher frequencies of cusp 6, whereas the frequencies for cusp 7 are mixed, depending on the molar examined. It is probably fair to assume that part of the difficulty with the reported frequencies for these accessory cusps is the different definitions of what constitutes a cusp. In some studies expressions that would usually be assigned a "large" category are only reported; others that make use of the standardized plaques report a much wider range of variation.

One should be aware that all of the cusps have names based on the theories of molar evolution. Generally, these follow the names assigned by Osborn, Gregory, and Cope (see Jordan et al., 1992: 302–304, for a brief summary). For a detailed examination of molar evolution and the names assigned to the cusps Peyer's (1968) description is one of the most complete. In the mandibular molars the mesiofacial cusp is termed the protoconid, the distofacial is the hypoconid, the distal is the hypoconulid, the mesiolingual is the metaconid and the distolingual is the entoconid. In the maxillary molars the mesiofacial cusp is termed the paracone, the distofacial is the

metacone, the mesiolingual is the protocone, and the distolingual is the hypocone. Names ending in –cone refer to the maxillary cusps and those ending in –id refer to the mandibular cusps. It should be kept in mind that there is general agreement on the nomenclature for the mandibular molars but there are varying opinions about the correctness of the nomenclature for the maxillary ones.

The maxillary cusp number is much simpler than the mandibular. The greatest amount of variation is found in the distolingual cusp. Again the standardized plaques are useful in identifying the range of variation. The hypocone may be well developed (4), somewhat smaller (4-), vestigial (3+), or absent (3) (Dahlberg, 1945). The first molars almost always display a well-developed cusp, while the second and third molars are more varied. As a broad generalization, Mongoloid populations are more conservative with larger expressions found on all molars, whereas Caucasoids tend toward a reduction in the hypocone size in the second and third molars. The hypocone tends to reduce in size as one goes distally in the molar series.

The volume of cusps has been described recently by Mayhall and Alvesalo (1991). They used the moiré technique and then determined the area within each contour line on each cusp of the maxillary molars of a Finnish population and combined these areas by multiplying by the "thickness" of the contour lines to achieve a true volumetric determination. This has the advantage not only of demonstrating the three dimensions of a cusp but also of identifying the actual growth of the cusp by using its volume, since growth is not two dimensional. These investigators found that there is little sexual dimorphism in the basal area and volume of the hypocone, but the other major cusps (trigon) do show significant differences in these two determinations. They suggest that growth of the later-developing hypocone slows down in relation to the growth of the rest of the crown.

Another area of interest to dental anthropologists is the artificial deformation of teeth, either intentional (Fastlicht, 1976; Migraine, 1987; Romero, 1958; Singer, 1953) or unintentional (Brown and Molnar, 1990; Patterson, 1984; Schulz, 1977), which can provide clues

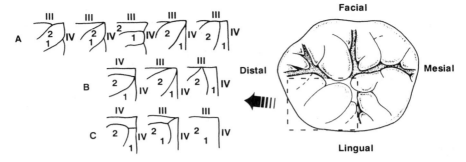

Fig. 11. Possible positions of furrows 1 and 2 on the entoconid. A. The patterns for the independent furrows can be written as: 1(IV)2(III), 1(IV)2(fc), 1(IV)2(IV), 1(fc)2(III). B. The patterns for the diradii would be written as DIV, Dfc, and DIII. C. The triradii would be represented as TIV, Tfc, and TIII. Adapted from Zubov (1977).

to cultural practices and relationships. Romero's classic monograph includes illustrations for the identification of the various alterations of tooth form he found in North America.

Finally, there is odontoglyphics, a neglected area of study. Zubov (1977) studied the groove patterns on molars and noted that they were as individualistic as dermatoglyphics. These groove patterns are important because, as Zubov notes, they are a result of the calcification waves meeting during ontogenesis of the teeth, a phenomenon that is genetically determined. He also points out that most of the furrows on the occlusal surface of the teeth are set prior to the formation of the enamel cap. Another advantage of this system is the usefulness of the groove patterns when the cusps have been worn away, although many of the superficial furrows may also be lost to investigation. Zubov proposed several "Laws and Principles of Odontoglyphics," which divided the furrows into "intertubercular furrows" (those that completely isolate cusps and are deep) and "tubercular furrows" (those passing over cusps and providing incomplete differentiation of the elements). The description of the patterns can be converted into symbols based on the intersections of the furrows (Fig. 11).

There are varying patterns in different populations and ethnic groups but little has been published in English. This technique has rarely been used outside the Soviet Union, but it appears to hold promise for individual identification (Zubov and Nikityuk, 1974, 1978), since

all skeletal biologists know the teeth are the part of the body that is usually best preserved.

This section on morphology has been brief and has discussed only the major traits that are most often reported. It is not unusual when conducting a study to find that "your" sample contains other traits, or expressions of the above traits, that are not identified by any of the usual works or standards. This is the chance to have a cusp or a pit named after you! As in the section on size of the teeth, the same general questions can be asked about the usefulness of these traits. In the case of the traits discussed above there has been a broad description of the range of expressions of the traits and the frequency of occurrence of them in different populations. These data suggest that there is a genetic determination for the traits but we do not understand the complex interaction between the environment and heredity in producing the expressions that can be observed. Berry (1976) has cautioned that before morphological traits are used for biological distance statistics, it is necessary to ascertain how the effects of the environment, such as diet, affect their expression. If there are effects from the interaction of pathological conditions and the traits, these might render large numbers of teeth unscorable. This last point is important, because it has been shown that the expression of a trait can have an effect on the amount of pathology seen in an individual or a population (Mayhall, 1972). This pathology may obliterate the trait or cause a tooth to be lost. Thus, morphological traits can affect the mortality of teeth, thereby skewing the results of morphological studies.

The sexual dimorphism of dental traits has been reported for the foregoing traits but these have been inconclusive. Canadian Inuit groups show no sexual dimorphism (Mayhall, 1976); there is no sexual difference in Japanese shovel-shaping but there are differences in the other traits above (Mizoguchi, 1985); and Lapps (Kirveskari, 1974) demonstrate an inconsistent pattern with no dimorphism for shoveling or protostylid but moderate dimorphism for Carabelli's and cusps 6 and 7. North American whites (Mayhall et al., 1982) revealed no dimorphic expressions. Harris (1980), in a study of 38 samples of living populations found that Caucasian, Asian, Polynesian, Melanesian, and Native American females possess significantly higher frequencies of shoveling on maxillary central incisors than do males. U.S. blacks did not display a sex difference in the frequency of shoveling. This varying amount of sexual dimorphism poses a problem for those who are examining unattributed teeth. However, the literature is full of studies that have not taken sex into consideration. The differences in expression and incidence are small even in those populations that are dimorphic and it is generally permissible to combine the sexes if it is not possible to report them separately.

The genetics of morphological traits is not well understood. Kirveskari and Alvesalo (1982) have examined the dental morphology of 45,X females and compared it with that of their normal relatives and the general population. The reduced expressions of nonmetric dental traits in their study suggests that there is a size-independent reduction in tooth crowns that is associated with the loss of an X chromosome. It is still too early to tell if these results are generally valid but there is some indication that the reductions seen in Turner's syndrome patients are not as uniform as first suspected (Mayhall and Alvesalo, 1991). Sofaer (1970) noted that the Hardy–Weinberg Law has been applied to population data and that the claims by these analyses that various morphological characters were controlled by single autosomal genes were flawed. He concluded by emphasizing that "the nature of the genetic control can only be derived from a study of related individuals" (Sofaer, 1970: 1508).

Asymmetry of morphological traits on the antimeres has historically been assumed to be negligible. Most studies that have examined only one side of the jaw have used the other side if a particular trait could not be scored on the side under study. The reasoning was that the there were few examples that contradicted the assumption of antimere symmetry and thus sample size could be increased. But as early as 1954, Meredith and Hixon stressed that there was a noticeable difference in the expression of the Carabelli's trait between sides of the maxilla. Biggerstaff (1973) and Harris (1977) reported relatively high levels of asymmetry for traits as well. In their study of Australian aboriginals, Townsend and Brown (1980, 1981) found almost 10% asymmetry in the deciduous second molar and about 9% asymmetry in the first molar for Carabelli's trait.

The comparisons in different groups of the amount of dental asymmetry in nonmetric traits are recent phenomena (Baume and Crawford, 1980; Perzigian, 1977). If these are to be reported one must be careful (1) to carefully specify how the asymmetry was scored, (2) to ensure that the sample sizes are adequate (Garn et al., 1979; Smith et al., 1982), (3) to take into account population differences in overall trait presence, and (4) to take into account the duration of the development of the trait (Saunders and Mayhall, 1982).

ORAL PATHOLOGY
Dental Caries and Periodontal Disease

The pathological condition of the teeth and maxillae has been of value to the skeletal biologist as it is directly related to the gathering of data about the morphology and size of the teeth and the diet and culture of the individuals being studied. Many studies have used pathological manifestations to indicate dietary differences based on modern studies that indicated that diets high in carbohydrates were cariogenic or that diets that were fibrous were less likely to produce generalized periodontal disease. It is impossible to completely cover the use of oral pathology in skeletal biology. However, the reader should refer to any of the comprehensive oral pathology texts or the more specialized texts on particular oral conditions to discover the wide variety of conditions and techniques that are of value to the study of teeth from archaeological sites. One work that has a detailed description of pathological conditions in skeletal materials, and of the problems of accurate description of them is Patterson's work (1984) on the pre-Iroquois and Iroquois populations of Ontario. A recent volume covering some of these topics is Kelley and Larsen (1991).

Dental caries. The most common and obvious pathological condition that has been studied in skeletal series is dental caries (a singular and plural form). Dental caries can be characterized as the number of teeth decayed, missing, or filled per individual. This is an important descriptive method if the study is to compare skeletal samples with living populations. However, this is rarely possible, because seldom are all of the teeth recovered in archaeological contexts. This means that the researcher must improvise: usually counting the number of teeth decayed and then determining the percentage of teeth in each tooth group (incisors, canines, premolars, and molars) that are affected by caries.

The determination of dental caries can be difficult. The researcher may be satisfied by simply counting the number of affected teeth, or it may be of interest to provide a more detailed description of the carious lesions. In the latter situation the study must indicate what is meant by a carious lesion. Is it one that can be seen by the naked eye and may be indicated by the discolorization of the crown? Or are lesions included that are identifiable only with the use of a sharp dental probe and/or radiographs? The study should indicate the locations of the lesions on the tooth surface. Location of lesions may vary by population and age (Keene and Keene, 1985; Parfitt, 1955; Zadik, 1976). Root caries are more prevalent in older individuals (Keene, 1986; Nikiforuk, 1985). The modern Native American populations of North America apparently have fewer interproximal lesions, but they may demonstrate more occlusal lesions because of their complex crown morphology (Mayhall, 1972; Pedersen, 1949). The skeletal biologist who wants in-depth knowledge of all aspects of dental caries is referred to the volumes by Nikiforuk (1985).

Periodontal disease. Periodontal disease is an area of controversy when we examine skeletal material (Alexandersen, 1967). The most benign form of periodontal disease is gingivitis, which is an inflammation of the gingiva with no obvious effects on the underlying bone. On the other hand, there are generalized periodontal diseases that may be observed on the alveolar bone of the maxillae. One of the possible signs of periodontal disease is a blunting of the alveolar crest bone. The crest appears porous and notched on the facial and lingual portions. This is probably due to inflammatory processes.

Normally, the alveolar crest is about 1–2 mm apical to the cementoenamel junction (CEJ) of the tooth it surrounds. It is impossible to meaningfully measure the distance of the crest from the cusps or incisal edges of the teeth, since they are subject to attrition. Mellquist and Sandberg (1939) have suggested that horizontal bone loss can be characterized by measuring the distance from the CEJ to the bone and then recording the result on a four unit scale (0 = no atrophy; 1–3 mm = 1; 3 mm to one-half the length of the root = 2; more than one-half of the root = 3), but it may be just as easy to physically measure the distances and record these (Davies et al., 1969). It should be remembered that this measurement is subject to great diversity because teeth may overerupt if not in occlusion. It is still problematic whether the horizontal bone loss described is pathological or physiological. There is evidence that horizontal bone loss is associated with attrition, which may be considered physiological, and is age related. It is difficult to determine whether to attribute generalized bone loss to a pathological condition or directly to attrition (Barker, 1975).

There are conditions of the alveolar bone that indicate periodontal disease. These are isolated areas of bone loss around individual teeth. These may be caused by food impaction because of a lack of contact between adjacent teeth, by teeth that are malpositioned, although there is evidence to counteract this (Beagrie et al., 1970; Thompson and Beagrie, 1973), or by teeth that have extensions of the enamel onto the roots of the teeth (Masters and Hoskins, 1964; Tratman, 1950). Lee et al. (1968) also noted that palatal–gingival grooves in maxillary incisors could lead to localized periodontal disease. These pockets may become severe enough to destroy any bone support the tooth may have and cause the tooth to be lost.

This very brief summary of the two major pathological conditions should suggest to the skeletal biologist that oral pathological conditions may significantly influence the results of any dental morphological study. As was mentioned earlier, there is a close relationship between tooth size, discrete traits and pathology, and this relationship must be taken into consideration in any study.

THE FUTURE

Dental stone models can be obtained for almost any dentition, living or dead, and these accurate models can be used in the future when the material is reburied, moved to a new storage site, or lost. These dental casts have the advantage of being easily shipped, handled, and extensively studied without harm to the original material.

The use of dental morphology along with other important areas such as tooth wear, oral pathology, enamel hypoplasia, and other microscopic changes in the tooth structure allows the skeletal biologist to reconstruct much of the life-style of the individual being studied. It is clear that the teeth are a very important component in any in depth study of skeletal material, not only because of their endurance but because of their ability to record the biology of the body during an important time in the life of an individual. The dentition begins its formation very early in gestation and has not completed its development until the third decade of life. The insults that the body and the dentition have received may be recorded permanently in the teeth, whereas bone has the opportunity to remodel during the life of an individual, thus obliterating the earlier changes.

For many studies the insults of living may not be as important as being able to reconstruct the population affinities of the groups under examination. Here, the use of tooth size and shape are very important, since there is evidence of a genetic basis to much of the variation that is observed. In the future there is a strong possibility that we will understand the genetics of tooth size and shape and we will be able to use this knowledge to accurately determine the affinities of individuals and groups. Survey of the literature makes it clear that the major problems confronting dental anthropologists are ones of consistency in observation. These problems can be overcome and the skeletal biologist can use the techniques noted above to further identify the biological and cultural background of much of the skeletal material that is still relatively unstudied.

With the use of stone models it is now possible to examine the tooth in a truly three-dimensional manner (moiré contourography). The future of dental morphological studies appears to rest with more three-dimensional representations that are accurate and measurable and that can provide the researcher with a true picture of the racial affinities, the cultural and pathological processes that have affected the individual, and the biological influences on the developing, growing, and aging individual.

REFERENCES

Aas IH (1979): The depth of the lingual fossa in permanent maxillary incisors of Norwegian Lapps. Am J Phys Anthropol 51:417–420.

Aas IH (1983): Variability of a dental morphological trait. Acta Odontol Scand 41:257–263.

Aas IHM, Risness S (1979a): The depth of the lingual fossa in permanent incisors of Norwegians: I. Method of measurement, statistical distribution and sex dimorphism. Am J Phys Anthropol 50:335–340.

Aas IHM, Risness S (1979b): The depth of the lingual fossa in permanent incisors of Norwegians: II. Differences between central and lateral incisors, correlations, side asymmetry and variability. Am J Phys Anthropol 50:341–347.

Alexandersen V (1967): The pathology of the jaws and the temporomandibular joint. In Brothwell D, Sandison AT (eds): "Diseases in Antiquity". Springfield, IL: Charles C. Thomas, 46:1–45.

Alvesalo L (1985): Dental growth in 47,XXY males and in conditions with other sex-chromosome anomalies. In Sandberg AA (ed): "The Y Chromosome. Part B: Clinical Aspects of Y Chromosome Abnormalities." New York: Alan R. Liss, pp 227–300.

Alvesalo L, Portin P (1980): 47,XXY males: Sex chromosomes and tooth size. Am J Hum Genet 32:955–959.

Alvesalo L, Varrela J (1979): Permanent tooth sizes in 46,XY females. Am J Hum Genet 32:736–742.

Axelsson G, Kirveskari P (1981): Cusp number and groove pattern of lower molars in Icelanders. Acta Odontol Scand 39:361–366.

Barker BCW (1975): Periodontal disease and tooth dislocation in aboriginal remains from Lake Nitchie (N.S.W.), West Point (Tasmania) and Limestone Creek (Victoria). Arch Phys Anthropol Oceania 10:185–217.

Baume RM, Crawford MH (1980): Discrete dental trait asymmetry in Mexican and Belizean groups. Am J Phys Anthropol 52:315–321.

Beagrie GS, Thompson GW, Basu MK (1970): Tooth position and alveolar bone loss in skulls. Br Dent J 129:471–474.

Berry AC (1976): The anthropological value of minor variants of the dental crown. Am J Phys Anthropol 45:257–268.

Biggerstaff, RH (1970): "A Quantitative and Qualitative Study of the Post-Canine Dentition of Twins." Ann Arbor, MI: University Microfilms.

Biggerstaff RH (1973): Heritability of the Carabelli cusp in twins. J Dent Res 52:40–44.

Brabant H (1973): Étude odontologique des restes humains découverts dans la necropole Gallo-Romaine et Merovingienne de Dieue (Meuse) en France. Bull Group Int Rech Sci Stomat 16:239–261.

Brothwell DR (ed). (1963): "Dental Anthropology." New York: Pergamon, p 288.

Brown T, Molnar S (1990): Interproximal grooving and task activity in Australia. Am J Phys Anthropol 81:545–554.

Brown T, Margetts B, Townsend GC (1980): Comparison of mesiodistal crown diameters of the deciduous and permanent teeth in Australian aboriginals. Aust Dent J 25:28–33.

Buschang PH, Demirjian A, Cadotte L (1988): Permanent mesiodistal tooth size of French-Canadians. J Can Dent Assoc 54:441–444.

Butler PM, Joysey KA (eds). (1978): "Development, Function and Evolution of Teeth." London: Academic Press, p 523.

Campbell TD (1925): "Dentition and Palate of the Australian Aboriginal." Adelaide: Hassell Press, p 123.

Dahlberg AA (1945): The changing dentition of man. J Am Dent Assoc 32:676–690.

Dahlberg AA (1950): The evolutionary significance of the protostylid. Am J Phys Anthropol 8:15–25.

Dahlberg AA (1951): The dentition of the American Indian. In Laughlin WS (ed): "Papers on the Physical Anthropology of the American Indian." New York: Viking Fund, pp 138–176.

Dahlberg AA (1958): Rotated maxillary central incisors among various tribes of American Indians, [in Japanese]. J Jpn Orthod Soc 17:157–169.

Dahlberg AA (1963): Analysis of the American Indian dentition. In Brothwell DR (ed): "Dental Anthropology." New York: Pergamon, pp 149–177.

Dahlberg AA (1965): Geographic distribution and origin of dentitions. Int Dent J 15:348–355.

Dahlberg AA (ed) (1971): "Dental Morphology and Evolution." Chicago: University of Chicago Press, p 350.

Dahlberg AA (1986): Ontogeny and dental genetics in forensic problems. Forensic Sci Int 30:163–176.

Dahlberg AA (1990): The face and dentition of Australasian population: Preface and overview. Am J Phys Anthropol 82:245–246.

Dahlberg AA, Graber TM (eds) (1977): "Orofacial Growth and Development." The Hague: Mouton, p 354.

Davies DM, Picton DCA, Alexander AG (1969): An objective method of assessing the periodontal condition in human skulls. J Periodont Res 4:74–77.

DeSmet R, Brabant H (1969): Observations anthropologiques sur la denture des Indiens Javagos. Bull Soc R Belge Anthropol Prehist 80:97–123.

De Vito CIH, Saunders SR (1990): A discriminant function analysis of deciduous teeth to determine sex. J Forensic Sci 35:845–858.

Fastlicht S (1976): "Tooth Mutilations and Dentistry in Pre-Columbian Mexico." Berlin: Quintessence, p 164.

Garn SM, Lewis AB, Walenga AJ (1968): Crown-size profile pattern comparisons of 14 human populations. Arch Oral Biol 13:1235–1242.

Garn SM, Cole PE, Smith BH (1979): The effect of sample size on crown size asymmetry. J Dent Res 58:2012.

Goose DH (1963): Dental measurement: An assessment of its value in anthropological studies. In Brothwell DR (ed): "Dental Anthropology." New York: Pergamon, pp 125–148.

Goose DH, Lee GTR (1971): The mode of inheritance of Carabelli's trait. Hum Biol 43:64–69.

Hanihara K (1976): Statistical and comparative studies of the Australian Aboriginal dentition. Univ Mus Univ Tokyo Bull 11:1–57.

Hanihara K (1977): Distances between Australian Aborigines and certain other populations based on dental measurements. J Hum Evol 6:403–418.

Hanihara T (1989): Comparative studies of geographically isolated populations in Japan based on dental measurements. J Anthropol Soc Nippon 97:95–107.

Hanihara K, Ueda H (1979): Crown diameters in Japanese–American F1 hybrids. Ossa 6:105–114.

Hanihara K, Tamada M, Tanaka T (1970a): Quantitative analysis of the hypocone in the human upper molars. J Anthropol Soc Nippon 78:200–207.

Hanihara K, Tanaka T, Tamada M (1970b): Quantitative analysis of the shovel-shaped character in the incisors. J Anthropol Soc Nippon 78:90–98.

Hanihara K, Matsuda T, Tanaka T, Tamada M (1975): Comparative studies of dentition. In Watanabe S, Knodo S, Matsunaga E (eds): "Anthropological and Genetic Studies on the Japanese. Part III. Anthropological and Genetic Studies of the Ainu." Tokyo: University of Tokyo, pp 256–264.

Harris EF (1977): "Anthropologic and Genetic Aspects of the Dental Morphology of Solomon Islanders, Melanesia." Ann Arbor, MI: University Microfilms, p 465.

Harris EF (1980): Sex differences in lingual marginal ridging on the human maxillary central incisor. Am J Phys Anthropol 52:541–548.

Hartweg R (1966): La dentition des Esquimaux de Ungava et des Indiens Wabemakustewatsh de la côte Orientale de la Baie Hudson. Université de Laval Centre d'Etudes Nordiques Travaux Divers, 13:1–156.

Henderson AM, Greene DL (1975): Dental field theory: An application to primate evolution. J Dent Res 54:344–350.

Hillson S (1986): "Teeth." Cambridge: Cambridge University Press, p 376.

Hinton RJ, Smith MO, Smith FH (1980): Tooth size changes in prehistoric Tennessee Indians. Hum Biol 52:229–242.

Jablonski S (1982): "Illustrated Dictionary of Dentistry." Philadelphia: Saunders, p 919.

Jacobson A (1982): "The Dentition of the South African Negro." Birmingham: Alexander Jacobson, p 365.

Jordan RE, Abrams L, Kraus BS (1992): "Kraus" Dental Anatomy and Occlusion." St. Louis: Mosby Yearbook, p 371.

Jorgensen KD (1956): The deciduous dentition: A descriptive and comparative anatomical study. Acta Odontol Scand 14 (Suppl 20):1–202.

Kajava Y (1912): Die Zahne der Lappen. Suomen Toimistuksia 10:1–64 (as cited by Pedersen, 1949).

Kanazawa E (1980): Principal component analysis of three–dimensional coordinates of landmarks on the Japanese skull, [in Japanese]. J Anthropol Soc Nippon 88:209–228.

Kanazawa E, Sekikawa M, Ozaki T (1983): Three-dimensional measurements of the occlusal surface of upper first molars in a modern Japanese population. Acta Anat 116:90–96.

Kanazawa E, Sekikawa M, Ozaki T (1984): Three-dimensional measurements of the occlusal surfaces of upper molars in a Dutch population. J Dent Res 63:1298–1301.

Kanazawa E, Morris DH, Sekikawa M, Ozaki T (1988): Comparative study of the upper molar occlusal table morphology among seven human populations. Am J Phys Anthropol 77:271–278.

Kari M, Alvesalo L, Manninen K (1980): Sizes of deciduous teeth in 45,X females. J Dent Res 59:1382–1385.

Keene HJ (1986): Dental caries prevalence in early Polynesians from the Hawaiian Islands. J Dent Res 65:935–938.

Keene HJ, Keene AJ (1985): Dental caries prevalence in early Hawaiian children. Pediatr Dent 7:271–277.

Kelley MA, Larsen CS (1991): "Advances in Dental Anthropology." New York: Wiley-Liss, p 389.

Kirveskari P (1974): Morphological traits in the permanent dentition of living Skolt Lapps. Proc Finn Dent Soc 70 (Suppl 2):1–90.

Kirveskari P and Alvesalo L (1981): Shovel shape of maxillary incisors in 47,XYY males. Proc Finn Dent Soc 77: 79–81.

Kirveskari P, Alvesalo L (1982): Dental morphology in Turner's syndrome (45,X females). In Kurtén B (ed): "Teeth: Form, Function and Evolution." New York: Columbia University Press, pp 298–303.

Kraus BS (1951): Carabelli's anomaly of the maxillary molar teeth. J Hum Gen 3:348–355.

Kurtén B (1982): "Teeth: Form, Function and Evolution." New York: Columbia University Press, p 393.

Lavelle CLB (1970): Comparison of the deciduous teeth between caucasoid, negroid, and mongoloid population samples. Dent Pract 21:121–124.

Lavelle CLB (1971): Mandibular molar tooth dimensions in different human racial groups. Bull Group Int Rech Sci Stomat 14:273–289.

Lee KW, Lee EC, Poon KY (1968): Palato-gingival grooves in maxillary incisors: A possible predisposing factor to localized periodontal disease. Br Dent J 127:14–18.

Lukacs JR (1984): Cultural variation and the evolution of dental reduction: An interpretation of the evidence from south Asia. In Basu A, Malhotra KC (eds): "Human Genetics and Adaptation, Vol 2." New Delhi: Indian Statistical Institute, pp 252–269.

Lukacs JR (1988): Dental morphology and odontometrics of early agriculturalists from neolithic Mehrgarth, Pakistan. In Russell DE, Santoro J-P, Sigogneau-Russell D (eds): "Teeth Revisited: Proceedings of the VIIth International Symposium on Dental Morphology." Mem Mus Natl Hist Nat, Paris, Ser C 53:285–303.

Lysell L, Myrberg N (1982): Mesiodistal tooth size in the deciduous and permanent dentitions. Eur J Orthod 4: 113–122.

Masters DH, Hoskins SW (1964): Projection of cervical enamel into molar furcations. J Periodont 35:49–53.

Mayhall JT (1972): Dental morphology of Indians and Eskimos: Its relationship to the prevention and treatment of caries. J Can Dent Assoc 38:152–154.

Mayhall JT (1976): "The Morphology of the Permanent Dentition of Prehistoric and Modern Central Arctic Eskimoid Peoples: A Study of Their Biological Relationships." PhD thesis, Chicago: University of Chicago.

Mayhall JT (1977): Cultural and environmental influences on the Eskimo dentition. In Dahlberg AA, Graber TM (eds): "Orofacial Growth and Development." The Hague: Mouton, pp 216–227.

Mayhall JT (1979): The biological relationship of Thule culture and Inuit populations: An odontological investigation. In McCartney AP (ed): "Thule Eskimo Culture: An Anthropological Retrospective." Archaeol Survey Can, 88:448–473.

Mayhall JT, Alvesalo L (1991): Sexual dimorphism in the three-dimensional determinations of the maxillary first molar: Cusp height, area, volume and position. In Smith P (ed): "Structure Function and Evolution of Teeth." Tel Aviv: Freund Publishing House. (in press).

Mayhall JT, Kanazawa E (1989): Three-dimensional analysis of the maxillary first molar crowns of Canadian Inuit. Am J Phys Anthropol 78:73–78.

Mayhall JT, Karp SA (1983): Size and morphology of the permanent dentition of the Waorani Indians of Ecuador. Can Rev Phys Anthropol 3:55–67.

Mayhall JT, Saunders SR (1985): Dimensional and discrete dental trait asymmetry relationships. Am J Phys Anthropol 69:403–411.

Mayhall JT, Saunders SR, Belier PL (1982): The dental morphology of North American Whites: A reappraisal. In Kurtén B (ed): "Teeth: Form, Function and Evolution." New York: Columbia University Press, pp 245–258.

Mayhall JT, Alvesalo J, Townsend G (1991): Tooth crown size in 46,X,i(Xq) human females. Arch oral Biol 36:411–414.

McKeown M (1981): A method of analyzing the form of individual human teeth. J Can Dent Assoc 47:534–537.

Mellquist C, Sandberg T (1939): Odontological studies of about 1400 medieval skulls from Halland and Scania in Sweden and from the Norse colony in Greenland and a contribution to the knowledge of their anthropology. Odontol Tidskr. Suppl 3B.

Meredith HV, Hixon EH (1954): Frequency, size, and bilateralism of Carabelli's tubercle. J Dent Res 33:435–440.

Middleton Shaw JC (1931): "The Teeth, the Bony Palate and the Mandible in Bantu Races of South Africa." London: John Bale & Sons, p 134.

Migraine D (1987): Les mutilations dentaires dans les civilisations exotiques et leur signification. J Can Dent Assoc 53:831–834.

Mizoguchi Y (1985): Shovelling: A statistical analysis of its morphology. Univ Mus, Univ Tokyo Bull 26:1–176.

Mizoguchi Y (1988): Tooth crown diameters of the permanent teeth of the Epi-Jomon people from the Usu-10 and other sites in the Seaside region of Funkawan Bay, Hokkaido, Japan [in Japanese]. Mem Natl Sci Mus 21:211–220.

Moorrees CFA (1957): "The Aleut Dentition." Cambridge: Harvard University Press, p 196.

Nikiforuk G (1985): "Understanding Dental Caries." Basel: Karger (2 vols).

Osborn JW (1981): "Dental Anatomy and Embryology." Oxford: Blackwell, p 447.

Ozaki T, Kanazawa E (1984): An application of the moiré method to three-dimensional measurements of the occlusal aspects of molars. Acta Morphol Neerl-Scand 22: 85–91.

Parfitt GJ (1955): The distribution of caries on different sites of the teeth in English children from the age of 2–15 years. Br Dent J 99:423–427.

Patterson DK (1984): A diachronic study of dental palaeopathology and attritional status of prehistoric Ontario pre-Iroquois and Iroquois populations. Ottawa: Archaeol Sur Can 122:1–428.

Pedersen PO (1949): The East Greenland Eskimo dentition. Medd øm Grönland 142(3):1–244.

Pedersen PO, Dahlberg AA, Alexandersen V (eds) (1967): Proceedings of the International Symposium on Dental Morphology. J Dent Res 46(pt 1):769–992.

Perzigian AJ (1975): Natural selection on the dentition of an Arikara population. Am J Phys Anthropol 42:63–69.

Perzigian AJ (1976): The dentition of the Indian Knoll skeletal population: Odontometrics and cusp number. Am J Phys Anthropol 44:113–122.

Perzigian AJ (1977): Fluctuating dental asymmetry: Variation among skeletal populations. Am J Phys Anthropol 47:81–88.

Perzigian AJ (1984): Human odontometric variation: An evolutionary and taxonomic assessment. Anthropologie 22: 193–198.

Peyer B (1968): "Comparative Odontology." Chicago: University of Chicago Press, p 347.

Romero J (1958): Mutilaciones dentarias prehispanicas de Mexico Y America en general. Inst Nac Anthropol Hist Invest Ser 3:1–326.

Rosenzweig KA (1970): Tooth form as a distinguishing trait between sexes and human populations. J Dent Res 49: 1423–1426.

Rosenzweig KA, Smith P (1971): Dental variability in isolates. J Dent Res 50:155–160.

Russell DE, Santoro J-P, Sigogneau-Russell D (eds) (1988): Teeth Revisited: Proceedings of the VIIth International Symposium on Dental Morphology. Mem Mus Natl Hist, Paris Ser C 53:462.

Saunders SR, Mayhall JT (1982): Developmental patterns of human dental morphology traits. Arch oral Biol 27:45–49.

Schulz PD (1977): Task activity and anterior tooth grooving in prehistoric California Indians. Am J Phys Anthropol 46:87–92.

Sekikawa M, Kanazawa E, Ozaki T. (1988): Cusp height relationships between the upper and lower molars in Japanese subjects. J Dent Res 67:1515–1517.

Selmer-Olsen R (1949): "An Odontometrical Study on the Norwegian Lapps." Oslo: I Kommisjon Hos Jacob Dybwad, p 167.

Singer R (1953): Artificial deformation of teeth: A preliminary report. S Afr J Sci 50:116–122.

Singh IJ, Savara BS (1964): A method for making tooth and dental arch measurements. J Am Dent Assoc 69:719–721.

Smith BH, Garn SM, Cole PE (1982): Problems of sampling and inference in the study of fluctuating dental asymmetry. Am J Phys Anthrop 58:281–289.

Sofaer JA (1970): Dental morphologic variation and the Hardy–Weinberg Law. J Dent Res 49:1505–1508.

Suzuki M, Sakai T (1955): On the "tuberculum accesorium (sic) mediale internum" in recent Japanese. [in Japanese] Anthropol Soc Nippon J 64:135–139.

Takasaki H (1970): Moiré topography. Appl Optics 9:1457–1472.

Takasaki H (1973): Moiré topography. Appl Optics 12:845–850.

Ten Cate AR (1989): "Oral Histology: Development, Structure, and Function" (3rd ed). St. Louis: Mosby, p 466.

Thompson GW, Beagrie GS (1973): Tooth irregularity and the height of the alveolar process in skulls. J Periodont Res 8:37–41.

Thomsen S (1951): Dental morphology and occlusion in the people of Tristan da Cunha. Results of the Norwegian Scientific Expedition to Tristan Da Cunha 1937–1938, 25:1–61.

Townsend GC (1981): Fluctuating asymmetry in the deciduous dentition of Australian Aboriginals. J Dent Res 60: 1849–1857.

Townsend GC, Brown T (1980): Dental asymmetry in Australian Aboriginals. Hum Biol 52:661–673.

Townsend G, Brown T (1981): The Carabelli trait in Australian Aboriginal dentition. Arch oral Biol 26:809–814.

Townsend G, Alvesalo A, Jensen B, Kari M (1988): Patterns of tooth size in human chromosomal aneuploidies. In Russell DE, Santoro J-P, Sigogneau-Russell D (eds): "Teeth Revisited: Proceedings of the VIIth International Symposium on Dental Morphology." Mem Mus Natl Hist Nat, Paris Ser C 53:25–45.

Tratman EK (1950): A comparison of the teeth of people: Indo-European racial stock with the Mongoloid racial stock. Dent Rec, 70:31–53, 63–68.

Tsuji T (1958): Incidence and inheritance of the Carabelli's cusp in a Japanese population. Jpn J Hum Genet 3:21–31.

Turner CG (1967): "The Dentition of Arctic Peoples." Ann Arbor, MI: University Microfilms, p 284.

Weidenreich F (1937): "The Dentition of *Sinanthropus pekinensis.* A Comparative Odontography of the Hominids." Palaeon Sin New Ser D, No 1, p 180.

Williams LR (1979): "A Photogrammetrical Analysis of Pongid Molar Morphology." PhD dissertation, University of Toronto, p 211.

Woelfel JB (1984): "Dental Anatomy: Its Correlation With Dental Health Service" (3rd ed). Philadelphia: Lea and Febiger.

Wolpoff MH (1971): Metric trends in hominid dental evolution. Case West Reserve Univ Stud Anthropol 2:1–244.

Yamada H, Brown T (1988): Contours of maxillary molars studied in Australian Aboriginals. Am J Phys Anthropol 76:399–407

Zadik D (1976): Caries experience in deciduous and permanent dentition of the same individuals. J Dent Res 55: 1125–1126.

Zubov AA (1977): Odontoglyphics: The laws of variation of the human molar crown microrelief. In Dahlberg AA, Graber TM (eds): "Orofacial Growth and Development." The Hague: Mouton. pp 269–282.

Zubov AA, Nikityuk BA (1974): New odontological methods of twin types diagnostics [in Russian]. Vopr Anthropol 46:108–128.

Zubov AA, Nikityuk BA (1978): Prospects for the application of dental morphology in twin type analysis. J Hum Evol 7:519–524.

Skeletal Biology of Past Peoples: Research Methods
pages 79–103 © 1992 Wiley-Liss, Inc.

Chapter 5

A Reconsideration of Trace Element Analysis in Prehistoric Bone

Mary K. Sandford

Department of Anthropology, The University of North Carolina at Greensboro, Greensboro, North Carolina 27412

INTRODUCTION

The completion of two doctoral dissertations during the 1970s signaled the beginnings of a new era in the anthropological applications of bone chemistry. The pioneers in this regard were Brown (1973) and Gilbert (1975), who first demonstrated the potential of trace element analysis of human bone toward the reconstruction of prehistoric diets. Exploring different approaches to this end, Brown relied on the use of bone strontium concentrations and strontium/calcium ratios in a geographically diverse sample, while Gilbert determined levels of five elements in human remains from prehistoric Illinois.

Interest in trace element analysis is certainly no less intense at present. Over a relatively brief period, diverse aspects of this dynamic and controversial field have been addressed through the publication of edited volumes (Price, 1989a; Grupe and Herrmann, 1988), doctoral dissertations (Radosevich, 1989; Edward, 1987; Katzenberg, 1984; Sandford, 1984; Sillen, 1981a; Bisel, 1980; Schoeninger, 1980; Szpunar, 1977), and numerous articles (Aufderheide, 1989; Sillen et al., 1989; Hancock et al., 1989; Lambert et al., 1989; Pate and Hutton, 1988; Grupe, 1988; Hanson and Buikstra, 1987; Byrne and Parris, 1987).

Of greater importance than the mere quantity of publications is the growing sense, evident in recent literature, that trace element research in anthropology has reached a pivotal phase (see especially Sillen et al., 1989; Hancock et al., 1989; Radosevich, 1989; Pate and Hutton, 1988). This sentiment, born out of controversy surrounding some of the most basic assumptions of elemental analysis, may well be marking the beginning of a new era, characterized by basic research that encompasses extensive use of experimental designs and laboratory investigations. Sillen and coworkers (1989: 510), for example, recently called for a "more aggressively experimental" approach to confront such fundamental problems in archaeological bone chemistry as diagenesis, or postmortem alterations in the elemental constituents of bone. This tactic has already been initiated by some researchers in the field (Pate and Hutton, 1988; Lambert et al., 1985), who have conducted laboratory experiments to explore such phenomena as ionic exchange processes between soil solutions and the mineral component of bone.

This chapter provides a historical framework for evaluating the current status of this exciting, dynamic, and controversial field. Beginning with a discussion of the biochemical structure of bone, the processes governing elemental deposition in both ante– and postmortem contexts, termed the biogenic–diagenetic continuum, are explored. Against this background, previous anthropological applications of trace element analyses and current information concerning the choice of appropriate analytical procedures and technical instrumentation are presented. In this light, the final section delineates ongoing trends and recommendations for future research.

THE BIOGENIC-DIAGENETIC CONTINUUM

Skeletal biologists often emphasize the dynamic nature of bone, a characteristic that may not be readily apparent, given its rather rigid macroscopic appearance (Stout, 1989; Shipman et al., 1985; Von Endt and Ortner, 1984; McLean and Urist, 1955). This characteristic should be underscored in the present discussion, as it refers to the ability of bone to exist in a dynamic relationship with its immediate environment. This feature, coupled with its unique microscopic structure, is central to understanding the elemental composition of bone, both in living individuals and soil-buried contexts.

Throughout life the skeletal system plays a vital role in maintaining mineral homeostasis (Neuman, 1980; Posner, 1969; Neuman and Neuman, 1958; McClean and Urist, 1955). Bone serves essentially as a mineral reservoir, where ions are deposited and released in accordance with physiological demands. Similarly, other dynamic processes, including elemental absorption and excretion and such physiological states as growth, pregnancy, and lactation, act with and upon dietary constituents to shape "biogenic" concentrations of major, minor, and trace elements (Blakely, 1989; Sillen and Smith, 1984; Parker and Toots, 1980).

Bone is no less dynamic in soil-buried, archaeological contexts, however (Von Endt and Ortner, 1984). While physiological input is obviously no longer present, processes involving skeletal chemistry and microstructure virtually ensure that elemental exchange between bone and the surrounding environment will continue. It is this propensity for ionic exchange that makes the skeleton especially vulnerable to postmortem alteration in elemental composition through contact with most soils (Pate and Hutton, 1988; Radosevich, 1989).

Such considerations illustrate that although the specific, external factors governing elemental composition may differ between living and archaeological bone, there is almost invariably a biogenic–diagenetic continuum along which the chemical makeup of skeletal tissues is continually altered both in antemortem and postmortem contexts. Thus, whether minerals are ultimately of dietary, physiological, or diagenetic origin, their presence in bone is a product of the interaction between the chemical properties of this tissue and its environmental milieu. A very similar perspective was expressed by Von Endt and Ortner (1984: 248), who noted that

> This tissue (bone) is chemically active during life, and after death continues to be reactive in response to extrinsic and intrinsic conditions as both the protein and mineral phases of bone as well as the association between the two components begins to break down, potentially resulting in complete dissolution of the tissue.

Bone structure and reactivity were among the important "intrinsic conditions" identified by these authors, while "extrinsic conditions" include the immediate postmortem environment of bone. Since the chemical structure of bone is a common denominator to pre– and postmortem mechanisms of elemental deposition, this topic is considered before further discussion of specific processes that operate along the biogenic–diagenetic continuum.

Bone Chemistry

Structurally, bone is composed of an organic component and a mineral component. The former makes up around 20%–25% of the dry weight of bone and consists chiefly of Type I collagen (Hare, 1980; Triffitt, 1980). This connective-tissue protein is arranged in fibrous bundles that, because of their elasticity and flexibility, confer upon bone properties of tensile and torsional strength. Collagen alone accounts for approximately 90% of the dry weight of the organic matrix, while other compounds, including noncollagenous proteins, proteoglycans (glycosaminoglycans), and lipids, make up the remaining fraction (Molleson, 1990; Triffitt, 1980: 47; McLean and Urist, 1955: 24–27). These are, in turn, important constituents of the organic "ground substance" that is interspersed among the collagen fibers.

While a few essential trace elements, such as iron and copper, appear to be deposited chiefly in the organic matrix (Spadaro et al., 1970a,b), most anthropological trace element studies assay the inorganic or mineral fraction, the primary location for elements of paleodietary relevance. Calcium phosphate, the most prevalent component of the mineral phase, is found in both crystalline and amorphous forms (Sillen, 1989; Neuman, 1980; Posner, 1969; Neuman and Neuman, 1958), a distinction based on the level of structural organization displayed by the constituents of a chemical solid (Goffer, 1980; Miller, 1978). Crystalline solids are, for example, composed of groups of regularly repeating "unit cells," arranged in a three–dimensional pattern or "crystal lattice." Structural units of amorphous solids, in contrast, are configured in a more disorganized fashion, although such solids may contain localized areas of more orderly arrangement.

In its crystalline form, skeletal calcium phosphate is commonly known as hydroxyapatite and has a unit cell formula which approximates the following: $Ca_{10}(PO_4)_6(OH)_2$ (Sillen, 1989: 213; Neuman and Neuman, 1958: 41). However, both the structural form and chemical nature of this compound are subject to great variation. Because such deviations involve the uptake and loss of elements in both living and soil-buried bones, they constitute an important, underlying mechanism of the biogenic–diagenetic continuum. Moreover, because the chemical constituents of living bone vary so markedly, studies aimed at delineating its normal properties, structure, and elemental concentrations (e.g., Hancock et al., 1989, 1987) are essential to our ability to accurately interpret ancient skeletal material.

Perhaps the most important property in this respect is the ability of skeletal hydroxyapatite to exist in a nonstoichiometric form (Sillen, 1989; Pate and Hutton, 1988; Neuman and Neuman, 1958: 41). Stoichiometric variations in the hydroxyapatite formula are due largely to the phenomenon of heteroionic exchange, whereby various ions are incorporated into bone by displacing its normal chemical constituents (Neuman and Neuman, 1958: 63–64; Neuman, 1980: 90; Molleson, 1990: 343). Although the timing and location of this phenomenon are influenced by numerous factors,

which are outlined below, it generally involves exchange of various cations for calcium (Ca^{2+}) and replacement of phosphate (PO_4^{3-}) and hydroxide (OH^-) by anions including carbonate (CO_3^{2-}) and fluoride (F^-), respectively. Most important, a fundamental premise of anthropological trace element investigations is derived from this property, as dietary intakes are assumed to be an important source of these chemical impurities (Klepinger, 1984: 76; Parker and Toots, 1980: 203). Thus, in theory, elemental analyses of bone provide a quantitative reflection of past intakes of elements through food and drink.

Ionic exchange processes are often conceptualized through descriptions of the structural complexes of bone mineral (Buikstra et al., 1989; Wing and Brown, 1979; McLean and Urist, 1955: 35–39; Neuman and Neuman, 1958: 61). While the numerous complexes share basic similarities, they are not necessarily identical. Most important, each three-dimensional complex is made up of four components, representing different propensities and locations for the uptake and/or release of ions. These essential components are (1) interior unit cells, (2) surface unit cells, (3) surface ions, and (4) a surface hydration shell.

The degree of and location for ionic exchange are regulated by a host of limiting factors, ranging from thermodynamic forces to the developmental stages of the individual crystals. In general, however, ions are, for several reasons, more readily exchanged at surface positions than interior unit cells. In particular, ionic exchange is most readily accomplished at the surface hydration shell (Buikstra et al., 1989; McLean and Urist, 1955: 35), a structure that possesses ions in equilibrium with other surfaces and the surrounding aqueous medium. Among the ions that tend to concentrate in the hydration shell are those of magnesium (Mg^{2+}), strontium (Sr^{2+}), radium (Ra^{2+}), and carbonate (CO_3^{2-}) (Wing and Brown, 1979: 78; Neuman and Neuman, 1958: 82–83). In addition, surface areas are more accessible to ions in body fluids by virtue of the microcrystalline nature of individual bone crystals (Neuman, 1980: 90). This characteristic endows crystals with large, highly charged surface areas, which present numerous opportunities for ionic substitutions.

Owing to their propensity for ionic exchange, surface regions have a chemical nature that has been characterized as a highly "dynamic system" with a "labile structure" (McLean and Urist, 1955: 35). This may well reflect the important role played by the skeletal system as a whole in maintaining mineral homeostasis. For example, skeletal calcium is readily mobilized to perform a variety of essential metabolic functions when serum calcium concentrations fall below a certain level (Ortner and Putschar, 1985; Shipman et al., 1985). Similarly, carbonate, the third most prevalent ion in inorganic bone, may reside primarily on the surfaces of bone crystals, largely as an available source of alkaline during times of acidotic stress (Posner, 1969: 766–767).

In contrast, the elemental constituents of interior unit cells, circumscribed within crystals, are more stable, having resulted primarily from contact with fluids during their formation (Buikstra et al., 1989; McLean and Urist, 1955). Ionic exchanges that may transpire during crystal development include (1) the substitution of strontium (Sr^{2+}), lead (Pb^{2+}), magnesium (Mg^{2+}), and sodium (Na^{2+}) for calcium (Ca^{2+}); (2) the replacement of hydroxyl ions (OH^-) by fluoride (F^-) and chloride (C^-) ions, and (3) the exchange of phosphate (PO_4^{3-}) by carbonate (CO_3^{2-}) ions (Posner, 1969: 765; McLean and Urist, 1955: 35). After crystal formation, however, dissolution of the crystal itself or its surface boundaries are requisite to such exchanges (McLean and Urist, 1955). Moreover, the amount of substitution that can transpire during crystal formation is further limited by thermodynamic and metabolic factors. For example, a maximum strontium/calcium ratio, mediated by the ability of the lattice to discriminate against impurities, places quantitative limits on exchanges involving these two elements (Buikstra et al., 1989; Klepinger, 1984; Parker and Toots, 1980). In this manner, chemical purity of crystals is enhanced by their increasing maturity.

Aside from fluctuations in chemical composition due to ionic exchange, another important property of bone lies in the ability of calcium phosphate to exist as different chemical phases, ranging from crystalline to amorphous forms (Neuman, 1980: 87–90). While substantial quantities of amorphous calcium phosphate ($Ca_9(PO_4)_6$) were inferred from early experimental investigations (Neuman and Neuman, 1958), more recent research supports a more conservative view (Neuman, 1980: 89). Additional evidence suggests that other compounds, including dicalcium phosphate dihydrate and octacalcium phosphate, may represent intermediate phases in the formation of crystalline hydroxyapatite.

While many aspects of the different phases of bone mineral await clarification, variation in their quantities appears to be influenced to some degree by the age of the calcified structures. Immature, less-calcified bone contains a higher proportion of amorphous mineral (Neuman, 1980; Posner, 1969), while the presence of this phase in adults is restricted to specific zones including surfaces of the endosteum, periosteum, trabeculae, and Haversian canals (Buikstra et al., 1989). It has also been hypothesized that the amorphous phase, which is more soluble than crystalline bone mineral, plays an important homeostatic role. Ortner and Putschar (1985: 25), for example, have suggested that amorphous bone mineral might provide a "more reactive or labile source of mineral ions."

It is quite clear that variation in both the structure and chemical composition of inorganic bone may be directly related to maintaining mineral homeostasis in the living individual. But because both properties are fundamentally involved in the release and/or deposition of elements, they also play a crucial role in diagenetic processes. Thus, the theoretical, physiological basis for the use of elemental analyses in archaeological pursuits also is an underlying factor of diagenesis. Before exploring diagenetic processes further, however, other confounding factors that influence biogenic signals, and hence the interpretation of elemental concentrations, must be considered.

Biogenic Processes

Biogenic processes are responsible for the deposition and loss of chemical elements throughout life. While skeletal concentrations ultimately relate to mineral homeostasis, they are originally derived from dietary intakes and environmental prevalences (Parker and Toots, 1980) and are further influenced by such metabolic factors as absorption, excretion, pregnancy, lactation, and growth. These processes are discussed below in conjunction with the major groups of elements found in the human body.

Classification and functions of elements. Elements found in the human body are typically categorized as either major or trace elements. This distinction is primarily based on the internal quantity of a given element, those in the former category being most abundant and those in the latter group comprising less than 0.01% of the total body mass (Schroeder, 1973). Trace elements are further classified as (1) dietary essentials, (2) possible essentials, (3) nonessentials, and (4) toxic elements (Underwood, 1977). As most anthropological research tends to focus on essential and/or toxic trace elements, and frequently on some major elements as well, these groups will be the primary focus of this discussion.

Major elements, required in relatively large quantities by higher animals and human beings, include carbon, hydrogen, nitrogen, calcium, phosphorus, oxygen, potassium, sulfur, chlorine, sodium, and magnesium (Schutte, 1964). Although these elements perform a variety of essential functions, they all play a critical role in maintaining the structural integrity of organisms. While this function is perhaps best illustrated by the contributions of calcium and phosphorus to the inorganic component of bone, other elements, including carbon, hydrogen, nitrogen, and oxygen, have been termed "molecular building blocks," because they are essential to the formation of amino acids, fatty acids, nucleotides, purines, and pyrimidines (Frieden, 1972: 150). In addition, other major elements, such as chlorine, calcium, sodium, and potassium function as electrolytes in such processes as the maintenance of acid–base and blood volumes as well as in muscle contraction and nerve–impulse transmission.

While trace elements were once believed to be environmental contaminants lacking physiological functions, 15 such substances are currently classified as dietary essentials among higher animals (Underwood, 1977). These elements include iron, zinc, copper, manganese, nickel, molybdenum, chromium, selenium, iodine, and fluorine.

In contrast to major elements, essential trace elements function primarily in catalytic reactions and are often associated with specific enzymes either as metalloenzymes or metal-activated enzymes (Sandford, 1984; Prasad, 1978; Underwood, 1977; Reinhold, 1975; Schutte, 1964). Zinc, for example, is present in numerous metalloenzymes in human beings, while manganese serves chiefly as an activator of metal-enzyme complexes. In other cases, as in the contribution of iron to hemoglobin, trace elements are vital constituents of metalloproteins which, while lacking catalytic capability, nonetheless perform metabolic functions.

The category encompassing toxic trace elements is more ambiguous, as virtually all trace elements are toxic if taken up in excessive quantities over relatively long periods of time (Aufderheide, 1989; Underwood, 1977). From this perspective, the category is usually restricted to those elements that have toxic consequences at rather low levels. Underwood (1977:2) thus confines the category to a few elements including lead, mercury, and cadmium.

Elemental intakes. Concentrations of various chemical elements are distributed differentially both within and between the myriad sources of food exploited by human populations. Based on this knowledge, anthropological studies involving trace element analyses often seek to determine the relative proportions of animal and plant resources in prehistoric diets (Byrne and Parris, 1987; Hatch and Geidel, 1985; Lambert et al., 1979; Gilbert, 1975; Brown, 1973). In general, for example, foods of animal origin have inherently higher concentrations of certain elements, such as zinc and copper, than those derived from plants. Conversely, other elements including strontium, manganese, magnesium, and calcium are usually found in higher quantities in plant resources. Thus, by comparing concentrations of specific elements, paleonutritionists can, in theory, reconstruct the relative contributions of the two food categories.

Attempts to use trace element analysis to delineate such a seemingly simple dietary dichotomy have, however, encountered several major difficulties. First, predictions and interpretations of skeletal concentrations are often clouded by a dearth of information on the elemental content of prehistoric food items. An excellent discussion of this problem recently was provided by Buikstra and coworkers (1989: 177–183) who demonstrated difficulties in arriving at accurate expectations concerning the elemental contributions of nuts and maize to many prehistoric Amerindian diets. For example, values that have often been used to predict elemental concentrations of prehistoric maize (see Gilbert, 1975) may be far less appropriate than those based on more traditionally prepared Hopi cornmeal and bread. Moreover, the assertion that nuts provide significant amounts of such elements as strontium and zinc must be carefully qualified, as the varieties eaten by prehistoric Amerindians, unlike those from other regions, are not necessarily high in trace elements.

Similar problems stem from difficulties in assessing the effects of food preparation techniques and environmental variation on dietary intakes. With respect to the former concern, quantities of some trace elements may enter food as contaminants through cooking utensils. Among the best documented examples in this regard are associations between lead toxicity and widespread use of lead-based and/or pewter food and drink containers by Greek, Roman, Colonial American, and other populations (Aufderheide, 1989). Alternatively, some evidence suggests that preparation techniques and cooking utensils may contribute either harmful or beneficial quantities of such essential elements as iron (S Kent et al., 1990). For example, the use of iron cooking pots by South African Bantu to prepare *kaffir* beer may supply an additional 2-3 mg of iron each day and is most likely a causal factor in the incidence of siderosis among Bantu adults (Underwood, 1977; Bothwell and Finch, 1962). On the other hand, one study suggests that use of iron cooking vessels by !Kung to boil meat, vegetables, and nuts may be a factor contributing to the absence of both iron deficiency anemia and significant sex differences with respect to iron status (Baumslag and Petering, 1976).

Finally, environmental levels, as manifested in soil and water concentrations, may make substantial contributions to internal elemental stores. Intakes of zinc (Halsted et al., 1972) and magnesium (Aikawa, 1981; Schroeder et al., 1969), for example, can be greatly augmented by local water supplies. In other instances, symptoms suggestive of elemental deficiencies

have been associated with variations in drinking water and/or soil concentrations (Allaway, 1986).

Elemental concentrations of soils exhibit marked variation, influencing dietary intakes through both direct and indirect mechanisms. While fluctuations in soil concentrations are most directly reflected by elemental levels of plants, the impact of such variation will be felt at higher levels on the food chain. In addition, soil and its elemental constituents may become introduced into food secondarily through contamination. In parts of Ethiopia, for example, the chief cereal grain *teff* becomes heavily contaminated with iron during the processes of cultivation, grinding, and storage, accounting for much of the estimated 470 mg of iron consumed each day by inhabitants of the region (Underwood, 1977; Fritz, 1972). Although such individuals probably absorb considerably less iron than they ingest, it would be useful to know the contribution made by this indirect route to their internal iron status.

In short, past elemental intakes were undoubtedly influenced, as in contemporary populations, by many variables. While knowledge of the elemental constituents of prehistoric staples is the most basic concern, a host of other factors, ranging from food processing techniques to concentrations in soil and drinking water, also contribute to elemental intakes. Intakes are then shaped by other processes that underlie tissue concentrations of elements.

Elemental homeostasis. Internal processes of absorption and excretion, as well as those governing storage and mobilization of elements, all play roles in maintaining elemental homeostasis. As absorption and excretion influence elemental concentrations most directly, consideration of these processes is especially important in predicting and interpreting prehistoric tissue levels.

In this context, true absorption refers to the proportion of an element that is taken up by the body (O'Dell, 1985: 41–42; Prasad, 1978; Underwood, 1977). While the gastrointestinal tract constitutes the chief route of true absorption, the specific manner, location, and degree of this process are subject to great variation. Most important, factors including age, sex, health, and nutritional status as well as concomitant dietary components and chemicals can profoundly alter elemental absorption and utilization, processes that are important components of an element's bioavailability.

Among the most pervasive factors that influence elemental uptake are chemical interactions between the elements themselves as well as between elements and other chemicals. Such interactions can often be characterized as either antagonistic or synergistic. As antagonists, the presence of one or more elements inhibits the uptake of another, often reflecting intense competition for binding sites along specific compounds required for absorption. For example, potential zinc antagonists include calcium, copper, iron, cadmium, and chromium, while those of copper include molybdenum, zinc, iron, and cadmium (O'Dell, 1985: 51–54; Prasad, 1978; Underwood, 1977). While the consequences of such antagonisms may have little if any discernible effect, they can in other instances produce severe secondary elemental deficiencies. For example, ruminants subsisting on high molybdenum intakes have been known to develop an often fatal form of copper deficiency (Underwood, 1977; Schutte, 1964).

One of the best-documented examples of elemental antagonism on human nutrition is provided by phytate, the hexaphosphoric acid of inositol, which hinders absorption of several elements including zinc, iron, and magnesium. Widespread in cereal bran and the edible portion of various other plants, phytate deters elemental absorption by forming relatively insoluble complexes with several elements. For this reason, high phytate intakes have been implicated in the etiology of human zinc deficiency in several Middle Eastern regions where unleavened, wholemeal breads are major dietary staples (Halsted et al., 1972). While subsequent laboratory studies have verified the ability of phytate to complex zinc (Reinhold et al., 1973), the problem is exacerbated by the presence of excessive calcium and, possibly, fiber (O'Dell, 1985: 51).

Knowledge of chemical synergists, substances that enhance the absorption of specific elements, is equally important in predicting past tissue levels. Unfortunately, lists of synergists, and of their actual effects on nutritional status, have not been adequately delineated for all elements. Iron, for example, has a rather high number of potential synergists including

ascorbic acid and ethanol, which are very potent in promoting the uptake of non-heme iron (Kent et al., 1990; O'Dell, 1985; Sandford, 1984). In contrast, synergists to absorption of such elements as zinc and copper are less well defined (see discussions in Sandford, 1984 and Underwood, 1977).

Synergistic and antagonistic interactions are not limited to absorption and may occur in conjunction with elemental mobilization and/or storage. For example, copper and iron maintain a complicated synergistic relationship in which the former element is required for adequate intracellular utilization and mobilization of iron (Prasad, 1985: 26–27; Frieden, 1972). Thus, copper deficiencies in human beings (Graham and Cordano, 1976) and many other species are almost invariably accompanied by anemia and depressed erythropoiesis, despite sufficient iron stores.

The excretory process also plays an essential role in maintaining mineral homeostasis, serving in the case of such elements as magnesium (Aikawa, 1981) and manganese (Leach, 1976) as the primary mechanism for maintaining consistent internal concentrations. It should be noted, however, that two distinct activities are actually subsumed under the term excretion. The term often denotes the direct elimination of the unabsorbed fraction of an element from the body, most commonly in the feces (Reinhold, 1975). "True" or "endogenous" excretion, in contrast, refers to the elimination of previously absorbed quantities of an element. Losses of this variety are mediated not only through the gastrointestinal tract but also through such secondary routes as biliary and pancreatic secretions, urine, and sweat. As with absorption, however, there are many features of both types of excretion that are element-specific, including the relative importance of secondary excretion. Pertinent information on each individual element must therefore be obtained in anthropological trace element investigations.

While elemental intakes, absorption, and excretion are of the utmost importance in predicting and interpreting tissue concentrations, anthropological studies must also consider the potential impact of special physiological states including growth, pregnancy, and lactation, as there are some indications that certain types of physiological stress influence the manner and extent to which an element is absorbed and/or excreted (Hambidge, 1985:9).

One of the most familiar examples of this phenomenon is the probable impact of pregnancy and lactation on skeletal strontium and calcium concentrations of females (Sillen and Kavanagh, 1982; Blakely, 1989). Although pregnant and lactating females display enhanced intestinal absorption of both elements, discrimination against strontium in favor of calcium during uptake by the placenta and mammary glands are believed to underlie higher skeletal strontium and lower skeletal calcium in such women. Thus, these factors may be partially responsible for higher strontium/calcium ratios among females as compared with males and higher strontium levels among reproductive-age females at two late prehistoric sites in Georgia (Blakely, 1989). In addition, higher bone turnover rates in pregnant and lactating women (see Kent, et al., 1990) may also contribute to sex-specific differences in elemental concentrations. Similarly, several anthropological studies have documented excessive elemental concentrations in young infants (Radosevich, 1989; Sandford et al., 1988; Sandford, 1984; Lambert et al., 1979), a phenomenon that, as will be discussed in a later section, may partially reflect the accumulation of body stores during gestation. Yet, in spite of such intriguing observations, the effects of physiological processes on skeletal concentrations remain one of the least explored areas of anthropological trace element research.

Diagenetic Processes

The concept of diagenesis was developed in geology to refer to the many processes that modify sediments or sedimentary rocks following deposition in water (Berner, 1980:3). As adapted by anthropologists, the term is directed more specifically to postmortem alterations in the chemical constituents of bone following deposition in soil. Diagenesis is thus subsumed by taphonomy (literally "the laws of burial"), a much broader field that focuses on "all aspects of the passage of organisms from the biosphere to the lithosphere" (Olson, 1980: 5).

As skeletal material enters soil, the homeostatic relationship that once existed between this tissue and the living, physiological environment is supplanted by an equally dynamic interaction between bone and various geochemical forces. In this postdepositional milieu, bone can either gain or lose chemical constituents. Thus diagenesis encompasses the twin processes of contamination and leaching, which in turn result from a host of interrelated factors.

Diagenetic changes of inorganic bone are attributable to several mechanisms (Molleson, 1990; Sillen, 1989; Pate and Hutton, 1988: 730; Parker and Toots, 1980: 199). First, elements may be precipitated as separate "void-filling" mineral phases in the small cracks and pores of bone. Examples of such mineral phases include calcite ($CaCo_3$) and barite ($BaSO_4$) as well as oxides of such elements as iron and manganese (Pate and Hutton, 1988; Parker and Toots, 1980). In addition, soluble ions present in soils may be exchanged for those that normally occupy lattice positions in skeletal hydroxyapatite. Finally, diagenesis may, through several means, promote recrystallization and growth of apatite crystals. Because apatite can "seed" formation of new crystals, biogenic apatite actually serves as the foundation for crystals of diagenetic derivation (Sillen, 1989: 221–223).

Diagenesis is furthered during crystal precipitation by ionic substitution. As in ionic exchange (which takes place after precipitation), various cations and anions are substituted for those normally found in biogenic apatite. Typically, cations of such elements as strontium, barium, and lead take the place of calcium, while anionic substitutions involve hydroxyl (OH^-), phosphate (PO_4^{3-}) and crystalline surface positions (Sillen, 1989: 221–222). Through this phenomenon, flouride (F^-) often occupies hydroxyl sites (Parker and Toots, 1980: 199) while carbonate (CO_3^{2-}) may substitute for phosphate (Price, 1989b: 134). The incorporation of such changes may bring about greater crystallinity and closer stoichiometric agreement (as measured by Ca/P ratios) than is typical of skeletal hydroxyapatite (Sillen, 1989). Under these conditions, diagenesis can be viewed as a stage in fossilization, as it ultimately serves to transform biogenic apatite into geological varieties of the minerals (Pate and Hutton, 1988: 730).

The degree and direction of diagenetic changes are further influenced by the interplay of numerous factors. Such variables include both "extrinsic" and "intrinsic" forces (Von Endt and Ortner, 1984). Parker and Toots (1980: 198–199), in an early attempt to relate diagenesis to the interpretation of elemental levels in bone, identified several extrinsic variables that temper postmortem modifications. These include the "chemical environment of the burial site" and "properties of the enclosing sediment." Moreover, they envision these factors as acting in concert with intrinsic forces, which stem largely from the chemical characteristics of bone, in determining the extent of diagenetic change.

To begin with the chemical environment of soil-buried bone, soil pH is among the most important variables that influence diagenetic alteration of osseous tissue. While potential associations between pH and diagenesis were recognized by early researchers in the field (Gilbert, 1975: 148–150), the relationship between soil acidity and skeletal preservation in general was quantified by Gordon and Buikstra (1981) who demonstrated a highly significant negative correlation between the former and latter variables, constructing six categories to operationalize varying degrees of bone preservation. They then used soil pH, together with skeletal age, to derive regression equations aimed ultimately at predicting the physical condition of skeletal remains prior to excavation.

Aside from soil pH, additional extrinsic factors that influence skeletal diagenesis include temperature (Von Endt and Ortner, 1984; Hare, 1980), microorganisms (Grupe and Piepenbrink, 1988; White and Hannus, 1983), groundwater, and precipitation (Hare, 1980). Other important characteristics of the local geochemical environment include soil texture, mineralogy, and organic content (Buikstra et al., 1989: 172; Pate and Hutton, 1988: 730; Radosevich, 1989; Newesely, 1988: 3–4). Intrinsic factors, on the other hand, include the density, size, microstructure and biochemistry of bone (Grupe, 1988; Von Endt and Ortner, 1984).

Diagenesis of bone mineral is closely related to and further affected by breakdown of the organic component of bone (Molleson, 1990; Sillen, 1989; Von Endt and Ortner, 1984; Hare, 1980), a process that may be initiated by microbial activity (Grupe and Piepenbrink, 1988; White and Hannus, 1983). Microorganisms promote the release of elements not only by dissolution of collagen, but also through the destructive action of acid metabolites on hydroxyapatite. In addition, fungi may contribute to diagenesis by actively delivering specific elements to bone. In one series of laboratory experiments (Grupe and Piepenbrink, 1988: 110), fungi were especially effective in transporting barium to bone, which later becomes chemically bound in osseous tissue as barite.

Although many unanswered questions remain, several generalizations concerning diagenetic change can be made on the basis of recent investigations. Because additional research will undoubtedly enhance our understanding of diagenesis, such generalizations should be perceived merely as guidelines, subject to further study and revision. Their primary utility at present lies in the delineation of strategies to identify diagenetic change and interpret elemental concentrations.

First, while elements may differ in terms of their susceptibility to diagenesis, there is no element that is invulnerable to postmortem alteration. At one extreme, bone manganese concentrations are apparently extremely malleable in most geochemical contexts and often undergo substantial diagenetic change (Francalacci and Tarli, 1988; Byrne and Parris, 1987). On the other hand, zinc and strontium have been widely regarded by past researchers as less susceptible to diagenesis (Aufderheide, 1989; Runia, 1988). The latter element was in fact once believed to be completely resistent to diagenetic change (Parker and Toots, 1980: 199). Recently, however, postmortem alterations in skeletal strontium concentrations have been documented in vastly different regions and environments (Price, 1989b; Radosevich, 1989; Francalacci and Tarli, 1988; Klepinger et al., 1986; Sillen, 1981b).

Just as some elements may be more susceptible to diagenesis, the same may be true for certain categories of bones. Greater porosity, less bone density, and larger quantities of amorphous material may predispose bone for diagenetic change (Buikstra et al., 1989; Grupe, 1988; Lambert et al., 1982; Gordon and Buikstra, 1981). For example, juvenile bones, especially those of young infants, often display extremely high elemental concentrations (Radosevich, 1989, in press; Sandford et al., 1988; Lambert et al., 1979), a fact that may be partially due to the higher proportion of amorphous mineral (see discussion in Buikstra et al., 1989: 171). Although the greater susceptibility of subadult remains to diagenetic change is virtually certain, interpretation of their elemental values remains equivocal. In fact, such excessive elemental concentrations may also reflect physiological processes including, in individuals less than a year old, the accumulation of gestational body stores (Sandford 1988b; Sandford et al., 1988). In other words, diagenetic enrichment may, in some instances, augment or accentuate differences that are ultimately due to physiology. Similar processes may be reflected in the elemental concentrations of other tissues as well. Indeed, significantly lower iron levels were, documented, as predicted, in hair samples of Christian-era Nubian children who suffered from cribra orbitalia—despite the possibilities of both pre- and postmortem contamination (Sandford, 1984; Sandford et al., 1983).

Along the same lines, there are strong indications that cancellous bone has a greater propensity for diagenesis than cortical bone. Lambert and colleagues (1982) were among the first to explore this phenomenon by comparing elemental concentrations of ribs and femurs. While their initial results may have been in part due to interindividual variation, as the ribs and femurs were not necessarily from the same individuals, several elements previously associated with diagenetic contamination were found in higher concentrations in ribs. Controlling for this source of variation, reanalysis of their data (Buikstra et al., 1989) confirmed the presence of significantly higher levels of such contaminants as iron, aluminum, and manganese in ribs. Moreover, the superiority of compact bone for elemental investigations was further reinforced in another recent study (Grupe, 1988), which demonstrated that elemental concentrations of trabecular bone were poorly correlated with estimates of total skeletal content and showed dramatic differences between elemental values of trabecular samples.

Interpretation of rib–femur differences in elemental concentrations is far from resolved, however, as normal interbone variation in elemental deposition and remodeling rates may be confounding variables (Buikstra et al., 1989: 174; Price, 1989b: 130–131). Thus, as was hypothesized with respect to age–dependent differences in elemental concentrations, discrepancies between elemental concentrations of trabecular and cortical bone may be exacerbated by superimposition of diagenetic processes on physiological levels. Most important, the absence of diagenesis cannot be established solely on the failure to find interbone differences. In fact, through the process of equilibration, diagenesis could theoretically dissipate differences that were once quite pronounced (Price, 1989b: 131; Sillen, 1981b: 136).

In addition, the direction and intensity of diagenetic change is not necessarily spatially and temporally uniform. Several investigations have suggested that specific modes and mechanisms of diagenesis can be altered over time. Parker and Toots (1980) observed that magnesium and potassium could, following an initial phase of leaching, reenter bone through pores and cracks. Other researchers recently have noted similar phenomena. For example, in a multielement study of skeletal material from the Peruvian site of Paloma, Edward (1987) and Edward and Benfer, (in press) noted indications that at least one element (antimony) that initially entered bone as a contaminant was subsequently leached from skeletal material. Another element (magnesium), in contrast, may have accumulated in bone following an initial period of leaching, while still others (manganese, scandium, cobalt) accumulated as particles filling minute voids and cracks and were subject to little, if any, leaching. Similarly, Radosevich (1989, in press) hypothesized that skeletal diagenesis at the South Asian sites of Harrapa and Mehrgarh was essentially a two-stage process. The first phase apparently involved substitution and addition of strontium or flouride for calcium, the second consisted either of elemental leaching attendant to decomposition or, less commonly, fossilization.

As with the modes and mechanisms of diagenesis, uniformity cannot automatically be assumed for other aspects of this complicated process. In one of the first anthropological field investigations to focus specifically on the nature of diagenetic change, Klepinger and coworkers (1986) analyzed human remains from three distinct and well-dated cultural components from the site of Morgantina in Sicily. Although substantial diagenesis was detected for many of the analyzed elements (a surprising fact in view of the semiarid climate), no consistent and/or predictable associations between diagenesis and length of interment could be demonstrated. Still other researchers (Radosevich, 1989, in press; Runia, 1987, 1988) have stressed the potential for elemental concentrations and availability to vary markedly within and among soils of a single watershed or archaeological site. Such variation could result not only in variable antemortem ingestion of minerals, but also in additional and unpredictable sources of differential diagenesis.

In short, anthropological trace element researchers have developed a greater appreciation of the complexity, variability, and unpredictability of diagenesis. This recognition has led to many strategies to recognize and circumvent diagenesis. Because these techniques developed in concert with anthropological applications of trace element analysis, they are best introduced in the light of a brief historical review.

ANTHROPOLOGICAL APPLICATIONS OF TRACE ELEMENT ANALYSIS

Since its inception, most anthropological trace element research has been focused on assessing its potential applications to paleonutrition, where attempts are made to reconstruct dietary patterns and assess the nutritional status of prehistoric populations (Wing and Brown, 1979). To this end, trace element investigators have instituted three methodologies, the past contributions and current status of which are considered briefly below.

Strontium and Strontium/Calcium Ratios

Determination of strontium concentrations and strontium/calcium ratios from skeletal material represents the first anthropological application of trace element analysis. Following the apparently successful attempt by Toots and Voorhies (1965) to use strontium levels of Pliocene fauna for dietary discrimination, Brown (1973) analyzed a series of skeletal remains from archaeological sites in Michigan, Illinois, Iran, and Mexico. Though her investigation was subsequently criticized for failing to address the effects of diagenetic and physiological factors on skeletal strontium concentrations (Sillen and Kavanagh, 1982: 81), her investigation clearly delineated three potential applications of strontium analysis for anthropologists (Brown, 1973: 90). First and most important, strontium content of human bone, when compared with that of faunal remains from the same archaeological site, can theoretically determine dietary proportions of animal and plant resources. In addition, strontium analyses are used to investigate diachronic dietary changes as well as dietary differences based on gender or socioeconomic standing.

Use of skeletal strontium and calcium concentrations in this manner relates to an important underlying principle (Radosevich, 1989; Klepinger, 1984; Katzenberg, 1984; Sillen and Kavanagh, 1982). Stated simply, organisms take up strontium in quantities that vary inversely to their position on the trophic pyramid. While plants absorb strontium directly from the environment, mammals obtain the element from secondary sources such as plants or other animals. Moreover, strontium absorption in mammals is further lessened by internal discrimination against the element in favor of calcium. Thus, mammalian tissues contain less strontium than plants, while dietary patterns at higher positions on the trophic pyramid are theoretically discernible as differential skeletal concentrations of strontium and calcium. Thus, herbivores should display higher strontium concentrations than those of carnivores, while omnivores (including humans) should contain intermediate levels.

Brown's initial efforts in the field helped to inspire many subsequent studies that further assessed the utility of this technique for reconstructing dietary patterns as well as dietary differences attendant on social ranking and temporal change. Schoeninger (1979), for example, explored relationships between status and skeletal strontium levels at the prehistoric site of Chalcatzingo, Mexico, documenting lower concentrations of the element in skeletons interred with more grave goods. These results thus provided support for her hypothesis that higher–ranking individuals had greater access to animal protein, while lending additional credence to the efficacy of strontium analysis for dietary discrimination. Subsequent researchers (Geidel, 1982; Blakely and Beck, 1981) have similarly investigated associations between social stratification and differential dietary patterns by using strontium concurrently with multielement strategies.

Additional investigations have addressed questions pertaining to dietary reconstruction in general, and dietary changes in particular, by focusing largely, though not necessarily exclusively, on analyses of skeletal strontium (Radosevich, 1989; Runia, 1987; Katzenberg, 1984; Sillen 1981b; Schoeninger 1981, 1982). In an early study of this type, Sillen (1981b) compared strontium concentrations in human and animal bones from Natufian and Aurignacian strata. His study provided both support for and caution concerning strontium analyses, in that strontium/calcium ratios clearly distinguished between herbivores and carnivores from Natufian levels, but no such differences were apparent in Aurignacian fauna.

Other studies, focusing more directly on the ability of strontium to monitor dietary changes over time, compared preagricultural and agricultural Middle Eastern populations (Schoeninger, 1981) as well as archaic and modern *Homo sapiens* (Schoeninger, 1982), and documented changes in subsistence from Middle to Late Woodland times in southern Ontario (Katzenberg, 1984). Interpretation of skeletal strontium levels is also emphasized in more recent investigations of Bronze Age remains from The Netherlands (Runia, 1987) and prehistoric material from Alaska and southeastern Asia (Radosevich, 1989).

While outlining the potential of strontium analysis for understanding past dietary adaptations, these and other studies point to various interpretive difficulties. Although strontium is no longer thought invulnerable to diagenesis, mounting evidence suggests that ante– and postmortem deposition can be substantially altered by variations, often rather subtle, in environmental and geological distributions of the element (Price, 1989b; Radosevich, 1989; Sillen, 1989; Sillen et al., 1989; Runia, 1987, 1988). Moreover, contributions of such foods as nuts and seafood to prehistoric strontium intakes are still under study (Buikstra et al., 1989; Byrne and Parris, 1987; Kyle, 1986) as are the influences of physiological processes including weaning (Sillen and Smith, 1984) and pregnancy and lactation (Blakely, 1989; Radosevich, 1989).

Multielement Studies

Multielement studies focus on a broader array of analyzed elements for purposes of dietary discrimination. Generally, the applications of this technique are much the same as those in which strontium and strontium/calcium ratios are emphasized. Delineating proportions of food categories, gender– and status-based dietary differences, and dietary changes over time are major objectives of such studies.

As noted above, the multielement approach was initiated by Gilbert (1975, 1977, 1985) who analyzed skeletal material from Dickson Mounds for five elements, distributed differentially in animal and plant resources. As the three cultural horizons represented in his sample spanned the transition from hunting–gathering to agricultural subsistence, Gilbert sought to document this change by contrasting levels of elements that are more abundant in vegetation with those that are more prevalent in animal resources. Of all of the study elements, zinc emerged as the most promising dietary discriminator, demonstrating significantly higher levels in the hunting and gathering population and appearing to have been less subject to postmortem alteration.

Documentation of dietary changes attendant on the adoption of maize agriculture was also an objective of Lambert and coworkers (1979) in their initial analyses of human remains from prehistoric Illinois (see also Szpunar, 1977, and Szpunar et al., 1978). Diagnosis of diagenetic effects was also chief among their concerns. Consequently, their initial investigation emphasized analysis of associated soil samples for distinguishing between "soil" (contaminating) and "nonsoil" (dietary) elements (see also Lambert et al., 1984). More important, additional techniques for recognizing and, where possible, circumventing diagenetic effects unfolded during their subsequent investigations (Lambert et al., 1979, 1989). Such techniques have been used extensively by various other researchers and will be discussed below in conjunction with methodology.

More recently, Buikstra and coworkers (1989) have published an exhaustive evaluation of multielement studies from 1975 through 1985, making special note of methods used to control for diagenesis and of significant research results. Prehistoric dietary adaptations in the southeastern United States were a focal point for many such studies, which continued to use elemental analyses to investigate association between diet and status (Brown and Blakely, 1985; Geidel, 1982; Blakely and Beck, 1981) and the transition to agricultural subsistence (Beck, 1985).

Beginning around 1985, multielement studies evidenced a broader sphere of concern, as investigators began analyzing remains from a more diverse spectrum of geographical and cultural contexts. Although trace element investigations of diet in prehistoric southeastern and midwestern United States have by no means been abandoned (Lambert et al., 1989; Byrne and Parris, 1987), recent studies of past populations from Peru (Edward, 1987; Edward and Benfer, in press), Tunisia (Sandford et al., 1988), Germany (Grupe, 1988), Australia (Kyle, 1986), Greece (Edward et al., 1984), Sicily (Klepinger et al., 1986), and Italy (Francalacci and Tarli, 1988) attest to the wider applicability of multielement strategies. This trend is even more apparent when such studies are coupled with those specifically focused on strontium (Price, 1989b; Radosevich, 1989; Runia, 1987).

More important, recent trends also include an increasing awareness of diagenesis, as shown by the frequent inclusion of several independent diagnostic methods into a single research design. Byrne and Parris (1987) analyzed ancient and modern fauna along with contemporary human femora to evaluate skeletal concentrations displayed by inhabitants of the Middle Woodland site of Abbott Farm. Kyle (1986), investigating an ancestral Motu population near Papua, New Guinea, searched for diagenetic effects through X-ray diffraction studies, correlation matrices of skeletal concentrations, comparisons of skeletal and dental concentrations, soil analyses, and comparisons with elemental levels of ancient and modern populations.

Edward (1987) and Edward and Benfer (in press) initiated an even more exhaustive multifaceted strategy for recognizing diagenesis in analyzing 143 human bones from the Preceramic period site at Paloma, Peru. Stressing the importance of using complementary methods in diagnosing diagenesis, comparisons were conducted between the elemental constituents of soil and bone samples, ancient and modern bones, dark– and light–colored bones, and ribs and tibiae of children and adults. In addition, correlations between bone and soil concentrations as well as between the skeletal levels themselves afforded additional means to evaluate diagenetic effects.

The predominance of diagenesis among the concerns of trace element researchers is also apparent in other trends. The importance of field and laboratory studies for testing hypotheses concerning diagenetic processes, as demonstrated by Klepinger and coworkers (1986) and Lambert and associates (1985), has been illustrated more recently by a multielement investigation of archaeological soils from Roonka in South Australia (Pate and Hutton, 1988).

Finally, recent multielement studies have promoted an increased concern over the interplay between biogenic and diagenetic signals in skeletal concentrations. Evidence obtained by both Kyle (1986) and Byrne and Parris (1987) suggests that dietary inferences based on skeletal concentrations are nonetheless possible despite diagenetic effects. This is of special interest in light of additional evidence, cited above, that suggests that age– and gender-specific physiological processes may actually be apparent or even more obvious due to a similar mechanism (Radosevich, 1989, in press; Sandford et al., 1988; Edward, 1987).

Single-Element Studies

The single-element approach represents the third and least common anthropological application of trace element analysis. The element of interest is typically one that has otherwise been associated with a particular disorder or disease in the population in question. In theory, a wide variety of elemental deficiencies or toxicities could be addressed through such means.

This factor, together with the virtually inextricable relationship between nutrition and disease, would seem to make trace element analysis an appropriate adjunct for investigations that cut across paleodietary and paleopathological concerns. Although the potential relevance of elemental analyses for the latter realm is widely recognized and formed the basis for a recent scientific symposium (Sandford, 1988a), "few have attempted prediction of specific element deficiency syndromes based on archaeological trace element levels" (Aufderheide, 1989: 240). Moreover, most past attempts to address theoretical relationships between elemental concentrations and paleopathology (Waldron, 1987) have emphasized primary deficiencies of nutritionally essential elements of genetic or dietary etiologies (but see Klepinger, in press).

However, elemental analyses of both bone (Edward and Benfer, in press; Fornaciari et al., 1983; Zaino, 1968) and hair (Sandford, 1988b, 1984; Sandford et al., 1983) concentrations have been used to investigate iron status in past populations. Zaino (1968), for example, compared Anasazi skeletal iron levels with contemporary populations and judged them to be within the normal range. Similarly, Fornaciari and coworkers (1981) conducted bone iron analysis on Punic remains from Carthage to investigate the etiology of cribra orbitalia. Although their sample was rather small, individuals with such lesions were characterized by significantly lower iron levels, leading to the conclusion that iron deficiency anemia had been associated with this condition in ancient Carthage.

Despite the widespread distribution of iron deficiency anemia and the obvious applicability of using skeletal iron levels to investigate cribra orbitalia, lead, rather than iron, has been the focus of most single-element studies (Aufderheide, 1989; Aufderheide et al., 1981, 1985, 1988; Waldron, 1981, 1983, 1987; Jarcho, 1964), often in attempts to relate cultural practices to abnormal lead ingestion and/or toxicity. Preferential deposition of lead in osseous tissue, coupled with a relatively poor excretory capacity and a low adult turnover rate, enhance our ability to assess lead status in past populations (Aufderheide, 1989: 248–250; Waldron, 1987: 156–157).

Anthropological applications of skeletal lead analyses have been much more thoroughly explored than any other single element, (see especially Aufderheide, 1989, and Aufderheide et al., 1988) with the exception of strontium. In the first, and perhaps most apparent, use of such analyses, Jarcho (1964) sought to determine whether occupational lead exposure, acquired through the manufacture of lead-glazed pottery, would be reflected in skeletal lead concentrations. Comparing skeletal levels from two historic locales in the U.S. Southwest, Jarcho unexpectedly found higher lead concentrations in bones from Point of Pines than in those from Kinishba, where lead-glazed pottery was made.

Subsequent researchers report greater success in working with skeletal lead concentrations. Efforts by Aufderheide and coworkers (1981, 1985, 1988) are particularly noteworthy in this regard. For example, in working with Colonial American human remains, they have not only confirmed the past importance of pewter utensils and food containers but have also demonstrated the utility of such analyses to delineate socioeconomic differences within populations and the occupational categories of specific individuals. Other applications of skeletal lead analyses initiated by these researchers, including sorting commingled remains and differentiating between past and contemporary material, clearly have relevance to both forensic and paleopathological investigations.

Waldron (1981, 1983, 1987) has similarly analyzed skeletons from the United Kingdom in an effort to document excessive lead intakes of Romano-British and medieval populations. Lead toxicity appears to have been somewhat common in such populations, where extraneous sources of the element ranged from contaminated food and drink containers to water pipes. Unfortunately, lead, like other elements, is subject to diagenetic change. In samples taken from a Cistercian monastery in Worcestershire, correlations between soil and bone lead concentrations confirmed that lead is taken up by the skeleton in postmortem contexts (Waldron, 1983). However, diagenetic sources of the element are not necessarily limited to the soil. Using the electron microprobe to examine remains from Romano–British and medieval cemeteries at Poundbury and Priory, Waldron (1981) found bones buried in lead coffins to have accumulated lead on their external and internal surfaces, a pattern typical of diagenetic contamination.

METHODOLOGICAL CONCERNS

The methodological stages of elemental analyses follow procedures established in analytical chemistry. These steps, as outlined by Goffer (1980: 22), include (1) sampling, (2) sample preparation, (3) determination and quantification of chemical contents, and (4) evaluation and interpretation.

Sampling

Sampling entails removal of a relatively small, presumably representative quantity from a larger body of material (Goffer, 1980: 23). While sampling procedures can be rather straightforward, the chemical heterogeneity of bone, often stemming from age- and/or sex-specific physiological differences, requires some special considerations. The most important concerns in this respect include (1) proper selection of the specific bone or bones to be sampled, (2) obtaining sufficient quantities of bone for analysis and (3) using appropriate techniques for sample extraction.

For the purposes of most anthropological trace element investigations, samples consisting of cortical bone are far superior to those composed of trabecular bone. While trabecular bone samples such as ribs might be deemed more expendable and therefore more desirable in this context, greater susceptibility to diagenesis and higher metabolic turnover rates usually mitigate against their use for such purposes (Grupe, 1988; Edward et al., 1984; Gilbert, 1985: 350–351; Gilbert, 1975: 138). Cortical bone carries additional advantages. Such samples display substantially less intraindividual variation in elemental concentrations, while those of trabecular bone fluctuate dramatically, even when different sampling sites are very close together (Grupe, 1988: 128). Moreover, the greater thickness of cortical bone affords a means to counter some of the effects of diagenesis, as the inner– and outer-most surfaces, where contaminants tend to accumulate, can be physically removed prior to analysis (Lambert et al., 1982, 1989; Grupe, 1988; Edward, 1987).

With these factors in mind, representative cortical cross sections with intact periosteal and endosteal surfaces should be obtained for most elemental investigations. However, the actual amount needed for analysis varies somewhat, depending largely on the specific instrumentation to be used. Multielement studies involving atomic absorption spectrometry (AAS) generally prepare analytical solutions from ashed bone samples weighing from 0.5 g to 2.0 g (Buikstra et al., 1989; Szpunar et al., 1978; Gilbert, 1975). Analyses by inductively coupled plasma emission spectroscopy (ICP) or instrumental neutron activation analysis (INAA) can usually be achieved with a smaller sample, although investigators may elect to prepare a larger quantity than is actually needed. For example, Klepinger and coworkers (1986) selected 100–mg portions of ground, ashed bone from prepared samples weighing from 200 mg to 1 g to make up solutions for ICP. As their results suggested the presence of significant heterogeneities in cortical tissue, they advise grinding and blending approximately 5 g of bone prior to analysis to secure a sample that represents an average value and counters such heterogeneity.

Thus, sections of approximately 3–4 cm in length, taken from the middiaphyseal region of the femur or tibia should be more than adequate for most purposes and afford the retention of adequate bone for histological, electron microprobe (EMP) and other related studies, if desired. Cortical cross sections are usually extracted for elemental investigations with various types of saws, including hacksaws (Radosevich, 1989; Bryne and Parris, 1987), autopsy saws (Edward, 1987), and electric band saws (Runia, 1987; Gilbert, 1975). These may be used in combination with other implements, such as chisels, to extract the quantity and type of sample desired. Alternatively, other investigators (Grupe, 1988; Aufderheide et al., 1981) extract bone samples with neurosurgical or trephining bits.

No matter which technique is chosen, care must be taken to evaluate and avoid possible sources of contamination during sample extraction. For example, blades and other cutting implements should be rinsed or ultrasonically washed between uses with distilled-deionized water to avoid intersample contamination and to guard against introducing extraneous quantities of elements into bone samples. Some types of cutting tools, depending on their chemical composition, may be briefly rinsed first in a weak acid solution.

Sample Preparation

Following extraction, bone samples are prepared for analysis in a manner that renders them the most amenable to delineating and quantifying their elemental constituents. Because preparation procedures differ, depending on both the nature of the study material and the instrumentation to be employed (Goffer, 1980: 23), techniques used in preparing bone samples vary accordingly. In general, however, elemental analyses of bone are prefaced by cleaning, drying, pulverizing, ashing, and digesting the sample (Lambert et al., 1979: 117), although the last stage, in particular, is obviated by certain types of instrumentation (INAA). The reader is referred to the following excellent sources for information on instrumentation-specific considerations relating to the preparation and analysis of archaeological human bone: AAS (Lambert et al., 1979; Szpunar et al., 1978), INAA (Radosevich, 1989; Edward, 1987), ICP (Klepinger et al., 1986), X-ray fluorescence (XRF) (Katzenberg, 1984).

The porous nature of bone, together with its susceptibility to postdepositional changes, necessitates special attention to the cleaning process. Typically, bone is rinsed in distilled–deionized water, often with an ultrasonic cleaner used to dislodge soil particles and other contaminants from small pores and cracks. Prior to this stage, however, some investigators now elect to physically abrade the superficial periosteal and endosteal surfaces with silicon carbide sandpaper (Lambert et al., 1989) or hand-held electric grinders, such as the Dremel Moto-Tool, equipped with diamond-studded (Edward, 1987) or tungsten steel burrs (Edward et al., 1984). In addition to removing areas where contaminants are most heavily concentrated, this procedure may also help free the sample of soil particles, spongy bone or occasional fragments of preserved soft tissue (Edward and Benfer, in press). Precautions against intersample contamination should again be exercised by rinsing burrs subsequent to each use with distilled–deionized water and, in some instances, weak acid solutions as well.

Washing procedures may be modified somewhat if the organic phase of bone is extremely well preserved, as in naturally mummified material. Thus, Edward (1987) cleaned bone samples from Paloma, Peru in a hydrogen peroxide–ethanol mixture to ensure removal of fats and blood proteins. Chemical removal of the organic fraction should, if deemed appropriate, be used with caution, as Hancock and coworkers (1989) found bones defatted with a $CHCl_3$-ETOH solvent to become heavily contaminated with chlorine and bromine.

Following cleaning, bone samples are generally dried, pulverized, ashed, and digested, although the sequence of these procedures is subject to some modification. Drying is generally accomplished overnight by placing samples in an oven at 105 °C, while pulverization to a relatively homogenous bone powder has been achieved through a variety of techniques including use of a mortar and pestle (Radosevich, 1989; Szpunar et al., 1978), hydrolyic press (Edward, 1987), disk mill (Runia, 1987), or swing mill (Katzenberg, 1984).

Muffle or electric furnaces are usually employed for ashing, which removes the organic fraction of bone. This process generally takes from 6h (Runia, 1987) to 24h (Szpunar et al., 1978), at temperatures of 500 °C or 750 °C, respectively. However, researchers using INAA may elect not to dry ash samples, as recent investigations by Edward and coworkers (1990) have demonstrated that concentrations of several elements may be seriously affected by this procedure.

Digestion and complete dissolution are the last major stages in sample preparation when destructive forms of instrumentation such as AAS (Bryne and Parris, 1987; Szpunar et al., 1978; Lambert et al., 1979) and ICP (Klepinger et al., 1986) are used. The essential features of this stage involve the addition of some type of concentrated acid and distilled-deionized water, followed by administration of heat. Complete dissolution is then accomplished through the combination of additional acid, water, and heat. Filtration can then be used to remove silica residue from bone samples (Francalacci and Tarli, 1988; Szpunar et al., 1978).

Analytical Instrumentation

The most frequently used techniques for quantitative elemental analyses of archaeological bone are AAS, INAA, ICP, and XRF. The theoretical foundations of these types of instrumentation are reviewed briefly below, along with their advantages and disadvantages for anthropological studies (see also Aufderheide, 1989 and Gilbert, 1985).

The first two techniques, AAS and ICP, are forms of light or optical spectrometry (Aufderheide, 1989; Goffer, 1980; Hamilton, 1979), because they use line spectra to identify and quantify specific elements. Such spectra, composed of clearly delineated, element-specific wavelengths, are emitted by gaseous substances following the administration of heat. Normally, electrons of an element revolve around a nucleus, in a manner reminiscent of "miniature solar systems," without absorbing or emitting radiation (Goffer, 1980: 35). Following the introduction of energy, however, excited electrons are transported into orbits farther from the nucleus, giving off energy and generating characteristic spectra upon returning to their original positions.

Capitalizing on these basic principles, instrumentation based on light spectroscopy first induces an excited state among electrons from heat generated by either a flame or an electrothermal device such as a graphite furnace. In the emission mode, identification and quantification of specific elements rests on the ability to recognize and measure the emitted wavelengths. The absorption mode is derived from a similar principle, known as Kirchoff's Law, which observes that "matter absorbs light at the same wavelengths at which it emits light" (Hamilton, 1979: 231). With this method, a hollow cathode lamp, giving off spectra specific to the element in question, is often used as a light source. The degree to which such spectra are absorbed by excited electrons of the same element thus serves as a quantitative reflection of the element's presence in the sample.

The most frequently used technique in anthropological elemental research is AAS, as most researchers prefer to use electrothermal rather than flame-generated sources of heat (Aufderheide, 1989: 241; Gilbert, 1977: 94). The popularity of this technique is no doubt a function of its high sensitivity for many elements, coupled with more pragmatic considerations in that it is readily accessible on most college campuses and is relatively inexpensive

to use. In addition, the basic know-how needed to operate the instrumentation can be acquired through a minimum of training. On the other hand, the primary disadvantage of the technique is that it analyzes only one element at a time, a factor that should be considered if multielement studies are contemplated.

Despite this drawback, AAS is still widely used for elemental analyses of archaeological bone. In particular, the instrumentation is a very popular choice for investigations focusing on strontium and calcium because of its high sensitivity for these elements (Sillen, 1981a,b, 1988; Schoeninger, 1979, 1982; Brown, 1973). Various multielement investigations have also used AAS both exclusively (see especially Buikstra et al., 1989, Lambert et al., 1979, Szpunar et al., 1978, and Gilbert, 1975) and in conjunction with other types of instrumentation, including ICP (Runia, 1987; Byrne and Parris, 1987).

Because of its sensitivity and capability for simultaneous analysis of numerous elements, inductively coupled plasma emission spectrometry (ICP) is being used increasingly for elemental analyses of archaeological bone (Price, 1989b; Francalacci and Tarli, 1988; Runia, 1987; Byrne and Parris, 1987; Klepinger et al., 1986). As an emission-based technique, elements are identified by spectra given off by the sample solution following its injection into a heated chamber containing argon gas (Aufderheide et al., 1989: 241–242; Klepinger et al., 1986: 326). Quantification of the analyzed elements is then accomplished by measuring the intensities of the emitted spectra.

The preparation of bone samples for ICP analysis is relatively simple (see especially Klepinger et al., 1986)—a factor that, together with other advantages cited above, may eventually make ICP the technique of choice for multielement studies. At present, however, this instrumentation is less widely available than AAS and initial equipment costs are quite expensive (Aufderheide, 1989: 244).

Two nondestructive methods, which provide a means of reanalyzing the same samples, represent the remaining quantitative techniques used by anthropologists in elemental investigations. The first method, INAA, requires a nuclear reactor as it transforms nonradioactive isotopes into unstable, radioactive forms by bombarding the nuclei of samples with neutrons. As the artificially produced radioactive isotopes decay, they emit gamma rays (and a host of other particles), which, when detected and measured, permit quantification of various elements (Aufderheide, 1989; Goffer, 1980: 74–75). The major advantages of INAA lie in its capability for analyzing numerous elements simultaneously, and the relative ease of sample preparation. Unfortunately, sample analysis can be quite costly. Nevertheless, barring such limitations, INAA should be considered, particularly for multielement studies. Recently, several anthropological investigations have been conducted by INAA, and useful protocols for sample preparation and analysis have been provided (see especially Radosevich, 1989, Edward, 1987, and Edward and Benfer, in press).

Finally, quantitative analysis of bone samples can also be accomplished by X-ray fluorescence spectrometry (XRF). Briefly stated, elemental constituents of samples are energized following their bombardment with primary X rays. In a manner reminiscent of optical emission techniques, the sample atoms "fluoresce" as they lose this energy by giving off secondary X rays at characteristic, element-specific wavelengths (Katzenberg, 1984: 56–60; Goffer, 1980: 45–47; Hamilton, 1979: 314–331). Quantitative determinations are then derived from the intensities of the emitted wavelengths.

Although this technique is the least commonly employed for anthropological trace element studies, it was characterized by Katzenberg (1984: 56), who used XRF to analyze archaeological human bone from southern Ontario, as "one of the more precise and accurate techniques for quantitatively analyzing strontium." More recently, Kyle (1986) applied XRF to a multi-element investigation of human bone and teeth from Motupore Island. Both sources provide useful details concerning sample preparation and analysis.

Statistical Evaluation and Interpretation

Assuming that appropriate sampling, sample preparation, and instrumentation procedures have been followed, sound interpretation of elemental data rests on techniques used for both statistical analysis and assessing diagenesis. As with all aspects of elemental analyses, both spheres of the interpretive process are clouded by controversial issues.

The most pervasive controversy concerning statistical analyses of elemental concentrations pertains to the nature of their statistical distributions. This issue, first addressed by Klepinger (1984: 76), bears directly on whether such data are best analyzed by parametric or nonparametric statistics. While the more powerful parametric statistics are preferred and have been used by many trace element researchers (Lambert et al., 1979; Gilbert, 1975), their applicability in this regard is often precluded by such factors as extremely small sample sizes and the failure to establish the normality of trace element distributions. Klepinger advised using nonparametric methods pending clarification of the nature of elemental distributions.

The problem was more recently discussed by Buikstra and colleagues (1989: 188–207), who used principal components analyses to "discover the kinds and directions of relationships among various trace elements and between trace elements and carbon isotopes" (1989: 191). As this technique requires the assumption of normality, trace element data were first tested for this criteria and then subjected to lognormal transformations when it could not be met. Perhaps the greatest advantage of principal components analysis, however, is the ability to weigh concomitantly the impact of factors stemming from diet, diagenesis, physiology, and elemental interactions. This investigation thus provides a useful model for future multielement studies, as it demonstrates a rather powerful means to compensate for nonnormal data, together with a multivariate technique that affords simultaneous consideration of biogenic and diagenetic processes.

Methods that afford the means to diagnose and, possibly, circumvent diagenetic effects, listed on Table 1, should be an integral part of every research protocol involving elemental analyses of archaeological tissue. Although initial anthropological trace element studies recognized some of the potential interpretive complications posed by diagenesis and introduced individual techniques for assessing postmortem change (Lambert et al., 1979; Gilbert, 1975), documentation of such a complex phe-

TABLE 1. Methods for Identifying and Circumventing Diagenesis

Identification of diagenesis
  1. Soil chemistry studies
  2. Electron microprobe
  3. X-ray diffraction
  4. Osteological comparisons
    A. Intrabone
    B. Interbone
    C. Interspecies
    D. Interpopulational
Circumvention of diagenesis
  1. Indicator elements/correction factors
  2. Physical removal of contaminated surfaces
  3. Solubility profiles

nomenon requires a more systematic, multifaceted approach. An essential component of this strategy is the concurrent use of alternative but complementary methods to evaluate diagenesis. The most commonly used techniques in this regard are considered briefly below (see also reviews in Edward and Benfer, in press, Buikstra et al., 1989, and Edward, 1987).

The techniques used most frequently for assessing diagenetic effects are based on chemical analyses of soil. Most commonly, comparisons are made between the total elemental concentrations of associated bone and soil samples, following such basic assumptions as concentration gradient theory (see discussions in Radosevich, in press, 1989, Edward and Benfer, in press, Edward, 1987, Klepinger, 1984: 79, and Lambert et al., 1979: 119). According to this assumption, significant contamination of bone by soil is considered less likely if soil concentrations are disproportionately lower than those of the same elements in bone. On the other hand, significant postmortem contamination of skeletal tissue is suggested by greater quantities of an element in the soil than in bone.

While soil chemistry studies are unquestionably of paramount importance in diagnosing diagenetic change, strict adherence to the concentration gradient assumption may result in incorrect assessment of such alterations. Above all, the unpredictable nature and direction of diagenetic change (Klepinger, 1984: 79), as indicated above, render this assumption quite questionable. Subsequent studies by Lambert

and coworkers (1984, 1985) demonstrated that the anisotropic elemental distributions of soil and bone, which result from postmortem change, may in fact be in opposite directions to those predicted by concentration gradient theory. In other words, elevated levels in soil relative to bone may indicate prior leaching from bone to soil. Conversely, depressed soil concentrations relative to those of bone may indicate the prior passage of elements from soil to bone (Lambert et al., 1984: 131).

While soil analyses have their limitations with respect to assessing diagenesis, they are nonetheless mandatory. In this regard, several additional factors should be considered by anthropologists who are planning trace element studies. First, soil samples should be taken from both burial and nonburial contexts for comparative analysis purposes. Comparing elemental compositions of soils adjacent to bone with those that were not in contact with interred skeletal material provides an additional means to delineate diagenetic elements (Sandford et al., 1988). Second, soil analyses for total elemental abundances may be less useful than analyses for soluble and exchangeable ions because

> most inorganic chemical reactions in the soil environment will involve ions in solution, and the relative concentrations of elements in a soil will not reflect the ionic concentrations in solution due to the differential solubilities of the various mineral and salt constituents. (Pate and Hutton, 1988: 729)

While ionic exchange processes may not be significant diagenetic forces in extremely arid environments (Edward and Benfer, in press), they are highly relevant to most elemental studies of archaeological bone. Finally, soil analyses alone are not sufficient for interpreting either diagenetic processes or the interactions between such processes with biogenic factors. Therefore, soil chemistry studies should be used in combination with other techniques, whenever possible.

Several techniques involving specialized instrumentation have been largely successful at detecting diagenetic change. The first, involving application of the electron microprobe (EMP), was used by Gilbert (1975) in conjunction with elemental studies of prehistoric human bone and has been adapted by a number of subsequent researchers with varying degrees of success (Radosevich, 1989, in press; Klepinger et al., 1986; Lambert et al., 1983, 1984). Contaminants typically accumulate along the outer cortical surfaces, although some buildup may occur along the endosteum as well. This observation led to methods for physically removing the outer– and innermost cortical surfaces (Lambert et al., 1989; Edward, 1987), as discussed above. However, failure to find such heterogeneity in elemental distributions is not automatically indicative of the absence of diagenesis. Substantial losses of elements may accrue through leaching and yet escape detection by microprobe analysis (Lambert et al., 1983). Other researchers (Klepinger et al., 1986: 329) have been unable to document the characteristic profiles of contaminating elements in the face of apparent diagenesis.

X-ray diffraction (XRD) spectrometry, another specialized form of instrumentation, is also useful in documenting diagenesis (Sillen, 1989: 213–217; Kyle, 1986; Schoeninger, 1981, 1982). Focusing on differences in the microcrystalline structure of biogenic and geological hydroxyapatite, this technique provides a means to demonstrate the often interrelated diagenetic processes of increased crystallinity, recrystallization, ionic exchanges involving strontium and calcium, and the incorporation of various mineral phases in skeletal material.

The remaining methods for detecting diagenesis can be categorized as comparative skeletal studies, in which the elemental concentrations of excavated skeletal material are typically examined against baseline levels documented for other bones, species, or human populations. These techniques may be subdivided into intrabone, interbone, interspecies and interpopulational comparisons.

While most comparative skeletal studies evaluate mean differences in elemental concentrations, intrabone comparisons are typically based on correlations between the elements themselves and are viewed in conjunction with soil analyses (Edward, 1987, Edward and Benfer, in press, Edward et al., 1984; Kyle, 1986; Katzenberg, 1984). In this manner, statistically significant correlations between an element and a known contaminant or "indicator element," such as silicon (Kyle, 1986) or uranium (Edward et al., 1984), may be indicative of further diagenetic change. In other instances, correction factors based on interelement relationships may be generated. Thus, acting on a significant correlation between zirconium and strontium, Katzenberg (1984: 81–97) employed a formula to correct for those quantities of the latter element that were deposited as soil particles in the postmortem environment.

Interbone comparisons most often involve comparisons between different types of bones, such as femora and ribs (Edward, 1987; Lambert et al., 1982). This procedure, as discussed earlier, is based on the assumption that the two types of bone should reflect varying degrees of diagenesis as they contain different proportions of cortical and trabecular bone, the latter being more susceptible to diagenesis. While this technique may be an appropriate adjunct to other, more direct methods for assessing diagenesis (Edward, 1987; Edward and Benfer, in press), it is not advisable to rely solely on information derived from this method because of questions concerning metabolic turnover and sex– and age-specific physiological differences.

Interspecies comparisons, in which elemental constituents of human bone are compared with those of fauna representing different dietary patterns, are of greater applicability (Radosevich, 1989, in press; Runia, 1987; Byrne and Parris, 1987; Kyle, 1986; Katzenberg, 1984; Sillen, 1981b). Faunal analyses serve a dual function: Diagenetic activity is suspected when elemental levels deviate from values predicted on the basis of dietary patterns, while biogenic concentrations of fauna facilitate reconstruction of prehistoric human diets (Buikstra et al., 1989: 176). Such studies most frequently use prehistoric species obtained from the same sites or regions as the human material, although data from modern fauna also may be instructive (Sillen, 1988; Price et al., 1985; Schoeninger, 1981). Inherent difficulties in the application of interspecies comparisons include recovery of sufficient representative material and dietary variability among animal species (Buikstra et al., 1989; Sillen et al., 1989; Runia, 1987, 1988). Finally, the paucity of comparative, baseline data from prehistoric and modern human populations is recognized as a significant problem in anthropological trace element research (Price et al., 1989: 248). While some data from contemporary populations have been available from the earliest anthropological studies (Lambert et al., 1979; Gilbert, 1975), their applicability is limited by the frequent lack of documentation of dietary and physiological factors (but see Byrne and Parris, 1987). Comparative archaeological data, while more abundant, present similar limitations. Moreover, researchers working with such data must consider that many variables, including subtle differences in the elemental compositions of soil and groundwater (Sillen et al., 1989; Runia, 1988; Radosevich, 1989) may lead to substantial interpopulational differences in biological and diagenetic deposition.

The present concerns about diagenesis are largely responsible for an increased emphasis on experimental/laboratory investigations in anthropological trace element research (Radosevich, 1989, in press; Sillen, 1989; Sillen et al., 1989; Pate and Hutton, 1988). Of special importance is the development of methods for circumventing diagenetic effects which, in addition to those already noted, include the recent development of solubility profiles (Sillen, 1989; Sillen et al., 1989). Based on differential solubilities of geological and biological apatites, the technique attempts to remove more soluble, diagenetic minerals with successive washes in acidic solutions. While the general applicability of the technique is not yet known, every set of strategies for recognizing and combating diagenesis must ultimately be individually tailored with site-specific, environment-specific, and culture-specific conditions in mind.

RESEARCH TRENDS, RECOMMENDATIONS, AND CONCLUSIONS

Investigations of diagenetic processes clearly dominate current anthropological trace element research—a trend that will almost certainly continue to grow and intensify throughout the present decade. The recognition that understanding diagenesis is requisite to accu-

TABLE 2. Ongoing and Future Research Trends in Anthropological Trace Element Research

1. Establish "normal" elemental concentrations for other tissues, including hair, teeth, nails.
2. Develop models to test basic assumptions concerning relationships between diet, physiology, and elemental concentrations.
3. Generate and test hypotheses concerning associations between elemental concentrations and pathology.
4. Investigate interactions between diagenetic and biogenic signals in determining elemental levels.
5. Initiate experiment-oriented field and laboratory research.

rate interpretation of elemental data underlies the current experimental/laboratory emphasis of trace element investigations. The multiplicity, unpredictability, and dynamic nature of diagenetic processes demand that diverse perspectives and research strategies be used to delineate more sophisticated methods for recognizing and, where possible, circumventing postmortem effects. Thus, we can expect increased attempts to discern the nature of diagenetic change by research originating both in the field and in the laboratory, along with intensified efforts to develop specific tactics for diagnosing and correcting for diagenesis, building on the pioneering efforts of earlier investigators.

As important as these considerations are, it is essential to remember that other processes operating on the biogenic–diagenetic continuum are sorely in need of additional study. Moreover, the future role of more traditionally focused trace element research should be addressed. In short, despite burgeoning interest in elemental analyses, several important avenues of investigation have been overlooked or given the most cursory treatment. These areas, some of which are delineated in Table 2, include both hypothesis–generating and hypothesis–testing designs and are cast in both field and laboratory settings.

Studies originating in the laboratory could fill several sizable gaps in our knowledge of elemental biochemistry, deposition, and metabolism. Although efforts to define normal ranges of elements in modern bone are currently under way (Hancock et al., 1989), similar initiatives with respect to hair and teeth should be intensified, as these tissues are also used, albeit less often, in anthropological research (Dorner, 1988; Vernois et al., 1988; Sandford, 1984; Sandford et al., 1983; Benfer et al., 1978).

In addition, experimental models should be used to further assess the degree to which elemental levels actually reflect differential dietary regimens and physiological processes. In this manner, some of our most fundamental underlying assumptions could be tested. Klepinger (1990) recently studied the effects of differential magnesium intakes on skeletal concentrations in swine, while earlier researchers (Price et al., 1986; Schoeninger, 1979) evaluated various features of skeletal strontium deposition, using experimental animals. Additional investigations of this kind are crucial if our knowledge of trace element metabolism is to keep pace with the expanding body of information on diagenesis.

While our understanding of associations between diet, physiology and trace element concentrations is, at best, fair, our knowledge of relationships between such levels and pathological conditions is in its infancy (see Klepinger, this volume, Chapter 7). Studies to date have focused only on two specific disorders and it appears quite likely that this avenue of investigation has been superseded, at least in the minds of most researchers, by more compelling concerns over diagenesis. Ironically, postmortem alterations in elemental values may, as indicated above, actually make variation due to biogenic processes more apparent. These and other suggestions of an intriguing interaction between biogenic and diagenetic signals certainly warrant further scientific scrutiny.

Finally, the present emphasis on experimental design need not be limited to such endeavors as laboratory studies involving tissue analyses or simulations of diagenetic forces. Rather, experiment–focused field investigations, as well as those aimed at the more traditional goal of dietary discrimination, have the potential for contributing substantially to the future of elemental analyses. Human remains excavated from historic contexts could prove to be especially valuable in this regard, as such material

affords the opportunity to document short-term, diagenetic and/or age-related physiological processes, concurrently with pursuit of more familiar objectives involving dietary reconstruction, paleopathology, and paleodemography.

Ultimately, however, the success of this work hinges on the ability to anticipate both potential applications and problems of elemental investigations prior to their inception. Most important, steps must be taken to ensure comparability with data and results generated experimentally, by following well–established protocols for the recovery and analyses of bone and related samples (see suggestions by Price et al., 1989).

In the final analysis, trace element studies over the past decade have probably taught us more about diagenesis than dietary adaptations. On a more positive note, the numerous unanswered questions demonstrate the potential, if properly investigated, for yielding pertinent information about the more anthropologically relevant end of the biogenic–diagenetic continuum, thereby enhancing our knowledge of diet, disease, and physiology among peoples of the past.

ACKNOWLEDGMENTS

I would like to thank Shelley Saunders and Annie Katzenberg for asking me to contribute this chapter to their volume. I also appreciate the helpful comments and suggestions made by David Weaver and Linda Klepinger to an earlier version of this manuscript.

REFERENCES

Aikawa JK (1981): "Magnesium: Its Biological Significance." Boca Raton, FL: CRC Press.

Allaway WH (1986): Soil-plant-animal and human interrelationships in trace element nutrition. In Mertz W (ed): "Trace Elements in Human and Animal Nutrition" (5th ed) Orlando, FL: Academic Press, pp 465–488.

Aufderheide AC (1989): Chemical analysis of skeletal remains. In İşcan MY, Kennedy KAR (eds): "Reconstruction of Life From the Skeleton." New York: Alan R Liss, pp 237–260.

Aufderheide AC, Neiman FD, Wittmers LE Jr, Rapp G (1981): Lead in bones II: Skeletal lead content as an indicator of lifetime lead ingestion and the social correlates in an archaeological population. Am J Phys Anthropol 55:285–291.

Aufderheide AC, Angel JL, Kelley JO, Outlaw AC, Outlaw MA, Rapp G Jr, Wittmers LE (1985): Lead in bone III: Prediction of social content in four Colonial American Populations (Catoctin Furnace, College Landing, Governor's Land and Irene Mound). Am J Phys Anthropol 66: 353–361.

Aufderheide AC, Wittmers LE, Rapp G, Wallgren J (1988): Anthropological applications of skeletal lead analysis. Am Anthropol 90:932–936.

Baumslag N, Petering AG (1976): Trace metal studies in Bushmen hair. Arch Environ Health 31:254–257.

Beck LA (1985): Bivariate analysis of trace elements in bone. J Hum Evol 14:493–502.

Benfer RA, Typpo JT, Gaff GB, Pickett EE (1978): Mineral analysis of ancient Peruvian hair. Am J Phys Anthropol 48:277–282.

Berner RA (1980): "Early Diagenesis: A Theoretical Approach." Princeton, NJ: Princeton University Press.

Bisel SLC (1980): A pilot study in aspects of human nutrition in the ancient Eastern Mediterranean, with particular attention to trace minerals in several populations from different time periods. PhD dissertation, University of Minnesota.

Blakely RI (1989): Bone strontium in pregnant and lactating females from archaeological samples. Am J Phys Anthropol 80:173–185.

Blakely RI, Beck LA (1981): Trace elements, nutritional status, and social stratification at Etowah, Georgia. Ann NY Acad Sci 376:417–431.

Bothwell TH, Finch CA (1962): "Iron Metabolism." Boston: Little, Brown.

Brown A (1973): Bone strontium content as a dietary indicator in human skeletal populations. PhD dissertation, University of Michigan. Ann Arbor, MI: University Microfilms, Publication No. 74–15.

Brown AB, Blakely RL (1985): Biocultural adaptation as reflected in trace element distribution. J Hum Evol 14:461–468.

Buikstra JE, Frankenberg S, Lambert JB, Xue L (1989): Multiple elements: Multiple expectations. In Price TD (ed): "The Chemistry of Prehistoric Human Bone." Cambridge: Cambridge University Press, pp 155–210.

Byrne KB, Parris DC (1987): Reconstruction of the diet of the Middle Woodland Amerindian population at Abbott farm by bone trace-element analysis. Am J Phys Anthropol 74:373–384.

Dorner K (1988): Trace element analysis of human hair. In Grupe G, Hermann B (eds): "Trace Elements in Environmental History." Heidelberg: Springer-Verlag, pp 113–123.

Edward J (1987): Studies of human bone from the Preceramic Amerindian site at Paloma, Peru by neutron activation analysis. PhD dissertation, University of Missouri.

Edward JB, Benfer RA (in press): The effects of diagenesis on the Paloma skeletal material. In Sandford MK (ed): "Investigations of Ancient Human Tissue: Chemical Analyses in Anthropology." Philadelphia: Gordon and Breach.

Edward J, Fossey JM, Yaffee L (1984): Analysis by neutron activation of human bone from the Hellenistic cemetery at Asine, Greece. J Field Archaeol 11:37–46.

Edward JB, Benfer RA, Morris JS (1990): The effects of dry ashing on the composition of human and animal bone. Biol Trace Element Res 25:219–231.

Fornaciari G, Mallegni F, Bertini D, Nuti Y (1983): Cribra orbitalia and elemental bone iron in the Punics of Carthage. Ossa 8:63–77.

Francalacci P, Tarli SB (1988): Multielementary analysis of trace elements and preliminary results on stable isotopes in two Italian prehistoric sites. Methodological aspects. In Grupe G, Hermann B (eds): "Trace Elements in Environmental History." Heidelberg: Springer-Verlag, pp 41–52.

Frieden E (1972): The chemical elements of life. In "Human Nutrition: Readings from Scientific American." San Francisco: WH Freeman, pp 148–155.

Fritz JC (1972): Iron and associated trace mineral problems in man and animals. In Cannon HL, Hopps HC (eds): "Geochemical Environment in Relation to Health and Disease." Geo Soc Am I 40:25–32.

Geidel AA (1982): Trace element studies from Mississippian skeletal remains: Findings from neutron activation analysis. MASCA J 2:13–16.

Gilbert RI (1975): Trace element analysis of three skeletal Amerindian populations at Dickson Mounds. PhD dissertation, University of Massachusetts. Ann Arbor, MI: University Microfilms, Publication No. 76–5854.

Gilbert RI (1977): Applications of trace element research to problems in archaeology. In Blakely RL (ed): "Biocultural Adaptations in Prehistoric America." Athens: University of Georgia Press, pp 85–100.

Gilbert RI (1985): Stress, paleonutrition, and trace elements. In Gilbert RI, Mielke JH (eds): "The Analysis of Prehistoric Diets." Orlando, FL: Academic Press, pp 339–358.

Goffer Z (1980): "Archaeological Chemistry: A Source Book on the Applications of Chemistry to Archaeology." New York: John Wiley & Sons.

Gordon CC, Buikstra JE (1981): Soil pH, bone preservation and sampling bias at mortuary sites. Am Antiq 46:566–571.

Graham CG, Cordano A (1976): Copper deficiency in human subjects. In Prasad AS (ed): "Trace Elements in Human Health and Disease," Vol 1. New York: Academic Press, pp 363–372.

Grupe G (1988): Impact of the choice of bone samples on trace element data in excavated human skeletons. J Archaeol Sci 15:123–129.

Grupe G, Herrmann B (eds) (1988): "Trace Elements in Environmental History." Heidelberg: Springer-Verlag.

Grupe G, Piepenbrink H (1988): Trace element contaminations in excavated bones by micro-organisms. In Grupe G, Herrmann B (eds): "Trace Elements in Environmental History." Heidelberg: Springer-Verlag, pp 103–112.

Halsted JA, Ronaghy HA, Abadi P, Haghshenass M, Amirhakemi GH, Barakat RH, Reinhold TC (1972): Zinc deficiency in man: The Shiraz experiment. Am J Med 53: 277–284.

Hambidge KM (1985): Clinical deficiencies: When to suspect there is a problem. In Chandra RK (ed): "Trace Elements in Nutrition of Children." New York: Raven Press, pp 1–15.

Hamilton EI (1979): "The Chemical Elements and Man: Measurements, Perspectives, Applications." Springfield, IL: Charles C Thomas.

Hancock RGV, Grynpas MD, Alpert B (1987): Are archaeological bones similar to modern bones? An archaeological assessment. J Radioanal Nucl Chem 110:283–291.

Hancock RGV, Grynpas MD, Pritzker KPH (1989): The abuse of bone analyses for archaeological dietary studies. Archaeometry 31:169–179.

Hanson DB, Buikstra JE (1987): Histomorphological alteration in buried human bone from the Lower Illinois valley: Implications for paleodietary research. J Archaeol Sci 14:549–563.

Hare PE (1980): Organic geochemistry of bone and its relation to the survival of bone in the natural environment. In Behrensmeyer AK, Hill AP (eds): "Fossils in the Making." Chicago: University of Chicago Press, pp 208–219.

Hatch JW, Geidel AA (1985): Status-specific dietary variation in two world cultures. J Hum Evol 14:469–476.

Jarcho S (1964): Lead in the bones of prehistoric lead-glaze potters. Am Antiq 30:94–96.

Katzenberg MA (1984): Chemical analysis of prehistoric human bone from five temporally distinct populations in Southern Ontario. National Museum of Man, Mercury Series. Archaeological Survey of Canada, Paper 129.

Kent GN, Price RI, Gutteridge DH, Smith M, Allen JR, Bhagat CI, Barnes MP, Hickling CJ, Retallack RW, Wilson SG, Devlin RD, Davies C, St. John S (1990): Human lactation: Forearm trabecular bone loss, increased bone turnover, and renal conservation of calcium and inorganic phosphate with recovery of bone mass following weaning. J Bone Min Res 5:361–369.

Kent S, Weinberg ED, Stuart-Macadam P (1990): Dietary and prophylactic iron supplements: Helpful or harmful. Hum Nature 1:53–79.

Klepinger LL (1984): Nutritional assessment from bone. Annu Rev Anthropol 13:75–96.

Klepinger LL (1990): Magnesium ingestion and bone magnesium concentrations in paleodietary research: Cautionary evidence from an animal model. J Archaeol Sci 17:513–517.

Klepinger LL (in press): Culture, health, and chemistry: A technological approach to discovery. In Sandford MK (ed): "Investigations of Ancient Human Tissue: Chemical Analyses in Anthropology." Philadelphia: Gordon and Breach.

Klepinger LL, Kuhn JK, Williams WS (1986): An elemental analysis of archaeological bone from Sicily as a test of predictability of diagenetic change. Am J Phys Anthropol 70:325–331.

Kyle JH (1986): Effect of post-burial contamination on the concentrations of major and minor elements in human bones and teeth. J Archaeol Sci 13:403–416.

Lambert JB, Szpunar CB, Buikstra JE (1979): Chemical analysis of excavated human bone from middle and late Woodland sites, Archaeometry 21:403–416.

Lambert JB, Vlasak SM, Thometz AC, Buikstra JE (1982): A comparative study of the chemical analysis of ribs and femurs in Woodland populations. Am J Phys Anthropol 59:289–294.

Lambert JB, Simpson SV, Buikstra JE, Hanson D (1983): Electron microprobe analysis of elemental distribution in excavated human femurs. Am J Phys Anthropol 62:409–423.

Lambert JB, Simpson SV, Szpunar CB, Buikstra JE (1984): Copper and barium as dietary discriminants: The effects of diagensis. Archaeometry 26:131–138.

Lambert JB, Simpson SV, Weiner SG, Buikstra JE (1985): Induced metal ion exchange in excavated human bone. J Archeol Sci 12:85–92.

Lambert JB, Xue L, Buikstra JE (1989): Physical removal of contaminative inorganic material from buried human bone. J Archaeol Sci 16:427–436.

Leach RM (1976): Metabolism and function of manganese. In Prasad AS (ed): "Trace Elements in Human Health and Disease," Vol II. New York: Academic Press, pp 235–247.

McLean FC, Urist MR (1955) "Bone: An Introduction to the Physiology of Skeletal Tissue." Chicago: University of Chicago Press.

Molleson T (1990): The accumulation of trace metals during fossilization. In Priest ND, Van De Vyver FL (eds): "Trace Metals and Fluoride in Bones and Teeth." Boca Raton, FL: CRC Press, pp 341–365.

Miller, GT (1978): "Chemistry: A Basic Introduction." Belmont, CA: Wadsworth Publishing Co.

Neuman WF (1980): Bone mineral and calcification mechanisms. In Urist MR (ed): "Fundamental and Clinical Bone Physiology." Philadelphia: JB Lippincott, pp 83–107.

Neuman WF, Neuman MW (1958): "The Chemical Dynamics of Bone Mineral." Chicago: University of Chicago Press.

Newesely H (1988): Chemical stability of hydroxyapatite under different conditions. In Grupe G, Herrmann B (eds): "Trace Elements in Environmental History." Heidelberg: Springer–Verlag, pp 1–16.

O'Dell BK (1985): Bioavailability of and interactions among trace elements. In Chandra RK (ed): "Trace Elements in Nutrition of Children." New York: Raven Press, pp 41–62.

Olson EC (1980): Taphonomy: Its history and role in community evolution. In Behrensmeyer AK, Hill AP (eds): "Fossils in the Making." Chicago: University of Chicago Press, pp 5–19.

Ortner DJ, Putschar WGJ (1985): "Identification of Pathological Conditions in Human Skeletal Remains." Washington, DC: Smithsonian Institution Press.

Parker RB, Toots H (1980): Trace elements in bones as paleobiological indicators. In Behrensmeyer AK, Hill AP (eds): "Fossils in the Making." Chicago: University of Chicago Press, pp 197–207.

Pate FD, Hutton JT (1988): The use of soil chemistry data to address postmortem diagenesis in bone mineral. J Archaeol Sci 15:729–739.

Posner AS (1969): Crystal chemistry of bone mineral. Phys Rev 49:760–792.

Prasad AS (1978): "Trace Elements and Iron in Human Metabolism." New York: Plenum Press.

Prasad AS (1985): Diagnostic approaches to trace element deficiencies. In Chandra RK (ed): "Trace Elements in Nutrition of Children." New York: Raven Press, pp 17–39.

Price TD (ed) (1989a): "The Chemistry of Prehistoric Human Bone." Cambridge: Cambridge University Press.

Price TD (1989b): Multielement studies of diagenesis in prehistoric bone. In Price TD (ed): "The Chemistry of Prehistoric Human Bone." Cambridge: Cambridge University Press, pp 126–154.

Price TD, Connor M, Parsen JD (1985): Bone chemistry and the reconstruction of diet: Strontium discrimination in white-tailed deer. J Archaeol Sci 12:419–442.

Price TD, Swick RW, Chase EP (1986): Bone chemistry and prehistoric diet: Strontium studies of laboratory rats. Am J Phys Anthropol 70:365–375.

Price TD, Armelagos GJ, Buikstra JE, Bumsted MP, Chisholm BS, Ericson JE, Lambert JB, Van Der Merwe NJ, Schoeninger MJ, Sillen A (1989): The chemistry of prehistoric human bone: Recommendations and directions for future study. In Price TD (ed): "The Chemistry of Prehistoric Human Bone." Cambridge: Cambridge University Press, pp 245–252.

Radosevich SC (1989): Diet or diagensis? An evaluation of the trace element analysis of bone. PhD dissertation, University of Oregon.

Radosevich SC (in press): The six deadly sins of trace element analysis: A case of wishful thinking in science. In Sandford MK (ed): "Investigations of Ancient Human Tissue: Chemical Analyses in Anthropology." Philadelphia: Gordon and Breach.

Reinhold JG (1975): Trace elements—A selective survey. Clin Chem 21:476–500.

Reinhold JG, Nasr K, Lahimgarzadeh A, Hedayati H (1973): Effects of purified phytate and phytate-rich bread upon metabolism of zinc, calcium, phosphorus, and nitrogen in man. Lancet 1:283–288.

Runia LT (1987): Analysis of bone from the Bronze Age site Bovenkarspel–Het Valkje, The Netherlands: A preliminary report. Archaeometry 29:221–232.

Runia L (1988): Discrimination factors on different trophic levels in relation to the trace element content in human bones. In Grupe G, Herrmann B (eds): "Trace Elements in Environmental History." Heidelberg: Springer–Verlag pp 53–66.

Sandford MK (1984): Diet, disease, and nutritional stress: An elemental analysis of human hair from Kulubnarti, a Medieval Sudanese Nubian population. PhD dissertation, University of Colorado. Ann Arbor, MI: University Microfilms, Publication No. DA 8428681.

Sandford MK (1988a): Trace element analysis: Implications for paleopathological research. Introduction to a symposium at the 15th annual meeting of the Paleopathology Association, March 23, Kansas City, Missouri.

Sandford MK (1988b): Elemental hair analysis: An application for paleopathology. Paper presented at the 15th annual meeting of the Paleopathology Association, March 23, Kansas City, Missouri.

Sandford MK, Van Gerven DP, Meglen RR (1983): Elemental hair analysis: New evidence on the etiology of cribra orbitalia in Sudanese Nubia. Hum Biol 55:831–844.

Sandford MK, Repke DB, Earle AL (1988): Elemental analysis of human bone from Carthage: A pilot study. In Humphrey JH (ed): "The Circus and a Byzantine Cemetery at Carthage," Vol 1. Ann Arbor: University of Michigan Press, pp 285–296.

Schoeninger MJ (1979): Diet and status at Chalcatzingo: Some empirical and technical aspects of strontium analysis. Am J Phys Anthropol 51:295–310.

Schoeninger MJ (1980): Changes in human subsistence activities from the Middle Paleolithic Period to the Neolithic Period in the Middle East. PhD dissertation, University of Michigan.

Schoeninger MJ (1981): The agricultural "revolution": Its effect on human diet in prehistoric Iran and Israel. Paleorient 7:73–92.

Schoeninger MJ (1982): Diet and the evolution of modern human form in the Middle East. Am J Phys Anthropol 58:37–52.

Schroeder HA (1973): "The Trace Elements and Man." Old Greenwich, CT: Devin-Adair.

Schroeder HA, Nason AP, Tipton IH (1969): Essential metals in man: Magnesium. J Chron Dis 21:815–841.

Schutte KM (1964): "The Biology of Trace Elements." Philadelphia: JB Lippincott.

Shipman P, Walker A, Bichell D (1985): "The Human Skeleton." Cambridge, MA: Harvard University Press.

Sillen A (1981a): Strontium and diet at Hayonim Cave, Israel. An evaluation of the strontium/calcium technique for investigating prehistoric diets. PhD dissertation, University of Pennsylvania.

Sillen A (1981b): Strontium and diet at Hayonim Cave. Am J Phys Anthropol 56:131–137.

Sillen A (1988): Elemental and isotopic analyses of mammalian fauna from Southern Africa and their implications for paleodietary research. Am J Phys Anthropol 76:49–60.

Sillen A (1989): Diagenesis of the inorganic phase of cortical bone. In Price TD (ed): "The Chemistry of Prehistoric Bone." Cambridge, MA: Cambridge University Press, pp 211–229.

Sillen A, Kavanagh M (1982): Strontium and paleodietary research: A review. Yearb Phys Anthropol 25:67–90.

Sillen A, Smith P (1984): Sr/Ca ratios in juvenile skeletons portray weaning practices in a medieval Arab population. J Archaeol Sci 11:237–245.

Sillen A, Sealy JC, van der Merwe NJ (1989): Chemistry and paleodietary research: No more easy answers. Am Antiq 54:504–512.

Spadaro JA, Becker RO, Bachman CH (1970a): The distribution of trace metal ions in bone and tendon. Calcif Tissue Res 6:49–54.

Spadaro JA, Becker RO, Bachman CH (1970b): Size-specific metal complexing sites in native collagen. Nature 225:1134–1136.

Stout SD (1989): Histomorphometric analysis of human skeletal remains. In İşcan MY, Kennedy KAR (eds): "Reconstruction of Life From the Skeleton." New York, Alan R. Liss, pp 41–52.

Szpunar CB (1977): Atomic absorption of archaeological remains: Human ribs from Woodland mortuary sites. PhD dissertation, Northwestern University.

Szpunar CB, Lambert JB, Buikstra JE (1978): Analysis of excavated bone by atomic absorption. Am J Phys Anthropol 48:199–202.

Toots H, Voorhies MR (1965): Strontium in fossil bones and reconstruction of food chains. Science 149:854–855.

Triffitt JT (1980): The organic matrix of bone tissue. In Urist MR (ed): "Fundamental and Clinical Bone Physiology." Philadelphia: J B Lippincott Company, pp 45–82.

Underwood EJ (1977): "The Trace Elements in Human and Animal Nutrition." 4th edition. New York: Academic Press.

Vernois V, Ung Bao M, Deschamps N (1988): Chemical analysis of human dental enamel from archaeological sites. In Grupe G, Herrman B (eds): "Trace Elements in Environmental History." Heidelberg: Springer-Verlag, pp 83–90.

Von Endt DW, Ortner DJ (1984): Experimental effects of bone size and temperature on bone diagenesis. J Archaeol Sci 11:247–253.

Waldron HA (1981): Postmortem absorption of lead by the skeleton. Am J Phys Anthropol 55:395–398.

Waldron HA (1983): On the postmortem accumulation of lead by skeletal tissues. J Archaeol Sci 10:35–40.

Waldron T (1987): The potential of analysis of chemical constituents of bone. In Boddington A, Garland AN, Janaway RC (eds): "Death, Decay, and Reconstruction: Approaches to Archaeology and Forensic Science." Manchester: Manchester University Press, pp 149–159.

White EM, Hannus LA (1983): Chemical weathering of bone in archaeological sites. Am Antiq 48:316–322.

Wing E, Brown AB (1979): "Paleonutrition." New York: Academic Press.

Zaino EC (1968): Elemental bone iron in the Anasazi Indians. Am J Phys Anthropol 29:433–435.

Skeletal Biology of Past Peoples: Research Methods
pages 105–119 © 1992 Wiley-Liss, Inc.

Chapter 6

Advances in Stable Isotope Analysis of Prehistoric Bones

M. Anne Katzenberg

Department of Archaeology, University of Calgary, Calgary, Alberta T2N 1N4

INTRODUCTION

The potential for reconstructing prehistoric human diets was significantly enhanced in the 1970s by two new approaches to analyzing human bone. Sandford (this volume, Chapter 5) reviews the historical developments in the analysis of trace elements in bone mineral; this chapter focuses on developments in the analysis of stable isotopes, primarily in protein preserved in bone.

The use of stable isotope data from bone collagen for the reconstruction of prehistoric human diet began in the late 1970s with the pioneering work of Vogel and van der Merwe (1977), van der Merwe and Vogel (1978), and DeNiro and Epstein (1978). Using stable carbon isotope ratios, Vogel and van der Merwe demonstrated a method for detecting the consumption of maize directly from human skeletal remains. Their work generated considerable excitement, as the consumption of maize represents the introduction of domesticated plants into the diet throughout much of North America. At the same time, DeNiro and Epstein showed the relationship between diet and animal tissues with respect to carbon isotope values in their controlled feeding experiments of laboratory animals. Since the publication of these studies, there has been a tremendous volume of data on stable carbon isotope ratios in human bone generated from skeletal collections all over the world (reviewed by Chisholm, 1989, and Schwarcz and Schoeninger, in

press). The potential for using stable isotopes to reveal prehistoric environments and lifestyles has now developed far beyond the detection of maize in the diet to include the determination of human reliance on marine versus terrestrial foods (Chisholm et al., 1982; Tauber, 1981; Schoeninger, 1985; Walker and DeNiro, 1986), environmental reconstructions including plant cover and climate (Ambrose and DeNiro, 1987, 1989; Sealy et al., 1987; van der Merwe, 1989), reliance on animal versus vegetable protein (Schwarcz et al., 1985; Ambrose and DeNiro, 1986a,b; Spielmann et al., 1990), and possibly patterns of human migration (Sealy and van der Merwe, 1986; Katzenberg, 1989a, 1991a). In addition, recent work on the determination of stable carbon isotopes on fossilized material, using carbonate from tooth enamel, suggests the potential for using stable isotopes to reconstruct early hominid diets (Lee-Thorp et al., 1989).

It is the purpose of this chapter to present basic background information in chemistry, biochemistry, and analytical techniques needed to understand isotope studies in physical anthropology and archaeology. In addition, applications to prehistoric problems are presented for the areas of carbon isotopes and photosynthesis, marine and terrestrial systems, nitrogen isotopes, and the reconstruction of food chains. Problems with the techniques such as diagenesis, differential uptake of isotopes by amino acids and analytical difficulties are discussed. Finally the most recent work in isotope analysis in prehistoric materials is viewed with a look to future applications. It is the goal of this work to provide advanced students and professionals in physical anthropology and archaeology with enough background to be able to critically evaluate research that employs stable isotope techniques.

Basic Chemical Concepts

Isotopes are chemical elements with the same number of protons, but different numbers of neutrons. Stable isotopes do not transmute into other elements as do radioactive isotopes. Isotopes of a given element behave similarly in chemical reactions but they react at different rates because of their different atomic weights. Biologically important elements such as carbon, nitrogen, sulphur, and oxygen occur in different isotope forms. For example, carbon occurs as ^{12}C, ^{13}C, and ^{14}C with abundances of 98.9%, 1.1%, and 10^{-12}%, respectively. During the process of photosynthesis, ^{12}C is incorporated into plant tissues preferentially relative to ^{13}C such that the ratio of ^{13}C to ^{12}C in the atmosphere is greater than the ratio of these two isotopes in plant tissue. This is termed *fractionation*.

Isotope ratios are expressed in delta δ units as follows:

$$\delta X_{std} = [(R_{sample}/R_{std}] - 1) \times 1,000,$$

where δX_{std} is the ratio of two isotopes in delta units relative to a standard, and R_{sample} and R_{std} are the absolute ratios of sample and standard (Ehleringer and Rundel, 1989). For carbon, the isotope ratio of the two stable isotopes is expressed:

$$\delta^{13}C\text{‰} = \left[\frac{^{13}C/^{12}C_{sample}}{^{13}C/^{12}C_{standard}} - 1 \right] \times 1,000.$$

The standard for carbon is a marine carbonate fossil from the Peedee formation in South Carolina and is referred to as PDB (for Peedee Belemnite). The standard for nitrogen is atmospheric air, which is referred to as AIR. Other isotope standards are SMOW (standard mean ocean water) for oxygen and hydrogen, and CD (Canyon Diablo meteorite) for sulphur.

While the range of $\delta^{13}C$ values in nature is over 100‰, the tissues of plants and animals normally range from -28 to -5. $\delta^{13}C$ values are negative relative to the PDB standard, since the process of photosynthesis results in fractionation of the stable isotope abundances in the air ($\delta^{13}C = -7$‰) and in seawater ($\delta^{13}C = 0$‰) such that less ^{13}C relative to available ^{12}C is incorporated into the organism. Nitrogen isotope values in plants and animals are positive relative to the standard and generally range from near 0‰ in legumes to $+15$ in animals in higher trophic levels.

Isotope Values in Plants and the Relationship Between Diet and Isotope Values in Animal Tissues

Carbon. Plant tissues were first analyzed for stable carbon isotopes in the 1950s (Craig, 1954). While the C_4, or Hatch-Slack photosynthesis pathway was not discovered until the 1960s, differences in $\delta^{13}C$ values among plants were noted earlier by Craig (1953). Bender (1968) and Smith and Epstein (1971) investigated the difference in stable carbon isotopes between C_3 (those utilizing the Calvin-Benson photosynthesis pathway) and C_4 plants. C_4 plants discriminate less against the heavier isotope, ^{13}C, when taking in CO_2 from the atmosphere. Therefore they have heavier, or less negative, $\delta^{13}C$ values than do C_3 plants (Deines, 1980). A third photosynthesis pathway, Crassulacean acid metabolism (CAM), is used by cacti and succulents which have $\delta^{13}C$ values intermediate between those of C_3 and C_4 plants.

The relationship of stable carbon isotope values in animals and their diets was investigated by DeNiro and Epstein (1978) and Teeri and Schoeller (1979). Chisholm and colleagues (1982) and van der Merwe (1982) have reported a fractionation factor of approximately 5‰ between diet and bone collagen. There is an additional fractionation factor of approximately 1‰ between herbivores and carnivores (Schoeninger 1985; Tieszen et al., 1983). Given a knowledge of $\delta^{13}C$ for various components in human diets, fractionation factors between food and collagen, and $\delta^{13}C$ for human bone collagen, it is possible to reconstruct prehistoric diet. Schoeninger (1989) has demonstrated this for several prehistoric situations including the people of Pecos Pueblo and Dutch whalers from Spitzbergen. For Pecos Pueblo, dietary components, as described from the faunal and paleobotanical evidence, were weighted as to their $\delta^{13}C$ values and the caloric values of each food. These data were then combined to make up proposed diets, which varied in the amounts of each food. The resulting $\delta^{13}C$ values of the proposed diets were then compared with the actual bone collagen values for humans. In this particular example, Schoeninger concluded that the proposed diet based on faunal and plant remains probably underestimated the amount of maize and meat from mixed grazers (herbivores consuming both C_3 and C_4 grasses) in the diet. Further refinements in diet reconstruction should be possible with current research on isotope values in individual dietary constituents such as lipids, carbohydrates, and protein (Ambrose, 1990) and isotope values in individual amino acids (Hare et al., 1991; Stafford et al., 1991). Specifically, with a better understanding of how the carbon in foods is used in the production of collagen it should be possible to improve diet reconstructions.

Nitrogen. Nitrogen is taken up by plants from the soil, and by some plants, directly from atmospheric nitrogen. Because the $\delta^{15}N$ value of atmospheric nitrogen is approximately 0‰ (Mariotti, 1983) and the $\delta^{15}N$ value of soils averages around 10‰ (Shearer and Kohl, 1989) plants which fix atmospheric nitrogen (i.e., legumes) have lower $\delta^{15}N$ values than non-nitrogen fixing plants. Herbivores show a trophic level shift of approximately +3‰ from the plants they consume, thus while all herbivores have higher $\delta^{15}N$ values than the plants they consume; herbivores that eat legumes will have lower $\delta^{15}N$ values than those that eat predominantly nonleguminous plants. Carnivores show a further trophic level shift of approximately 3‰ (Schoeninger and DeNiro 1984).

Schoeninger (1989) uses nitrogen isotopes along with the carbon isotope data mentioned above to reconstruct diets for Pecos Pueblo and Dutch whalers from Spitzbergen. However, weighting factors for nitrogen isotopes are based on the amount of protein in foods rather than the amount of calories, since the nitrogen in collagen is obtained from protein.

Recent studies by Heaton and colleagues (1986), Ambrose and DeNiro (1987), and

Sealy and colleagues (1987) indicate that nitrogen isotope values may also be influenced by climate in arid regions. It has not yet been determined if higher than expected $\delta^{15}N$ values in animals in arid regions are due to physiological factors related to water conservation in animals or to environmental factors such as soil salinity (Ambrose and DeNiro, 1989). Nevertheless, environment must be considered when applying nitrogen isotope data to the reconstruction of diet in arid regions such as south and east Africa (Ambrose and DeNiro, 1986b; Sealy et al., 1987) and the U.S. Southwest (Spielmann et al., 1990; Katzenberg and Kelley, 1991).

APPLICATION OF ISOTOPE RATIOS TO PREHISTORIC BONE
Composition of Bone

Bone is composed of an organic matrix of the structural protein collagen, which is studded with crystals of calcium phosphate in the form of hydroxyapatite. Dry bone is approximately 70% inorganic and 30% organic by weight. About 85%–90% of the organic material is collagen. The majority of research on the stable isotopes in prehistoric bone has been done with collagen since this protein has been found in fossils dating as far back as the Devonian (Wyckoff, 1980). Because of the intimate structural relationship between collagen and hydroxyapatite, collagen may survive for a very long time with variation that depends on the burial environment (Hedges and Wallace, 1980). While some degradation may occur, the characteristic amino acid composition and 640 Å (angstrom) banding pattern are retained.

There was a debate in the 1980s regarding the use of carbon contained in the carbonate of apatite for stable isotope analysis (Sullivan and Krueger 1981; Schoeninger and DeNiro, 1982; Sullivan and Krueger, 1983). Research into the processes of diagenesis (e.g., Nelson et al., 1986 and reviewed by Sandford, this volume, Chapter 5) demonstrates that while bone mineral is subject to numerous chemical substitutions and alterations, collagen, if preserved at all, is relatively unaffected by postmortem exchange with the burial environment. However, recent studies (Lee-Thorpe n.d.; Lee-Thorpe and colleagues, 1989, Lee-Thorpe and van der

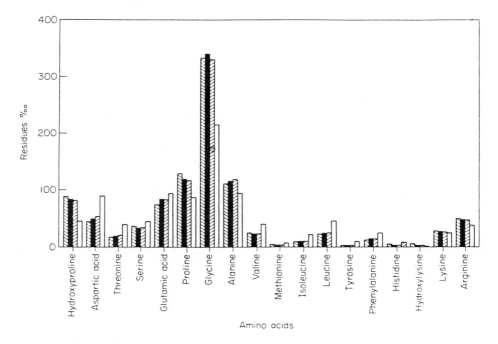

Fig. 1. Amino acid profile of type 1 collagen (left) and human bone from a seventeenth century horticultural village site in Ontario. Human bone was prepared with (center left) and without (center right) a 20-h soak in NaOH. The material precipitated from the NaOH soak is represented on the far right Reproduced from Katzenberg (1989b), with permission of the publisher.

Merwe, 1987) have been directed toward isolating carbon isotopes from the inorganic phase, which is the only hope of extending the application of stable carbon isotope analysis to reconstruct the diet of early hominids.

Amino Acid Composition of Collagen

Collagen is a structural protein that provides mechanical strength to bone, tendon, cartilage, skin, and blood vessels. It occurs as a triple helix with approximately 1000 amino acids per chain. In order to coil into a helix, every third amino acid is glycine, thus approximately one third of the amino acids of collagen are glycine. Another feature which distinguishes collagen from other proteins is the presence of two amino acids, hydroxyproline (89/1000 residues) and hydroxylysine (5/1000 residues) (Bornstein and Piez, 1964). The profile of amino acids for collagen is unique and may be used to verify the nature of the substance isolated from prehistoric bone. An example of this

is provided in Figure 1, which shows the results of an experiment to determine whether two different treatments used in collagen extraction resulted in different products. Sodium hydroxide (NaOH) is used to remove base-soluble humic substances but it was suggested that the treatment results in loss of collagen as well. There is little difference between the results for the prehistoric bone (two center bars for each amino acid) and values for the standard profile (left bars). The bars on the far right for each amino acid indicate the amino acid composition of the normally discarded material from the NaOH soak, and it is apparent, from the presence of hydroxyproline and hydroxylysine, that some collagen is lost when the NaOH soak is used (Katzenberg, 1989b).

Masters (1987) has demonstrated characteristic amino acid profiles for collagen and noncollagenous proteins extracted from bone. As collagen degrades, the amino acid profile for noncollagenous proteins becomes apparent. The most common contaminants in prehistoric buried remains are humic acids, which consist of decayed plant matter. The presence of humic acids can be demonstrated by amino acid analysis and, more simply, by precipitating base-soluble humic acids from a base soak and analyzing for $\delta^{13}C$ (Boutton et al., 1984; Katzenberg, 1989b).

Diagenesis

Diagenesis is a term that refers to chemical and physical alteration in sediments during and after their deposition. It is used in bone chemistry to refer to chemical and physical changes that occur in the burial environment, and it is of considerable significance, since such changes may entirely mask the biological information sought by prehistorians. Sandford (this volume, Chapter 5) details many of the concerns in the context of trace element analysis. The problem appears to be less serious in bone collagen from subfossil populations. It is an important subject of study for those attempting to use isotopes from carbonate in fossilized hard tissues such as enamel, dentin, and bone. Nelson and colleagues (1986) studied the effects of diagenesis on trace elements and stable isotopes in bone and concluded that collagen stable isotope values were not altered by postmortem change, whereas strontium and stable isotopes values in apatite were altered. It appears that postmortem degradation of collagen results in an absence of stable isotope data (i.e., too little CO_2 or N_2 for analysis) in most cases rather than an erroneous result, as is the case with some trace elements. However, Schoeninger and colleagues (1989) have noted that a low yield of collagen is often associated with aberrant stable isotope values. Recent work by Stafford and colleagues (1991) demonstrates that bone with a protein content of less than 5% has a noncollagenous amino acid composition and is severely altered. DeNiro (1985) proposed that the atomic ratio of carbon to nitrogen in protein extract be used to identify preserved collagen. On the basis of studies of modern and prehistoric bones of the same species he proposed that atomic C/N ratios outside the range 2.9–3.6 are sufficiently altered to make their stable isotope values suspect. Modern bone atomic C/N ratios are 3.2–3.3. In collagen samples contaminated with humic ac-

ids the C/N ratio is higher than expected and the stable carbon isotope value reflects the combined value of collagen and the plant cover in the area at the time the soil was formed (Katzenberg 1989b).

While research into diagenetic changes that affect protein is ongoing, at present it appears that checks such as C/N ratios and amino acid analysis can identify altered samples so that they are omitted from stable isotope data sets. Ambrose (1990) suggests that collagen from samples where collagen yields are very low should be suspected of alteration. Of the two checks, C/N ratios and amino acid analysis, the former is easily accomplished at the time of analysis but amino acid analysis requires additional laboratory set-up and is more costly and time-consuming. However, amino acid analysis is more reliable and should be considered for a subset of samples.

INSTRUMENTATION
Collagen Extraction

Chisholm (1989) provides a step-by-step review of techniques for extracting collagen from bone. A recent comparative study by Schoeninger and colleagues (1989) also provides procedures and a critical analysis of results. Most researchers use one of three methods. Bone chunks can be decalcified in 1 M HCl until all mineral is dissolved, leaving the insoluble protein, which is rinsed to neutrality and then freeze-dried (Sealy, 1986). Bone can also be demineralized in EDTA (ethylenediaminetetraacetic acid, a sodium salt that is a strong chelating agent) as described by Tuross and colleagues (1989a: 270). This method also isolates protein from bone mineral and a preliminary step removes soluble proteins. A third method involves gelatinization of bone powder by demineralization in hydrochloric acid, followed by slow hydrolysis in weakly acidic hot water. This was first presented by Longin (1971) and has since been modified with respect to additional steps for the removal of humic acids and lipids (DeNiro and Epstein 1981; reviewed in Chisholm et al., 1983a) and with respect to laboratory apparatus (Schoeninger and DeNiro, 1984).

In each of these procedures the objective is to remove the inorganic portion of bone, then

DOUBLE COLLECTOR STABLE ISOTOPE
MASS SPECTROMETER

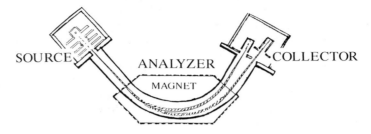

Fig. 2. Diagram of the three main components of a mass spectrometer showing source, where gas from a sample is introduced and molecules are ionized then accelerated; analyzer, where ions of different masses are separated; and detector, where the abundances of ions of different masses are measured relative to the standard. Courtesy of H.R. Krouse.

to isolate the protein collagen, without including organic materials from the burial environment. Masters' (1987) research on collagen and noncollagenous protein from prehistoric remains suggests that stable isotope values are similar for noncollagenous proteins and collagen. However, Hare and Estep (1982) and others (Hare et al., 1991) have demonstrated that stable isotope values vary among individual amino acids. Since noncollagenous proteins have a different amino acid composition than does collagen, the ideal situation is to isolate the purest possible collagen from bone. There are a number of highly sophisticated methods for isolating individual amino acids for stable isotope analysis and such analyses may prove more revealing of diet than current research on collagen. However, as Ambrose (1990) points out, these methods are extremely time-consuming and not feasible in many labs where such fine resolution is not required. It is important to balance feasibility and cost with resolution and results for routine analyses. It may become apparent that the additional resolution gained through analyzing individual amino acids justifies the extra effort. In any event it should be obvious that students of prehistory need to be conversant, if not skilled themselves, in biochemical concepts and techniques.

Mass Spectrometry

Mass spectrometry has been used in analytical chemistry for over 80 years and stable iso-topes have been studied since the early 1900s. Therefore details of analysis by mass spectrometry are rarely given, beyond stating the type and make of mass spectrometer used. Because most students of anthropology are not familiar with the basic principals of this method of analysis, the following brief summary is intended to demystify the process.

The mass spectrometer measures the abundances and masses of stable isotopes in the form of ions. There are three sections to the mass spectrometer: the source, in which the sample gas is ionized and the ions are accelerated; the analyzer, wherein the accelerated ions are separated according their mass, either by a magnetic field, an electrostatic analyzer, or a combination of these; and a detector, where the separated ions are counted (Figure 2).

For carbon and nitrogen isotope analysis of collagen, approximately 5 mg of freeze-dried collagen is loaded into quartz tubes with cupric oxide, silver, and elemental copper, following the procedure of Stump and Fraser (1973), as modified by Sofer (1980) and described by Chisholm (1989). The tubes are evacuated and sealed, then combusted in a furnace at 800°C for 3 hrs, producing CO_2 and N_2 gas. The gas (CO_2 for $\delta^{13}C$ analysis and N_2 for $\delta^{15}N$ analysis) is introduced into the mass spectrometer by an inlet system, which takes up the gas as the tube is cracked within the system. The gas is then ionized and the accelerated ions are passed through a mass analyzer, which may be a magnet or an electrical field. The ions are dispersed in curved trajectories depending on their mass and are focused prior to reaching the detector (Bauer et al., 1978). The detector picks up the number of ions of different masses and the abundance is indicated by the height of the peak for a given mass.

The mass spectrometer alternately lets in sample and standard gases; a computer program prints out the ratio of stable isotopes in the sample and in the standard and then prints out a δ value, as described earlier in this chapter. The ratio of stable isotopes in the sample and standard (usually an in-house standard) is normally given relative to the international standard so that the final value for carbon, for example, will be $\delta^{13}C‰PDB$.

STANDARDS, PRECISION, AND ACCURACY

Samples for stable isotope analysis are run in conjunction with standards that are materials of known value. In-house standards are used to check consistency of results during a run and to calculate precision, and international standards insure accuracy and comparability of results among different laboratories. The United States National Bureau of Standards (NBS) and the International Atomic Energy Commission (IAEC) supply materials for interlaboratory standardization. For collagen, some labs use Sigma Chemical Corporation type 1 insoluble collagen from bovine tendon (Ambrose, 1990; Stafford et al., 1991). Precision (i.e., the closeness of repeated measurement) varies depending on equipment. It is generally $\pm 0.1‰$ or less for $\delta^{13}C$ and $\pm 0.2‰$ or less for $\delta^{15}N$.

Expected Variation in Biological Samples

It is important to be aware of the normal variation expected in $\delta^{13}C$ and $\delta^{15}N$ values for individuals consuming the same foods. Studies addressing this concern have been conducted in controlled feeding experiments (DeNiro and Schoeninger, 1983) in prehistoric human groups (Lovell et al., 1986a) and in prehistoric animals (Katzenberg, 1990, unpublished data). DeNiro and Schoeninger (1983) analyzed bones of mink and rabbits and compared different skeletal elements within the same individual, males versus females, and all individuals for each species (30 mink and 21 rabbits). In

each case the standard deviation for $\delta^{13}C$ and for $\delta^{15}N$ values is less than 1‰. They conclude that small sample sizes in archaeological studies should not present a problem, because variation is so small within a group of animals eating the same diet. Lovell and coworkers (1986a) found similar results for prehistoric human hunter-gatherers from the northern Plains with $\sigma = 0.3‰$ on a sample of 50 individuals. Bumsted (1984) found a standard deviation of 0.7‰ in a sample of 32 adults (17 females and 15 males) from a prehistoric horticultural site in South Dakota. In a study of stable isotope values of animal bones from archaeological middens, Katzenberg found standard deviations of less than 1‰ for both $\delta^{15}N$ and $\delta^{13}C$ in 22 deer bones, 13 bear bones and 12 beaver bones. Fifteen dog bones had a standard deviation of slightly greater than 1‰ for $\delta^{13}C$, probably owing to the fact that they are opportunistic scavengers who consumed a significant amount of C_4 plant food. As a general rule, differences of less than 1‰ are not considered to reflect dietary differences in isotope studies (Fogel, 1990).

APPLICATIONS OF STABLE ISOTOPE RESULTS TO RECONSTRUCTING PREHISTORIC DIET

In recent years, several reviews of stable isotope studies, as applied to prehistoric diet, have been published, including works (or articles) by van der Merwe (1982) and Ambrose (1987) specifically on North America, and by DeNiro (1987) specifically on nitrogen isotopes, as well as Keegan (1989) and the edited volume by Price (1989), which includes chapters by Chisholm, Schoeninger and van der Merwe. A very recent review is by Schwarcz and Schoeninger (in press). Rather than duplicate these works which are readily available to the interested researcher, this review will highlight published studies that pertain to various applications of stable isotope data to reconstructing human diet, health and migration.

Identification of C_3 and C_4 Plants in the Diet

This early application of stable carbon isotopes to human prehistory developed from research in radiocarbon dating by which it was found that maize remains gave younger dates than did wood from the same site (Bender, 1968; van der Merwe, 1982). Concurrently, the discovery of photosynthesis pathways other than the Calvin, or C_3, pathway provided the explanation for the difference in stable carbon isotope ratios in C_3 versus C_4 plants (Bender, 1968; Hatch et al., 1967). C_4 plants include a number of tropical grasses such as maize, sorghum, millet, and sugar cane, which are adapted to hot and/or dry conditions. They discriminate less against the heavier stable isotope of carbon and therefore have less-negative $\delta^{13}C$ values, which range from -9 to $-14‰$ as compared to C_3 plants which have $\delta^{13}C$ values ranging from -20 to $-35‰$. C_3 plants include trees, shrubs, and most plants that grow in temperate regions (Deines, 1980).

Controlled feeding experiments by DeNiro and Epstein (1978) demonstrated the relationship between the stable isotope ratio of diet and animal tissues. Thus the necessary information for reconstructing human diets in which a diet of almost exclusively C_3 plants was altered to include increasing amounts of the C_4 plant, maize, was in place in the late 1970s when Vogel and van der Merwe published two papers demonstrating the elegant application of stable isotope data to the detection of plant domestication in northeastern North America (Vogel and van der Merwe, 1977; van der Merwe and Vogel, 1978). Other researchers soon applied this approach for detecting maize in the diet to studies of other regions. Such studies include those by Bender and colleagues (1981) on Hopewell agriculture, Boutton and colleagues (1984) and Lynott and colleagues 1986) on the central Mississippi valley, Buikstra and colleagues (1988) on Tennessee, Decker and Tieszen (1989) on southwestern Colorado, DeNiro and Epstein (1981) on the Tehuacan Valley of Mexico, Ericson and colleagues (1989) on Peru, Katzenberg and Kelley (1991) on New Mexico, Schwarcz and colleagues (1985) on southern Ontario, Spielmann and colleagues (1990) on New Mexico, Stothers and Bechtel (1987) on the lower Great Lakes, van der Merwe and colleagues (1981) on Venezuela, and White and Schwarcz (1989) on Belize. Murray and Schoeninger (1988) have applied stable carbon isotope studies to reconstructing the use of millet in eastern Europe.

Distinguishing Diets Based on Marine and Terrestrial Foods

Another application of stable carbon isotopes to the reconstruction of human diets relates to the difference in $\delta^{13}C$ values between foods obtained from marine versus terrestrial environments. Tauber (1981) and Chisholm and colleagues (1982, 1983b) demonstrated this application, which is based on the fact that dissolved carbonate in seawater, the main carbon source for marine plants and animals, has a $\delta^{13}C$ value of approximately 0‰ whereas CO_2 in the atmosphere, the main source of carbon for terrestrial plants and animals, has a $\delta^{13}C$ value of $-7‰$. This 7 ‰ difference in $\delta^{13}C$ is maintained in plants and animals from marine and terrestrial environments. In regions with no C_4 plants, it is possible to detect marine foods in C_3-plant-based diets since $\delta^{13}C$ values for terrestrial diets should be -19 or less (more negative), while $\delta^{13}C$ values for people dependent in large part on marine resources will be -14.5 to $-16‰$, as suggested by Johansen and colleagues (1986).

Studies of prehistoric subsistence based on the maintenance of the 7‰ difference between marine and terrestrial carbon sources include those by Johansen and colleagues (1986) on terrestrial- versus marine-based diets from inland and coastal regions in Norway spanning the Stone Age to the 17th century; by Walker and DeNiro (1986) on prehistoric peoples of the Santa Barbara Channel area comparing sites on the Channel Islands, the mainland coast, and the mainland interior; by Tauber (1981) on Mesolithic and Neolithic diet change in Denmark; by Keegan and DeNiro (1988) on diet in the Bahama Islands and the peculiarities of stable isotope data in coral-reef communities; by Sealy and van der Merwe (1988) on the role of marine foods in the southwestern Cape, South Africa over a span of several thousand years; by Hobson and Collier (1984) on Australian aboriginal diets; and by Lovell and colleagues (1986b) on salmon consumption among interior British Columbia peoples spanning 2,000 years. Generally stable carbon isotopes are effective in distinguishing consumption of marine foods. For example, in the study by Walker and DeNiro (1986), $\delta^{13}C$ values decrease from those for peoples living on the Channel Islands, to those for peoples living on the mainland coast, and to those, the lowest values, for peoples living inland. Similarly, Lovell and co-workers (1986b) found decreasing $\delta^{13}C$ values moving upstream along major salmon-producing rivers in interior British Columbia.

Distinguishing Marine and Terrestrial Foods With Nitrogen Isotopes

One of the problems with using stable carbon isotopes alone is that in areas with some C_4 plant component to the diet, the carbon isotope signals for marine foods and C_4 plants are indistinguishable. Such is the case, for example, among early historic coastal agriculturalists of northeastern North America. Stable nitrogen isotopes also distinguish marine from terrestrial diets but are not influenced by the type of terrestrial plants consumed, with the exception of leguminous versus nonleguminous plants. Therefore in many studies of marine and terrestrial subsistence, both carbon and nitrogen isotopes are used. The potential for using nitrogen isotopes to distinguish marine from terrestrial food sources in prehistoric peoples was first suggested by DeNiro and Epstein (1981) in their report of their controlled feeding experiments for nitrogen isotopes in diet and animal tissues. Their suggestion was based on results from isotope ecology studies. Schoeninger et al. (1983) tested the idea on a worldwide sample of prehistoric skeletal remains representative of diverse diets and found that coastal peoples had higher $\delta^{15}N$ values than inland peoples. Subsequently others have used nitrogen isotopes to determine the relative proportions of terrestrial versus marine foods in the diet (Walker and DeNiro, 1986; Keegan and DeNiro, 1988).

Nitrogen Isotopes and Trophic Level Distinctions

Another use of nitrogen isotope data is the determination of trophic level (i.e., the placement of organisms in the food web). Studies in ecology on food webs show a progressive increase in $\delta^{15}N$ values (around 3‰) in successively higher trophic levels (DeNiro and Epstein, 1981; Schoeninger et al., 1983; Minagawa and Wada, 1984; and Schoeninger, 1985). Terrestrial and marine systems cannot be compared directly, since terrestrial organisms generally have lower $\delta^{15}N$ values at every trophic level in comparison with marine organisms (Schoeninger and DeNiro 1984). Studies of prehistoric food webs are consistent in showing a trophic level difference of approximately 3‰ (Ambrose and DeNiro, 1986a; Sealy et al., 1987; Katzenberg, 1989b; Katzenberg and Kelley, 1991). Figures 3 and 4 provide examples of combined results of stable carbon and nitrogen isotope analysis from the last two studies cited above. Figure 3 is plotted from data on mammals, birds, and fish from a seventeenth century Ontario Iroquois site. Woodchucks, which eat legumes, have the lowest $\delta^{15}N$ values; bear, beaver, and deer eat primarily nonleguminous plants, while raccoon, dog, and humans (from a neighboring site) are all omnivores. For fish, suckers are bottom feeders while pickerel and walleye are omnivorous. Migratory birds such as geese, have $\delta^{15}N$ values that are higher than those of terrestrial animals, such levels being indicative of their diet, which is derived from both marine and terrestrial foods. Figure 4 is from data on mammals recovered from sites dated A.D. 800 to A.D. 1400 from the American southwest. Deer are more positive for nitrogen here than in Ontario. Dogs and humans have higher $\delta^{15}N$ values than the herbivorous mammals, deer, antelope, bison, cottontail, and jackrabbit.

A very interesting addition to the literature on the trophic level shift for nitrogen isotopes is a study by Tuross and co-workers (1989b, and in preparation) in which the fingernails of modern mothers and their infants were analyzed throughout the period of breast feeding and weaning. The nursing infants showed $\delta^{15}N$ values approximately 3‰ higher than their mothers'. Infant values fell to adult levels shortly after weaning. Similar results were obtained in a prehistoric group. Subsequently, others (Katzenberg and Saunders, submitted; Katzenberg 1991b; Katzenberg and Pfeiffer, in preparation) have found similar results in a prehistoric group from southern Ontario and two historic cemetery groups. In one case (1991b) bones of a mother and her infant (documented through historic records) had a $\delta^{15}N$ difference of 2.2‰. This appears to be a very promising area of research, since the determination of weaning age is crucial to understanding patterns of health and disease and

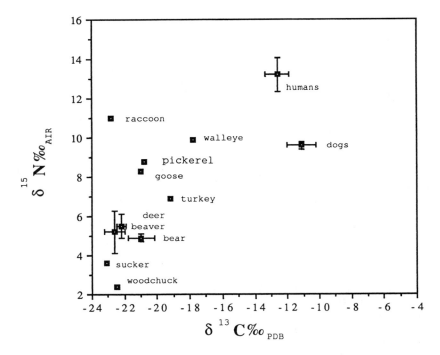

Fig. 3. $\delta^{13}C$ and $\delta^{15}N$ values plotted for faunal bone samples from the Kelly-Campbell site, a Seventeenth century Ontario Iroquois site. Human bone samples are from the neighboring ossuary at Ossossané. Reproduced from Katzenberg, (1989b), with permission of the publisher.

demography in prehistoric peoples (see Saunders, Skinner and Goodman, and Jackes, this volume, Chapters 1, 9, and 11).

Climatic Influence on Nitrogen Isotope Values

Not all variation in $\delta^{15}N$ values within a particular ecosystem can be attributed to trophic level differences. Heaton and co-workers (1986) have demonstrated a climatic influence on nitrogen isotope ratios in mammals, including humans, from southwestern Africa. $\delta^{15}N$ values are negatively correlated with annual rainfall. Ambrose and DeNiro (1987) responded to Heaton and colleagues' report by pointing out that metabolic factors, specifically urea output and urine concentration, in water-conserving mammals would cause the same pattern of results for $\delta^{15}N$ values in arid regions. In either case, nitrogen isotope data from animals in arid regions cannot be interpreted strictly as reflecting trophic level differ-

ences and climate is related to $\delta^{15}N$ values (Ambrose and DeNiro, 1989). In other studies from dry regions nitrogen isotope values for herbivorous mammals are unexpectedly high, based on a trophic level interpretation (Katzenberg and Kelley, 1991).

PROBLEMS AND NEW DIRECTIONS

Current research efforts are largely directed toward sorting out some of the problems with interpreting stable isotope data. These include the differential incorporation of carbon and nitrogen from specific dietary sources such as protein and carbohydrate; differential stable isotope values in specific amino acids, diagenesis, particularly with respect to carbon in apatite; and the composition of noncollagenous proteins. At the same time new applications are being developed, including the identification of migrants from areas with different diets, the extension of paleodiet studies using stable carbon isotopes to fossilized remains of bones and

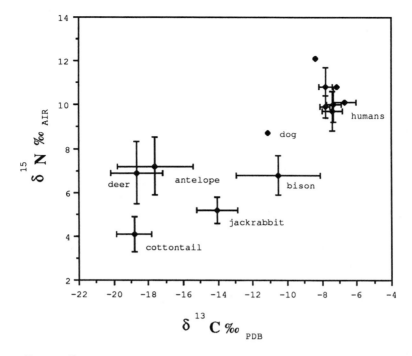

Fig. 4. $\delta^{13}C$ and $\delta^{15}N$ values plotted for human and faunal bone samples from sites in the Sierra Blanca region of New Mexico dating from A.D. 800 to A.D. 1400. Reproduced from Katzenberg and Kelley (1991), with permission of the publisher.

teeth, and the detection of weaning age. Also, stable isotopes of other elements, such as strontium, sulfur, hydrogen, and oxygen, are being used to address new questions.

Research into the biochemical incorporation of carbon and nitrogen from specific food sources into specific amino acids is centered on controlled feeding experiments with laboratory animals. Such studies, in which the proportion of C_3 and C_4 plants are varied in the feed, are currently under way but results are not yet available (Ambrose, personal communication). Recent work on reconstructing actual proportions of specific foods in the diet has shown that stable isotope values frequently contradict other archaeological evidence about diet. In her study of the people from Pecos Pueblo, Schoeninger (1989: 46) points out that the source of nitrogen from food is protein, whereas the source of carbon may be a combination of protein, carbohydrates, and lipids. Schoeninger uses weighting factors for nitrogen based on the amount of protein in

specific foods, and for carbon based on the amount of calories in the foods. By doing so she achieves results more in line with those from other sources of information on diet for the region and, at the same time, presents a model for use in other regions.

The analysis of specific amino acids has already been discussed. This line of research is important because it should be possible to trace specific foods that contribute specific amino acids to collagen (Hare et al., 1991). Some amino acids are formed from various products of metabolism, while others are directly incorporated into collagen molecules. Therefore it may be possible to detect food sources more specifically by using this approach. Stafford and co-workers provide (1991: 44–46) a detailed explanation of the chemical methods for isolating individual amino acids.

Problems associated with degradation of collagen and the isolation of collagen from noncollagenous protein have also been mentioned previously. Isolation of individual amino acids is one way around these problems, but is not a practical one for routine analyses, given the time and cost involved. The problem of diagenesis is not unique to stable isotope and trace element analyses. Research into the extraction of DNA from prehistoric bone (Rothschild, this volume, Chapter 8) and the preservation of histological structures (Stout, this volume, Chapter 2) also must take into account the changes that occur after death and burial. Thus there is a substantial emphasis on experimental studies that provide information on how, and under what circumstances, changes occur. Hopefully these will lead to the ability to predict which materials are altered, and to a knowledge of how to separate biogenic from diagenetic signals (see Sandford, this volume, Chapter 5).

The repeated findings of narrow ranges of variation for carbon and nitrogen isotope values of adults suggests that, within groups, individuals with values outside the main cluster of values did have different diets. In some regions there is evidence from the archaeological record of migration of peoples with different diets. An example is the prehistoric southwestern United States, where Spielmann (1983) has discussed interactions between Plains hunter–gatherers and Pueblo agriculturalists. Speth (1987) has suggested that Plains women were marrying Pueblo men and moving into the farming society. Katzenberg and Kelley (1991), in an analysis of stable isotope values in south-central New Mexico, found three individuals with unexpectedly low $\delta^{13}C$ values, suggesting a lower intake of maize. In a follow-up study (Smith et al., 1990) four individuals from one site were identified as outliers with isotope values indicating a lower intake of maize, as would be expected of Plains peoples. Unfortunately, owing to poor preservation of diagnostic features, sex could not be determined for any of the four individuals, thus the specific hypothesis put forward by Speth could not be tested. In another study that addressed the question of place of residence (Katzenberg, 1991a) U.S. soldiers from the War of 1812, discovered in Fort Erie, Ontario, were analyzed for stable isotopes of carbon and nitrogen and compared with native North Americans from the area (Schwarcz et al., 1985; $\delta^{13}C$ and $\delta^{15}N$)

and with British sailors (Kennedy, 1989; $\delta^{13}C$ only). The variation in values for the sample of 29 individuals is greater than that usually observed in archaeological samples. During this time U.S. soldiers could have been from various regions in the northeast and midwest, recent immigrants from Europe, or Native Americans. Indeed one individual was isotopically similar to the earlier Ontario Iroquois (less negative $\delta^{13}C$ value, indicating a greater consumption of maize), while another was similar to British sailors (more negative $\delta^{13}C$ value, indicating greater consumption of Old World cultigens such as wheat, barley and oats). Other lines of evidence also identified the latter individual as an outlier (Pfeiffer and Williamson, 1991). A more sensitive indicator of a move from one environment to another is stable isotopes of strontium. Ericson (1985) first presented the potential of strontium isotopes for this purpose and applied it to determining residence patterns in prehistory. Schwarcz and colleagues (1991) have applied oxygen isotope data to identifying place of residence in the Snake Hill sample. Katzenberg and Krouse (1989) have completed a preliminary study that demonstrates the potential for using isotope ratios from several elements, including carbon, nitrogen, and sulfur, for identifying place of residence. They collected hair samples from living individuals with known residence and found that although there is considerable overlap in isotope values for individual elements, a multi-element model distinguishes geographical regions.

Sealy and van der Merwe (1986) used stable carbon isotope data to test the hypothesis of seasonal migration of humans during the Holocene in the southwestern Cape, South Africa. Their results indicate that seasonal population movement did not occur, because coastal peoples reflected a coastal diet, and interior peoples reflected a terrestrial diet, contrary to expectations of intermediate $\delta^{13}C$ values, which would be expected with regular movement between the two regions.

One especially exciting prospect for stable isotope studies is the refinement of techniques for analyzing fossilized remains such as the Australopithecines. Van der Merwe (1991) has preliminary results on fossil tooth enamel from South African robust and gracile Australopithecines that appear promising. Lee-Thorpe and co-workers (1989) have analyzed carbonate in tooth enamel from two species of extinct baboons in South Africa and were able to distinguish C_3– from C_4–based diets.

From the earlier applications of stable carbon isotopes to charting the development of plant domestication in the New World to the present use of isotopes of a number of elements to address problems in the prehistory of *Homo sapiens* as well as earlier hominids, the potential for this line of research has developed considerably in a relatively short period of time.

The literature on this subject has become vast, especially since around 1987. This chapter has presented basic background information on the methods and their applications to reconstructing past human diet. The potential for detecting weaning age, residence patterns, and migration in combination with the ability to detect diet, dietary shifts, and intragroup differences results in a technique that, when used in conjunction with other sources of information, enables the peoples of the present to learn a great deal about the lives of peoples of the past.

REFERENCES

Ambrose SH (1987): Chemical and isotopic techniques of diet reconstruction in eastern North America. In Keegan, WF (ed): "Emergent Horticultural Economies of the Eastern Woodlands." Occasional Paper No. 7. Southern Illinois University; Center for Archaeological Investigations, pp 87–107.

Ambrose SH (1990): Preparation and characterization of bone and tooth collagen for isotopic analysis. J Archaeol Sci 17: 431–451.

Ambrose SH, DeNiro MJ (1986a): Reconstruction of African human diet using bone collagen carbon and nitrogen isotope ratios. Nature 319:321–324.

Ambrose SH, DeNiro MJ (1986b): The isotopic ecology of East African mammals. Oecologia 69:395–406.

Ambrose SH, DeNiro MJ (1987): Bone nitrogen isotope composition and climate. Nature 325:201.

Ambrose SH, DeNiro MJ (1989): Climate and habitat reconstruction using stable carbon and nitrogen isotope ratios of collagen in prehistoric herbivore teeth from Kenya. Quat Res 31:407–422.

Bauer HH, Christian GD, O'Reilly JE (1978): "Instrumental Analysis." Boston: Allyn and Bacon.

Bender MM (1968): Mass spectrometric studies of carbon 13 variation in corn and other grasses. Radiocarbon 10: 468–472.

Bender MM, Baerreis DA, Steventon AL (1981): Further light on carbon isotopes and Hopewell agriculture. Am Antiq 46:346–353.

Bornstein P, Piez KA (1964): A biochemical study of human skin collagen and the relation between intra- and intermolecular cross-linking. J Clin Invest 43:1813–1823.

Boutton TW, Klein PD, Lynott MJ, Price JE, Tieszen LL (1984): Stable carbon isotope ratios as indicators of prehistoric human diet. In Turnlund JR, Johnson PE (eds): "Stable Isotopes in Nutrition." ACS Symposium Series 258. Washington, DC: American Chemical Society, pp 191–204.

Buikstra JE, Autry W, Breitburg E, Eisenberg L, van der Merwe N (1988): Diet and health in the Nashville Basin: Human adaptation and maize agriculture in middle Tennessee. In Kennedy BV, LeMoine GM (eds): "Diet and Subsistence: Current Archaeological Perspectives." Proceedings of the Nineteenth Annual Chacmool Conference, University of Calgary Archaeological Association pp 243–259.

Bumsted MP (1984): "Human Variation: $\delta13C$ in Adult Bone Collagen and the Relation to Diet in an Isochronous C4 (Maize) Archaeological Population." Publication LA10259T Los Alamos, New Mexico: Los Alamos National Laboratory.

Chisholm BS (1989): Variation in diet reconstructions based on stable carbon isotopic evidence. In Price TD (ed): "The Chemistry of Prehistoric Human Bone." School of American Research Advanced Seminar Series. Cambridge: Cambridge University Press, pp 10–37.

Chisholm BS, Nelson DE, Schwarcz HP (1982): Stable carbon isotope ratios as a measure of marine versus terrestrial protein in ancient diets. Science 216:1131–1132.

Chisholm BS, Nelson DE, Hobson KA, Schwarcz HP (1983a): Carbon isotope measurement techniques for bone collagen: Notes for the archaeologist. J Archaeol Sci 10:355–360.

Chisholm BS, Nelson DE, Schwarcz HP (1983b): Marine and terrestrial protein in prehistoric diets on the British Columbia coast. Curr Anthropol 24:396–398.

Craig H (1953): The geochemistry of stable carbon isotopes. Geochim Cosmochim Acta 3:53–92.

Craig H (1954): Carbon-13 in plants and the relationship between carbon-13 and carbon-14 variations in nature. J Geol 62: 115–149.

Decker KW, Tieszen LL (1989): Isotopic reconstruction of Mesa Verde diet from Basketmaker III to Pueblo III. Kiva 55:33–47.

Deines P (1980): The isotopic composition of reduced organic carbon. In Fritz P, Fontes JC (eds): "Handbook of Environmental Isotope Geochemistry." Amsterdam: Elsevier, pp 329–406.

DeNiro MH (1985): Postmortem preservation and alteration of in vivo bone collagen isotope ratios in relation to palaeodietary reconstruction. Nature 317:806–809.

DeNiro MJ (1987): Stable isotopy and archaeology. Am Sci 75:182–191.

DeNiro MJ, Epstein S (1978): Influence of diet on the distribution of carbon isotopes in animals. Geochim Cosmochim Acta 42:495–506.

DeNiro MJ, Epstein S (1981): Influence of diet on the distribution of nitrogen isotopes in animals. Geochim Cosmochim Acta 45:341–351.

DeNiro MJ, Schoeninger MJ (1983): Stable carbon and nitrogen isotope ratios of bone collagen: variations within individuals, between sexes, and within populations raised on monotonous diets. J Archaeol Sci 10:199–203.

Ehleringer JR, Rundel PW (1989): Stable isotopes: History, units and instrumentation. In Rundel PW, Ehleringer JR, Nagy KA (eds): "Stable Isotopes in Ecological Research." New York: Springer-Verlag, pp.1–16.

Ericson JE (1985): Strontium isotope characterization in the study of prehistoric human ecology. J Hum Evol 14:503–514.

Ericson JE, West M, Sullivan CH, Krueger HW (1989): The development of maize agriculture in the Viru valley,

Peru. In Price TD (ed): "The Chemistry of Prehistoric Bone". Cambridge: Cambridge University Press, pp 68–105.

Fogel M (1990): Introduction to light isotope ratio mass spectrometry: The basics. Paper presented to the Sixth International Conference of the International Council for Archaeozoology, Washington, DC, May.

Hare PE, Estep M (1982): Carbon and nitrogen isotopic composition of amino acids in modern and fossil collagens. Carnegie Inst Washington Yearb, 82:410–414.

Hare PE, Fogel MF, Stafford TW, Mitchell AD, Hoering TC (1991): The isotopic composition of carbon and nitrogen in individual amino acids isolated from modern and fossil protein. J Archaeol Sci 18:277–292.

Hatch MD, Slack CR, Johnson HS (1967): Further studies on a new pathway of photosynthetic carbon dioxide fixation in sugar cane, and its occurrence in other species. Biochem J 102:417–422.

Heaton THE, Vogel JC, Chevallarie G, Collett G (1986): Climatic influence on the isotopic composition of bone nitrogen. Nature 322:822–823.

Hedges REM, Wallace CJA (1980): The survival of protein in bone. In Hare PE, Hoering TC, King K (eds): "Biogeochemistry of Amino Acids." New York: John Wiley and Sons, pp 35–41.

Hobson KA, Collier S (1984): Marine and terrestrial protein in Australian Aboriginal diets. Curr Anthropol 25:238–240.

Johansen OS, Gulliksen S, Nydal R (1986): δ13C and diet: Analysis of Norwegian human skeletons. Radiocarbon 28:754–761.

Katzenberg MA (1989a): Determination of diet and residence from stable isotopes. Am Anthropol Assoc, Abstracts of the 88th Annual Meeting, p 201.

Katzenberg MA (1989b): Stable isotope analysis of archaeological faunal remains from southern Ontario. J Archaeol Sci 16:319–329.

Katzenberg MA (1990): Stable isotope analysis of faunal bone and the reconstruction of human paleodiet. Unpublished Final Report submitted to the Social Sciences and Humanities Research Council of Canada, Ottawa.

Katzenberg MA (1991a): Analysis of stable isotopes of carbon and nitrogen. In Pfeiffer S, Williamson R (ed): "Snake Hill: An Investigation of a Military Cemetery from the War of 1812." Toronto: Dundurn Press, pp 247–255.

Katzenberg MA (1991b): Isotopic analysis. In Saunders SR, Lazenby R (eds): "The Links that Bind: The Harvie Family Nineteenth Century Burying Ground." Dundas: Copetown Press.

Katzenberg MA, Kelley JH (1991): Stable isotope analysis of prehistoric bone from the Sierra Blanca region of New Mexico. In Beckett PH (ed): "Mogollon V: Proceedings of the 1988 Mogollon Conference, Las Cruces, New Mexico." La Cruces, NM: COAS Publishing and Research, pp 207–219.

Katzenberg MA, Krouse HR (1989): Application of stable isotope variation in human tissues to problems in identification. Can Soc Forensic Sci 22:7–19

Katzenberg MA, Pfeiffer S (in preparation): Stable isotope analysis of the skeletal remains from Prospect Hill, a 19th century Methodist cemetery from Newmarket, Ontario.

Katzenberg MA, Saunders SR (submitted) Age differences in stable carbon and nitrogen isotope ratios in a population of prehistoric maize horticulturalists. Am J Phys Anthropol.

Keegan WF (1989) Stable isotope analysis of prehistoric diet. In İşcan MY, Kennedy KAR (eds): "Reconstruction of Life from the Skeleton." New York: Alan R. Liss, pp 223–236.

Keegan WF, DeNiro MJ (1988): Stable carbon- and nitrogen-isotope ratios of bone collagen used to study coral-reef and terrestrial components of prehistoric Bahamian diet. Am Antiq 53:320–336.

Kennedy BV (1989): Variation in δ13C values of post-medieval Europeans. Unpublished doctoral dissertation, University of Calgary, Department of Archaeology.

Lee-Thorpe JA (n.d.) Stable carbon isotopes in deep time. Unpublished doctoral dissertation, University of Cape Town, Department of Archaeology.

Lee-Thorpe JA, van der Merwe NJ (1987) Carbon isotope analysis of fossil bone apatite. S Afr J Sci 83:712–715.

Lee-Thorpe JA, van der Merwe NJ, Brain CK (1989): Isotopic evidence for dietary differences between two extinct baboon species from Swartkrans. J Hum Evol 18:183–190.

Longin R (1971): New method of collagen extraction for radiocarbon dating. Nature 230:241–242.

Lovell NC, Nelson DE, Schwarcz HP (1986a): Carbon isotope ratios in palaeodiet: Lack of age or sex effect. Archaeometry 28:51–55.

Lovell NC, Chisholm BS, Nelson DE, Schwarcz HP (1986b): Prehistoric salmon consumption in interior British Columbia. Can J Archaeol 10:99–106

Lynott MJ, Boutton TW, Price JE, Nelson DE (1986): Stable carbon isotopic evidence for maize agriculture in southeast Missouri and northeast Arkansas. Am Antiq 51:51–65.

Mariotti A (1983): Atmospheric nitrogen is a reliable standard for natural 15N abundance measurements. Nature 303:685–687.

Masters PM (1987): Preferential preservation of noncollagenous protein during bone diagenesis: Implications for chronometric and stable isotopic measurements. Geochim Cosmochim Acta 51:3209–3214.

Minagawa M, Wada E (1984): Stepwise enrichment of 15N along food chains: Further evidence and the relation between δ15N and animal age. Geochim Cosmochim Acta 48:1135–1140.

Murray ML, Schoeninger MJ (1988): Diet, status, and complex social structure in Iron Age Central Europe: some contributions from bone chemistry. In Gibson B, Geselowitz M (eds): "Tribe and Polity in Late Prehistoric Europe." New York: Plenum, pp 155–176.

Nelson BK, DeNiro MJ, Schoeninger MJ, DePaolo DJ, Hare PE (1986): Effects of diagenesis on strontium, carbon, nitrogen and oxygen concentration and isotopic composition of bone. Geochim Cosmochim Acta 50:1941–1949.

Pfeiffer S, Williamson R (1991): "Snake Hill: An Investigation of a Military Cemetery from the War of 1812." Toronto: Dundurn Press.

Price TD (ed) (1989): "The Chemistry of Prehistoric Bone." Cambridge: Cambridge University Press.

Schoeninger MJ (1985): Trophic level effects on 15N/14N and 13C/12C ratios in bone collagen and strontium levels in bone mineral. J Hum Evol 14:515–525.

Schoeninger MJ (1989): Reconstructing prehistoric human diet. In Price TD (ed): "The Chemistry of Prehistoric Human Bone." School of American Research Advanced Seminar Series. Cambridge: Cambridge University Press, pp 38–67.

Schoeninger MJ, DeNiro MJ (1982): Carbon isotope ratios of apatite from fossil bone cannot be used to reconstruct diets of animals. Nature 297:577–578.

Schoeninger MJ, DeNiro MJ (1984): Nitrogen and carbon isotopic composition of bone collagen from marine and terrestrial animals. Geochim Cosmochim Acta 48:625–639.

Schoeninger MJ, DeNiro MJ, Tauber H (1983): Stable nitrogen isotope ratios of bone collagen reflect marine and terrestrial components of prehistoric human diet. Science 220:1381–1383.

Schoeninger MJ, Moore KM, Murray ML, Kingston JD (1989): Detection of bone preservation in archaeological and fossil samples. Appl Geochem 4:281–292.

Schwarcz HP, Schoeninger MJ (in press): Stable isotope analyses in human nutritional ecology. Yearb Phys Anthropol 35.

Schwarcz HP, Melbye FJ, Katzenberg MA, Knyf M (1985): Stable isotopes in human skeletons of southern Ontario: reconstructing paleodiet. J Archaeol Sci 12:187–206.

Schwarcz HP, Gibbs L, Knyf M (1991): Oxygen isotopic analysis as an indicator of place of origin. In Pfeiffer S, Williamson R (eds): "Snake Hill: An Investigation of a Military Cemetery from the War of 1812". Toronto: Dundurn Press, pp 263–268.

Sealy J (1986): "Stable Carbon Isotopes and Prehistoric Diets in the South-Western Cape Province, South Africa". Cambridge Monographs in African Archaeology 15: BAR International Series 293.

Sealy JC, van der Merwe NJ (1986): Isotope assessment and the seasonal-mobility hypothesis in the southwestern Cape of South Africa. Curr Anthropol 27:135–150.

Sealy JC, van der Merwe NJ (1988): Social, spatial and chronological patterning in marine food use as determined by δ13C measurements of Holocene human skeletons from the south- western Cape, South Africa. World Archaeology 20:87–102.

Sealy JC, van der Merwe NJ, Thorp JA, Lanham JL (1987): Nitrogen isotopic ecology in southern Africa: Implications for environmental and dietary tracing. Geochim Cosmochim Acta 51:2707–2717.

Shearer G, Kohl DH (1989): Estimates of N2 fixation in ecosystems: The need for and basis of the 15N natural abundance method. In Rundel PW, Ehleringer JR, Nagy KA (eds): "Stable Isotopes in Ecological Research." New York: Springer-Verlag pp 342–374.

Smith BN, Epstein S (1971): Two categories of 13C/12C ratios for higher plants. Plant Physiol 47:380–384.

Smith J, Katzenberg MA, Kelley JH (1990): Identification of population differences through stable isotope analysis in the American Southwest (abstract). Newsl of the Can Assoc Phys Anthropol, Spring, p 26.

Sofer Z (1980): A simplified method for the preparation of CO2 for stable carbon isotope analysis of petroleum fractions. Analytical Chemistry 52:1389–1391.

Speth JD (1987): Some unexplored aspects of mutualistic Plains/Pueblo food exchange. Paper presented at the 1987 Conference on "Interaction: Plains and Pueblo Interaction." Fort Burgwin Research Center, Taos, New Mexico.

Spielmann KA (1983): Late prehistoric exchange between the southwest and southern plains. Plains Anthropol 28: 257–272.

Spielmann KA, Schoeninger MJ, Moore K (1990): Plains-Pueblo interdependence and human diet at Pecos Pueblo, New Mexico. Am Antiq 55:745–765.

Stafford TW, Hare PE, Currie L, Jull AJ T., Donahue DJ (1991): Accelerator radiocarbon dating at the molecular level. J Archaeol Sci 18:35–72.

Stothers DM, Bechtel SK (1987): Stable carbon isotope analysis: An inter-regional perspective. Archaeol Eastern N Am 15:137–154.

Stump RK, Fraser JW (1973): Simultaneous determination of carbon, hydrogen, and nitrogen in organic compounds. Nucl Sci Abstr 28:746.

Sullivan CH, Krueger HW (1981): Carbon isotope analysis of separate chemical phases in modern and fossil bone. Nature 292:333–335.

Sullivan CH, Krueger HW (1983): Carbon isotope ratios of bone apatite and animal diet reconstruction. Nature 301: 177–178.

Tauber H (1981): 13C evidence for dietary habits of prehistoric man in Denmark. Nature 292:332–333.

Teeri JA, Schoeller DA (1979): δ13C values of an herbivore and the ratio of C3 to C4 plant carbon in its diet. Oecologia 39:197–200.

Tieszen LL, Boutton TW, Tesdahl KG, Slade NA (1983): Fractionation and turnover of stable carbon isotopes in animal tissues: Implications for δ13C analysis of diet. Oecologia 57:32–37.

Tuross N, Behrensmeyer AK, Eanes ED, Fisher LW, Hare PE (1989a): Molecular preservation and crystallographic alterations in a weathering sequence of wildebeest bones. Appl Geochem 4:261–270.

Tuross N, Fogel ML, Owsley D (1989b): Tracing human lactation with stable nitrogen isotopes. 2: Studies with subfossil human skeletal tissue. American Anthropological Association Abstracts of the 88th Annual Meeting, pp 180–181.

van der Merwe NJ (1982): Carbon isotopes, photosynthesis, and archaeology. Am Sci 70:596–606.

van der Merwe NJ (1989): Natural variation in 13C concentration and its effect on environmental reconstruction using 13C/12C ratios in animal bones. In Price TD (ed): "The Chemistry of Prehistoric Human Bone." School of American Research Advanced Seminar Series. Cambridge: Cambridge University Press, pp 105–125.

van der Merwe NJ (1991): Carbon isotopes and the diets of early hominids (abstract). Newsl Can Assoc for Phys Anthropol 49.

van der Merwe NJ, Vogel JC (1978): 13C content of human collagen as a measure of prehistoric diet in Woodland North America. Nature 276:815–816.

van der Merwe NJ, Roosevelt AC, Vogel JC (1981): Isotopic evidence for prehistoric subsistence change at Parmana, Venezuela. Nature 292:526–538.

Vogel JC, van der Merwe NJ (1977): Isotopic evidence for early maize cultivation in New York State. Am Antiq 42: 238–242.

Walker PL, DeNiro MJ (1986): Stable nitrogen and carbon isotope ratios in bone collagen as indices of prehistoric dietary dependence on marine and terrestrial resources in southern California. Am J Phys Anthropol 71:51–61.

White CD, Schwarcz HP (1989): Ancient Maya diet: As inferred from isotopic and elemental analysis of human bone. J Archaeol Sci 16:451–474.

Wyckoff RWG (1980): Collagen in fossil bones. In Hare PE, Hoering TC, King K (eds): "Biogeochemistry of Amino Acids." New York: John Wiley and Sons, pp 17–22.3

Skeletal Biology of Past Peoples: Research Methods
pages 121–130 © 1992 Wiley-Liss, Inc.

Chapter 7

Innovative Approaches To The Study of Past Human Health and Subsistence Strategies

Linda L. Klepinger

Department of Anthropology, University of Illinois, Urbana, Illinois 61801

To dwell upon bone is to contemplate the fate of Man. Bone is the keepsake of the earth, all that remains of a man when everything else has long since crumbled away.

–Richard Selzer

INTRODUCTION

Whereas subsistence patterns, nutritional status and pathology of prehistoric groups have long been approached by artifact analysis, floral and faunal remains, and morphological traits of the skeleton, the decade of the 1970s brought the application of materials science to these same problems. The heady enthusiasm for the new methodologies was soon accompanied by a series of cautionary tales, which tempered some of the original assumptions and conclusions. Nevertheless, there is no doubt that chemical approaches to calcified tissues can offer additional valuable new routes for uncovering the dormant evidence of physiological variables in the past.

Paleodietary analysis is not simply an end in itself, but is also an avenue to inferring evolution and variation in subsistence strategies, adequacy of nutrition, and differential diagnosis of skeletal lesions. Conversely, the pathology of malnutrition may reveal previously unexpected dietary practices. For the most part, analyses of skeletal pathology have focused on nutritional status whereas analyses of bone chemistry have been directed at paleodiet, and for the most part these two types of studies have been separate. Although paleodiet and paleonutrition clearly are not identical (there are a variety of dietary paths to both good and imbalanced nutrition), there are just as clearly some areas of overlap.

It is not the intention of this chapter to review relevant studies of bone chemistry or paleopathology as dietary and nutritional indicators, since this has been done elsewhere (e.g., Price et al., 1985; Price, 1989a; Gilbert, 1985; Klepinger, 1984; Huss-Ashmore et al., 1982; Steinbock, 1976; Ortner and Putschar, 1981; Martin et al., 1985; Rose et al., 1985; Powell, 1985; Buikstra et al., 1989). Instead, it will focus on studies that have taken a somewhat different tack. These studies are distinguished by the comparative rarity of their approach. They are characterized by either or both of two features: combining morphological/pathological and chemical analyses, and focusing on an excess rather than a deficiency of a certain nutrient. Some complexities of diet–disease interaction will be explored. Finally, several hypotheses will be presented about the effects of a high meat diet on the skeleton, and ways will be suggested of inferring such a diet from analysis of bone—or, to take the Popperian twist, ways in which the hypotheses can by falsified.

POROTIC HYPEROSTOSIS AND IRON DEFICIENCY

Differential Diagnoses

It has long been suspected that porotic hyperostosis and cribra orbitalia result from anemia, and the morphological case for this etiology has been recently strengthened (Stuart-Macadam, 1987a, 1987b, 1989). Both conditions result from a reactive hyperplasia of the hemopoetic marrow and the osseous response to that hyperplasia. Orbital lesions represent the earliest skeletal signs and vault lesions characterize the more advanced cases (Stuart-Macadam, 1989). A number of hematological and circulatory disorders may result in porotic hyperostosis, and while they might be responsible for a few individual, sporadic occurrences, they cannot account for any significant population frequencies. Prevalences above about 1% must be due either to one of the hereditary hemolytic anemias or to iron deficiency anemia. Diagnostic choice between the two may be based on other skeletal indicators, but it is often aided by other factors such as geographic origin of the specimens. Of course, the two classes of anemia need not be mutually exclusive in those areas of the world where the hereditary anemias are frequent.

Iron deficiency anemia may result from dietary causes such as high intake of iron-poor foods and/or high intake of other dietary substances, such as phytate, that can decrease the bioavailability of iron. Iron deficiency anemia may also be the sequela of obvious or occult blood loss, which may result from parasitic infection or other diseases of the gastrointestinal tract. Although blood loss is by far the predominant cause of iron deficiency anemia in the modern developed countries, dietary factors may have played a more significant role in the past. Prehistoric cases of porotic hyperostosis in the New World generally have been attributed to iron deficiency anemia, but even in these cases, diagnoses were less than certain. Two studies have applied chemical analysis of bone to the etiology of specific cases of porotic hyperostosis/cribra orbitalia, but have done so in very different ways.

Fornaciari and coworkers (1981) noted that 54% of skulls recovered from a Punic tomb in Carthage (third century B.C.) showed some evidence of cribra orbitalia. Gross features of the cranial lesions and their distribution according to age and sex suggested that they were more likely to have been the result of iron deficiency anemia than of thalassemia major or minor or sickle cell anemia. To test this hypothesis they used atomic absorption spectroscopy to determine the bone iron levels in seven skulls with cribra orbitalia and five skulls without the lesion. Skulls with the lesions were significantly ($0.01 > p < 0.005$) lower in iron concentration than normal skulls. Since all skeletons were recovered from a single tomb filled with sandy soil in a very arid environment, they assumed that iron contamination from the soil was low and that what contamination there was would have affected all the bones equally. It is interesting to note that these soil conditions are quite similar to those described by Pate and Hutton (1988), in which one could expect low exchangeable iron concentrations; this may explain why apparent physiological differences were not overwhelmed by diagenetic contamination. The results of the iron analysis support the hypothesis that the cribra orbitalia was brought about by iron deficiency anemia, since the hemolytic anemia would have, if anything, increased the iron content of bone.

This study's apparently successful application of skeletal iron analysis to a pathology problem should not overshadow uncertainties that must be taken into account when interpreting the results of such an approach. The basic biological parameters of skeletal iron and their responsiveness to hematological disease have not been firmly established by clinical or controlled animal studies. Included in this list of unknowns are (1) what the normal range of iron concentration is in various skeletal sites, (2) what percentage of body iron stores are located in the skeleton, and (3) to what extent and how rapidly skeletal iron concentration reflects changes in body iron status. The uncertainties surrounding these biological parameters along with those resulting from diagenesis tend to overshadow the potential error inherent in any analytical technique. A variety of analytical techniques (e.g., atomic absorption, neutron activation, X-ray fluorescence, inductively coupled plasma emission spectroscopy—ICP) are applicable to iron (see Sandford, Chapter 6). The analytical method of choice usually depends on such factors as availability, cost, preparation time, and total number of elements to be analyzed.

Von Endt and Ortner (1982) took a different approach to detecting a potential effect of iron deficiency anemia in bone: an investigation of amino acid composition. Collagen makes up 85%–90% of the organic material in bone. The most common amino acid residue in collagen is glycine, which makes up about one third of collagen. Collagen differs from most other common proteins in that it contains significant amounts of hydroxyproline (8.9%) and hydroxylysine (0.5%) (Hare, 1980). These two amino acids have no genetic triplet code; instead they are formed from the precursors proline and lysine, after these parent amino acids have been inserted into the polypeptide chain. Since iron is a cofactor for enzymes catalyzing the hydroxylation of lysine and proline during collagen formation, Von Endt and Ortner reasoned that iron deficiency might be reflected in altered collagen synthesis. To investigate this possible relationship, they analyzed the amino acid content of a prehistoric child with severe porotic hyperostosis from Pueblo Bonito in the U.S. Southwest, along with bone from two children from the same pueblo who were morphologically normal and one modern child who also showed no bone pathology and had died accidentally. These results were compared with literature values for amino acid analyses of collagen, noncollagenous protein, and bone. The amino acid profile of the two unaffected prehistoric children agreed quite closely with that of the modern child, indicating that protein hydrolysis was minimal in the arid climate of the pueblo. The relative proportion of amino acids from the diseased child differed from the other three, showing a greater than expected proportion of collagen relative to noncollagenous proteins. Specifically, the diseased child had high levels of glycine and low levels of acidic and hydroxy amino acids compared with levels for the three unaffected children. Von Endt and Ortner interpreted the lower levels of hydroxy amino acids as compatible with the thesis that iron deficiency anemia is responsible for porotic hyperostosis in the U.S. Southwest.

While both of these creative approaches to differential diagnosis strongly implicated iron deficiency anemia as the agent responsible for the porotic hyperostosis/cribra orbitalia, neither was able to distinguish the cause of the anemia. Attempts to understand the origins of, and the interrelationships among diseases, can greatly improve our comprehension of past pathology.

Porotic Hyperostosis and Infectious Disease

The connection between porotic hyperostosis and skeletal evidence of infectious disease has received considerable attention (e.g., Lallo et al., 1977; Mensforth et al., 1978; Cohen and Armelagos, 1984). Although several investigators have noted such a relationship, the nature of that relationship varies considerably from one population to another, ranging from a strong positive to a strong negative correlation. The varying associations between porotic hyperostosis and skeletal inflammatory lesions probably reflect, at least in part, the complex interactions between iron levels and susceptibility to infectious disease. Weinberg's review (1974) has pointed out that since iron is essential for the growth of most microorganisms, hyperferremia and/or hypotransferrinemia predispose individuals to bacterial and fungal attack. When iron is absorbed from the small intestine, it immediately combines with transferrin, with which it is transported in the blood plasma. The iron is very loosely combined with the globulin molecule and consequently can be released to any of the tissue cells at any point in the body. Excess iron is stored mainly in the liver, where it combines with apoferritin to form ferritin. When the total quantity of iron is more than the apoferritin storage pool can accommodate, some of it is stored in an insoluble form in the body cells. At some point then, transferrin can become highly saturated and cannot accept any more iron from the mucosal cells. Therefore, highly saturated transferrin will facilitate a microorganism's acquisition of iron from the host and both frequency and severity of attack are increased. Normal, healthy hosts respond to pathogen invasion by lowering intestinal absorption of iron and sequestering increased amounts of plasma iron in their livers. But hyperferremic episodes in persons suffering from liver disease, hemolytic anemia, or excess dietary iron produce high levels of saturated

transferrin, rendering them especially susceptible to microorganismic attack.

On the basis of these considerations only,
one would expect individuals with porotic hyperostosis due to one of the hemolytic anemias
to be more susceptible than normal persons to
infection. On the other hand, as Stuart-Macadam (1988) has also noted, individuals with
porotic hyperostosis due to iron deficiency
anemia should be less susceptible to infection
than iron-replete peers. But in the latter case
there may be other considerations or conditions that would negate any protective effect.
For example, although children with kwashiorkor are usually hypoferremic, they also
suffer a deficiency of transferrin, which results
in high transferrin saturation (a condition favorable to pathogen extraction of host iron).
The consequence is a much higher rate of bacterial infection in children with kwashiorkor,
and administration of iron to hypotransferrine-
mic patients can lead to terminal exacerbation
of infection (Weinberg, 1974). Moreover, studies of rat pups, made iron-deficient by the feeding of iron-deficient diets to their dams
throughout gestation and lactation, demonstrated severe detrimental effects on the immune system produced by iron deficiency
(Lockwood and Sherman, 1988). If this same
situation holds true for humans, then maternal
iron status during pregnancy and lactation may
be at least as important to immunocompetence
of the offspring as the weaning diet itself.
Whether maternally induced neonatal iron deficiency results in porotic hyperostosis is unknown. However, in Lockwood and Sherman's
(1988) study the pups of iron-deficient dams
had significantly lower hemoglobin and hema-
tocrit levels than controls, a condition that is
likely to stimulate hyperplasia of hemopoetic
tissues. If it does, it might constitute an etiological factor that contributes to the high frequency of the cribra orbitalia in Mississippian
infants under 6 months old reported by Cook
(1984).

In any event, the intricate relationship between iron and disease susceptibility may offer
partial explanation for the seemingly paradox-
ical correlations between porotic hyperostosis
in the New World (generally regarded as due
to iron deficiency anemia) and skeletal evidence of infectious disease: sometimes a positive correlation, sometimes negative. Just as
cases of porotic hyperostosis resulting from
one of the hemolytic anemias (in the Old
World) should be associated with increased
frequencies of skeletal infectious lesions, so
should any cases stemming from maternal iron
deficiency during pregnancy and lactation and
cases in which iron deficiency is coupled with
protein calorie malnutrition. In contrast, cases
of porotic hyperostosis attributable to postweaning acquired iron deficiency anemia, un-
accompanied by other pertinent nutritional or
physiological disorders, should be coupled
with decreased frequencies of infectious lesions. Typically, skeletal lesions attributable to
infection are the result of chronic bacterial or
mycotic disease. Positive associations between
porotic hyperostosis and skeletal evidence of
chronic infectious disease have been attributed to the anemia of chronic infections (Lallo
et al., 1977). However, the anemia of chronic
infection would not result in porotic hyperostosis, because in this form of anemia the bone
marrow typically does not exhibit compensatory hyperplasia, but instead is usually normal
(Gale, 1983).

Iron deficiency anemia, when of dietary origin, is but one example of many nutritional
deficits that have been investigated in prehistoric populations. But there is also another im-
pediment to adequate and well-balanced diet.
The other side of the malnutrition coin is excess of one or more dietary components. Even
in the case of iron, excess can produce deleterious health effects (Weinberg, 1974). Although nutrient excess is widely regarded as a
problem of modern times consequent upon the
overindulgence in fatty fast food and commercial vitamin and mineral supplements, the
problem may also have existed from time to
time in the past.

NUTRITIONAL EXCESS
Hypervitaminosis

From a historical point of view evidence for
vitamin toxicity may be present at a startlingly
remote time. The earliest prehistoric case is a
Homo erectus skeleton from East Turkana
dated at approximately 1.6 million years ago
(Walker et al., 1982). The adult skeleton of a
presumed female showed a marked subperi-

osteal deposition of coarse woven bone on the diaphyseal appendicular bones. The most likely diagnosis was chronic hypervitaminosis A, presumably resulting from high dietary intake of carnivore liver. Differential diagnosis was based entirely on gross and microscopic pathology, which is probably the only reliable approach. Although high liver ingestion should also result in high body stores of iron, the highly mineralized nature of the bone probably precludes the usefulness of chemical analysis for additional evidence. This is regrettable since corroborative evidence of vitamin A poisoning in this case would have remarkable implications for *Homo erectus* subsistence strategies.

On the other hand, it was stable carbon isotope analysis of human bone from the Northwest Coast that led Lazenby and McCormack (1985) to hypothesize that an age-specific dietary specialization arose in response to hypervitaminosis D in children. They noted that carbon isotope values indicated that dependence on marine-based protein was significantly greater for adults than for children (Chisholm et al., 1983) in aboriginal groups known to be heavily dependent on salmon. Comparing the vitamin D content of salmon, literature values for toxic intake of vitamin D in children, and estimates of average daily salmon consumption, Lazenby and McCormack calculated that if children were eating half the amount of salmon as the average adult, visible signs and symptoms of vitamin D toxicity in children could have resulted. They argued that high salmon consumption had been recognized as a cause of the clinical symptoms in children and that, as a result, terrestrial resources came to play a more important role in the diets of children. They extended their hypothesis to suggest that pregnant and lactating women would have strongly reduced their consumption of salmon, since levels of vitamin D that were not toxic for the adult would have been toxic for the fetus. However, they were uncertain as to whether theoretical isotopic differences between males and females would be detectable.

High protein. Although the problems of protein-deficient diets have been emphasized in the anthropological literature, the possible deleterious effects of high-protein diets have received much less consideration. Speth (1987) and Speth and Speilmann, (1983) have proposed that seasonal protein overload may have been a problem for hunter–gatherers in a variety of climatic settings. More recently Noli and Avery (1988) and Speth (1989) have stressed the dire physiological consequences of protein poisoning and have concluded that prolonged protein intake cannot exceed 50% of daily caloric intake without rapid appearance of toxicity and, eventually, death. As these authors emphasize, diets with a higher protein contribution could have been sustained only on a relatively short-term, desperation basis. Altough such extremes of protein consumption are incompatible with long-term survival, lesser, but still high, percentages of protein intake can be sustained on a long-term basis. Traditional populations with high daily protein consumption include some foragers, pastoralists, coastal resource exploiters, and (highest of all) Eskimos (Speth, 1989; Noli and Avery, 1988; Lazenby and McCormack, 1985).

There is evidence that sustainable high-protein diets, while avoiding acute, frank toxicity, have more subtle metabolic costs. In 1974 Mazess and Mather proposed that a high meat, high protein diet might be an etiological factor in the high prevalence of osteoporosis among Eskimos. This suggestion is supported by animal experimentation in which high protein diet induced severe bone loss (Whiting and Draper, 1980). There is evidence that the osteoporosis problem among Eskimos has been long-standing, predating any of the confounding factors that result from acculturation (Thompson et al., 1983). Some of the pertinent studies relating protein consumption to premature bone loss in Eskimo and other groups and a critical appraisal of these studies can be found in Beall (1987). The question then arises of how to detect the effects of a high-meat (or high-seafood), high-protein diet in archaeological bone.

Richman and coworkers (1979) reported differences in intracortical bone remodeling among three aboriginal North American populations with different subsistence patterns. They noted differences in what they labeled type II osteon remodeling. This particular type of remodeling appears to be limited to the walls of Haversian canals in highly mineralized osteons and creates an osteon-within-an-osteon appearance (see Stout, Chapter 2). The frequency of type II structures was significantly higher among the Eskimo sample than among the Pueblo sample. The frequency among an Arikara sample fell between the other two, although it was not significantly different from either. Thus, the number of type II osteon structures increased with increased contribution of meat to the diet, and it was significantly different between the two extremes: Pueblo and Eskimo. The authors speculated that this effect was the result of an increased frequency with which bone mineral was mobilized to buffer the acidotic effect of the high-meat diet of Eskimos. Although type II osteons have been reported to be significantly associated with such diseases as cancer, senile osteoporosis, diabetes mellitus, heart disease, and immobilization (Stout, 1989), none of these etiological factors better explains the populational distribution found by Richman and coworkers, nor do they necessarily contradict the hypothesized acidotic cause in this case.

Chemical Correlates of High-Protein Diet

Stable nitrogen isotope ratios of bone collagen offer a view of protein consumption that is a logical first step in analysis (see Katzenberg, this volume, Chapter 6). All other variables being roughly equal, there is an enrichment of $\delta^{15}N$ values of about 3–4‰ for each step up the trophic level ladder from herbivore to omnivore to carnivore (Schoeninger, 1985; Schoeninger and DeNiro, 1984). Since increase in protein consumption tends to increase directly with trophic level, $\delta^{15}N$ values can provide an indication of high protein consumption. It should be noted, however, that other factors can cause significant variation in the nitrogen isotope values that may interfere with or obliterate trophic level signals; these have been reviewed in Ambrose (in press). While nitrogen isotope data can often supply good approximations of the level of meat consumption, one might explore whether there might be some further chemical methods for assessing the physiological effects of very high meat diets. In other words, might it be possible to also discover nutritionally detrimental effects of such diets?

It is known that prolonged consumption of a high meat diet results in chronic metabolic ac-

idosis that is due in large part to the sulfuric acid generated from the metabolism of sulfur-containing amino acids of protein. Decreased bone carbonate has long been recognized as a sequela to metabolic acidosis (Pellegrino and Farber, 1960, and references therein). Apparently this is the consequence of the mobilization of alkaline salts from bone to buffer the serum. Thus, decreased bone carbonate may, in appropriate circumstances, serve as a signal reflecting metabolic acidosis that is consequent upon high-protein diet. For a discussion of this relationship and an appraisal of the potential for carbonate analysis in archaeological bone see Klepinger (in press).

In addition to bone carbonate, there may be another potential clue to chronic metabolic acidosis, and that is bone sodium content. Pellegrino and Farber (1960) reported that both of two patients who were known to be acidotic for at least 3 months prior to death showed significantly depressed bone sodium levels compared with a 15-member control group. In five other patients who had acidosis of relatively shorter duration, bone sodium values were not significantly different from the mean of the controls. Since the bone samples were taken from the tibial cortex, which is metabolically less active than trabecular bone, it is not surprising that some period of time in acidosis was required for significant alteration in sodium values. Except for the two cases of chronic acidosis, the authors found no evident correlation between bone sodium and serum sodium levels. This, too, is not surprising, since serum sodium values need not reflect body stores of sodium; instead, they often reflect the state of body water.

The usefulness of bone sodium concentration in detecting periods of chronic metabolic acidosis in the past may be compromised, however, by diagenetic alteration. There is evidence that sodium has some tendency to leach from the skeleton (Parker et al., 1974; Lambert et al, 1985) but may occasionally be increased over time (Price, 1989b); indeed, the effect of diagenesis over time may be hard to predict (Klepinger et al., 1986).

However, there may be an analytical technique that would sidestep the tendency of hydroxyapatite to undergo diagenic change. In a preliminary study samples of cortex from six human cadaver long bones (five femora, one tibia) were taken for analysis. Each sample was crushed and divided into two. The first set of whole bone samples was digested in hot ($\sim$70°C) concentrated HCl, diluted and analyzed by atomic absorption spectroscopy for six elements: magnesium, copper, iron, potassium, sodium and calcium. Prior ashing of the whole bone samples was not part of the procedure; current evidence suggests that several elements including sodium and potassium are affected by ashing (Edward et al., 1990). In the second set collagen was extracted and gelatinized and similarly analyzed. (Since possible humic acid contamination was not an issue, no NaOH wash was used.) An apparent correlation between whole bone element concentration and collagen element concentration existed only for sodium. A linear regression model generated a coefficient of correlation of 0.81 and a coefficient of determination of 0.66. A quadratic model yielded a coefficient of correlation of 0.93 and a coefficient of determination of 0.86. Both models suggested a relationship between collagen concentration and whole bone concentration that was significant at the 0.05 level. But 0.05 is not a true measure of the probability of chance occurence of the relationship. In this study linear correlations were run for six elements (a modest example of data dredging). If each test were independent, the risk of finding a false-positive association due to random chance is $1-(.95)^6 = .26$ (Glantz, 1987). Since these association tests are probably not totally independent, the risk of a random significance error is probably somewhat lower. Nevertheless, a 20% chance of error is likely a minimal estimate. Under these circumstances such a study cannot be considered hypothesis testing; it can, however, be considered hypothesis generating. In other words, although it would be premature to declare that 86 percent of the variance in collagen sodium concentration is accounted for by variance in whole bone sodium concentration, a significant association between the two variables is a hypothesis to be tested in future research. If total bone sodium load can be predicted from the collagen sodium content in archaeological bone, then the uncertain effects of diagenetic change can be minimized. Although collagen alteration cannot be completely ignored, the effects of diagenesis seem to be less pernicious than for apatite. Judging from the conditions of the pilot experiment, a proportion of physiological sodium is tightly bound to the collagen and would be unlikely to easily leach out.

SOME DIRECTIONS FOR FUTURE RESEARCH

The fluctuating correlation between porotic hyperostosis and skeletal evidence of chronic infectious disease is salient to the inferences of paleopathology. Clearly the two conditions do not always represent the results of a positive synergism between malnutrition and infection. Depending on the accompanying circumstances, iron deficiency anemia may serve either as a protective factor or a risk factor for pathogen attack. The latter alternative should be operative if protein calorie malnutrition complicated the picture. The extent to which current analytical technology can help sort out possible risk factors and associations between porotic hyperostosis and infection is uncertain, but one approach might be useful when protein calorie malnutrition is suspected (e.g., Cassidy, 1984).

High frequencies of porotic hyperostosis in many Mississippian site children contrast with the healthier appearance of earlier foragers, and poor nutrition has been implicated as one of the dominant causes (Cohen and Armelagos, 1984). If, as many surmise, the Mississippian culture conformed to the pattern of many agrarian societies, then weanlings were fed a gruel prepared from the starchy staple of the diet. At the same time, the adult males may have been the first in the household to eat and have received the greatest portion of protein rich food such as meat, while the weanling received the least. This cultural practice would place the young child at risk for diet generated anemia. Not only is heme iron, the form in which bioavailability is independent of other dietary constituents, severely restricted, but those on low meat and low-vitamin C diets may be unable to increase iron absorption in response to iron deficiency (Finch, 1989).

In those groups in which kwashiorkor is suspected, stable carbon isotope analysis may provide supporting evidence. In Mississippian culture the starchy staple (maize) is isotopically distinct from the principal protein and iron source (game meat). Do bone collagen and carbonate from young Mississippian children and adult males reflect the hypothesized difference in diet? In other words, is bone carbon from the two- to five-year age group isotopically enriched in carbon-13 in comparison with of adult males? If so, then protein calorie malnutrition may have accompanied iron deficiency, rendering the children more, not less, susceptible to infection.

If, as some workers posit, seasonal protein and habitual high-protein diets were not negligibly rare, then testing that hypothesis in some situations may be feasible. The chronic metabolic acidosis generated by a high protein diet may have left its chemical imprint on the bone. Although any physiological cause of chronic metabolic acidosis would produce the same effect, only dietary factors would be responsible for widespread, as opposed to sporadic, occurrences. Depressed levels of bone sodium and carbonate, as well as elevated $\delta^{15}N$ values, may be expected to accompany a high protein diet. The feasibility of detecting seasonal shifts to high-protein diets is problematic. The slow rate of bone turnover, even the more rapid metabolic pace of trabecular compared with compact bone, suggests that seasonality effects would be subtle, especially if the periodic dietary stress were a matter of only a couple of months. Interpretation of chemical data could be equivocal. In groups intensively exploiting coastal resources, such as salmon, the dual perils of high protein and high vitamin D may have threatened health.

The diagenetic alteration of bone mineral is a potential pitfall in such investigation. Worse yet, sodium and carbonate enrichment may be coupled as the two ions substitute for calcium and phosphate, respectively (Sillen, 1989). Under such circumstances diagenetic enrichment could swamp the original biogenic signal and produce misleading false negatives. The problem of extraneous carbonate may be surmountable by pretreatment with acetic acid or use of solubility profiles (Lee Thorp and van der Merwe, 1987; Sillen, 1989). Although not yet demonstrated, the use of solubility profiles might be applicable to extraneous sodium as well. The postmortem loss of sodium (Parker

et al., 1974; Lambert et al., 1985) is not a negligible risk and would result in false-positives. This presents a thornier problem for apatite analysis, and the potential use of collagen analysis should be further investigated. Should that approach ultimately fail, recognition of sodium, and for that matter carbonate, loss becomes the predominant goal in order to identify material unsuitable for analysis. Parenthetically, it should be noted that if depressed bone sodium content is being used as an indicator of acidosis, it should be accompanied by lowered carbonate content. Lowered bone sodium values could also be a response to sodium deprivation (Denton, 1982), although sodium stress is not characteristic of individuals consuming a high-meat diet.

CONCLUSIONS

Clearly, chemical analyses of fossil and subfossil bones, in conjunction with more traditional morphological and archaeological analyses, can offer insights not only into paleodietary reconstruction, but also into a variety of pathological conditions arising wholly or in part from nutritional imbalances, even if the nutritional imbalances are not strictly dietary in origin (as may be frequently the case for iron deficiency anemia). But the new technologies are not in themselves guidebooks to the past; the degree of success or failure of the whole reconstructive endeavor ultimately rests on the anthropological interpretation of the data. "The data speak for themselves" with all the ambiguity of the Delphi oracle. The most perilous part of the work may be the search for a valid explanation of the quantitative data in archaeological context. Sadly, we cannot look up problem answers in the back of the book. If an assumption or conclusion is incorrect, the error may go unnoticed and be used as the foundation for further models or hypotheses. For instance, to what extent do overpopulated peasant societies in contemporary underdeveloped countries provide a valid model for nutrition and disease in prehistory? Although we cannot be certain of the answer, we can be cognizant of the question. The new methodologies are adding considerably to our data base, and a whole new set of variables must now be sifted. Some previous conceptions have been strengthened, others weakened. No scenario is beyond refinement or revision, and only to the extent that competing explanations have been eliminated or minimized can anthropologists claim to have made a given case. Of course, there could always be another explanation of which we are unaware.

REFERENCES

Ambrose SH (nd) Isotopic analysis: Methodological and interpretive considerations. In Sandford MK (ed): "Investigations of Ancient Human Tissue: Chemical Analyses in Paleoanthropology." New York: Gordon and Breach.

Beall CM (1987) Nutrition and variation in biological aging. In Johnston FE (ed): "Nutritional Anthropology." New York: Alan R. Liss, pp 197–221.

Buikstra JE, Frankenberg S, Lambert JB, Xue L (1989) Multiple elements: Multiple expectations. In Price TD (ed): "The Chemistry of Prehistoric Bone." Cambridge: Cambridge University Press, pp 155–210.

Cassidy CM (1984): Skeletal evidence for prehistoric subsistence adaptation in the central Ohio River Valley. In Cohen MN, Armelagos GJ (eds): "Paleopathology at the Origins of Agriculture." New York: Academic Press, pp 307–345.

Chisholm BS, Nelson DE, Schwarcz HP (1983) Marine and terrestrial protein in prehistoric diets on the British Columbia coast. Curr Anthropol 24:396–398.

Cohen MN, Armelagos GJ (eds) (1984): "Paleopathology at the Origins of Agriculture." New York: Academic Press.

Cook DC (1984): Subsistence and health in the Lower Illinois Valley: osteological evidence. In Cohen MN, Armelagos GJ (eds): "Paleopathology at the Origins of Agriculture." New York: Academic Press, pp 235–269.

Denton D (1982): "The Hunger for Salt." Berlin: Springer-Verlag.

Edward JB, Benfer RA, Morris JS (1990): The effects of dry ashing on the composition of human and animal bone. Biol Trace Elem Res 25:219–231.

Finch CA (1989): Regulation of iron exchange. In Halsted CH, Rucker RB (eds): "Nutrition and the Origins of Disease." New York: Academic Press, pp 57–67.

Fornaciari G, Mallegni F, Bertini D, Nuti V (1981): Cribra orbitalia and elemental bone iron in the Punics of Carthage. Ossa 8:63–77.

Gale RP (1983): Bone marrow failure. In Stein JH (ed): "Internal Medicine." Boston: Little, Brown, pp 1575–1584.

Gilbert RI (1985): Stress, paleonutrition, and trace elements. In Gilbert RI, Mielke JH (eds): "The Analysis of Prehistoric Diets." New York: Academic Press, pp 339–358.

Glantz SA (1987): "Primer of Biostatistics" (2nd ed). New York: McGraw-Hill.

Hare PE (1980): Organic geochemistry of bone and its relation to the survival of bone in the natural environment. In Behrensmeyer AK, Hill AP (eds): "Fossils in the Making." Chicago: University of Chicago Press, pp 208–219.

Huss-Ashmore R, Goodman AH, Armelagos GJ (1982): Nutritional inference from paleopathology. In Schiffer MB (ed): "Advances in Archaeological Method and Theory," Vol. 5. New York: Academic Press, pp 395–474.

Klepinger LL (1984): Nutritional assessment from bone. Annu Rev Anthropol 13:75–96.

Klepinger LL (nd): Culture, health and chemistry: A technological approach to discovery. In Sandford MK (ed): "Investigations of Ancient Human Tissue: Chemical Analyses in Paleoanthropology." New York: Gordon and Breach.

Klepinger LL, Kuhn JK, Williams WS (1986): An elemental analysis of archaeological bone from Sicily as a test of predictability of diagenetic change. Am J Phys Anthropol 70:325–331.

Lallo J, Armelagos GJ, Mensforth RP (1977): The role of diet, disease and physiology in the origin of porotic hyperostosis. Hum Biol 49:71–483.

Lambert JB, Simpson SV, Weiner SG, Buikstra JE (1985): Induced metal-ion exchange in excavated human bone. J Archaeol Sci 12:85–92.

Lazenby RA, McCormack P (1985): Salmon and malnutrition on the Northwest Coast. Curr Anthropol 26:379–384.

Lee Thorp J, van der Merwe NJ (1987): Carbon isotope analysis of fossil bone apatite. S Afr J Sci 83:712–715.

Lockwood JF, Sherman AR (1988): Spleen natural killer cells from iron-deficient rat pups manifest an altered ability to be stimulated by interferon. J Nutr 118:1558–1563.

Martin DL, Goodman AH, Armelagos GJ (1985): Skeletal pathologies as indicators of quality and quantity of diet. In Gilbert RI, Mielke JH (eds): "The Analysis of Prehistoric Diet." New York: Academic Press, pp 227–279.

Mazess RB, Mather W (1974): Bone mineral content of North Alaskan Eskimos. Am J Clin Nutr 27:916–925.

Mensforth RP, Lovejoy CO, Lallo JW, Armelagos GJ (1978): The role of constitutional factors, diet and infectious disease in the etiology of porotic hyperostosis and periosteal reactions in prehistoric infants and children. Med Anthropol 2:1–59.

Noli D, Avery G (1988): Protein poisoning and coastal subsistence. J Archaeol Sci 15:395–401.

Ortner DJ, Putschar WGJ (1981): "Identification of Pathological Conditions in Human Skeletal Remains." Washington, DC: Smithsonian Institution Press.

Parker RB, Toots H, Murphy JW (1974) Leaching of sodium from skeletal parts during fossilization. Geochim Cosmochim Acta 38:1317–1321.

Pate FD, Hutton JT (1988): The use of soil chemistry data to address post-mortem diagenesis in bone mineral. J Archaeol Sci 15:729–739.

Pellegrino ED, Farber SJ (1960): Mineral composition of human bone in various clinical disorders. J Clin Lab Med 56:520–536.

Powell ML (1985): The analysis of dental wear and caries for dietary reconstruction. In Gilbert RI, Mielke JH (eds): "The Analysis of Prehistoric Diets." New York: Academic Press, pp 307–338.

Price TD (ed) (1989a): "Chemistry of Prehistoric Bone." Cambridge: Cambridge University Press.

Price TD (1989b): Multi-element studies of diagenesis in prehistoric bone. In Price TD (ed): "The Chemistry of Prehistoric Bone." Cambridge: Cambridge University Press, pp 126–154.

Price TD, Schoeninger MJ, Armelagos GJ (1985): Bone chemistry and past behavior: An overview. J Hum Evol 14:419–447.

Richman EA, Ortner DJ, Schulter-Ellis FP (1979): Differences in intracortical bone remodeling in three aboriginal American populations: Possible dietary factors. Calcif Tissue Int 28:209–214.

Rose JC, Condon KW, Goodman AH (1985): Diet and dentition: Developmental disturbances. In Gilbert RI, Mielke JH (eds): "The Analysis of Prehistoric Diet." New York: Academic Press, pp 281–306.

Schoeninger MJ (1985): Trophic level effects on $^{15}N/^{14}N$ and $^{13}C/^{12}C$ ratios in bone collagen and strontium levels in bone mineral. J Hum Evol 14:515–525.

Schoeninger MJ, DeNiro MJ (1984): Nitrogen and carbon isotope composition of bone collagen from marine and terrestrial animals. Geochim Cosmochim Acta 48:625–639.

Sillen A (1989): Diagenesis of the inorganic phase of cortical bone. In Price TD (ed): "The Chemistry of Prehistoric Bone." Cambridge: Cambridge University Press, pp 211–229.

Speth JD (1987): Early hominid subsistence strategies in seasonal habitats. J Archaeol Sci 14:13–29.

Speth JD (1989): Early hominid hunting and scavenging: the role of meat as an energy source. J Hum Evol 18:329–343.

Speth JD, Spielmann KA (1983): Energy source, protein metabolism and hunter-gatherer subsistence strategies. J Anthropol Archaeol 2:1–31.

Steinbock RT (1976): "Paleopathological Diagnosis and Interpretation: Bone Diseases in Ancient Human Populations." Springfield, IL: Charles C Thomas.

Stout SD (1989): Histomorphometric analysis of human skeletal remains. In İşcan MY, Kennedy KAR (eds): "Reconstruction of Life from the Skeleton." New York: Alan R. Liss, pp 41–52.

Stuart-Macadam P (1987a): A radiographic study of porotic hyperostosis. Am J Phys Anthropol 74:511–520.

Stuart-Macadam P (1987b): Porotic hyperostosis: New evidence to support the anemia theory. Am J Phys Anthropol 74:521–526.

Stuart-Macadam P (1988): Nutrition and anaemia in past human populations. In Kennedy BV, LeMoine GM (eds): "Diet and Subsistence: Current Archaeological Perspectives." Calgary: University of Calgary Archaeological Association pp 284–287.

Stuart-Macadam P (1989): Porotic hyperostosis: Relationship between orbital and vault lesions. Am J Phys Anthropol 80:187–193.

Thompson DD, Posner AS, Laughlin WS, Blumenthal NC (1983): Comparison of bone apatite in osteoporotic and normal Eskimos. Calcif Tissue Int 35:392–393.

Von Endt DW, Ortner DJ (1982): Amino acid analysis of bone from a possible case of prehistoric iron deficiency anemia from the American Southwest. Am J Phys Anthropol 59:377–385.

Walker A, Zimmerman MR, Leakey REF (1982): A possible case of hypervitaminosis A in Homo erectus. Nature 296:248–250.

Weinberg ED (1974): Iron and susceptibility to infectious disease. Science 184:952–956.

Whiting SJ, Draper HH (1980): The role of sulfate in the calcuria of high protein diets in adult rats. J Nutr 110:212–222.

Skeletal Biology of Past Peoples: Research Methods
pages 131–151 © 1992 Wiley-Liss, Inc.

Chapter 8

Advances in Detecting Disease in Earlier Human Populations

Bruce M. Rothschild
The Arthritis Center of Northeast Ohio, Youngstown, Ohio 44512

THE TESTABLE HYPOTHESIS AND INHERENT ASSUMPTIONS

Paleopathology, the study of disease in prehistory, attempts not only to describe the appearance of alterations, but also to identify their cause. Such speculation may involve flights of fantasy, as the evidence that remains allows only a glimpse of the problem. Recalling the imagery of the blind men and the elephant, paleopathology examines residual evidence (often only the skeleton, rarely mummies) at one point in time (death). As death represents only one point in the natural history of disease, different criteria must be applied for diagnosis of prehistoric phenomena than those applied to the living patient, whose soft tissues are available for assessment and whose mind can provide a history of the disease events.

Paleopathologic research has at times led to intriguing diagnoses, which must be considered in the category of untested hypotheses. Although specimens have been examined and the most reasonable diagnoses suggested, rigorous testing of such hypotheses has been limited. Methodology has progressed to the point where such diagnostic perspectives can and probably should be tested. Several assumptions underlie this approach. Recognition of disease in antiquity relies on the following assumptions:

1. Diagenesis does not sufficiently alter the residual skeletal tissue to preclude meaningful assessment. Diagenesis includes factors in the burial environment, such as moisture, plant roots, and animal gnawing, which may produce artifactual changes (see Sandford, this volume, Chapter 5).

2. The disease has not changed sufficiently to preclude its recognition.

3. No other disease process existed that had a similar appearance but now no longer exists.

A major avenue for advancement of paleopathology lies in coordinated efforts to form testable hypotheses and then to identify valid techniques for testing them. If a testable hypothesis cannot be generated, perhaps the problem should be placed on hold or an interdisciplinary council formed for determining new technologies appropriate to its assessment. While isolated finds are occasionally of value, approaches that analyze paleopathological phenomena in a population context are essential (Ortner and Putschar, 1981; Paine, 1989; Rothschild and Woods, 1988). In addition, the biases inherent in the deposition or acquisition of the skeletal samples must be identified.

Testable hypotheses are the key. The relatively common occurrence of a subchondral erosion in the third metatarsal tarsal joint is an intriguing observation in skeletal collections. Unfortunately, no method has been identified to recognize this phenomenon in the living individual. Therefore it is extremely difficult to establish a cause. If skeletal material is to be analyzed in a diagnostic manner, it must be comparable with "clinical material." As clinicians rarely have the opportunity to examine diseases in defleshed skeletons, the "gold standard" for recognition of disease has not been fully established. Therefore a common ground is sought. The X-ray offers that common ground for diseases that cause recognizable radiographic changes. Herein a new concept is introduced: epidemiological radiology. Not only is the nature of a lesion and its radiological appearance important, the sample frequency and distribution is also critical to the analysis. Also, the sources for "clinical material" must be unbiased population samples if they are to be compared with anthropological populations (Medsger and Masi, 1989; Paine, 1989; Woods and Rothschild, 1988).

Ideally, the anthropological sample should be from the same population as the clinical sample. This approach acknowledges regional variation in disease manifestations as well as regional differences in diagnostic approach (Martio et al., 1980; Moran et al., 1987). Unfortunately, it is often not possible to accurately identify comparable biological populations. Therefore, radiological studies of many, relatively unbiased clinical samples are the best available standard for comparison (Rothschild and Woods, 1989; Rothschild et al., 1988). If comparisons are to be made with contemporary clinical "specimens," then the alignment of the skeletons being studied must be the same as that in the intact clinical "specimen." The effect of burial, maceration, and "retrieval" must be assessed to assure that none of these processes alter the radiological appearance. How representative are skeletons of the population? Is there evidence of postdepositional disturbance, postdepositional decay (e.g., loss of certain bones owing to soil conditions), incomplete excavation (sampling artifact), spatial variability (sample bias), differential burial (excluding or overrepresenting certain classes (e.g., infants), excavation and postexcavation loss (Boddington, 1987; see Saunders, this volume, Chapter 1). Comparison of clinical intact "specimens" with macerated bones from individuals with clearly documented disease is an essential step in this process.

Common sense is an important tool in assessment of paleopathology. The issue of ochronosis in Egyptian mummies is an excellent example. Black pigmentation of intervertebral disks

in many Egyptian mummies (Stenn et al., 1977) raised the question of whether ochronosis was present. X-rays of the mummies revealed apparent disk calcification. Infrared examination of the material showed a spectrum that appeared to match that of homogentisic acid, the accumulation product in ochronosis (Stenn et al., 1977). The proof seemed solidly established. However, 50% of mummies manifested this alteration. Since ochronosis is an autosomal recessive disease, its population frequency could not be expected to exceed 25% (Stanbury et al., 1983). Therefore a reexamination of the evidence was required. Use of computed axial tomography (CAT scanning) techniques revealed that the apparent disk calcification was actually an artifact of overlapping shadows (Wallgren et al., 1986). The source of the shadows was shown to be nodules of a calcium salt, and review of Egyptian burial procedures revealed the presence of Nubian sand. Evaluation of this sand showed its concretions to be the source of the shadows. The mystery of the black pigment was solved when the embalming technique was further explored and found to be the source of the black pigment. Nuclear magnetic resonance spectroscopic examination of disk material (embalmed by Egyptian technique) demonstrated that the Egyptian disk material had a different spectral pattern from that of homogentisic acid (Wallgren et al., 1986). While scientific method was used in the first assessment, it was common sense that led to recognition of the limitations of the technique orginally applied.

The optimal technique for examination of specimens would be nondestructive, easily accessible, and amenable to interpretation. Collaborative investigations by specialists in structure–function relationships (e.g., anthropologists/paleontologists) and specialists in disease (e.g., health care providers) need to be encouraged. Sigerist (1951) suggested such an approach to disease with cooperation among physicians, veterinarians, botanists, geographers, meteorologists, agronomists, entomologists, and geologists. Understanding of the vocabulary pertinent to each discipline and an emphasis on the development of testable hypotheses would allow significant progress. "Pattern recognition" (the pattern of findings suggestive of a specific diagnosis) may yield hypothetical diagnoses. More commonly a hypothesis will represent a best guess at the disease in paleopathological cases.

ARTIFACTS

Tissue (e.g., bone) preservation after death is affected by the removal of proteins and minerals, substitution, infiltration, and adsorption of ions (Henderson, 1987). The assumption is made that the tissue of interest and its anatomic relationships are preserved or replaced in a representative manner. An important premise is that the matrix of the tissue of interest is preserved, such that the features that are inherent in the tissue are retained. The assumptions of biochemical or immunological integrity of the preserved tissue, however, require substantiation (Blakely, 1989).

Confounding factors must also be considered. Strontium calcium ratios have been of interest in dietary meat intake analysis (Brown, 1973; Sillen, 1981). Although diagenesis and disease may affect ratios (Sillen, 1981; Sillen and Kavanagh, 1982; Price et al., 1985), so too may pregnancy and lactation (Blakely, 1989; Kostial et al., 1969; see Sandford, this volume, Chapter 5).

Major factors that affect diagenesis are water, soil, temperature, and air (Goffer, 1980; Klinkhammer and Lambert, 1989; Weigelt, 1927). While preservation of inorganic matrix is better in neutral or slightly alkaline soil, salts also compromise bone preservation (Henderson, 1987). Soil pressure (Henderson, 1987) may also induce significant modification of shape (warping). For example, Wells (1967) noted misdiagnoses of rickets because of postmortem distortion of long bones. Silt in long bones can even produce a radiopaque pattern of lines perpendicular to the diaphysis, mimicking growth arrest lines (Wells, 1967).

Not only are chemical reaction (decomposition) rates doubled for each temperature rise of 10 degrees centigrade (Henderson, 1987; Ortner et al., 1972; von Endt and Ortner, 1984), but burrowing and scavenging animals become more active as temperature rises. Exposure to oxygen (e.g., from burial in porous soils) accelerates decomposition (Rentoul and Smith, 1973). Similarly, the more porous the bone, the more susceptible it is to destruction

Fig. 1. Carapace of *Protostega* RMM 2249. Conical depressions identify sites of mosasaur bite.

(Boddington et al., 1987). Collagen matrix degradation further accelerates diagenesis by increasing the surface area for deposition and providing voids for precipitation (Pate and Hutton, 1989).

Plant roots, bacteria, fungi, protozoans, insects, snails, and mammals may mimic pathology. They often produce focal destructive lesions (Ascenzi and Silvestrini, 1984; Ascenzi, 1963; Garland, 1987; Hackett, 1981; Henderson, 1987; Wells, 1967) and allow leaching of elements from the bone or deposition of elements from the burial environment (Grupe and Herrmann, 1988). Animal activities that alter bone include breakage, destruction and disturbance. Punctures (Fig. 1) are discernible as circular, or elongated depressions surrounded by adherent jagged-edged cortical fragments typically oriented perpendicular to the bone surface and the center of the defect (Milner and Smith, 1989; Rothschild, 1991). Linear U-shaped bands of crushed cortex or short, broad grooves result if only "skidding" and not tooth penetration occur. Hand and foot involvement is notably absent from the osseous record, probably secondary to complete scavenger-related destruction or dispersal (Milner and Smith, 1989). Cranial lesions caused by beetles have been misdiagnosed as syphilis (Henderson, 1987). Peri- or postmortem environmental interactions may themselves be of interest. Cut marks on bone may reveal pertinent "interactions" with humans (Sledzik, 1989). While the latter is often clarified by scanning electron microscope (SEM) examination, this is often not possible because of the "preservative cover" (Russell and LeMort, 1986). Sandpaper "striae" or the use of sharp metal tools in specimen processing (from restoration or molding techniques) may artifactually induce cut marks (White and Toth, 1989).

Staining artifacts may compromise analysis of both contemporary stored specimens and those from antiquity. Formalin is stained by silver impregnation techniques, precipitating as distinctive rod-like structures resembling bacteria. Calcific deposits become stained by the glycogen- and fungi-identifying periodic acid–Schiff (PAS) stain (Gorelkin and Chandler, 1988).

MICROSCOPIC TECHNIQUES

Persistence of histological structure over geological time has long been recognized (Ascenzi, 1963; Pander, 1856; Schaffer, 1889; Williamson, 1849). Cyanobacteria are recognizable histologically in sediment 3.3 billion years old (Schopf and Packer, 1987). Romer (1964) described bone structure in 300-million-year-old Devonian fish as did Broili (1922) and Dollo (1887) for dinosaurs. Subcellular details were visible in 40-million-year-old amber-enclosed insects (Paabo et al., 1989; Poinar and Hess, 1982) Randall et al. (1952) extracted collagen from an *Elephas primigenius* tusk dated at 10,000–15,000 years found frozen in Siberia. X-ray diffraction (measuring the path alteration of the X-ray photon, as it passes through the test substance) revealed that periodic (identical repeating amino acid groupings) structures had been preserved (Rowley and Rich, 1986), but preservation may be quite variable. Oakley (1955) isolated collagen fibrils from an Upper Pleistocene rhinoceros, but they were in a poor state of repair, electron microscopy revealing no visible periodic structure.

The nature of normal histological structure, and its modification by underlying disease states, are major factors in its preservation. Putschar (1966) suggested that some disorders (e.g., fibrous dysplasia and osteoblastic metastases) are associated with very "frail" trabeculations, making them "probably often not sturdy enough to survive long burial." Such fragile trabeculae appear to be responsible for the disproportionate survival of severe spondyloarthropathy lesions compared with those of rheumatoid arthritis (Rothschild et al., 1988; Woods and Rothschild, 1988). Spondyloarthropathy is a type of erosive arthritis that affects fewer joints than rheumatoid but is associated with new bone formation and a tendency to affect the spine and sacroiliac joints.

Routine microscopy and use of polarizing optics allow recognition of normal structure and its disruption. Normal light is composed of waves oriented in all directions. Polarizing optics filter normal light, allowing passage of only those component waves that are parallel to the grid of the polarizer. Use of a second polarizer, at right angles to the first, will therefore block all light transmission, since none is parallel to the second grid. Any object placed between the two polarizers will not be visible, unless it can bend the light from the first polarizer sufficiently so that it becomes parallel to the grid of the second. Production of thin sections allows recognition with transmitted light. Ground specimens of undecalcified material embedded in plastic or resin have been the standard approach (Putschar (1966). Specimens are sectioned and (following one protocol) are polished with #600 grit paper and then polished with graded (1.0–0.3 μm) alumina powders on standard metallographic polishing wheels, using aqueous lubrications (Swedlow et al., 1975). Etching with 0.01 N HCl for 15–25 min enhances surface visualization of lamellar patterns.

Tetracycline-induced fluorescence is a standard clinical technique for assessment of bone growth rate. Fluorescent patterns in bone (apparently due to tetracycline labeling in antiquity) may well relate to consumption of tetracycline in life, although metabolites from soil microorganisms (e.g., *Strachybotrys*) can produce similar patterns (Cook et al., 1989). Ingestion during life suggests exposure to stored grain contaminated with *Streptomycetes*, the bacteria from which the antibacterial agent was first obtained.

If one wishes to minimize damage to the specimen, an alternative approach is epi-illumination. Whereas routine transmitted light microscopy requires an ultrathin specimen, in epi-illumination only a surface of the specimen is required for imaging; hence minimal processing is necessary and the specimen can be relatively preserved.

Specimens can of course be examined by transmission electron microscopy, which requires preparation of ultrathin slices, or by scanning electron microscopy, which examines surface phenomena. Scanning electron microscopes are currently available that will accept specimens as large as coffee cups, allowing relatively nondestructive analysis. As osseous structures are fairly nonconductive, charging artifact may be a problem. Scanning electron microscopy, even on fresh bone, is often associated with severe electrostatic charging. This build-up of electrons (from the electron microscope) results in loss of image resolution. This is partially controlled in contemporary skeletal material by soaking the specimen in commercial antistatic agents and reducing the electron microscope beam current or voltage (Whitehouse and Dyson, 1974). Vacuum-coating with carbon and gold or palladium to 20-nm thickness is usually required. However, the coating does not always penetrate into all areas of the specimen, leaving exaggerated contrast between coated and uncoated parts. Furthermore, it is impossible to remove the coating. Carbon cannot be removed without damaging the finer bony structures. Vacuum-generating time (electron microscopy requires that the specimen be placed in a chamber from which the air is extracted, to create a vacuum) is also prolonged by porous specimens. Specimen dehydration with alcohol and storage over phosphorus pentoxide in a vacuum is thus required, to avoid long delays in initiating the electron microscope study.

The SEM also makes available X-ray diffraction (electron probe) techniques, which allow identification of contained elements and their relative concentrations. Small localized sites can be assessed, and it is possible to identify cystic structures (holes) that are invisible from the exterior of the bone.

While grinding and peels have long been part of analysis, it is now possible to digitize (represent as a numerical value at a precise site in three dimensions) the information and have it regenerated from any angle with any portion of it "dissected away" to leave the area of interest. A three-dimensional image can be generated of the structure of interest.

MOLECULAR TECHNIQUES

The ability of "biological molecules" to survive geological time allows intriguing molecular approaches. Bone collagen has been detected in 200-million-year-old dinosaur bones (Wyckoff, 1980), Pleistocene avian and mammalian fossils (Randall et al., 1952; Rowley and Rich, 1986), and 1.8-million-year-old hominids (Lowenstein, 1980, 1981). Collagen extracted from a 15,000-year-old *Elephas primigenius* tusk even retained its periodic helical structure (by X-ray diffraction), and sensitivity to collagenase and to heat denaturation (Randall et al., 1952; Rowley and Rich, 1986). Weser et al. (1989) even report extraction of an "enzymatically active component" of a superoxide dismutase from a 3,000-year-old mummy.

While preservation may be surprisingly good—as documented by the homology of 360-million-year-old fossil shell proteins with those of contemporary mollusks (Abelson, 1954)—Weiner et al. (1979) found dramatic change in the character of the protein (fossil shell was almost completely soluble, whereas shell protein from extant mollusca was more than 90% insoluble). They did not observe any relationship between amino acid composition of the fossil and that of contemporary shell proteins, suggesting that the amino acid composition of this fossil is probably an artifact related to diagenesis.

The study of changes in albumin structure provides an excellent tool for phylogenetic analysis of fossils (Ibrahimi et al., 1979). Albumin is resistant to denaturation (Nakanishi et al., 1969; Peters, 1975; Sensabaugh et al., 1971), is present in high concentration (Peters, 1975; Nakanishi et al., 1969), and has been defined structurally in 2,000 living species (Sarich, 1977; Wilson et al., 1977). The amount of albumin extracted from mammoth muscle was approximately 50 times less than that found on extraction from extant elephants, and only 20% of this retained its original charge, size, and antigenicity (Prager et al., 1980). Prager et al. (1980) suggest that postmortem albumin modification is responsible for the major differences in amino acid composition. These caveats considered, the survival of proteins in ancient bone allows for application of immu-

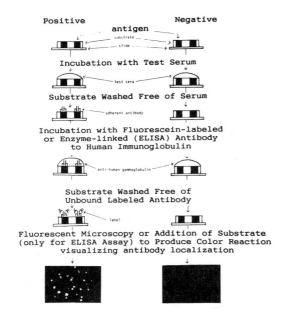

Fig. 2. Illustration of fluorescence and ELISA assay techniques.

nological techniques in assessment of phylogenetic relationships and confirmation of disease processes.

IMMUNOLOGICAL TECHNIQUES

Antigens present in tissues can be recognized by use of specific antibodies. If the appropriate site in the tissue has been chosen for analysis, if the antigen is still present, and if the appropriate antisera are applied, fixation of the antibody to the specimen can be detected. One technique frequently used in contemporary specimens links an enzyme to the antibody of interest (Fig. 2). The chosen enzyme metabolizes a colorless material to a form recognized because of the deposition of a colored product. This enzyme-linked immunologic saturation assay (ELISA) is not applicable to most anthropological/paleopathological applications because bone and bone powder extracts have significant background color in the 400- to 500-nm wavelength range, which ELISA requires for visibility (Ascenzi et al., 1985). The use of a fluorescent label is the premise of the immunofluorescence technique (Collins, 1986). Incident light filtered to 450–490 nm

causes acridine orange molecules (which bind to bacterial nucleic acid) to fluoresce (Yeh et al., 1987). Other histological techniques are available for labeling antisera, enabling documentation of a reaction with antigen at the "test site." The choice of the technique is somewhat determined by the background "coloration" or fluorescence of the specimen. One chooses a technique with minimal background interference. Of course, adequate controls must be run to rule out artifacts and to verify that the antisera will detect the antigen when it is present.

Blood group typing of bone and ancient tissues has been of long-standing interest in anthropology (Abelson, 1954; Alciati and Bosman, 1978; Allison et al., 1976, 1978; Barraco, 1978; Berg et al., 1975; Boyd and Boyd, 1939; Candela, 1936, 1940; Ezra-Cohn and Cook, 1961; Gray, 1958; Tarli, 1979; Thieme et al., 1956). In one example, blood group typing was applied by Llopp and Rothhammer (1988) to 5,000-year-old mummies from northern Chile. Unfortunately, cross-reactivity of blood group antigens with bacterial liposaccharides and susceptibility to enzymatic degradation compromise ABO blood group analysis in paleopathology (Lengyel, 1975; Mandrell et al., 1988; Springer et al., 1961). A and B blood types are transformed to O and O to the null determinant state (Llopp and Rothhammer, 1988). Since plant and microbial antigen contaminants cross-react or bind to blood group determinants (Mandrell et al., 1988), the ABO system is probably not appropriate to pursue in archaeological specimens.

Prager and colleagues (1980) used an immunological approach to analyze the relationship of extinct Pleistocene mammoth to extant elephants. Antibody to mammoth muscle albumin "reacted strongly" with muscle albumin from extant elephants but only weakly with that from a sea cow. The immunological test revealed shared antigens, but also evidence of variation. Near, but not absolute, identity was found. In another study, rabbit-derived, anti-chicken collagen antibodies showed reactivity with emu or rhea of 70%–80% of that with chicken, compared with 50% reactivity with mammalian collagen (Rowley and Rich, 1986). The oldest material (mid-Miocene) gave a "weak but definite signal."

Ascenzi et al. (1985) attempted to identify the presence of an inherited defect of hemoglobin production called thalassemia in the bones of ancient Romans. The amount of hemoglobin detected was only 1/10 of what is usually detectable in modern samples and the immunological technique (immunodiffusion) they chose for analysis was found to be insensitive.

The potential identification of the disease *Blastomycosis* from a case of osteomyelitis in Ohio (Paul Scuilly, personal communication) exemplifies the diversity of quality controls that must be built into immunological analyses. Although blastomycetes are certainly likely offending organisms, they are also common in the soil in this area of the country. To prove their role in the etiology of the bone infection, one would have to show their presence only in the affected area of bone and their absence in unaffected bones and in unaffected individuals from the same geographic region.

In another example, an attempt was made to distinguish brucellosis and/or tuberculosis in Native Americans, based on the suggestion that ingestion of infected bison may have been the source (Jakubowski et al., 1988). Certain Plains animals had a form of erosive joint disease compatible with such diagnoses, and the lesions are characteristic of granulomatous disease of the tubercular or brucellosis variety. If the organism could be identified in the lesion, then the hypothesis would be strongly supported, or perhaps proven. But if an immunological technique is to be utilized to identify the organism, the specificity of that reaction must be established. While tuberculosis or brucellosis are not generally considered soil organisms, nonpathogenic mycobacteria (tuberculosis is caused by mycobacteria) are found in the soil. Confidence in specificity of antisera for *Mycobacterium tuberculosis* or *Mycobacterium bovis* would be established only if the antisera were documented not to react with these nonpathogenic varieties of mycobacteria.

Immunological tests for mycobacterial infections have been compromised by the antigenic cross-reactivity among the mycobacteria and other organisms, including *Coccidiomycosis* (Daniel and Debanne, 1987; Fifis et al., 1989; Humphrey and Weiner, 1987; Oftung et al., 1987; Papa et al., 1988). Antibodies to myco-

bacteria even cross-react with DNA (Shoenfeld et al., 1986). While Raja et al. (1988), utilizing a specific *M. tuberculosis* antigen, found somewhat increased sensitivity in contemporary humans, as did Chand et al. (1988), using *Brucellosis* antigens, the antisera are not sufficiently specific and the diagnosis in Pleistocene plains animals must remain conjecture.

Establishment of specificity of any antisera applied in the study of paleopathology is essential. Monoclonal antibodies are not the answer, as they are not necessarily monospecific in their reactivity (Dardenne et al., 1987). Srinivasappa et al. (1986) noted cross-reactivity of monoclonal antiviral antibodies with normal mouse pituitary, heart, stomach, salivary duct, and testes. Polyclonal antibodies of assured specificity are quite acceptable. Polycolonal antisera to Rotavirus identified five times more viral particles (in contemporary specimens) than monoclonal antibodies and 10% additional viral strains (Gerna et al., 1989). As polyclonal antibodies have multiple target reactivity sites, they are more likely to be effective in paleopathology since they are less dependent upon the survival of a single antigen.

The antiquity of treponemal disease has now been addressed by identification of the antigen in the prehistoric record. Suspicion that the gummatous lesions and peculiar spiculated periosteal reaction in *Arctodus simus* (Pleistocene bear) were related to treponemal disease was confirmed on examination of sections of involved vertebrae (Rothschild and Turnbull, 1987). Direct immunofluorescent examination, using antisyphilis, *Treponeme phagedenis*-absorbed antisera, revealed focal clumps of treponemal antigen in the margins of the vertebral erosion. Examination of unaffected bony surfaces and use of antibodies with other specificities confirmed the specificity of the reaction. Thus the oldest example of treponemal disease (11,500 years before the present) was verified in what is now called Indiana.

DNA Techniques

The genetic code is present in a reproducible form apparently from the origins of life (Eigen et al., 1989). The human genome is composed of 100,000 genes (exons or coding regions), comprising 3%–5% of 1 billion base pairs (Bishop, 1974; O'Brien, 1973). A given gene may be 2 million base pairs long. The intervening sequences are referred to as introns. Preservation of DNA has been documented in an aqueous environment, as well as the arid environments of mummification (Doran et al., 1986). Survival of DNA allows potential application of other molecular biology techniques.

This has major applications for the study of paleopathology. If the techniques can be further validated, it might be possible to identify particular bacteria or even inherited diseases from the past. Although Paabo and colleagues (1989) detected both nuclear and mitochondrial DNA in an Egyptian mummy, they point out that less than 1% of DNA in museum or archaeological specimens is undamaged. Mitochondrial DNA is a valuable tool because of the constancy of its coding sequence, with gene order differing only among major taxonomic groups (Vawter and Brown, 1986). Vertebrate mitochondrial DNA evolves 5 to 10 times faster than nuclear DNA.

The first step in analyzing DNA is extraction from the ancient or contemporary specimen. Ability to isolate DNA is actually quite variable. While Rowley and Rich (1986) were unable to extract any detectable DNA from 1 g of bird and mammal bone samples (rich in identifiable collagen); Higuchi et al. (1984) extracted 5 µg of DNA per gram of dried muscle from an ancient horse (which became extinct in 1883). Isolation from antiquity was approximately 1% of that extracted from fresh muscle. Curiously, DNA has been recovered from a 40,000-year-old frozen Siberian mammoth (Higuchi and Wilson, 1984) and apparently from 25-million-year-old amber-preserved insects (Poinar and Hess, 1982). Salvo et al. (1989) identified and cloned DNA from 500- to 8,000-year-old pre-Columbian mummies. Individuals 700 (Maitas) and 500 (Camarones) years before present had recoverable high-molecular-weight DNA (>12,000 base pairs) of both genomic and mitochondral origin. However, yields were low and the DNA had to be "repaired" to allow replication.

One technique involves proteinase K and detergent "tissue" treatment (Robbins et al., 1979). An alternative denaturation process (Fig. 3) breaks the hydrogen bonds by physical

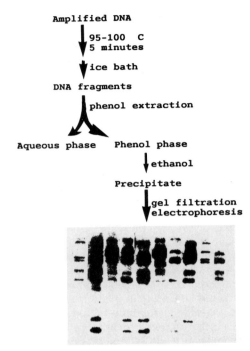

Fig. 3. Illustration of DNA extraction and separation technique.

or chemical means, the most efficient of which is heating to 95–100°C (Schochetmann et al., 1988). This involves boiling (30 µl of amplified DNA) for 5 min with ice-bath quenching. The denatured material is then subjected to purification with phenol extraction, ethanol precipitation, gel filtration, and electrophoresis (Robbins et al., 1979). Quantification of extracted DNA by the traditional measurement of absorbance ratio at 260/280 nm may be compromised by pigment absorption in some archaeological material (Paabo, 1989), often requiring innovative approaches.

As the amount of extracted DNA is below the limits of resolution of characterization techniques, methods have been explored to amplify and replicate that which is present. The major approaches have involved bacterial cloning or polymerase techniques.

Molecular cloning ligates (binds) DNA fragments to a plasmid or other vector that is subsequently introduced into bacteria (Maniatis et al., 1982). The hybrid plasmid-infected bacteria are grown under conditions that are selective to the particular plasmid. Subsequent colonies are then cloned and the colonies of interest are grown and subjected to sequencing. The clones of interest are identified by a specific DNA probe.

The mitochondrial DNA of the Quagga, an extinct striped horse-like animal, was analyzed by this technique. It appeared to have two replacement substitutions compared with the zebra (Higuchi et al., 1984, 1987). These were located in the genes for cytochrome oxidase I and NADH dehydrogenase I. As these substitutions would cause amino acid replacements at sites conserved in all other tested vertebrates (Paabo and Wilson, 1988), common sense suggests an artifact. Paabo (1989) found low cloning efficiency in an analysis of Quagga, perhaps related to the amount of DNA damage. The segments were found to be identical to other vertebrates when studied by the polymerase amplification technique that is described below (Paabo and Wilson, 1988). Cloning efficiency was probably low because of ligation of the vector molecule to damaged ancient DNA, precluding replication. Repair mechanisms, inherent in cellular DNA replication, introduce variation or error, as the modified DNA may then resemble an alternative nucleotide (Paabo et al., 1989). Salvaging altered molecules introduces significant cloning artifacts. Other researchers have been more effective at DNA cloning. Robbins and colleagues (1979) examined 229-base-pair (bp) mitochondrial sequences of the goat, finding only 12 substitutions in relation to the contemporary mountain zebra. Most of the substitutions represented nucleic acid "transitions" or alternative DNA sequences, coding for the same amino acid. They felt the material showed no determinable postmortem modification of the sequences and interpreted the obtained information as evidence that the two species were derived 3–4 million years ago from a common ancestor, thus confirming implications of the fossil record (George and Ryder, 1983). This approach, however, has been generally abandoned in favor of the polymerase technique.

As the retrieved materials are quite limited in quantity, the development of the DNA polymerase technique has provided a methodology for replicating this limited material to "workable" amounts. This is a test-tube technique for copying the two complementary DNA strands that compose genetic information. A single target area in the DNA can be amplified by use of a specific DNA polymerase that amplifies segments containing 20–1,000 bp. One of the advantages of the DNA polymerase reaction is that the DNA being cloned "does not have to be in good shape" (Marx, 1988).

The polymerase technique eliminates the low cloning efficiency and ancient DNA modification-induced cloning artifact problems (Paabo et al., 1989). Most damaged DNA fragments will not be replicated, as they contain inter- and intramolecular cross-links. Presence of baseless sites (damaged DNA lacking the adenine, cytosine, guanine, thymine component) reduces the rate of replication, providing less damaged fragments and hence a production advantage. Such baseless fragments will replicate well, but may not accurately represent the original fragment. As each error was initially present in only one molecule, it will probably minimally affect the final population of molecules (by the polymerase technique), as selective cloning is not employed.

Gene amplification (Fig. 4) makes use of a polymerase chain reaction that amplifies the DNA more than a millionfold. Some details are provided here as this technique has tremendous implications not just for paleopathology but for archaeology and anthropology in general. *Thermus aquaticus* (Taq bacteria) heat-stable DNA polymerase is the catalyst (Saiki et al., 1988), which utilizes a defined DNA segment as the template for assembling a complementary strand. Treatment cycles of 3- to 5-min duration are repeated 20–40 times (Mullis and Faloona, 1987; Schochetmann et al., 1988). Each cycle heats the sample (from 72° to 95° for 1 min, to denature DNA), cools it (for 1 min to 55°) to allow it to reanneal, and heats it again (to 72° for 2.5 min) to extend the annealed primers. Once the primer DNA fragment has been replicated, the material is heated to separate the DNA strands. Lowering the temperature allows the polymerase to again utilize the strands to produce additional complementary sequences. This approach allows 30 amplification cycles in 2.5 h, using a programmable heat block (DNA Thermal Cycler, PECI). As the number of DNA strands dou-

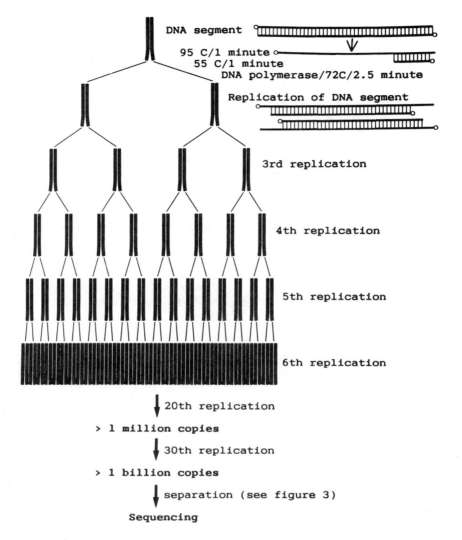

Fig. 4. Illustration of DNA polymerase amplification technique.

bles with each cycle, one million copies are replicated in as few as 20 cycles and one billion in 30 cycles. The automated polymerase technique may result in a millionfold amplification in as little as 4 h (Landegren et al., 1988). Applying the technique to antiquity, however, appears to require large amounts of enzyme, because of "an inhibitory activity present in the ancient DNA extract" (Paabo, 1989). The Taq polymerase has an error frequency of 0.25% in this application (Saiki, 1988).

Once amplified, the DNA is amenable to a variety of analyses including actual sequencing. Short DNA segments of 300–600 nucleotides can be sequenced by chemical degradation (Church and Kieffer-Higgins, 1988; Maxam and Gilbert, 1963) or chain termination (Sanger and Thompson, 1977) techniques. These techniques electrophoretically separate DNA fragments, terminating at every G, A, T, or C throughout the sequence. The size order of fragment bands distinguishes single nucleotide differences in length (Landegren et al., 1988).

An automated technique can actually complete 24 sequencing reactions in as little as 45 min.

The weak hydrogen bond linkage of the DNA double helix, which is amenable to denaturation to single strands and to reannealing, forms the basis for DNA molecular hybridization techniques. Although the match-up of DNA strands does not have to be perfect, the more homologous the strands, the stronger their attraction and the more stable the resultant DNA hybrid. Temperature sensitivity of the hydrogen bonds is a major determinate of denaturation of such hybrids. Varying the temperature selects the stringency of a hybridization reaction (the degree of homology necessary for two strands of DNA to anneal) from no annealing if there is a single mismatch to some degree of flexibility (Saiki et al., 1988; Shoemaker et al., 1985). Musial et al. (1988) relate reliability and cost effectiveness of the technique to the likelihood of positivity.

Amplified DNA can be hybridized with a synthetic labeled DNA probe that possesses a restriction enzyme recognition site. Application of the restriction enzyme releases the radiolabeled fragment, which can then be recognized on polyacrylamide gel electrophoresis (Schochetmann et al., 1988). Fragments of DNA can be separated by size on agarose gel and blotted (transferred) onto a nitrocellulose or nylon membrane (Meinkoth, 1984; Southern, 1975). Labeling the probes with radioisotopes or biotin/avidin sandwich methods (similar to the ELISA assay illustrated in Fig. 2) allows recognition of very small amounts of the requisite DNA (Barrows, 1989). Hybridization of these probes with DNA isolated from cells allows recognition of the nuclear material of interest.

Control extracts must be analyzed in parallel with replicates of samples from antiquity to verify absence of reagent contamination. Contamination from handling during excavation or by reagents or glassware must be stringently avoided and controlled for. Verification of the antiquity of the specimen is possible by evaluating several parameters:

1. Archaeological remains cannot be amplifiable beyond the 150-bp size and museum specimens not beyond 500. Longer specimens should be considered contaminants (Paabo et al., 1989).

2. Because of cross-linking, old DNA is resistant to enzymatic digestion, in contrast with modern contaminating materials (Doran et al.,

1986). The amplification efficiency for contemporary DNA is uniform in the 100- to 500-bp fragment range, which contrasts with an inverse efficiency in ancient specimens. Successful amplication of longer fragments has "invariably yielded contemporary human sequences" (Paabo et al., 1988). Contamination with small amounts of exogenous human DNA (e.g., from excavators, preparators, or lab workers) is one major problem.

Paabo (1989) noted that DNA can be retrieved from desiccated, macroscopically well preserved ancient soft tissue remains. While its molecular weight was reduced, the reduction did not correlate with specimen age. Specimens that were 4 years old and 13,000 years old showed similar degrees of degradation. As nuclear DNA is rapidly degraded after death, Paabo (1989) suggests that the major factor determining DNA size is the rapidity of postmortem desiccation. Postmortem damage is substantial. Cytosine and thymine were substantially underrecognized (<5%), which is not unexpected, since pyrimidines (especially thymine) are more sensitive to oxidative damage (than are purines) (Teoule and Cadet, 1978). Paabo (1989) found ancient DNA to be highly sensitive to alkali, estimating that one alkali-sensitive site per 20 bp was present. Such increased alkali sensitivity can be (Hutchinson, 1985), and in the Paabo (1989) study appeared to be, related to modification of sugar residues or the actual purine/pyrimidines. At least one pyrimidine in ten was so modified, further documenting the significant oxidative damage in archaeological material.

Analysis of variation of mitochondrial DNA in contemporary humans has yielded support for the contention that all humans today are descended from an African "mitochondrial Eve," 200,000 years ago (Marx, 1988). Mitochondrial polymorphisms in brain tissue from an 8,000-year-old Floridian revealed a 9-bp segment known to occur in Asians, as well as North Americans (Paabo et al., 1988; Wrischnik et al., 1987). Marx (1988) suggests, on the basis of this and gene deletion data, that Native Americans derived from East Asian populations (Marx, 1988).

Specificity of probes for a particular diagnosis is critical. If a diagnosis of tuberculosis in ancient bovids could be documented, the relationship of the food chain to Native American disease could be pursued. While a DNA probe for the avian mycobacterium *M. avium* (Gen-Probe Inc., San Diego) has been developed (du Moulin et al., 1988), its specificity is unclear. DNA probes for *Mycobacterium tuberculosis, avium,* and *intracellulare* were unfortunately distinguishable only by variation in titer, a phenomenon that cannot be quantified in archaeological specimens (Shoemaker et al., 1985; Sherman et al., 1989). Peterson et al. (1989) feel that the DNA probe for *Mycobacterium tuberculosis* lacks sufficient specificity for paleopathological application. The DNA probe for *Chlamydia trachomatis* is felt to be quite specific (Horn et al., 1988), and may lend itself to analysis of some cases of Reiter's syndrome (Rothschild, 1982). The latter is a disease recognized today by inflammation of the mouth, genitalia, and skin and by an arthritis of the spondyloarthropathy variety.

RADIOLOGICAL TECHNIQUES
X-ray

X-ray assessment facilitates analysis, with less specimen compromise, than that available with conventional preparation and surface assessment techniques (Horner and Weishampel, 1988). Routine X-rays offer a great deal of information but some radiological techniques may be compromised by overlapping shadows. Conventional X-ray techniques are also compromised by scatter radiation, which reduces image contrast and resolution (Floyd et al., 1989). Direct techniques for limiting such scatter interference include the use of grids (Rothschild, 1982; Rothschild et al., 1985), airgaps (Rothschild et al., 1985; Sorenson and Floch, 1985), or moving, tightly collimated photon beams (Barnes et al., 1977; Plews, 1983; Plews and Vogelstein, 1983; Sorenson et al., 1980). The airgap technique simply places the specimen at a distance from the X-ray film, rather than lying immediately adjacent to it. Postexposure or indirect techniques (Floyd et al., 1989) designed to reduce the impact of scatter radiation include Fourier transformation algorithms with two exposures (Boone, 1986) or one standard exposure in digital format (Naimuddin et al., 1987; Shaw et al., 1982). Routine radiological techniques can offer 0.1-mm resolution, and satellite photograph en-

hancement techniques are quite applicable to routine images to increase the information obtained. Kodak Kodabrome IIRC F2M (normal contrast) black-and-white paper and Kodak high-speed calcium tungstate intensifying screens are reported by Fairgrieve and Bashford (1988) to provide the best combination of contrast, resolution, exposure time, and film range. These techniques are required when the specimens are fossilized or when the structures of interest are smaller than 1 mm.

While routine X-rays are not particularly helpful in assessing overall bone density, density of the various parts of a given bone do lend themselves to analysis. The failure of routine radiology to allow assessment of bone density is not actually a problem, as even techniques that validly assess bone density in contemporary individuals (e.g., radioabsorption, CAT scans) cannot be applied to most anthropological materials because of diagenesis. If diagenesis were not a factor in assessing bone density, diagnostic implications of reduction in bone density are still quite complicated (even when you can talk to the individual). Documentation of variation of bone density among individuals in a given population may, however, be amenable to interpretation on a comparative basis.

Osteopenia or reduction in bone density may have a variety of interacting causes (Resnick and Niwayama, 1989; Rothschild, 1982). Osteoporosis related to reduction in osseous support structures may be idiopathic or related to malnutrition, hypovitaminosis C, reduction of estrogen or thyroid function, excess endocrine function (e.g., Cushing's syndrome with corticosteroid excess, acromegaly with growth hormone excess, hyperthryroidism, or hyperparathyroidism), alcoholism, or liver disease. Disuse or immobilization may produce an identical picture. Evaluation of a single bone is not adequate, as regional osteopenia or reflex sympathetic dystrophy may affect isolated joints or limbs. Osteomalacia (vitamin D deficiency) must also be considered. Vitamin C deficiency (scurvy) interferes with removal of calcified cartilage and new trabecula formation with resultant osteopenia. The osteopenia of hypovitaminosis C is recognizable in children from the presence of a very characteristic metaphyseal white line. The occurrence of a linear band of rarefaction parallel to the white line is occasionally noted. Vitamin C deficiency is typically associated with subperiosteal hemorrhage that results in elevation of the periosteum. Cushing's syndrome and acromegaly are often associated with pituitary fossa enlargement and may, in the latter instance, entail associated osseous hypertrophy. Hypothyroidism is often associated with osteopenia, and only rarely with periosteal reaction. Hyperthyroidism increases bone turnover rates, with resultant osteopenia. Hyperparathyroidism also produces a pattern of bone resorption characterized radiologically as subperiosteal. It is highly specific, but has not, to this author's knowledge, been correlated with gross skeletal changes. Resorption of the lamina dura (the radio-dense line paralleling the tooth surface) of the tooth socket is also highly characteristic, though not a pathognomonic *in vivo* sign. Again, this author is unaware of any analyses in skeletal remains.

Osteomalacia results in osteopenia because of failure of bone osteoid to mineralize. Distinguishing osteomalacia from osteoporosis on a histological basis requires evaluation of undecalcified bone with preserved osteoid. Osteoid is generally not preserved in archaeological materials (with the possible exception of mummies). Osteomalacia results in poorly defined, coarse trabeculae and it often produces enlargement of the costochondral junction. While such enlargement is difficult to visualize radiologically in intact individuals, it should be recognizable on gross skeletal examination. Failure of calcification of distal diaphyses results in cupping, widening, and fraying of the metaphyses. Thread-like calcified distal diaphyseal shadows produce a frayed appearance. This may also be seen with vitamin C deficiency and in congenital syphilis. Epiphyseal displacement may even occur. The lower end of the femur is too thick and its epiphyseal–diaphyseal junction too irregular for changes of osteomalacia to be recognizable. However, the distal radius and ulna appear to be the optimal sites to survey. Failure of osteoid to calcify results in general skeletal softening, which may lead to diaphyseal bowing (often with thickening of the concave surface). Failure of osteoid ossification may occur in linear diaphyseal lines, producing a "pseudofracture" appearance.

Softening of bones may also be manifested as alterations in vertebral structure. Compression fractures of vertebrae with reduction of anterior (compared with posterior) height is a classic change of osteoporosis, but they may occur with replacement processes such as malignancy. Malignancy typically produces focal or diffuse decreases or increases in vertebral density, often with planar vertebral collapse. Osteoporotic softening of the vertebral body, with preservation of the annular ring, often produces a "fish"-shaped or biconcave vertebra when viewed radiologically from a lateral projection. This must be distinguished from the H-shaped vertebrae noted with sickle cell anemia or Gaucher's disease, an inborn error of metabolism.

Increased bone density may also be noted in archaeological samples (Resnick and Niwayama, 1988; Rothschild, 1982). Lead poisoning produces dense metaphyseal sclerotic lines. Fluorosis produces thickening and coarsening of trabecular and cortical bone. Enthesial (tendon, ligament, or joint capsule attachment) areas may become calcified. Fluorosis is associated with diffuse osteosclerosis, irregular periosteal thickening, spinal osteophytosis, and disorganization of osseous lamellar structure (Faccini and Teotia, 1974). A similar pattern of enthesial ossification is characteristic of hypervitaminosis A, which may even manifest metaphyseal cupping and splaying, and epiphyseal hypertrophy or premature closure (Pennes et al., 1985; Seawright and English, 1965; Singh et al., 1962). While cortical hyperostosis has been reported, general bony density is not increased. While Walker and colleagues (1982) have proposed a diagnosis of hypervitaminosis A in *Homo erectus* on the basis of "subperiosteal diaphyseal" deposition "of woven bone," the diagnosis must be considered suspect. As the more characteristic lesion of enthesial ossification is not mentioned, an alternative diagnosis such as hypertrophic osteoarthropathy is likely.

Nonuniform widening of the diploic space of the skull has several origins. Radially oriented trabeculae produce a "hair-on-end" appearance under conditions of accentuated production of bone marrow red cells (Jaffe, 1972; Ortner and Putschar, 1981; Resnick and Niwayama, 1988; Rothschild, 1982; Steinbock, 1976). While hemolytic anemias (especially thalassemia) and sickle cell anemia are probably the most common causes, iron deficiency anemia may also be responsible. The hair-on-end phenomenon is very rarely noted in studies of populations with iron deficiency anemia. It is much more common in those groups where inherited hemolytic anemias are common. While iron deficiency anemia is more prevalent than the inherited hemolytic anemias, at least in some groups, even if all individuals in a population had iron deficiency anemia, the hair-on-end phenomenon would only rarely be seen. Rare manifestations of common diseases are still rare. Frequent occurrence of the hair-on-end phenomenon in a population would not be compatible with a diagnosis of iron deficiency anemia, rather it would imply that the population has a special predisposition (e.g., inherited hemolytic anemia).

Tomograms and CAT Scans

A specimen can be "cut" radiologically by making tomograms without harming the specimen. Computerized axial tomograms (CAT scans) are more sophisticated, computerized versions of tomograms offering an eloquent approach to the same "cutting" process, but they are limited in resolution. Computerized axial tomography offers an opportunity to obtain cross-sectional information, without sacrificing the specimen. It has been used in assessment of endocranial volume (Conroy and Vannier, 1985) and for analyzing specific intracranial relationships. Dental development, often determined through "dissection" of the fossil mandible and maxilla, is easily demonstrated by CAT scan techniques. Routine radiological analysis of the Taung skull (type specimen of *Australopithecus africanus*) had previously been limited because of the dense mineralization and interference by the calcified matrix (Skinner and Sperber, 1982). A CAT scan revealed maturational affinities with a 3- to 4-year-old pongid, suggesting a more transitional role for this species (Conroy and Vannier, 1987).

Standard CAT scan resolution, however, is only 1 mm (Poelmann and Verbout, 1987). A relatively new technique is microscopic CT scanning. A 5-μm X-ray beam source (FeinFo-

cus, Wunstorf, FRG) was used by Ford Motor Company Scientific Research Laboratory (Dearborn, MI) to examine specimens rotated through 129 positions on a rotational stage (Layton et al., 1988). They subsequently reconstructed the images into three-dimensional arrays.

Magnetic Resonance Imaging

Magnetic resonance imaging (MRI) may be applicable to specimens with adequate water/fluid content, offering an alternative method for assessment of the noncortical structures. This expensive technique ($1,000 per hour, the typical specimen requiring approximately 1 h for equipment adjustment and performance of the scan) analyzes the environment of individual hydrogen atoms by noting their response to variously applied magnetic fields. The specimen is in effect magnetized. Timing of the response of a given part of the specimen to magnetic field changes results in a spatial (two-dimensional) image that allows identification of internal structures. This technique, based upon alterations in the proton (hydrogen) environment, is essentially dependent upon water, the major hydrogen-containing component of tissue. Dehydrated specimens do not become visualized with such MRI or NMR techniques. Nonuniform field-induced variable image brightness produces significant variation in image localization (Farrell and Zappulla, 1989). Regenerating images along viewing angle variations of 6°–9° even allows for stereo representation of the structure.

THREE-DIMENSIONAL IMAGING

Three-dimensional imaging was apparently initiated by Sir Charles Wheatstone in the 1830s (Wade, 1983). Subsequent stereoscopes have utilized mirrors, prisms, and, most recently, lenses and partitions. Lenticular and differently colored or polarized lenses and holography have also been utilized (Moseley et al., 1989). It has been this author's experience that bone pathology is difficult to identify and analyze with a two-dimensional image. Erosions, easily recognized *in situ*, are often difficult to characterize when seen in two dimensions. Three-dimensional representation appears essential. The images are obtained with 7° of camera angulation between images. Placing the specimen on a board balanced on a dowel is one approach to obtaining such images. Because of the parallax problem, long focal distances (e.g., 4–6 ft) are required. Unfortunately, the inability of 5% of the normal population to visually fuse stereo images limits its use to some extent (Morgan and Symmes, 1982).

More sophisticated techniques have been attempted in the assessment of osseous and even microscopic structures. Stacking techniques (Feldkamp et al., 1989; Poelmann and Verbout, 1987) are quite time intensive and are susceptible to compromise by distortion and discontinuity. Other approaches to three- dimensional reconstruction have included models derived from clay or plastic sheets, tracing for subsequent computer or mechanical spatial representation (Johnson and Capowski, 1983), and computer reconstructions (Sato et al., 1986).

Direct conversion by Fourier transformation of two- dimensional information to three-dimensional images is feasible with the same technology as that inherent in CAT scan and MRI applications (Farrell and Zappulla, 1989; Hadley et al., 1987). As data from different measurements (e.g., actual measurement, scanning instruments) vary in format, preprocessing of data to a "conventional" format is often useful (Farrell and Zappulla, 1989) and allows elimination of artifactual information (Farrell and Zappulla, 1989). However, the 2–20 megabytes involved requires large amounts of computer memory. Use of these techniques requires recognition that they are averaging techniques. Trabeculae may be "lost" to visual recognition if they fall below the resolution threshold of the technique and even the "average density" of the pixel underestimated (Feldkamp et al., 1989).

These techniques produce derived images and have several disadvantages: The software is expensive, and time requirements for data acquisition, reconstruction, and image manipulation are significant. Slice reconstruction techniques produce significant image degradation because of averaging artifacts (Moseley et al., 1989). This is especially problematic when there is an abrupt change in density (e.g., at bone interfaces) (Farrell and Zappulla, 1989).

Three-dimensional computer imaging techniques allow visualization of interior structures, removing the portion of the structure blocking the view (Farrell, 1983; Frank et al., 1987; Totty and Vannier, 1984; Virapongse et al., 1986; Woolson et al., 1986). Alternatively, the object can be "split" on a plane and the two portions rotated to "open" the image (Artzy and Herman, 1981; Artzy et al., 1980; Farrell and Zappulla, 1989). The material can also be displayed by means of a graded transparency (Batnizky et al., 1979; Farrell and Zappulla, 1989). The latter technique produces a perspective not unlike that of stereo images. A novel approach is to use three-dimensional modeling, generating molds from the three-dimensional image (Roberts et al., 1984; Sundberg et al., 1986).

More specific three-dimensional images can be derived by "dissecting" the area of interest free of "overlying" structures in two-dimensional images. These can be combined to generate an image that illustrates only the area of interest. The specimen can thus be rotated (Conroy and Vannier, 1984); therefore, specimens can be examined without removal of matrix and measurements can be made that would not be accessible without damaging the specimen. Marx and D'Auria (1988) applied this approach to visualization of head and neck structures in linen- and plaster-wrapped mummies. Such techniques have been applied to generating three-dimensional images of primate skulls and even of microscopic images (Brankenhoff et al., 1985; Farrell and Zappulla, 1989; Jimenez et al., 1986; Mazziotta and Hamilton, 1977).

Laser scanning microscopy allows microscopic tomography and three-dimensional reconstruction of microstructures (Hansen et al., 1985; Takamatsu and Fujita, 1988; Valkenberg et al., 1985). Holography has been applied to the study of fossil cephalopods (Illert and Reverberi, 1988), as well as to three-dimensional representation of CT and MRI images (Benatar et al., 1988; Fujioka et al., 1988). Reproduction quality is sufficient for accurate measurements of object relationships (Benatar et al., 1988).

Three-dimensional imaging has also been applied to electron microscopy (Crowther et al., 1970). Serial sectioning to obtain a three-dimensional image sacrifices the specimen and the technique itself changes the structure being examined. Alignment may also be problematic. An alternative is using angular range of rotation of the electron microscope with Fourier transformation of evenly spaced angular planes (Frank, 1989). The object is positioned through a series of "tilts." A replica is preferred, as the large accumulated electron dose often damages the specimen and up to 50% mass loss/shrinkage has been noted (Luther et al., 1988). Cryoelectron microscopy may make this a more practical technique (Dubochet et al., 1982; Taylor and Glaeser, 1974). For example, assessment of ciliary structure abnormalities is a potential application in paleopathology.

PREDICTION OF DIRECTION OF FUTURE RESEARCH

The study of paleopathology has entered a new era in which diagnostic impressions can be confirmed and diseases can be placed in historical perspective. Biological invasions (macro- and microorganisms), for example, can be divided into phases: chance initiation, establishment, spread, and persistence (Mollison, 1986; Sattenspiel, 1988). Chance initiation of a process requires that the environment (e.g., host) and biological agent (e.g., microorganism) be brought into juxtaposition. Establishment requires that the environment be sufficiently fertile (e.g., that sufficient susceptible hosts be present) to allow the organism to grow and multiply. Spread requires that the organism has access to additional supportive (susceptible) environments. Persistence requires that the organism not be so aggressive as to eliminate all supporting factors (e.g., kill off all susceptible hosts) and that the organism develops a mechanism of overcoming the environment's ability to resist the organism (e.g., host's ability to develop protective antibodies).

Sattenspiel (1988) has enumerated a series of assumptions about infectious processes:

1. The population size is constant, with births equaling deaths.

2. There is no permanent movement of individuals between regions.

3. The infection of interest has no latency period.

4. Recovering percentage is proportional to the number of infected individuals.

5. The number of new cases is proportional to the number of contacts between infected and susceptibles.

There is a unique threshold for stability of any given infection. An aggressive, fatal disorder would quickly affect all susceptible individuals, leaving little opportunity for its persistence. Diseases of low infectivity require a critical population size for their persistence. The same approach is pertinent for noninfectious disorders.

The analysis of diseases, as represented in the archaeological record, is predicated on comparison with contemporary samples. Such analysis is meaningful only if the biases inherent in the deposit or in the acquisition of those samples can be identified. A common error in human clinical studies that invalidates statistical analysis is comparing individuals that make up biased groups. If it is not recognized that only the affluent of a group are buried, or if "diseased" individuals are not buried with their community, a false impression of the occurrence and severity of disease will result.

Nondestructive, easily accessible techniques are now available and amenable to interpretation. Recognition of the value of collaborative investigations (as suggested by Sigerist, 1951) by specialists in structure/function relationships (e.g., anthropologists/paleontologists) and specialists in disease (e.g., health care providers) should lead to new perspectives. Assessment of testable hypotheses of course requires consideration of the sensitivity and specificity of the applied technique. These concepts in turn must be applied with the predicted prevalence rate of a given disease in the population kept in mind. Common sense and collaborative efforts will allow the advantages and limitations of technology and epidemiological approaches to be held in focus in a most productive manner.

REFERENCES

Abelson PH (1954): Organic constituents of fossils. Carnegie Inst Washington Yearb 53:97–101.
Alciati G, Bosman C (1978): An attempt toward blood grouping in thin bone section. J Hum Evol 7:111–114.

Allison MJ, Hossaini AA, Castro N, Munizaga J, Pezzia A (1976): ABO blood groups in Peruvian mummies. I. An evaluation of techniques. Am J Phys Anthropol 44:55–62.

Allison MJ, Hossaini AA, Munizaga J, Fung R (1978): ABO blood groups in Peruvian mummies. II. Results of agglutination–inhibition technique. Am J Phys Anthropol 49:139–142.

Artzy E, Herman GT (1981): Boundary detection in three dimensions with a medical application. Comput Graphics 15:92–136.

Artzy E, Frieder G, Herman GT (1980): The theory, design, implementation and evaluation of a three-dimensional surface detection algorithm. Comput Graphics Image Processing 15:1–91.

Ascenzi A (1963): Microscopy and prehistoric bone. In Ascenzi A (ed): "Science and Archaeology: A comprehensive Survey of Progress and Research." New York: Basic Books, pp 526–538.

Ascenzi A, Silvestrini G (1984): Bone-boring marine microorganisms: An experimental investigation. J Hum Evol 13:531–536.

Ascenzi A, Brunori M, Citro G, Zito R (1985): Immunological detection of hemoglobin in bones of ancient Roman times and of Iron and Neolithic Ages. Proc Natl Acad Sci 82:7170–7172.

Barnes GT, Brezovich IA, Witten DM (1977): Scanning multiple slit assembly: A practical and efficient device to reduce scatter. Am J Radiol 129:497–501.

Barraco RA (1978): Preservation of proteins in mummified tissues. Am J Phys Anthropol 48:487–491.

Barrows GH (1989): Application of DNA probes to hematology: An overview with selected examples. Ann Clin Lab Sci 19:139–145.

Batnizky S, Price HI, Lee KR, Cook PN, Cook LT, Fritz SL, Dwyer SJ III, Watts C (1979): Three-dimensional computer reconstructions of brain lesions from surface contours provided by computed tomography: A prospectus. Neurosurgery 11:73–84.

Benatar M, Wynchank S, Adams LP (1988): Three-dimensional magnetic resonance image representation using reflection holography. Phys Med Biol 33:1469–1472.

Berg K, Rosing FW, Schwazfischer F, Wischerath H (1975): Blood grouping of old Egyptian mummies. Homo 26:148–153.

Bishop JO (1974): Three abundant classes in HeLa cell messenger RNA. Nature 250:199–201.

Blakely RL (1989): Bone strontium in pregnant and lactating females from archaeological samples. Am J Phys Anthropol 80:173–185.

Boddington A (1987): From bones to population: The problem of numbers. In Boddington A, Garland AN, Janaway RC (eds): "Death, Decay and Reconstruction: Approaches to Archaeology and Forensic Science." Manchester: Manchester University Press, pp 180–197.

Boddington A, Garland AN, Janaway RC (1987): Flesh, bones dust and society. In Boddington A, Garland AN, Janaway RC (eds): "Death, Decay and Reconstruction: Approaches to Archaeology and Forensic Science." Manchester: Manchester University Press, pp 3–8.

Boone JM (1986): Scatter correction algorithm for digitally acquired radiographs: Theory and results. Med Phys 13:319–328.

Boyd WC, Boyd LG (1939): Blood group reactions of preserved bone and muscle. Am J Phys Anthropol 25:421–434.

Brankenhoff GJ, van der Voort HT, van Spronsen EA, Linnemans WA, Nanninga N (1985): Three-dimensional chromatin distribution in neuroblastoma nuclei shown by confocal scanning laser microscopy. Nature 317:748–749.

Broili F (1922): Über den feineren Ban der "Verknocherten Sehnen" (=Verknocherten Muskeln) von Trachodon. Anat Anz 55:464–475.

Brown AB (1973): Bone strontium as a dietary indicator in human skeletal populations. PhD dissertation. University of Michigan, Ann Arbor.

Candela PG (1936): Blood group reactions in ancient human skeletons. Am J Phys Anthropol 21:429–432.

Candela PG (1940): Reliability of blood group tests on human bones. Am J Phys Anthropol 27:365–381.

Chand P, Khanna RN, Sadana JR (1988): Counterimmunoelectrophoresis for the detection of *Brucella* antigen and antibodies in the diagnosis of brucellosis in buffaloes. J Appl Bacteriol 64:445–450.

Church GM, Kieffer-Higgins S (1988): Multiplex DNA sequencing. Science 240:185–188.

Collins MT (1986): *Legionella* infections in animals. Israel J Med Sci 22:662–673.

Conroy GC, Vannier MW (1984): Noninvasive three-dimensional computer imaging of matrix-filled fossil skulls by high-resolution computed tomography. Science 226:456–458.

Conroy GC, Vannier MW (1985): Endocranial volume determination of matrix-filled fossil skulls using high-resolution computed tomography. In Lawrence KS (ed): "Hominid Evolution: Past, Present and Future." New York: Alan R. Liss, pp 419–426.

Conroy GC, Vannier MW (1987): Dental development of the Taung skull from computerized tomography. Nature 239:625–627.

Cook M, Molto E, Anderson C (1988): Possible case of hyperparathyroidism in a Roman period skeleton from the Dakhleh Oasis, Egypt, diagnosed using bone histomorphometry. Am J Phys Anthropol 75:23–30.

Cook M, Molto E, Anderson C (1989): Fluorochrome labelling in Roman Period skeletons from Dakhleh Oasis, Egypt. Am J Phys Anthropol 80:137–143.

Crowther RA, DeRosier DJ, Klug A (1970): The reconstruction of a three-dimensional structure from projections and its application to electron microscopy. Proc R Soc Lond A 317:319–340.

Daniel TM, Debanne SM (1987): The serodiagnosis of tuberculosis and other mycobacterial diseases by enzyme-linked immunosorbent assay. Am Rev Resp Dis 135:1137–1151.

Dardenne M, Savino W, Bach J-F (1987): Thymomatous epithelial cells and skeletal muscle share a common epitope defined by a monoclonal antibody. Am J Pathol 126:194–198.

Dollo L (1887): Note sur les ligaments ossifiés des dinosauriens de Bernissart. Arch Biol 7:249–264.

Doran GH, Dickel DN, Ballinger WE Jr, Agee OF, Laipis PJ, Hauswirth WW (1986): Anatomical, cellular and molecular analysis of 8,000-year-old human brain tissue from the Windover archaeological site. Nature 323:803–806.

Dubochet J, Lepault J, Freeman R, Berriman JA, Homo JC (1982): Electron microscopy of frozen water and aqueous solutions. J Microsc 128:219–237.

duMoulin GC, Stottmeier KD, Pelletier PA, Tsang AY, Hedley-Whyte J (1988): Concentration of *Mycobacterium avium* by hospital hot water systems. JAMA 260:1599–1601.

Eigen M, Lindemann BF, Tietze M, Winkler-Oswatitsch R, Dress A, von Haeseler A (1989): How old is the genetic code? Statistical geometry of tRNA provides an answer. Science 244:673–679.

Ezra-Cohn HE, Cook SF (1961): Blood typing compact human bone tissue. Nature 191:1267–1268.

Faccini JM, Teotia SP (1974): Histopathological assessment of endemic skeletal fluorosis. Calcif Tissue Res 16:45–47.

Fairgrieve SI, Bashford J (1988): A radiographic technique of interest to physical anthropologists. Am J Phys Anthropol 77:23–26.

Farrell EJ (1983): Color display and interactive interpretation of three-dimensional data. IBM J Res Dev 27:356–366.

Farrell EJ, Zappulla RA (1989): Three-dimensional data visualization and biomedical applications. CRC Crit Rev Biomed Eng 16:323–363.

Feldkamp LA, Goldstein SA, Parfitt AM, Jesion G, Kleerekoper M (1989): The direct examination of three-dimensional bone architecture in vitro by computed tomography. J Bone Mineral Res 4:3–11.

Fifis T, Packettt P, Corner LA, Wood PR (1989): Purification of a major *Mycobacterium bovis* antigen for the diagnosis of bovine tuberculosis. Scand J Immunol 29:91–101.

Floyd CE, Beatty PT, Ravin CE (1989): Scatter compensation in digital chest radiography using Fourier deconvolution. Invest Radiol 24:30–33.

Frank J (1989): Three-dimensional imaging techniques in electron microscopy. BioTechniques 7:164–173.

Frank J, McEwen BF, Radermacher M, Turner JN, Rieder CL (1987): Three-dimensional tomographic reconstruction in high voltage electron microscopy. J Electron Microsc Technique 6:193–205.

Fujioka M, Ohyama N, Honda T, Tsujinchi J, Suzuki M, Hashimoto S, Ikeda S (1988): Holography of 3-D surface reconstructed CT images. J Comput Assist Tomogr 12:175–178.

Garland AN (1987): A histological study of archaeological bone decomposition. In Boddington A, Garland AN, Janaway RC (eds): "Death, Decay and Reconstruction: Approaches to Archaeology and Forensic Science." Manchester: Manchester University Press, pp 121–126.

George M, Ryder OA (1983): Mitochondrial DNA evolution in the genus Equus. Genetics 104:27S.

Gerna G, Passarani N, Unicomb LE, Parea M, Sarasini A, Battaglia M, Bishop RF (1989): Solid-phase immune electron microscopy and enzyme-linked immunosorbent assay for typing of human rotavirus strains by using polyclonal and monoclonal antibodies: A comparative study. J Infect Dis 159:335–339.

Goffer Z (1980): "Archaeological Chemistry." New York: John Wiley and Sons.

Gorelkin L, Chandler FW (1988): Pseudomicrobes: Some potential diagnostic pitfalls in the histopathologic assessment of inflammatory lesions. Hum Pathol 19:954–959.

Gray MP (1958): A method for reducing non-specific reactions in the typing of human skeletal material. Am J Phys Anthropol 16:135–138.

Grupe G, Herrmann B (1988): Trace Elements in Environmental History. New York: Springer-Verlag.

Hackett CJ (1981): Microscopical focal destruction (tunnels) in exhumed human bones. Med Sci Law 21:243–265.

Hadley MN, Sonntag VK, Amos MR, Hodak JA, Lopez LJ (1987): Three-dimensional computed tomography in the diagnosis of vertebral column pathological conditions. Neurosurgery 21:186–192.

Hansen EW, Allen RD, Strohbehn JW, Chaffee MA, Farrington DL, Murray WF (1985): Laser scanning phase modulation microscope. J Microsc 140:371–381.

Henderson J (1987): Factors determining the state of preservation of human remains. In Boddington A, Garland AN, Janaway RC (eds): "Death, Decay and Reconstruction: Approaches to Archaeology and Forensic Science." Manchester: Manchester University Press, pp 43–54.

Higuchi R, Wilson AC (1984): Recovery of DNA from extinct species. Fed Proc 43:1557.

Higuchi R, Bowman B, Freiberger M, Ryder OA, Wilson AC (1984): DNA sequences from the quagga, an extinct member of the horse family. Nature 312:282–284.

Higuchi RG, Wrischnik LA, Oakes E, George M, Toyng B, Wilson AC (1987): Mitochondrial DNA of the extinct quagga: Relatedness and extent of postmortem changes. J Mol Evol 25:283–287.

Horn JE, Kappus EW, Falkow S, Quinn TC (1988): Diagnosis of *Chlamydia trachomatis* in biopsied tissue specimens by using in situ DNA hybridization. J Infect Dis 157:1249–1253.

Horner JR, Weishampel DB (1988): A comparative embryological study of two ornithischian dinosaurs. Nature 332:256–257.

Humphrey DM, Weiner MH (1987): Mycobacterial antigen detection by immunohistochemistry in pulmonary tuberculosis. Hum Pathol 18:701–708.

Hutchinson F (1985): Chemical changes induced in DNA by ionizing radiation. Prog Nucleic Acids Res Mol Biol 32:115–154.

Ibrahimi IM, Prager EM, White TJ, Wilson AC (1979): Amino acid sequence of California quail lysozyme. Effect of evolutionary substitutions on the antigenic structure of lysozyme. Biochemistry 18:2736–2744.

Illert CR, Reverberi D (1988): Holography reveals the soft anatomy of ancient cephalopods. Bull Math Biol 50:19–34.

Jaffe HL (1972): "Metabolic, Degenerative, and Inflammatory Diseases of Bone and Joints." Philadelphia: Lea and Febiger.

Jakubowski A, Elwood RK, Enarson DA (1988): Clinical features of abdominal tuberculosis. J Infect Dis 158:687–692.

Jiminez J, Santisteban A, Carazo JM, Carrascosa JL (1986): Computer graphic display method for visualizing three-dimensional biological structures. Science 232:1113–1115.

Johnson EM, Capowski JJ (1983): A system for the three-dimensional reconstruction of biological structures. Comp Biomed Res 16:79–87.

Klinkhammer GP, Lambert CE (1989): Preservation of organic matter during salinity excursions. Nature 339:271–274.

Kostial IK, Gruden N, Durakovic A (1969): Intestinal absorption of calcium-47 and strontium-85 in lactating rats. Calcif Tissue Res 4:13–19.

Landegren U, Kaiser R, Caskey CT, Hood L (1988): DNA diagnostics—Molecular techniques and automation. Science 242:229–237.

Layton MW, Goldstein SA, Goulet RW, Feldkamp LA, Kubinski DJ, Bole GG (1988): Examination of subchondral bone architecture in experimental osteoarthritis by microscopic axial tomography. Arthritis Rheum 31:1400–1405.

Lengyel Y (1975): "Paleoserology. Blood Typing with the Fluorescent Antibody Method." Budapest: Akademiai Kiado.

Llopp E, Rothhammer F (1988): A note on the presence of blood groups A and B in pre-Columbian South America. Am J Phys Anthropol 75:107–111.

Lowenstein JM (1980): Species-specific proteins in fossils. Naturwissenschaften 67:343–346.

Lowenstein JM (1981): Immunological reactions from fossil material. Phil Trans R Soc London B 292:143–149.

Luther PK, Lawrence MC, Crowther RA (1988): A method for monitoring the collapse of plastic sections as a function of electron dose. Ultramicroscopy 24:7–18.

Mandrell RE, Griffiss JM, Macher BA (1988): Lipooligosaccharides (LOS) of *Neisseria gonorrhoea* and *Neisseria meningitidis* have components that are immunochemically similar to precursors of human blood group antigens. J Exp Med 168:107–126.

Maniatis T, Fritsch EF, Sambrook J (1982): "Molecular Cloning: A Laboratory Manual." Cold Spring Harbor, NY: Cold Spring Harbor Laboratory.

Martio J, Kiviniemei P, von Essen R (1980): Early rheumatoid arthritis in the USSR and in Finland. Scand J Rheumatol 9:39–43.

Marx J (1988): Multiplying genes by leaps and bounds. Science 240:1408–1410.

Marx M, D'Auria SH (1988): Three-dimensional CT reconstructions of an ancient human Egyptian mummy. Am J Radiol 150:147–149.

Maxam AM, Gilbert W (1977): A new method for sequencing DNA. Proc Natl Acad Sci USA 74:560–564.

Mazziotta JC, Hamilton BL (1977): Three-dimensional computer reconstruction and display of neuronal structure. Comput Biol Med 7:265–279.

Medsger TA Jr, Masi AT (1989): Epidemiology of the rheumatic diseases. In McCarty DJ (ed): "Arthritis and Allied Conditions" (11th ed). Philadelphia: Lea and Febiger, pp 16–54.

Meinkoth J, Wahl G (1984): Hybridization of nucleic acids immobilized on solid supports. Anal Biochem 138:267–284.

Milner GR, Smith VG (1989): Carnivore alteration of human bone from a late prehistoric site in Illinois. Am J Phys Anthropol 79:43–49.

Mollison D (1986): Modelling biological invasions: Chance, explanation, prediction. Phil Trans R Soc London B:1–28.

Moran H, Chen S-L, Muirden KD, Jiang S-J, Gu Y-Y, Hopper J, Jiang P-L, Lawler G, Bai M-X (1987): A comparison of changes seen on radiographs of rheumatoid arthritis patients in Australia and in China. Arthritis Rheum 30:1298–1302.

Morgan H, Symmes D (1982): Amazing 3-D. Boston: Little, Brown.

Moseley ME, White DL, Wang S-C, Wikstrom M, Gobbel G, Roth K (1989): Stereoscopic MR imaging. J Comput Assist Tomogr 13:167–173.

Mullis KB, Faloona FA (1987): Specific synthesis of DNA in vitro via a polymerase-catalyzed chain reaction. Methods Enzymol 155:335–350.

Musial CE, Tice LS, Stockman L, Roberts GD (1988): Identification of mycobacteria from culture by using the Genprobe rapid diagnostic system for *Mycobacterium avium* complex and *Mycobacterium tuberculosis* complex. J Clin Microbiol 26:2120–2123.

Naimuddin S, Hasegawa B, Mistretta CA (1987): Scatterglare correction using a convolution algorithm with variable weighting. Med Phys 14:331–334.

Nakanishi M, Wilson AC, Nolan RA, Gorman GC, Bailey GS (1969): Phenoxyethanol: Protein preservation for taxonomists. Science 163:681–683.

Oakley KP (1955): The associated implements and mammalian remains and the composition of the hominoid remains. Br Mus Nat Hist Bull Geol 2:254–265.

O'Brien SJ (1973): On estimating functional gene number in eukaryotes. Nature 242:52–54.

Oftung F, Mustafa AB, Husson R, Young RA, Godal T (1987): Human T cell clones recognize two abundant *Mycobacterium tuberculosis* protein antigens expressed in *Escherichia coli*. J Immunol 138:927–931.

Ortner DJ, Putschar WGJ (1981): "Identification of Pathological Conditions in Human Skeletal Remains." Washington, DC: Smithsonian Institution Press.

Ortner DJ, von Endt DW, Robinson MS (1972): The effect of temperature on protein decay in bone; its significance in nitrogen dating of archaeological specimens. Am Antiq 37:514–520.

Paabo S (1989): Ancient DNA: Extraction, characterization, molecular cloning, and enzymatic amplification. Proc Natl Acad Sci USA 86:1939–1943.

Paabo S, Wilson AC (1988): Polymerase chain reaction reveals cloning artifacts. Nature 334:387–388.

Paabo S, Gifford JA, Wilson AC (1988): Mitochondrial DNA sequences from a 7000-year old brain. Nucleic Acids Res 16:9775–9787.

Paabo S, Higuchi RG, Wilson AC (1989): Ancient DNA and the polymerase chain reaction. J Biol Chem 264:9709–9712.

Paine RR (1989): Model life table fitting by maximum likelihood estimation: a procedure to reconstruct paleodemographic characteristics from skeletal age distributions. Am J Phys Anthropol 79:51–61.

Pander CH (1856): Monographie der fossilen Fische des silurischen Systems der russisch-baltischen Gouvernements. St. Petersburg: Buchdruk d keis Akad d Wiss.

Papa F, Laszio A, David HL (1988): Specificity of *Mycobacterium tuberculosis* phenolic glycolipid (PGL-Tb1) antiserum. Ann Inst Pasteur Microbiol 139:535–545.

Pate FD, Hutton JT (1989): Identification of postmortem diagenetic phases in archaeological bone. Am J Phys Anthropol 78:282.

Pennes DR, Martel W, Ellis CN (1985): Retinoid-induced ossification of the posterior longitudinal ligament. Skeletal Radiology 14:191–193.

Peters T Jr (1975): In Putnam FW (ed): "The Plasma Proteins—Structure, Function, and Genetic Control" (2nd ed). New York: Academic Press, 50:133–181.

Peterson EM, Lu R, Floyd C, Nakasone A, Friedly G, de la Maza, LM (1989): Direct identification of *Mycobacterium tuberculosis, Mycobacterium avium,* and *Mycobacterium intracellulare* from amplified primary cultures in BACTEC media using DNA probes. J Clin Microbiol 27:1543–1547.

Plews DB (1983): A scanning system for chest radiography with regional exposure control: Theoretical considerations. Med Phys 10:646–654.

Plews DB, Vogelstein E (1983): A scanning system for chest radiography with regional exposure control: Practical implementation. Med Phys 10:655–663.

Poelmann RE, Verbout AJ (1987): Computer-aided three-dimensional graphic reconstructions in a radiological and anatomical setting. Acta Anat 130:132–136.

Poinar GO, Hess R (1982): Ultrastructure of 40-million-year-old insect tissue. Science 215:1241–1242.

Prager EM, Wilson AC, Lowenstein JM, Sarich VM (1980): Mammoth albumin. Science 209:287–289.

Price TD, Schoeninger MJ, Armelagous GJ (1985): Bone chemistry and past behavior: An overview. J Hum Evol 14:419–447.

Putschar WG (1966): Problems in the pathology and paleopathology of bone. In Jarcho S (ed): "Human Palaeopathology." New Haven, CT: Yale University Press, pp 57–65.

Raja A, Machicao AR, Morrissey AB, Jacobs MR, Daniel TM (1988): Specific detection of *Mycobacterium tuberculosis* in radiometric cultures by using an immunoassay for antigen 5. J Infect Dis 158:468–470.

Randall JT, Fraser RD, Jackson S, Martin AW, North AC (1952): Aspects of collagen structure. Nature 169:1029–1033.

Rentoul E, Smith H (1973): "Glaister's Medical Jurisprudence and Toxicology" (13th ed). Edinburgh: Churchill Livingstone.

Resnick D, Niwayama G (1988): "Diagnosis of Bone and Joint Disorders." Philadelphia: Saunders.

Robbins J, Rosteck P Jr, Haynes JR, Freyer G, Cleary ML, Kalter HD, Smith K, Lingrel JB (1979): The isolation and partial characterization of recombinant DNA containing genomic sequences from the goat. J Biol Chem 254:6187–6195.

Roberts D, Pettigew J, Udupa JK, Ram C (1984): Three-dimensional imaging and display of the temporomandibular joint. Oral Surg, Oral Med, Oral Pathol 58:461–474.

Romer AS (1964): Bone in early vertebrates. In Frost HM (ed): "Bone Biodynamics." Boston: Little, Brown, pp 13–37.

Rothschild BM (1982): "Rheumatology: A Primary Care Approach." New York: Yorke Medical Press.

Rothschild BM (1991): Stratophenetic analysis of avascular necrosis in turtles: Affirmation of the decompression syndrome hypothesis. Comp Biochem Physiol (in press).

Rothschild BM, Turnbull W (1987): Treponemal infection in a Pleistocene bear. Nature 329:61–62.

Rothschild BM, Woods R (1988): Old World spondyloarthropathy: The gorilla connection. Arthritis Rheum 31:934–935.

Rothschild BM, Woods RJ (1989): Spondyloarthropathy in gorillas. Semin Arthritis Rheum 18:267–276.

Rothschild BM, Sebes JI, DeSmet AA (1985): Radiologic assessment of bone and joint disease. I. Magnification radiology. Semin Arthritis Rheum 14:274–279.

Rothschild BM, Turner KR, DeLuca MA (1988): Symmetrical erosive peripheral polyarthritis in the Late Archaic Period of Alabama. Science 241:1498–1501.

Rowley MJ, Rich PV (1986): Immunoreactive collagen in avian and mammalian fossils. Naturwissenschaften 73:620–622.

Russell MD, LeMort F (1986): Cut marks on the Engis 2 calvaria? Am J Phys Anthropol 69:317–323.

Saiki RK (1988): Primer-directed enzymatic amplification of DNA with a thermostable DNA polymerase. Science 239:487–494.

Saiki RK, Chang C-A, Levenson CH, Wadwarren TC, Boehm CD, Kazazian HH Jr, Erlich HA (1988): Diagnosis of sickle cell anemia and B-thalassemia with enzymatically amplified DNA and nonradioactive allele-specific oligonucleotide probes. N Engl J Med 319:537–541.

Salvo JJ, Allison MJ, Rogan PK (1989): Molecular genetics of pre-Columbian South American mummies. Am J Phys Anthropol 78:295.

Sarich VM (1977): Albumin phylogenetics. In Rosenoer VM, Oratz M, Rothschild MA (eds): "Albumin Structure, Function and Uses." Oxford, UK: Pergamon, pp 85–111.

Sato AG, Yasuda M, Sato Y, Nakamae E (1986): Stereographic semitransparent images reconstructed by computer graphics from serial microscopic sections. In Ishizaka S (ed): "Science on Form." Tokyo: KTK Publishers, pp 305–311.

Sattenspiel L (1988): Spread and maintenance of a disease in a structured population. Am J Phys Anthropol 77:497–504.

Schaffer J (1889): Uber den feineren Bau fossiler Knochen. Sber Akad Wiss Wien 98:319–382.

Schochetmann G, Ou C-Y, Jones WK (1988): Polymerase chain reaction. J Infect Dis 158:1154–1169.

Schopf JW, Packer BM (1987): Early Archean (3.3-billion to 3.5-billion-year-old) microfossils from Warrawoona Group, Australia. Science 237:70–73.

Seawright AA, English PB (1965): Hypervitaminosis A and hyperostosis of the cat. Nature 206:1171–1172.

Sensabaugh GF, Wilson AC, Kirk PL (1971): Protein stability in preserved biological remains. 1. Survival of biologically-active proteins in an 8 year old sample of dried blood. Int J Biochem 2:545.

Shaw CG, Ergun DL, Myerowitz PD (1982): A technique of scatter and glare correction for videodensitometric studies in digital subtraction videoangiography. Radiology 142:209–213.

Sherman I, Harrington N, Rothrock A, George H (1989): Use of a cutoff range in identifying mycobacteria by the Gen-probe rapid diagnostic system. J Clin Microbiol 27:241–244.

Shoemaker SA, Fisher JH, Scoggin CH (1985): Techniques of DNA hybridization detect small numbers of mycobacteria with no cross-hybridization with nonmycobacterial respiratory organisms. Am Rev Resp Dis 131:760–763.

Shoenfeld Y, Vilner Y, Coates AR, Rauch J, Lavie G, Shaul D, Pinkhas J (1986): Monoclonal anti-tuberculosis antibodies react with DNA, and monoclonal anti-DNA autoantibodies react with *Mycobacterium tuberculosis*. Clin Exp Immunol 66:255–261.

Sigerist HE (1951): "A History of Medicine." New York: Oxford University Press.

Sillen A (1981): Strontium and diet at Hayonim Cave. Am J Phys Anthropol 56:131–137.

Sillen A, Kavanagh M (1982): Strontium and paleodietary research: A review. Yearb Phys Anthropol 25:67–90.

Singh A, Dass R, Singhhayreh S, Jolly SS (1962): Skeletal changes in endemic fluorosis. J Bone Joint Surg 44B:806–815.

Skinner MF, Sperber GH (1982): "Atlas of Radiographs of Early Man." New York: Alan R. Liss.

Sledzik P (1989): "How sharper than a serpent's tongue": Cutmarks on bone and the instruments that make them. Am J Phys Anthropol 78:304.

Sorenson JA, Floch J (1985): Scatter rejection by air gaps: An empirical model. Med Phys 12:308–316.

Sorenson JA, Nelson JA, Niklason LT, Jacobsen SC (1980): Rotating disk device for slit radiography of the chest. Radiology 134:227–231.

Southern EM (1975): Detection of specific sequences among DNA fragments separated by gel electrophoresis. J Mol Biol 98:503–517.

Spector WS (1956): "Handbook of Biological Data." Philadelphia: Saunders, p 343.

Springer G, Villiamson P, Brandes W (1961): Blood group activity of gram negative bacteria. J Exp Med 113:1077–1093.

Srinivasappa J, Saeugsa J, Prabhakar BS, Gentry MK, Buchmeier MJ, Wiktor TJ, Koprowski H, Oldstone MB, Notkins AL (1986): Molecular mimicry: Frequency of reactivity of monoclonal antiviral antibodies with normal tissues. J Virol 57:397–401.

Stanbury JB, Wyngaarden JB, Fredrickson DS, Goldstein JL, Brown MS (1983): "The Metabolic Basis of Inherited Disease" (5th ed). New York: McGraw-Hill.

Steinbock RT (1976): "Paleopathological Diagnosis and Interpretation." Springfield, IL: Charles C Thomas.

Stenn FF, Milgram JW, Lee SL, Weigand RJ, Veis A (1977): Biochemical identification of homogentisic acid pigment in an ochronotic Egyptian mummy. Science 197:566–568.

Sundberg SB, Clark B, Foster BK (1986): Three-dimensional reformation of skeletal abnormalities using computed tomography. J Pediatr Orthoped 6:416–420.

Swedlow DB, Frasca P, Harper RA, Katz JL (1975): Scanning and transmission electron microscopy of calcified tissues. Biomat Med Devices Artif Organs 3:121–153.

Takamatsu T, Fujita S (1988): Microscopic tomography by laser scanning microscopy and its three-dimensional reconstruction. J Microsc 149:167–174.

Tarli SM (1979): Paleoserology—General bibliography. J Hum Evol 8:735–740.

Taylor K, Glaeser RM (1974): Electron diffraction of frozen, hydrated protein crystals. Science 186:1036–1037.

Teoule R, Cadet J (1978): In BertinchampsAJ, Hutterman J, Kohnlein W, Teoule R (eds): "Effects of Ionizing Radiation on DNA." Berlin: Springer, pp 171–203.

Thieme FP, Otten CM, Sutton HE (1956): A blood typing of human skull fragments from the Pleistocene. Am J Phys Anthropol 14:437–443.

Totty WG, Vannier MV (1984): Complex musculoskeletal anatomy: Analysis using three dimensional surface reconstruction. Radiology 150:173–177.

Valkenberg JA, Woldringh CL, Brakenhoff GJ, van der Voort HT, Nanninga N (1985): Optical fluorescence microscopy in three dimensions: Microtomoscopy. J Microsc 138:29–34.

Vawter L, Brown WM (1986): Nuclear and mitochondrial DNA comparisons reveal extreme rate variation in the molecular clock. Science 234:194–196.

Virapongse C, Shapiro M, Gmitro A, Sarwar M (1986): Three-dimensional computed tomographic reformation of the spine, skull, and brain from axial images. Neurosurgery 18:53–58.

von Endt DW, Ortner DJ (1984): Environmental effects of bone size and temperature on bone diagenesis. J Archaeol Sci 11:247–253.

Wade NJ (1983): Brewster and Wheatstone on vision. New York: Academic Press.

Wallgren JE, Caple R, Aufderheide AC (1986): Contributions of nuclear magnetic resonance studies to the question of alkaptonuria (ochronosis) in an Egyptian mummy. In David RA (ed): "Science in Egyptology." Manchester: Manchester University Press, pp 321–327.

Walker A, Zimmerman MR, Leakey RE (1982): A possible case of hypervitaminosis A in *Homo erectus*. Nature 296: 248–250.

Weigelt J (1927): "Rezente Wirbeltierleichen und ihre palaeobiologische Bedeutung." Leipzig: Verlag von Max Weg. Translated by J Schaefer as Vertebrate Carcasses and Their Paleobiological Implications. Chicago: University of Chicago Press.

Weiner S, Lowenstam HA, Taborek B, Hood L (1979): Fossil mollusk shell organic matrix components preserved for 80 million years. Paleobiology 5:144–150.

Wells C (1967): Pseudopathology. In Brothwell DR, Sandison AT (eds): "Diseases in Antiquity." Springfield, IL: Charles C Thomas, pp 5–19.

Weser U, Miesel R, Hartman H-J (1989): Mummified enzymes. Nature 341:696.

White TD, Toth N (1989): Engis: Preparation damage, not ancient cutmarks. Am J Phys Anthropol 78:361–367.

Whitehouse WJ, Dyson ED (1974): Scanning electron microscope studies of trabecular bone in the proximal end of the human femur. J Anat 118:417–444.

Williamson W (1849): On the microscopic structure of the scales and dermal teeth of some ganoid and placoid fish. Phil Trans R Soc London 140:435–475.

Wilson AC, Carlson SS, White TJ (1977): Biochemical evolution. Annu Rev Biochem 46:573.

Woods RJ, Rothschild BM (1988): Population analysis of symmetrical erosive arthritis in Ohio Woodland Indians (1200 years before the present time). J Rheumatol 15: 1258–1263.

Woolson ST, Dev P, Fellingham LL, Vassiliadis A (1986): Three-dimensional imaging of bone from computerized tomography. Clin Orthop Rel Res 202:239–248.

Wrischnik LA, Higuchi RG, Stoneking M, Erlich HA, Arnheim N, Wilson AC (1987): Nucleic Acids Res 15:529–542.

Wyckoff RW (1980): In Hare PE (ed): "Biogeochemistry of Amino Acids." New York: Wiley, pp 17–23.

Yeh TY, Godshalk JR, Olson GJ, Kelly RM (1987): Use of epifluorescence microscopy for characterizing the activity of *Thiobacillus ferrooxidans* on iron pyrite. Biotech Bioeng 30:138–146.

Skeletal Biology of Past Peoples: Research Methods
pages 153–174 © 1992 Wiley-Liss, Inc.

Chapter 9

Anthropological Uses of Developmental Defects of Enamel

Mark Skinner and Alan H. Goodman

*Department of Archaeology, Simon Fraser University, Burnaby, British Columbia, Canada V5A 1S6 (M.S.);
School of Natural Science, Hampshire College, Amherst, Massachusetts 01002 (A.H.G.)*

INTRODUCTION

The study of disturbed dental development is a bit like reading a newspaper—it is the bad news we find most fascinating. The durability of enamel makes it a particularly informative hard tissue for studying the adaptations of ancient and contemporary peoples to their physical and sociocultural environments. Unlike bone, dental enamel does not remodel once it is formed and consequently can retain a complete record of physiological disturbance for an individual from the second trimester to puberty. Humans have potentially a particularly rich record of such developmental disturbance because they mature so very slowly. Developmental defects of enamel can be readily observed on the external surfaces of the teeth or through relatively simple microscopic examination of histological thin sections.

BASIC HISTOLOGY AND DENTAL MATURATION

While the general pattern of enamel development is well understood (Boyde, 1989, Moss-Salentijn and Klyvert, 1980, Osborn, 1981, Provenze, 1986 and Warshawsky, 1985, provide general reviews), the fine points of tooth formation and the appearance of histological structures are not readily expressed nor is their meaning agreed upon. This may be due to variation in analytical techniques, which range widely from radiography and scanning electron microscopy to tissue staining. Uncertainties as to the precise mode and rates of formation of teeth (e.g., crown elongation) and structures within teeth (e.g., enamel prisms), and population differences in these processes, inhibit our ability to understand the meaning of developmental defects of enamel and their application to anthropological problems.

Enamel and dentin secretion begins at the dentinoenamel junction of cusp tips at a time that is genetically prescribed for each tooth type (Garn, 1961). Ameloblasts, enamel-forming cells, secrete a protein matrix that forms the basic structure of the enamel crown. Subsequently, ameleoblast cells take on a resorptive and transport function that hardens the enamel until it is approximately 96% mineral by weight (Reith and Cotty, 1967). Enamel formation is usually described as occurring in two steps: the secretion of an organic matrix, including primary calcification, followed by a maturation phase of progressive mineralization (Diamond and Weinmann, 1940). However, the attainment of full mineralization is a protracted process that involves three waves of calcification from the surface to the dentinoenamel junction and back again, resulting in a highly mineralized outermost layer (Suga, 1989). This process can span years, occurring even posteruptively (Fearnhead et al., 1982). Immature (i.e., newly deposited) enamel is formed of tiny crystallites of mineral, akin to hydroxyapatite, composed mainly of calcium

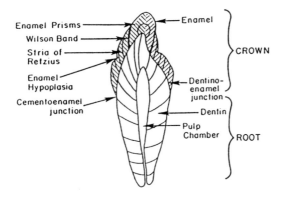

Fig. 1. Diagrammatic representation of longitudinal section through a human mandibular canine, showing major incremental features of crown. Reproduced from Rose et al. (1985), with permission of the publisher.

and phosphorus. Enamel maturation occurs through growth in size of crystallites, deposited upon initial mineralization, which largely replace the organic matrix.

Enamel is a hard layer of mineralized tissue on the chewing surfaces of teeth that is composed of thousands of tightly packed prisms. These primary structures are created by the combined activities of four adjacent ameloblasts, which secrete a keyhole-shaped rod that elongates away from the dentinoenamel junction (Shawashy and Yaeger, 1986). Dental crowns grow outward for a time as enamel rods (prisms) until the normal thickness of enamel (about 1–2 mm in humans) has been attained (Gantt, 1986). The enamel is deposited in successive increments that cover the previously deposited layer completely, but later the increments are deposited only on the sides of the crown as overlapping sleeves that extend cervically (Fig. 1). Active, secretory ameloblasts differ in the length of time they have been functional, the more cervical ameloblasts having secreted enamel matrix for the shortest period of time. The "front" of new enamel matrix is therefore tangential or curved in relation to the dentinoenamel junction. It is furthest away from the dentinoenamel junction occlusally and closest at the cervical end. The shape of this forming front is maintained in the pattern of striae of Retzius, normal incremental

structures of enamel. There is general agreement that they are an exaggerated version of the same physicochemical alteration that causes cross-striations. For example, Osborn (1973) accounts for striae of Retzius as reflecting hydrostatically mediated changes in secretory rate that result in major changes in prism direction. Dental crowns grow in height by recruitment of differentiated ameloblasts that extend the dentinoenamel margin in a cervical direction. Dentin, which constitutes the bulk of a human tooth, continues to be deposited to form the root after the enamel crown thins to completion at the cervical margin. Cementum formation commences at the neck of the tooth and eventually covers the root.

It is commonly accepted that enamel prisms grow with a circadian rhythm of about 2 to 6 μm, creating a characteristic series of constrictions or cross-striations (e.g., Boyde, 1976; Osborn, 1981). Under certain conditions of specimen preparation and lighting, layering is observable within individual prisms, as cross-striations, and across prisms as striae of Retzius (Fig. 2). Indeed, it is often claimed that the latter are simply a series of accentuated cross-striations (Gohdo, 1982). However, the developmental processes of cross-striations and striae of Retzius are not well understood. Boyde has suggested that there is a daily interval of decreased rate of matrix and mineral secretion that permits the deposition of more crystallites on the sides of the Tomes's process pit (Boyde, 1989). This produces a localized swelling in the prism that alternates with a narrowing of the prism as the ameloblasts' activity speeds up. In this scheme, the result is varicosities along the prism's length with a periodicity of 4–8 μm. Osborn (1973) believes, rather, that prism diameter remains constant but develops kinks, which bend the light, owing to episodic buckling of the cell as hydrostatic forces recommence after an interval of quiescence.

For almost three decades, Boyde (1963, 1976, 1979) has reaffirmed observations by Asper (1916), half a century before, that cross-striations with a repeat interval of 4 μm exist and that these are deposited daily. Several recent workers have linked counts of perikymata (easily discerned ridges on the dental crowns) to absolute rates of crown formation in differ-

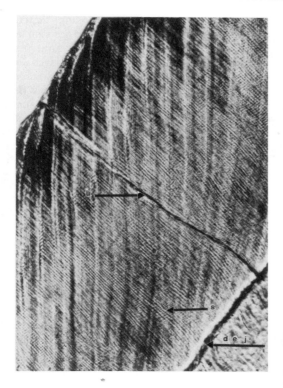

Fig. 2. Incremental features of enamel: Most obvious layers are physiological striae (s), of which some are accentuated as dark pathological striae (bottom left); cross-striations produce fine banding parallel to dentinoenamel junction (dej); nonincremental structure is a lamella (L) Reproduced from Kraus et al. (1969), with permission of the publisher.

ent hominine species. They claim to be able to show in histological thin sections that perikymata are separated by 7 or 8 cross-striations and hence take about a week to form (Beynon and Wood, 1987; Bromage and Dean, 1985). However, the basis for this methodology has not gone unchallenged (Weber and Glick, 1975; Warshawsky and Bai, 1983; Warshawsky, 1988). Actually, there is no unequivocal evidence that the rate of "banding" is circadian. The latter assumption arose historically through a methodological error in the optical microscopy of sectioned teeth. Only recently has it been realized that because enamel prisms, which undulate significantly in their course from the dentinoenamel junction to the surface, are so very long and thin, there is virtually no chance that a sectioned surface would parallel a prism throughout its length. In fact, prisms, which are deposited in adjacent rows, are inevitably sectioned more or less obliquely across their width. This can create the optical illusion of cross-striations, which are in reality the ends of transversely or obliquely sectioned adjacent prisms (Weber and Glick, 1975); a conclusion acknowledged by Boyde in 1979. Alternatively or additionally, Warshawsky (1989) has suggested that as a specimen is sectioned or fractured, spiralling crystallites, ranged along the prism, are plucked differentially, depending on the degree of crystal edge that is exposed to the cleaving surface; this creates a banded appearance. For the nonspecialist the uncertainty surrounding this fundamental aspect of enamel formation is worrisome. The prospect of uniform time markers in the enamel is tantalizing, since it bears directly on so many important issues in dental anthropology, ranging from the evolution of the human growth curve (Mann et al., 1990) to reconstruction of seasonality (Skinner, 1986b). For the moment the case is unproven and we should direct our research efforts to resolution of the problem.

TERMINOLOGY

The process of enamel formation involves the protracted replacement of a soft tissue matrix by mineral ions at varying rates; consequently, disturbed formation takes several characteristic forms.

Enamel Hypoplasia

Enamel hypoplasia occurs on the external surface of teeth as reduced enamel thickness macroscopically visible as more or less confluent horizontal pits or as actual grooves (Fig. 3). This change is usually attributed to an initial deficit in matrix formation during the secretory phase of enamel formation (Spouge, 1973; Suckling, 1989).

Enamel Hypocalcification

Enamel hypocalcification is also visible on dental surfaces, where it usually appears as dull-white opacities or stained areas of reduced mineralization (Fig. 4). Often termed simply a problem of matrix mineralization, hypocalcifi-

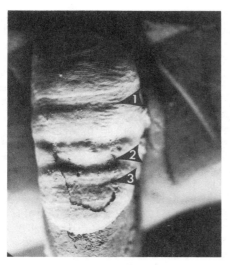

Fig. 3. Example of linear enamel hypoplasia. Three examples are indicated by numbers. Reproduced from Goodman and Rose (1990), with permission of the publisher.

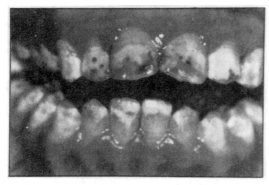

Fig. 4. Example of enamel hypocalcification. Opacities are present on all the teeth in the form of white patches. Reproduced from King and Wei (1986), with permission of the publisher.

cation is perhaps better understood as impaired functioning of ameloblasts (Suga, 1989). In that mineralization is a protracted process that continues even after eruption of the tooth, the timing of enamel hypocalcification is not readily inferred. Also, since staining from soils can occur in buried remains, hypocalcification has been relatively neglected by dental anthropologists.

Pathological Striae

Pathological striae of enamel reflect disturbances of the normal incremental pattern of enamel deposition on the growing dental crown (Massler et al., 1941). These are visible in low-power, transmitted-light microscopy as optically distinct lines that mark changes in mineral ion density and/or crystal orientation at the forming enamel front (Rose, 1973; Wilson and Schroff, 1970) (Fig. 2). Hypoplastic enamel is usually associated directly with a pathological stria (Condon, 1981), but the reverse is less often true. Unfortunately, enamel striae can only be observed, currently, through destructive thin-sectioning techniques.

IDENTIFICATION AND RELIABILITY

Enamel hypoplasias are regions of decreased enamel thickness produced by cessation or slowing of secretion by the ameloblast. In that an actual absence of enamel, exposing the dentin, is rarely observed, it seems that regardless of the severity of systemic stress involved, it is only ameloblasts that are approaching the end of their secretory life that are actually halted in their activity. In this case, the floor of the hypoplastic area may reveal prismatic enamel (there is normally an aprismatic layer laid down in the final stages of forming surface enamel). More usual, however, is a diminution of ameloblast activity that produces more closely spaced striae of Retzius, which terminate, in thin section, in a slight depression on the enamel surface (Condon, 1988). In either case, the ameloblasts that were depositing the more cervically located enamel are less affected and recover sufficiently from the stress episode to deposit the normal thickness of enamel. As a result, typically, a hypoplastic groove is formed somewhat occlusally but in association with an accentuated (pathological) stria of Retzius that marks the full height of the enamel front forming at the time of the stress.

Several authors distinguish between "pathological" striae and "rhythmic" or "physiological" striae. To avoid confusion, Rose (1973, 1977) has redefined pathological striae as Wilson bands in which there is a combination of altered prism elongation and abnormal structure (Condon, 1981). The cause of physiological striae is unknown. They are evenly spaced incremental features, most visible in the gingival enamel (Moss-Salentijn and Klyvert, 1980; Gustafson and Gustafson, 1967; Wilson and Schroff, 1970). Warshawsky (1985, 1988) has posited that physiological striae are due to recruitment of a cohort of approximately seven ameloblasts at a time during cervical elongation. It must be stressed, however, that there is no clear distinction between the two forms of striae at the customary levels of magnification employed by anthropologists, since Wilson bands appear simply as accentuated physiological striae.

Turning now to surface defects, they can be described fairly unequivocally in terms of defect type, number or demarcation, and location. These have been standardized by the Commission on Oral Health, Research and Epidemiology (Ainamo, 1982) and recently modified by Clarkson (1989) (see Table 1). The term *enamel hypoplasia* describes any deficiency of enamel thickness, including a pit, line, groove, or other form of missing enamel of various depths. A pit is comparable to Federation Dentaire Internationale (FDI) type 3 and may be linearly arranged or nonlinear, singular or multiple. *Linear enamel hypoplasia* (LEH), that most commonly encountered by anthropologists, is comparable to FDI type 4. LEH is distinguished by a marked horizontal groove or undulation due to decreased enamel thickness (Goodman et al., 1980). An enamel opacity or hypocalcification (FDI types 1 and 2) refers to a change in color and opacity of enamel without change in thickness.

The current classification of surface defects is inadequate. Particularly, anthropologists need to be able to classify the variety of pits and grooves encountered, both for descriptive and etiological purposes. For example, a horizontal arrangement of pits (a mere subtype of type 3) is far more commonly encountered than type 5 (a vertical groove whose etiology is quite obscure). Similarly, since the FDI classification was created, a new class of enamel hypoplasia with combined local and systemic factors, termed *localized hypoplasia of the primary canine* (LHPC) (Skinner, 1986a; Skinner and Hung, 1986, 1989), has been described (LHPC is described later in this chapter).

A pervasive problem is the lack of a means for describing a gradient of severity. For example, there is little to distinguish reliably normal perikymata from mild hypoplasia. Similarly, the meaning of differences in defect width and depth is unclear. They may vary with the se-

TABLE 1. Scoring Codes for Developmental Defects of Enamel (Federation Dentaire Internationale)

Defect category	Code (deciduous/ permanent)
Index of developmental defects of enamel (Ainamo, 1982)	
A. Type of defect	
Normal	A/0
Opactiy	
White/cream	B/1
Yellow/brown	C/2
Hypoplasia	
pits	D/3
Grooves (horizontal)	E/4
Grooves (vertical)	F/5
Missing enamel	G/6
Discolored enamel	H/7
Any other defect	I/8
B. Number or demarcation	
Single defect	A/1
Multiple defects	B/2
Diffuse opacities (paralleling perikymata)	C/3
Diffuse patchy opacities	D/4
C. Location of defect	
Gingival half of crown	1
Incisal half of crown	2
Gingival and incisal halves	3
Occlusal	4
Cuspal	5
Whole surface	6
Other combinations	7
Modified DDE index for use in general purpose epidemiological studies (Clarkson, 1989)	
Normal	0
Demarcated opacities	
White/cream	1
Yellow/brown	2
Diffuse opacities	
Lines	3
Patchy	4
Confluent	5
Confluent/patchy + staining + loss of enamel	6
Hypoplasia	
Pits	7
Missing enamel	8
Any other defects	9
Extent of Defect	
Normal	0
Less than < 1/3	1
At least 1/2 < 2/3	2
At least 2/3	3

verity and/or duration of the stress (Guita, 1984; Shklar and McCarthy, 1976). These are significant problems that require clarification as soon as possible if surface defects are to be interpreted with confidence. There are few published tests of intra- and interobservor error in recording the presence, location, or size of enamel defects. Murray et al. (1984) report 86.4% intraobservor agreement and Goodman et al. (1987) report 80.8% interobservor agreement in studies of living individuals from England and Mexico, respectively. Staining and adherent deposits on prehistoric teeth can create further uncertainties, as can a sheen of moisture on the teeth of living subjects [directed air will rapidly dry the teeth (King, 1989)]. Goodman and Rose (1990) discuss strategies for recording surface details including casting, coating with ammonium chloride vapor, and photography. Despite these problems, recourse to the FDI classification has proved useful in field studies of contemporary groups (e.g., Goodman et al., 1987) and should enhance communication among specialists. Bioarchaeologists should examine the utility of this epidemiological tool for their own work.

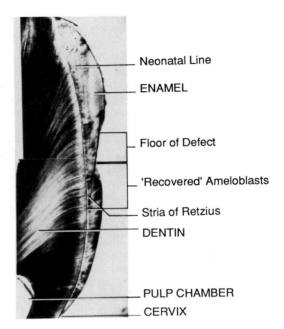

Fig. 5. Localized hypoplasia of the primary canine and associated pathological stria. Reproduced from Skinner and Hung (1989), with permission of the publisher.

ANTHROPOLOGICAL STUDIES OF ENAMEL DEFECTS

Most reports emphasize either the primary or secondary dentition but seldom both. Several earlier studies of the primary teeth from prehistoric Amerindians allegedly showed prenatal locations of both hypocalcifications and hypoplasia, with frequent involvement of the primary canine (e.g., Cook and Buikstra, 1979; Blakey and Armelagos, 1985; Storey, 1988). Increased stress at younger ages among these groups is usually attributed to the nutritional consequences of a subsistence shift associated with the introduction of maize agriculture. Recent research by Skinner (1986a; Skinner and Hung, 1986, 1989) indicates the need for caution regarding interpretations in these studies. It now seems apparent that hypoplasias form somewhat occlusally on the surface, since there is recovery of the secretory function of more cervically located ameloblasts (Fig. 5). This has resulted in a tendency to significantly underestimate the age of occurrence of hypoplasias in the primary dentition (e.g., by several months for the primary canine) and to identify hypoplasias that are probably perinatal or even later as prenatal defects.

Also, it is clear from contemporary epidemiological studies that the primary canine owes most of its hypoplasia to a different cause than do the other primary teeth (Skinner and Hung, 1986). Localized hypoplasia of the primary canine (LHPC) is caused by minor trauma to ameloblasts through fenestrated cortical bone overlying the canine crypt that is due, it is thought, to some form of nutritional stress (Skinner and Hung, 1989). Thus LHPC, which is caused by a combination of local and systemic factors, tends to be far more common than hypoplasia of the remaining primary dentition that is due to systemic factors. This results in a strong bias to our interpretation of comparative prevalence of enamel hypoplasia in the primary dentition. For example, in a Californian study (Nation et al., 1987) the proportion of children with enamel hypoplasia of the primary canine was 18%, a figure that increased only to 20.7% when the entire primary dentition was included; in other words 25% of the teeth accounted for 87% of the enamel defects. Consequently, the meaning of the comparative prevalence of enamel hypoplasia in the primary dentitions of prehistoric samples is no longer clear.

A similar caution applies to the interpretation of the timing of hypocalcified areas in the primary dentition. While it is widely recognized that full mineralization is a post-matrix-secretion phenomenon, there is no agreement, nor much research, on the actual lag time reflected by a hypocalcified area, primarily because the mineralization process is quite protracted. Mineralization can be visualized as taking place in two directions: cervically, and between the dentinoenamel junction and surface. Crown elongation in a cervical direction is accomplished, as described earlier, through a biphasic process of matrix secretion followed closely by initial mineralization. Deutsch and Pe'er (1982) show that the rate of mineralization (along the tooth's longitudinal axis) is twice the rate of matrix formation, so that the relatively mineralized portion of a crown catches up, to a degree, with crown elongation. Enamel hypoplasia is attributed to disturbed matrix secretion at this early stage in the process of crown formation. Enamel hypocalcification, on the other hand, is due to undermineralization, possibly at this early stage but more likely during the protracted mineralization of the enamel thickness. In experimental work with goat and sheep molars, the results of which were generalized to humans, Suga (1982) found that after the initial secretion of matrix, accompanied immediately by mineralization to about 20%, there followed three waves of progressive mineralization (maturation stage) from the surface to the dentinoenamel junction and back to the surface, ending with hypermineralization of the outermost layer. While hypomineralization could potentially occur at any time until the end of the mineralization phase, it appears that the bulk of mineralization occurs in stage 2 (the first wave of mineralization from surface to depth). Deutsch and Pe'er (1982) show that stage 2 mineralization of anterior primary human enamel lags at least 3 months behind initial matrix secretion (i.e., is not demonstrable in concepti of age 8 months intrauterine). In-

deed, even after 5 months of crown formation, which corresponds to the time of birth, the earliest secreted enamel has yet to attain full mineralization.

As to the total duration of not fully mineralized human enamel, Fearnhead and colleagues (1982) have observed that porosity and the potential for continued mineralization are present even in teeth that have erupted (which for the anterior primary teeth would be at postnatal ages from 6 to 20 months); indeed they conclude that "there appears to be no clear fixed timing for the completion of maturation" (p. 1528). Consequently, it is not known whether a hypocalcified area has been produced by lack of available minerals at the beginning, middle, or end of the mineralization process. Suckling and Thurley (1984) remark that

At present, there is no information available on the duration of the secondary and tertiary stages of mineralization (the maturation phase) of the human permanent teeth. Thus it is not possible to diagnose the age of a child at which an enamel [hypocalcification] defect was formed from the appearance of the defect and its location on the surface of the erupted teeth. (p. 358)

There is no reason to doubt that this gloomy conclusion also applies to hypomineralized areas of the primary teeth.

In summary, the timing of hypomineralization areas of enamel seems difficult to determine, but it can be assumed that the probable minimum time lag between matrix formation and completed mineralization (and therefore its potential for hypomineralization) is 5 months for the primary dentition [based on rapidly forming incisor teeth (Deutsch and Pe'er, 1982)] and could be as long as a year or more. Consequently, in view of the latter comments and the earlier conclusion that timing hypoplasias in primary teeth tends to be underestimated because of their placement on the dental crown, it is difficult to accept assertions of prenatal-onset hypomineralization and hypoplasia. Support for this position has recently appeared in Cook (1990). Demonstration that a hypoplastic defect actually has occurred prenatally will require that teeth be sectioned to disclose placement of the defect relative to the neonatal line.

Much research on enamel hypoplasia is devoted to permanent teeth, which disclose developmental disturbance from age 1 year to around puberty. Most studies show that there is considerable variation in the proportion of affected individuals and teeth within individuals from particular samples exhibiting enamel hypoplasia (Table 2). While this tabulation is necessarily crude because it involves comparison of a wide range of studies, there appears to be a tendency for technologically more advanced peoples, particularly agricultural and industrial groups, to show increased prevalence of enamel hypoplasia, and presumably stress, which is a pattern remarked upon by several other workers (e.g., articles in Cohen and Armelagos, 1984; Smith and Peretz, 1986; Lanphear, 1990). An allied phenomenon is the demonstration that the prevalence of enamel hypoplasia and/or microdefects (striae) varies inversely with socioeconomic level in both contemporary and prehistoric societies (e.g., Cook, 1981). It is at the level of the latter sort of study, which compares samples from similar socioecological settings, that meaningful differences will be revealed. Perhaps the most convincing research, as to the meaning of developmental defects of enamel, is that which provides good documentation of a correlation of enamel defects with reduced life expectancy (Cook and Buikstra, 1979; Goodman and Armelagos, 1988).

SCOPE AND LIMITATIONS

A clear distinction must be drawn between events at the individual and cellular levels. Questions of validity and time (previously addressed), and specificity and sensitivity (discussed below), depend upon a solid understanding of cellular activity.

Specificity

It is not entirely clear how malnutrition and fever, for example, affect the normal secretory activities of ameloblasts; consequently, we cannot predict which particular stressors will produce enamel hypoplasia. The two broad categories of stress that appear to account for enamel defects are (1) insufficient materials for matrix formation or mineralization (malnutrition) and (2) disturbed cellular function. Ni-

kiforuk and Fraser (1981) have concluded that low serum calcium is a common factor in many conditions that are associated with enamel hypoplasia, whether attributable to a mineral deficit in ingestion or absorption, or to impaired cellular calcium secretion. Support for this view has been provided in an important study by Seow et al. (1989), who show that enamel hypoplasia among prematurely born, low-birthweight infants is associated with a 29% reduction in cortical thickness in the humerus. In other words, both the bones and teeth are reduced in normal thickness owing to a mineral deficiency (not reflected, however, in differences in serum calcium values (contra Nikiforuk and Fraser, 1981). Seow and colleagues conclude that the ameloblast is extremely sensitive to calcium changes of even a few hours duration. A myriad of contemporary conditions are known to disturb enamel formation, including cerebral disorders (Via and Churchill, 1959), rickets, tetany, measles, whooping cough, pneumonia, severe gastrointestinal disease, prematurity, defective nutrition, convulsion, scurvy, syphilis, heredity, hormonal imbalance, hypovitaminosis A, exanthematous diseases (Sweeney et al., 1969; Herman and McDonald, 1963); cerebral palsy, birth trauma, allergy (Rattner and Myers, 1962); primary maternal hyperparathyroidism, maternal diabetes mellitus, neonatal asphyxia, hemolytic disease of the newborn, and reduced sunlight (Purvis et al., 1973).

Only slight acquaintance with the conditions of life in disadvantaged societies shows that the main stressors on children are malnutrition and infectious disease (Martorell, 1980). While it is recognized that these are broad and not mutually exclusive categories of stress, it does not necessarily follow that enamel hypoplasias are poor indicators of dietary stress, as suggested by Neiburger (1990). Interpretations of defects in ancient hard tissues are inferences rather than precise diagnoses. They are probability statements based on the best available scientific evidence.

In modern epidemiological studies, particularly in Guatemala, the pioneering works of Sweeney (e.g., Sweeney and Guzman, 1966; Sweeney et al., 1969, 1971) and Infante (Infante, 1974; Infante and Gillespie, 1974) have shown a consistent association between

TABLE 2. Comparative Prevalence of Enamel Hypoplasia in the Permanent Dentition of Selected Samples

Sample	Percentage of affected teeth		Percentage of affected individuals		Source
Nonhuman primates					
Pan troglodytes	16	$(n = 748)^a$	58	$(n = 110)$	1
Male	18	$(n = 208)$	66	$(n = 35)$	
Female	15	$(n = 540)$	55	$(n = 75)$	
G. gorilla	20	$(n = 849)^a$	76	$(n = 119)$	
Male	24	$(n = 386)$	81	$(n = 53)$	
Female	17	$(n = 463)$	71	$(n = 66)$	
Plio-Pleistocene hominines					
Australopithecus					
Sterkfontein	8	$(n = 166)^g$	12	$(n = 66)^g$	2
Swartkrans	17	$(n = 304)^g$	31	$(n = 143)^g$	
robustus	29	$(n = 47)$			16
Pre-Neanderthal Ibeas, Spain	24	$(n = 21)$			15
Late Pleistocene					
Homo s. neanderthalensis	42	$(n = 565)$	57	$(n = 165)$	3
Homo s. sapiens (West. Europe)					
Middle Paleol.	19	$(n = 157)$	34	$(n = 64)^b$	4
Upper Paleol.	30	$(n = 160)$	45	$(n = 53)^b$	
Early Holocene or preagricultural					
Scandinavia			53	$(n = 58)$	13
Natufian Levant			25	$(n = 135)$	5
Aust. aborigines	31	$(n = 521)^c$			6
Males	33	$(n = 393)$			
Females	24	$(n = 128)$			
Illinois Woodland			58	$(n = 130)$	8
Dickson Mound			45	$(n = 20)$	9
Ohio River Valley	21	$(n = 97)$			10
Cent. California			11–20	$(n = 3610)$	11
Ecuador (Sta. Elena)	0.4	$(n = 1989)$			12
Neolithic or agricultural					
Scandinavia			45	$(n = 102)$	13
Levant			40	$(n = 37)$	5
Iran/Iraq			6	$(n = 49)$	7
Illinois Miss.[d]			56	$(n = 94)$	8
Dickson Mound Miss.[e]			70	$(n = 91)$	9
Ohio River Valley	60	$(n = 494)$			10
Ecuador	3	$(n = 3625)$			12
Metal ages/Roman/Medieval					
Levant			70	$(n = 282)$	5
Iran/Iraq			17	$(n = 327)$	7
Poundbury			38	$(n = 457)$	17
Historic					
19th Cent. Poorhouse			72	$(n = 537)^f$	14
African Baptist Church			82	$(n = 73)$	18
Caribbean slave			54[h]	$(n = 103)$	19

[a]Mandibular lefts only.
[b]Immature specimens only.
[c]Canines and third molars only.
[d]Includes Late Late Woodland.
[e]Includes Mississippian Acculturated Late Woodland.
[f]No sex differences, incisors and canines only.
[g]Includes some primary teeth.
[h]Clearly underestimated in authors' opinion.

Sources
1. Skinner (1986b).
2. White (1978).
3. Ogilvie, Curran, and Trinkaus (1989).
4. Skinner (1989).
5. Smith, Bar-Yosef, and Sillen (1984).
6. Webb (1989).
7. Rathbun (1984).
8. Cook (1984).
9. Goodman et al. (1984).
10. Perzigian, Tench, and Braun (1984).
11. Dickel, Schulz, and McHenry (1984).
12. Ubelaker (1984).
13. Alexandersen 1988 (cited in Meiklejohn and Zvelebil (manuscript)).
14. Lanphear (1990).
15. de Castro (1987).
16. Robinson (1956).
17. Stuart-Macadam (1985).
18. Rathbun (1987).
19. Corruccini, Handler, and Jacobi (1985).

enamel hypoplasias and socioeconomic status, especially malnutrition. Goodman and colleagues (1987) studied the frequency and chronological distribution of enamel hypoplasias in 300 Mexican children from five rural communities in which mild to moderate malnutrition was endemic (children were about 60%–95% of weight for age). Almost 47% of the children were affected, and most deciduous tooth defects were attributed by the authors to the last trimester and birth (but see our caveats, expressed earlier, that timing of enamel defects in the primary teeth tends to be underestimated by several months). The peak timing of stress for the permanent dentition was 18–36 months (linked possibly to weaning). Longitudinal study is under way in a highland Mexican community where the children of nutritionally supplemented adolescents show only half the frequency of enamel hypoplasias compared with controls in the same village (Goodman et al., 1989; Goodman and Rose, 1991). It should be noted, however, that the improved nutrition was associated with a reduced number of days of illness with gastroenteritis and respiratory infection (Chavez and Martinez, 1982); so the contribution of the variables of nutrition and disease to enamel hypoplasia is still uncertain.

Nevertheless, this situation is not as disappointing as it might seem at first glance. If one is seeking to elucidate the adaptive and functional consequence of stressors, then a nonspecific indicator might be quite useful, in much the same manner that reduced stature acts as a good guide to chronic nutritional stress (Martorell and Ho, 1984). If enamel hypoplasias are rather nonspecific but sensitive, they will be an important medium for anthropological research, especially since they can be used to refine an understanding of the timing of hypoplastic lesions.

An experimental basis for linking the occurrence of enamel developmental defects to malnutrition was established through numerous rodent studies in the 1930s and 1950s. The development of rodent incisor enamel is continuous, however, and differs signficantly from that of other mammals (Fejerskov, 1979). The most important recent experimental work on enamel defect etiology has been undertaken by Suckling and coworkers on New Zealand sheep

(Suckling and Thurley, 1984; Suckling, 1986). Induced parasitism showed a clear dose-related response in the form of increased enamel hypoplasia (Suckling et al., 1983, 1986) but not hypocalcification. In that sheep with the highest parasite load experienced severe weight loss and debilitation, it may be concluded that nutrient robbing by the parasite results in an inability of the host's ameloblasts to secrete sufficient matrix.

Traditionally, systemic or localized disruptions of enamel integrity have been recognized. As noted above, a new class of enamel hypoplasia—localized hypoplasia of the primary canine (LHPC)—that is due to both factors has recently been described (Skinner, 1986a). Epidemiological study of this condition in Burnaby, British Columbia (Skinner and Hung, 1989) implicates nutritional factors in thinning of the facial bone in affected infants. Cortical bone being deposited superficial to the unerupted primary canine crown thins to the point of fenestration. This exposes the enamel-forming cells to minor impacts as the infant learns to mouth objects. Mothers of affected infants (2.4% of the general population) usually belong to low-income, ethnic minorities (East Asians and Indo-Asians) with reduced consumption of cow's milk and/or duration of breast feeding.[1] In the United States, the most commonly affected sector consists of mildly malnourished black children (Silberman et al., 1989).

To conclude, disturbed enamel formation is a relatively nonspecific marker of physiological stress, usually caused in traditional societies by malnutrition and infection. Despite uncertainty as to the precise cause of the observed stress, it is valid and informative to compare the relative prevalence of disturbed enamel formation among various prehistoric and modern samples.

Sensitivity

It is important to distinguish between susceptibility of the individual, or classes of individuals, to stress as a function of biosocial factors such as status or prior infection from

---

1. The reasons for avoidance of milk among certain ethnic groups (e.g., lactose intolerance) were not investigated.

TABLE 3. Age of Onset and Completion of Enamel Deposition (Mid-sex Ages in Years)

Tooth type	Upper			Lower		
	Start	Stop	Duration	Start	Stop	Duration
Primary[a]						
Central incisor	−0.37[b]	0.09[c]	0.46	−0.42[b]	0.02[c]	0.44
Lateral incisor	−0.42[b]	0.15[c]	0.57	−0.42[b]	0.21[c]	0.63
Canine	−0.33[b]	0.77[c]	1.10	−0.33[b]	0.96[c]	1.29
First molar	−0.33[b]	0.50[b]	0.83	−0.33[b]	0.51[d]	0.84
Second molar	−0.25[b]	0.50[b]	0.75	−0.25[b]	0.76[d]	1.01
Permanent						
Central incisor	0.42[f]	3.65[e]	3.23	0.25[g]	3.60[e]	3.35
Lateral incisor	0.83[g]	3.90[e]	3.07	0.25[g]	3.85[e]	3.60
Canine	0.33[g]	4.50[e]	4.17	0.61[d]	4.45[e]	3.84
First premolar	1.50[g]	5.45[e]	3.95	2.06[d]	5.30[e]	3.24
Second premolar	3.80[e]	6.10[e]	2.30	3.95[e]	6.10[e]	2.15
First molar	0.00[g]	3.80[e]	3.80	0.10[d]	3.70[e]	3.60
Second molar	3.75[e]	6.50[e]	2.75	3.75[e]	6.50[e]	2.75
Third molar	9.35[e]	13.00[e]	3.65	9.40[e]	13.05[e]	3.65

Duration values are approximate since calculations are based on observations from different studies.
[a]gestation is presumed to be 9.5 months.
[b]Levine, Turner, and Dobbing (1979).
[c]Deutsch, Tam, and Stack (1985).
[d]Fanning (1971).
[e]Anderson, Thompson, and Popovich (1976).
[f]Mellanby in footnote g.
[g]Massler, Schour, and Poncher (1941).

susceptibility of the individual's tissues to record stress. There appear to be considerable, but little understood, differences in the sensitivity of different teeth and different parts within teeth to stress. For example, it seems that lingual enamel, thin enamel, and smaller teeth are less vulnerable (Suga, 1989). Smith and Peretz (1986) found maxillary teeth from a Byzantine Arab sample more commonly hypoplastic, which they tentatively attributed to a better blood supply in the lower jaw—an intriguing speculation. Even though enamel formation is of uncertain sensitivity to various stressors, we can conclude with confidence that enamel hypoplasias are less sensitive indicators of stress than are pathological striae of enamel. Not only are internal striae much more common than external hypoplasias, it is well known that almost all primary enamel crowns will exhibit internally an accentuated stria known as the neonatal line, while only rarely is this expressed on the surface of the tooth as a hypoplastic groove. In that perinatal physiology and birth traumata are well-documented phenomena, the severity of the neonatal line provides an unappreciated guide to ameloblast sensitivity to stressors of documentable duration and type. For example, Eli and colleagues (1989) have shown that the neonatal line is wider than normal in children born by difficult operative delivery and thinner than normal in children born by cesarean section.

Consideration of the problem of patterned susceptibility suggests that the timing of enamel formation is of paramount importance. In other words, enamel has to be forming for hypoplasia to occur, while the number of crowns forming throughout childhood varies in characteristic ways. Consequently, we have attempted to develop a critique of the current understanding of dental chronology (Table 3). On the population level, enamel defects potentially record developmental disturbances from approximately 5 months in utero until about age 7 years with a hiatus from age 8 to 9 years, when typically no enamel is being formed, followed by third-molar enamel deposition from about age 10 to 13 (Anderson et al., 1976) or 16 years (Goodman et al., 1980). The richest period of enamel formation is around ages 2 to

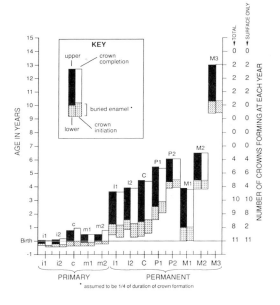

Fig. 6. Age-related susceptibility of dentition to surface defects of enamel. One side of both upper and lower jaws is included.

effect" in which only those adults who die young, perhaps as a consequence of heightened childhood stress, will be selected for analysis—a choice that would result in the false inference of high levels of childhood stress for that population. The solution to this problem, where samples are sufficiently large, is to compare the prevalence of enamel defects in a homologous tooth (likely third molars as these will be least worn) from an adult sample partitioned into younger and older individuals. If no difference is found in defect prevalence between younger and older adult cohorts, then worn teeth from the older adults can be included in the analysis.

WITHIN-TOOTH CONSIDERATIONS

There is a difference between the potential of the tooth surface (enamel hypoplasia) and that of the interior (pathological striae) to disclose stress. Enamel is initially deposited as successive, roughly conical increments that completely cover enamel formed earlier. Because of buried formational increments at the occlusal surface, only stress episodes experienced in the latter stages of crown formation produce hypoplastic depressions on the tooth surface. Clearly, pathological striae can, however, be deposited throughout the entire span of crown formation. Although not adequately documented, it would appear from examination of a small number of longitudinally sectioned dental crowns that between one-quarter (anterior teeth) and one-third (posterior teeth) of crown formation time, depending on the tooth type, is not expressed on the outside of the tooth (Skinner and Anderson, 1991).[2] This phenomenon seriously weakens previous efforts to infer timing of occurrence, since customarily the most occlusal level has been taken to coincide temporally with initial mineralization that is detectable radiologically.

Figure 7 shows that the first year to year and a half of incisor and canine crown formation (respectively) were not expressed on the surface of the tooth from a single individual in the

3 years (Fig. 6). Primary teeth record stress up to approximately age 1 year, whereas the secondary dentition brackets the interval from a few months after birth to middle childhood and, later, around puberty.

In that the potential of the individual to record stress in the form of enamel defects fluctuates as a function of the number of enamel crowns forming, it is important, when using the tooth as the unit of analysis, not to translate a peak or trough in occurrences of enamel hypoplasia directly into a time of heightened or lessened stress. Ogilvie and colleagues (1989) concur that this may be the reason for the lack of stress between ages 5–10 years in Neanderthals. This problem can be reduced by using a few, selected teeth or, preferably, the individual as the unit of analysis (Goodman and Armelagos, 1985).

As crowns wear down with use, earlier episodes of stress will be lost from study; consequently, in most samples of prehistoric remains older adults with severely worn teeth are not suitable for analysis of developmental defects of enamel. This could result in a "cohort

---

2. Very severe stress, e.g., birth anoxia, may halt enamel formation totally on the occlusal crown surface. While this observation contradicts the previous contention that "buried" enamel cannot record early-onset enamel hypoplasia, such severe enamel hypoplasia is very rare in prehistoric populations.

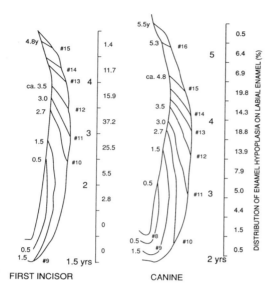

FIRST INCISOR   CANINE

Fig. 7. Reconstructed age at occurrence of internal and surface defects of maxillary central incisor and canine. Each tooth outline records the age of stress episodes experienced by an individual. To the right of each tooth is shown the percentage distribution of hypoplastic enamel defects observed by Lanphear (1990) in equal segments of crown height. Modified from Lanphear (1990) and Skinner and Anderson (1991).

Skinner and Anderson study. It appears that the maxillary canine crown records stress from 2 years (not 6 months) to about 5 years. Furthermore, in that crown formation slows markedly in the cervical region, there must be an increased susceptibility of this part of the tooth to the occurrence of stress episodes; yet one suspects that, as the enamel thins to nonexistence, it becomes difficult to discern and score hypoplasia with confidence in the final millimeter or so of crown formation. This latter area spans a significant amount of time, perhaps as much as 6 months to a year.

Goodman and Rose (1991) have acknowledged that "perhaps the most important factor in determination of the chronology of enamel hypoplasia relates to the choice of developmental standard and how it is interpreted and employed" (p. 287). As Skinner (1986b) has shown for the African ape canine, a single tooth with prolonged formation can, by itself, potentially record ≥95% of all hypoplastic episodes. Students of human enamel hypoplasia have cus-

tomarily chosen the maxillary central incisor and mandibular canine for this purpose (e.g., Goodman et al., 1980; Lanphear, 1990). However, the correctness of this choice depends on whether there are reliable standards of development for these teeth.

There are very few studies of anterior crown formation from birth to 3 years of age because of a reluctance to radiograph young children and the unsatisfactory nature of autopsy data. For example, Logan and Kronfeld (1933) produced an oft-cited report (Goodhart and Shils, 1973) of 33 terminally ill children, of whom more than half were less than 3 months of age, and who were used to represent the entire span of formation up to 15 years. It is likely that the latter report influenced Massler, Schour, and Poncher, as Kronfeld published several articles at this time with the first two authors. Anthropologists have been forced to select the only standards that included observations on the early stages of crown formation for the anterior dentition, of which those in Massler, Schour, and Poncher (1941) seemed the best. Unfortunately, these authors did not provide the source of their own sample, which allowed them to revise earlier work by Mellanby (1927, 1934) and Swanson (1931a,b).

It seems that additional standards of tooth formation are sorely needed. In the meantime investigators can continue to reconstruct age at occurrence from the standards of Massler and colleagues (1941) as long as they retain their raw data for recalibration as new standards come along. Already there is recourse to new radiological standards that are based on modern criteria for sample representativeness, some of which are based on longitudinal data (e.g., Anderson et al., 1976; Demirjian et al., 1973; Fanning, 1971; Haavikko, 1969). Regretably, current radiological standards lack information about early stages of anterior crown formation (but see Nystrom et al., 1977) and may fail to detect the earliest stages of mineralization. Nevertheless they seem to provide age estimates for crown formation that are consistent and significantly different from those provided by earlier workers. As can be seen in Table 4, selected to illustrate crown formation times for the two teeth most commonly used in enamel defect studies, the mandibular canine completes its crown at an approximate mean

TABLE 4. Comparative Prevalence of Enamel Hypoplasia in the Permanent Dentition of Selected Samples

	Maxillary central incisor		Mandibular canine	
	Start	Stop	Start	Stop
1. Goodman et al. (1980) (after Massler et al., 1941)	0	4.5	0.5	6.5
2. Anderson et al. (1976) (Canada)				
Male	?	$3.7 \pm .59^c$	?	4.8 ± 1.18^a
Female	?	$3.6 \pm .28^c$	?	$4.1 \pm .98^a$
3. Haavikko (1969) (Finland)				
Male	?	$3.3 \pm .8$	?	4.3 ± 1.6^b
Female	?	3.3 ± 1.4	?	4.1 ± 1.6^b
4. Fanning (1971) (USA)				
Male	—	—	0.7(.37–1.02)	$4.53(3.37–5.72)^c$
Female	—	—	.52(.29–1.21)	$4.39(3.54–5.47)^c$

[a] 2 SD.
[b] 10–90th percentile.
[c] 3rd–97th percentile.

age of 4.2 years—substantially less than the 6–6.5 years claimed by Massler and colleagues (1941) and 6–7 years claimed by Logan and Kronfeld (cited in Schour, 1953). For two reasons it seems likely that the true interval of developmental time for the canine, for example, for which stress can be recorded, is closer to 3 years, not 5 or more years as commonly supposed: The first year or so of enamel deposition is hidden by later increments (so-called "buried" enamel). Secondly, crown formation time for this tooth ends about a year and a half earlier than was thought.

MULTITOOTH CONSIDERATIONS

There is a problem occasioned by the use of multiple teeth, such as canines and incisors, to infer age at stress. These teeth, as currently studied, yield two different peak ages of stress in a single population; for example, 2.5 years for the maxillary central incisor and 3.5 years for the mandibular canine (Goodman and Armelagos, 1985). These authors held the difference to be possibly attributable to systematic error in the mineralization standard but more likely to differential intertooth susceptibility. The latter explanation is favored also by Lanphear (1990), who found peak stress times of 2.5–3 years for the incisor versus 3.5–4 years for the canine.

Recent consideration of this problem in light of revised estimates of canine crown formation and histological study of homologous striae from a single stressed individual (Skinner and Anderson, 1991) suggests a different interpretation. Tracings of, in this case, a maxillary central incisor and canine (Fig. 7) show that accepted crown formation intervals are not accurate for the purposes of reconstructing the timing of enamel hypoplasia episodes, primarily because of the fact of buried striae and the degree that this varies among teeth. When allowance is made for this change in methodology, it is clear that similar proportions (65%–80%) of stress episodes recorded in Lanphear's study (1990) of nineteenth century workhouse poor occur in those homologous portions of the incisor and canine crowns that form between 3 and 4 years of age. The important point here is that when a study seems to show different classes of teeth yielding different ages at peak stress, we should question our methods rather than the sample. Furthermore, two samples composed of different proportions of late-forming (canine) versus early-forming (incisor) teeth will provide different mean ages of peak stress if current estimates of crown formation timing are incorrect.

There is a further problem for multitooth comparisons in that most of the permanent crowns cease formation around age 6–7 years. From about age 6 years there will appear to be a sudden diminution in stress that in actuality simply reflects a sharp decline in scorable enamel.

BETWEEN-INDIVIDUALS CONSIDERATIONS

Since there is normal individual variation in the ages at which crowns start and stop formation, a cross-sectional study such as the kind anthropologists have to undertake on prehistoric remains results in an overestimation of the range during which characteristic stressors, such as weaning, occur. For example, according to Haavikko (1969) the age range (from 10th to 90th percentiles) for stages of crown formation is normally about 2 years. This includes variation in the onset and completion as well as the duration of crown formation. Even though estimates of average timing of peak stress will have a comparable uncertainty, one can determine the minimum difference necessary to demonstrate a statistically significant difference between two samples—the so-called least significant difference (Arkin and Colton, 1970). For example, a difference of three months in age at peak stress will be significant at the .05 level in two samples of 50 individuals each with a standard deviation of crown formation rates of 6 months. Thus, a reduction of 6 months in age of peak stress at Dickson Mounds, Illinois, with the adoption of intensive maize agriculture (Goodman et al., 1984) is a culturally (and statistically) significant finding.

There is a fundamental problem of methodology that has affected virtually all studies of the chronological distribution of enamel hypoplasias. These studies show consistently a peak age of stress of around 2–4 years, which is almost invariably attributed to weaning.

It is important to note that although each of these studies shows variation for age of insult, most stress periods indicate peak insult during the period from 1 to 4 yr. Most authors conclude that this period with higher evidence of morbidity is probably associated with the weaning age interval, a period of time when the individual is subjected to an increase in stress. . . . This period in the growing young preadult is especially precarious in that there is an increase in nutritional stress due to the sudden loss of nutrients provided by human milk, a decrease in immunity due to the decreased immunoglobulin levels during the 1.5–2.5 yr. period . . . , as well as the loss of immunity provided by the mother's milk. . . . The infant is also subjected to the first real extramaternal contact with the environment and new pathogens. (Larsen, 1987, p. 375)

All archaeological graphs follow a roughly normal, single-peaked distribution. We suggest that these delayed central tendencies in the archaeological samples are the result of increased infection and nutritional stress in the postweaning period. (Huss-Ashmore et al., 1982, p. 448)

These quotations are fairly typical of conclusions drawn from anthropological studies of enamel hypoplasia timing. However, for reasons explained below it may be that, in most such studies, methodological problems are creating the perceived pattern.

In that there is normal variation in the age of crown initiation and completion and in that the human dentition matures as a series of overlapping episodes of maturing teeth, there will inevitably be a "heaping up" of observations of stress at the time of peak enamel formation. The consequence of this is shown in Figure 8, where it can be seen that despite an assumption of constantly maintained stress starting from age 1 year, there appears to be a peak of stress occurring at age 3.0. The situation is actually worse than this. If one accepts that enamel hypoplasia can be expressed only in approximately the latter three-fourths of a crown's formation, the peak of enamel formation remains at 3 years of age but is much more accentuated at this age (Fig. 6).

A partial solution to this problem would be to restrict analysis of stress timing for each individual to a major occurrence on a single tooth, since only individual variation in formation for that tooth would spread out the estimated age of peak stress. Thus as long as the period of enamel formation includes that of peak stress, it would be discernible. One such study by Corruccini et al. (1985) suggests that the weakness alleged here is correct. These authors initially used all the teeth and obtained a clear unimodal distribution centering on age 3.5 years. Analysis by single individuals yielded a more uniform distribution of age at stress al-

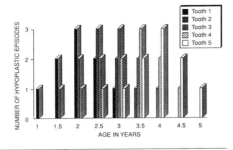

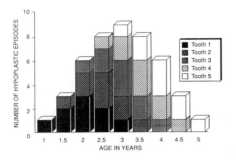

Fig. 8. Top: Distribution of stress occurrences under conditions of constant stress in separate teeth whose timing of formation varies. Bottom: Cumulative distribution of stress occurrences under conditions of constant stress in combined sample (see text for further details).

though still with higher frequency around age 3 years. The latter analysis is still methodologically flawed in that for individuals with multiple events (i.e., two or more events per tooth) they calculated a mean age at occurrence. This results in a central tendency concentrating on the average age when a tooth forms its crown. Fortunately, however, they provided a novel type of analysis, one that seems best suited for detecting weaning stress (should it exist)—age of earliest hypoplasia in each individual. In this case they noted a "markedly platykurtic distribution with mode almost evenly spread over the 1.75–3.5 year range" (Corruccini et al., 1985, p. 705). The latter pattern of stress distribution is consistent with a fairly uniform level of stress postnatally that is unassociated with weaning, or with great individual variation in the age of weaning. It is the present authors' opinion that the alleged peak episodes of stress (e.g., due to weaning) that have been

found in previous studies of the timing of enamel hypoplasia are most likely to be a statistical artifact of flawed methodology.

There are both biological and anthropological reasons for suspecting that weaning stress concentrated at age 36 months or thereabouts is unlikely. While we recognize that weaning can occur at very late ages, it is commonly observed in nonindustrialized societies in the second year of life (Cassidy, 1980), that is, 13–24 months. Anthropologists apparently assume a lag exists between weaning and onset of stress. For example, Corruccini and colleagues (1985) find the historically documented weaning age among Carribbean slaves (2–3 years) to be consistent with their age at peak stress, as reconstructed from enamel hypoplasia (3–4 years)—as much as a year later. It is worth noting that a normal age to begin supplementation, which would partially mitigate the effects of abrupt weaning, is probably about 9 months, when the primary incisor teeth are in place, milk volume starts to wane, and mineral (calcium and zinc) concentration stabilizes (Stini et al., 1980). Also, supplementation begins among the San at age 6 months even though they breast-feed frequently and for a number of years (Gaulin and Konner, 1977). For these reasons it is suggested that dental reconstruction of age at weaning is uncertain.

SUMMARY AND CONCLUSIONS

Of the three basic types of developmental defects of enamel, hypocalcification remains of limited utility owing to our current uncertainty regarding the timing of such defects. Systematic collection of exfoliated primary teeth or extracted permanent teeth from individuals with medical histories (e.g., children in institutions or enrolled in longitudinal health programs) may be the only means of documenting the timing of hypocalcification defects. While it appears unlikely that hypocalcification occurs prenatally, as is commonly claimed, this defect has clear anthropological relevance for revealing stress in early infancy. A more inclusive approach to the study of developmental defects of enamel is suggested, especially in the integration of results from the study of pathological striae and enamel hypoplasia. Striae, while difficult to observe, are more sensitive and record fairly precise episodes of stress over a longer interval than do enamel hypoplasias. Comparative studies that report only the prevalence of affected teeth or individuals are usually too crude to be very informative. A fine-grained picture of relative adaptive success will be revealed when age-specific defect frequencies are compared among populations that differ in social, temporal, ecological, or geographic circumstances.

The limitations of the medium have to be more widely appreciated. Early stages of crown formation embracing up to one-third of the formation span do not usually manifest hypoplasias. For this reason, enamel hypoplasias cannot provide a good record of stress until well into the second year of life unless the primary dentition and/or pathological striae are included in the analysis. A serious methodological flaw persists in the attempts to determine whether and when there may be ages of peak stress, particularly weaning. "Weaning stress," commonly reconstructed for skeletal samples at 3 years, is primarily if not entirely a reflection of the age at which the maximum amount of enamel is being formed. Similarly, there is an apparent decline in stress in middle childhood as the amount of enamel being deposited wanes.

How, then, shall the age of stress in different populations be determined? First of all, the unit of analysis for between-sample comparisons should be the individual not the tooth. Second, the age of occurrence must be determined more accurately. This can be accomplished in several ways:

1. Create new normative standards of crown formation; designed particularly to determine whether crown elongation varies characteristically in speed (for example, slowing markedly in the cervical third).

2. Link the timing of hypoplasia (externally) to crown formation through recourse to sectioned hypoplastic teeth where a corresponding pathological stria (when present) intersects the dentinoenamel junction.

3. Tie the formation of a particular tooth to the moment of birth so as to avoid a free-floating chronology. This can be done in selected cases by obtaining from individual children up to the age of 9 years the primary and permanent teeth from which there was crown formation overlap

and by matching striae from tooth to tooth (Skinner and Anderson, 1991). Probably the best combination of teeth to obtain would be the primary and permanent canines (and possibly the maxillary incisor to ensure covering the time of overlap in formation between the previous two teeth).

4. Combine the results from both waves of dentition so as to compare the timing of pre-weaning stress episodes in early infancy with later stress recorded on the permanent teeth (remembering that the majority of permanent enamel does not start to form until age 6 months or later and that permanent enamel does not record the timing of stress events on the surface of the tooth until about 12 months after crown initiation).

5. Separate the analyses of first and subsequent hypoplasias on single teeth from individuals, and compare the chronological distributions of each. If lactation does afford protection, then a narrow distribution of ages at first occurrence of hypoplasia might indicate a culturally sanctioned age at weaning. A decidedly platykurtic distribution of age at subsequent occurrences would reflect stress levels subsequent to weaning. A platykurtic distribution throughout early childhood that lacks a weaning peak would suggest either that there was no marked stress or that its age of occurrence is not recorded in the surface enamel. Combined studies of internal and external defects could examine the latter possibility.

Students of prehistoric adaptation who are concerned with etiology can probably discount the majority of clinical causes of disturbed enamel formation; rather the major tasks will be to determine whether the prevalence and timing of developmental defects of enamel are common to the group or have a more severe impact on particular social sectors or individuals, for example, pregnant females. Similarly, the relative contribution of malnutrition and infection to the stress load can be expected to vary with age and sex classes in ways that will illuminate the effects of cultural elaboration and shifts in subsistence. However, it seems likely that prehistorians will have to turn increasingly to epidemiological studies of their own devising among contemporary samples in order to lay the empirical foundation for theories of the impact of culture change on ancient peoples.

In the immediate future, some anthropological problems can be approached through the study of developmental defects of enamel. Episodic stress phenomena such as late-spring starvation have considerable potential for anthropological studies. Hypoplasia that is due to semiannual stressing associated with seasonal moisture cycles has been suggested for West African apes (Skinner, 1986b). Like apes and unlike other mammals, fossil hominines probably matured so slowly that several annual cycles would be recorded in their hard tissues; consequently their dental enamel potentially contains a valuable record of seasonal patterns and a guide to their own absolute maturation rates. The evolution of subsistence behaviors in the Middle Pleistocene could be reconstructed through the study of episodic striae or hypoplasias in fossil enamel; for example, variation in enamel quality, calibrated against internal episodic markers, might reveal the absence or advent of food storage techniques.

It is widely accepted that although humans show the longest gestation length of primates in absolute time, relative to our overall rate of maturation we are born early (Gavan and Swindler, 1966); estimates of our relative prematurity range from 2 months to as much as 12 months (Trinkaus, 1984; Portman, cited in Gould, 1977). Clearly birth in human beings normally occurs when maturation of the brain has attained a level commensurate with the balance between environmental pressures on the young and the degree of developed social care. Socially assisted labor and postpartum care of the mother and premature infant by other group members is a mechanism of cultural selection that can account for the relatively short gestation of modern humans. This hypothesis is testable in part because the timing of birth is recorded as a neonatal line in dental enamel forming at birth. It is possible to show the location (timing) of the neonatal line in a nondestructive manner in a cracked, but otherwise unimproved dental crown by strong backlighting (Skinner, 1990). This means that, in principle, the timing of birth in Neanderthals and other fossil forms could be investigated on cracked primary teeth in a nondestructive fashion.

While we have serious reservations about the timing of perikymata formation (Beynon

and Wood, 1987; Bromage and Dean, 1985), the potential of incremental structures of uniform periodicity to solve anthropological problems is considerable. For example, the precise timing of crown formation and stress events within the crown could be determined. Whether enamel prisms slow down their formation naturally in different parts of a tooth or in response to stress could also be investigated. The significant problem of variation in tooth size, particularly the evolutionary trend towards dental reduction among Late Pleistocene humans (Brace et al., 1987) could also be reexamined in light of the time required to deposit the enamel thickness as well as to grow crown height.

Given the time control afforded by enamel formation, research effort can be directed in the future to ontogenetic variation in major and minor elemental composition in association with enamel defects. The exciting potential of this line of effort is shown by Schneider and Blakeslee's recent demonstration (1990) that the elemental composition of normal enamel from prehistoric Arikara males is more variable than that of females, a pattern that is attributed to males' leaving their natal group upon marriage. Weaning related rises in strontium/calcium ratios in the bones of young infants from a Byzantine graveyard have been demonstrated by Sillen and Smith (1984). Uncertainty as to the precise timing of dietary supplementation in this group persists because of rapid bone turnover in infants; clearly this problem could be avoided by performing the same analysis on dental enamel. Instrumentation capabilities can be developed to permit examination within and between microdefects, such as pathological striae. For example, Noren and colleagues (1981) performed ion probe analysis of discolored enamel on either side of the neonatal line from primary teeth of infants from diabetic mothers. With this technique one can examine areas about $2.5 \times 10^3 \ \mu m^2$. They found that only postnatally did the composition of discolored enamel vary significantly. Such a technique has clear relevance for understanding the meaning of pathological enamel striae for an individual's well-being. Such studies should be allied with the collection of clinical samples of teeth from children with documented stress at known age. Extrapolation of the technique to the study of prehistoric remains (e.g., Molleson, 1988) can benefit from the extensive literature on the effect of diagenetic changes in enamel composition in buried teeth (e.g., Bell, 1990). Familiarity with the normal range of variation in biological processes suggests that the most fruitful level of analysis of trace element composition in dental enamel will be intrapopulational, that is, looking at differences between social classes and age/sex cohorts from a single locale rather than comparing samples from widely different times or geographic locales.

Lastly, an article by Skinner and Anderson (1991) has shown that pathological striae can be matched for timing and severity with detailed health records. Not only does this have potential for individualization of otherwise unidentifiable immature remains in forensic contexts, it shows, once again, that an understanding of prehistoric adaptation can be improved through recourse to the study of enamel defects in contemporary subjects.

REFERENCES

Ainamo J (1982): An epidemiological index of developmental defects of dental enamel (DDE Index). Commission on Oral Health, Research and Epidemiology. Intern Dent J 32:159–167.

Anderson DL, Thompson GW, Popovich F (1976): Age of attainment of mineralization stages of the permanent dentition. J Forensic Sci 21:191–200.

Arkin H, Colton RR (1970): "Statistical Methods" (5th ed). San Francisco: Barnes and Noble.

Asper, H (1916): Über die braune Retzius'sche Parallelstreifung im Schmelz der Menschlichen Zähne. Schweiz Vjschr Zahnheilk 26:275–314.

Bell, LS (1990): Palaeopathology and diagenesis: An SEM evaluation of structural changes using backscattered electron imaging. J Archaeol Sci 17:85–102.

Beynon AD, Wood BA (1987): Patterns and rates of enamel growth in the molar teeth of early hominids. Nature 326:493–496.

Blakey ML, Armelagos GJ (1985): Deciduous enamel defects in prehistoric Americans from Dickson Mounds: Prenatal and postnatal stress. Am J Phys Anthropol 4:371–380.

Boyde A (1963): Estimation of Age at Death of Young Human Skeletal Remains from Incremental Lines in the Dental Enamel. Paper presented at the Third International Meeting in Forensic Immunology, Medicine, Pathology, and Toxicology, Plenary Session IIA, London, April 1963.

Boyde A (1976): Amelogenesis and the Structure of Enamel. In Cohen B, Kramer IRH (eds): "Scientific Foundations of Dentistry." London: Heinemann, pp 335–352.

Boyde A (1979): Carbonate Concentration, Crystal Centers, Core Dissolution, Caries, Cross Striations, Circadian Rhythms and Compositional Contrast in the SEM. J Dent Res 58B(Special issue B)981–983.

Boyde A (1989): Enamel. In Berkowitz BKB, Boyde A, Frank RM, Hohling HJ, Moxham BJ, Nalbandian J, Tonge CH (eds): "Teeth." Berlin: Springer-Verlag, pp 309–473.

Brace CL, Rosenberg KR, Hunt KD (1987): Gradual change in human tooth size in the Late Pleistocene and Post-Pleistocene. Evolution 41:705–720.

Bromage T, Dean MC (1985): Re-evaluation of the age at death of Plio-Pleistocene fossil hominids. Nature 317:981–983.

Cassidy CM (1980): Benign neglect and toddler malnutrition. In Greene LS, Johnston FE (eds): "Social and Biological Predictors of Nutritional Status, Physical Growth and Neurological Development." New York: Academic Press, pp 109–139.

Chavez A, Martinez C (1982): "Growing Up in a Developing Community." Mexico: Instituto Nacional de la Nutricion.

Clarkson J (1989): Review of terminology, classifications, and indices of developmental defects of enamel. Adv Dent Res 3(2):104–109.

Cohen MN, Armelagos GJ (1984): "Paleopathology at the Origins of Agriculture." Orlando, FL: Academic Press.

Condon KW (1981): Correspondence of Developmental Enamel Defects Between the Mandibular Canine and the First Premolar. Unpublished doctoral dissertation, University of Arkansas.

Condon KW (1988): Histological structure of enamel surface defects (abstract). Am J Phys Anthropol 75:198.

Cook DC (1981): Mortality, age-structure, and status in the interpretation of stress indicators in prehistoric skeletons: A dental example from the Lower Illinois valley. In Chapman R, Kinnes I, Randsborg K (eds): "The Archaeology of Death." London: Cambridge University Press, pp 133–144.

Cook DC (1984): Subsistence and health in the Lower Illinois Valley: Osteological evidence. In Cohen MN, Armelagos GJ (eds): "Paleopathology at the Origins of Agriculture." Orlando, FL: Academic Press, pp 235–269.

Cook DC (1990): Epidemiology of circular caries: A perspective from prehistoric skeletons. In Buikstra JE (ed): "A Life in Science: Papers in Honor of J. Lawrence Angel." Scientific Papers Number 6. Center for American Archaeology.

Cook DC, Buikstra JE (1979): Health and differential survival in prehistoric populations: Prenatal dental defects. Am J Phys Anthropol 51:649–664.

Corruccini RS, Handler JS, Jacobi KP (1985): Chronological distribution of enamel hypoplasias and weaning in a Caribbean slave population. Hum Biol 57:699–711.

de Castro JMB (1987): Dental diseases and Harris lines in the fossil human remains from Atapuerca-Ibeas (Spain). J Paleopathol 1:131–146.

Demirjian A, Goldstein H, Tanner JM (1973): A new system of dental age assessment. Hum Biol 45:211–227.

Deutsch D, Pe'er E (1982): Development of enamel in human fetal teeth. J Dent Res 61(Special issue):1543–1551.

Deutsch D, Tam O, Stack MV (1985): Postnatal changes in size, morphology and weight of developing postnatal deciduous anterior teeth. Growth 49:202–217.

Diamond M, Weinmann JP (1940): "The Enamel of the Human Teeth." New York: Columbia University Press.

Dickel PN, Schulz PD, McHenry HM (1984): Central California: Prehistoric subsistence changes and health. In Cohen MN, Armelagos GJ (eds): "Paleopathology at the Origins of Agriculture." Orlando, FL: Academic Press, pp 439–461.

Eli I, Sarnat H, Talmi E (1989): Effect of the birth process on the neonatal line in primary tooth enamel. Pediatr Dent 11:220–223.

Fanning EA, Brown T (1971): Primary and permanent tooth development. Australian Dent J 67:41–43.

Fearnhead RW, Kawasaki K, Inoue K (1982): Comments on the porosity of human tooth enamel J Dent Res 61 (Special issue):1524–1530.

Fejerskov O (1979): Human dentition and experimental animals. J Dent Res 58(Special issue B):725–731.

Gantt DG (1986): Enamel thickness and ultrastructure in hominoids: With reference to form, function and phylogeny. In Swindler DR, Erwin J (eds): "Comparative Primate Biology (Vol. 1) Systematics, Evolution and Anatomy." New York: Alan R. Liss, pp 453–475.

Garn SM (1961): The genetics of dental development. In Garn SM (ed): "The Genetics of Normal Human Growth. Genetica Humana Normalis—de Genetica Medica—Pars II." Rome: Apud Mendelianum Institutum, pp 413–434.

Gaulin SJC, Konner M (1977): On the natural diet of primates, including humans. In Wurtman RJ, Wurtman JJ (eds): "Nutrition and the Brain" (Vol. 1). New York: Raven Press, pp 1–86.

Gavan JA, Swindler DR (1966): Growth rates and phylogeny in primates. Am J Phys Anthropol 24:181–190.

Gohdo S (1982): Differential rates of enamel formation on human tooth surfaces deduced from the striae of Retzius. Arch Oral Biol 27:289–296.

Goodhart RS, ME Shils (1973): "Modern Nutrition in Health and Disease. Dietotherapy" (5th ed). Philadelphia: Lea and Febiger.

Goodman AH, Armelagos GJ (1985): The chronological distribution of enamel hypoplasia in human permanent incisor and canine teeth. Arch Oral Biol 30:503–507.

Goodman AH, Armelagos GJ (1988): Childhood stress and decreased longevity in a prehistoric population. Am Anthropol 90:936–944.

Goodman AH, Rose JC (1990): The assessment of systemic physiological perturbations from developmental defects of enamel and histological structures. Yearb Phys Anthropol 33:59–110.

Goodman AH, Rose JC (1991): Dental enamel hypoplasias as indicators of nutritional status. In Kelley M, Larsen C (eds): "Advances in Dental Anthropology." New York: Wiley-Liss, pp 279–293.

Goodman AH, Armelagos GJ, Rose JC (1980): Enamel hypoplasias as indicators of stress in three prehistoric populations from Illinois. Hum Biol 52:515–528.

Goodman AH, Lallo J, Armelagos GJ, Rose JC (1984): Health changes at Dickson Mounds, Illinois (A.D. 950–1300). In Cohen MN, Armelagos GJ (eds): "Paleopathology at the Origins of Agriculture." Orlando, FL: Academic Press, pp 271–305.

Goodman AH, Allen LH, Hernandez GP, Amador A, Arriola LV, Chavez A, Pelto GH (1987): Prevalence and age at development of enamel hypoplasias in Mexican children. Am J Phys Anthropol 72:7–19.

Goodman AH, Martin DL, Perry A, Martinez C, Chavez A, Dobney K (1989): The effect of nutritional supplementation on permanent tooth development and morphology (abstract). Am J Phys Anthropol 78:129–130.

Gould SJ (1977): "Ontogeny and Phylogeny." London: Belknap Press.

Guita JL (1984: "Oral Pathology" (2nd ed). Baltimore: Williams & Wilkins.

Gustafson G, Gustafson A-G. (1967): Microanatomy and histochemistry of enamel. In Miles AEW (ed): "Structure and Chemical Organization of Teeth (Vol. 2). New York: Academic Press, pp 75–133.

Haavikko K (1969): The formation and the alveolar and clinical eruption of the permanent teeth. Finn Dent J 65: 103–170.

Herman SC, McDonald RE (1963): Enamel hypoplasia in cerebral palsied children. J Dent Child 30:46–49.

Huss-Ashmore R, Goodman AH, Armelagos GJ (1982): Nutritional inference from paleopathology. Adv Archaeol Method Theory 5:395–474.

Infante PF (1974): Enamel hypoplasia in Apache Indian childhood. Ecol Food Nutr 2:155–156.

Infante PF, Gillespie GM (1974): An epidemiologic study of linear enamel hypoplasia of deciduous anterior teeth in Guatemalan children. Arch Oral Biol 19:1055–1061.

King NM (1989): Developmental defects of enamel in Chinese girls and boys in Hong Kong. Adv Dent Res 3(2): 120–125.

King NM, Wei SH (1986): Developmental defects of enamel: A study of 12-year-olds in Hong Kong. J Am Dent Assoc 112:835–839.

Kraus BS, Jordan RE, Abrams L(1969): "Dental Anatomy and Occlusion: A Study of the Masticatory System." Baltimore: Williams & Wilkins.

Lanphear KM (1990): Frequency and distribution of enamel hypoplasias in a historic skeletal sample. Am J Phys Anthropol 81:35–43.

Larsen CS (1987): Bioarchaeological interpretations of subsistence economy and behavior from human skeletal remains. Adv Archaeol Method Theory 10:339–445.

Levine RS, Turner EP, Dobbing J (1979): Deciduous teeth contain histories of developmental disturbances. Early Hum Dev 3/2:211–220.

Logan WHG, Kronfeld R (1933): Development of the human jaws and surrounding structures from birth to the age of fifteen years. J Am Dent Assoc 20:379–427.

Mann A, Lampl M, Monge J (1990): Patterns of ontogeny in human evolution: Evidence from dental development. Yearb Phys Anthropol 33:111–150.

Martorell R (1980): Interrelationships between diet, infectious disease and nutritional status. In Greene L, Johnston FE (eds): "Social and Biological Predictors of Nutritional Status, Physical Growth and Neurological Development." New York: Academic Press, pp 81–106.

Martorell R, Ho T (1984): Malnutrition, morbidity and mortality. Pop Dev Rev 10(Suppl):49–68.

Massler M, Schour I, Poncher HG (1941): Developmental pattern of the child as reflected in the calcification pattern of the teeth. Am J Dis Child 62:33–67.

Meiklejohn C, Zvelebil M (nd): Health status of European populations at the agricultural transition and the implications for the adoption of farming. In Bush H, Zvelebil M (eds): Biocultural Approaches to Human Bones (submitted).

Mellenby M (1927): The structure of human teeth. Brit Dent J 48:737—751.

Mellenby M (1934): Diet and the teeth. An experimental Study. London: His Majesty's Stationary Office, Med Res Coun Sp Rep Ser 191.

Molleson T (1988): Trace elements in human teeth. In Grupe G, Herrman B (eds): "Trace Elements in Environmental History." London: Springer-Verlag, pp 67–82.

Moss-Salentijn L, Klyvert M (1980): "Dental and Oral Tissues." Philadelphia: Lea and Febiger.

Murray JJ, Gordon PH, Carmichael CL, French AD, Furness JA (1984): Dental caries and enamel opacities in 10-year old children in Newcastle and Northumberland. Br Dent J 156:255–258.

Nation WA, Matsson L, Peterson JE (1987): Developmental enamel defects of the primary dentition in a group of Californian children. J Dent Child 54:330–334.

Neiburger EJ (1990): Enamel hypoplasias: Poor indicators of dietary stress. Am J Phys Anthropol 82:231–232.

Nikiforuk G, Fraser D (1981): The etiology of enamel hypoplasia: A unifying concept. J Pediatr 98:888–893.

Noren JG, Odelius H, Magnusson BO (1981): Ion probe analysis of discolored areas in the enamel of deciduous teeth: A pilot study. Acta Odontol Scand 39:97–100.

Nystom M, Kilpinen E, Kleemola-Kajula E (1977): A radiographic study of the formation of some teeth from 0.5 to 3.0 years of age. Proc Finn Dent Soc 73:167–172.

Ogilvie MD, Curran BK, Trinkaus E (1989): Incidence and patterning of dental enamel hypoplasia among the Neandertals. Am J Phys Anthropol 79:25–41.

Osborn JW (1973): Variations in structure and development of enamel. Oral Sci Rev 3:3–83.

Osborn JW (1981): Enamel. In Osborne J (ed): "Dental Anatomy and Embryology" (Vol. 1, Book 2). Oxford: Blackwell, pp 174–187.

Perzigian AJ, Tench PA, Braun DJ (1984): Prehistoric health in the Ohio River Valley. In Cohen MN, Armelagos GJ (eds): "Paleopathology at the Origins of Agriculture." Orlando, FL: Academic Press, pp 347–366.

Provenze DV (1986): "Oral Histology. Inheritance and Development." Philadelphia: Lea and Febiger.

Purvis RJ, Mackay GS, Cockburn F, Barrie WJMcK, Wilkinson EM, Belton NR, Forfar JO (1973): Enamel hypoplasia of the teeth associated with neonatal tetany: A manifestation of maternal vitamin D deficiency. Lancet 2:811–814.

Rathbun TA (1984): Skeletal pathology from the Paleolithic through the Metal Ages in Iran and Iraq. In Cohen MN, Armelagos GJ (eds): "Paleopathology at the Origins of Agriculture." Orlando, FL: Academic Press, pp 137–167.

Rathbun TA (1987): Health and disease at a South Carolina Plantation: 1840–1870. Am J Phys Anthropol 74:239–254.

Rattner LJ, Myers HM (1962): Occurrence of enamel hypoplasia in children with congenital allergies. J Dent Res 41:646–649.

Reith EJ, Cotty E (1967): The absorptive activity of ameloblasts during maturation of enamel. Anat Rec 157:577.

Robinson JT (1956): "The Dentition of the Australopithecinae." Transvaal Museum Memoir 9. Pretoria: Transvaal Museum.

Rose JC (1973): Analysis of Dental Microdefects of Prehistoric Populations from Illinois. Unpublished doctoral dissertation, University of Massachusetts.

Rose JC (1977): Defective enamel histology of prehistoric teeth from Illinois. Am J Phys Anthropol 46:439–446.

Rose JC, Condon K, Goodman AH (1985): Diet and dentition: Developmental disturbances. In Gilbert RI, Mielke JH (eds): "The Analysis of Prehistoric Diets." New York: Academic Press, pp 281–306.

Schneider KN, Blakeslee DJ (1990): Evaluating residence patterns among prehistoric populations: Clues from dental enamel composition. Hum Biol 62:71–83.

Schour I (1953): "Noyes' Oral Histology and Embryology." Philadelphia: Lea and Febiger.

Seow WK, Masel JP, Weir C, Tudehope DI (1989): Mineral deficiency in the pathogenesis of enamel hypoplasia in prematurely born, very low birthweight children. Pediatr Dent 11:297–302.

Shawashy M, Yaeger J (1986): Enamel. In Behaskar SN (ed): "Orban's Oral Histology and Embryology." St. Louis: C.V. Mosby, pp 45–100.

Shklar G, McCarthy PL (1976): "Oral Manifestations of Systemic Disease." Boston: Butterworths.

Silberman SL, Duncan WK, Trubman A, Meydrech EF (1989): Primary canine hypoplasia in Head Start children. J Public Health Dent 49:15–18.

Sillen A, Smith P (1984): Weaning patterns are reflected in strontium–calcium ratios of juvenile skeletons. J Archaeol Sci 11:237–245.

Skinner MF (1986a): An enigmatic hypoplastic defect of the deciduous canine. Am J Phys Anthropol 69:59–69.

Skinner MF (1986b): Enamel hypoplasia in sympatric chimpanzee and gorilla. Hum Evol 1:289–312.

Skinner MF (1989): Developmental stress in immature hominids from the Late Pleistocene of Western Europe: Evidence from dental attrition and enamel hypoplasia (abstract). Am J Phys Anthropol 78:303–304.

Skinner MF (1990): Models of growth and form in hominine evolution (abstract). Am J Phys Anthropol 81:296.

Skinner MF, Anderson G (1991): Individualization and enamel histology: Case report in forensic anthropology. J Forensic Sci 36:393–948.

Skinner MF, Hung, JTW (1986): Localized enamel hypoplasia of the primary canine. J Dent Child 53:197–200.

Skinner MF, Hung JTW (1989): Social and biological correlates of localized enamel hypoplasia of the human deciduous canine tooth. Am J Phys Anthropol 79:159–175.

Smith P, Peretz B (1986): Hypoplasia and health status: A comparison of two lifestyles. Hum Evol 1:535–544.

Smith P, Bar-Yosef O, Sillen A (1984): Archaeological and skeletal evidence for dietary change during the Late Pleistocene/Early Holocene in the Levant. In Cohen MN, Armelagos GJ (eds): "Paleopathology at the Origins of Agriculture." Orlando, FL: Academic Press, pp 101–136.

Spouge JD (1973): "Oral Pathology." St. Louis: C.V. Mosby.

Stini WA, Weber CW, Kemberling SR, Vaughan LA (1980): Lean tissue growth and disease susceptibility in bottle-fed versus breast-fed infants. In Greene LS, Johnston FE (eds): "Social and Biological Predictors of Nutritional Status, Physical Growth and Neurological Development." New York: Academic Press, pp 61–79.

Storey R (1988): Prenatal enamel defects in Teotihuacan and Copan (abstract). Am J Phys Anthropol 75:275–276.

Stuart-Macadam P (1985): Porotic hyperostosis: Representative of a childhood condition. Am J Phys Anthropol 66:391–398.

Suckling GW (1986): Sheep—and research into developmental defects of dental enamel. N Z Dent J 82:68–71.

Suckling GW (1989): Developmental defects of enamel: Historical and present-day perspectives of their pathogenesis. Adv Dent Res 3(2):87–94.

Suckling GW, Thurley DC (1984): Developmental defects of enamel: Factors influencing their macroscopic appearance. In Fearnhead RW, Suga S (eds): "Tooth Enamel IV." Elsevier Science Publishers, pp 357–362.

Suckling GW, Elliott DC, Thurley DC (1983): The production of developmental defects of enamel in the incisor teeth of penned sheep resulting from induced parasitism. Arch Oral Biol 28:393–399.

Suckling GW, Elliott DC, Thurley DC (1986): The macroscopic appearance and associated histological changes in the enamel organ of hypoplastic lesions of sheep incisor teeth resulting from induced parasitism. Arch Oral Biol 31:427–439.

Suga S (1982): Progressive mineralization pattern of developing enamel during the maturation stage. J Dent Res 61(Special issue):1532–1542.

Suga S (1989): Enamel hypomineralization viewed from the pattern of progressive mineralization of human and monkey developing enamel. Adv Dent Res 3(2):188–198.

Swanson JH (1931a): Age incidence of lines of Retzius in the enamel of human permanent teeth. J Am Dent Ass 18:819–826.

Swanson JH (1931b): The relation of growth velocity to the quality of enamel. J Am Dent Ass 18:2174—2176.

Sweeney EA, Guzman M (1966): Oral conditions in children from three highland villages in Guatemala. Arch Oral Biol 11:687–698.

Sweeney EA, Cabrera J, Urrutia J, Mata L (1969): Factors associated with linear hypoplasia of human deciduous incisors. J Dent Res 48:1275–1279.

Sweeney EA, Saffir JA, de Leon R (1971): Linear enamel hypoplasias of deciduous incisor teeth in malnourished children. Am J Clin Nutr 24:29–31.

Trinkaus E (1984): "The Shanidar Neandertals." New York: Academic Press.

Ubelaker DH (1984): Prehistoric human biology of Ecuador: Possible temporal trends and cultural correlations. In Cohen MN, Armelagos GJ (eds): "Paleopathology at the Origins of Agriculture." Orlando, FL: Academic Press, pp 491–513.

Via Jr WF, Churchill JA (1959): Relationship of enamel hypoplasia to abnormal events of gestation and birth. J Am Dent Assoc 59:702–707.

Warshawsky H (1985): Ultrastructural studies on amelogenesis. In Butler WT (ed): "The Chemistry and Biology of Mineralized Teeth." Birmingham, AL: Ebsco Media, pp 33–44.

Warshawsky H (1988): Formation of enamel and dentin: A critical review. CRC Crit Rev Anat Cell Biol 1(4): 425.

Warshawsky H (1989): Are Linear Markings on Dental Enamel Valid Indicators of Time? Paper presented at the Symposium on "Biomechanics of Bones and Teeth," 17th Annual Meeting, Canadian Association for Physical Anthropology, Vancouver, BC, November 2–4.

Warshawsky H, Bai P (1983): Knife chatter during thin sectioning of rat incisor enamel can cause periodicities resembling cross-striations. Anat Rec 207:533–538.

Webb S (1989): Prehistoric Stress in Australian Aborigines: A Paleopathological Study of a Hunter–Gatherer Population. Oxford: British Archaeological Reports International Series 490.

Weber DF, Glick PL (1975): Correlative microscopy of enamel prism orientation. Am J Anat 144:407–420.

White TD (1978): Early hominid enamel hypoplasia. Am J Phys Anthropol 49:79–83.

Wilson DF, Shroff FR (1970): The nature of the striae of Retzius as seen with the optical microscope. Aust Dent J 15:162–171.

Skeletal Biology of Past Peoples: Research Methods
pages 175–188 © 1992 Wiley-Liss, Inc.

Chapter 10

Applications of Demographic Models to Paleodemography

Eric Abella Roth

Department of Anthropology, University of Victoria, Victoria, British Columbia, Canada V8W 2Y2

INTRODUCTION

In the past three decades paleodemography moved from the fringe to the forefront of prehistoric research. A major impetus in this movement was the seminal work of Ester Boserup (1965), whose text, *Conditions of Agricultural Growth*, argued that population should be viewed as an independent variable capable of initiating cultural evolution. Although anthropologists differed with some of Boserups's premises (Spooner, 1972) the overall concept of population as a "prime mover" of cultural evolution was adopted by anthropologists to explain such diverse phenomena as the onset of the Neolithic (Cohen, 1977) and the collapse of the Classic Mayan Empire (Cowgill, 1975).

Against this background of cultural change paleodemography emerged as an approach to delineating prehistoric biological patterns. Most recently, this field was defined by Buikstra and Koningsberg (1985: 316) as "the study of vital rates, population distribution and density in extinct human groups, especially those for which there are no written records." Today this subject occupies a central position in undergraduate and graduate teaching of physical anthropology as well as representing a major research focus. Despite this new prominence, recent controversies have raised doubts concerning the validity of paleodemography as a scientific endeavor. While examining these controversies, this chapter takes the position that paleodemography is a valid, specialized subfield of demography. As such, the following stresses areas of common ground where the current methodological approaches of paleodemography can be integrated with demographic models based on contemporary human populations.

Perhaps the major link between paleodemography and classical demography is through the specialized subfield of anthropological demography. Traditionally demographers studied the three essentials of population change—mortality, fertility, and migration—for large national samples. Anthropological demography is concerned with these same parameters, but in the context of what Howell (1973: 249) originally termed "anthropological populations," designating small, nonliterate groups lacking Western calendrical systems. Later Leslie and Gage (1989: 20), noting the trying field conditions usually associated with these groups, referred to them as "demographically inconvenient" populations. Certainly no population can be more demographically inconvenient than those studied by paleodemographers. All population members are, by definition, dead, thus making even basic reconstruction of the population's age–sex profile damnably inconvenient.

Demographers share the problem of difficult, or as one classical manual (Brass, 1975) termed them, "incomplete or defective" data. In response, demographers developed a large battery of indirect demographic rate estimations (Brass and Coale, 1968; United Nations,

1983) based on mathematical models of age-specific fertility and mortality patterns. Likewise, anthropological demographers devised and tested ingenious methodologies for age estimation, notably age ranking (Howell, 1979), historical event calendars (Dorjahn, 1986), and development stage definition (Cleveland, 1988). Paleodemographic methodologies of age and sex assessment are also indirect techniques, since they are invariably based on known age patterns of skeletal growth and/or wear or sex-specific morphological characteristics.

All such methodologies are grounded in an implicit position of "biological uniformitarianism." As proposed by Howell (1976: 26):

A uniformitarian position in paleodemography implies that the human animal has not basically changed in its direct biological response to the environment in processes of ovulation, spermatogenesis, length of pregnancy, degree of helplessness of the young, and rates of maturation and senility over time.

With this viewpoint in mind the chapter first briefly reviews important advances and controversies in paleodemography, follows this with a search for areas of articulation between this field and the "proximate variables" models of mortality and fertility presently featured in demographic analyses, and concludes with suggestions for future research.

PALEODEMOGRAPHY: RECENT HISTORY AND PRESENT STATE

The current prominence of paleodemography is grounded in advances in osteological methodology made during the 1960s and 1970s. Foremost among these was the development of microscopic techniques for skeletal age determination (Kerley, 1965; Ahlqvist and Damsten, 1969; Ubelaker, 1974; see also Stout, this volume, Chapter 2), permitting accurate age assessment of later-aged adults and allowing construction of life tables that feature standardized age intervals. During this same time period Angel (1969) attempted to relate morphological changes in the female os pubis to absolute number of parities, thus directly approaching the estimation of prehistoric fertility as well as

mortality. Simultaneously physical anthropologists successfully adapted demographic theory to paleodemographic research. Most influential of these pioneering works was the series of life tables constructed by Weiss (1973). Unlike other life table series based on either historic or contemporary human populations (Coale and Demeny, 1982), Weiss's was derived in part from prehistoric skeletal samples. In conjunction with Ascadi and Nemeskeri's (1970) classic text, *History of Human Life Span and Mortality*, Weiss's work illustrated the usefulness of a uniformitarian approach to prehistoric demography. Physical anthropologists were quick to realize the potential of this approach, as demonstrated in a series of works in demographic anthropology that featured paleodemography (Swedlund, 1975; Ward and Weiss, 1976).

So promising was paleodemographic work during the 1960s and 1970s that its critics were few. However, Petersen (1975) noted carelessness and confusion in paleodemographic analyses in general, and Spring et al. (1989) noted that Angel's attempt to calculate fertility directly from osteological material did not account for the wide range of variation evident in known-parity skeletal samples. However, it was not until the 1980s that the field faced its first systematic challenge. In a 1982 article entitled "Farewell to Paleodemography," Bocquet-Appel and Masset pronounced paleodemography a "still-born science" and stated that

Save unforeseen developments—unpredictable in the future at least—it would be futile to expect to have a working knowledge of the demography of ancient populations if we start only from the estimations of age at death. The scholars who persist in this course will only obtain artefacts; the information conveyed by the age indicators is so poor that the age distributions thus available can hardly reflect anything but random distributions and errors of method. (Bocquet-Appel and Masset, 1982: 329)

As summarized by Buikstra and Konigsberg (1985: 317), Bocquet-Appel and Masset leveled five specific charges against paleodemography: (1) Paleo-populations' age-at-death distributions so closely reflect underlying reference populations that true age distributions remain unknown; (2) standards derived from samples with uneven age class representation will result in biased age estimates of death; (3) biases will also be incurred from standards that are population-specific, ignore sexual dimorphism, and omit older adults; (4) available methodologies for age estimation are not sufficiently precise to accurately classify age at death; and as a result of the first four charges, (5) variation among populations reflects imperfect methodologies and stochastic "noise" rather than true biological differences.

Paleodemographers responded quickly and effectively to these charges. Van Gerven and Armelagos's (1983) analysis of a prehistoric Nubian skeletal series demonstrated significant differences between their population's mortality profile and the reference series used. Buikstra and Konigsberg (1985) reviewed the literature and concluded that microscopic age determination appears to be influenced neither by sex nor by population. As for bias arising from uneven age classes, the same authors noted that Bocquet-Appel and Masset's claim was based on the use of cranial suture closure, a technique out of favor in North American studies for over a century. However, through computer simulation and principal components analysis these authors did find evidence for imprecision in age-at-death estimation, particularly for older adults, and noted that these errors can significantly affect mortality profiles.

Another, indirect challenge to paleodemography was offered at this time by Howell's (1982) computer simulation analysis of a life table reported for a large prehistoric North American cemetery, the Libben Site (Lovejoy et al., 1977). Noting that the life table yielded a distinctive mortality profile, with low infant/child mortality and extremely high adult mortality, Howell used the life table in association with fertility assumptions as input schedules for the stochastic microsimulation program AMBUSH (Howell and Lehotay, 1978). Capable of detailing kinship networks as well as simulating demographic events, AMBUSH revealed that a highly unusual society resulted from the paleodemographic data. Peculiarities included (1) unstable marriage patterns, due to high adult mortality that resulted in a large proportion of widows and remarried partners; (2) a two-human rather than the usual three-human

generation system, once again because of high adult mortality; (3) an unusually high proportion of orphaned children; and (4) a high dependency ratio (defined in standard demographic terms as people aged 0–14 plus those 60+/people aged 15–59). The overall picture was one of a society facing the dual problems of disproportionately high per capita labor requirements in combination with constantly high childcare provision. Both would have to be solved within a two-generation kinship system unlike any known today. This innovative "fleshing out" of a prehistoric population led, as Howell states, to making the choice between accepting that the biology, and concomitantly the basic society, of prehistoric populations were distinctly different from those of modern groups, or envisioning continuing problems in accurately assessing human age at death from skeletons.

Despite these challenges, or perhaps because of them, paleodemography emerged a stronger, more introspective field of study. Evidence that rejects most of Bocquet-Appel and Masset's charges, coupled with new and revised methods of skeletal aging and sexing (Meindl et al., 1985a,b), represent the continued evolution of paleodemography. Yet the very nature of paleodemographic data, human skeletons, and their context, prehistoric archaeological sites, form persistent difficulties. First and foremost, the demographic analyses of human skeletal material have remained focused almost entirely on mortality. Paleodemography is then a misnomer, in reality the field is represented by paleomortality alone. This unidimensional view of prehistoric demography is exacerbated by archaeological problems of preservation. Although environmental and/or cultural factors can bias the recovery of skeletal material (see Jackes, this volume, Chapter 11, for a full discussion), a more widespread problem is the loss of infant and child skeletal material. Poorly preserved owing to incomplete ossification (see Saunders, this volume, Chapter 1), this material represents the most demographically variable and sensitive portion of the human life cycle, while constituting the best estimator of a population's health and well-being. Although it acknowledges the importance of such material, Buikstra and Konigsberg's (1985) principal components analysis of 26 life tables from prehistoric North American skeletal series omits probability of dying (qx) in life table notation) values for ages 0, 1, 5, and 10 because "these often reflect not only probability of death, but also probability of burial, recovery, and curation" (Buikstra and Konigsberg, 1985: 327). That is undoubtedly true, but omission of these valuable data result in a sophisticated statistical analysis of a biased sample, leading to conclusions that are difficult to interpret.

In spite of such obstacles Bocquet-Appel and Masset's view that paleodemography simply be abandoned is both pessimistic and premature. As Weiss (1982) notes, difficult and flawed as paleodemography remains, it is a valid approach to hearing the biological "voices of our ancestors" no matter how faintly. Therefore it may prove worthwhile to search for demographic models and data that can profitably be applied to the specialized field of paleodemography.

DEMOGRAPHY AND PALEODEMOGRAPHY

One area where anthropology and demography converge is the study of nutrition (Mosley, 1978; Gilbert and Mielke, 1985; Johnston, 1987). This subject also has a long history in osteological research, ranging from macroscopic study of malnutrition (e.g., rickets, scurvy) through radiographic (Harris lines) and microscopic (bone remodeling) analyses to the present emphasis on biochemical studies (trace elements and stable isotopes). The following section examines the role of nutrition for demography and paleodemography studies via the intermediate, or proximate, models of fertility and mortality currently featured in demography (Bongaarts, 1978, 1982; Chen, 1983; Mosley and Chen, 1984; Wood, 1990).

Mortality

These constitute frameworks for identifying and assessing the "midrange" determinants of fertility and mortality, with birth and death events viewed as the final biological outcomes of cultural, social, and economic higher-order variables. Intermediate, or proximate, variables take their names from their assumed intermediate position, between higher-order variables

and the immediate processes of death and birth. Figure 1 presents one model of the proximate determinants of child mortality as envisioned by Chen (1983). In this framework child mortality is the result of interaction between four groups of proximate variables: (1) parental factors, (2) nutritional factors, (3) infection factors, and (4) childcare factors. Nutrition is explicit in the form of maternal and child nutritional regimes and implicit in infection factors, where its importance lies in the synergism between infection and nutrition. Recent research on the relationships between infection and nutrition indicates that infections reduce the efficiency of nutrient metabolism, utilization, and absorption, and dietary intakes are reduced by as much as 20%−40% during infections as a result of appetite loss (Gordon et al., 1968; Chen and Schrimshaw, 1983; Martorell and Ho, 1984).

The maturation approach taken by this model stresses the longitudinal role of nutrition in child survival. This role begins before birth; Pebley et al. (1985) found maternal nutritional status, measured both as preconception weight and weight gain during pregnancy, to be highly associated with intrauterine mortality for a poorly nourished Bangladeshi sample. Research on national (Puffer and Serrano, 1988) and ethnic (Habict et al., 1974; Rogers, 1989) samples repeatedly demonstrates low-birthweight full-term babies suffering significantly higher neonatal mortality. Such research has identified a "threshold effect" centering on 2,500 g, with lighter infants associated with much higher mortality.

For early childhood similar threshold values are sought through the use of standard anthropometric measurements, with the goal of utilizing these as prospective indicators of morbidity and mortality, thereby identifying those most at risk within study populations (Chen et al., 1980, 1981; Trowbridge and Sommer, 1981). Table 1 presents data from Bangladesh on relative risk for differing anthropometric measurements. Dividing the study population into classes based on the measurements yields evidence for a curviliner relationship with mortality over time, again suggesting threshold effects.

These findings and their relevance to demography within a proximate mortality frame-

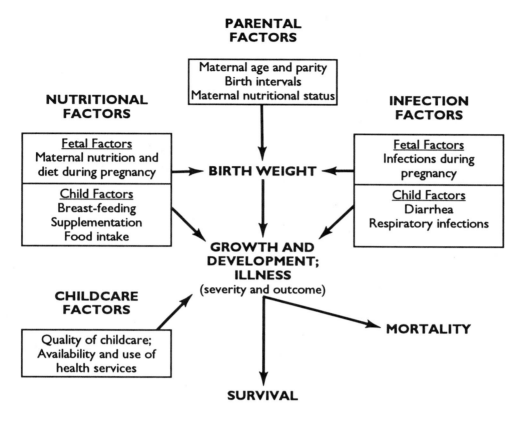

Fig. 1. The proximate determinants of child mortality. Reproduced from Chen (1983: 206), with permission of the publisher.

work having been briefly outlined, the question arises as to their applicability to paleodemography. The answer is that human osteologists have also demonstrated measures of prospective mortality risk and nutrition–infection synergisms. Both are exemplified by Cook and Buikstra's (1979) study, which correlates dental defects occurring during the fetal stage with later increased weaning mortality for skeletal series in the Lower Illinois Valley. In doing so the authors drew upon data from contemporary populations that linked malnutrition to fetal dental defects. Finding significantly higher childhood mortality for skeletons with these characteristics led them to interpret the relationship as nutritional insults that led to increased susceptibility to future infections. Similar results are reported for syn-

ergistic relationships between porotic hyperostosis, representing nutritional stress, and infection in the form of periosteal reaction (Lallo et al., 1977; Mensforth et al., 1978).

Correspondence between demography and paleodemography confirms the uniformitarian approach and suggests future research directions. For instance, demography has developed sophisticated multivariate models to delineate and evaluate sociocultural economic, and biological determinants of infant and child mortality (Farah and Preston, 1982; Trussell and Menken, 1984). These models are capable of assessing the relative roles of biological and social variables associated with age-specific mortality in human skeletal remains. In addition, the discrete data emphasized in paleopathological investigations (e.g., presence/ab-

TABLE 1. Percentage Mortality (M)[a], Relative Risk (R)[b], and Number of Children at Risk (C) 0–11 Months and 12–23 Months After Nutritional Assessment, Bangladeshi Data, Harvard Standard (After Chen et al., 1980)

| Nutritional status | Definition (percentage of standard) | C | Follow-up period | | | | | |
| | | | 0–11 months | | 12–23 months | | 0–23 months | |
			M	R	M	R	M	R
Weight for age								
Normal/mild	≥75	546	2.38	1.0	1.28	1.0	3.66	1.0
Moderate	60–74	1,046	2.68	1.1	1.53	1.2	4.21	1.2
Severe	<60	427	4.68	2.0	6.56	5.1	11.24	3.1
Weight for height								
Normal	≥90	399	3.51	1.0	1.75	1.0	5.26	1.0
Mild	80–89	979	2.66	0.8	2.66	1.5	5.32	1.0
Moderate	70–79	566	2.83	0.8	2.12	1.2	4.95	0.9
Severe	<70	75	6.67	1.9	8.00	4.6	14.67	2.8
Height for age								
Normal	≥95	182	1.65	1.0	1.65	1.0	3.33	1.0
Mild	90–94	656	2.29	1.4	1.68	1.0	3.96	1.2
Moderate	85–89	713	2.80	1.7	0.98	0.6	3.79	1.1
Severe	<85	468	5.13	3.1	6.22	3.8	11.32	3.4

[a]M = Percentage of children at risk of dying in interval. [b]R = Mortality rate decided by that of category III in same age group.

sence of porotic hyperostosis) pose no problems for categorical data analysis models such as logistic regression, and log-linear models, which, unlike ordinary least squares multiple regression, are designed for nonlinear data. Even with nutrition-related paleopathology as outlined by Huss-Ashmore et al. (1982) retained as the primary focus, cultural factors including status and subsistence base could be incorporated in these models. Table 2 presents a dummy table representing a logistic regression analysis of a hypothetical skeletal series to illustrate this approach. The model's dependent variable is the dichotomy "died/survived" for the specified age period 1–4 years, representing childhood mortality. Independent variables include sex, age, stature, status, subsistence base, as well as present/absent information for porotic hyperostosis, periosteal reaction, and osteoporosis. Additional columns indicate the individual variable's chi-squared values, corresponding probability levels, and maximum likelihood estimation coefficients. In this case logistic regression would serve to identify key variables associated with childhood mortality. Subsequent analysis, for instance via log-linear modeling, could best search for interactive relationships between

independent variables and mortality (e.g., sex and status, age and subsistence base, porotic hyperostosis, periosteal reaction and stature).

Fertility

Unlike mortality, nutrition is not stressed in the major intermediate fertility model developed by Bongaarts (1978, 1982). This model defines eight variables: the proportion of reproductive period spent in marriage, contraception, induced abortion postpartum nonsusceptibility, frequency of intercourse, sterility, spontaneous intrauterine mortality, and duration and viability of ova and sperm. On a population level, with some notable exceptions, only the first four are deemed important (for a physiologically derived variation on this basic model see Campbell and Wood, 1988, and Wood, 1990).

For noncontracepting populations that feature long birth intervals, an intense debate concerning the role of nutrition as an underlying force in delaying the resumption of regular ovulatory cycles and the end of the postpartum nonsusceptibility period has existed for the past two decades. The major proponent of nutrition as a central agent in natural fertility reg-

TABLE 2. Dummy Table for Logistic Regression Analysis of Childhood Mortality

Dependent variable
01 = Died
02 = Survived

Independent variables	Maximum likelihood coefficient	Chi-squared	Prob-ability
Sex			
01 = male			
02 = female			
Age			
01 = 1–2 years			
02 = 3–4 years			
Stature			
01 = <Median			
02 = ≥Median			
Status			
01 = low			
02 = high			
Subsistence base			
01 = foraging			
02 = agricalutural			
Porotic hyperostosis			
01 = absent			
02 = present			
Periosteal reaction			
01 = absent			
02 = present			
Osteoporosis			
01 = absent			
02 = present			

ulation remains Frisch (1977, 1978, 1981), the developer of the so-called critical fat hypothesis. This posits a necessary minimum ratio of body fat to lean body weight to initiate menarche and continue regular ovulatory cycles. Failure to maintain these ratios would result in a lengthening of the postpartum nonsusceptibility period and consequently in lowered fertility levels. Although based on longitudinal and cross-sectional growth and development data, supported by secondary historical findings on famine periods, Frisch's theory has nevertheless been disputed on methodological grounds (Menkan et al., 1981) and criticized for its potential relevance to food aid programs (Scott and Johnston, 1985). The best-known critique of this position emanates from Bongaarts's (1980) review of field data from Guatemala, Mexico, and Bangladesh, all of

which report increasing, but statistically nonsignificant, postpartum nonsusceptibility periods with progressively poorer maternal nutrition. In reviewing these data, Bongaarts (1980: 568) noted that chronic malnutrition "could make a difference of only a few percent between the fertility levels of poorly and well-nourished women with caloric differences of the order of several hundred calories a day."

Rather than chronic malnutrition, Bongaarts cited breast-feeding patterns, measured in terms of frequency, intensity and duration as the primary determinant of postpartum nonsusceptibility. In doing so he noted the apparent relationship between the production of the hormone primarily responsible for lactation, prolactin, and the delay of regular ovulatory cycles. Later, Bongaarts (1983) examined 20 populations to derive a formula for the relationship between mean/median duration of postpartum amenorrhea and breast-feeding, given as

$$A = 1.75e^{0.1396B - 0.001872B^2} \quad (1)$$

where A = mean or median duration of postpartum amenorrhea in months, and B = mean or median duration of breast-feeding in months. The high R^2 value for this equation (0.96) led to the widespread acceptance of breast-feeding patterns as the primary determinant of postpartum nonsusceptibility.

However, there are still grounds for not completely dismissing the role of nutrition in natural fertility regimes. The first is the lengthening in birth intervals that is associated with poor maternal nutrition. While not statistically significant by itself, this lengthening was found in all field studies cited by Bongaarts (1980), and it assumes new importance in relation with other factors. One such factor is the aforementioned association between poor maternal nutrition and intrauterine mortality (Pebley et al., 1985). However, the most important advance in the nutrition/breast-feeding debate is the recognition that rather than representing an either/or dichotomy, these two factors may be another example of a synergism, as described for nutrition and infection. Evidence for such a claim comes from the Prentice et al. (1983a,b) study of lactating Gambian women, in which declines in serum prolactin levels and a 6-

month decrease in postpartum amenorrhea were recorded in association with a maternal supplementation program. Since culturally defined breast-feeding patterns did not change during the study period, investigators hypothesized that high prolactin levels in malnourished women might reflect channeling of nutrients to the breast for milk production. With maternal supplementation, milk output levels may be achieved with correspondingly less stress on the mother, leading to earlier resumption of ovulatory cycles.

This recent research suggests that, in combination with other factors, maternal nutrition can influence birth intervals. Since this variable is of primary interest to paleodemographers, the question is, Can it be assessed from human skeletons? The answer appears to be yes, although tentatively and indirectly. Sillen and Smith (1984), noting that the introduction of solid foods, representing weaning, should result in distinct strontium–calcium (Sr/Ca) ratios for juveniles, utilized trace element analysis to determine weaning patterns in a prehistoric Mediterranean skeletal population. In view of the observation that human milk is exceptionally low in Sr/Ca, but that solid foods are relatively high, the authors searched for evidence of changes in these ratios in juvenile skeletal material. The result was the detection of a shift in ratios for the age group 1.5–3.0 years. These figures concur with ethnographic data collected on traditional Palestinian Arab communities that noted weaning at 2–3 years of age. While the authors stress caution in the application of this approach because of difficulties in distinguishing age at death versus age of bone calcification, their innovative analysis is a first approximation at estimating weaning times and consequently birth intervals from prehistoric skeletal populations. Subsequent studies by Tuross et al. (1989) and Katzenberg and Saunders (n.d.) successfully used stable nitrogen isotope analysis in the detection of weaning age, further pointing to the potential usefulness of this approach.

BEYOND LIFE TABLES: FUTURE DIRECTIONS FOR PALEODEMOGRAPHY

In summary, demographic research indicates that nutrition is an important intermediate variable for mortality and fertility. Recent

TABLE 3. Environmental Variation and Population (After Howell, 1976: 36)

Food supply	E_o^o	Pathogens	
		Low 30	High 20
Rich (TFR[a] = 8)		Type 1	Type 3
Poor (TFR = 5)		Type 2	Type 3

[a]TFR = Total fertility rate

advances in the reconstruction of prehistoric diets (Sandford, Katzenberg, and Klepinger, this volume, Chapters 5, 6, and 7) and the analysis of human skeletal material highlight the potential of nutritional information in paleodemography. Howell (1976) provided a general framework for utilizing this information, as shown in Table 3. Her model calls for placing prehistoric populations along a continuum form by life expectancy at birth values (E_o^0) derived from skeletal analysis and ranges of total fertility levels (denoted here as Total Fertility Rates (TFR)) recorded for contemporary natural fertility populations. Nutrition, explicit in the role of food supply, was intended primarily as a fertility determinant. It is also applicable to mortality, both as an independent variable and in synergism with infection, which is represented here by the presence of pathogens. To place populations into one of the four classifications that arise from the interaction of fertility and mortality, Howell suggested considering environmental factors such as food supply in relation to population density and reconstructed stature. To these can be added the measures of paleonutrition outlined by Huss-Ashmore et al. (1982).

Above all, the model attempts consideration of fertility, mortality, and their interaction to form a dynamic view of prehistoric demography. In doing so, it goes beyond the static view of prehistoric demography that results from consideration of mortality alone. Of course, this emphasis on mortality stems from the aforementioned inability to directly determine fertility levels from osteological remains. One advance in this area is the Sattenspiel and Harpending (1983) study noting a strong association between death statistics derived from skeletal populations and crude birth rates. These authors showed that the crude birth rate is approximately equal to the inverse of the mean age at death of a skeletal population, regardless of its true intrinsic rate of growth. On the basis of this initial finding Buikstra et al. (1986) developed a modified methodology for estimating fertility and applied it to prehistoric populations from the Midwestern United States. Their major modification was to replace mean age at death, a measure prone to errors in age assessment and underenumeration of infants (see also Horowitz et al., 1988), by a ratio of deaths over 30 years of age divided by the number of deaths over age 5 (denoted as D_{30+}/D_{5+} in life table notation). Coale and Demeny (1982) Model West Female stable populations were used to generate regression equations for the crude birth and death rates based on these proportions. Applying the resulting equations to eight skeletal series from west-central Illinois, the authors demonstrated an increase in fertility, as measured by the crude birth rate. In addition, on the basis of the observation that populations featuring high juvenile mortality are characterized by high childhood mortality levels (ages 1–4), they constructed a ratio of deaths at age 1–5 to those at age 1–10 (D_{1-5}/D_{1-10}). Calculation of this ratio over the time span represented by the skeletal series indicated constant mortality levels. The combined findings of increased fertility and stable mortality led to a convincing picture of increased population growth over time.

These innovative approaches move paleodemography past sole reliance on life table construction. To further highlight prehistoric population dynamics, it is suggested that paleodemography make more use of computer simulation methodologies featured in demographic and anthropological research for the past two decades (for reviews see Dyke and MacCluer, 1973; Dyke, 1981; and Hammel, 1980). Within these fields simulations have performed tasks ranging from the estimation of vital rates for small populations (Dyke and MacCluer, 1975; Roth, 1981a), through the testing of adherence to complex social rules and patterns of inheritance (Legesse, 1973; Wachter et al., 1978), to examination of family and household formation (Bongaarts, 1981; Wachter, 1988).

Yet with notable exceptions (Bocquet-Appel and Masset, 1982; Howell, 1982; Buikstra and Konigsberg, 1985) paleodemography has made little use of simulations. The rationale for this reluctance lies in the nature of simulations and paleodemography. The former can be divided into deterministic macrosimulations, sometimes called projections, and stochastic microsimulations. Macrosimulations employ linear equations to project an entire start population, segregated by age and sex classes, over a specified period. Since the controlling equations are deterministic age-specific fertility and mortality schedules, the use of a particular set of schedules produces one set of summary statistics.

In contrast, stochastic microsimulations derive their name from two different characteristics: First, demographic decisions are made individually on an annual basis. For example, for each person in the simulation an annual decision is made concerning death, survival, marriage, and childbirth on the basis of probability schedules. As a result, different runs using the same input schedules yield multiple, nonidentical outcomes. In this way individual runs and their corresponding results are viewed as samples in a universe of outcomes. This universe is bounded by the original schedules, so that changing schedules result in differences in both the mean and variance of the results. Means produced in this manner may be likened to the "signal" given by a population's vital rates over time, while the variation represents the "noise" arising from stochastic fluctuations characteristic of small populations.

Of the two, stochastic microsimulations hold the most promise for paleodemographers working with small groups. Despite the ready availability and widespread use of at least two microsimulation programs—SOCSIM, developed by Hammell (1976), and AMBUSH (Howell and Lehotay, 1978)—the prerequisites for these, and all other simulations, have been difficult for paleodemographers to meet. These are essentially threefold: (1) an initial start population divided by age and sex, (2) an age- and sex-specific mortality schedule, and (3) an age- and sex-specific fertility schedule.

The third factor remains most difficult for paleodemographers to estimate. Applying once again the principal of demographic uniformi-

TABLE 4. Age-Specific and Total Fertility Rates for Natural Fertility Populations

Group/country	Reference	Age-specific fertility							Total fertility rate
		15–19	20–24	25–29	30–34	35–39	40–44	45–49	
I. Hunter–gatherers									
!Kung San—Botswana	Howell, 1979	0.135	0.242	0.203	0.152	0.119	0.071	0.016	4.691
Inuit—Alaska, USA	Brainard and Overfield, 1986	0.074	0.242	0.276	0.295	0.194	0.121	0.000	6.010
N. Athapascan, Yukon, Canada	Roth, 1981b	0.120	0.337	0.320	0.263	0.126	0.109	0.046	6.605
II. Pastoralist/agropastoralists									
Fulani, Mali (Delta Region)	Hill, 1985	0.141	0.338	0.303	0.238	0.210	0.069	0.119	7.090
Fulani, Mali (Seno Region)	Hill, 1985	0.172	0.282	0.276	0.256	0.195	0.098	0.051	6.650
Delta Tamasheg, Mali	Hill, 1985	0.136	0.234	0.288	0.267	0.216	0.105	0.065	6.555
Gourma Tamasheg, Mali	Hill, 1985	0.152	0.259	0.248	0.168	0.105	0.062	0.046	5.200
Somali, Somalia	Somalia, 1981	0.070	0.286	0.333	0.271	0.224	0.149	0.096	7.145
Toposa, Southern Sudan	Roth, 1986	0.055	0.296	0.324	0.294	0.238	0.122	0.019	6.740
III. Horticulturalists									
Juang, Orissa, India	Ray and Roth, 1984	0.174	0.336	0.259	0.165	0.119	0.060	0.044	5.785
Koya Dora, Orissa, India	Roth et al., 1984	0.102	0.275	0.234	0.209	0.194	0.155	0.122	6.455
Gainj, New Guinea	Wood et al., 1985	0.000	0.180	0.234	0.208	0.158	0.073	0.010	4.315
Trio, Surinam	Gage et al., 1984	0.252	0.250	0.154	0.120	0.072	0.033	0.018	4.495
Semai, Malaysia	Fix, 1982	0.107	0.289	0.291	0.278	0.141	0.032	0.000	5.690
IV. Farmers									
Bambara, Mali	Hill, 1985	0.183	0.351	0.323	0.271	0.303	0.130	0.061	8.110
Rural Chinese	Barclay et al., 1976	0.107	0.268	0.262	0.221	0.156	0.674	0.011	5.550

tarianism, a list of age-specific and total fertility rates for 14 populations is given in Table 4, grouped according to subsistence base. Intended to supplement rates for the 14 natural fertility populations collected by Weiss (1973) and used in paleodemographic studies (Hassan, 1981), these have benefited from the advent of indirect vital rate estimation techniques developed by Brass and Coale (1968) and later fine-tuned (United Nations, 1983), plus anthropological techniques such as age ranking (Howell, 1979) and computer simulation of internal consistency (Roth, 1981a). Consequently, they represent demographic analogies of prehistoric fertility. While it is hoped that these schedules can be utilized to power computer simulation programs, care and caution must be exercised in their application. For example, although grouped according to subsistence base, they do not reflect particular fertility levels associated with a particular economic adaptation. That such associations do not exist was driven home by Campbell and Wood's (1988) examination of 70 natural fertility populations' total fertility levels. Analysis of variance revealed no significant differences between subsistence patterns (e.g., hunter–gatherers, tribal horticulturalists and pastoralists, and peasants). In recognition of these findings the fertility patterns represented in Table 4 are primarily intended to exemplify the possible range of natural fertility regimes contained within Howell's (1976) model. Selection of specific patterns and levels of fertility should be tied to archaeological and/or pathological evidence concerning the study population.

The second requisite factor, age– and sex-specific mortality schedules is of course the strength of paleodemography, since they can be derived directly from life tables. Recognition of potential problems and pitfalls in both skeletal preservation and identification can be addressed through model life tables, such as the Coale and Demeny (1982) or Weiss (1973) series previously mentioned. More recently Gage (1988, 1989, 1990) developed a three-parameter hazard model of human mortality, which has been successfully tested on both contemporary and prehistoric (Libben Site) populations. For paleodemographers this approach has several potential advantages over current model life tables. First, it does not impose an age structure on mortality data, allowing its use to smooth and correct inconsistent and/or defective data without making underlying assumptions concerning the pattern of mortality. Thus, its flexibility permits more variation in human mortality patterns. In constructing a new set of model life tables based on this approach, Gage (1990) derived seven clusters of mortality patterns, four of which have no equivalent in the Coale and Demeny model life table families (although the Coale and Demeny "West" Series is equivalent to the average mortality pattern of all seven clusters). Particularly important for paleodemographers is the finding that Gage's (1990) cluster analysis indicated that the greatest source of variation between clusters lies in adult mortality. This is the opposite of previously constructed life tables and constitutes that portion of the human life cycle most commonly preserved in skeletal series. Unfortunately, like all model life tables, the fit between raw and smoothed data attained by this approach deteriorates when the study population features life expectancies at birth of less than 20 years, a feature of many prehistoric populations.

Where model life tables series currently retain an advantage is in the construction of an initial start population. Coale and Demeny's (1982) series give age and sex profiles for stable populations with a wide range of negative and positive growth rates. As exemplified by Howell (1982), archaeological data pertaining to the time span of prehistoric cemeteries can be utilized to infer an initial population size and composition.

Some suggested uses for prehistoric demography, once the constituent parts have been assembled, include the following. First, testing of the internal consistency of aging, sexing, and

mortality patterns can be accomplished by the dynamic view of population provided by simulations. Howell's analysis of the social concomitants of the Libben Site life table can be considered a model for this type of investigation. Similarly, simulation may help estimate the chronic problem of infant underenumeration in paleodemography through exploration of population viability of a small start population with a low number of surviving infants. Simulations could also explore the effects of demographic change over time on kinship ties and family formation. The analysis by Buikstra and colleagues (1986) of increased fertility linked to constant high levels of juvenile mortality provides a prime example of questions that simulations could address concerning these demographically induced parameters. Likewise, simulations could examine the possible effects of sex-specific mortality differentials found within skeletal, as well as contemporary, populations. For example, what would be the effect of marriage patterns, both with respect to age and availability of nonconsanguine partners, in the face of higher female than male death rates?

SUMMARY

Fifteen years ago the demographer Petersen (1975) delivered a scathing review of prehistoric demography. In contrast, the present review acknowledges the validity of paleodemography as a specialized branch of demography, notes significant advances made within the field both in osteological methodology and demographic applications, and favorably examines the relevance of recent demographic research to paleodemography. Undoubtedly a large part of this reaction is due to the author's being an anthropological demographer, with training and roots in anthropology. At the same time, this positive outlook stems from the end of what Howell (1986: 221) terms, "the bad old days," when standard demographic techniques were poorly understood and applied, resulting in exaggerated and distorted claims.

Today, while paleodemography is exciting in its methodological innovations, it remains conservative in its interpretation. Perhaps this reflects the introspection arising from paleodemography's recent challenge by Bocquet-

Appel and Masset (1982). Yet, in this observer's opinion, these charges seemed to strengthen the field, refutation of most charges being possible, and critical assessment of others making paleodemography more viable. What is needed now is for paleodemography to move beyond the merely descriptive examination of prehistoric mortality and to assert itself as a more complete study of prehistoric demography. To this end this chapter suggests that paleodemography would benefit from adopting multivariate models to analyze mortality differentials, use ethnographic analogies to indirectly estimate age-specific fertility levels for skeletal populations, and make more extensive use of computer simulation methodology.

REFERENCES

Alhqvist J, Damsten O (1969): Modification of Kerley's method for the microscopic determination of age in human bone. J Forensic Sci 14:205–212.

Angel JL (1969): The bases of paleodemography. Am J Phys Anthropol 30:427–437.

Ascádi G, Nemeskeri J (1970): "History of Human Life Span and Mortality." Budapest: Akademia Kaido.

Barclay G, Coale A, Stoto M, Trussell J (1976): A reassessment of the demography of traditional rural China. Popul Index 42:606–635.

Bocquet-Appel J, Masset C (1982): Farewell to paleodemography. J Hum Evol 11:321–333.

Bongaarts J (1978): A framework for analyzing the proximate determinants of fertility. Popul Dev Rev 4:105–132.

Bongaarts J (1980): Does malnutrition affect fecundity: A summary of the evidence. Science 208:564–569.

Bongaarts J (1981): "Simulation of the Family Life Cycle." Center for Policy Study Working Paper, No. 70. New York: The Population Council.

Bongaarts J (1982): The impact on fertility of traditional and changing child-spacing patterns. In Lesthaeghe R, Page H (eds): "Child-Spacing in Tropical Africa: Tradition and Change." New York: Academic Press, pp 111–132.

Bongaarts J (1983): The proximate determinants of natural fertility. In Bulatao R, Lee R (eds): "Determinants of Fertility in Developing Countries (Vol. 1): Supply and Demand for Children." New York: Academic Press, pp 103–138.

Boserup E (1965): "Conditions of Agricultural Growth." Chicago: Aldine.

Brainard J, Overfield T (1986): Transformation in the natural fertility regime of Western Alaska Eskimo. In Handwerker WP (ed): "Culture and Reproduction: An Anthropological Critique of Demographic Transition Theory." Boulder, CO: Westview Press, pp 112–134.

Brass W (1975): "Methods for Estimating Fertility and Mortality from Limited and Defective Data." Chapel Hill, NC: Laboratories for Population Studies.

Brass W, Coale A (1968): Methods of analysis and estimation. In Brass W et al. (eds): "The Demography of Tropical Africa." Princeton, NJ: Princeton University Press, pp 88–139.

Buikstra J, Konigsberg L (1985): Paleodemography: Critiques and controversies. Am Anthropol 87:316–333.

Buikstra J, Konigsberg L, Bullington J (1986): Fertility and the development of agriculture in the prehistoric Midwest. Am Antiq 51:528–546.

Campbell KL, Wood JW (1988): Fertility in traditional societies. In Diggory P, Potts M, Teper S (eds): "Natural Human Fertility: Social and Biological Determinants." London: MacMillan, pp 36–69.

Chen L (1983): Child survival: Level, trends, and determinants. In Bulatao R, Lee R (eds): "Determinants of Fertility in Developing Countries." New York: Academic Press, pp 199–232.

Chen L, Scrimshaw N (1983): "Diarrhea and Malnutrition." New York: Plenum Press.

Chen L, Chowdhury A, Huffman S (1980): Anthropometric assessment of energy-protein malnutrition and subsequent risk of mortality among preschool aged children. Am J Clin Nutr 33:1836–1845.

Chen L, Huq E, Huffman S (1981): A prospective study of the risk of diarrheal diseases according to the nutritional status of the child. Am J Epidemiol 114:284–292.

Cleveland D (1988): Developmental stage age groups and African population structure: The Kusasi of the West African savannah. Am Anthropol 90:401–413.

Coale A, Demeny P (1982): "Regional Model Life Tables and Stable Populations" (2nd ed). Princeton, NJ: Princeton University Press.

Cohen M (1977): "The Food Crisis in Prehistory: Overpopulation and the Origin of Agriculture." New Haven: Yale University Press.

Cook D, Buikstra J (1979): Health and differential survival in prehistoric populations: Prenatal dental defects. Am J Phys Anthropol 51:649–664.

Cowgill G (1975): On causes and consequences of ancient and modern population change. Am Anthropol 77:505–525.

Dorjahn V (1986): Temne fertility: Rural continuity, urban change, rural–urban differences and public policy problems. In Handwerke WP (ed): "An Anthropological Critique of Demographic Transition Theory." Boulder, CO: Westview, pp 321–350.

Dyke B (1981): Computer simulation in anthropology. Annu Rev Anthropol 10:193–207.

Dyke B, MacCluer J (1973): "Computer Simulation in Human Population Studies." New York: Academic Press.

Dyke B, MacCluer J (1975): Estimation of vital rates by means of Monte Carlo simulation. Soc Biol 10:383–403.

Farah A-A, Preston S (1982): Child Mortality differentials in Sudan. Popul Dev Rev 8:365–383.

Fix A (1982): Genetic structure of the Semai. In Crawford M, Mielke J (eds): "Current Developments in Anthropological Genetics" (Vol. 2). New York: Plenum Press, pp 179–204.

Frisch R (1977): Critical weights, a critical body composition, menarche and the maintenance of menstrual cycles. In Watts E, Johnston F, Lasker G (eds): "Biosocial Interrelationships in Population Adaptation." The Hague: Mouton, pp 319–352.

Frisch R (1978): Population, food intake and fertility. Science 199:22–30.

Frisch R (1981): Population, nutrition, and fecundity: Significance for interpretation of changes in fertility. In Eberstadt N (ed): "Fertility Decline in the Less Developed Countries." New York: Praeger, pp 319–336.

Gage T (1988): Mathematical hazards models of mortality: An alternative to model life tables. Am J Phys Anthropol 86:429–441.

Gage T (1989): Bio-mathematical approaches to the study of human variation in mortality. Yearb Phys Anthropol 32:185–214.

Gage T (1990): Variation and classification of human age patterns of mortality: Analysis using competing hazards models. Hum Biol 62:589–617.

Gilbert R, Mielke J (1985): "The Analysis of Prehistoric Diets." New York: Academic Press, p 182.

Gordon J, Ascoli W, Mata L, Guzman M, Scrimshaw N (1968): Nutrition and infection field study in Guatemalan villages, 1959–1964: VI: Acute diarrheal diseases and nutritional disorders in general disease incidence. Arch Environ Health 16:424–437.

Habict J-P, Lechtig A, Yarbrough C, Klein R (1974): Maternal nutrition, birth weight and infant mortality. In Ciba Foundation (ed): "Size at Birth." Amsterdam: Ciba Foundation Symposium, pp 353–370.

Hammell E (1976): "The SOCSIM Demographic sociological Microsimulation Program Operating Manual." Berkeley, CA: Institute of International Studies.

Hamel E (1980): Experimental history. J Anthropol Res 35:274–292.

Hassan F (1981): "Demographic Archaeology." New York: Academic Press.

Hill A (1985a): "Population, Health and Nutrition in the Sahel: Issues in the Welfare of Selected West African Communities." London: Routledge and Kegan Paul.

Hill A (1985b): The recent demographic surveys in Mali and their main findings. In Hill A (ed): "Population Health and Nutrition in the Sahel: Issues in the Welfare of Selected West African Communities." London: Routledge and Kegan Paul, pp 41–64.

Horowitz S, Armelagos G, Wachter K (1988): On generating birthrates from skeletal populations. Am J Phys Anthropol 76:189–196.

Howell N (1973): The feasibility of demographic studies in "anthropological" populations. In Crawford M, Workman P (eds): "Methods and Theories of Anthropological Genetics." Albuquerque, NM: University of New Mexico Press, pp 249–262.

Howell N (1976): Toward a uniformitarian theory of human paleodemography. J Hum Evol 5:25–40.

Howell N (1979): "Demography of the Dobe !Kung." New York: Academic Press.

Howell N (1982): Village composition implied by a paleodemographic life table: The Libben Site. Am J Phys Anthropol 59:263–269.

Howell N (1986): Demographic anthropology. Annu Rev Anthropol 15:219–246.

Howell N, Lehotay V (1978): AMBUSH: A computer program for stochastic microsimulation of small human populations. Am Anthropol 80:905–922.

Huss-Ashmore R, Goodman A, Armelagos G (1982): Nutritional inference from paleopathology. Adv Archaeol Methods Theory 5:395–474.

Johnston F (1987): "Nutritional Anthropology." New York: Alan R. Liss.

Katzenberg MA, Saunders S (1991) Age differences in stable carbon and nitrogen isotope ratios in a population of prehistoric horticulturalists. Am J Phys Anthropol 81:247, (Abstract).

Kerley E (1965): The microscopic determination of age in human bone. Am J Phys Anthropol 23:149–169.

Lallo J, Armelagos G, Mensforth P (1977): The role of diet, disease and physiology in the origin of porotic hyperostosis. Hum Biol 49:471–483.

Legesse A (1973): "Gada: Three Approaches to the Study of African Society." New York: Free Press.

Leslie P, Gage T (1989): Demography and human population biology: Problems and progress. In Little M, Haas JD (eds): "Human Population Biology: A Transdisciplinary Science." New York: Oxford University Press, pp 15–44.

Lovejoy CO, Meindl R, Pryzbeck T, Barton T, Heiple K, Kotting D (1977): Paleodemography of the Libben Site, Ottawa Country, Ohio. Science 198:241–293.

Martorell R, Ho T (1984): Malnutrition, morbidity and mortality. In Mosley W, Chen L (eds): "Child Survival: Strategies for Research." New York: The Population Council.

Meindl RS, Lovejoy CO, Mensforth RP, Don Carlos L (1985a): Accuracy and direction of error in the sexing of the skeleton: Implications for paleodemography. Am J Phys Anthropol 68:15–25.

Meindl RS, Lovejoy CO, Mensforth RP, Walker RA (1985b): A revised method of age determination using the os pubis, with a review and tests of accuracy of other current methods of pubic symphyseal aging. Am J Phys Anthropol 68:29–45.

Menken J, Trussell J, Watkins S (1981): The nutrition–fertility link: An evaluation of the evidence. J Interdiscip Hist 11:425–441.

Mensforth R, Lovejoy CO, Lallo J, Armelagos G (1978): The role of constitutional factors, diet and infectious disease in the etiology of porotic hyperostosis and periosteal reactions in prehistoric infants and children. Med Anthropol 2:1–59.

Mosley W (1978): "Nutrition and Human Reproduction." New York: Plenum Press.

Mosley W, Chen L (1984): "Child Survival: Strategies for Research." New York: The Population Council.

Pebley A, Huffman S, Chowdhury A, Stupp P (1985): Intrauterine mortality and maternal nutritonal status in rural Bangladesh. Popul Stud 39:425–440.

Petersen W (1975): A demographer's view of prehistoric demography. Curr Anthropol 16:227–245.

Prentice A, Lunn P, Watkinson M, Whitehall R (1983a): Dietary supplementation of lactating Gambian women. I: Effect on breastmilk volume and quantity. Hum Nutr Clin Nutr 37(C):53–63.

Prentice A, Lunn P, Watkinson M, Whitehall R (1983b): Dietary supplementation of lactating Gambian women. II: Effect on maternal health, nutritonal status and biochemistry. Hum Nutr Clin Nutr 37(C):65–74.

Puffer RR, Serrano CV (1988): "Patterns of Birthweights." New York: Pan American Scientific Publication No. 504.

Ray AK, Roth E (1984): Demography of the Juang tribal population of Orissa. Am J Phys Anthropol 65:193–197.

Rogers R (1989): Ethnic and birth weight differences in cause-specific mortality. Demography 26:335–343.

Roth EA (1981a): Sedentism and changing fertility patterns in a Northern Athapaskan isolate. J Hum Evol 10:413–425.

Roth EA (1981b): Community demography and computer simulation methodology in historic village population reconstruction. J Anthropol Res 37:279–301.

Roth E (1986): Demography of Toposa Agro-pastoralists of Kapoeta District, Southern Sudan. Unpublished manuscript, UNICEF-Sudan.

Roth E, Ray AK, Mohanty B (1984): Computer simulation of an Indian tribal popultion. Curr Anthropol 25:347–349.

Sattenspiel L, Harpending H (1983): Stable populations and skeletal age. Am Antiq 48:489–498.

Scott E, Johnston F (1985): Science, nutrition, fat and tests of the critical fat hypothesis. Curr Anthropol 26:463–473.

Sillen A, Smith P (1984): Weaning patterns are reflected in strontium–calcium ratios of juvenile skeletons. J Archaeol Sci 11:237–246.

Somalia, Central Statistical Department (1981): "Report on the Demographic Survey of Banadir, Bay and Lower Shebelle Regions of Somalia, 1981." Mogadishu, Somali Democratic Republic.

Spooner B (1972): "Population Growth: Anthropological Implications." Cambridge: MIT Press.

Sprint D, Lovejoy CO, Bender G, Duerr M (1989): The radiographic pre-auricular groove: Its non-relationship to past parity. Am J Phys Anthropol 79:247–252.

Swedlund A (1975): "Population Studies in Archaeology and Biological Anthropology: A Symposium." Soc Am Archaeol Mem No. 30.

Trowbridge F, Sommer A (1981): Nutritional anthropometry and mortality risk. Am J Clin Nutr 34:2591–2592.

Trussell J, Menken J (1984): Estimating levels, trends and determinants of child mortality in countries with poor statistics. In Mosley W, Chen L (eds): "Child Survival: Strategies for Research." New York: The Population Council.

Tuross N, Fogel ML, Owsley D (1989) Tracing human lactation with subfossil human skeletal tissue. Abstracts of the Annual Meeting of the 88th American Anthropological Association, pp 180–181.

Uberlaker D (1974): "Reconstruction of Demographic Profiles from Ossuary Skeletal Samples: A Case Study from the Tidewater Potomac." Smithsonian Contrib Anthropol No. 15.

United Nations, Department of Economic and Social Affairs (1983): "Manual X: Indirect Techniques of Demographic Estimation." U.N. Population Studies No. 83.

Van Gerven DP, Armelagos G (1983): Farewell to paleodemography? Rumours of its death are exaggerated. J Hum Evol 12:353–360.

Wachter K (1988): Microsimulation of household cycles. In Bongaarts J, Burch TK, Wachter K (eds): "Family Demography: Methods and Their Applications." Oxford: Clarendon Press, pp 215–228.

Ward R, Weiss K (1976): "The Demographic Evolution of Human Populations." New York: Academic Press.

Weiss K (1973): "Demographic Models for Anthropology." Am Antiq 38(Pt 2), Mem. 27.

Weiss K (1982): Voices of our ancestors. In Crawford M, Mielke J (eds): "Current Developments in Anthropological Genetics." New York: Plenum Press, pp 3–16.

Wood JW (1990): Fertility in anthropological populations. Annu Rev Anthropol 19:211–242.

Wood JW, Johnson PL, Campbell KL (1985): Demographic and endocrinological aspects of low natural fertility in highland New Guinea. J Biosoc Sci 17:57–79.

Skeletal Biology of Past Peoples: Research Methods
pages 189–224 © 1992 Wiley-Liss, Inc.

Chapter 11

Paleodemography: Problems and Techniques

Mary Jackes

Department of Anthropology, University of Alberta, Edmonton, Alberta, Canada T6G 2H4

INTRODUCTION

Paleodemographic studies based on human skeletal remains excavated by anthropologists and archaeologists seek to reconstruct basic biological and social facts of human life in the past—population structure, life expectancy, and mortality and fertility rates. The first step in such a study is to establish the distribution of ages at death, and by the 1970s this became a mandatory part of any anthropological report on a cemetery site.

Interest in paleodemography began slowly in the United States with the work of Hooton (1920, 1930), then picked up through the 1960s (Angel, 1968, 1969; Biraben, 1969; Churcher and Kenyon, 1960; Johnston and Snow, 1961; Swedlund and Armelagos, 1969). Paleodemography reached its apogee in central Europe with the publication of *The History of Human Life Span and Mortality* (Acsádi and Nemeskéri, 1970), and the 1970s saw paleodemography emerging as a topic for theses in several American graduate schools (e.g., Asch, 1976). While paleodemographic methods were studied in broad terms (Swedlund, 1975; Swedlund and Armelagos, 1976; Weiss, 1973, 1976), the techniques underlying the data on which the demographic parameters were based received little consideration.

Analysis of the large Libben sample led to the fullest expression of paleodemography based on methods developed in the United States between 1920 and the mid-1970s (Lovejoy et al.,

1977). But it also contributed to increasingly trenchant questioning of this traditional paleodemography (Petersen, 1975; Howell, 1976). Howell's paper on Libben demography (1982) forcefully pointed out that the results of paleodemographic research were not in accord with the knowledge accumulated by demographers over 200 years.

In Europe, Masset arrived at a similar position through a consideration of age estimates (1971, 1973, 1976a,b,c). His work was continued by Bocquet-Appel (Bocquet, 1977); their jointly published doubts about the accuracy of age estimates (Bocquet and Masset, 1977; Bocquet-Appel and Masset, 1982) elicited a strong reaction on behalf of paleodemography in the United States (Van Gerven and Armelagos, 1983; Buikstra and Konigsberg, 1985; and Greene et al., 1986).

New histological techniques developed in forensic science during the 1960s and 1970s were expected to provide more accurate age estimates and during the 1980s they were tested on archaeological samples. At the same time, traditional methods of assessment continued to be refined (Katz and Suchey, 1986, 1989), and the methods used to age the Libben sample were published in great detail (e.g., Meindl et al., 1980, 1983, 1985; Meindl and Lovejoy, 1989). Such detail is desirable, a departure from the norm of the previous two decades, when aging techniques were generally accepted without question and, in the obligatory paragraph on "methods," were described in reports in the most general terms or not at all.

This chapter will summarize what has been learned over the last decade and propose methods of research that allow not so much a resurrection of paleodemography (cf. Bocquet-Appel and Masset, 1985), but its reincarnation in a humbler but wiser form. Paleodemographic methods must be suited to a foreseeable future of limited access to skeletal materials and of funding restraints.

With this in mind, there must be attempts to develop techniques that allow comparisons of data among sites and over time. Comparison alone can help identify sites that are biased by differential burial practices and/or by partial excavation. Comparison alone will allow researchers to differentiate among archaeological sites and see the relationship of archaeological mortality to historical, modern, and model mortality rates.

The primary concern in this chapter is with the techniques of adult age assessment, as well as a focus on the crux of the 1980s disagreements between European and North American paleodemographers, that is, on the basic question: How reliable are these age assessment techniques? If age estimates turn out to be inaccurate, there is no foundation on which to build "biological" paleodemography. Paleodemography will then become completely "archaeological," relying on such data as size and density of sites, houses, and hearths.

Throughout the discussion some of the techniques described are evaluated in the context of a sample of several hundred burials from Portugal dating from the Mesolithic and Neolithic (Jackes, 1988; Lubell and Jackes, 1988; Lubell et al., 1989).

MORPHOLOGICAL TECHNIQUES OF AGE ASSESSMENT
Pubic Symphyses

Todd (1920) first demonstrated the systematic changes on the face of the pubic symphysis. A new schema was drawn up by McKern and Stewart (1957) on the basis of their work on the young conscripts killed in the Korean War. Gilbert (1973) pointed out that the application of male standards to females was

bound to introduce error, and Gilbert and McKern (1973) proposed a new system for aging the female os pubis. Work has continued on the Todd system (Brooks, 1955), and Suchey, after testing the accuracy of the 1973 female aging system of Gilbert and McKern and finding it wanting (Suchey, 1979), has refined the Todd schema in order to increase the accuracy of age estimates on male (Katz and Suchey, 1986) and female (Brooks and Suchey, 1990) pubes.

In Europe Nemeskéri independently developed a system of pubic symphysis age assessment (Nemeskéri et al., 1960). In seeking to apply it, European researchers noted that different results derived from U.S. and European techniques. Masset (1976c) pointed out that each method would give a different age for the same stage and, citing a study comparing the Todd and Nemeskéri methods on a Czech known-age sample, he concluded that each method is most applicable to a group with an age structure equivalent to that used to develop the method (Masset, 1976a: 334). Bocquet-Appel and Masset (1982) based their "Farewell to Paleodemography" on the opinion that the results of a technique depend on the age-at-death distribution of the sample used in developing the technique.

This was restated slightly by Jackes (1985) in demonstrating that each technique does in fact give different results. It was shown that, in cases where pubic symphyses alone are used in age estimates, it is sometimes possible to determine the technique used from the resulting age-at-death distribution. During the 1960s and 1970s the mean ages of the pubic symphysis stages were used for age assessment: the mean age was used as the age of the individual assessed at a given stage. In sites in which multiple aging techniques could not be used (e.g., ossuaries consisting of disarticulated remains), characteristic age-at-death curves were produced.

This replication of age-at-death distributions became clear in the comparison of North American sites of the period just before and after contact with Europeans, a period of extreme demographic change. Expected differences in mortality patterns were masked by the use of pubic symphysis age estimates (Jackes, 1986). Ten years earlier the interpre-

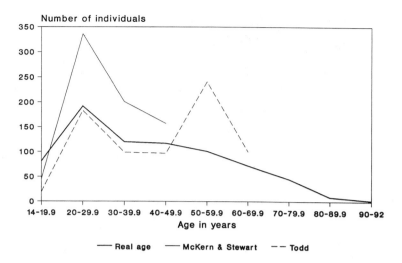

Fig. 1. Age estimations of males based on McKern and Stewart and Todd pubic symphysis techniques compared with known ages derived from data from Katz and Suchey (1986).

tation of this phenomenon of "similar results from dissimilar sites" had been quite different: "archeological data from different sites or different times at the same site produce similar demographic results, so we can have confidence that whatever we are doing, we are doing consistently" (Weiss, 1976: 357). And yet Acsádi and Nemeskéri (1970) had already shown that the European and American methods of age assessment gave fundamentally different pictures of past mortality.

We now have clearer evidence that different techniques produce different results. Katz and Suchey's work (1986) on a large sample of males of known age, clearly demonstrates the characteristic distribution of ages at death that results from the McKern and Stewart technique (see Fig. 1). We can now understand why, for many sites, "everyone is reported to have died before age 45 or 50" (Weiss, 1973: 59). This relative absence of the elderly is still accepted, although with acknowledgments that compensatory adjustments must be applied.

The Todd method also underages those over 60 (Fig. 1; see also Meindl et al., 1983, and Jackes, 1985). Nevertheless, Brooks (1955: 571) obtained quite high correlations of assessed and known age in her tests of Todd's system. However, the tests utilized a sample derived from Todd's original series selected so

that "each pubic phase has approximately the same number of individual skeletons whose known age falls within that span." Meindl and colleagues (1983) also tested the Todd method. They obtained a correlation of .57 for males and females combined, on samples selected from the Todd collection to reflect the supposed age structure of archaeological populations (i.e., very few old people). Neither the Brooks nor the Meindl and colleagues test is thus independent of the age distributions imposed by the method, nor was either carried out on a sample other than the reference sample.

The Nemeskéri method results in assigning far too many individuals an age of 45–60 years (Jackes, 1985), and Bocquet et al. (1978) found a very low correlation with real age in testing the Nemeskéri pubic method on a known-age population. Brooks and Suchey (1990) advise against the use of the method, after testing it on 1,000 modern pubes.

Examination of the pubic symphysis was the basic method of choice for every skeletal biologist through much of the past three decades (e.g., Blakely, 1971: 45; Bender, 1979: 185). U.S. researchers (Meindl et al., 1983: 81; Lovejoy et al., 1985a: 12; Meindl et al., 1985) drew attention to the inaccuracy of pubic indicators, but the strong negative responses from others

(Buikstra and Konigsberg, 1985; Van Gerven and Armelagos, 1983) to the paper of Bocquet-Appel and Masset (1982) persuaded paleodemographers to continue using traditional methods (e.g., Storey, 1985: 527). The pubis has been regarded as the mainstay of ossuary aging techniques, and a major contributor to multiple-factor age assessment.

One important factor is often overlooked. Pubic symphyseal techniques are not applicable to all sites: numbers of adults evidenced by the MNI (minimum number of individuals) counts may not be represented by pubic symphyses. Waldron (1987) has shown that the rate of survival of the pubic symphysis may be only around 30%. Pfeiffer (1986) reported over 400 adult individuals in the Kleinburg Ossuary but only 51 adults (12.5%) were given ages by pubic symphyses (Jackes, 1985, 1986). Similarly, only 95 of some 312 adults (30%) could be aged on pubic symphyses in the Uxbridge Ossuary (Pfeiffer, 1986). Of the several hundred adults in recently analyzed Portuguese Mesolithic and Neolithic sites (e.g., Jackes, 1988; Lubell and Jackes, 1988; Lubell et al., 1989) only two or three were represented by analyzable symphyses. The exclusion of adults of indeterminate age from paleodemographic analyses has profound effects on the results obtained.

Auricular Surfaces

Lovejoy and colleagues (1985b) proposed an age-estimating technique based on the auricular surface of the ilium, which changes with age in specific ways that are highly correlated with changes in the pubic symphysis (Lovejoy et al., 1985a). The method requires a large series of clean and well-preserved auricular surfaces and controlled seriation. Both the Koyabashi (1967) form of this observation and the Lovejoy method, applied to Portuguese Mesolithic samples, were found to be unsatisfactory owing to the condition of the auricular surfaces and constant interobserver disagreements. However, a test on an independent known-age sample has suggested that the auricular surface is of more value than the pubis, producing interobserver correlations of 0.8 or more and a correlation with age of 0.6 (Bedford et al., 1989). Lovejoy and colleagues (Lovejoy, 1985b; Meindl and Lovejoy, 1989)

have tested the technique, but because the exact age/sex/race/parity breakdown of the two samples tested (which make up 75%–82% of the test samples described in Lovejoy and colleagues, 1985a) is unknown, the utility of the method cannot be judged. The technique has been applied to a known age European sample (Rogers, 1990) and was found to be accurate only for young adults.

The technique may be inappropriate for females. Ullrich (1975) demonstrated marked changes in the corresponding sacral joints of multiparous females, and Lovejoy et al. (1985b: 27) have noted that female innominates with preauricular sulci cannot be judged on the apical and inferior margins.

Additional Morphological Age Criteria

Several other methods by which adult age can be estimated have been proposed: atrophy of the scapula (Graves, 1922), which is rarely useful for archaeological material, since the scapular blade is fragile; fusion of the sternum, judged of no value by Jit and Bakshi (1986); fusion of the cranial sutures, which is highly variable and the subject of considerable literature (e.g., McKern and Stewart, 1957; Nemeskéri et al., 1960; Meindl and Lovejoy, 1985; Masset, 1989); degenerative changes (Stewart, 1958), which are activity-, sex-, and population-specific in ways not fully documented; fusion of the maxillary suture, found to be of limited value by Gruspier and Mullen (1991); and the sternal end of some ribs (İşcan et al., 1984, 1985).

Only the last of these techniques appears potentially useful to skeletal biologists for aging large collections of skeletons. Unfortunately, it requires excellent preservation, identification and sex assignment of the third, fourth, or fifth rib, limiting its value in sites with disarticulated, mixed, or incomplete individuals. Furthermore, racial differences appear to be marked.

Sex, Race, and Morphological Age Assessment

Early work on pubic age estimation was restricted to males. Todd (1921) included females, but his sample was too small for analysis of variability. Stewart (1957: 18) stated that "until more reliable pubic age standards are available for females the sex difference in mortality curves for ancient populations will be suspect." Gilbert and McKern's (1973) system for females was later shown to be inadequate, and Suchey (1979) demonstrated that a pubic symphysis of a female aged 60 or more years had no more than a 10% chance of being assigned to the correct 5-year age category. It is the variability in female pubes that leads to these unsatisfactory results (Gilbert and McKern, 1973; Gilbert, 1973; Suchey, 1979; Katz and Suchey, 1986; Angel et al., 1986; Stewart, 1957). While Brooks and Suchey (1990) have now provided a schema for female age assessment based on 273 Los Angeles forensic cases, they acknowledge that the variability of older female pubic symphyses limits the value of the technique. It must be used in conjunction with other methods.

Sex has been a recognized problem in morphological studies, but racial differences have rarely been discussed in the context of morphological age assessments. Todd (1921) concluded that differences between black and white pubic symphyses existed but were unimportant. In further work on the same collection, Meindl and colleagues (1985: 33) acknowledged that their technique results in greater underaging of 60- to 69-year-old blacks than whites.

Buikstra and Konigsberg (1985) cited Hanihara and Susuki (1978; a test limited to individuals between 18 and 38) to prove that pubic symphysis age distributions are not population-specific. At the time, only one good test of this existed. Koyabashi (1967) tested the age estimation techniques on a sample of 142 adolescent and adult Japanese skeletons of known age; age changes in Japanese pubes seemed less obvious after age 35 than Todd or Brooks would suggest on the basis of U.S. blacks and whites.

Katz and Suchey (1989) have now shown that significant differences exist between white, black, and Mexican males in their Los Angeles pubes sample. The average age of a stage VI pubis in a white is 64 years (probability range 53–75 years), while an equivalent Mexican pubis would be about 47 years (±2 σ = 39–55 years). However, since only 2% of the Suchey sample of individuals over age 50 were Mexican, (none over 59 years), there is

no clear idea yet of the age changes taking place in the Mexican pubis.

In sum, after about 70 years of studying morphological age indicators, researchers are only beginning to grapple with population differences, and new methods for aging females are acknowledged to have limitations. Even for a sample of males of European origin, the accuracy of age estimates depends directly on the age distribution of the dead, precisely the unknown factor in archaeological populations. All that can be determined with certainty is that the older the adult sample, the less accurate the age estimates.

RADIOGRAPHIC TECHNIQUES IN AGE ASSESSMENT

The cortical width and density of bone and the arrangement of trabeculae undergo changes with age that have been identified by radiographers and clinicians searching for techniques by which osteoporosis can be diagnosed or predicted. Anthropologists attempting to assess skeletal age in adults have recently used X-rays, especially to examine changes in trabeculae in femoral and humeral heads (summary in Sorg et al., 1989). Other techniques have either not been attempted on archaeological bone (calcaneus: Walker and Lovejoy, 1985) or have been tried and rejected (radius: Lovejoy et al., 1977, 1985a; clavicles: Jhamaria et al., 1983; Meiklejohn, personal communication).

Alteration in Femoral Trabeculae

The Singh Index, systematizing changes in the proximal femur, is used in clinical studies as a method of evaluating osteoporosis (Singh, 1972). Detailed literature on this index indicates that accurate ages cannot be assigned on the basis of femoral radiographs and that, generally, femoral scores have lower correlations with age than the index of second metacarpal cortical bone (e.g., Nordin et al., 1966). High correlations with age have been found ($r = .91$; Jhamaria et al., 1983), but the sample used could be regarded as biased. By contrast, Singh's data for female femora suggest a correlation with age of .6 (Singh, 1972, data extracted from Fig. 3, p. 65).

The first important use of radiography for anthropological age determination was by Nemeskéri and colleagues (1960; see also Acsádi and Nemeskéri, 1970), when they added age changes in the trabeculae of the proximal humerus and femur to pubic symphyseal face modification and ectocranial suture closure.

Bergot and Bocquet (1976) redefined the six stages of trabecular change. Subsequently Bocquet and his colleagues (1978) tested a method of estimating age by multiple regression, by using pubes, cranial sutures, and humeral and femoral radiographs on the known-age collection at the University of Coimbra, Portugal. The results based on humeri were very unsatisfactory, but at $r = .7$ for males and .6 for females, the trabecular stage of the proximal femur showed a more encouraging correlation with real age.

Walker and Lovejoy (1985) have proposed a fourth schema for analyzing femoral trabecular changes with age. They initially used an optical densitometer to avoid subjectivity in reading radiographs, but found it of no value. Their results are therefore based on a seriation of X-ray images, with emphasis on morphological changes in trabeculae and relative translucency of the various areas in the proximal femur as in other methods.

A series of inter- and intraobserver tests by five researchers on a large number of Portuguese Mesolithic and Neolithic femoral radiographs has been undertaken. Many radiographs are unreadable because of damage to the bone or heavy matrix in the medullary canal, and the lack of standardization enforced by differing burial conditions has been shown to bias results. Paired t tests demonstrated that interobserver differences are most significant when the Walker–Lovejoy technique is used ($n = 73$; 63% disagreement) and least with the Nemeskéri method ($n = 80$; 52% disagreement).

The Bergot–Bocquet and Nemeskéri methods generally correlate at higher levels, and the Walker–Lovejoy method consistently has lower correlations with other methods, irrespective of observer or site. Interobserver differences are less significant for Neolithic site radiographs, demonstrating the importance of X-ray clarity and bone preservation. Only the Walker–Lovejoy technique produces significant interobserver differences when these are tested by cultural period, and this is found only with the Neolithic material, indicating that it performs least well on the best preserved material.

No single method stands out as consistently performing better than the others, although the Walker–Lovejoy is in general the least satisfactory. The Walker–Lovejoy stages derive from seriation and are therefore often imprecisely defined in terms such as "more," "less," "greater," and "significant increase." This compounds the subjectivity inherent in reading radiographs (Bergot and Bocquet, 1976).

A number of problems must be resolved before a useful application of techniques of scoring femoral trabecular involution to archaeological material is possible. The comparability of grades among methods is questionable, and in several cases the descriptions of stages are ambiguous. Moreover, the stages may not be comparable between populations (e.g., in many of the Portuguese radiographs, subcapital rarefaction appears advanced over the formation of a clear Ward's Triangle, making Singh Grade 6 inappropriate as a description of observed changes).

On the basis of the work on Portuguese radiographs, this author proposes a scheme by which seven radiographic characteristics of the femoral head are deemed to pass through eight phases. Each area (the apex of the canal, Ward's Triangle, subcapital area, fovea capital area, the greater trochanter, the arciform bundle, the cephalic bundle) is observed in order to clarify whether all pass through the equivalent stage at the same time in all individuals. Age is assessed on the basis of clustering of the scores on each of the seven areas.

Of the 126 or so individuals represented by the Portuguese radiographs, few are taken to represent older people (determined on the basis of clustering trabecular stage with cortical variables, to be described below). This is almost inevitable, as less dense proximal femora do not survive. Thus radiography underrepresents the elderly on the basis of preservation, and because some elderly present "young" proximal femora, they will be underaged. Poor preservation of femoral heads suggests that it is worthwhile to consider another radiographic technique: measurement of cortical thickness.

Cortical Thickness

Cortical thickness is determined from radiographs for diagnostic purposes by two midshaft measurements, especially on femora: the Nordin Index (Barnett and Nordin, 1960) is the width of the femoral cortex expressed as a percentage of the shaft diameter. Other cortex widths are also measured, especially the second metacarpal (Barnett and Nordin, 1960; Morgan, 1973). Measurement of the cortex width in long bones has been applied by anthropologists to determine bone loss associated with disease or nutritional stress (summary in Macchiarelli, 1988).

Humeri have been suggested as preferable to femora, in that they are not weight-bearing (Smith et al., 1984). Walker and Lovejoy (1985) propose radiography of the clavicle, and their phases for the clavicle and for the proximal femora both refer to cortical thinning. Kaur and Jit (1990) have shown by direct measurement that the clavicular cortex is reduced markedly with age.

Measurement of the medial femoral cortex, just above the lesser trochanter, has been discussed by radiologists (e.g., Horseman et al., 1982). This area, the calcar femorale, extends to just below the lesser trochanter, where it is often complete in archaeological bone and is readily identifiable. Intraobserver error on the external measurement at this point is less than that for the midshaft external measurement in tests on Portuguese femora. Measurement of the medullary width at the subtrochanteric level is less accurate than simple measurement of the lower calcar femorale, judged on the basis of correlations with proximal femoral trabecular scores. One test has shown that the average difference between the subtrochanteric index (expressing the width of lower calcar femorale in relation to the external subtrochanteric diameter) on multiple X-ray films of the same bones is half that of the average difference for Nordin's Index. We can assume that Nordin's Index is much more sensitive to variations in radiographs. An index that expresses the breadth of the calcar femorale may be of value as an additional variable in analyses of the seven characteristics of proximal femoral trabeculae discussed above.

Intraobserver error and multiple interobserver error on radiographic indices have been tested on the Portuguese bones and found to be high—often significantly high. Direct measurement of the cortex on midfemoral bone samples is preferable. The ratio of bone sample cortical thickness to anterior posterior midfemoral diameter has low correlations with Nordin's Index (below .5 even on the Neolithic femora) based on multiple tests on the Portuguese femora. Radiographic cortical measurement error has been found to be high under the more ideal conditions of clinical trials: it seems reasonable to assume that Nordin's Index will have a very high error for archaeological material.

THE MULTIFACTORIAL APPROACH

Whenever complete individuals are available for analysis, multiple age assessment methods can be used. Nemeskéri et al. (1960) were the first to attempt a systematization of multiple aging techniques.

Acsádi and Nemeskéri (1970) have proposed that four age indicators be used in age estimation. First, the pubic symphysis is used to determine whether the individual is young, about 50 years, or old. On this basis, cranial sutures and trabeculae in the proximal humerus and femur are analyzed, and the pubis is reexamined. Age ranges for each point of observation are fixed, and age is determined by choosing the low, middle, or high end of each range, according to the initial information given by the symphysis pubis. The four ages thus derived are then averaged to give the final estimated age for the individual. Acsádi and Nemeskéri (1970: 123) claim that, on the basis of their study with individuals of known age, "actual, chronological age can be approximated fairly well." Accuracy is 80%–85% with a margin of error of ±2.5 years in individual cases and a lower error if ages of a sample are distributed (1970: 131; but see Sjøvold 1978: 111).

Concluding that three people died at age 18–20 requires drawing up the age-at-death distribution on the assumption that 1.0 (3 years/3 individuals) person died at each of ages 18, 19 and 20. But as Sjøvold (1978) pointed out, equal distribution is only one of a number of possible ways of combining 3 dead and 3 years; in fact it has a 0.1 probability, and for each individual the probability of death at a given age is only .33. Sjøvold, however, maintains that the confidence limits for methods of age determination are unknown and that a normal distribution of ages cannot be assumed for every age class of every age indicator, a contention which receives some support from Brooks and Suchey (1990: Fig. 4).

The accuracy of the method of Acsádi and Nemeskéri has been further tested on the Coimbra sample by Bocquet et al. (1978), who used six age indicators (including humeral and femoral cortical widths) on 194 males and 161 females. Of the six techniques, none showed high correlations with the actual population; the humeral cortical index for females, at −.688 (Boquet et al., 1978: 140) was the highest. The use of a theoretical population in which all age classes were equally represented provided correlations of .71 for both the male proximal femur and the female humeral cortical index. Combining all age indicators generates correlation coefficients of .829 for males and .789 for females. The combined method does not give results much better than the single indicator results, and Bocquet-Appel would maintain that only results in the $r = .9$ range can be used in paleodemography.

It is appropriate to enquire whether we know the true correlation of multiple techniques with age, since some have a linear relationship with age and others (e.g., cortical widths) do not. The method of computing ages in the face of this problem has not been discussed.

Another proposal for multiple techniques derives from the analysis of the Libben site (Lovejoy et al., 1977). Age estimates were based on pubis, proximal femur and distal radius radiography, dental attrition, cranial sutures, and auricular changes. Vertebral osteophytosis had been one of the original age indicators, but it was not used in the final assessments of age. The estimate of the reliability of the other six indicators and the weight assigned them was derived from a principal components analysis. Each indicator was weighted according to its contribution to the first principal component. The contribution to the first principal component, which accounted for 74% of the variance, was taken as an estimate of reliability. The weightings have not been published.

The accuracy of the technique was post facto tested on the basis of three samples chosen from among 500 specimens with "reliable records of age at death" (Meindl et al., 1980) in the Todd collection. Meindl et al. (1983) subsequently published an account of testing on two samples of 130 each. The skeletons were carefully chosen: in order "to mimic archaeological conditions two adult life tables were selected from the literature and two samples of 130 cases each . . . were chosen . . . to correspond to the two tables" (1983: 76–77). Sample 1 appears similar to Point of Pines (Bennett, 1973), while a distribution like that of Indian Knoll (Johnston and Snow, 1961) may have provided the basis for sample 2. Both sites were aged by McKern and Stewart pubic indicators and by dental attrition, although attrition coding methods differed between the two sites.

The composition of the two Todd Collection samples is shown in Figure 2. Sample 1 has fewer young adults and non-Europeans than sample 2. As "accuracy of age assessment is greatest in the younger age categories" (Lovejoy et al., 1985a: 9) and as pubic indicators are more likely to underage Europeans than Africans or Asians, it is predictable that correlations between indicators and known age will be higher for sample 2 than for sample 1. Mensforth and Latimer (1989) have shown that osteoporotic fracture rates are much lower among Todd Collection blacks than whites (e.g., among women in their fifties the black fracture rate is one quarter that of the rate for white women), so a young age given to a black on the basis of radiographs is most likely to be correct for a sample in which there are many young individuals. Again sample 2 should produce higher correlations between known age and estimated age than sample 1.

Methods and the results of age estimations of the two samples are discussed in Meindl et al. (1983) and Lovejoy et al. (1985a). Correlations between dental, auricular, and femoral ages and real age remain the same, but the correlation of the pubic symphysis, in its revised form, rises to .78 for sample 2.

The assumption outlined above, that accuracy would increase on the second test, holds true only for the pubis, and yet the results of the sample 2 tests have been published as im-

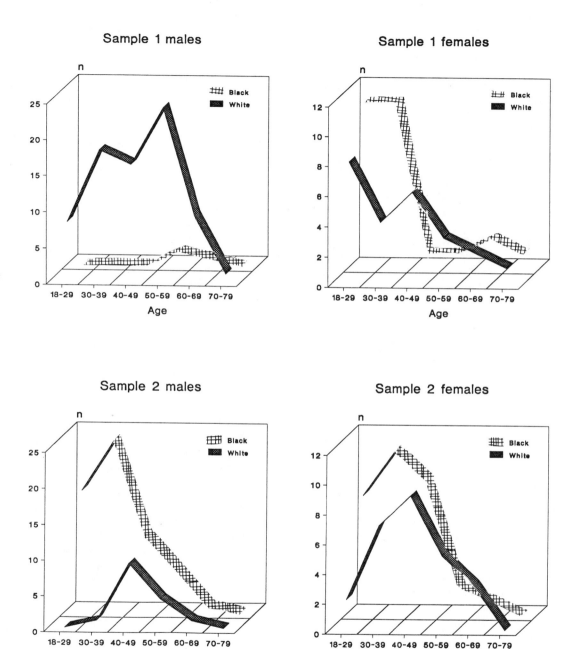

Fig. 2. Composition of the Hamann–Todd Collection samples used to test age indicators (Lovejoy et al., 1985a: Table 1).

provements over the methods used for sample 1. The reason for this is the opinion that "the value of age indicators cannot be judged on the correlation coefficient which in fact is only an indication that a relationship between indicator and chronological age exists" (Walker and Lovejoy, 1985: 77; see also Lovejoy et al., 1985a: 9). They propose instead the use of the mean absolute error and average bias. These "normalized" values are described as less "highly sensitive to the age range and distribution in the test population" than the correlation coefficient (Lovejoy et al., 1985a: 9).

Inaccuracy and bias are much reduced in the sample 2 tests. Is this the result of improved methods or does it relate to the range and age distribution of the samples? The answer is that the two samples are different, not that the methods give more accurate results.

There are phases of inaccuracy, shown most clearly by sample 1, in which there are four such phases. The first phase ranges from age 18 to 44 (mean inaccuracy ca. 4); the second, from 45 to 56 (mean inaccuracy ca. 8); the third, from 57 to 66 (ca. 13); and the fourth from 67 to 78 (mean inaccuracy ca. 22). Inaccuracy is therefore dependent on the age structure of the sample, and the two samples must be tested over comparable areas of their distributions: individuals of real age 50 and under provide samples with homogeneous means for inaccuracy ($p = .182$: tested as large but unequal samples with unequal variances).

The only real change is that the inaccuracy of the Todd pubis technique has been reduced for the age group 50–59. Since the number of individuals between 50 and 59 falls from 30 to 17 and the proportions of blacks and females rise from 13% to 47% and 13% to 41%, respectively, it is impossible to say that inaccuracy has been dramatically reduced while all other factors are held constant between sample 1 and sample 2.

While it may be assumed that more age indicators are better than fewer age indicators, the Libben investigators have not yet provided confidence in their "multifactorial approach." Apart from the pubic symphysis, which is not reliable, they emphasize the value of the auricular surface, which is highly correlated with the pubic symphysis and not universally applicable to archaeological material. They consis-

tently note dental attrition as the most unbiased indicator of age. A description of the Libben attrition scale has been published (Lovejoy, 1985), and it is significant that "extreme wear" is given an age of 45–55 years. Libben attrition is most highly correlated with the pubic age indicators. It is clear that the multifactorial approach, in this case, is not increasing accuracy but, rather, bolstering inaccurate assessments. The intercorrelation of features that are all variously age-dependent is to be expected, but it does not prove the accuracy of age estimates.

Meindl and colleagues (1990: 356) have now questioned the attempt to systematize age estimation by the development of "standardized morphotypes" of age changes in the pubic symphysis. They propose, however, that examination of pubes should continue, in conjunction with "the systematic use of other adult age indicators."

Brooks and Suchey (1990) have stated that multiple indicators should not be averaged to produce an age estimate. They propose that the technique that gives the narrowest age range should be given most weight as the age indicator for each individual. Since younger ages provide the narrowest ranges, the proposal is likely to increase underaging.

Probability distributions over pubic stages was suggested as a method of smoothing (Jackes, 1985) that is preferable to those previously used—for example, running averaging, equal distribution over age ranges, regression, or seriating by dental attrition levels. The overall method that may give the best results for paleodemography is to chose several disparate age estimation techniques, distribute the age estimates according to tables of probability (Table 1, for example), and average the results within each 5-year age category. The estimated age-at-death distributions will still be partly determined by the techniques of age determination, but allowance will have been made for the variability of adult age indicators. Such a technique could give us no assurance of accuracy, merely a reduction of inaccuracy.

Finally, multiple techniques can be applied in a controlled way only in sites with complete skeletons and excellent preservation. Under the circumstances obtaining for most archaeological skeletal collections, published ages will

TABLE 1. Probability Distributions for Pubic Symphysis Stages Based on Data in Brooks and Suchey (1990)

Age range	I	II	III	IV	V	VI
Females						
10–14	0.022		0.003			
15–19	0.545	0.131	0.067	0.025	0.004	
20–24	0.386	0.346	0.148	0.065	0.030	
25–29		0.346	0.225	0.113	0.051	
30–34		0.131	0.236	0.159	0.077	
35–39			0.172	0.181	0.105	0.030
40–44			0.087	0.168	0.126	0.060
45–49			0.016	0.126	0.136	0.097
50–54				0.078	0.130	0.133
55–59				0.039	0.110	0.157
60–64					0.084	0.157
65–69					0.057	0.133
70–74					0.034	0.097
75–79					0.010	0.060
80–84						0.030
Males						
10–14	0.025					
15–19	0.714	0.149	0.067	0.030		
20–24	0.215	0.500	0.195	0.086	0.001	
25–29		0.295	0.294	0.151	0.043	
30–34		0.010	0.255	0.202	0.087	
35–39			0.125	0.203	0.141	0.018
40–44			0.018	0.156	0.182	0.051
45–49				0.091	0.187	0.087
50–54				0.035	0.153	0.127
55–59					0.100	0.155
60–64					0.052	0.161
65–69					0.008	0.143
70–74						0.106
75–79						0.067
80–84						0.036
85–90						0.003

have been variously assessed by a variety of techniques. Skeletal preservation, age- and sex-dependent though it may be, will be controlling our techniques of age assessment.

HISTOLOGICAL METHODS

Conceding that morphological age indicators are of problematic value for individuals over age 50, Buikstra and Konigsberg (1985) proposed histological data as the likely salvation for paleodemography.

Teeth

Cemental annulation. Gustafson (1950) first noted that the thickness of cementum increases with age in human beings. While age estimation based on cemental annulations, an-

nual depositions being distinguished by a darkly staining resting line, has been used for some time for other mammals, in which cementum is normally laid down at fairly constant rates, the method was not used for human beings until the 1980s. Naylor et al. (1985) discuss the early techniques, pointing out that the number and clarity of annuli vary within one root.

Charles and colleagues (1986) found that canines display lower intratooth count variability than do premolars, but equal intraobserver variability. However, higher interobserver variability for canines than premolars led them to conclude that premolars give better results. They did not discuss the accuracy of age estimates for canines, and although they hypothesized that an excess of annuli may be counted in poorly defined areas of cementum when the cementum is thicker (as in canines), this was not evaluated.

Condon and coworkers (1986) found a correlation of premolar annuli with age of .7 for males and .95 for females. However, since the mean age of the females in their sample is lower than that of the males, their conclusion that cemental annuli are more accurate predictors of age in females than in males cannot be evaluated.

The results of a study by Miller and colleagues (1988) confirm the finding of Condon and coworkers (1986) that cemental annulation techniques can be used only for young individuals: they report a correlation of .78 between annuli counts and age for individuals under 35, but .01 for those over 35 years. Kay and Cant (1988) studied cemental annulation and attrition in *Macaca mulatta* lower first molars. Age could be predicted accurately for individuals under 10 years, but with increasing error beyond that, especially after age 14. Age was predicted more accurately in males than in females. Kay and Cant conclude that environmental factors may affect the formation of resting lines in cementum.

Neither the preferred tooth nor the technique by which annulations should be examined has been settled. Charles and colleagues (1986, 1989) stress the importance of $7\mu m$ decalcified stained sections, but recent attempts to produce these sections from archaeological material (from the Portuguese Neolithic ossuary cave, Casa da Moura, ca. 6877–5735 B.P.) have been unsuccessful. Decalcification and staining after embedding was also unsuccessful; the cementum is reduced to a wisp of discontinuous network, separated from the shredding dentin in a number of places— which was not unexpected, since cementum is much less mineralized than dentin (Furseth and Mjør, 1973).

The Portuguese Neolithic annuli are best visualized directly under polarized light with a lambda compensator wedge to enhance weak birefringence. The incremental lines are often obscured or fade out so that many counts must be abandoned. Both bacterial and fungal destruction are seen, occasionally resulting in almost complete obliteration of the incremental lines. Work on cementum has highlighted a factor that is of critical importance to paleodemography: poor bone preservation may make histological and chemical age assessment less valuable than morphological and radiological age assessment in archaeological samples.

Casa da Moura is in a limestone area and the deposits are therefore alkaline. While the chemistry of such sediments normally promotes tooth and bone preservation (Gordon and Buikstra, 1981), it may also destroy collagen (Protsch, 1986). Since the difference between annuli and their bounding resting lines is that the resting lines have less collagen and more mineral (Furseth and Mjør, 1973), collagen decomposition reduces the contrast between the two areas.

Literature on cementum diagenesis is minimal (see Hillson, 1986: 157, for summary). Sognnaes (1955) and Werelds (1961, 1962, 1967) report microbial damage in teeth and Beeley and Lunt (1980) document the loss of collagen and a decrease in the Ca/P ratio in dentin.

Mineralization increases with age (Fraysse and Kerebel, 1982), so microradiography rather than polarizing microscopy may assist in visualizing adult cemental annuli. The technique has been used successfully on herbivore teeth (Koike and Ohtaishi, 1985), but human annuli may require magnifications above those satisfactorily achieved with microradiographs. The use of reflecting microscopy with acid etched thick sections is now being attempted.

Root transparency and combined methods of age assessment. Gustafson (1950) proposed a technique of dental age assessment based on attrition, amount of root exposed above the gingiva, cemental thickness, root resorption, secondary dentin deposited in the pulp cavity, and transparency of the root. Miles (1963) tested root transparency on incisors and reports a correlation of .73 with known age. Philippas and Applebaum (1967, 1968) discussed age-dependent variations in maxillary lateral incisors and canines.

Burns and Maples (1976) warn that periodontal disease, dental pathology, and diet may alter the rate of dentin mineralization. Their tests of Gustafson's method give correlations of .76 with real age. Maples (1978) showed that root transparency was the best predictor of age, followed by secondary dentin, while multiple regression gives correlations with real age of better than .90 in all teeth except the first molars. The use of root transparency and secondary dentin alone provides fairly high correlations, especially for the central (.89) and lateral incisors and the second molar (.88).

Hillson (1986) and Costa (1986) provide short reviews of methods that have been used to observe root transparency, and Cook (1984) critically evaluates the work of Gustafson and of Johanson (1971) and several of their successors. Kilian and Vlček (1989) summarize Czech research on root transparency. Their own work on the anterior teeth of 116 adults of known age suggests that the relation between dental biological age and chronological age is linear in males, but not in females.

Although transparency of root dentin may be altered during diagenesis (Vlček and Mrklas, 1975), this author has observed transparency in Neolithic maxillary canines. The distribution of transparency is similar to that described by Philippas and Applebaum (1968), rather than the simple advance of transparency from the root tip to half way up the root; some authors (e.g., Bang and Ramm, 1970) have stressed the need to concentrate on the lower root area.

On the basis of the literature summarized above, the oldest tooth in our sample of sectioned Portuguese canines is estimated to be well over 80 years of age, and all ages for the canine sample accord with the sequence of wear levels established for the Portuguese Neolithic. The combined method has potential for archaeological age assessment, especially if annulation counts are used in conjunction with all other indicators. There is a need to define which teeth are best used for both root transparency and cemental annulation studies, taking into account that anterior teeth may be more affected by trauma and nondietary functions, and posterior teeth by pathology. Most importantly, the effect of heavy attrition must be studied (e.g., Neolithic canines display complete infilling of the pulp chamber at an early age), and tests must be undertaken to establish whether age estimates are equally reliable in populations in which dental attrition rates and pathology differ.

Cortical Bone Microstructure

Femoral cortical remodeling. Osteon counting techniques are well summarized in several review articles (Stout, 1989a,b; Ubelaker, 1986) and by Stout (this volume, Chapter 3). Some tests on modern forensic and dissecting room material have shown formidable accuracy: for example, Uytterschaut's (1985) test of the Ahlqvist and Damsten (1969) method produced a correlation with age of .959.

On the other hand, Bocquet-Appel et al. (1980) had poor results from the Coimbra sample. Their best results ($r = .7$) were based on the number of osteons and osteon fragments. They hypothesize that their results may be disappointing because they took 6-mm cores slightly above, rather than at, the femoral midshaft. However, the site of coring is within the range of error likely to occur on incomplete archaeological femora.

Lazenby (1984), finding both inadequate sample sizes and bias in the reference samples, doubts the accuracy of all cortical remodeling age estimates. Others (Bouvier and Ubelaker, 1977; Stout, 1978; Stout and Gehlert, 1980) have compared techniques, and their conclusion that Kerley's technique (1965) provides more accurate results is supported in part by Drusini (1987). Pfeiffer's (1985) analysis of the Kleinburg Ossuary demonstrated that estimates obtained by the Ahlqvist and Damsten method differ from those obtained by the Thompson (1979) method.

The Thompson method has been tested on an independent sample, though still largely from the same general population (forensic cases in the United States) as the original reference group, and been analyzed by the same researchers using the same microscopes: the definition of the structures observed and the optics involved are important considerations in tests of histomorphological age assessment techniques. In this test, Thompson (1981) and Thompson and Gunness-Hey (1981) found a correlation of .83 between real and estimated age. However, only 54% of individuals were placed in the correct 5-year age intervals, and the resulting differences in demographic parameters are considerable. Moreover, Americans, black or white, are more likely to be aged correctly than those representing disparate dietary regimes and/or environments.

Drusini (1987) has a number of criticisms of the Thompson technique and found it inaccurate in a test of Italian specimens. Similarly, the correlations between real age and age estimated by eight variables from the Thompson technique are quite low (.75 in females and .58 in males) for middle-aged to elderly Japanese (Narasaki, 1990).

Martin and colleagues (1981) argue that many environmental factors affect cortical remodeling rates (see also Stout, this volume, Chapter 2). Ericksen (1980), Richman and colleagues (1979), Thompson and Gunness-Hey (1981), and Thompson and colleagues (1984) have all reported population differences attributed to genetic and/or environmental factors (see also Pfeiffer, 1980, and Stout and Simmons, 1979). Stout (1983) implicates diet as a major variable. It seems unlikely that the differences between femora from Ledders (agricultural) and Gibson and Ray (preagricultural) can be attributed to differences in the age assessment techniques used by Buikstra (1976), but clarification is needed, since the bone formation rates for Ledders are consonant with an older age range. The differentiating factors for femoral cortical remodeling could be as fundamental as the level of physical activity (Ubelaker, 1974).

Consequently, the universal application of regression formulas based on North American forensic cases must be questioned. Ubelaker (1986:246) has applied Kerley's technique to 158 poor from the Dominican Republic and has shown that "the rate of age change in the San Domingo sample is somewhat different from the sample used in the original Kerley study." Population differences may also explain the unsatisfactory results in the Portuguese and Italian analyses (Bocquet-Appel et al., 1980; Drusini, 1987).

However, the problems are even more basic: the recognition of forming and resorbing osteons, of cement lines, of osteon fragments, even in some cases of the osteons themselves, since bone histomorphology is not maintained in all archaeological bone.

The histology of ancient bone has been studied by Baud (1987) and Garland and colleagues (Garland, 1987, 1989; Garland et al.,

1987, 1988). Both have found that the attack on bone by microorganisms is of major importance. Garland et al. (1987) state that 100% of their sections contain exogenous material in bone spaces and 73% of archaeological bone may be destroyed by physical weathering or (in most cases) by microbial activity.

Stout (Stout and Teitlebaum, 1976) studied archaeological rib and found 39% of the Ledders sections were unreadable (Hanson and Buikstra, 1987). Differential preservation of the ribs of older and younger individuals must be considered in this context. Only Masset (1973) has considered differential preservation in any detail. Its importance has been clearly stated by Boddington and colleagues (1987: 4):

The more porous the bone and the less dense the bone, the more susceptible it is to destruction. Porosity and density are factors which depend upon age, sex and health of the individual as well as varying between individual bones of the body. Hence, the nature and rate of decay is as much a product of the buried skeleton as the burial environment.

No research has focused on the relationship of diagenesis and age at death (but see Walker et al., 1988, on age-related preservation bias favoring young adults).

Research on the effect of the burial environment has barely begun. Archaeological bone may be exceptionally well preserved in dry environments (Martin et al., 1981; Cook et al., 1989), and perfect preservation is possible in permafrost (Amy et al., 1986). Ubelaker (1974) appears to have had a 100% success rate sectioning precontact American ossuary material, but well-preserved material is the exception, not the rule. Pfeiffer has made several attempts at osteon counting methods of age assessment. Her success rates ranged from 100% for a Late Archaic site (Pfeiffer, 1980), through 27%–37%, depending on the technique employed, for a late sixteenth century site (Pfeiffer, 1985), to 11% for an early nineteenth century site (Pfeiffer, 1989). Black (1979) abandoned cortical remodeling age assessment after producing no readable thin sections. Samson and Branigan (1987) also abandoned the attempt to count osteons in favor of quantifying porosity, as did Palmer (1987).

Histomorphological age estimation has been attempted on femora from Portuguese archaeological sites: two Mesolithic open-air estuarine middens dated 7929 and 7604 B.P. (calibrated weighted averages) and six Neolithic sites dated 6877–4638 B.P. (Lubell and Jackes, 1988). The Neolithic sites include deep limestone caves in the interior mountains and open sandy caves near the coast. One additional sample comes from a medieval rock grave burial.

Results of cortical remodeling techniques on the Portuguese sample. The Portuguese femoral sections exhibit physical, chemical and microbial destruction (Fig. 3). Unless thin sections are cleared with, for example, hydrogen peroxide (xylene is of no value here, cf. Stout, 1989a: 43), structures appear to be obscured by a dark granular congestion. In sections where this granulation is pronounced, fluorescence is increased and birefringence under polarized light is markedly reduced. In some cases, only a few birefringent areas can be discerned over a half section of femur. Histomorphology may be completely disrupted. While a few "ghost" areas of lamellae may be seen, most often near Haversian canals, the lamellae are often discontinuous and disintegrate into multiple circular or ovoid forms (Fig. 3A,B). Hackett (1981) has called these forms "lamellate foci," since they lie roughly oriented with the concentric lamellae surrounding the Haversian canals. The foci are surrounded by rims of bright (dense) reprecipitated bone 2–5μm wide (described by Hackett, 1981, as "cuffs"). At high magnifications it can be seen that within each larger focus there exist multiple small foci each just under 1μm in diameter (Fig. 3B). Lamellate foci are evidence that bone has undergone bacterial attack (Jackes, 1990).

Material from the earliest site (Moita do Sebastião) has been cleared with hydrogen peroxide, thus allowing observation in light microscopes. Of 31 sections, most show complete destruction of the morphology; only six retain any microstructure, and only in the midcortical third. The four femora that retain the most structure still have a great deal of lamellar bone and the least endosteal porosity; the mean number of empty spaces in the endosteal third of these sections range from 5.83 to 7.00. All other sections have a mean endosteal porosity count of 7.25 to 13.25 (Palmer, 1987:

150). Only these younger individuals allow examination of histomorphology and they could not provide age estimates by techniques that require examination of the periosteal third of a section.

Even when morphology has been partially maintained, the sections cannot be read. Cement lines do not show up clearly under transmitted, polarized, or fluorescent light and attempts at staining cement lines have been unsuccessful. Reduced birefringence, particularly of the outer lamellae of osteons, ensures that osteon area and osteon fragments cannot be observed accurately. In many sections every space is filled with calcite (see Fig. 3A) derived from the burial environment (Pate and Hutton, 1988). The calcite makes it impossible to examine the canal edges to see whether they are forming or resorbing. Calcite commonly fills cracks (Fig. 3A) that emanate from the periosteal border, thus precluding periosteal osteon counts. Attempts to remove the calcite with triammonium citrate result in almost complete destruction of the bone within a few hours.

It is no doubt valuable to continue research into techniques of preparing bone samples and observing microstructure. The extreme difficulty of preparing thin sections of archaeological bone has suggested the use of several alternatives, for example, reflected light microscopy (Bennike, 1990) and microradiography (Boivin and Baud, 1984; Garland, 1989; Stout and Simmons, 1979).

The reduced birefringence of osteons in archaeological specimens makes it impossible to distinguish among the various types of osteons visible under polarized light. Since the osteon types may have some association with age, this is particularly unfortunate for paleodemographers. But osteon type seems also to have a relationship with mineralization (Martin and Burr, 1989: 71), and degrees of mineralization are picked up by microradiography. Older osteons will be more mineralized; younger individuals with a higher rate of remodeling will have less mineralized osteons and older individuals with slower resorption and refilling rates should have more mineralized osteons. Detailed work on osteon types may help to answer Lazenby's major criticism, that by considering all osteons within a certain area, we

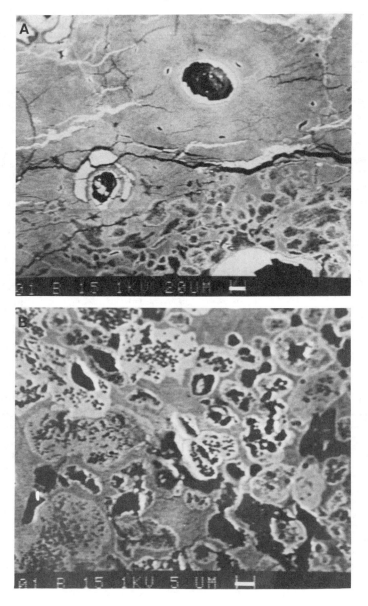

Fig. 3. **A:** Backscattered electron image of an undecalcified embedded endosteal midfemoral section from Cabeço da Arruda F, showing dessication cracks, calcite in spaces, and focal destruction in the lower third of the picture. ×210. **B:** Backscattered electron image of the midendosteal area of a femur from Caldeirão (P11/155), undecalcified and embedded, illustrating lamellate foci. 1,000×.

are including osteons formed years before, with the result that "our mean value will be more reflective of the younger age than of the true age at death" (Lazenby, 1984: 99).

Bone Density, Porosity, and Bone Mineral Content

Porosity of bone increases with age: there are more Haversian canals (there are more osteons per square millimeter and the osteons have a smaller area); the Haversian canal diameters are larger; there are more resorption spaces and incompletely refilled osteons, since the resorptive and refilling phases are slower in the elderly (Martin and Burr, 1989). But, while the volume of bone (excluding spaces) may decrease with age, the density and mineralization of bone may increase.

In archaeological bone, studies of porosity, density, and mineralization are almost impossible. Porosity has been studied in the Portuguese sample (Palmer, 1987) by fluorescing microscopy, but backscattered electron imaging demonstrates that not all calcite filled spaces can be visualized under fluorescing light. Image analysis with polarized light is possible, but calcite lies over bone as well as within spaces (Fig. 3A). Microbial activity introduces many false spaces into the bone that are surrounded by reprecipitated bone of increased density. Bone density values may be falsified when calcite is present in bone spaces and cannot be removed from a bone sample without destroying it. The calculation of density, as weight/volume bone, is an element in the Thompson technique, but it cannot be calculated for a bone that has undergone decomposition and in which many of the voids and cracks are filled with extraneous minerals. Portuguese midfemoral cortex samples have a mean bone density of 1.51 ($\sigma = .38$ $n = 105$ adults only), a value so low that it is unlikely to be a reliable indicator of in vivo bone density.

Bone Chemistry

There are changes in bone chemistry with age; a decrease of calcium, phosphate, and collagen and an increase of carbonate (Beattie, 1982; Lengyel and Nemeskéri, 1965; Lengyel, 1978), but there is little possibility that age trends can be discerned in archaeological bone.

Calcium and phosphorus. The Ca/P molar ratio of human bone mineral is 1.67, although microprobe analyses can show differences in Ca/P ratios across a single osteon (Ortner and von Endt, 1971). The ratio may be maintained throughout life (Mellors et al., 1966), or may increase after age 30 (Ascenzi, 1983). Deviations from a Ca/P ratio of 1.67 in archaeological bone can never be taken to indicate changes in bone chemistry that have resulted from age. Ratios in buried bone can be altered markedly (Sillen, 1989; Acsádi and Nemeskéri, 1970: 136–137; Lengyel, 1978; Salomon and Haas, 1967) and ratios in $1 \mu m^2$ areas of bone reprecipitated by bacterial action are particularly variable (Jackes, 1990).

It appears that bone apatite retains its chemical composition after death, although crystals may enlarge during diagenesis (Schoeninger et al., 1989; Susini et al., 1987; Jackes, 1990). Despite this, analyses that are not pinpointed on a few microns of bone will certainly find highly altered bone chemistry, solubility, and crystallinity because of the occurrence of brushite (Piepenbrink, 1986; Susini et al.,1987) and calcite in dead bone, and because of carbonate substitution.

Carbonate. Carbonates may substitute for phosphates in bone apatite during life (Le-Geros et al., 1967), leading to altered crystal forms and increased solubility: the bones of the elderly will withstand diagenesis less well than those of young individuals.

While carbonate levels in bone may be related to age at death, it seems unlikely that the *in vivo* carbonate content of bone mineral could be measured accurately. As discussed, removal of diagenically introduced carbonates with triammonium citrate in one test resulted in the total destruction of samples. Baud (1987) has summarized information on the minerals that are formed by the reprecipitating activities of bacteria. These minerals are primarily calcite (i.e., pure $CaCO_3$). Groundwater carbonates may be added to bone carbonate without the intervention of bacteria (Pate and Hutton, 1988). At the same time, leaching in the soil may lead to a loss of apatite carbonates (Susini et al., 1987).

Collagen. Collagen is markedly reduced from the time growth is complete. However, collagen is also reduced in buried bone. The

dense bright rims of lamellate foci lack collagen (Jackes, 1990), presumably utilized by
bacteria. The mean percentage collagen of 22
Portuguese ribs sampled for stable isotope analyses and radiocarbon dating is 5.4% (range
2%–10%), compared with the 18%–20% expected in modern bones. Collagen levels are
reduced even in areas with low soil temperatures (Nelson et al., 1986: 1945), and a loss of
at least 60% collagen seems general (Lengyel
and Nemeskéri, 1965; Lengyel, 1978; Pfeiffer,
1991).

Discussion. Bone decomposition depends
on the burial microenvironment, the temperature, the humidity, and the pH of the deposits.
Bone decomposition, as discussed above, also
depends on the age at death of the individual.
In spite of these considerations, Lengyel
(1968) assumes that all femora from one level
in a site will have equivalent bone decomposition, and that one can therefore reconstruct
population characteristics and interpret deviations as individual differences, not diagenetic
alterations. Pfeiffer (1991), on the other hand,
has demonstrated the surprising variations in
preservation of same-sex, same-age individuals,
buried at the same time within one small and
homogeneous area.

Lengyel has attempted chemical age assessment of 90 Mesolithic individuals from Vlasac
(Nemeskéri, 1978). The remains were seriated
on the basis of reduced phosphorus and increased carbonate and the ages were estimated
by a regression formula that takes into account
the difference between the Vlasac mean values
and those of a sample of 700 autopsied individuals. Chemical ages were compared with morphological ages determined by Nemeskéri with
the following results: in 54% ages were within
the range of the morphological age; in 29.5%
ages were contradictory. The published results
do not allow us to determine which ages provided discrepant results.

Analyses of the micromorphology, density
and chemistry of archaeological bone must
start with the assumption that diagenesis has
occurred. The hope that histomorphology will
give us accurate age estimates for complete
samples from a large variety of archaeological
populations is vain; paleohistology and pa-
leochemistry will not give paleodemography a
new lease on life.

AGE DISTRIBUTIONS BASED ON DENTITION

Dental Wear

Wear is age-dependent, although factors
such as type of diet and methods of food preparation will control the rate of attrition. Furthermore, wear is caused not only by the mastication of food but by individual idiosyncrasies
(bruxism rather than age may determine attrition rates among modern European and North
American adults) and by the use of teeth as
tools. The normal pattern and rate of wear may
be altered by malocclusion and pathology.

Opinions vary as to the importance of dental
wear in age determination. Blakely (1971: 44)
stated that "continued reliance on dental attrition as an accessory means of age estimation is
a questionable practice," in contrast to the
view that wear is "the best single indicator for
determining age at death" (Lovejoy et al.,
1985a: 12). Some of the many schemas upon
which the observation of wear have been based
are reviewed in Costa (1986), Hillson (1986),
and Brothwell (1989). Seriation by dental wear
(e.g., Lovejoy, 1985) can be followed by analysis of wear gradients (see e.g., Miles, 1963,
1978) and estimates of chronological age.
Other researchers have developed quite different techniques (Molnar et al., 1983a,b; McKee
and Molnar, 1988), which demonstrate, among
other things, that different techniques can lead
to different conclusions, for example with regard to sex differences in rates and patterns of
wear.

Kieser and colleagues (1985) have shown
that wear follows a linear progression up to 39
years of age, and then slows down (see also
Hillson, 1986: 185). The fairly high correlations with age discerned by Lovejoy and colleagues (1985a: 9, $r = .7$) in studies of samples
from the Todd Collection may result from the
age distributions of those samples (Fig. 2).
Molleson and Cohen (1990) demonstrated that
attrition stages do not represent a series
through which all dentitions pass in ordered
and steady sequence. In fact, they suggest that
the analysis of attrition stages produces underaging in archaeological samples. Testing of the
Brothwell system showed that, while early
stages are passed through rapidly, the later
stages last for many years of an individual's life.

Lubell and colleagues (1989) and Lubell and Jackes (1988) have modified the dental wear grading categories of Smith (1984); the modified wear stages allowed consistent coding among three researchers. Nevertheless, the results of separate analyses of the Portuguese Mesolithic lower molar wear stages are discouraging. Attrition levels coded within a month of the time when the original schema was drawn up show no significant differences between observers. Observations made 1 year and 2 years later give a clear indication that observers altered criteria over time, yet the methods and detailed written criteria for scoring remained the same.

Other tests of interobserver and intraobserver error have been undertaken on large samples of loose upper and lower molars from the Portuguese Neolithic ossuary cave site of Casa da Moura. On the basis of random shifts of significance and nonsignificance among sets of teeth (from one molar to another, and from side to side), it appears that intraobserver error is as important as interobserver error. Even in higher wear categories in which distinctions were made on what seemed to be "objective" criteria (pattern of dentin exposures) agreement reached only around 50%.

All upper molars with no more than a pinpoint of dentin have now been further observed under a microscope. This study showed that even in the early stages of wear, when assessments are based on fairly objective categorizations (presence and absence of scratching, polishing, facetting, blunting, pinpoint dentin exposures), surprisingly little agreement is reached.

Other Dental Observations and Age Estimation

Attempts are under way to supplement wear scores with metrical data to reduce the subjectivity of wear assessment (Jackes, 1988). Kieser and colleagues (1985) showed the relation of crown height, occlusal slope, and interproximal facet width to age in a known age population. Measurements of cusp height are also possible (Tomenchuk and Mayhall, 1979; Molnar et al., 1983a), but cusp height is rapidly reduced in archaeological populations, and various crown height measurements have proven adequate in recent analyses.

Cementoenamel junction height above the alveolar margin (CEJ height). Tal (1984) analyzed CEJ heights on 100 mandibles of known age and found that the mean differences between the decades from those in their twenties to those in their forties were significant. Later age groups did not show significant differences, perhaps because of tooth loss.

CEJ height has been recorded on the Portuguese Mesolithic dentitions (Jackes, 1988). Three observers measured the CEJ height on the same set of mandibles, and one intraobserver test was carried out. Comparisons among the measurements showed unexpected lack of error. It appears that the CEJ height of first molars can be measured with very little error; but damage and periodontal disease will reduce the sample size and the value of the variable in some archaeological samples.

Occlusal angles and crown heights (Fig. 4A,D). Crown height measurements allow the calculation of angles of wear by trigonometry (Jackes, 1988). Two separate buccal height and lingual height measurements of 879 upper molars have been made. Paired sample *t* tests show that significant differences exist, as might be expected for surfaces with complex topography, but interobserver measurement differences are reduced in measuring teeth in which dentin is already exposed. Buccal measurements are reliable ($p = .806$ $n = 339$), but lingual measurement error remains significant.

Smith (1984) has shown the relationship of the angle of wear (measured differently) to attrition grades, and work by Jackes (1988) has also demonstrated the value of calculating the angle of the occlusal surfaces of lower and upper molars. The coefficients of variation of angles are excessively high, even for the controlled technique proposed here. The buccolingual occlusal angle of the mesial cusps has the lowest coefficient of variation on first lower molars, and future work should perhaps concentrate on the mesial half of lower molars.

Interproximal facets (Fig. 4C,E,F). Some studies have utilized the form and/or width of the interproximal facets (Hinton, 1982; Kieser et al., 1985; Jackes, 1988). The metrical analysis of interproximal facets has been emphasized in the Portuguese samples both because the form of the contact area (straight, concave–convex, or sinuous; Kieser et al., 1985; Whit-

A: Occulusal Angle

Mean degrees

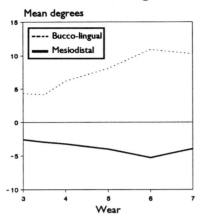

B: Length/Breath Ratio

Mean length/breadth

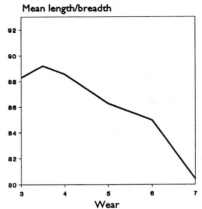

C: Crown Height Above IP Facets

Mean height (mm)

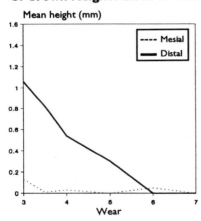

D: Buccal & Lingual Crown Heights

Mean height (mm)

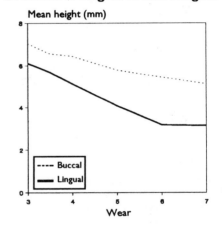

E: Interproximal Facet Shape

Mean height/width

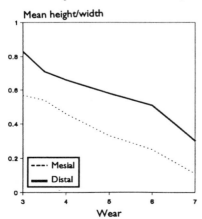

F: Interproximal Facet Area

Mean height x width (mm)

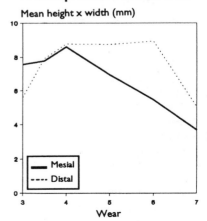

taker et al., 1987) may not be an error-free observation and because work on loose molars allows more detailed analysis. The height of the facets is recorded as well as their width and the midpoint depth of the facet below the occlusal margin. In the expectation that facet width on upper molars would be inaccurate, two sets of measurements were made by the same individual, but the results of paired t tests were nonsignificant (mesial width, $p = .14$; distal width, $p = .47$; $n = 879$). A test on the depth of facets below the occlusal surface, using 277 first lower molars, gave equivalent results.

Length/breadth ratio and crown area (Fig. 4B). Reduction in the mesiodistal diameter of teeth is a result of interproximal wear (demonstrated for the Casa da Moura loose lower molars; Jackes, 1988). Upper molars show the same pattern (see also Mayhall, this volume, Chapter 4, for a discussion of dental measurement).

Tests on *In Situ* and Loose First Molars

A number of metrical variables can be used with or without wear scores to assign molars to categories. Of prime importance is the demonstration that variables can be grouped and that intercorrelations between variable groups are low. The lower molar variable groups generally sort out to express (1) the size and shape of the mesial facet; (2) the size and shape of the distal facet; (3) the buccolingual angles; (4) the length–breadth ratio of the crown or the crown area; (5) most crown and cusp heights and the height of the CEJ above the alveolar margin; and (6) the mesiodistal occlusal angles and the mesial crown heights. Variables from

various groups can be combined in multivariate analyses to test the wear categories.

Subjectively, it appeared that the wear levels 2 and 3 (Smith, 1984) as used in the Portuguese project were inadequate for the range of wear at those levels, and this was confirmed objectively by discriminant analysis using the metrical variables defined above. It was demonstrated that wear level 3 performed unsatisfactorily; discriminant analysis indicated a low level of correct predictions of membership in wear level 3. Wear levels 2.5 and 3.5 were therefore added to the wear scores.

By using the means of three trial scorings of loose first lower molars as the grouping variable, 65% correct classification by discriminant analysis was achieved; the result was an improvement over the use of separate trial scores. In this test, 99% of the discrimination was achieved by the first two functions. The first expressed the mean of the crown heights at the four main molar cusps, the second the area of the mesial interproximal facet, the third the mesiodistal occlusal angle, and the fourth the buccolingual occlusal angle; the ratio of crown length to crown breadth weighed heavily on the fifth canonical discriminant function. Such analyses show that the wear of enamel and exposure of dentin form but one aspect of dental changes with increased age. Since, furthermore, wear is subject to observer error and the choice of factors defining a certain wear level is arbitrary, dental wear is not an ideal variable. Less subtle problems also arise: dental trauma and cupped wear (commonly over a millimeter deep in Neolithic lower molars) may lead to overestimation of attrition levels, and pathology may introduce variation.

For all these reasons, observations of dental wear should be balanced by the addition of dental measurements. When analyzed by wear categories, the coefficients of variation for many of these measurements are excessively high for biological data. Human dental wear may be so variable that measurements have little discriminating value, but it is more likely that the wear categories used to group the measurements are too coarse and inexact.

Cluster analysis (rather than analysis relying only on wear levels) can provide clear groupings of upper molars (Fig. 5) and leads to re-

---

Fig. 4. Upper first molar metrical changes plotted against a set of attrition scores. Sample ($n = 113$) consists of molars with both interproximal facets and dentin exposure. **A:** Buccolingual and mesiodistal occlusal slope. **B:** Ratio of length to breadth of the molar crown. **C:** Distance between the top of the facet and the occlusal surface of the tooth changes as the tooth wears down. **D:** Buccal and lingual crown heights. **E:** Shape of the facet alters as the facet height is lost and breadth increased. **F:** Interproximal facet area increases and then decreases as crown height is lost.

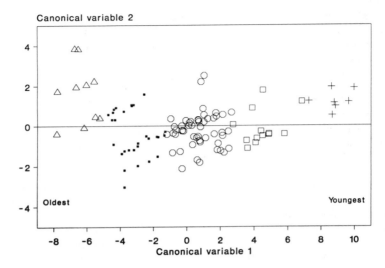

Fig. 5. Clustering of Casa da Moura upper first molars in which dentin is exposed, based on attrition score and three metrical variables (buccolingual angle, crown area, distal facet shape). Symbols indicate different clusters.

duced coefficients of variation for most of the metrical variables. However, the coefficients of variation for the angles and the facet variables remain beyond levels normally acceptable for biological data, and care should be taken that discrimination does not rely too heavily on these variables.

Sorting Teeth Into Age Categories

First, the sequence of crown and root calcification is identified (Moorrees et al., 1963; Anderson et al., 1976; Trodden, 1982) in conjunction with the early stages of occlusal wear and the appearance of interproximal attrition. Root formation scores are not error-free: tests on upper molars have shown marked differences between observers. Agreements reached only 47.6% ($n = 84$ incomplete roots, excluding cases considered broken in either or both observation runs). Agreement was highest for crown complete (59%) and initial root formation (100%), since these are the least subjective; but unequal sample sizes preclude valid analysis of each formation score for error.

In teeth with complete roots, the progress of occlusal wear and changes in the form of the interproximal facets up to the wear stage at which dentin is exposed are noted. Next, changes in the crown dimensions and occlusal

angles, together with alterations in the interproximal facets, are identified. This permits the recognition of five levels of wear in which there is more than minimal dentin exposure.

Summary on Dentition

Dental wear alone will not provide a high correlation with real age (Kieser et al., 1985; Kay and Cant, 1988). Wear stages are arbitrarily defined and subject to inter- and intraobserver error. Wear is not a linear progression or, rather, dental anthropologists have not yet defined a series of wear stages that allows a linear progression with age to be identified on the basis of a large known-age, traditional diet sample. The Miles method has been tested on the known-age Lengua sample (Kieser et al., 1983), and although the correlation between real age and estimated age was high for mandibular samples (low for maxillary teeth), age estimates were less accurate in older adults (after age 27).

Detailed studies of enamel wear and dentin exposure, controlled by reference to cemental annulation and combined- method age estimates of individual teeth, and also incorporating analyses of metrical variables, may make age estimates more accurate. Grouping dentitions on the basis of multivariate analyses may

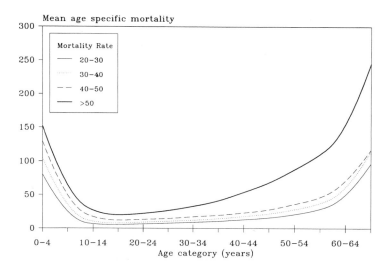

Fig. 6. Age-specific mortality curves for Finland, A.D. 1751 to 1868 based on data in Turpeinen (1979). The average age-specific mortalities are plotted for those years in which the mortality rates fell between 20 and 30, 30 and 40, 40 and 50, and 50 to 77.5.

well assist in assigning broad age categories that would be of value in discerning trends in rates of attrition and dental pathology. They may provide age categories for the study of cortical width, porosity, and degenerative changes. But the age estimates will not be accurate enough for full paleodemographic studies, since attrition is so strongly variable beyond young adulthood and paleodemographic analyses ideally require that ages at death be accurately ascribed to set 5-year age categories.

Furthermore, in populations with extreme dental pathology (e.g., North American maize agriculturalists), the dentition cannot be used to estimate adult age. Premortem tooth loss and high caries rates will make it impossible to observe many teeth, and the wear on the remaining teeth will not fall into the standard pattern. Similarly, in populations with extreme wear and/or extensive use of the teeth for functions other than eating, teeth will be worn too rapidly to provide the possibility of age estimations for older adults.

PALEODEMOGRAPHY

Paleodemography has been plagued by controversy over the last decade. The basis of the controversy is a very simple question: can anthropologists give accurate ages to the dead? Those who defend paleodemography state that the demographic curves generated by their data are meaningful (Van Gerven and Armelagos, 1983; Greene et al., 1986; Piontek and Weber, 1986). Buikstra and Konigsberg (1985) acknowledge that older adults may be underaged, but maintain that adult q values (probability of death curves) carry demographic information. The basis of this statement is a principal components analysis with unrotated component scores, specifically the second principal component, which explains only 18.5% of the total variance and to which q_{15} is the major contributor, that is, the probability of dying between 15 and 20 years of age.

Those who question the value of paleodemography state that the archaeological demographic parameters fall outside known values or curves and thus must be determined by inaccuracies in age assessment and biases in the data (Bocquet-Appel and Masset, 1982, 1985; Bocquet-Appel, 1986; Masset and Parzysz, 1985). Comparison of Figures 6 and 7 illustrates the point.

The age-specific mortality curves for Finland between 1751 and 1868 (Turpeinen, 1979) illustrate that human mortality (even in periods

A

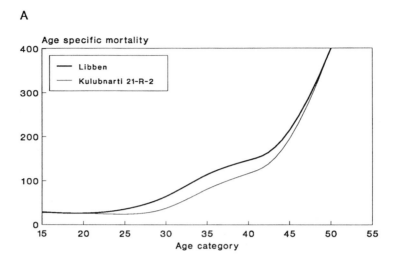

B

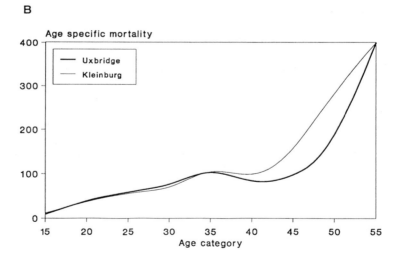

Fig. 7. Comparison of age-specific mortality curves. **A:** Libben and Kulubnarti aged by Todd pubic indicators smoothed on the basis of dental attrition scores. **B:** Uxbridge and Kleinburg aged by the McKern and Stewart method for males and the Gilbert and McKern method for females, and smoothed by equal distribution.

of extreme distress in which the death rate far exceeds the birth rate) follows curves of well-defined shape (Fig. 6). This has been established for all known human populations: although infant deaths may be underregistered and people may make errors in stating adult ages, the overall pattern of human mortality is clear (Coale and Demeny, 1966; United Nations, 1982; Gage, 1990) and supported by the findings of historical demographers.

Archaeological mortality, however, is different. Figure 7A shows the smoothed age-specific mortality curves derived from a Sudanese Nubian medieval Christian cemetery, Kulubnarti 21-R-2 (Greene et al., 1986) and the Late Woodland site of Libben in Ohio. Kulubnarti and Libben were aged by the same methods: major emphasis on Todd pubic indicators and dental attrition (the use of the Todd–Brooks method is confirmed by Greene et al., 1986: 197; Libben techniques are clearly stated in Lovejoy et al., 1977: 292 and note 10, and further outlined in later publications by the same team of researchers showing that the pubis and the dentition were most highly correlated with each other and with the assessed ages). The two curves are identical (G = 8.4, p = .3, 7 df). Figure 7B shows the age-at-death distributions derived from two precontact Ontario Huron ossuaries (see Jackes, 1986, for details). Both were given ages based on equal distribution of McKern–Stewart ages for males and Gilbert–McKern ages for females. Since Uxbridge showed a much higher level of skeletal tuberculosis (Pfeiffer, 1984) than the later site, Kleinburg (Jackes, 1977; Jackes, nd), identical age-specific mortality curves in young adulthood are best explained by identical age estimation techniques.

The Kleinburg curve is only one of a number of possible curves. Different age-at-death distributions will be generated by different treatments of the same 100 pubes (see Jackes, 1985). Different curves again are based on a sample of 112 femoral cores (Pfeiffer, 1984, since the Kleinburg site is an ossuary it is impossible to compare directly between osteonal and pubic ages or to use multifactorial age techniques). There is no basis for assuming that any curve best represents the true Kleinburg mortality. It is only known that the shape of the curve (whatever demographic parameter is used: age at death, probability of death, age-specific mortality, and so on) is partly determined by the "great unknown" of archaeological samples (the real age distribution) and partly by the technique(s) of age assessment.

The discussion here has highlighted the difficulties surrounding paleodemography. What hope is there for paleodemography?

Paleodemographic Comparisons and Trends

Even in its heyday when no symposium was complete without a paper on paleodemography (e.g., Angel, 1968, 1969; Brothwell, 1971), Angel argued that the most reliable basis for comparison was a child:adult death ratio. Nevertheless, life tables were increasingly used and in 1973 model paleodemographic tables were published (Weiss, 1973), which were intended to expand fragmentary data. They were used by Lovejoy and colleagues (1977) to calculate age-specific birth rates based on the Libben life expectancy and survivorship at age 15 (although the accuracy of survivorship depends on the completeness of the sample up to age 15). The Weiss tables are still used today (e.g., Corruccini et al., 1989).

There is little correspondence between the Weiss tables and other model or historical data. The lack of correspondence results from the way in which the 72 tables were constructed; the probability-of-death values fluctuate slightly according to a fixed pattern between 0 and 14 years, but not thereafter, in each of the nine tables per set of life expectancies at 15 years. The Weiss tables assume low mortality in infants and young children and high adolescent and early adult mortality—often characteristics of biased or misaged samples. The Weiss tables reflect this pattern simply because they derive most importantly from archaeological data. Predictive values calculated on the basis of some Weiss tables lie beyond the range of valid data, as determined by methods to be discussed below.

Anthropologists have also attempted to show trends by calculating either "the crude mortality rate" or "the crude birth rate": each of these values is actually 1 divided by the average age at death ($1/e_0$). The average age at death can be calculated through the use of a life table (as life expectancy at birth), or it can be derived by multiplying the number of dead in each age category (e.g., 5.0–9.9 years) by the midpoint of the age category (i.e., 7.5) and then summing the resulting figures for all age categories. The crude mortality or death rate, $1e_0$, has been cited for comparative purposes (Bass et al., 1971; Hassan, 1981; Owsley and Bass, 1979; Ubelaker, 1974; Weiss, 1973).

As the crude birth rate, $1/e_0$ has been used to show trends through time (Sattenspiel and Harpending, 1983). However, the high mortality level model life tables constructed by Coale and Demeny (1966) show that $1/e_0$ will provide an accurate crude birth rate only in populations that are either near zero growth or in decline. In populations with growth, $1/e_0$ will be higher than the birth rate.

Major Biases in Paleodemographic Data

Unfortunately, $1/e_0$ cannot be used for comparative purposes, for it has a number of inbuilt biases when derived from paleodemographic samples. The first bias is widely recognized: in many archaeological samples children, and especially infants (0–12 months), are not fully represented (for a further discussion see Saunders, this volume, Chapter 2). For North America, judging from the archaeological samples, it seems probable that Arikara villagers of South Dakota buried all infants or that most infants have been recovered during excavation (Bass et al., 1971; Owsley and Bass, 1979). At the opposite end of the pole, Huron ossuaries in southern Ontario provide fair certainty of complete excavation of all individuals within the sharply delimited burial area, but very few infants seem to have been buried in the general community burial area (Thwaites, 1898, Vol. 10: 273; Saunders and Spence, 1986). It is true that "changes in infant representation affect only infant life table values and survivorship values; life expectancy . . . [is] mathematically unaffected" (Moore et al., 1975: 60). However, life expectancy at birth (the demographic parameter on which comparison is usually based) is strongly affected.

The second bias results from the fact that average age at death (e_0) depends on the representation in older age categories. Assignment of skeletons to these categories in an age distribution has been accomplished by using running averages or by extending curves to some chosen final age. This is no more than a choice, one that is based on the preconceptions of the anthropologist. Van Gerven and Armelagos (1983), while contending that skeletal biologists can accurately estimate age from human archaeological bone, state that it is impossible to assign correct ages to those over 55 or so. By this view, which is widely accepted by those who use Todd or McKern and Stewart pubic indicators, there is no way of knowing whether the oldest individual in a group was 65 or 85. Opinions on the longevity of archaeological populations determine the final age category chosen. Since the choice of final age is arbitrary, Howell (1973) is perfectly correct in accusing paleodemographers of employing "a rubber yardstick." Life tables that end at 50, and in which the final age calculations are made on the assumption that all people die by 55 have reduced mean age-at-death values.

A third source of error in the calculation of the average age at death relates to the overall accuracy of estimating age from skeletons of individuals over the age of about 25, as discussed above. It is worth reemphasizing, since even recent literature (e.g., Paine, 1989) ignores the possibility of adult underaging and assumes that deviation from model tables is a result of cultural or postdepositional processes.

A fourth source of error can be identified in the calculation of e_0 and thus of $1/e_0$. Not all adult skeletons in an archaeological population can be given an estimated age. Beyond the statement that there are so many indeterminate adults older than age 25 or so, there is nothing to be done about estimating the age of a number of adults. Although there has been little work on this subject, much of the evidence covered in this chapter indicates that the older individuals in a sample are most likely to be given indeterminate age. Exclusion of these individuals from calculation of the average age at death will naturally depress the average age at death, giving the same result as does underrepresentation of adults. Such individuals have often been excluded from life table calculations. Equal distribution over all age categories, and, better yet, cumulative graphing, which is no doubt the best method of redistribution, are possible solutions. Distribution over adult age groups proportionate to the percentage membership of each age category (Biraben, 1969;

Asch, 1976) simply compounds age estimation errors.

The literature has emphasized the problem of infant underrepresentation, but in fact adult underrepresentation is far more important. Adults contribute more to the average age at death than do young children. It would require a $_5D_0$ value of 360 (that is, 360 children under 5 in a site) to equal the contribution of 20 adults in a "25–65" adult category, and if it were a "25–75" category, 400 individuals of 0–5 years would be necessary. This is despite the fact that early childhood deaths are here taken to be equally distributed between 0 and 4.9 years, as compensation for infant underrepresentation. In the same way, adult deaths are treated as though evenly distributed, to avoid the problem of left or right skewing of adult age-at-death distributions.

These four sources of error all have marked effects on e_0 and thus militate against the use of $1/e_0$ for comparative studies. Nevertheless, comparison is vital to the study of paleodemography. For example, an obvious question is How were American indigenous mortality and fertility rates altered by contact with Europeans and with the infectious diseases of the Old World? If this question cannot be answered on the basis of methods presently used in paleodemography, then one must either admit paleodemography to be a futile exercise (Bocquet-Appel and Masset, 1982), or work to change the methods.

The recent emphasis on the value of fertility rates (Sattenspiel and Harpending, 1983; Buikstra et al., 1986) must not be misconstrued to suggest that sites should be compared by using life table fertility rates (general or total fertility, or child:woman ratios). Sites at which infant underrepresentation and adult age estimate errors inflate the age classes between age 15 and age 45 (these are the age categories that determine life table fertility rates) result in erroneous fertility rates. It is occasionally possible to demonstrate the errors by comparison with ethnohistorical evidence. Jackes (1986) showed that Ossossané, a postcontact Huron site with a life table total fertility rate of 5.6 (total fertility = general fertility × 30), contradicted the ethnohistorical evidence of fertility rates below 4.4 (see also Engelbrecht, 1987). Adjusting the life table for infant under-

representation simply increases total fertility to well over 6.0. Life table values (apart from the q values) are too dependent upon infant representation to be useful. Fertility estimates are too dependent on correct age estimates of females aged 15–45 to be considered.

Circumventing the Problems

There have been several proposals that avoid the problem of the underrepresentation of those below age 5 and the inaccurate aging of adults. The first was that of Bocquet and Masset (1977), who suggested that estimators could overcome some paleodemographic problems, specifically the estimator 5–14.99/20+ (termed the Juvenile:Adult Ratio or JA; Jackes, 1986). Jackes (1986, 1988) proposed comparing pre- and postcontact mortality in North America and the transition to horticulture in Portugal by basing the analysis on childhood q values (mean childhood mortality or MCM, the mean of $_5q_5$, $_5q_{10}$, and $_5q_{15}$). Although the q values of a life table are markedly affected by the representation of adults (i.e., indeterminate adults must be included in one broad adult age category, say 25–65, if q values are to be analyzed), they are not in any way determined by infant representation. Mortality based on q values (mortality quotients) from age 1 to age 15 is equally valuable, but since young children as well as infants may be underrepresented in archaeological sites, ages 5–25 are preferable.

MCM is highly correlated with the JA because both depend on the relative representation of those under and those over 20 in a buried population. Their correlation is .97, based on 52 presumably unbiased archaeological samples with $n > 100$, or .95 based on 17 samples from the literature on historical demography (France, Switzerland, Quebec, Poland). Model life table correlations (Coale and Demeny, 1966) are .997 (the relationship is linear).

Buikstra and colleagues (1986) proposed that the statistic 30+/5+, published by Coale and Demeny (1966: 39), be used as an estimate of fertility. This value does have good predictive power but the question of the source of adult age variations arises. Konigsberg and coworkers (1989) have acknowledged that a demographic parameter based on assignment of

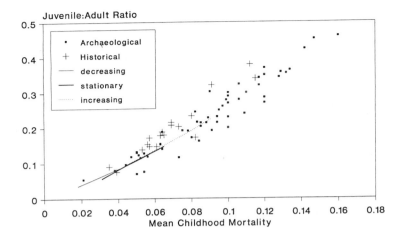

Fig. 8. Juvenile:Adult ratio plotted against mean childhood mortality for 60 archaeological sites compared with data drawn from 17 historical life tables. Trends shown are those based on Coale and Demeny (1966), West Model Life Tables 1–10, for populations that were decreasing, stationary, and increasing at low levels.

adult skeletal age to under 30 and over 30 categories is unsuitable for some sites and recommend use of 20+/5+ in the future. The correlation of MCM with log 20+/5+ is −.99986, the relationship being very slightly nonlinear.

The utility of the three proposed estimators is judged on the basis of 18 Model West tables from levels 1 to 10, for stationary, increasing (but only up to r = .01%), and declining populations (Coale and Demeny, 1966), calculated for pooled sexes (r = the crude birth rate minus the crude death rate = the rate of natural increase). For stationary populations JA is the best predictor, correlated with log general fertility at .9999 (general fertility calculated from C_x values: infants/half the population aged 15–45 years). For increasing populations the best predictor is MCM, which is correlated with log general fertility at .9987. For declining populations the best predictor is log 20+/5+, which is correlated with log general fertility at −.9995. Overall, 20+/5+ and MCM will give equivalent results: r = .9970 with log general fertility and log total fertility.

The conjoint use of MCM and JA has been proposed (Jackes, 1986, 1988) because together they provide additional demographic information (Fig. 8). It can be seen which sites fall far from the line and might be considered biased in some way. For example, "high mor-

tality sites" may actually be those in which there are more children than expected or fewer adults than expected. Sites that fall high on the line must be checked for possible sources of bias: (1) preferential burial of children, (2) incomplete excavation that has bypassed an area of adult burial, (3) exclusion of indeterminate adults from analysis. For example, the abnormal q curve presented by Kulubnarti 21-S-46 (Van Gerven et al., 1981) can be brought closer to other paleodemographic data simply by increasing the proportion of adults in the site. But this and other extreme outliers (beyond the range shown in Fig. 8: Kulubnarti 21-S-46, JA = 1.173 and Nea Nikomedia, JA = .683) could also be checked for evidence of extraordinarily rapid population increase. Analyses have concentrated on low levels of population increase, since extremely high rates of increase have been considered unlikely (Hassan, 1981).

High values may well represent populations that are expanding; included within the high value group of sites (JA above .3 and MCM above .12 on Fig. 8) are some that could represent increasing populations (e.g., Schild and Ledders; see Buikstra et al., 1986). Nevertheless, high values are also characteristic of sites that are known to have been in decline (Jackes, 1986).

It is possible to distinguish increasing from declining populations (and perhaps also biased populations) by considering not simply the level of childhood mortality, but the shape of mortality. For example, clustering of samples on the four q values from 5 to 20 indicates that sites of populations under stress (Larson, Grimsby: Jackes, 1983) may group separately from increasing populations. In other words, the shape of juvenile mortality quotient curves (q curves) can be considered, as well as the level of mortality, when one seeks to interpret paleodemographic evidence (Jackes, 1988).

Carrier's (1958) method of adjustment allows the calculation of life tables for nonstationary populations, and for this purpose standardized life tables have been proposed (Jackes, 1986; with figures published for r). The figures used give r values approximating those of Coale and Demeny (1966) very closely. The correction for nonstationary populations does not radically alter the shape of the mortality curves; it simply increases the calculated mortality quotients when $r < 0$ (population decline) and decreases the quotients when $r > 0$ (population increase). With an adjustment for population increase, the shape of the curve is altered only slightly, but the JA and MCM are reduced and a site like Ledders, which falls above the regression line, is brought to the line.

Ossossané, the Huron ossuary already referred to, provides good evidence for avoiding the assumption that predictions of fertility will be accurate once they have been adjusted for the rate of natural increase. The Ossossané life table (Katzenberg and White, 1979) total fertility rate of 5.6 has already been shown to be too high. If decline ($r = -.005\%$) is adjusted for and total fertility predicted by regression based on $20+/5+$, the result is an impossible 8.5. It can only be assumed that the ossuary does not contain all the dead. The addition of 150 adults to the life table would bring the JA and MCM into line, at high mortality in a declining population with a total fertility of 3.3. The picture would then accord with ethnohistorical evidence, including the possibility that not all adult males were buried in the ossuary.

It thus seems possible to determine whether a site is biased or nonstationary, and adjust accordingly in calculating mortality and fertility

TABLE 2. Crude Birth Rate (CBR) Estimates for Barbados Slave Population

Basis for estimate[a]	CBR	SE
West 3, female, $r = 0$	40	—
Historical life table[b]	39.5	—
MCM (log CBR): Historical	39.49	0.007
JA (linear): Historical	50.37	1.11
JA (log CBR): Historical	51.88	0.007
$20+/5+$ (log CBR): Historical	40.37	0.006
JA derived from skeletons[c]	24.2	0.006

[a]JA—Juvenile:Adult ratio; MCM—Mean childhood mortality.
[b]Konigsberg et al. (1989).
[c]Corruccini et al. (1989).

rates. Caution is necessary, however, since the usefulness of the estimators themselves may be limited. Masset and Parzysz (1985) have calculated the 33% confidence limits of JA (which they confusingly call "r") and have shown that, even in cemeteries containing 1,000 individuals aged 5–14 and over 19 years, fertility estimates cannot be considered accurate.

Corruccini and colleagues (1989) have questioned fertility predictors of the type discussed above by comparison of Barbados slave historical records with skeletal evidence. The historical life table, as calculated by Konigsberg and colleagues (1989), gives a mean age at death and MCM that are in general accord with the pooled West level 3 at $r = 0$ age-at-death distribution (Table 2). The data provided by Corruccini and coworkers (1982, 1989) do not allow calculation of any values, so this second example of paired skeletal and ethnohistoric data cannot be analyzed. There must be full publication of ages at death and methods of age assessment to test bias in a skeletal sample. However, it is possible to demonstrate (Table 2) that estimators such as MCM can be completely accurate and that the Barbados skeletal series is probably incomplete and a poor choice upon which to base a trial of estimators.

SUMMARY

It has been shown that adult ages at death cannot yet be estimated with satisfactory accuracy from skeletal data.

Estimates based on morphological and radiographic methods do not appear to be reliable.

Chemical methods, although hardly tried, are probably too affected by diagenesis to be useful unless very uneconomic methods of point analysis are used. Histomorphology is possible only for material from sites with exceptional preservation.

On the other hand, it may be possible to produce higher correlations with real age by using a complex system based on dentition. Attrition, although shown to be variable and error-prone, can be made less subjective by the addition of metrical variables. In combination with histological techniques, teeth may provide age estimates where diagenesis, pathology, and trauma are limited.

Although the accuracy of age estimation may be improved, the degree of that accuracy will almost always be an unknown. Tests on modern samples cannot ensure accurate age assessment of past populations whose environment and life-style are imperfectly understood. Nevertheless, the minimum number of individuals count (MNI) can be based on teeth and extremely detailed analyses of sets of dentition of individuals aged 5–25 years can be undertaken. On the assumption that childhood age at death can be accurately estimated, childhood mortality and the proportion of children to adults in a cemetery sample can be used to assess the biases, to suggest whether the population is nonstationary, and to compare trends through time.

If the paleodemographic parameters discerned do not accord with model or historical data, the accuracy of the paleodemographic data should be questioned. One should not assume that the human experience of mortality and fertility has altered dramatically, from place to place and time to time (Howell, 1976; and see Roth, this volume, Chapter 10).

On the assumption that childhood mortality levels reveal something about a population, and that human mortality follows a discernible pattern irrespective of place and time, research in paleodemography can continue. But the limits of paleodemography are clear. If those limits are acknowledged, we can still trace human mortality and fertility through time.

ACKNOWLEDGMENTS

This research was done in association with Dr. David Lubell and was funded by the Social Sciences and Humanities Research Council of Canada (Grants 810-84-0030 and 410-86-2017) to Lubell, Jackes, and Dr. Christopher Meiklejohn (University of Winnipeg) and by the Central Research Fund, University of Alberta (to Lubell). I am grateful to Meiklejohn for sharing his data, and to Dr. Miguel Ramalho of the Geological Survey of Portugal, Lisbon, for allowing us to work on the skeletal collections under his care (Moita, Arruda, Casa da Moura, Melides, Furninha, and Fontainhas) and for facilitating our research. We thank our colleagues (Drs. Miguel Ramos, Henry Schwarcz, Gerd Weih, João Zilhão), students (Cidália Duarte, Kirsten Jackes, Pamela Mayne, Esther Palmer, Gary Tait), and technicians (Peter Black, Dennis Carmel, Malti Nikrad, José Severino Rodrigues, Paul Wagner). The long-term work of Carmel, Mayne, and Palmer has been especially important. Radiography was done in Portugal at the Santiago do Caçem Hospital, and by Paulo de Deus Machado at the Janares Clinic, Sintra.

REFERENCES

Acsádi G, Nemeskéri J (1970): "History of Human Life Span and Mortality." Budapest: Akademiai Kiadó.

Ahlqvist J, Damsten O (1969): A modification of Kerley's method for the microscopic determination of age in human bone. J Forensic Sci 14:205–212.

Amy R, Bhatnagar R, Damkjar E, Beattie O (1986): The last Franklin expedition: Report of a postmortem examination of a crew member. Can Med Assoc J 135:115–117.

Anderson DL, Thompson GW, Popovich F (1976): Age of attainment of mineralization stages of the permanent dentition. J Forensic Sci 21:191–200.

Angel JL (1968): Ecological aspects of palaeodemography. In Brothwell DR (ed): "The Skeletal Biology of Earlier Human Populations." London: Pergamon Press, pp 263–270.

Angel JL (1969): The bases of paleodemography. Am J Phys Anthropol 30:427–438.

Angel JL, Suchey JM, İşcan MY, Zimmerman MR (1986): Age at death from the skeleton and viscera. In Zimmerman MR, Angel JL (eds): "Dating and Age Determination in Biological Materials." London: Croom Helm, pp 179–220.

Ascenzi A (1983): Microscopic dissection and isolation of bone constituents. In Kunin AS, Simmons DJ (eds): "Skeletal Research," Vol 2. New York: Academic Press, pp 185–236.

Asch DL (1976): "The Middle Woodland Populations of the Lower Illinois Valley: A Study in Paleodemographic Methods." Northwestern University Archaeological Program, Scientific Papers No. 1.

Bang G, Ramm E (1970): Determination of age in humans from root dentine transparency. Acta Odontol Scand 28:3–35.

Barnett E, Nordin BEC (1960): The radiological diagnosis of osteoporosis: A new approach. Clin Radiol 11:166–174.

Bass WM, Evans DR, Jantz RL (1971): "The Leavenworth Site Cemetery." University of Kansas Publications in Anthropology, No. 2.

Baud C-A (1987): Altérations osseuses post-mortem d'origine fongique ou bactérienne. In Duday H, Masset C (eds): "Anthropologie Physique et Archéologie: Méthodes d'étude des Sépultres." Paris: Centre National de la Recherche Scientifique, pp 135–146.

Beattie O (1982): An assessment of x-ray energy spectroscopy and bone trace element analysis for the determination of sex from fragmentary human skeletons. Can J Anthropol 2:205–215.

Bedford ME, Russell KF, Lovejoy CO (1989): The utility of the auricular surface aging technique (abstract). Am J Phys Anthropol 78:190–191.

Beeley JG, Lunt DA (1980): The nature of the biochemical changes in softened dentine from archaeological sites. J Arch Sci 7:371–377.

Bender SJ (1979): Paleodemographic analysis of a Late Woodland site in southwestern Michigan. Mid-Cont J Archaeol 4:183–208.

Bennett KA (1973): "The Indians of Point of Pines, Arizona." Anthropological Papers of the University of Arizona, No. 2.

Bennike P (1990): A simplified preparation of undecalcified bone for osteoanalyses (abstract). Populations of the Nordic Countries: Human Population Biology From the Present to the Mesolithic. Second Seminar of Nordic Physical Anthropology, Institute of Archaeology, University of Lund.

Bergot C, Bocquet JP (1976): Étude systématique de l'os spongieux et de l'os cortical du femur et de l'humerus en fonction de l'âge. Bull Mém Soc d'Anthropol (Paris): (Série XIII) 3:215–242.

Biraben JN (1969): Durée de la vie dans la population de Columnata (épipaléolithique oranais). Population 3:487–500.

Black JK III (1979): "The Biological and Social Analyses of a Mississippian Cemetery From Southeast Missouri." Anthropol Pap Mus Anthropol Univ Mich, No. 68.

Blakely RL (1971): Comparison of the mortality profiles of Archaic, Middle Woodland and Middle Mississippian populations. Am J Phys Anthropol 34:45–53.

Bocquet J-P (1977): Paléodémographie: Ce que nous apprend de la Nubie soudanaise. Annales: Économies, Sociétés, Civilisations 32:54–96.

Bocquet J-P (1978): Estimation methods of age at death in adult skeletons and demographic structure of the populations of the past. In Garralda MD, Grande RM (eds): "I Simposio de Antropologia Biologica de Espana." Madrid: Facultad de Biología Cuidad Universita, pp 37–47.

Bocquet J-P, Masset C (1977): Estimateurs en paléodémographie. L'Homme 7:65–70.

Bocquet J-P, Maia Neto MA, Tavares da Rocha MA, Xavier de Morais MH (1978): Estimation de l'âge au décès des squellettes d'adultes par régressions multiples. Contribuçónes para o Estudo da Antropologia Portuguesa 10(3): 107–133.

Bocquet-Appel J-P (1986): Once upon a time: Palaeodemography. In Herrmann B (ed): "Innovative Trends in der prähistorischen Anthropologie." Mitt Berl Ges Anthropol Ethnol Rugesch 7:127–133.

Bocquet-Appel J-P, Masset C (1982): Farewell to palaeodemography. J Hum Evol 11:321–333.

Bocquet-Appel J-P, Masset C (1985): Palaeodemography: Resurrection or ghost. J Hum Evol 14:107–111.

Bocquet-Appel J-P, Tavares da Rocha MA, Xavier de Morais MH (1980): Peut-on estimer l'âge au décès à l'aide du remaniement osseux? Biom Hum (Paris) 15:51–56.

Boddington A, Garland AN, Janaway RC (1987): Flesh, bones, dust and society. In Boddington A, Garland AN, Janaway RC (eds): "Death, Decay and Reconstruction." Manchester: Manchester University Press, pp 3–9.

Boivin G, Baud CA (1984): Microradiographic methods for calcified tissues. In Dickson GR (eds): "Methods of Calcified Tissue Preparation." Amsterdam: Elsevier, pp 391–410.

Bouvier M, Ubelaker DH (1977): A comparison of two methods for the micrscopic determination of age at death. Am J Phys Anthropol 46:391–394.

Brooks ST (1955): Skeletal age at death: The reliability of cranial and pubic age indicators. Am J Phys Anthropol 13:567–598.

Brooks ST, Suchey JM (1990): Skeletal age determination based on the os pubis: A comparison of the Acsádi–Nemeskéri and Suchey–Brooks methods. Hum Evol 5:227–238.

Brothwell DR (1971): Palaeodemography. In Brass W (ed): "Biological Aspects of Demography." Society for the Study of Human Biology, Symposium No. 10, pp 111–130.

Brothwell D (1989): The relationship of tooth wear to aging. In İşcan MY (ed): "Age Markers in the Human Skeleton." Springfield, IL: Charles C Thomas, pp 303–316.

Buikstra JE (1976): "Hopewell in the Lower Illinois Valley: A Regional Approach to the Study of Human Biological Variability and Prehistoric Behavior." Evanston, IL: Northwestern University Archaeological Program, Scientific Papers No. 2.

Buikstra J, Kongisberg LW (1985): Paleodemography: critiques and controversies. Am Anthropol 87:316–333.

Buikstra J, Konigsberg LW, Bullington J (1986): Fertility and the development of agriculture in the prehistoric midwest. Am Antiq 51:528–546.

Burns KR, Maples WR (1976): Estimation of age from individual adult teeth. J Forensic Sci 21:343–356.

Carrier, NH (1958): A note on the estimation of mortality and other population characteristics given death by age. Popul Stud (London) 12:149–163.

Charles DK, Condon K, Cheverud JM, Buikstra JE (1986): Cementum annulation and age determination in *Homo sapiens*. I. Tooth variability and observer error. Am J Phys Anthropol 71:311–320.

Charles DK, Condon K, Cheverud JM, Buikstra JE (1989): Estimating age at death from growth layer groups in cementum. In İşcan MY (ed): "Age Markers in the Human Skeleton." Springfield, IL: Charles C Thomas, pp 277–301.

Churcher CS, Kenyon WA (1960): The Tabor Hill ossuaries: A study in Iroquios demography. Hum Biol 32:249–273.

Coale AJ, Demeny P (1966): "Regional Model Life Tables and Stable Populations." Princeton: Princeton University Press.

Condon K, Charles DK, Cheverud JM, Buikstra JE (1986): Cementum annulation and age determination in *Homo sapiens*. II. Estimates and accuracy. Am J Phys Anthropol 71:321–330.

Cook DC (1984): Adult age determination from the dentition. In Rathbun TA, Buikstra JE (eds): "Case Studies in Forensic Anthropology." Springfield, IL: Charles C Thomas, pp 307–328.

Cook M, Molto EL, Anderson C (1989): Fluorochrome labelling in Roman period skeletons from Dakhleh Oasis, Egypt. Am J Phys Anthropol 80:137–143.

Corruccini RS, Handler JS, Mutaw RJ, Lange FW (1982): Osteology of a slave burial population from Barbados, Indies. Am J Phys Anthropol 59:443–459.

Corruccini RS, Brandon EM, Handler JS (1989): Inferring fertility from relative mortality in historically controlled cemetery remains from Barbados. Am Antiq 54:609–614.

Costa RL (1986): Determination of age at death: Dentition analysis. In Zimmerman MR, Angel JL (eds): "Dating and Age Determination of Biological Materials." London: Croom Helm, pp 248–269.

Drusini A (1987): Refinements of two methods for the histomorphometric determination of age in human bone. Z Morphol Anthropol 77:167–176.

Engelbrecht W (1987): Factors maintaining low population density among the prehistoric New York Iroquois. Am Antiq 52:13–27.

Ericksen MF (1980): Patterns of microscopic bone remodeling in three aboriginal American populations. In Browman DL (ed): "Early Native Americans: Prehistoric Demography, Economy and Technology." The Hague: Mouton, pp 239–270.

Fraysse C, Kerebel B (1982): Aspects histologiques du vieillissement cementaire chez le chien. Bulletin du groupement international pour la recherche scientifique en stomatologie et odontologie 25:13–34.

Furseth R, Mjör IA (1973): Cementum. In Mjör IA, Pindborg JJ (eds): "Histology of the Human Tooth." Copenhagen: Munksgaard, pp 97–119.

Gage TB (1990): Variation and classification of human age patterns of mortality: Analysis using competing hazards models. Hum Biol 62:589–617.

Garland AN (1987): A histological study of archaeological bone decomposition. In Boddington A, Garland AN, Janaway RC (eds): "Death, Decay and Reconstruction." Manchester: Manchester University Press, pp 109–126.

Garland AN (1989): Microscopical analysis of fossil bone. Appl Geochem 4:215–229.

Garland AN, Freemont AJ, Stoddart RW, Jayson MIV (1987): Post-mortem histological changes and their implications for the study of exhumed human remains (abstract). Acta Anat 10:36.

Garland AN, Janaway RC, Roberts CA (1988): A study of the decay processes of human skeletal remains from the parish Church of Holy Trinity, Rothwell, Northamptonshire. Oxford J Archaeol 7:235–252.

Gilbert BM (1973): Misapplication to females of the standard for aging the male os pubis. Am J Phys Anthropol 38:39–40.

Gilbert BM, McKern TW (1973): A method for aging the female os pubis. Am J Phys Anthropol 38:31–38.

Gordon CC, Buikstra JE (1981): Soil pH, bone preservation, and sampling bias at mortuary sites. Am Antiq 46:566–571.

Graves WW (1922): Observations on age changes in the scapula. Am J Phys Anthropol 5:21–33.

Greene DL, Van Gerven DP, Armelagos GJ (1986): Life and death in ancient populations: Bones of contention in paleodemography. Hum Evol 1:193–207.

Gustafson G (1950): Age determinations of teeth. J Am Dent Assoc 41:45–54.

Hackett CJ (1981): Microscopical focal destruction (tunnels): In exhumed human bones. Med Sci Law 21:243–265.

Hanihara H, Suzuki T (1978): Estimation of age from the pubic symphysis by means of multiple regression analysis. Am J Phys Anthropol 48:233–239.

Hanson DB, Buikstra JE (1987): Histomorphological alteration in buried human bone from the Lower Illinois Valley: Implications for paleodietary research. J Archaeol Sci 14:549–563.

Hassan FA (1981): "Demographic Archaeology." New York: Academic Press.

Hillson S (1986): "Teeth." Cambridge: Cambridge University Press.

Hinton RJ (1982): Differences in interproximal and occlusal tooth wear among prehistoric Tennessee Indians: Implications for masticatory function. Am J Phys Anthropol 57:103–115.

Hooton EA (1920): "Indian Village Site and Cemetery near Madisonville, Ohio." Pap Peabody Mus, Archaeol Ethnol Harvard Univ 8(1).

Hooton EA (1930): "The Indians of Pecos Peublo: A Study of Their Skeletal Remains." New Haven: Yale University Press.

Horseman A, Nordin C, Simpson M, Speed R (1982): Cortical and trabecular bone status in elderly women with femoral neck fracture. Clin Orthop Related Res 166:143–151.

Howell N (1973): The feasibility of demographic studies in "anthropological" populations. In Crawford MH, Workman PL (eds): "Methods and Theories in Anthropological Genetics." Albuquerque, NM: University of New Mexico Press, pp 249–262.

Howell N (1976): Toward a uniformitarian theory of human paleodemography. In Ward RH, Weiss KM (eds): "Demographic Evolution and Human Populations." London: Academic Press, pp 25–40.

Howell N (1982): Village composition implied by a paleodemographic life table: The Libben site. Am J Phys Anthropol 59:263–269.

İşcan MY, Loth SR, Wright RK (1984): Age estimation from the rib phase analysis: White males. J Forensic Sci 29:1094–1104.

İşcan MY, Loth SR, Wright RK (1985): Age estimation from the rib by phase analysis: White females. J Forensic Sci 30:853–863.

Jackes MK (1977): "The Huron Spine." University of Toronto: PhD thesis.

Jackes MK (1983): Osteological evidence of smallpox: A possible case from seventeenth century Ontario. Am J Phys Anthropol 60:75–81.

Jackes MK (1985): Pubic symphysis age distributions. Am J Phys Anthropol 68:281–299.

Jackes MK (1986): Mortality of Ontario archaeological populations. In Pfeiffer (ed): "The Skeletal Biology of Ontario Populations." Can J Anthropol 5:33–48.

Jackes MK (1988): Demographic change at the Mesolithic–Neolithic transition: Evidence from Portugal. Riv Antropol (suppl) 66:141–158.

Jackes MK (1990): Diagenetic change in prehistoric Portuguese human bone (4000 to 8000 BP). Eighteenth annual meeting of the Canadian Associan for Physical Anthropology, Banff, Alberta.

Jackes MK (nd): The Osteology of the Grimsby Cemetery. Unpublished manuscript.

Jhamaria NL, Lal KB, Udawat M, Banerji P, Kabra SG (1983): The trabecular pattern of the calcaneum as an index of osteoporosis. J Bone Joint Surg 65-B:195–198.

Jit I, Bakshi V (1986): Time of fusion of the human mesosternum with manubrium and xiphoid process. Indian J Med Res 83:322–331.

Johanson G (1971): Age determination from human teeth: A critical evaluation with special consideration of changes after fourteen years of age. Odontol Rev 22(Suppl 21):1–126.

Johnston FE, Snow CE (1961): The reassessment of the age and sex of the Indian Knoll skeletal population: Demographic and methodological aspects. Am J Phys Anthropol 19:237–244.

Katz D, Suchey JM (1986): Age determination of the male os pubis. Am J Phys Anthropol 19:237–244.

Katz D, Suchey JM (1989): Race differences in pubic symphyseal aging patterns in the male. Am J Phys Anthropol 80:167–172.

Katzenberg MA, White R (1979): The os coxae from Ossossané ossuary: A paleodemographic analysis. Can Rev Phys Anthropol 1:10–28.

Kaur H, Jit I (1990): Age estimation from cortical index of the human clavicle in northwest Indians. Am J Phys Anthropol 83:297–305.

Kay RF, Cant JGH (1988): Age assessment using cementum annulus counts and tooth wear in a free-ranging population of Macaca mulatta. Am J Primatol 15:1–15.

Kerley ER (1965): The microscopic determination of age in human bone. Am J Phys Anthropol 23:149–163.

Kieser JA, Preston CB, Evans WG (1983): Skeletal age at death: An evaluation of the Miles method of ageing. J Archaeol Sci 10:9–12.

Kieser JA, Groeneveld HT, Preston CB (1985): Patterns of dental wear in the Lengua Indians of Paraguay. Am J Phys Anthropol 66:21–29.

Kilian J, Vlček E (1989): Age determination from teeth in the adult. In İşcan MY (ed): "Age Markers in the Human Skeleton." Springfield, IL: Charles C Thomas, pp 255–275.

Koike H, Ohtaishi N (1985): Prehistoric hunting pressure estimated by the age composition of excavated sika deer (Cervus nippon) using the annual layer of tooth cement. J Archaeol Sci 12:443–456.

Konigsberg LW, Buikstra JE, Bullington J (1989): Paleodemographic correlates of fertility. Am Antiq 54:626–636.

Koyabashi K (1967): Trend in length of life based on human skeletons from prehistoric to modern times in Japan. J Fac Sci Univ Tokyo: Sect V, 3(Pt2):107–162.

Lazenby RA (1984): Inherent deficiencies in cortical bone microstructural age estimation techniques. Ossa 9/11: 95–103.

LeGeros RZ, Trautz OR, LeGeros JP, Klein E, Shirra WP (1967): Apatite crystallites: Effects of carbonate on morphology. Science 155:1409–1411.

Lengyel I (1968): Biochemical aspects of early skeletons. In Brothwell D (ed): "The Skeletal Biology of Earlier Human Populations." Oxford: Pergamon Press, pp 271–288.

Lengyel I (1978): Laboratory examination of the Vlasac human bone finds. Vlasac Mesolitiko Naselje na Djerdapu Tom II. Serbian Academy of Sciences and Arts, Monographs Vol. 512, Department of Historical Sciences, 5: 261–283.

Lengyel I, Nemeskéri J (1965): Investigation of the chemical composition of aged human bones belonging to recent and subfossil periods. In "International Conference on Gerontology, Separatum." Budapest: Akadémiai Kiadó, pp 141–146.

Lovejoy CO (1985): Dental wear in the Libben population: Its functional pattern and role in the determination of adult skeletal age at death. Am J Phys Anthropol 68:47–56.

Lovejoy CO, Meindl RS, Pryzbeck TR, Barton TS, Hemple KG, Kotting D (1977): Paleodemography of the Libben Site, Ottawa County, Ohio. Science 198:291–293.

Lovejoy CO, Meindl RS, Mensforth RP, Barton TJ (1985a): Multifactorial determination of skeletal age of death: A method and blind tests of its accuracy. Am J Phys Anthropol 68:1–14.

Lovejoy CO, Meindl RS, Pryzbeck TR, Mensforth RP (1985b): Chronological metamorphosis of the auricular surface of the ilium: A new method for the determination of adult skeletal age at death. Am J Phys Anthropol 68: 15–28.

Lubell D, Jackes MK (1988): Portuguese Mesolithic–Neolithic subsistence and settlement. Riv Antropol 66 (Suppl):231–248.

Lubell D, Jackes MK, Meiklejohn C (1989): Archaeology and human biology of the Mesolithic–Neolithic transition in southern Portugal. In Bonsall C (ed): "The Mesolithic in Europe: Papers Presented at the Third International Symposium, Edinburgh 1985." Edinburgh: John Donald, pp 632–640.

Macchiarelli R (1988): Age-related rates and patterns of cortical bone involution in past human populations: A protohistorical Italian example. Riv Antropol 66(Suppl): 55–76.

Maples WR (1978): An improved technique using dental histology for estimation of adult age. J Forensic Sci 23: 764–770.

Martin RB, Burr DB (1989): "Structure, Function, and Adaptation of Compact Bone." New York: Raven Press.

Martin DL, Armelagos GJ, Mielke JH, Meindl RS (1981): Bone loss and dietary stress in an adult skeletal population from Sudanese Nubia. Bull Mém Soc Anthropol Paris (Ser 13) 8:307–319.

Masset C (1971): Erreurs systématiques dans la détermination de l'âge par les sutures crâniennes. Bull Mém Soc Anthropol Paris (Ser 12) 7:85–105.

Masset C (1973): Influence du sexe et de l'âge sur la conservation des os humains. In Sauter M (ed): "L'Homme, Hier et Aujourd'hui: Recueil d'études en Hommage à André Leroi-Gourhan." Paris: Cujas, pp 333–343.

Masset C (1976a): Sur quelques fâcheuses méthodes de détermination de l'âge des squelettes. Bull Mém Soc Anthropol Paris (Sér 13) 3:329–336.

Masset C (1976b): Sur des anomalies d'ordre démographique observées dans quelques sepultures néolithiques. In "IXe Congrès, Union Internationale des Sciences Préhistoriques et Protohistoriques, Nice." Prétirage, Thémes specialisés, pp 78–105.

Masset C (1976c): Sur la mortalité chez les anciens Indiens de l'Illinois. Curr Anthropol 17:128–131.

Masset C (1989): Age estimation on the basis of cranial sutures. In İşcan MY (ed): "Age Markers in the Human Skeleton." Springfield, IL: Charles C Thomas, pp 71–105.

Masset C, Parzysz B (1985): Démographie des cimetières? Incertitude statistique des estimateurs en paléodémographie. L'Homme 94, XXV, pp 147–154.

McKee JK, Molnar S (1988): Measurements of tooth wear among Australian Aborigines: II. Intrapopulational variation in patterns of dental attrition. Am J Phys Anthropol 76:125–136.

McKern TW, Stewart TD (1957): Skeletal age changes in young American males. Quartermaster Research and Development Command Technical Report EP-45.

Meindl TW, Lovejoy CO (1985): Ectocranial suture closure: A revised method for the determination of skeletal age at death based on the lateral-anterior sutures. Am J Phys Anthropol 68:57–66.

Meindl RS, Lovejoy CO (1989): Age changes in the pelvis: Implications for paleodemography. In İşcan MY (ed): "Age Markers in the Human Skeleton." Springfield, IL: Charles C Thomas, pp 137–168.

Meindl RS, Lovejoy CO, Mensforth RP (1980): Multifactorial determination of skeletal age at death: A double blind test on a population of known age (abstract). Am J Phys Anthropol 52:255.

Meindl RS, Lovejoy CO, Mensforth RP (1983): Skeletal age at death: Accuracy of determination and implications for human demography. Hum Biol 55:73–87.

Meindl RS, Lovejoy CO, Mensforth RP, Walker RA (1985): A revised method of age determination using the os pubis, with a review and tests of accuracy of other current methods of pubic symphyseal aging. Am J Phys Anthropol 68:29–45.

Meindl RS, Russell KF, Lovejoy CO (1990): Reliability of age at death in the Hamann–Todd collection: Validity of subselection procedures used in blind tests of the summary age technique. Am J Phys Anthropol 83:349–357.

Mellors RC, Carroll KG, Solberg T (1966): Quantitative analysis of CA/P molar ratios in bone tissue with the electron probe. In "The Electron Microprobe." New York: Wiley, pp 834–840.

Mensforth RP, Latimer BM (1989): Hamann–Todd Collection aging studies: Osteoporosis fracture syndrome. Am J Phys Anthropol 80:461–479.

Miles AEW (1963): The dentition in the assessment of individual age in skeletal material. In Brothwell DR (ed): "Dental Anthropology." New York: Pergamon, pp 191–209.

Miles AEW (1978): Teeth as an indicator of age in man. In Butler PM, Joysey KA (eds): "Development, Function, and Evolution of Teeth." London: Academic Press, pp 455–462.

Miller CS, Dove SB, Cottone JA (1988): Failure of use of cemental annulations in teeth to determine the age of humans. J Forensic Sci 33:137–143.

Molleson TI, Cohen P (1990): The progression of dental attrition stages used for age assessment. J Archaeol Sci 17:363–371.

Molnar S, McKee JK, Molnar IM, Przybeck TR (1983a): Tooth wear rates among contemporary Australian Aborigines. J Dent Res 62:562–565.

Molnar S, McKee JK, Molnar I (1983b): Measurements of tooth wear among Australian Aborigines: 1. Serial loss of the enamel crown. Am J Phys Anthropol 61:51–65.

Moore JA, Swedlund AC, Armelagos GJ (1975): The use of life tables in paleodemography. In Swedlund AC (ed): "Population Studies in Archaeology and Biological Anthropology: A Symposium." Society of American Archeology: Memoir No. 30, pp 57–70.

Moorrees CFA, Fanning EA, Hunt EE (1963): Age variation of formation stages for ten permanent teeth. J Dent Res 42:1490–1502.

Morgan DB (1973): The metacarpal bone. Clin Radiol 24:77–82.

Mullen G, Gruspier K (1991): Maxillary suture obliteration: A test of the Mann method. J Forensic Sci 36:512–519.

Narasaki S (1990): Estimation of age at death by femoral osteon remodeling: Application of Thompson's core technique to modern Japanese. J Anthropol Soc Nippon 98:29–38.

Naylor JW, Miller WG, Stokes GN, Stott GG (1985): Cemental annulation enhancement: A technique for age determination in man. Am J Phys Anthropol 68:197–200.

Nelson BK, DeNiro MJ, Schoeninger MJ, Paolo DJ, Hare PE (1986): Effects of diagenesis on strontium, carbon, nitrogen and oxygen concentration and isotopic composition of bone. Geochim Cosmochim Acta 50:1941–1949.

Nemeskéri J (1978): Demographic structure of the Vlasac epipaleolithic population. Vlasac Mesolitiko Naselje na Djerdapu Tom II. Serbian Academy of Sciences and Arts, Monographs Vol. 512, Department of Historical Sciences, 5:97–133.

Nemeskéri J, Harsányi L, Acsádi G (1960): Methoden zur diagnose des Iebensalters von skelettfunden. Anthropol Anz 24:70–95.

Nordin BEC, MacGregor J, Smith DA (1966): The incidence of osteoporosis in normal women, its relation to age and the menopause. Q J Med 35(137):25–38.

Ortner DJ, Von Endt DW (1971): Microscopic and electron microprobe characterization of the sclerotic lamellae in human osteons. Israel J Med Sci 7:480–482.

Owsley DW, Bass WM (1979): A demographic analysis of skeletons from the Larson Site, Walworth County, South Dakota. Am J Phys Anthropol 51:145–154.

Paine RR (1989): Model life table fitting by maximum likelihood estimation: A procedure to reconstruct paleodemographic characteristics from skeletal age distributions. Am J Phys Anthropol 79:51–61.

Palmer E (1987): Micromorphology of prehistoric human bone from the Mesolithic site of Moita do Sebastião, Portugal. Unpublished MA thesis, Department of Anthropology, University of Alberta.

Pate FD, Hutton JT (1988): The use of soil chemistry data to address postmortem diagenesis in bone mineral. J Archaeol Sci 15:729–739.

Petersen W (1975): A demographer's view of prehistoric demography. Curr Anthropol 16:227–246.

Pfeiffer S (1980): Bone remodeling age estimates compared with estimates by other techniques. Curr Anthropol 21:793–794.

Pfeiffer S (1984): Palaeopathology in an Iroquoian ossuary, with special reference to tuberculosis. Am J Phys Anthropol 64:181–189.

Pfeiffer S (1985): Comparison of adult age estimation techniques using an ossuary sample. Can J Anthropol 4:13–17.

Pfeiffer S (1986): Morbidity and mortality in the Uxbridge ossuary. Can J Anthropol 5:23–31.

Pfeiffer S (1989): Characterization of archaeological bone decomposition in a sample of known length of interment (abstract). Am J Phys Anthropol 78:283.

Pfeiffer S (1991): An Exploration of Possible Relationships Between Bone Structure and Chemical Composition. First International Congress of Mummy Studies, Tenerife.

Philippas GG, Applebaum E (1967): Age changes in the permanent upper lateral incisor. J Dent Res 46:1002–1009.

Philippas GG, Applebaum E (1968): Age change in the permanent upper canine teeth. J Dent Res 47:411–417.

Piepenbrink H (1986): Two examples of biogenous dead bone decomposition and their consequences for taphonomic interpretation. J Archaeol Sci 13:417–430.

Piontek J, Weber A (1986): Controversy on paleodemography. Int J Anthropol 5:71–83.

Protsch RRR (1986): Radiocarbon dating of bone. In Zimmerman MR, Angel JL (eds): "Dating and Age Determination of Biological Materials." London: Croom Helm, pp 3–38.

Richman EA, Ortner DJ, Schulter-Ellis FP (1979): Differences in intracortical bone remodeling in three aboriginal American populations: Possible dietary factors. Calc Tissue Int 28:209–214.

Rogers T (1990): A test of the auricular surface method of estimating age-at-death and a discussion of its usefulness in the construction of paleodemographic lifetables. Eighteenth annual meeting of the Canadian Association of Physical Anthropology, Banff, Alberta.

Salomon CD, Haas N (1967): Histological and histochemical observations on undecalcified sections of ancient bones from excavations in Israel. Israel J Med Sci 3:747–754.

Samson C, Branigan K (1987): A new method for estimating age at death from fragmentary and weathered bone. In Boddington A, Garland AN, Janaway RC (eds): "Death, Decay and Reconstruction." Manchester: Manchester University Press, pp 101–108.

Sattenspiel L, Harpending H (1983): Stable populations and skeletal age. Am Antiq 48:489–498.

Saunders SR, Spence MW (1986): Dental and skeletal age determinations of Ontario Iroquois infant burials. Ontario Archaeol 46:45–54.

Schoeninger MJ, Moore KM, Murray ML, Kingston JD (1989): Detection of bone preservation in archaeological and fossil samples. Appl Geochem 4:281–292.

Sillen A (1989): Diagnosis of the inorganic phase of cortical bone. In Price TD (ed): "The Chemistry of Prehistoric Human Bone." Cambridge: Cambridge University Press, pp 211–229.

Singh IJ (1972): Femoral trabecular pattern of the upper end of the femur as an index of osteoporosis. J Bone Joint Surg 52-A:457–467.

Sjøvold T (1978): Inference concerning the age distribution of skeletal populations and some consequences for paleodemography. Budapest: Anthropol Kozlemenyek 22:99–114.

Smith BH (1984): Patterns of molar wear in hunter–gatherers and agriculturalists. Am J Phys Anthropol 63:39–56.

Smith P, Bloom RA, Berkowitz J (1984): Diachronic trends in humeral cortical thickness of Near Eastern populations. J Hum Evol 13:603–612.

Sognnaes RF (1955): Postmortem microscopic defects in the teeth of ancient man. Am Med Assoc Archaeol Pathol 59:559–570.

Sorg MH, Andrews RP, İşcan MY (1989): Radiographic aging of the adult. In İşcan MY (ed): "Age Markers in the Human Skeleton." Springfield, IL: Charles C Thomas, pp 169–193.

Stewart (1957): Distortion of the pubic symphyseal surface in females and its effect on age determination. Am J Phys Anthropol 15:9–18.

Stewart TD (1958): The rate of development of vertebral osteoarthritis in American whites and its significance in skeletal age identification. The Leech (Johannesburg) 28:114–151.

Storey R (1985): An estimate of mortality in a Pre-Columbian urban population. Am Anthropol 87:519–535.

Stout SD (1978): Histological structure and its preservation in ancient bone. Curr Anthropol 19:601–604.

Stout SD (1983): The application of histomorphometric analysis to ancient skeletal remains. Anthropos (Greece) 10:60–71.

Stout SD (1989a): Histomorphometric analysis of human skeletal remains. In İşcan MY, Kennedy KAR (eds): "Reconstruction of Life From the Skeleton." New York: Alan R. Liss, pp 41–52.

Stout SD (1989b): The use of cortical bone histology to estimate age at death. In İşcan MY (ed): "Age Markers in the Human Skeleton." Springfield, IL: Charles C Thomas, pp 195–207.

Stout SD, Gehlert SJ (1980): The relative accuracy and reliability of histological aging methods. Forensic Sci Int 15:181–190.

Stout SD, Simmons D (1979): Use of histology in ancient bone research. Yearb Phys Anthropol 22:228–249.

Stout SD, Teitlebaum SL (1976): Histological analysis of undecalcified thin sections of archaeological bone. Am J Phys Anthropol 44:263–270.

Suchey JM (1979): Problems in the aging of females using the os pubis. Am J Phys Anthropol 44:263–270.

Susini A, Baud CA (1988): Altérations osseuses dues à l'action de la chaux. Journées Anthropol 24:69–75.

Susini A, Baud CA, Lacotte D (1987): Bone apatite crystals alterations in Neolithic skeletons and their relations to burial practices and soil weathering. Riv Antropol 66(Suppl):35–38.

Swedlund AC (1975): Population studies in archaeology and biological anthropology: A symposium. Soc Am Arch Mem 30 (issued as Am Antiq 40(2), Pt. 2).

Swedlund AC, Armelagos GJ (1969): Une recherche en paléo-demographie: La Nubie soudanaise. Annales: Economies, Sociétés, Civilisations 24:1287–1298.

Swedlund AC, Armelagos GJ (1976): "Demographic Anthropology." Dubuque, IA: Brown.

Tal H (1984): The prevalence and distribution of periodontal bone loss in dry mandibles of Bantu-speaking South African Blacks. Ossa 9/11:181–188.

Thompson DD (1979): The core technique in the determination of age at death in skeletons. J Forensic Sci 24:902–915.

Thompson DD (1981): Microscopic determination of age at death in an autopsy series. J Forensic Sci 26:470–475.

Thompson DD, Gunness-Hey M (1981): Bone mineral–osteon analysis of Yupik–Inupiag skeletons. Am J Phys Anthropol 55:1–8.

Thompson DD, Laughlin SB, Laughlin WS, Merbs C (1984): Bone core analysis and vertebral pathologies Sadlermiut Eskimo skeletons. Ossa 9/11:189–193.

Thwaites RG (ed) (1898): "The Jesuit Relations and Allied Documents." Cleveland: Burrows.

Todd TW (1920): Age changes in the pubic bone, I: The male white pubis. Am J Phys Anthropol 3:285–334.

Todd TW (1921): Age changes in the pubic bone. II–IV. Am J Phys Anthropol 4:1–70.

Tomenchuk J, Mayhall JT (1979): A correlation of tooth wear and age among modern Igloolik Eskimos. Am J Phys Anthropol 51:67–77.

Trodden BJ (1982): A Radiographic Study of the Calcification and Eruption of the Permanent Teeth in Inuit and Indian Children. Archaeological Survey of Canada, Paper 112, Mercury Series. Ottawa: National Museums of Canada.

Turpeinen O (1979): Fertility and mortality in Finland since 1750. Popul Stud 33:101–114.

Ubelaker DH (1974): Reconstruction of demographic profiles from ossuary skeletal samples. A case study from the Tidewater Potomac. Smithsonian Contributions to Anthropology 18.

Ubelaker DH (1986): Estimation of age at death from histology of human bone. In Zimmerman, Angel JL (eds): "Dating and Age Determination of Biological Materials." London: Croom Helm, pp 240–247.

Ullrich H (1975): Estimation of fertility by means of pregnancy and childbirth alterations at the pubis, the ilium, and the sacrum. Int J Skel Res 2:23–39.

United Nations (1982): "Model Life Tables for Developing Countries." New York: United Nations.

Uytterschaut HT (1985): Determination of skeletal age by histological methods. Z Morphol Anthropol 75:331–340.

Van Gerven DP, Armelagos GJ (1983): "Farewell to paleodemography?" Rumours of its death have been exaggerated. J Hum Evol 12:353–360.

Vlček E, Mrklas L (1975): Modifications of the Gustafson method of determination of age according to teeth on prehistorical and historical osteological material. Scripta Med 48:203–208.

Waldron T (1987): The relative survival of the human skeleton: Implications for palaeopathology. In Boddington A, Garland AN, Janaway RC (eds): "Death, Decay and Reconstruction." Manchester: Manchester University Press, pp 55–64.

Walker RA, Lovejoy CD (1985): Radiographic changes in the clavicle and proximal femur and their use in the determination of skeletal age at death. Am J Phys Anthropol 68:67–78.

Walker PL, Johnson JR, Lambert PM (1988): Age and sex biases in the preservation of human skeletal remains. Am J Phys Anthropol 76:183–188.

Weiss KM (1973): Demographic models for anthropology. Mem Soc Am Archaeol No. 27.

Weiss KM (1976): Demographic theory and anthropological inference. Annu Rev Anthropol 5:351–381.

Werelds R-J (1961): Observations macroscopique et microscopique sur certaines altérations postmortem des dents. Bull Group Int Rech Sci Stomatol 4:7–60.

Werelds R-J (1962): Nouvelles observations sur les dégradations postmortem de la dentine et du cément des dents inhumées. Bull Group Int Rech Sci Stomatol 5:554–591.

Werelds R-J (1967): Du moment ou apparaissent dans les dents humaines les altérations postmortem en forme d'évidements canaliculaires: Présence de lesions dentaires identiques *in vivo* chez les poissons. Bull Group Int Rech Sci Stomatol 10:419–477.

Whittaker DK, Ryan S, Weeks K, Murphy WM (1987): Patterns of approximal wear in cheek teeth of a Romano-British population. Am J Phys Anthropol 73:389–396.

Skeletal Biology of Past Peoples: Research Methods
pages 225–257 © 1992 Wiley-Liss, Inc.

Chapter 12

Advances in the Quantitative Analysis of Skeletal Morphology

G.N. van Vark and W. Schaafsma

*Anatomy and Embryology Laboratory, University of Groningen, 9713 EZ Groningen, The Netherlands
(G.N.v.V) Department of Mathematical Statistics, University of Groningen, 9700 AV Groningen,
The Netherlands (W.S.)*

1. INTRODUCTION

When comparing samples from different populations or classifying specimens on the basis of their skeletal morphology, one can either rely on visual comparison or follow a mathematical approach that involves the use of numerical characterization and subsequent computation (see also Ruff, this volume, Chapter 3). In both instances one will consider various characteristics of the skeletal parts under study. The multivariate statistical aspect of the situation is not generally realized if one uses analyses based on visual comparison of morphology. Also, in the latter case, researchers use information that is present in a number of metric and/or nonmetric forms though they are less restricted in the choice of variables, and by their precise numerical values. Therefore, it may be said that both approaches involve multivariate statistical considerations though not only the data but also their analyses are very different. The student who uses visual diagnosis attaches, as in the mathematical approach, a certain weight to the variables. However, this is done on the basis of professional training and intuition rather than on the basis of a quantitative analysis. By means of a mathematical approach, the intercorrelations between the variables can be taken into account in a much more explicit way. This has several advantages. For example, in classification of specimens, the mathematical approach will in principle (if sample sizes are suffi-ciently large) lead to a smaller probability of misclassification. Besides, it allows the construction of (interval) estimates for the posterior probability that a particular specimen belongs to a certain group. An additional advantage is that it may reveal biological structures that cannot easily be revealed otherwise. On the other hand, the visual approach may use morphological details that might not be expressed in a set of quantitative variables. The following discussion shows why the results of visual and mathematical approaches may be different and, at the same time, show how both approaches have their own specific value. It is still too early to evaluate their relative usefulness because anthropologists, as far as they use the mathematical multivariate statistical approaches at all, tend to rely on standard statistical packages. As a consequence, the advantages that specifically designed approaches might offer are insufficiently recognized.

In this chapter discriminant analysis techniques will be emphasized, together with accessory classification procedures. These techniques are by far the most important ones for the skeletal research of past peoples. By restricting the scope of the chapter in this way, two purposes are served: first, to provide a survey of recently developed methodology that is applicable to some of the most essential problem areas, along with directions on how to use this methodology; and, second, to provide insight into the advantages, the limitations, and possible future developments in the use of the techniques described here.

The chapter begins with a brief description of some essential ingredients. Next modifications of standard techniques are discussed as well as some supplementary procedures for making existing techniques more useful for anthropological practice. In the process, the limitations of the multivariate methodology will also become clear. A few remarks are made about misinterpretations found in the current literature. The chapter concludes with a discussion of the measures that should be taken for making the mathematical multivariate methodology more generally accessible.

2. MATHEMATICAL MULTIVARIATE ANALYSIS; THE CONCEPT OF POPULATION AND SAMPLE

Mathematical multivariate statistical analysis deals with problems that involve the employment of scores on a set of p metrical and/or nonmetrical variables, $X_1,...,X_p$ ($p \geq 2$), that are taken from specimens from one or more populations. An important common characteristic is that the variables are dependent, and that the techniques to be used take these dependencies into account. This would, strictly speaking, exclude Penrose's distance statistic as well as a number of other distances which are used in the study of nonmetrical variables. In actual practice, however, it is not necessarily true that such simple techniques are outperformed by the more complicated ones. Much will depend on the magnitude of the correlations between the variables, and on the sizes of the available samples.

Any introduction to multivariate statistical methods should start from considerations about population and sample (Blackith and Reyment, 1971). The concept of population is used in both biology and statistics. Current biological definitions do not necessarily correspond with the statistical one. In the present chapter the concept of population is used in the statistical sense to characterize individuals living in a certain area at a certain time. As the area and time may vary widely, a population may contain individuals of varying taxonomic origins. A population may consist, for example, of all the individuals who died in the first half

of a certain century in a certain town, or it may comprise all Neanderthal individuals. In the latter case a whole subspecies, or possibly even a whole species, is looked upon as a population. Often one will have only a vague idea of the range of area and time in which the population lived. This certainly is true in the case of prehistoric populations. In sex diagnosis, the male and female subpopulations are regarded as populations in the statistical sense.

A sample is defined as a subgroup of a population. We shall treat the samples as if the individuals involved are chosen independently and at random. In practice, these assumptions are violated in a number of instances. Without making such assumptions, however, statistical investigations like the ones described below are not feasible.

3. DISCRIMINANT ANALYSIS

3.1. Basic Concepts; Two Populations

The most important multivariate statistical method for skeletal studies is discriminant analysis. This analysis was first applied in a study by Barnard (1935), and then formally described by Fisher (1936). Various topics are involved, the major ones being (1) expressing morphological distance, (2) expressing the constellation of groups in a lower-dimensional space via cluster analysis or multiple discriminant functions, and (3) classifying individuals. Fisher demonstrated that a linear compound $Y = \lambda_1 X_1 + \lambda_2 X_2 + ... + \lambda_p X_p$ can be constructed from p measurements $X_1, X_2,...,X_p$, such that the populations A and B are optimally separated and that the discriminatory value $(\eta_A - \eta_B)/\sigma$ is greater than that of any other linear combination of the variables $X_1, X_2,...,X_p$. Here the following notations are used: η_A expected value (population mean) of Y for population A, η_B expected value of Y for population B, and σ^2 variance of Y for each of the two populations.

The optimum value corresponds with the Mahalanobis distance $\Delta = \{(\mu_A - \mu_B)^T \Sigma^{-1}(\mu_A - \mu_B)\}^{1/2}$, where μ_A = mean vector of scores on $X_1, X_2,...,X_p$ in population A, μ_B = mean vector of scores on $X_1, X_2,...,X_p$ in population B, and Σ = the common covariance matrix.

The concept of maximum separation holds for normally distributed variables. For binary, ordinal, and qualitative variables, and for com-

TABLE 1. Comparison of Design Sample Discriminatory Values D Calculated From Nontransformed (Col. A) and Transformed (Cols. B, C, and D) Scores[a,b]

		Discriminatory values (D)			
Numbers of selected measures	n_{δ}, n_{φ}	A: Non transformed scores	B: Scores used are the logaritms of scores used in A	C: Scores used are the square roots of scores used in A	D: Scores used are the square roots of scores used in B
2 4 5	23,18	3.65	3.72	3.72	3.76
2 3 5	23,21	3.10	3.20	3.19	3.23
1 4 5	25,18	2.92	2.93	2.93	2.94
1 3 5	24,22	2.59	2.73	2.69	2.75
2 3 4	19,16	3.60	3.62	3.65	3.65
1 3 4	18,17	3.30	3.33	3.31	3.31

[a]Scores were taken by Gejvall (1947) from a modern cremated skeletal series from Stockholm of known sex. Measurements were the following: (1) Humerus, vertical diameter of the head (M10). (2) Humerus, transversal diameter of the head (M9). (3) Humerus, thickness of the cortex in the middle of the diaphysis. (4) Radius, thickness of the cortex in the middle of the diaphysis opposite the interosseous line. (5) Femur, thickness of the cortex in the middle of the diaphysis opposite the linea aspera. [b]Reproduced from Van Vark (1970), with permission of the publisher.

binations of these, the theory is also applicable, although in these cases the assumption of a common covariance matrix Σ is questionable. If all variables are assumed to be normally distributed and the covariance matrices from which the function is calculated are assumed to be equal, then Fisher's linear discriminant function provides the best discrimination among all possible discriminant functions, not only the linear ones. This linear combination is obtained by calculating the weights λ_j from

$$\lambda_j = \sigma^{1j}\delta_1 + \sigma^{2j}\delta_2 + \ldots + \sigma^{pj}\delta_p \ (j = 1, \ldots, p) \tag{3.1}$$

or, in matrix notation, $\lambda = \Sigma^{-1}\delta$, where σ^{jb} is the (j,b) element of the inverse Σ^{-1} of the covariance matrix Σ, and $\delta_j = \mu_{A,j} - \mu_{B,j}$ is the difference between the expected values of variable X_j in the two populations.

If it is assumed that the measurements are distributed normally, then a classification procedure can be based simply on Y such that the maximum probability of misclassification is minimized. In the course of skeletal investigation one will usually work with measurements whose distributions deviate from normality to a greater or lesser extent. As long as these deviations are not "large," there will be no serious objections to applying the intended classi-

fication procedure. For practical application it will suffice to assume that the distributions of the y values calculated from the measurements do not deviate significantly from normality at the 5% level, if the samples are "large." This may very well be the case if the variables themselves are far from being normally distributed. The general rule is that the more variables entered in the function, the more the distribution of discriminant function scores will tend to normality. A test in which the distributions of Y in both populations are simultaneously tested for normality is given in Van Vark (1971).

Square root and logarithmic transformation of the scores or a combination of these transformations may approximate normality and equality of the variances and covariances more closely. The effect of these transformations is that the discriminatory value is usually only slightly increased (Andrews et al., 1971). Examples are given in Table 1.

3.2. More Than Two Populations

In the event that $k > 2$ populations are compared, or a specimen has to be assigned to one out of k ($k > 2$) populations, more than one discriminant function can be calculated. In general, if k populations are compared, $k - 1$ mutually uncorrelated linear discriminant functions can be constructed—or p functions, when this number is less. In the literature these functions are often referred to as canonical variates. In fact, canonical variates are a special case of multiple discriminant functions. The property of uncorrelatedness of the functions is often used to construct an orthogonal coordinate system, each axis representing a discriminant function. By considering two or three functions at a time, it is possible to visualize distance relationships between samples and to study possible deviations from the underlying idea that distributions are normal with equal covariance matrices. In theory, the isodensity contours are circles or spheres. In practice, isodensity contours—ellipses in the case of two dimensions, ellipsoids in the case of three—may be computed from the discriminant function scores of the various samples. This may give a visual impression of the actual dispersion of the samples under consideration (cf. Fig. 3 on page 231).

4. SAMPLING EFFECTS; VARIABLE SELECTION

4.1. Discriminatory Values in Design Samples, Populations, and Test Samples

In actual practice, one always works with samples so that only estimates of the population parameters are available. Sampling effects may play a very important role, particularly if the sample sizes are small relative to the number of variables. Neglect of these effects may easily lead to a loss of diagnostic power, biased results, and misinterpretations.

This is demonstrated by discussing procedures for selecting variables in a discriminant analysis. Contrary to first impressions, the inclusion of as many variables as possible does not always lead to the best performance. The nature of this phenomenon is illustrated in Figure 1. The curves presented refer to three different concepts of discriminatory value in a series of discriminant functions, calculated from two samples that develop when variables are added one by one to the preceding selection.

The solid line represents the curve of true, that is, population discriminatory values (Mahalanobis distances), Δ. This is a well-defined concept, but for a given set of variables its value is an unknown parameter. The curve presented is nothing more than a suggestive guess. In practice, estimates are needed.

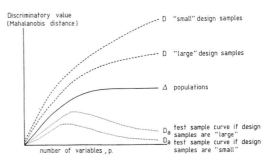

Fig. 1. Theoretical comparison of discriminatory values. Δ: Theoretically calculated Δ curve from two populations. D: Curves calculated from design samples taken from these populations. D_a: Curves calculated from test samples taken from these populations (actual discriminatory values).

Note the difference between the two design sample curves, which implies that if no appropriate corrections are applied, the bias of the usual Mahalanobis distance estimates is positive and tends to increase as the sample sizes are decreased and/or the number of variables is increased.

Further note the difference between the two test sample curves, which implies that if design sample sizes are increased, more variables may be used effectively and, consequently, more actual discriminatory capacity becomes available.

The upper, broken lines denote the curves of the usual estimates D for Δ, calculated from two samples that in the literature are often called the *design* or *training* samples. These are the samples of individuals from which the functions are calculated. If the sample sizes are increased, the estimation errors $D - \Delta$ (or rather their absolute values) will decrease and the (broken) line of estimates D will approach the curve of true values. The figures correctly suggest that the bias is positive and increases with the number of variables (p). This bias may be partially removed by modifying the estimate D according to $\hat{\Delta}$, where

$$\hat{\Delta}^2 = \frac{n_A + n_B - p - 3}{n_A + n_B - 2} \cdot D^2 - \frac{n_A + n_B}{n_A \cdot n_B} \cdot p \ (4.1)$$

The line of estimated "true" values Δ has actually been obtained by plotting these modified, almost unbiased estimates ($\hat{\Delta}^2$ is an unbiased estimator of Δ^2).

The lower, dotted lines are the most intriguing ones. They refer to the actual discriminatory value D_a of the sample-based discriminant function, that is, the discriminatory value which applies to individuals that are to be diagnosed—that is, to samples of individuals that belong to the same populations but have not taken part in the construction of the discriminant functions. These include so-called test samples of known origin, which can be used to estimate the actual discriminatory values of the functions used. This is why the discriminatory values concerned are sometimes denoted by D_t, and their maximum values by $D_{t\ max}$. These D_t are estimates of the actual performance D_a of the sample-based discriminant function. Estimates of D_a can also be obtained on the basis of the original design samples. This is explained in greater detail below. The dotted curves suggest that there exists an "optimum" number of variables, p^*, which depends on the sizes of the samples from which the functions are calculated: As these sizes decrease, the number of effective variables also decrease.

4.2. Three Stages in Variable Selection

Inherent in the problem of variable selection is that one will wish to order the variables somehow, for example, "according to their independent contribution to the discrimination." Obviously it is most important to incorporate as much diagnostic capacity in as few a number of variables as is practically possible, since the role of adverse sampling effects is then minimized. This implies that the procedure for selecting variables essentially contains three stages:

1. Make a first choice of variables.

2. Order these variables such that the most important ones come first.

3. Make a final selection by deciding upon the number p^* of variables to be introduced in the discriminant function(s).

4.3. Stage 1: The First Choice of Variables

There is no clearcut answer to the question of which set of variables should be chosen first in a multivariate situation. This may be illustrated by Figure 2, which shows a specific variable (X_1) that has exactly the same mean and variance in both populations but contains a considerable amount of information for discriminating between these two populations in

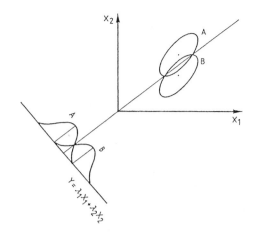

Fig. 2. Comparison of univariate and multivariate discriminatory capacities. Variable X_1, which displays the same distributions in population A and in population B (i.e., $\mu_1^A = \mu_1^B$, and $\sigma_1^A = \sigma_1^B$) and consequently has no discriminatory capacity when considered separately, nevertheless provides additional discriminatory information in a multivariate situation. The overlap of the distributions of discriminant function scores is smaller than that of the distribution of X_2 (the latter not drawn in the figure) owing to the correlation between X_1 and X_2. This additional information is not directly available in a visual diagnosis.

addition to that provided by X_2. The cause of this phenomenon lies in the correlation between the specific variable X_1 and the other variables. Similar and other complications caused by correlations are as follows:

1. Variables that have considerable discriminatory value when considered separately may hardly contribute, or not contribute at all, to the performance of a discriminant function; the additional information for the discrimination may be negligible. This, of course, depends on the variables already included.

2. Distance statistics, and misclassification probability estimates based on them or on related statistics, may give a biased impression of the actual situation if the intercorrelations between variables are neglected.

3. If an adequate concept (Mahalanobis distance) is chosen as the basis of analysis, the researcher has a certain freedom in choosing variables. Quite different sets of variables may provide approximately the same distance pattern. This becomes important when the mate-

rial under investigation is in poor condition. The choice of variables can then be adapted to the remaining possibilities for scoring.

4.4. Stage 2: The Ordering of the Variables

Various methods for ordering variables have been developed. Although they may be very useful in actual practice, none of them is completely satisfactory. The most popular procedure is to perform "stepwise discriminant analysis." This procedure is implemented in computer program packages such as BMDP or SPSS. The procedure runs as follows.

The variable selected first from a set of variables is the one having the highest discriminatory value or, in other words, the one for which the ratio of the within-group to the total variance is highest. After that, the influence of the first selected variable on the matrix of the remaining variables is eliminated; that is, a new matrix of variables is built up, comprising variables whose correlation with the variable selected first is nil. Next, a second variable is selected, which has the next highest F value, and so on. Variables are entered into the function only if their partial F values are larger than a certain value that is chosen by the investigator, the so-called F-to-enter value. The procedure also allows for discarding at a later stage variables that were chosen previously. The underlying argument is that a variable that may have appeared to be very important at an early stage may, at a later stage, become redundant because of the correlation between it and variables selected later. To that end, at each successive step, the partial F value of each variable already in the function is calculated. If for a variable the corresponding partial F value (in this context called the F-to-delete) has become lower than a certain value chosen by the investigator, the variable concerned is removed. The procedure stops when no further significant gain in discrimination can be achieved by the inclusion of more variables.

It is clear that, quite apart from the fact that any ordering is sample-specific, different orderings may result, depending on the choice of the values F-to-enter and F-to-delete. Though Rao's test for additional information (Rao, 1965) has some bearing on the problem, there are no conclusive statistical criteria for this choice, so the ordering of the variables is partly a matter of personal preference. A certain evaluation of this preference can be obtained by trying out various values for F-to-enter and F-to-delete and judging the stability of the calculated ordering (see Fig. 3).

The result of this procedure is that a certain ordering of the variables is chosen that is not necessarily optimal in any respect but may be substantially superior to that of a random ordering. Although the procedure theoretically requires that assumptions of normality of the distributions of the variables and equality of the covariance matrices be satisfied, it can also be applied successfully to the construction of discriminant functions if nonmetrical variables are involved.

A second customary ordering procedure is to use principal component function scores calculated from design samples instead of the raw scores. The rationale behind this approach is that, because of the variance-absorbing properties of principal component functions, it might be possible to use them to obtain a small number of variables that contain considerable discriminatory capacity. However, the performance of this approach tends to be less than that of approaches using the original raw scores. Examples are given in Van Vark and Van der Sman (1982).

A third obvious ordering procedure is to use the coefficients of the standardized variables in the overall discriminant function. Assuming that the confidence intervals of these coefficients do not overlap (implying that relatively large samples should be available), one could order the variables according to the decreasing value of their respective coefficients. This solution may seem attractive at first sight, but several problems are involved, such as the fact that, because of possible variable collinearity, the coefficients may be very imprecise. As an example, if intercorrelations between two variables are high, the magnitude of the statistical error in estimating the two corresponding weights may be enormous. As Huberty (1984) points out in a discussion of ordering criteria, the problem of ordering variables is troublesome.

The employment of such coefficients for interpretation becomes even more questionable if multiple discriminant functions are considered, because there are no formulas for calcu-

A

#	Series	$n\male$	$n\female$
1.	Northern Europe: Medieval Norse, Oslo	$n\male = 55$	$n\female = 55$
2.	Central Europe: Zalavar, Hungary	$n\male = 54$	$n\female = 45$
3.	Central Europe: Berg, Carinthia, Austria	$n\male = 56$	$n\female = 53$
4.	Egypt: 26th–30th Dynasties	$n\male = 58$	$n\female = 53$
5.	East Africa: Teita, Kenya	$n\male = 34$	$n\female = 49$
6.	West Africa: Dogon, Mali	$n\male = 48$	$n\female = 53$
7.	South Africa: Zulu	$n\male = 55$	$n\female = 46$
8.	South Africa: Bushman	$n\male = 41$	$n\female = 49$
9.	Australia: Lake Alexandrina tribes	$n\male = 52$	$n\female = 49$
10.	Tasmania: general	$n\male = 45$	$n\female = 42$
11.	Melanesia: Tolai, New Britain	$n\male = 55$	$n\female = 55$
12.	Polynesia: Mokapu, Oahu, Hawaii	$n\male = 51$	$n\female = 49$
13.	Siberia: Buriats	$n\male = 54$	$n\female = 55$
14.	Greenland: Inugsuk Eskimo	$n\male = 54$	$n\female = 54$
15.	South America: Yauyos, Peru	$n\male = 55$	$n\female = 55$
16.	Andaman Islands: general	$n\male = 26$	$n\female = 28$
17.	North America: Early Arikara	$n\male = 42$	$n\female = 27$
18.	Eastern Asia: Ainu, Hokkaido, Japan	$n\male = 48$	$n\female = 38$
19.	Eastern Asia: Hokkaido, N. Japan	$n\male = 55$	$n\female = 32$
20.	Eastern Asia: Kyushu, S. Japan	$n\male = 50$	$n\female = 41$
21.	Eastern Asia: Han Chinese, Hainan	$n\male = 45$	$n\female = 38$
22.	Eastern Asia: Anyang, Shang Dyn., China	$n\male = 42$	
23.	Eastern Asia: Atayal, Taiwan	$n\male = 29$	$n\female = 18$
24.	Eastern Asia: Philippines	$n\male = 50$	
25.	Marianas: Guam	$n\male = 30$	$n\female = 27$
26.	North America: Santa Cruz Island, California	$n\male = 42$	$n\female = 38$
27.	Easter Island	$n\male = 49$	$n\female = 37$

B

F-to-enter	F-to-delete
0.01	0.005
0.05	0.01
0.1	0.05
0.5	0.1
1.5	1.0

C

	Ordering found. Variables numbered according to Howells's list.									
$\male\male$	9	29	4	5	18	37	56	55	1	63
	13	44	48	58	10	70	31	66	24	68
	6	7	15	35	17	32	12	22	14	38
	8	41	53	49	2	51	36	20	21	57
	39	33	11	54	47	46	43	28	16	42
	67	30	65	34	19	23	45	26	50	52
	62	3	27	64	69	59	25	61	40	60

D

	Ordering found. Variables numbered according to Howells's list.									
$\female\female$	9	55	37	18	29	48	1	5	70	59
	63	13	44	66	6	10	31	32	68	53
	17	24	41	35	7	22	15	2	20	49
	56	12	36	42	14	38	51	8	43	30
	16	50	39	46	57	21	11	19	52	34
	27	67	33	26	54	47	65	28	58	62
	4	60	23	45	40	64	69	3	61	25

Fig. 3. Ordering of variables. Seventy cranial variables, defined in Howells (1973), were ordered according to their independent contribution to discrimination by the stepwise discriminant analysis program and various values for F-to-enter and F-to-delete. **A.** Series compared. First run: 27 $\male$ cranial series. Second run: 25 $\female$ female cranial series. All series measured by Howells, and in part described in Howells (1973). **B.** Five pairs of F-to-enter and F-to-delete tried out. **C.** Resulting ordering for the 27 $\male$ series found for all five pairs of F values. **D.** Resulting ordering for the 25 $\female$ series found for all five pairs of F values. The covariance matrices are based on pooling.

It is seen that, in the present instance, the choice of F values has no influence on the resulting ordering, whereas sex and/or sampling has. In subsequent calculations, in which all series were split up into (almost) equal parts, sampling was found to be an important factor. Note that once a different variable has been selected, subsequently selected variables will also be different so that no general conclusions can be drawn as to the relative importance of the variables for the diagnosis at issue.

In the present example, variable no. 9, biauricular breadth, is an exception, having been selected as the first variable in the range in all instances, is an exception.

Numbers of the variables correspond with those in Howells (1973).

lating standard errors. Moreover, as Oxnard (1979: 205) has remarked, "there is no prior reason why biological information should be bound by such a statistical straitjacket." The difficulties seem to be less serious in the event that interpretations based on these coefficients correspond with interpretations based on the correlations of the variables with the multiple discriminant functions (Corruccini, 1984). Although it appears that even these interpretations remain difficult and rather speculative, the precise ordering of the variables is not that important; it suffices to have a reasonably good one.

4.5. Stage 3: The Ultimate Selection of the Variables

As mentioned above, the stepwise discriminant analysis procedure stops when "no further significant gain" in discrimination can be achieved by the inclusion of more variables. This criterion does not necessarily lead to the selection of the optimal number of variables such that the actual discriminatory value (D_a) is maximized. Consequently, it is not advisable to use this procedure for selecting the variables in the ultimate analysis. It is obvious that the stopping criterion should depend on the aim of the investigator. The most interesting ones are the following.

   1. Testing for differences between the populations under study.

   2. Constructing procedures for classifying individuals.

   3. Constructing procedures for estimating the posterior probabilities (see Section 7.1) of individuals (probabilistic classification).

Assuming that it is obvious that considerable differences exist, one can concentrate on aims 2 and 3. The procedures to be used will essentially make use of certain discriminant functions or classification statistics. The performance of such functions can be characterized more easily than that of the entire procedure.

Consider the aim to differentiate between two populations on the basis of two samples by constructing a discriminant function. Assuming that an ordered set of variables is available, it is possible to follow at least two different methods for specifying the number p^* of variables to be used.

Method a. Calculate approximate values for D_a directly from the design samples and, subsequently, select the number p^* that provides the largest approximate value. For the purpose of optimizing p in the sense mentioned, the following formula might be applied:

$$E(D_a) \approx \left\{ \Delta^2 - \Delta^2 \cdot \frac{(p-1)\{1+(n_A+n_B-3)(n_A+n_B)/(n_A \cdot n_B \cdot \Delta^2)\}}{(n_A+n_B-3)\{1+p(n_A+n_B)/(n_A \cdot n_B \cdot \Delta))^2} \right\}^{1/2}$$

$$(4.2)$$

Here n_A and n_B are the respective design sample sizes. The true value of $\hat{\Delta}^2$ in this expression has to be replaced by some estimate. The unbiased estimate $\hat{\Delta}^2$ obtained from Mahalanobis's D^2 by applying the correction formula (Eq. 4.1) discussed earlier is recommended. Equation 4.2 and similar ones (Schaafsma, 1982) show that the actual discriminatory value to be expected in test samples (i.e., $E(D_a)$) is lower than the theoretically optimal value Δ.

If the aim is to assign unknown individuals, it is possible to proceed by calculating the estimated sectioning point, $\hat{\mu} = (\hat{\mu}_A + \hat{\mu}_B)/2$ of the scores of the design sample individuals on the discriminant function with the largest estimated value for Equation 4.2. This sectioning point separates the individuals to be assigned to population A from those to be assigned to population B.

Method b. Calculate estimates of the expected values of D_t (corresponding with the actual discriminatory value) from test samples. The simplest way is to use part of the original samples as test samples, also called holdout samples. One simply computes $D_t = \hat{\sigma}_t^{-1}|\hat{\mu}_t^{(A)} - \hat{\mu}_t^{(B)}|$, where the parameters $\mu_t^{(A)}$ and $\mu_t^{(B)}$ and σ_t are estimated by substituting the scores of the test sample individuals on the variables used in the appropriate discriminant function that is calculated from the other part of the original samples (i.e., the design samples).

A difficulty of the holdout method is that the available samples have to be split up into design and test samples. This waste of information may be overcome by following the data analysis procedure described by Van Vark (1976, 1984), and Van Vark and Van der Sman (1982) and based on Lachenbruch's "leaving one out" (LOO) method (Lachenbruch, 1967). By this procedure all available individuals are subsequently employed as design as well as test sample individuals.

It has already been shown that both the analytical approach based on Equation 4.2 and the LOO approach focus on the same concept of actual performance. For $k = 2$ the two meth-

TABLE 2. Sex Diagnosis of Skulls by Means of Discriminant Analysis

Number of variables	1	2	3	4
20	2.256	2.172	2.096	1.984
21	2.265	2.167	2.096	1.971
22	2.271	2.177	2.094	1.968
23	2.297	2.199	2.112	1.971
24	2.312	2.209	2.118	1.975
25	2.312	2.205	2.110	1.972
26	2.438	2.326	2.226	2.087
27	2.438	2.322	2.218	2.077
28	2.503	2.382	2.273	2.126
29	2.511	2.386	2.273	2.125
30	2.511	2.382	2.265	2.114
31	2.573	2.438	2.317	2.168
32	2.574	2.434	2.309	2.160
33	2.577	2.433	2.304	2.152
34	2.609	2.460	2.326	2.177
35	2.632	2.470	2.332	2.187
36	2.650	2.491	2.349	2.212
37	2.653	2.491	2.345	2.206
38	2.666	2.498	2.348	2.216
39	2.825	2.650	2.493	2.376
40	2.852	2.672	2.511	2.395
41	2.867	2.682	2.516	2.404
42	2.870	2.681	2.511	2.398
43	3.008	2.811	2.633	2.530
44	3.028	2.825	2.643	2.536
45	3.067	2.859	2.672	2.565
46	3.072	2.859	2.667	2.559
47	3.104	2.885	2.689	2.562
48	3.113	2.889	2.689	2.563
49	3.148	2.918	2.713	2.584
50	3.151	2.917	2.707	2.575
51	3.183	2.943	2.728	2.591
52	3.196	2.951	2.731	2.537
53	3.205	2.954	2.730	2.503
54	3.212	2.956	2.728	2.504
55	3.217	2.956	2.723	2.499
56	3.217	2.951	2.714	2.492
57	3.218	2.947	2.707	2.473
58	3.218	2.943	2.698	2.484

Discriminatory values were calculated from scores on measurements according to Broca's system (Broca, 1875) taken from 300 male and 300 female specimens of a Lisbon skull series collected by Ferraz de Macedo (Masset, 1982). Discriminant functions were calculated by successively adding variables one by one to the preceding selection, the first function using 20 variables, the last one 58. Variables were not previously ordered.
Col. 1. D values calculated from design samples.
Col. 2. Estimates for population discriminatory values, calculated according to Equation 4.1.
Col. 3. Estimated actual discriminatory values D_a, calculated according to Equation 4.2.
Col. 4. Estimated actual discriminatory values D_a, calculated according to the LOO-based procedure.
Note that the discriminatory values of Col. 3 are systematically larger than those of Col. 4. However, the optimum number of variables, being 51 and 52 respectively, is almost the same. On comparison with Table 4 where a different skull series consisting of two smaller skull samples was used, and where variables were previously ordered, differences between D and estimated D_a values are, quite according to expectation, smaller. Differences between discriminatory values of the four respective columns will disappear as $n \rightarrow \infty$.

ods might be compared by performing a simulation study. For $k > 2$ the LOO method has the advantage that it exists (in Van Vark and Van der Sman, 1982), whereas the analytical approach seems to be too difficult. For $k = 2$ the latter approach, based on Equation 4.2, has some theoretical advantage; moreover it requires no excessive computation (see Tables 2 and 3).

An attractive alternative is to select a number of variables, p^*, such that the number of correctly assigned test sample individuals is maximized. It will be clear that for this variant both the holdout and LOO-based procedures may be used. For $k = 2$ there is also an analogue of the analytical approach.

Whatever method one uses there is a tendency to overestimate D_a and to underestimate the misclassification probabilities if the information used for the calculation of these statistics has previously been used for ordering the variables. This holds true for all variable selection procedures discussed. In using the LOO approach, it might be possible to eliminate this kind of bias by applying a super LOO procedure by which the method is modified in such a way that, with one individual deleted, the entire procedure is repeated. This should then be repeated with all other individuals as the successively deleted ones. This super LOO procedure, however, is impractical and possibly also misleading. Since using the same samples for stages 2 and 3 will introduce a bias, it is advisable, if possible, to order the variables with other samples than the ones under investigation. These may even be samples from quite different populations. For example, for sex diagnosis, it appears that the direction and size of sexual dimorphism is sufficiently constant within *Homo sapiens sapiens*. This implies that variables that are important sex discriminators in one *Homo sapiens sapiens* population will also be so in other *Homo sapiens sapiens* populations. If the subject is to compare the morphology of recent populations, the literature provides examples of variables that are useful for that purpose.

That in any discriminant analysis bias may result from reusing the design samples for estimating performance (unless adequate corrections are made; see Section 4.2) is also illustrated in Figure 4, where isodensity ellipses

TABLE 3. Comparison of European (Polish; n = 99) Versus African (Ugandan; n = 66) Skulls

Number of variables	1	2	3	4
2	2.641	2.607	2.594	2.527
3	2.944	2.895	2.869	2.781
4	5.889	5.061	4.947	4.889
5	5.254	5.114	5.070	5.053
6	5.897	5.756	5.656	5.616
7	5.935	5.772	5.652	5.631
8	5.975	5.790	5.649	5.639
9	6.036	5.829	5.666	5.656
10	6.166	5.934	5.748	5.784
11	6.170	5.915	5.709	5.648
12	6.350	6.066	5.835	5.747
13	6.364	6.058	5.805	5.713
14	6.427	6.096	5.820	5.715
15	6.442	6.086	5.790	5.687
16	6.448	6.069	5.752	5.646
17	6.682	6.268	5.920	5.720
18	6.685	6.247	5.878	5.625
19	6.697	6.234	5.844	5.570
20	6.709	6.221	5.810	5.543
21	6.717	6.205	5.772	5.527
22	6.749	6.210	5.755	5.494
23	6.750	6.186	5.710	5.471

Data from Krzyzaniak and Miszkiewicz (1955).
Col. 1. Discriminatory values calculated from design samples.
Col. 2. Estimated population discriminatory values, calculated according to Equation 4.1.
Col. 3. Estimated actual discriminatory values D_a, calculated according to Equation 4.2.
Col. 4. Estimated actual discriminatory values D_a, calculated according to the LOO-based procedure. Variables were previously ordered with the aid of other samples from the same populations, by the stepwise discriminant analysis program. Discriminant functions were calculated by successively adding variables one by one to the preceding selection. Maximum values for D_a were found with 10 variables by means of the LOO-based procedure, and with 17 variables by means of Equation 4.2 (corresponding with a local maximum of the LOO-based procedure). However, it was found that from six variable functions onward all specimens were classified correctly. This would imply that, apart from the knowledge of how to score a small number of variables, no professional knowledge is required for diagnoses of this nature. The function using the first six variables (with the exception of the fifth variable denoted by their Martin numbers), is $Y = -0.088$ (M26) $+ 0.078$ (M8) $- 0.136$ (M11) $+ 0.121$ (M13) $- 0.039$ (1-ba) $+ 0.108$ (M2).

constructed on the basis of bivariate design sample scores are compared with corresponding scores of test samples of the same population.

The same statistical rule is applicable here, that is, the bias will be larger, the smaller the quotient of the total design sample size and the number of variables entered in the functions. In

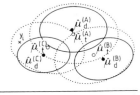

Fig. 4. Comparison of design and test sample isodensity ellipses. Continuous lines: Isodensity ellipses representing cross-sections of normal density surfaces, calculated from design samples taken from populations A, B, and C, respectively. Dotted lines: Corresponding ellipses calculated from three test samples taken from the same respective populations.

It is seen that the ellipses calculated from the design samples are smaller and farther apart than those calculated from the test samples, and they thus form an unreliable basis for classifying unknown specimens. Also note that an individual i with score vector y_i (denoted by an asterisk in the figure) does not seem to stem from any of these populations mentioned, on using design sample ellipses as a basis for comparison. However, it falls within the range of population C if (as should be done) the test sample ellipses are used instead.

the present instance, this means that the design sample centroids are further apart and the ellipses smaller than those of corresponding test samples. Thus, misinterpretations are easily made, in particular if one uses the method for getting some idea of the relative location of a single specimen. An additional problem is that an incorrect idea of this location may be obtained by restricting the attention to one plane. It may very well be that the differences between the series used for the calculation of the functions (being the design samples) and a single specimen primarily lie in different planes. That is, though it may look as if the specimen belongs to one of the series concerned, it might in fact be remote from it, if other canonical variates are taken into account.

4.6. Estimating the Population Mahalanobis Distance

A variable selection problem of a quite different nature arises if the aim is to estimate the population Mahalanobis distance Δ. Since Δ is an increasing function of p^*, no optimum number of variables, p, in the sense mentioned above, exists. However, if the ordering is not too bad, Δ will hardly increase after a certain number of variables have been included. The inclusion of further variables then will not make much sense. In fact, it can be harmful, because many additional parameters have to be estimated and this may have the effect of increasing the confidence intervals around the estimated value for Δ. Such interval estimates might be much more appropriate elsewhere. The unbiased point estimator $\hat{\Delta}^2$ (see Equation 4.1 for $k = 2$) for $\hat{\Delta}^2$, generalized for $k > 2$, is

$$\hat{\Delta}^2 = \frac{n - k - p - 1}{n - k} \cdot D^2 - \frac{n_A + n_B}{n_A + n_B} \cdot p. \quad (4.3)$$

Here k = total number of samples involved (possibly including one or more large reference samples, i.e., samples that are used for obtaining a better estimation of the underlying covariance matrix), n is the total sample size, and n_A and n_B are the sizes of the samples whose squared Mahalanobis distance is calculated. The variance of this estimator can be expressed as follows:

$$var\hat{\Delta}^2 = \frac{1}{n - p - k - 3}$$

$$\left\{ 2\hat{\Delta}^4 + 4 \frac{n_A + n_B}{n_A \cdot n_B}(n - k - 1)\hat{\Delta}^2 + \frac{2p(n - k - 1)(n_A + n_B)^2}{n_A^2 \cdot n_B^2} \right\} \quad (4.4)$$

(W.H.V. de Goede, unpublished result).

Calculating this variance is worth the trouble because it gives an idea of the reliability of one's findings.

The construction of a confidence interval for a parameter like Δ is relatively easy, but that of a "prediction" interval for the actual discriminatory value D_a is extremely complicated (unless bias terms are ignored by focusing on asymptotic results), because this is also dependent on the data. There is a need for simulation studies to be carried out.

4.7. Checking the Results by Several Calculation Runs

It is clear that the preliminary choice of variables (step 1, Section 4.3) is very important. All that follows is dependent on this choice. Investigators will want to know how far their

results might deviate if their first choice (for which, as we have seen, there are no clearcut criteria) had been different. An obvious (however, rather rarely followed) procedure is then to compare the results obtained with those of other sets and subsets of variables, if possible sets consisting of variables that are all different from the original set. (A further consequence is that in this way the effect of measurement errors, though usually not a point of much concern in skeletal studies, is reduced.) One may then find that, after the inclusion of a certain number of variables, the resulting distances are approximately the same or, at least, suggest a similar pattern in all instances. The value of this number is codetermined by the nature of the bone(s) under study. For something as complex as the cranium, this number is relatively large (see Table 2).

Laborious as this procedure may be, it forms in many instances an important and necessary extension to the investigation. In fact, it is advisable to carry this idea one step further and to apply various multivariate procedures, using different programs, and so on, whenever possible. Thus, by making various evaluations along different but not unrealistic lines, one will obtain a variety of results. The idea is that these should be combined by presenting only those results for which some kind of consensus exists. Doubt should be expressed whenever results are contradictory. Note that this approach is still less conservative than a stringent mathematical statistician might wish, especially if no adequate attention is paid to the statistical uncertainties. Most research workers tend to focus on point estimates, point predictions, and so forth. The systematic errors are investigated by varying the types of analysis, but the statistical uncertainties are usually not adequately expressed. It should be emphasized that the analyses discussed here are attempts to express these uncertainties in some way. Statistical uncertainties, systematic errors, and other factors may lead to very different results. This holds in particular if, as is not uncommon in anthropological studies, sample sizes are "small." In the context of hominid investigations, where samples may consist of just one specimen, very diverse results have been found. However, not multivariate methodology but the way it is used is to blame for this diversity.

A

II	Late Upper Paleolithic	5.8			
III	Early Upper Paleolithic	7.1	7.5		
IV	Qafzeh 6	22.1	12.3	21.3	
V	Qafzeh 9	9.4	6.7	4.1	17.5
		Recent	L.U.P.	E.U.P.	Qaf.6	Qaf.9
		I	II	III	IV	V

D²-VALUES

B

II	Late Upper Paleolithic	7.8			
III	Early Upper Paleolithic	11.7	9.0		
IV	Qafzeh 6	35.6	19.1	29.2	
V	Qafzeh 9	14.3	8.6	4.3	22.2
		Recent	L.U.P.	E.U.P.	Qaf.6	Qaf.9
		I	II	III	IV	V

Fig. 5. Comparison of Mahalanobis D^2 Values, Using the Same Set of Facial Measurements and Data but Different Covariance Matrices. **A.** Covariance matrix calculated according to Equation 5.1. Twenty-five recent subpopulations that by and large cover the variation of the present world population are weighted according to their respective contributions in numbers to the recent world population. **B.** Covariance matrix pooled over 25 samples from these 25 subpopulations. D^2 values were calculated from scores on the first 8 principal components extracted from 13 facial measurements. For codes and short names of measurements see Figure 6. For full description of measurements see Howells (1973).

Groups: I. Recent *H.sapiens, n* = 2,361 (Howells series, see Fig. 3). II. Late Upper Paleolithic *H.sapiens, n* = 10. III. Early Upper Paleolithic *H.sapiens, n* = 7. IV. Qafzeh 6. V. Qafzeh 9.

5. ABOUT THE COVARIANCE MATRIX
5.1. The Equality Assumption

One may take from Section 3 that the population Mahalanobis distance Δ is theoretically calculated from two types of parameters: the p-dimensional vector of differences between the population means, μ_A and μ_B, and the p-dimensional covariance matrix.

In actual practice, these population characteristics are not available, and it is customary to plug in the estimates for these unknown parameters taken from design samples. This implies in particular that the sample covariance matrices of the samples are pooled, if possible with the inclusion of reference samples so as to remove biases due to small sample size (cf. Equation 4.3, and Sections 5.3 and 6.5).

The underlying assumption of equality of covariance matrices will never be completely satisfied in actual practice. However, it is obvious that the degree of deviations from equality will vary in intensity. Uytterschaut and Wilmink (1983: 347) concluded in an article that compared crania of recent human populations that "the equality of Σ_g between the sexes and between subraces was not questionable, whereas the results warrant some caution as to the equality of Σ_g among the main racial groups." In the literature various opinions have been expressed about the systematic errors caused by the heterogeneity of population covariance matrices. Campbell (1963), Gilbert and Dunn (1969), and Marks and Dunn (1974) are of the opinion that inequality of the Σ_g affects results only mildly, whereas others like Corruccini (1975) and Reyment (1962) suggest that this inequality may have serious effects.

Testing the equality of Σ_g is easy from a mathematical–statistical point of view. From a practical point of view, however, the meaning of this approach is very limited because the basic heterogeneity of Σ_g is usually beyond doubt. Consequently, significant differences will be found once the samples employed are sufficiently large. However, if one feels that the standard model should not be used, then one is faced with the need to employ more complex models, which may very well be counterproductive in the sense that discriminatory performances decrease rather than increase due to lack of robustness. It is advisable to ignore this type of statistical significance unless the actual estimates suggest that the deviations are "considerable." Using the same samples and sets of variables for comparison, there are many situations where several calculation runs can be made on the basis of varying assumptions about the covariance matrices. One may, for example, in the first run employ a pooled sample covariance matrix taken just from the samples under investigation. In a second run, covariance matrices of one or more large reference samples may be used, and in a third, the covariance matrices of both reference samples and samples being diagnosed may be pooled. Several other approaches are conceivable. The rationale is that by using several different but not unrealistic estimates for the underlying covariance matrix, one will obtain a good impression of the stability of the results. Interpretations are made only if most results point in the same direction. Preferably, one should also try to incorporate the statistical uncertainties into this type of discussion. The aim of the analysis may also be of interest. If one wants to characterize affinities or distances among populations, it is more pertinent to employ a common covariance matrix than it is if one studies a pattern recognition or probabilistic classification procedure. POSCON, a program developed by Van der Sluis et al. (1985), has options for computing confidence intervals for posterior probabilities even if covariance matrices are different. This is a completely natural extension of the more common idea of making assessments of (individual) probabilities. In Figure 5 it is seen how the choice of the covariance matrix underlying the calculations may affect the results. Differences are clearly marked though not to the extent that they will lead to differences in general interpretations.

5.2. Estimation of the Covariance Matrix of a Stratified Population

The estimation of a population covariance matrix may become a very complex matter if the population is a composite one and the random sampling hypothesis is inappropriate. An example is the present world population, which consists of various subpopulations of varying sizes. If random samples are available from these strata then an unbiased estimate for the population covariance matrix can easily be calculated according to

$$\hat{\Sigma} = \sum_{g-1}^{k} (n_g - 1)^{-1} \epsilon_g \hat{\mathbf{W}}_g \{1 - n_g^{-1}(1 - \epsilon_g)\}$$
$$+ \sum_{g=1}^{k} \epsilon_g (\hat{\mu}_g - \hat{\mu})(\hat{\mu}_g - \hat{\mu})^T, \qquad (5.1)$$

where

k = number of sampled recent sub-populations,

$\hat{\mu}_g$ = estimated centroid of the g-th sub-population,

$\mathbf{W}_g$ = estimated within-group SSCP matrix of the g-th recent sub-population,

ϵ_g = size of the g-th recent sub-population divided by the size of the total recent world population,

$\hat{\mu}$ = $\sum_{g-1}^{K} \epsilon_g \hat{\mu}_g$ = estimated centroid of the recent world population.

Note that the assumption of no bias holds only if various assumptions are made and samples are available from all subpopulations. In the event that the aim is to estimate the variances and covariances of cranial measures for the present day world population and one uses, for example Howells's well-known cranial series (Howells, 1973), then the resulting estimated covariance matrix is rather reliable in our opinion. In studies of past periods where nonrecent samples for the construction of the covariance matrix are used, the results will be much less reliable, because sample sizes are small and the stratification of the population is questionable. In hominid studies, it is advisable to use the estimate for the covariance matrix that belongs to the present world population as calculated by Equation 5.1, though this has been criticized by Professor Howells (personal communication), who notes that some of these subpopulations have expanded much more radically than others, so that their contributions to the present world population are not representative of their natural contribution to the total variance resulting from their evolutionary divergence from other (sub)populations generally. This criticism is valid, but it does not point to a clear proposal for performing a calculation. For practical purposes we often proceed by comparing the results of more than one calculation run. The first run is then based on an estimated covariance matrix in which best possible estimates of the proportions ε_g in the separate strata are incorporated into an overall estimate; the second one is based on pooling, or on assuming that all ε_g values are equal. Other views that would result in still other estimates are conceivable. Again, only results that point in the same direction are to be used for interpretations.

5.3. The Problem of Widely Separated Populations

One general principle is that the assumption of equality of the covariance matrices tends to become debatable the more widely populations are separated. This implies that the use of linear discriminant analysis is questionable if different hominid species are compared. In order to obtain useful information on this, the advice is again to employ different covariance matrices. If older hominids, especially *Australopithecus* specimens, are included, it is advisable to make one or more additional calculation runs while using covariance matrices taken from pongid samples, and then compare the results. Samples of older hominids are insufficiently large to build up a covariance matrix of their own, quite apart from the fact that their taxonomy may be a matter of debate.

In a well-known study, Cherry et al. (1982) investigated distinctions across three classes of vertebrates. They compared results obtained from the Mahalanobis distance with those obtained from distance statistics like the Manhattan distance and a statistic similar to Pearson's Coefficient of Racial Likeness. It was found that when small samples were used, the Mahalanobis distance was the most biased and was, contrary to the other distance statistics, not free from violating the triangle inequality. However, these conclusions were based on computations obtained by pairwise pooling of the sample covariance matrices of each pair of spe-

cies that was compared. In this way, the Mahalanobis distances were based on different covariance matrices. This would explain why various violations of the triangle inequality appeared. Cherry et al. suggested on the basis of these violations that the Mahalanobis-based methodology is less appropriate than other, easier approaches. If they had used a covariance matrix that pooled all samples, the violations would not have appeared. It is obvious that in situations in which widely divergent species are used any morphological distance is questionable. Heterogeneity of means and covariance matrices are so large that the differences cannot be satisfactorily condensed into a single number.

6. MAHALANOBIS'S D^2

6.1. The Mahalanobis Distance and Other Distance Statistics

Mahalanobis first proposed this statistic in 1925 and later elaborated on it (1930, 1936). Since the advent of computers it has become the most popular distance statistic in skeletal studies. It has the advantage that its value does not change if the set of measurements chosen is replaced by an equivalent one; that is, it is invariant under linear transformation of the measurement system. This does not mean, however, that everyone is pleased with the results, and quite a number of anthropologists still prefer to use the more simple Penrose distance statistic and the size and shape components derived from it (Penrose, 1954). Penrose himself suggested that the discredited Coefficient of Racial Likeness (Pearson, 1926) might, in a number of cases, be more useful than the "generalized" Mahalanobis distance.

A commonly heard argument for the use of the Penrose distance is that it requires much less computation, and that it tends to be highly correlated with the Mahalanobis distance. Quite apart from the fact that the correlations obtained will vary according to sample size and number and nature of the variables introduced (Knussman, 1967, for example, gave examples of correlations varying from 0.208 to 0.969), one should realize that a high correlation does not necessarily imply that distance relationships obtained from calculations with the Penrose and Mahalanobis distance and

TABLE 4. Sex Diagnosis of Skulls: Comparison of Results Obtained by Multivariate and Univariate Methodologies

Number of variables used	No., code, and short name of variables according to Howells (1973)	1	2	3	4	5
1	8 ZYB Bizygomatic breadth	5.8	5.8	5.8	5.8	5.8
2	20 MDH Mastoid height	7.2	7.2	6.9	8.3	6.7
3	36 SOS Supraorbital projection	8.4	8.3	7.8	9.6	7.5
4	44 PAF Bregma-subtense fraction	9.2	9.2	8.5	10.4	8.0
5	37 GLS Glabella projection	10.4	10.3	9.4	14.4	8.8
6	38 FOL Foramen magnum length	10.4	10.0	9.2	14.9	8.5
7	9 AUB Biauricular breadth	10.4	9.1	9.1	18.2	8.2
8	5 XCB Maximum cranial breadth	12.8	10.2	11.0	21.6	9.8
9	21 MDB Mastoid width	13.0	9.7	11.0	23.7	9.6
10	34 MLS Malar subtense	13.5	9.9	11.3	24.6	9.7
11	26 EKB Biorbital breadth	16.9	9.0	13.9	26.1	11.9
12	22 ZMB Bimaxillary breadth	17.1	8.7	13.9	27.8	11.6
13	24 FMB Bifrontal breadth	17.2	8.0	13.7	29.8	11.3
14	58 NAA Nasion angle	17.4	8.0	13.6	29.8	11.1
15	35 WMH Cheek height	17.4	8.1	13.8	30.1	10.7
16	15 OBH Orbit height, left	18.0	8.0	13.6	30.1	10.7
17	30 WNB Simotic chord	18.0	8.0	13.4	30.1	10.3
18	13 NPH Nasion-prosthion height	18.8	8.2	13.7	31.8	10.4
19	41 FRF Nasion-subtense fraction	18.8	8.2	13.5	32.9	10.0
20	28 DKB Interorbital breadth	18.8	8.0	13.2	33.3	9.6

Sex-diagnosis of Howells's Northern Japanese cranial series consisted of 55 male and 32 female specimens, all of known sex. Variables were previously ordered with the aid of stepwise discriminant analysis, using several of Howells's other male and female samples. Variables were successively added to the preceding selection on the basis of the ordering found.

Col. 1. Squared D-values (squared design sample Mahalanobis distances). These correspond to the squared discriminatory values of Fisher's linear discriminant function.

Col. 2. The analogue of Col. 1 but with Fisher's vector of weights replaced by the analogue where the off-diagonal elements are put equal to 0.

Col. 3. Estimates for the squared population discriminatory values, as calculated according to formula (4.1).

Col. 4. Estimates for the squared Euclidean population distances.

Col. 5. Estimates for the squared Mahalanobis test sample distances (actual distances D_a), calculated by pooling the two covariance matrices, and by applying formula (4.2).

Note that the distances of Col. 4 keep increasing with an increasing number of variables. This is due to the fact that when variables are added to the preceding function their univariate squared discriminatory value is incorporated as if it were an independent contribution. Consequently, these distances are not directly connected with the discriminatory power of the set of variables used.

For actual practice, the most interesting comparison is that between Cols. 2 and 5. For small values of p the values in Col. 2 exceed those in Col. 5, indicating that the discriminatory power of Fisher's linear discriminant function is increased if the off-diagonal elements in the covariance matrix involved in the computation of the vector of weights are put equal to 0. For values of p larger than or equal to 11 the situation is reversed.

which are calculated on the basis of the same scores, display a high degree of correspondence. Rightmire, for example, found in a study of Bushman, Hottentot, and African Negro crania a correlation between Penrose's C_H^2 and D^2 of 0.959, whereas on using D^2 he found Bushmen to be roughly three times as distant from Zulus as from Hottentots, while C_H^2 yielded a figure of over 6:1 for the same distance ratio (Rightmire, 1970).

A serious argument for not using D^2 in certain instances stems from the fact that unique to the calculation of Mahalanobis distances is the requirement of estimates for the $p(p-1)/2$ elements of the covariance matrix. This is an additional source of error that pertains to the Mahalanobis distance only. One consequence is that, when "small" samples are used, the Mahalanobis distance may be outperformed by metrics that do not try to correct for the correlations between the variables. However, performance does not refer to the population definition of some distance but rather to the separation that can be achieved if one uses some Mahalanobis or other distance-related procedures. One possibility is that of characterizing classificatory performance; another one is to consider the discriminatory value of the linear discriminant functions. The phenomenon is illustrated in Table 4.

6.2. Multivariate Normality

As was shown in Section 3.1, it is technically possible to calculate linear discriminant functions and Mahalanobis distances from metric and/or nonmetric variables. Classification procedures based on estimated Mahalanobis distances usually assume multivariate normality of the discriminant function scores or, more fundamentally, that the p-variate distributions involved are normal and have equal covariance matrices. The classification procedures (see Section 7) can be applied just as well if the assumptions are not satisfied, but their performance is questionable. A test for multivariate normality is to be found in Mardia (1975).

6.3. Size and Shape

In correspondence with all other distance statistics including that of Penrose, the Mahalanobis distance statistic does not allow the calculation of "size" and "shape" components in a satisfactory way. Technically, the splitting of D^2 in a way similar to Penrose's distance is feasible (Van Vark, 1970; Spielman, 1973), but it is easy to see that the components thus derived may have little to do with size or shape. Suppose that the original variables are all indices, and that scores on these variables are substituted in the formula in which size would be expressed. That would produce a score on this size statistic that would clearly have no relation with size whatsoever. Generally speaking, the degree to which such scores refer to size will depend on the set of measurements used. This means that "size" and "shape" components deduced from either the Penrose or the Mahalanobis distance statistic are only vaguely related to size and shape, whatever the biological meaning of such quantities may be.

Quite a number of other measures for size and shape have been proposed (see, e.g., Corruccini, 1987). However, the authors feel that none of these proposals is completely satisfactory. In a recent paper, Read (1990:428) remarked that "proposed systems for measuring and comparing the size and shape of forms make use of an imposed analytical space and so

they do not capture the underlying biological space in which development takes place." This conclusion is not unlike that of Healy and Tanner (1981:19), who remarked that "the distinction between size and shape is one of these intuitively obvious notions which become less and less clear the longer we look at them." This remark obviously refers not only to mathematical but also to visual comparison. At present, there is no consensus on the relative importance of size and shape, however defined, for taxonomic distinctions. This clearly reduces the relevance of the subject. However, this does not mean that the issue is unimportant. In fact, quite a number of anthropological studies are based on combinations of linear and other measures. It might be interesting to reanalyze everything by working with ratios and other dimension-free variables but it requires many choices that might ultimately affect the results (see also Howells, 1989).

6.4. What Does the Mahalanobis Distance Measure?

A basic question is: What are the D^2 values, calculated from skeletal metrical variables, really measuring? Obviously, morphological similarity is not the same as relatedness. Morphometric (and visually observed morphological) traits are subject to nongenetic variation, which can only weaken phylogenetic interpretations. Moreover, even genetic variation in these traits, if adaptive, may be misleading if used for reconstructing phylogenies (Guglielmino-Matessi et al., 1979).

Based on the authors' experience it is possible to trace historical events by studying patterns of Mahalanobis distances calculated from skull measurements. This was the case in an unpublished study in which inhabitants of several villages, all situated in the same Dutch province, were compared. On the basis of skull measurements significant differences between some of these groups could be established, and they were interpreted as the effect of a substantial influx of people from another country who settled in one of the villages several centuries earlier. This and many similar findings suggest that morphological differences in skeletal parts as measured by Mahalanobis distances are to a certain extent genetically based. For closely related populations it is expected that more refined results will become possible if nonmetric variables are involved in the calculation. This, however, requires analyses that are more sophisticated than those used at present (see also Section 10).

Studies by Crichton (1966), Mukerjee and coworkers (1955), Rightmire (1972), and Cavalli-Sforza and colleagues (1988), which deal with more widely divergent *Homo sapiens sapiens* populations, seem to confirm that Mahalanobis distances must, to a large extent, reflect underlying genetic distances. These and many other results (see, e.g., Nakata et al., 1974, and Jamison et al., 1989) make it plausible that, with some reservations, Mahalanobis distances calculated from skull measurements do indeed relate to actual phylogenetic structures.

Similar considerations hold for comparisons at the species level. For example, Lambert and Paterson (1982: 291) stated that "with genetical species no relationship exists between morphological difference and the two most common forms of genetic distance, chromosomal and electromorphic distance." If this is so, this will also hold for Mahalanobis distances calculated from skeletal variables. However, one should also note the following. Various authors (e.g., Andrews, 1987; Chakraborty, 1985; Friday, 1987) have pointed to the theoretical difficulties of distance models in molecular evolution. Besides, skeletal morphological differences will, at least in part, reflect other parts of the genetic spectrum than differences based on other data. Phenomena such as mosaic evolution strengthen this assertion. A further difficulty of any molecular approach is that suitable data are, as yet, unavailable for past populations (see Rothschild, this volume, Chapter 8). On the other hand, multivariate statistical methodology shares with other diagnostic methods that are based on the study of the morphology the difficulty that there are no satisfactory criteria for recognizing species and other taxa on morphological grounds. Consequently, it cannot provide a clearcut answer to the question, How many species are present in the hominid fossil record? However, a substantial reduction in the prevailing variety of opinions in this realm could be achieved if advanced multivariate statistical methodology were employed. For example, convergent evolution may lead to an explanation of morpho-logical similarities between certain taxa that, on visual comparison, may easily be mistaken for relatedness. It would seem that genetically distinct taxa displaying such apparent similarities will nevertheless have relatively large Mahalanobis distances which would correspond better with their actual phylogenetic position (Van Vark, 1985b). This suggests that visual comparison may easily distinguish between evolutionary grades, whereas mathematical comparison may distinguish, in addition, certain genetic dissimilarities that remain unnoticed by visual comparison alone. In fact, a comparison of visual and mathematical affinity patterns has led to the hypothesis that convergence plays a role at all taxonomic levels, and is much more common in hominid phylogeny than one would conclude on the basis of visual comparison (of morphology) alone (Van Vark, 1990a,b).

6.5. A Possible Application: Interindividual Distances

An interesting alternative to calculating between-groups squared Mahalanobis distances is to calculate squared distances between the individuals of the k groups under investigation, and then compare the interindividual within-groups variabilities, $\bar{D}_g^2$, of each of the k groups. In the same fashion, one can calculate the interindividual between-groups variabilities, $D_{gh}^2 = \Sigma_i \Sigma_j D_{ij}^2/n_g \cdot n_h$, between individuals from group g and individuals from group h. Accordingly, a matrix can be built up with diagonal elements $\bar{D}_g^2$ and off-diagonal elements D_{gh}^2. Interindividual squared Mahalanobis distances are found by first calculating principal component functions from the covariance matrix of a (preferably large) reference sample, transforming the individuals' raw scores into principal component function scores for each individual, and finally calculating squared interindividual Mahalanobis distances from $D_{ij}^2 = \sum_{b=1}^{p} (Y_{ib} - Y_{jb})^2$, p being the number of principal components employed.

An example is given in Figure 6. Squared interindividual Mahalanobis distances were calculated from 13 measurements of the face plus 13 measurements of the braincase, by using a covariance matrix based on scores of 2,216 recent specimens, which for the most part cover

		I	II	III	IV	V
I	Recent *Homo sapiens* n = 2361	52.1				
II	Late Upper Paleolithic *Homo sapiens* n = 12	70.7	69.7			
III	Early Upper Paleolithic *Homo sapiens* n = 7	84.5	90.5	89.3		
IV	Qafzeh 6	142.5	152.2	141.6	—	
V	Qafzeh 9	46.3	58.8	75.1	124.3	—

Measurements of the face.
Code and short name.

13. NPH—Nasion prosthion height
15. OBH—Orbit height, left
16. OBB—Orbit breadth, left
17. JUB—Bijugal breadth
18. NLB—Nasal breadth
19. MAB—Palate breadth, external
22. ZMB—Bimaxillar breadth
26. EKB—Biorbital breadth
35. WMH—Cheek height
51. PPR—Prosthion radius
54. FMR—Frontal malar radius
57. AVR—Molar alveolus radius
58. NAA—Nasion angle

Measurements of the brain case.
Code and short name.

1. GOL—Glabello-occipital length
2. NOL—Nasio-occipital length
5. XCB—Maximum cranial breadth
7. STB—Bistephanic breadth
9. AUB—Biauricular breadth
11. ASB—Biasterionic breadth
36. SOS—Supraorbital projection
39. FRC—Nasion-bregma chord (Frontal chord)
40. FRS—Nasion-bregma subtense (Frontal subtense)
41. FRF—Nasion-subtense fraction
43. PAS—Bregma-lambda subtense (Parietal subtense)
44. PAF—Bregma-subtense fraction
48. VRR—Vertex radius

Fig. 6. Interindividual within-group (diagonal elements) and between-group (off-diagonal elements) squared Mahalonobis distances.

the variation of the present world population. If two individuals are taken at random from the same populations and the covariance matrix of these populations is assumed to be equal to that incorporated into the computations, then the corresponding value of $\frac{1}{2}D_{ij}^2$ is the outcome of a χ_p^2 distributed random variable. The expectation of D_{ij}^2 is $2p = 52$ and the standard deviation is $(8p)^{1/2} = 14.4$.

The two following interpretations are possible.

Situation a. By means of a χ^2 test of the difference between the skulls of Qafzeh 6 and Qafzeh 9, these skulls were found to be significantly different at the 5% level. It should also be noted that the average squared distance between Qafzeh 9 and the recent sample is smaller than the average of the squared distances between the individuals of that sample. This means that, at least as far as its skull mor-

phology is concerned, this individual can be considered as fully modern. For Qafzeh 6 this does not hold.

It will be clear that the calculation procedures discussed here are generally useful in situations in which there is no a priori knowledge of whether all individuals investigated belong to the same population (a related approach is that by Key and Jantz, 1990). If the variability of an unknown *Homo sapiens* sample turns out to be relatively large, then there is evidence that this sample belongs to more than one population, or to a population that is for some reason more heterogeneous than the reference population. In hominid studies, the number of populations (genera, species, or subspecies) in the material at hand usually cannot be regarded as sufficiently known. This implies that the investigator is faced with a cluster analysis problem. For this kind of analysis interindividual squared Mahalanobis distances, calculated on the basis of a covariance matrix taken from a large reference sample, may form a useful starting point. Since the size of the reference sample is "large," the number of variables that may be effectively used will also be "large." From the discussion of variable selection in Section 4 it will be clear that the use of such a large reference sample is indispensable for defining the Mahalanobis distance in the present situation, in which samples of a very small number of individuals are available (Van Vark, 1984, 1985a,b). It may be inferred from Section 5 that it is advisable with this type of study to check the stability of the procedure by repeating the calculations with covariance matrices taken from other populations.

Situation b. In the event that, as in the first example, 2,216 specimens from one population are available for the construction of a 26-dimensional covariance matrix, it is reasonable to assume that the population covariance matrix is known. Following this assumption, one can easily test whether the European Upper Paleolithic populations from which the samples of Figure 6 were taken are more variable than the total recent world population. To that end one may use the test statistic $T = 1/2$ $(n_g - 1)\bar{D}_g^2$. The null hypothesis of equal variability is rejected if $T \geq \chi^2_{(n_g-1)p;\alpha}$. For the Late Upper Paleolithic sample it holds that $1/2 (n_g - 1)\bar{D}_g^2 = \frac{1}{2}*11*69.7 = 383.4$, and $\chi^2_{(n_g-1)p;\alpha} = \chi^2_{286;\alpha} = 326.2$. For the Early Paleolithic samples these figures are 267.9 and 186.0 respectively; thus it was found that both Upper Paleolithic European populations were, as far as cranial morphology is concerned, more variable than the total recent world population. One may wonder how far this is due to the fact that both Upper Paleolithic samples span, in contrast to the recent samples, a time period of several thousands of years. However, in a further analysis it was found that the reduction of variability observed was with facial measures; braincase variability remained fairly constant over time. Consequently, the time factor certainly does not provide a complete explanation. With further analyses a reduction of variability over time was found to be a more general phenomenon in hominid evolution. Various explanations might be envisaged.

6.6. A Second Possible Application: A Simulation Study

Recent extensions of statistical methodology (based on new possibilities that have arisen owing to the introduction of high-speed computers) are several simulation techniques amongst which so-called bootstrap procedures (Efron, 1979). The principle is that given a single sample, artificial samples can be generated so as to obtain a reliable impression of the statistical accuracy of the estimate for a certain parameter.

A related resampling procedure is as follows. Assume that one wants to estimate the correlation between two variables X_1 and X_2, and that the correlation coefficient is estimated from a sample of 20 individuals. New samples can now be generated, for example, by keeping the scores of the 20 individuals in X_1 fixed and by randomly reshuffling the scores in X_2 of the individuals a very large number of times. In this way, a correspondingly large number of estimated correlation coefficients may be generated that together provide a frequency distribution of this coefficient which can be used to test the null hypothesis of independence. This makes it possible, for example, to calculate the interval for the 5% highest scores of the distribution, and subsequently check whether the observed actual score, say 0.72, falls within that interval. If that is the case, one can conclude that there is, if tested at the 5% level, a positive correlation between X_1 and X_2. In this simple example one could equally well have applied the standard t test for testing the null hypothesis of independence. Resampling is not needed here.

However, procedures of this nature offer interesting possibilities for anthropological studies. Assume that one wants to investigate whether two distance matrices are correlated. One distance matrix may, for example, refer to Mahalanobis distances based on skull measurements, the other one to quite different distance statistics, such as statistics used for comparing blood group data. It is also possible that distance matrices are involved that pertain to variables that, like climatic variables, have a more or less constant score for a certain population. In all these instances one may employ some obvious modification of the above-mentioned simulation study for testing whether the interpopulation distances contained in one data set are correlated with those contained in another set. For the comparison of distance matrices the simulation principle provides a way out for a problem that cannot be solved satisfactorily with standard statistical methods, since distance scores within each matrix are partially correlated.

This procedure has been applied to establish the association between recent *Homo sapiens* skull morphology and climatic conditions. It was found that 12 variables that express various aspects of temperature differences and 6 variables related to humidity differences were all significantly correlated with skull morphology, whereas 2 variables referring to differences in precipitation were not (Van Vark et al., 1985).

Note that establishing the existence of an association as indicated above is quite different from providing a more complete description by using a so-called Procrustes analysis (Sibson, 1978). With the aid of the latter approach one can investigate the nature and degree of correspondence. By carrying out a transformation of the data, the distance information contained in the two matrices is combined so as to obtain more complete insight into the distance relationships of the populations concerned (Gower and Digby, 1984). The transformation proceeds along optimization criteria that may lead to an overestimation of the fit of the two sets of data. As Gower and Digby (1984) pointed out, the statistical theory about various types of uncertainty associated with the method is still largely unknown. It seems reasonable to assume that such Procrustes analyses should not be carried out unless some testing procedure, such as the one discussed above, has made clear that at least some relationship between the two matrices is present.

6.7. Other Possibilities for Application

It should be clear from the above discussion that numerous other applications of the Mahalanobis distance are possible. Several of these are due to recent developments in statistical theory. Some obvious extensions were developed by Steerneman and colleagues (1990). With the aid of one of their tests one can investigate whether two populations, A and B, are

more different than two populations C and D (Variant 1), or more different than two populations A and C, population A being the same in both pairs, whence the procedure is called the triangle test (Variant 2). The first variant is useful in situations in which the sexual dimorphism of various populations is compared (Van Vark et al., 1989a), the latter one in evolutionary studies. A second test developed by Steerneman and coworkers investigates whether the vector of differences between two populations, A and B, is in the same direction as the vector of differences between two populations, C and D. With the aid of this procedure one can test for differences in direction of sexual dimorphism, or whether phylogenetic lines display evolutionary changes in the same direction (Steerneman et al., 1990). It is expected that with the continuous development of multivariate statistical theory the applicability of the Mahalanobis distance will increase accordingly.

7. CLASSIFICATION

7.1. The Posterior Probability

The customary concept for discussing group membership of individual specimens is the posterior probability. Estimates for this probability can be calculated on the basis of Bayes's theorem. If we write the Bayes equation in terms of the Mahalanobis distance, we may for $k = 2$ obtain a point estimate for the posterior probability that an individual i, given its discriminant function score, y_i, belongs to a population A. The point estimate is given by

$$\hat{P}(A|y_i) = \frac{\hat{\pi}_A \cdot e^{-\frac{1}{2}D_A^2}}{\hat{\pi}_A \cdot e^{-\frac{1}{2}D_A^2} + \hat{\pi}_B \cdot e^{-\frac{1}{2}D_B^2}} \quad (7.1)$$

where

y_i = the discriminant function score of individual i,

$\hat{\pi}_A$ = the estimated prior probability of population A,

$D_A^2 = D_{(iA)_t}^2$ = the squared Mahalanobis distance between individual i and the mean of a test sample from population A.

TABLE 5. Comparison of Some Upper Paleolithic Skulls With Recent Series on the Basis of Three Different Statistics[a]

	Cro-Magnon 1	Dolni Vestonice 3	Oberkassel ♂
Assigned to:	Mokapu ♂	South Japan ♂	South Australia ♂
With posterior probability	0.9885	0.5033	0.9918
Accessory standard deviation	0.0351	0.6085	0.0241
With typicality probability			
Lower bound	<0.0000	0.0009	<0.0000
Upper bound	<0.0000	0.0398	0.0017
Probability of exceedance Hotelling's F test	<0.0000	0.0095	0.0003

[a]Using the 26 measurements described in Figure 6, three Upper Paleolithic skulls were compared with 14 of Howells's cranial series, viz. Norse ♂, Norse ♀, Zulu ♂, Zulu ♀, South Australia ♂, South Australia ♀, Mokapu ♂, Mokapu ♀, Peru ♂, Peru ♀, South Japan ♂, South Japan ♀, Bushman ♂, Bushman ♀. In all 14 samples sizes were equal to 40.

In this table, for each skull there are listed only scores that refer to the series to which the skull would have been assigned on forced allocation, using the posterior probability statistic. It can be seen that all three skulls are significantly different from these respective series, the upper bounds of the typicality probabilities and the probabilities of exceedance Hotelling's F test all being smaller than 0.05.

Of course, D_B^2 is defined similarly, and $\hat{\pi}_B = 1 - \hat{\pi}_A$ while $\hat{P}(B|Y_i) = 1 - \hat{P}(A|Y_i)$. The individual i will be assigned to the population for which it has the largest probability; doubtful cases can be excluded by defining some appropriate interval in the middle. If more than two populations are involved, the Bayes formula can be generalized in a straightforward manner.

Usually it will not be possible to obtain reliable estimates for prior probabilities. In that case it is customary to use equal prior probabilities. This is also done in sex diagnosis. Here, however, the choices of estimates $\pi_{\female} = 0.5$ and $\pi_{\male} = 0.5$ are rather compelling.

7.2. The Typicality Probability

Commonly a researcher does not know whether an individual to be classified belongs to any of the populations under consideration. It may very well belong to another, unknown, $k + 1$st, population. This is, as we have seen, one of the basic questions in hominid investigations. It is also a common problem with archaeological skeletal material. In such instances the typicality probability statistic can be used (Aitchinson and Dunsmore, 1975; Campbell, 1980; Ambergen and Schaafsma, 1984). The definition chosen by Ambergen and Schaafsma is as follows: Let $\Delta_{i,A}^2$ be the squared population distance between individual i and population A, then the typicality

probability of this individual with respect to population A is the probability that an individual randomly chosen from population A has a larger squared Mahalanobis distance than that of the population. Since the squared Mahalanobis distance between a randomly chosen individual and the population mean follows a χ^2 distribution with p degrees of freedom, the typicality probability is equal to

$$P(\chi_p^2 \geq \Delta^2).\qquad(7.3)$$

It will be seen that as the typicality probability of an individual for a certain population becomes smaller, the less typical this individual is for that population. If the individual is located in the centroid of the population, its typicality probability with respect to that population is equal to 1. If the individual is, at the 5% level, statistically different from that population, the probability concerned will have a value of ≤ 0.05. In practice, the (population) value Δ^2 has to be estimated from the data. The elaboration by Ambergen and Schaafsma allows the construction of approximate 95% confidence intervals for the k estimated typicality probabilities of an individual. With the aid of these intervals, which are nothing but transformed confidence intervals for Δ^2, one may locate the approximate position of the individual under investigation and decide whether the individual may belong to one of the k populations

TABLE 6. Sex Diagnosis of Skull Series With the Aid of Maximum Likelihood Estimation[a]

	n_{δ}, 1	n_{φ}, 2	D_a, 3	Expected percentage of misclassifications, 4	Actual numbers and percentage of misclassification		
					δ, 5	φ, 6	%, 7
North Japan (reference series)	55	32	3.49	4.9			
Norse	55	55	3.29	5.7	8	3	10.0
Berg	56	53	3.18	6.2	4	3	6.4
Bushman	41	49	2.94	7.5	8	11	18.8
Ainu	48	38	2.95	7.5	5	2	8.1
Arikara	42	27	2.81	8.5	6	1	10.1
Mokapu	51	49	3.06	6.9	6	1	7.0

[a]For the North Japanese reference series, the sex of all specimens was known a priori. $D_{t\ max}$ was attained with 11 variables. These variables form a previously ordered selection from Howells's 70 variables. The estimated discriminant function using these 11 variables is

$Y = 0.940\,(ZYB) + 0.638\,(MDH) + 1.651\,(SOS)$
$\quad + 0.140\,(PAF) + 1.359\,(GLS) + 0.119\,(FOL)$
$\quad + 0.330\,(AUB) + 0.493\,(XCB) - 0.817\,(MDB)$
$\quad + 0.860\,(MLS) - 0.860\,(EKB).$

Initial values for the maximum likelihood estimation procedure were obtained with the aid of PROC8. The number of actual misclassified individuals was determined by using Howells's visual sexing as a standard. Actual numbers of misclassifications may therefore be somewhat different.

The values of D_a suggest that the present procedure may provide percentages of correct classification for prehistoric series that are higher than those obtained for recent series if visual diagnosis was used. It should also be noted, however, that some series, not mentioned here, display a lower sexual dimorphism, which may be due to sampling and/or particularities of the population (Cunha and Van Vark, 1991). It is expected that values for D_a would become larger if the reference series could be enlarged. (For further explanation see text.)

with which it is compared or is from a different population.

7.3. Hotelling's Two-Sample Test

The typicality probability of an individual i with respect to a certain population can also be evaluated by applying a modification of Hotelling's two-sample test, one sample consisting of individual i, the other samples consisting of individuals from the population with which it is compared. This statistic follows an F distribution with p and another large number of degrees of freedom, under the null hypothesis that the individual is from the population with which it is compared. The F test thus obtained is particularly useful in those cases in which the confidence interval for the typicality probability, discussed in Section 7.2 and Table 5, contains the point 0.05. The basic difference with the statistic discussed in Section 7.2 is that the aim of the statistic is to locate a specimen i on a typicality–atypicality scale, whereas Hotelling's statistic is the appropriate tool for testing the indicated null hypothesis. Table 5 gives an example.

8. SEX DIAGNOSIS

8.1 Problems and Possibilities

When comparing *Homo sapiens sapiens* populations on the basis of skeletal remains, it is necessary to determine the sex of the individuals because morphological differences between the males and females of one population can markedly exceed the morphological differences between individuals of the same sex of different populations. Disregarding the sex might therefore result in quite misleading values for the distance statistics used in a morphological comparison. Until quite recently, similar considerations held for the estimation of an individual's stature. Sjøvold (1990), however, has demonstrated that formulas for the estimation of stature can be developed that are valid both for males and females of *Homo sapiens*, regardless of the populations to which the individuals belong.

In particular if "large" samples from the population being investigated are available, mathematical multivariate analysis may be a helpful tool for diagnosing the sex from skeletal re-

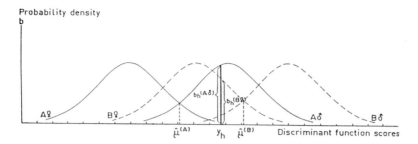

Fig. 7. The male and female distributions of discriminant function scores of population A, to which individual b with score y_b, belongs, are given by continuous lines. The proportion of the ordinates $b_h{}^{(A\,\female)}/b_h{}^{(A\,\male)}$ at the value of y_b, of the respective curves, is about 0.05. Starting from this figure one will classify b as a male. The probability that the classification is correct is 19 to 1.

The curves of the male and female distributions of discriminant function scores of a second population, population B, are given by broken lines. The proportion of the ordinates $b_h{}^{(B\,\female)}/b_h{}^{(B\,\male)}$ at the value of y_b, is about 5.5. Starting from this proportion, one would rather classify b as a female, and (as will be seen, since b belongs to population A) the probability that this is an incorrect decision is 19 to 1.

The figures in this example may be found in practice with skulls, cremated remains, and other skeletal material. The message is that "classical" discriminant analysis procedures do not suffice for the sex diagnosis of prehistoric skeletal material. Reliable diagnosis can usually be obtained only by adding supplementary procedures as discussed in the text. (In order to avoid confusion with discriminant function scores, denoted by y, the x and y axes are called a and b axes, respectively).

Reproduced from Van Vark (1970), with permission of the publisher.

mains. In hominid studies, the situation is more complex not only because of the small sample sizes but also because the species designation of many specimens is uncertain. This implies that, in many instances, it is unclear whether observed morphological differences are due to sex and/or species differences (Leutenegger and Shell, 1987). In fact, the possibilities for a mathematical statistical diagnosis of sex are rather marginal in this subject area.

If appropriately collected male and female *Homo sapiens sapiens* samples are available, then it may be relatively easy to construct mathematical procedures that outperform visual sex diagnosis. This holds for skulls, but although experience on this subject is minimal, it is likely that this will also hold for postcranial skeletal parts.

The special problem of sex determination of past *Homo sapiens sapiens* is that there are no male/female reference samples from which to construct a sex discriminant function (Figure 7). Given a sufficiently large number of individuals to be diagnosed, two quite different procedures can be used for coping with this

complication. It is suggested here that, where possible, both procedures be used for mutual checking of results.

8.2. Sex Diagnosis by Means of Iterative Discriminant Analysis (IDA)

The first procedure, IDA (Van Vark, 1970, 1971, 1974), consists of the following successive steps.

1. From the skeletal material those cases are selected that leave no doubt as to the sex to which the individuals belong (these will be the most feminine and masculine specimens and/or relatively complete specimens).

2. A discriminant function, in which the individuals mentioned in 1 are used exclusively, is calculated.

3. The function is applied to the whole sample to be investigated, that is, the score on the function is calculated for every individual; the estimated sectioning point, separating individuals being classified as males from those being classified as females, $\hat{\mu} = (\hat{\mu}_\male + \hat{\mu}_\female)/2$, is calculated.

TABLE 7. Comparison of Results Obtained With Fisher's Discriminant Analysis (FDA) and IDA, Using Three Postcranial Measurements[a]

| Measures used | Number of misclassified individuals, Amsterdam[b] | | Number of misclassified individuals, Stockholm[c] | | $n_\delta^{(A)} = n_\delta^{(S)}$ | $n_\circ^{(A)} = n_\circ^{(S)}$ |
	FDA	IDA	FDA	IDA		
2,4,5	6	5	2	2	23	18
1,4,5	4	5	2	13	25	18
2,3,5	2	11	3	3	23	21
1,3,5	4	5	3	3	24	22
2,3,4	2	2	1	2	19	16
1,3,4	1	2	1	1	18	17

[a]It is seen that, with the exception of two cases, the results of the two methods differ little, although only three measurements are used which certainly do not form a combination that is "optimum" in any sense.

It seems likely that in the two cases where large differences are found the iteration has degenerated. Note that FDA is based on samples of known sex, whereas IDA uses the sex of the individuals in the initial samples only.

For measurement definitions see Table 1.

[b]Amsterdam: Noncremated skeletal series of known sex from a nineteenth century burial place. Scores are given in Van Vark (1975).

[c]Stockholm: Cremated skeletal series of known sex (see Table 1). Scores are given in Van Vark (1975).

4. A second discriminant function is calculated, in which the individuals from 1 are used, but now the individual is included whose discriminant function score on the first function is furthest removed from the estimated sectioning point $\hat{\mu}$, mentioned in 3. This individual is assigned to the nearest population.

5. The process is repeated until all the individuals have been included in the calculation of a discriminant function. An example is given in Table 7.

For theoretical reasons the number of both male and female individuals with which the calculation procedure is started (individuals of step 1) must be at least equal to $(p + 2)/2$. It is advisable, however, to start with a larger number of individuals because the iteration degenerates in certain instances, with the result that many cases are incorrectly classified. Clearly, the possibility of a degeneration will become larger the smaller the percentage of individuals chosen in step 1. If it is not possible to obtain $(p + 2)/2$ male and $(p + 2)/2$ female individuals who can be visually sexed a priori, then one may first calculate a sex discriminant function by means of a reference sample that consists of individuals of both sexes. Next, calculate the scores of the sample based on this function and finally, compose two subsamples, one of $\geq (p + 2)/2$ highest and one of $\geq (p + 2)/2$ lowest-scoring individuals. These subsam-

ples can then be used in step 1. Another possibility that may be used if no such reference sample is available is to register the p univariate scores for all individuals being diagnosed, and then select for step 1 the individuals with the highest and lowest standardized scores summed over the p variables.

8.3. Sex Diagnosis by Means of Maximum Likelihood Estimation

An alternative method for determining sex in archaeological samples is to apply maximum likelihood estimation. Assuming that the size of the sample being diagnosed is "large" and that a pair of "large" reference samples is available (one consisting of male and the other of female specimens) one may proceed as follows.

1. Estimates for the weights $\lambda_1, \lambda_2, ..., \lambda_p$ of a discriminant function Y are calculated from the reference samples.

2. Discriminant function scores $Y_1, Y_2, ..., Y_p$, on the function Y are calculated for the individuals of the sample to be investigated. This series is regarded as a random sample from the mixture of two normal distributions, the $N(\mu_\delta, \sigma)$ and $N(\mu_\circ, \sigma)$ distributions, with mixing proportion $\zeta = n_\delta/(n_\delta + n_\circ)$. In some cases $\zeta = 0.5$ will be postulated, in other cases it is considered an unknown parameter.

3. The parameters defined in μ_δ, $\mu_\circ$, σ and if necessary ζ are estimated from the scores

$Y_i, Y_2, ..., Y_p$ with the aid of the maximum likelihood principle.

4. The individuals investigated are classified by substituting the estimated parameters μ_δ, μ_φ, σ, and $\zeta = n_\delta/(n_\delta + n_\varphi)$, and the individual's discriminant function scores in Bayes's Equation 7.1 (Van Vark, 1970, 1974).

In practice, it has become clear that the direction and size of sexual dimorphism within populations of *Homo sapiens sapiens* are sufficiently similar to produce a discriminatory value $| (\hat{\mu}_\delta - \hat{\mu}_\varphi)/\hat{\sigma} |$ in the samples being diagnosed that is, with use of "large" reference series, only slightly less than the corresponding value $| (\hat{v}_\delta - \hat{v}_\varphi/\hat{\sigma}) |$ of the reference sample. The difference between mixed samples of different anatomically modern populations is mainly in the sectioning points separating males and females. As a consequence, sex discriminant functions calculated from a pair of samples from one population are not directly applicable to a mixed sample from other populations without using the supplementary procedures discussed here.

As mentioned, the procedure is applicable only if both the reference samples and the sample being diagnosed are "large." Note that the discriminatory capacity of the set of variables employed also has to be "large," since otherwise the iteration procedure may easily degenerate, that is, it may find local maxima for the parameters to be estimated, or it may not converge at all.

However, the efficiency of the method can be increased in two ways. The first is to use additional information from the reference sample by postulating $\mu_\delta = \gamma \cdot v_\delta$ and $\mu_\varphi = \gamma \cdot v_\varphi$. As a consequence, the number of parameters to be estimated is reduced to three: (γ, σ, and ζ) and if one assumes $\zeta = 0.5$, even to two.

A second method is to obtain better initial values for the parameters being estimated by applying a procedure that is called PROC8 (Uytterschaut, 1983). The essentials of the procedure are as follows.

1. Individuals are ordered according to their discriminant function scores.

2. A small portion of n' individuals are assigned to the female sex, the remaining $n - n'$ individuals to the male sex.

3. From these samples a discriminatory value is calculated.

4. The number of supposedly female individuals is increased by 1, and the accessory discriminant value is calculated.

5. The procedure is continued so that a range of discriminatory values is obtained.

6. Estimates for the parameters μ_δ, μ_φ, σ, and ζ associated with the highest discriminatory value are calculated.

This procedure can substantially improve the performance of the maximum likelihood estimation. Examples are given in Figure 8.

8.4. Comparing the Pros and Cons of Both Procedures

The main pros and cons of the two alternative procedures can be listed as follows.

1. IDA does not require the scores of "large" reference samples, so it is unnecessary to take into account the qualities of reference material from other populations when selecting the most suitable sets of measures for the sample to be diagnosed.

2. IDA works only if the sets of variables to be employed have a theoretically large discriminatory value. This is so because an incorrect classification of one individual produces an incorrect starting point for all the following functions, which are calculated on the basis of that individual's scores, among other things. However, acceptable results are found if one uses a set of measures to construct a discriminant function that separates males and females such that the misclassification probabilities are smaller than, say, 90%.

3. A valuable addition to the maximum likelihood procedure is to apply a likelihood ratio test. This test pertains to situations in which the investigator is uncertain whether one or both sexes are present in the skeletal material. The test can be described as follows: If L_ω is the maximum likelihood of the model ω with one normal distribution (one sex), while L_Ω is the maximum likelihood of model Ω with two normal distributions (both sexes), then it holds that if the one-sex model is correct,

$$-2 \log L_\omega / L_\Omega \sim \hat{\chi}_f^2.$$

where f is the additional number of parameters in the two-sex model in comparison with the null hypothesis.

A

I	Recent *Homo sapiens n* = 14	16.7					
II	Upper Palaeolithic *Homo sapiens n* = 29	21.7	17.7				
III	Asiatic *Homo erectus n* = 5	63.0	62.0	21.9			
IV	Broken Hill	114.3	98.8	61.3	—		
V	Petralona	107.9	93.2	55.9	2.3	—	
VI	Steinheim	111.7	109.4	50.0	13.3	16.8	—
		I	II	III	IV	V	VI

B

Predmost 3	1.5
Mladec 1	1.1
Dolni Vestonice 3	1.5
Cro-Magnon 2	1.8
Combe Capelle	1.8
Broken Hill	0.3
Petralona	0.1

Measurements used.
Code and short name.

1. GOL—Glabello-occipital length
2. NOL—Nasio-occipital length
5. XCB—Maximum cranial breadth
6. XFB—Maximum frontal breadth
7. STB—Bistephanic breadth
11. ASB—Biasterionic breadth
36. SOS—Supraorbital projection
37. GLS—Glabella projection
39. FRC—Nasion-bregma chord (Frontal chord)
40. FRS—Nasion-bregma subtense (Frontal subtense)
41. FRF—Nasion-subtense fraction
42. PAC—Bregma-lamdba chord (Parietal chord)
43. PAS—Bregma-lambda subtense (Parietal subtense)
44. PAF—Bregma-subtense fraction
48. VRR—Vertex radius
49. NAR—Nasion radius
54. FMR.—Frontomalare radius

Fig. 8. Estimation of the effect of missing scores on D^2 values. **A.** Interindividual within-group (diagonal elements) and between-group (off-diagonal elements) squared Mahalanobis distances calculated from 17 cranial variables. **B.** Squared Mahalonobis distances, based on the same set of variables, and calculated between two vectors of scores (one "real," the other one artificial) of the same specimen.

    Missing scores on variables 11 (ASB) and 36 (SOS) were artificially generated for the listed seven hominid specimens who actually score completely on all 17 variables. Using the data analysis technique mentioned in the text (which is completely described in Van Vark, 1974, 1985a), the incomplete vectors of raw scores were transformed into complete vectors of principal components scores. Consequently, each of the seven specimens could be represented by two sets of principal components scores, viz. one set of "real" principal components scores, and one obtained by means of regression. Next, Mahalonobis distances were calculated between the two vectors of scores for each of the seven specimens. As can be seen, these distances turned out to be all lower than 2.0.

    This suggests that the estimation of a complete vector of 17 principal components scores for the Steinheim skull, the only skull in the present calculation whose scores on variables 11 and 36 are missing, will not lead to D^2 values for this skull that are very different from those that would have been obtained if all scores of this skull had been available. Consequently this suggests that, in the present instance, general interpretations to be taken from Panel A are not affected by the two missing scores mentioned.

Theoretically, a similar test could be used for finding out whether individuals from one population or from more than one population are present in the material. However, this appears to be impracticable since, even on applying the reduction mentioned above, six parameters will have to be estimated in this case and, as was shown above, one might be faced with some difficulties in the estimation of only four parameters. Van Vark (1970: 59–60) presents an analytical procedure that may cope with such situations.

The IDA and maximum likelihood procedures share the difficulty that the iteration procedure may degenerate, so it is best to carry out several calculation runs. Both methods are limited in their scope. They are restricted to two samples to be diagnosed with sizes of, say, $n_\delta \geq 10$ and $n_\varphi \geq 10$, depending on the separating value of the sets of measures used. For lower sample sizes sex diagnosis by means of mathematical multivariate methods is impossible. On the other hand, under favorable conditions, that is, with "large" sample sizes, and "large" D, the mathematical procedures will outperform visual ones. An example is shown in Table 8, where IDA was applied to cremated skeletal remains of known sex.

Finally it should be noted that IDA may also be used if the aim is to differentiate between populations. The procedure was carried out on 298 European (Polish) skulls and 58 skulls of Australian Aborigines. With 30 cranial variables (and for IDA 36 starting individuals), it was found that by both IDA and Fisher's standard method all specimens but one were classified correctly.

8.5. Age Effects

An important confounding factor in sex determination, and also in defining morphological distances in general, is age. It is known from various studies (Corruccini, 1974; Carpenter, 1976) that the adult skeleton is subject to change due to progressive age. Consequently, a biased impression of the sex-diagnosing capacity of a set of variables might be obtained if male and female design samples have quite different age distributions. Depending on these distributions the discriminatory value may be over- or underestimated. Age effects can be dealt with in several ways.

a. A researcher can take the view that it is preferable to make use of age effects to increase the discriminatory value of a discriminant function. In this case, one should attempt to express biological age effects (the chronological age is not available for most skeletal samples) in one or more variables, and to introduce them into the discriminant function. In order to avoid a bias, the age distributions in the male and female samples will be made equal so that age alone will have no discriminatory value. Due to the correlation of the age variables with the morphological variables, age will nevertheless contribute to the discrimination. Figure 2 in Section 4.3 is an illustration of a similar phenomenon.

b. One can also regard age effects as a disturbing element. In this case, there should be an attempt to eliminate them as much as possible.

c. It seems, however, that the most sensible approach is to combine the two points of view mentioned above. The introduction of age effects will be attempted in so far as it proves feasible to express them in appropriate measures, as variables in the discriminant function, and to eliminate them when this is not possible.

An obvious difficulty with age effects is that biological aging processes vary with populations (e.g., Katz and Myers Suchey, 1989) and it is far from clear how large these variations are with respect to past peoples. Future studies in which various populations are compared, by regressing biological age variables on chronological age, may provide some insight into this question.

9. MISSING DATA

One of the most serious problems in studying skeletal material of past peoples with the aid of mathematical multivariate methods is that the bones under investigation are often incomplete and sometimes fragmentary. This implies that it may be difficult to find variable sets that both have a large discriminatory value and can be scored from a sufficiently large number of specimens.

Theoretically, two different approaches (to be used separately or in combination) can be followed that may be helpful in coping with this problem. The first approach is to use standard multivariate methodology. This requires scores of all specimens on all variables selected. Several sets of variables can be considered, each one involving a particular set of specimens. An obvious advantage of this approach is that no supplementary procedures are needed and, consequently, additional errors associated with these procedures are avoided. The second approach implies that values for missing scores are estimated by some regression technique. The performance of multivariate functions partly calculated from estimated scores tends to be lower than that of similar functions calculated from complete sets of real scores, but this effect may be small or even negligible under favorable conditions. Sample sizes should not be too small, and the percentage of estimated scores should be kept limited.

For cases in which the population covariance matrix of all variables is known beforehand, elegant optimization procedures have been developed (De Goede, 1984). In other cases, when this prior information is not available, one has to rely on simulation studies in order to obtain a clear impression of the effects of substituting real scores by estimated ones. Missing scores are then artificially generated for individuals that actually score completely on the set(s) of variables selected. The corresponding results (classifications or Mahalanobis distances) can then be compared with similar results obtained from using the original, complete score vectors. In this way one can obtain the most direct answer to the question of how far incompleteness of the skeletal material under investigation will affect the results and their interpretation.

An example of such a computer-assisted data analysis technique is based on the idea that the set of principal components scores, calculated from a large reference sample, can be predicted from the set of raw scores of an incomplete specimen by proceeding as if this specimen was randomly drawn from the reference population (Van Vark, 1974, 1984). By carrying out a number of simulation studies one can test the usefulness of this regression technique for the problems at hand. For calculation of Mahalanobis distances, missing scores are artificially generated for specimens that actually score com-

pletely on all variables. Thus such specimens are characterized by (1) a complete and (2) an incomplete vector of raw scores. By the data analysis technique mentioned, the incomplete vector of raw scores is transformed into a complete vector of principal components function scores. Consequently, each of these specimens can finally be represented by two sets of principal components scores: one set of "real" principal components scores, and one obtained by means of regression. Finally, Mahalanobis distances are calculated between two vectors of scores for each of the specimens concerned.

In a study in which squared Mahalanobis distances were calculated between hominid groups, and in which the between-groups squared distances ranged from about 16 to 112, it was found that squared Mahalanobis distances that fell between the correct and the estimated vectors of principal components scores were on the order of magnitude of 2.0 (Van Vark, 1985b). This suggests that, in this instance, general interpretations were not affected by the fragmentary status of many of the sample specimens (see Figure 8). A thorough review of the literature on missing data problems is given by Kariya and colleagues (1983).

10. NONMETRICAL VARIABLES

The use of nonmetrical skeletal traits in anthropological studies has acquired a certain popularity since Berry and Berry (1967) drew attention to them in their classic article. However, the results of these studies have not led to a clear idea of the value of these variables for physical anthropology. The cause of this lies with some of the particular characteristics of nonmetric traits: They tend to be only slightly correlated; their scores are not (even approximately) normally distributed; and it is not realistic to assume that the covariance matrices of their scores are equal in different populations. As a consequence, although several distance statistics are currently used for these traits, none of them is really satisfactory. This, in turn, has led to the impression that there is little correspondence between distance patterns based on metrical variables, on the one hand, and on nonmetrical variables, on the other.

Opinions vary widely about the usefulness of nonmetrical traits. Rightmire's (1972) study of

East African Negro crania compared the efficiency of nonmetric and metric distance techniques and found equivalent patterns of group similarities (or differences) as deduced on independent grounds from archaeological, linguistic, and historical sources. However, the results obtained with D^2 and continuous cranial measurements did a significantly better job and led to much the same conclusions as those reached from a study of eye-witness accounts and analysis of oral tradition of the peoples concerned than did the nonmetric results. Another contribution was made by Corruccini (1974: 425), who noted that "discrete traits in isolation are not of paramount value to skeletal genetic studies, but may be vital in comparison and conjunction with other types of data in analyzing the population genetics of extinct groups."

More work is required to fully evaluate the usefulness of these traits. There are a number of reasons for this, which include the following (see also Van Vark and Van der Sman, 1982, and Van Vark et al., 1989b).

1. An unknown percentage of the differences found between metrical and nonmetrical distances are mathematical artefacts that are due to differences in calculation technique. With use of the same calculation technique, for example, discriminant analysis, for both kinds of variables, the comparability between metrical and nonmetrical variables will increase but will, nevertheless, remain limited. This is because by imposing a model that is well adapted to metrical variables, the nonmetrical variables are not given a fair chance.

2. The main reasons for the latter are that, for nonmetric variables, the covariance and correlation matrices are unequal, and in connection with this the estimation of these matrices is a difficult problem, in particular if samples are "small." Consequently, relatively large systematic errors and errors due to chance may result.

3. The general impression so far is that correlations between nonmetrical variables tend to be small. In the calculation of distances as well as classification functions this has led to the use of models that neglect correlations. However, it may very well be that the correlations between a pair of variables, X_1, X_2 and between the pair, X_2,X_3, are negligible or even

absent but that nevertheless the multiple correlation between X_1 and X_2, X_3 may be very large and even equal to $+1.0$ or -1.0 (examples are given in Van Vark et al., 1987:145). As a consequence very biased distance patterns may be found if such models are used. This has doubtlessly also contributed to the differences that were found between metrical and nonmetrical distances.

For the same reason, variables that do not correlate with sex when considered separately may very well do so when considered together with a battery of variables, and thus display in combination with these variables considerable sex discriminatory capacity. This implies that population analyses using nonmetric traits should separate the sexes.

4. However, if the correlations between nonmetric variables are taken into account other problems are encountered because this substantially increases the number of parameters that have to be estimated. Obviously, these problems will increase if inequality of the covariance matrices is postulated. Though this assumption will reflect biological reality more closely, it also implies that the number of correlation coefficients to be estimated is doubled on comparing samples of two populations.

5. Another point of interest is connected with the nature of the underlying genetic structure. Studies made by Czarnetzki (1992) seem to confirm earlier findings (Dempster and Lerner, 1950) that nonmetric traits are influenced by many genes that act in an additive way. Consequently, these traits have an underlying continuity, both genetic and environmental in origin, with one or more thresholds that impose a discontinuity on their visual impression (Hauser and De Stefano, 1989:5–8). If a trait has two or more thresholds, it is possible, in certain circumstances, to make a comparison between the variances of populations as well as between the means. The principles of these calculations are well known in quantitative genetics (Falconer, 1960). Mathematical statistical elaboration may be found, for example, in Fomby et al. (1984). It seems that once extensive studies based on the latter methods have been carried out, one may obtain better insight into the value of nonmetrical variables for anthropological practice. This is evident from the current literature (Saunders, 1989).

Recently, Ambergen (1989) designed formulas (implemented in the POSCON computer program; Van der Sluis et al., 1985) for estimating posterior probabilities and obtaining accessory confidence intervals if combinations of metrical and nonmetrical variables are used. Several other examples of ongoing developments could be given. Although heritability estimates tend to produce low figures, and some estimates are even not significantly different from zero (Sjøvold, 1984), it is clear that the main issue is to obtain more clarity as to underlying genetic structure. Twenty years ago Jantz stated, "It is clear that much more work is needed before nonmetric traits can afford a basis for definitive statements about population relationships" (Jantz, 1970: 100). This statement seems to have lost nothing of its relevance.

11. MATHEMATICAL MULTIVARIATE ANALYSIS: PROBLEMS AND PROSPECTS

It has been said that "physical anthropology is the nursery of multivariate methods" (Healy, 1985). More recently, it appears that the recent anthropological literature shows a certain lack of acceptance of these methods. This is all the more remarkable since, during this time, computer software has become available with such a wide range of applications of multivariate methods. There are a number of reasons for the neglect.

1. There is a tendency among anthropologists to apply standard methodology without paying adequate attention to systematic errors and errors due to chance. In connection with this, little attention is paid to the development of procedures that are specifically designed for the anthropological problems at issue. This has led to conflicting results.

2. The complexity of mathematical multivariate methodology tends to generate a certain fear among anthropologists, and this may easily lead to an a priori rejection of these methods. Anyone who has ever submitted a paper to an anthropological journal in which unconventional multivariate methods are used will know what is meant.

3. It must be admitted that the mathematical training of the average anthropologist is insufficient. One of the major consequences is that

he or she may have difficulty with the interpretation of the calculation results. Besides, more often than not the individual investigator lacks adequate support from mathematical statisticians and computer specialists. A consequence of the latter is that it becomes difficult or even impossible for the anthropologist to program or have programmed the specific methods needed.

4. Although several databanks are already at the disposal of anthropologists, there is a need for a more generally accessible databank that is based on uniformly accepted systems of measurement (Schwidetzky, 1984). With the aid of such a bank the quality and quantity of anthropological research would increase.

A specific example is the problem of sex determination. So far, it is not known how well the discriminant analysis procedures described above work for sex determination of past human skeletal samples (Cunha and Van Vark, 1991). Sections in this chapter on variable selection and sex diagnosis show that only if scores on a "large" number of variables are taken from "very large" male and female reference samples, can this question be answered satisfactorily.

5. For an efficient application of mathematical multivariate methods one often has to do a lot of work which takes time and money, especially if specific adaptations are necessary. The advice of, and cooperation with, a mathematical statistician may be needed. Part of the research may be "data-analytic" rather than statistical because no statistical solution is available, and no statistical consultant is able to develop a methodology that satisfies rigid mathematical statistical criteria. Examples are the IDA and the LOO-based procedures. Methods of this nature generally do not appeal to statisticians, which implies that anthropologists will have to develop them themselves and, subsequently, test their usefulness by means of simulation studies.

So much for the problematic side. A positive point is that it is unnecessary for every anthropologist to fully understand the mathematical background. The nonspecialist anthropologist could be compared with a skilled factory worker who successfully uses sophisticated tools without exact knowledge of how the tools are made. What this anthropologist needs is no more than a general understanding of the underlying rationale of these techniques as well as a knowledge of how and when to use them. Another positive point is that with increasing power and user-friendliness of personal computers and software, multivariate analyses will be easier and faster to carry out. Mathematical multivariate methodology can be far more rewarding than it has been so far. There is no doubt that future studies will contribute considerably to our understanding of past peoples and their evolution.

ACKNOWLEDGMENTS

The authors wish to thank Dr. W.H.M. Amesz-Voorhoeve, A. den Arend, J. Dijkema, Dr. W.G. Frederiks, Dr. S.K. Hazewindus, Dr. J.V. Jansen, and P.G.M. van der Sman for their assistance with computing; Mr. D. Kuizenga, Mrs. G.T. Hoogenberg, and Mrs. S.W. Nijdam for technical and secretarial assistance; and Mr. K. van Linschoten for making the drawings.

REFERENCES

Aitchinson J, Dunsmore IR (1975): "Statistical Prediction Analysis." Cambridge: Cambridge University Press.

Ambergen AW (1989): Statistical Uncertainties in Posterior Probabilities. Thesis, University of Groningen, the Netherlands.

Ambergen AW, Schaafsma W (1984): Interval estimates for posterior probabilities, applications to Border Cave. In van Vark GN, Howells WW (eds): "Multivariate Statistical Methods in Physical Anthropology." Dordrecht, the Netherlands: Reidel Publishing Co., pp 115–134.

Andrews DF, Gnanadesikan RG, Warner JL (1971): Transformations of multivariate data. Biometrics 27:825–840.

Andrews P (1987): Aspects of hominoid evolution. In Patterson C (ed): "Molecules and Morphology in Evolution." Cambridge: Cambridge University Press, pp 23–53.

Barnard MM (1935): The secular variations of skull characters in four series of Egyptian skulls. Ann Eug 6:352–371.

Berry AC, Berry RJ (1967): Epigenetic variation in the human cranium. J Anat 101:361–371.

Blackith RE, Reyment RA (1971): "Multivariate Morphometrics." London: Academic Press.

Broca P (1875): Instructions craniologiques et craniometriques. Mem Soc Anthropol 1/2.

Campbell BG (1963): Quantitative classification and human evolution. In Washburn SL (ed): "Classification and Human Evolution." Chicago: Aldine, pp 50–74.

Campbell NA (1980): On the study of the Border Cave remains: Statistical comments. Curr Anthropol 21/4:532–535.

Carpenter JC (1976): A comparative study of metric and nonmetric traits in series of modern crania. Am J Phys Anthropol 45:337–444.

Cavalli-Sforza LL, Piazza A, Menozzi P, Mountain J (1988): Reconstruction of human evolution: Bringing together genetic, archaeological, and linguistic data. Proc Natl Acad Sci USA 85:6002–6006.

Chakraborty R (1985): Genetic distance and gene diversity: Some statistical considerations. In Krishnaiah PR(ed): "Multivariate Analysis–VI." Amsterdam: Elsevier Publishers, pp 77–96.

Cherry LM, Case SM, Kunkel JG, Wyles JS, Wilson AC (1982): Body shape metrics and organismal evolution. Evolution 38(5):914–933.

Corruccini RS (1974): An examination of the meaning of cranial discrete human skeletal biological studies. Am J Phys Anthropol 40:425–446.

Corruccini RS (1975): Multivariate analysis in biological anthropology: Some considerations. J Hum Evol 4:1–19.

Corruccini RS (1984): Interpretation of metrical variables in multivariate analysis. In van Vark GN, Howells WW (eds): "Multivariate Statistical Methods in Physical Anthropology." Dordrecht, Netherlands: Reidel Publishing Co., pp 13–19.

Corruccini RS (1987): Shape in morphometrics: Comparative analyses. Am J Phys Anthropol 73:289–303.

Crichton JM (1966): A multiple discriminant analysis of Egyptian and African Negro crania. Pap Peabody Mus Archael Ethnol Harv Univ 57.

Cunha E, Van Vark GN (1991): The construction of sex discriminant functions from a large collection of skulls of known sex. Int J Anthropol 6(1):53–66.

Czarnetzki A (1992): Epigenetische Skeletmerkmale im Populationsvergleich. Eine Apologie (in preparation).

De Goede WHV (1984): Incomplete samples from multivariate normal distributions with the same, known covariance matrix. In van Vark GN, Howells WW (eds): "Multivariate Statistical Methods in Physical Anthropology." Dordrecht, Netherlands: Reidel Publishing Co., pp 37–48.

Dempster ER, Lerner M (1950): Heritability of threshold characters. Genetics 35:112–236.

Efron B (1979): Bootstrap methods: Another look at the jackknife. Am Statist 7:1–26.

Falconer DS (1960): "Introduction to Quantitative Genetics." Edinburgh: Oliver and Boyd.

Fisher RA (1936): The use of multiple measurements in taxonomic problems. Ann Eug 8:179–188.

Fomby Th, Hill B, Johnson SR (1984): "Advanced Econometric Methods." New York: Springer.

Friday AE (1987): Models of evolutionary change and the estimation of evolutionary trees. Oxford Surv Evolut Biol 4:61–88.

Gejvall N-G (1947): Bestaemning av braenda ben från forntida gravar. Fornvaennen 1:39.

Gilbert BE, Dunn OJ (1969): The effect of unequal variance–covariance matrices on Fisher's linear discriminant function. Biometrics 25:505–515.

Gower JC, Digby PGN (1984): Some recent advances in multivariate analysis applied to anthropometry. In van Vark GN, Howells WW (eds): "Multivariate Statistical Methods in Physical Anthropology." Dordrecht, Netherlands: Reidel Publishing Co., pp 21–36.

Guglielmino Matessi CR, Gluckman P, Cavalli-Sforza LL (1979): Climate and the evolution of skull metrics in man. Am J Phys Anthropol 50:549–564.

Hauser G, De Stefano GF (1989): "Epigenetic Variants of the Human Skull." Stuttgart: Schweizerbart.

Healy MJR, Tanner JM (1981): Size and shape in relation to growth and form. Symp Zool Soc London 46:19–35.

Healy MJR (1985): Review of "Multivariate Methods in Physical Anthropology." Biometrics 41(1):345.

Howells WW (1973): Cranial variation in man: A study by multivariate analysis of patterns of difference among recent human populations. Peabody Mus Pap Archaeol Ethnol Harv Univ 67.

Howells WW (1989): Skull shapes and the map. Craniometric analyses in the dispersion of modern Homo. Peabody Museum Paper. Archaeol. Ethnol. Harv. Univ, 79.

Huberty CJ (1984): Issues in the use and interpretation of discriminant analysis. Psychol Bull 95(1):156–176.

Jamison PL, Meier RJ, Thompson Jacob D (1989): Meaning of biodistance statistics: A test case using adult monozygotic twins. Am J Phys Anthropol 80:485–492.

Jantz RL (1970): Change and variation in skeletal populations of Arikara Indians. Thesis, University of Kansas, Lawrence.

Kariya T, Krishnaiah PR, Rao CR (1983): Inference on parameters of multivariate normal populations when some data is missing. In Krishnaiah PR (ed): "Developments in Statistics–III." New York: Academic Press, pp 137–184.

Katz D, Myers Suchey J (1989): Race differences in pubic symphyseal aging patterns in the male. Am J Phys Anthropol 80(2):167–172.

Key PJ, Jantz LR (1990): Statistical measures of intrasample variability. Hum Evol 5:457–469.

Knussman R (1967): Penrose–Abstand und Diskriminanzanalyse. Homo 18:134–140.

Krzyzaniak M, Miszkiewicz B (1955): "Crania Polonica." Materials and Anthropologial Monographs, No. 10. Wroclaw: Polska Akademia Nauk.

Lachenbruch PA (1967): An almost unbiased method of obtaining confidence intervals for the probabilities of misclassification in discriminant analysis. Biometrics 23:639–645.

Lambert DM, Paterson HE (1982): Morphological resemblance and its relationship to genetic distance measures. Evol Theory 5:291–300.

Leutenegger W, Shell B (1987): Variability and sexual dimorphism in canine size of *Australopithecus* and extant hominoids. J Hum Evol 19:359–367.

Mahalanobis PC (1930): On test and measures of group divergence. J Proc Asiat Soc Bengal 26:541–588.

Mahalanobis PC (1936): On the generalized distance in statistics. Proc Nat Inst Sci India 2(1):49–55.

Mardia KV (1975): Assessment of multinormality and the robustness of Hotelling's T-test. Appl Stat 24:163–171.

Marks S, Dunn OJ (1974): Discriminant functions when covariance matrices are unequal. J Am Stat Assoc 69:555–559.

Masset C (1982): Estimation de l'âge du deces par les sutures craniennes. Thesis, University of Paris, France.

Mukerjee R, Rao CR, Trevor JC (1955): "The Ancient Inhabitants of Jebel Moya, Sudan." Cambridge: Cambridge University Press.

Nakata M, Yu P, Davis B, Nance W (1974): Genetic determinants of craniofacial morphology: A twin study. Ann Hum Genet London 37:431–443.

Oxnard CE (1979): Some methodological factors in studying the morphological–behavioral interface. In Morbeck ME, Preuschoft H, Gomberg N (eds): "Environment, Behavior and Morphology: Dynamic Interactions in Primates." Fischer, pp 183–207.

Pearson K (1926): On the coefficient of racial likeness. Biometrika 18:105–117.

Penrose LS (1954): Distance, size and shape. Ann Eug 18:337–343.

Rao CR (1965): "Linear Inference and Its Applications." New York: Wiley.

Read DW (1990): From multivariate to qualitative measurements: Representation of shape. Hum Evol 5:417–429.

Reyment RA (1962): Observations on homogeneity of covariance matrices in paleontologic biometry. Biometrics 18:1–11.

Rightmire GP (1970): Bushman, Hottentot and South African negro crania studied by distance and discrimination. Am J Phys Anthropol 33:169–196.

Rightmire GP (1972): Cranial measurements and discrete traits compared in distance studies of African Negro skulls. Hum Biol 44:263–276.

Saunders SR (1989): Nonmetric skeletal variation. In İşcan MY, Kennedy KAR (eds): "Reconstruction of Life from the Skeleton." New York: Alan R. Liss, pp 95–108.

Schaafsma W (1982): Selecting variables in discriminant analysis for improving upon classical procedures. In Krishnaiah PR, Kanal LN (eds): "Handbook of Statistics," Vol. 2, Chapter 40. Amsterdam: North-Holland Publishing Co.

Schwidetzky I (1984): Data banks and multivariate statistics in physical anthropology. In Van Vark GN, Howells WW (eds):"Multivariate Statistical Methods in Physical Anthropology." Dordrecht, Netherlands: Reidel Publishing Co., pp 283–288.

Sibson R (1978): Studies on the robustness of multidimensional scaling: Procrustes statistics. J R Stat Soc (B) 40:234–238.

Sjøvold T (1984): A report on the heritability of some cranial measurements and nonmetrical traits. In Van Vark GN, Howells WW (eds): "Multivariate Statistical Methods in Physical Anthropology." Dordrecht, Netherlands: Reidel Publishing Co., pp 223–246.

Sjøvold T (1990): Estimation of living stature from long bone measurements utilizing the line of organic correlation. Hum Evol 5:431–447.

Spielman RS (1973): Do the natives all look alike? Size and shape components of anthropometric differences among Yanomama Indian villages. Am Nat 108/957:694–708.

Steerneman AGM, van der Meulen EA, Schaafsma W, van Vark GM (1990): Testing some hypotheses on human evolution and sexual dimorphism. Hum Evol 5:449–456.

Uytterschaut HT (1983): Affinity of Philippine Populations. Thesis, University of Groningen.

Uytterschaut HT, Wilmink W (1983): On the assumption of equality of variance–covariance matrices in the sex and racial diagnosis of human skulls. Am J Phys Anthropol 60:347–357.

Van der Sluis DM, Schaafsma W, Ambergen AW (1985): "POSCON User Manual." University of Groningen.

Van Vark GN (1970): Some Statistical Procedures for the Investigation of Prehistoric Human Skeletal Material. Thesis, University of Groningen.

Van Vark GN (1971): Eine Methode zur Geschlechtsbestimmung prahistorischer Individuen auf Grund von Skelettütberresten. Homo 22:76–84.

Van Vark GN (1974): The investigation of human cremated skeletal material by multivariate statistical methods. I. Methodology. Ossa 1:63–96.

Van Vark GN (1975): The investigation of human cremated skeletal material by multivariate statistical methods. II. Measures. Ossa 2:47–68.

Van Vark GN (1976): A critical evaluation of the application of multivariate statistical methods to the study of human populations from their skeletal remains. Homo 27(2):94–114.

Van Vark GN (1984): On the determination of hominid affinities. In van Vark GN, Howells WW (eds): "Multivariate Statistical Methods in Physical Anthropology." Dordrecht, Netherlands: Reidel Publishing Co., pp 323–349.

Van Vark GN (1985a): Some aspects of the reconstruction of human phylogeny with the aid of multivariate statistical methods. In "Proceedings of the Indian Statistical Institute: Golden Jubilee Conference on Human Genetics and Adaptation, Calcutta, February 1–5," pp 64–77.

Van Vark GN (1985b): Multivariate analysis in physical anthropology. In Krishnaiah PR (ed): "Multivariate Analysis–VI." Amsterdam: North Holland, pp 599–611.

Van Vark GN (1987): An anthropometric approach to the study of evolution. Acta Morphol Neerl-Scand 107–116.

Van Vark GN (1990a): Taxonomic problems with the reconstruction of hominid phylogeny. Proc 21. Arbeitstagung der Sektion Anthropologie der Biologischen Gesellschaft der DDR, Wittenberg, GDR, October 1989.

Van Vark GN (1990b): A study of Upper Paleolithic crania. Fame 2:7–15.

Van Vark GN, Howells WW (eds) (1984): "Multivariate Statistical Methods in Physical Anthropology." Dordrecht, Netherlands: Reidel Publishing Co.

Van Vark GN, van der Sman PGM (1982): New discrimination and classification techniques in anthropological practice. Z Morphol Anthropol 73(1):21–36.

Van Vark GN, van der Sman PGM, den Arend A, Hazewindus SK (1985): The statistical significance of an association between skull morphology and climatic conditions. Homo 36(4):232–241.

Van Vark GN, van der Sman PGM, Dijkema J, Buikstra JE (1989a): Some multivariate tests for differences in sexual dimorphism between human populations. Ann Hum Biol 16(4):301–310.

Van Vark GN, Steerneman AGM, Czarnetzki A (1989b): Some notes on the definition and application of nonmetrical skeletal variables. Homo 40(3):113–116.

Index